# Environmental Justice

# Environmental Justice
## *Law, Policy, and Regulation*

**Clifford Rechtschaffen**
Professor and Co-Director, Environmental Law and Justice Clinic
Golden Gate University School of Law

**Eileen Gauna**
Professor, Southwestern University School of Law

CAROLINA ACADEMIC PRESS
Durham, North Carolina

ISBN: 0-89089-412-4
LCCN: 2002105197

Carolina Academic Press
700 Kent Street
Durham, North Carolina 27701
Telephone: (919) 489-7486
Fax: (919) 493-5668
Email: cap@cap-press.com
www.cap-press.com

Printed in the United States of America.

To my dad, for his great example
Clifford Rechtschaffen


To my mom Josie, and to Ted, Jeanne, Loyola and Ruth
Eileen Gauna

# Summary of Contents

# Contents

# Preface

Environmental justice is arguably the most important and dynamic development in environmental law in the past decade. Drawing on principles from environmental law, civil rights law, and broader movements for economic and social justice, the environmental justice movement has focused attention on the disparate environmental harms and benefits experienced by low income communities and communities of color. Indeed, some of the claims presented by activists challenge some of the fundamental underpinnings of environmental law and policy. Environmental justice considerations arise in virtually all aspects of environmental law, including standard setting, program design, permitting facilities, enforcement, cleaning up contaminated sites, and redeveloping brownfields. And the environmental justice movement has generated an explosion of scholarship; since 1991, there have been close to 300 law review articles and over 30 books written on the subject.

This book is designed to provide students with a comprehensive introduction to environmental justice, whether or not they have prior background in environmental law. While its focus is oriented toward legal and regulatory issues, the book also draws considerably on non-legal disciplines; thus, it can be used in undergraduate or graduate courses as well. We have included frequent introductory notes to provide background for students unfamiliar with some of the environmental statutes and other materials. This book is designed for use in a single semester seminar course, and each of the 16 chapters roughly corresponds to a week's worth of reading. The book also can be easily used as a supplement in other environmental, land use, or civil rights classes in which the professor wishes to cover selected issues in environmental justice. The book also can serve as a reference for practitioners, government officials, and activists involved in environmental justice matters, as well as students wishing to engage in more focused research on environmental justice. On key areas of interest, we have included pathfinders for students and others wishing to undertake further research on specific topics

A note about the scope of the book's coverage. Environmental problems are far ranging, and environmental disparities implicate land use, transportation, civil rights, labor issues, international law, Native American law and other areas. A single casebook/reader of this nature cannot adequately cover all of these disparate and intricate legal specialties. Consequently, we have elected to limit the scope of this book to domestic environmental regulation and those subjects most closely related to and having an impact on environmental regulation, such as land use issues and constitutional or civil rights cases against environmental regulators. Other specialized areas such as labor law, transportation law, and international law are not within the scope of this book, although the health, quality of life and political issues that may implicate these legal subjects are briefly described. In a related vein, we have elected to focus upon federal environmental law, as implemented by federal, state, local, and tribal governments, rather than various state laws (although one chapter does contain a sampling of recent state law initiatives).

We do this for several reasons. First, the EPA was one of the first of the governmental institutions to respond to charges of environmental justice and it remains a key participant. Second, much of the controversy over environmental regulation and enforcement at the state and local level has involved dissatisfaction with the way the federal environmental statutes have been implemented. And third, state laws vary significantly and are only at the very beginning of their implementation phases. We look forward to articles and books on these important areas from our colleagues.

The editors of this book maintain the position that pursuing complete neutrality in these difficult and politically-charged issues is unrealistic. Although we are sympathetic to environmental justice struggles, we recognize that the issues are complex and raise hard questions that often generate compelling arguments from all perspectives. We strive to bring that complexity to the surface by choosing a range of materials that present different viewpoints. To further tease out the clash of interests and viewpoints, our notes often contain intentionally provocative questions. Those with a perspective different than ours may take issue with the way that some of the issues are framed and discussed. In response, we can only invite alternative ways to frame the debates and similar disclosures of the subject position of the author.

A note on the editing conventions we use: In general, we have omitted footnotes and other references from excerpted materials. We have left in citations from case excerpts that are directly discussed by the court or that we believe are important to understand the opinion. The few case footnotes that are included are numbered as they appear in the original opinions. We have indicated text that we omitted from the original sources with three ellipses, i.e. . . . . Text that was omitted in the original excerpts is indicated by three ellipses separated by a space, i.e. . . . .

We are deeply grateful to the following people who reviewed chapters of the book when they were in draft form: Tony Arnold, Denis Binder, Carl Cranor, Colin Crawford, Sheila Foster, Rachel Morello-Frosch, Casey Jarman, Steve Johnson, Alice Kaswan, Brad Mank, Catherine O'Neill, Marc Poirier, Rena Steinzor, and Rob Verchick. Thanks also to Diane Takvorian who reviewed portions of Chapter 15 dealing with Barrio Logan, and a special thanks is due to Bob Kuehn, who reviewed early drafts of multiple chapters. We are also grateful to Michael Gerrard for generously sharing materials with us. We are also deeply appreciative of the excellent research assistance provided by Golden Gate Law students Kristin Henry and Amy Cohen, and Southwestern University Law students Shannon Tool, Tony Foster, Alane Kumamoto, and Dan Bugay; thanks also to the administrative help provided by Pat Paulson of Golden Gate, and the assistance provided by Golden Gate law librarian Michael Daw. Karen Kramer provided unwavering support and terrific advice. The authors also thank Golden Gate University School of Law and Southwestern University School of Law for administrative and financial support.

Finally, we dedicate this book to activists from the grassroots. Their insight, courage, tenacity and wit constantly inspire.

# Acknowledgments

We gratefully acknowledge the permissions granted by the authors and publishers of the following works to reproduce excerpts in this book:

Douglas Anderton, et al., *Environmental Equity: The Demographics of Dumping*, 31 Demography 229 (May 1994). Reprinted by permission of the Population Association of America.

Craig Anthony Arnold, *Planning Milagros: Environmental Justice and Land Use Regulation*, 76 Denver University Law Review 1 (1998). Reprinted by permission of the Denver University Law Review.

Vicki Been, *What's Fairness Got To Do With It: Environmental Justice and the Siting of Locally Undesirable Land Uses*, 78 Cornell Law Review 1001 (1993). Reprinted by permission of the Cornell Law Review.

Vicki Been, *Locally Undesirable Land Uses in Minority Neighborhoods: Disproportionate Siting or Market Dynamics?*, 103 Yale Law Journal 1383 (1994). Reprinted by permission of the Yale Law Journal Company and William S. Hein Company.

Vicki Been, *Compensated Siting Proposals: Is it Time to Pay Attention?*, 21 Fordham Urban Law Journal 787 (1994). Reprinted by permission of the Fordham Urban Law Journal.

Vicki Been & Francis Gupta, Coming to the Nuisance or Going to the Barrios? A Longitudinal Analysis of Environmental Justice Claims, 24 Ecology Law Quarterly 1. Copyright 1997 by the Regents of the University of California. Reprinted by permission of the University of California, Berkeley.

Denis Binder, et al., *A Survey of Federal Agency Response to President Clinton's Executive Order 12,898 on Environmental Justice*, 31 Environmental Law Reporter 11,133 (2001). Reprinted by permission of the Environmental Law Institute.

Lynn E. Blais, *Environmental Racism Reconsidered*, 75 North Carolina Law Review 75 (1996). Reprinted by permission of the North Carolina Law Review.

Terry R. Bossert, *The Permit Applicant's Perspective*, 18 Temple Environmental Law and Technology Journal 135 (2000). Reprinted by permission of the Temple Environmental Law and Technology Journal.

Edward Patrick Boyle, *It's Not Easy Bein' Green: The Psychology of Racism, Environmental Discrimination, and the Argument for Modernizing Protection Analysis*, 46 Vanderbilt Law Review 937 (1993). Copyright 1993 by Vanderbilt Law Review. Reprinted by permission.

Robert Bullard, *A Model Environmental Justice Framework*, in Confronting Environmental Racism: Voices from the Grassroots 203 (1993). Reprinted by permission of South End Press.

Robert Bullard et al., *The Routes of American Apartheid*, 15 Forum for Applied Research and Public Policy 66 (2000). Reprinted by permission of the Forum for Applied Research and Public Policy.

Lloyd Burton & David Ruppert, *Bear's Lodge or Devil's Tower: Intercultural Relations, Legal Pluralism, and the Management of Sacred Sites on Public Lands*, 8 Cornell Journal of Law and Public Policy 201 (1999). Reprinted by permission of the Cornell Journal of Law and Public Policy.

William W. Buzbee, *Brownfields Environmental Federalism and Institutional Determinism*, 21 William and Mary Environmental Law and Policy Review 1 (1997). Reprinted by permission of the William and Mary Environmental Law and Policy Review.

Francis Calpotura, *Why the Law?* Third Force Magazine (May/June 1994). Reprinted by permission of the Center for Third World Organizing.

Luke Cole, *Empowerment as the Key to Environmental Protection: The Need for Environmental Poverty Law*, 19 Ecology Law Quarterly 619 (1992). Copyright 1992 by the Regents of the University of California. Reprinted by permission of the University of California, Berkeley.

Luke Cole & Sheila Foster, From the Ground Up: Environmental Racism and the Rise of the Environmental Justice Movement, 70–74 (2000). Reprinted by permission of New York University Press.

Robert Collin, *Environmental Equity: A Law and Planning Approach to Environmental Racism*, 11 Virginia Environmental Law Journal 495 (1992). Reprinted by permission of the Virginia Environmental Law Journal.

Richard Toshiyuki Drury & Flora Chu, *From White Knight Lawyers to Community Organizing: Citizens for a Better Environment-California*, 5 Race, Poverty and the Environment 52 (Fall/Winter 1995). Reprinted by permission of Race, Poverty and the Environment.

Richard Toshiyuki Drury, et al., *Pollution Trading and Environmental Injustice: Los Angeles' Failed Experiment in Air Quality Policy*, 9 Duke Environmental Law and Policy Forum 231 (Spring 1999). Reprinted by permission of the Duke Environmental Law and Policy Forum.

Joel B. Eisen, *Brownfields of Dreams?: Challenges and Limits of Voluntary Cleanup Programs and Incentives*, 1996 University of Illinois Law Review 883 (1996). Copyright 1996 by the Board of Trustees of the University of Illinois. Reprinted by permission of the University of Illinois Law Review and the Board of Trustees of the University of Illinois.

Joel B. Eisen, *Brownfields Policies for Sustainable Cities*, 9 Duke Environmental Law & Policy Forum 187 (1999). Reprinted by permission of the Duke Environmental Law and Policy Forum.

Kirsten H. Engel, *Brownfield Initiatives and Environmental Justice: Second-class Cleanups or Market-based Equity?*, 13 Journal of Natural Resources and Environmental Law 317 (1998). Reprinted by permission of the Journal of Natural Resources and Environmental Law.

Daniel A. Farber, *Taking Slippage Seriously: Noncompliance and Creative Compliance in Environmental Law*, 23 Harvard Environmental Law Review 297 (1999). Copyright 1999 by President and Fellows of Harvard College and the Harvard Environmental Law Review. Reprinted by permission.

Christopher H. Foreman, Jr., The Promise and the Peril of Environmental Justice (1998). Reprinted by permission of the Brookings Institution Press.

Sheila R. Foster, *Meeting the Environmental Justice Challenge: Evolving Norms in Environmental Decisionmaking*, 30 Environmental Law Reporter 10,992 (2000). Reprinted by permission of the Environmental Law Institute.

Jody Freeman, *Collaborative Governance in the Administrative State*, 45 University of California Law Review 1 (1997). Copyright 1997, the Regents of the University of California. All rights reserved. Reprinted by permission of the author.

William Funk, *Bargaining Toward the New Millennium: Regulatory Negotiation and the Subversion of the Public Interest*, 46 Duke Law Journal 1351 (1997). Reprinted by permission of the author.

Robert Garcia, *Mean Streets*, 15 Forum for Applied Research and Public Policy 75 (2000). Reprinted by permission of the Forum for Applied Research and Public Policy and the author.

Eileen Gauna, *Federal Environmental Citizen Provisions: Obstacles and Incentives on the Road to Environmental Justice*, 22 Ecology Law Quarterly 1 (1995). Copyright 1995 by the Regents of the University of California. Reprinted by permission of the University of California, Berkeley.

Eileen Gauna, *The Environmental Justice Misfit, Public Participation and the Paradigm Paradox*, 17 Stanford Environmental Law Journal 3 (1998). Reprinted by permission of the Stanford Environmental Law Journal.

Eileen Gauna, *EPA at Thirty: Fairness in Environmental Protection*, 31 Environmental Law Reporter 10,528 (2001). Reprinted by permission of the Environmental Law Institute.

Michael B. Gerrard, *Building Environmentally Just Projects: Perspectives of a Developers' Lawyer*, 5 Environmental Law News 33 (Environmental Law Section, State Bar of California, 1996). Reprinted by permission of the author.

Robert Hersh & Kris Wernstedt, *Out of Site, Out of Mind: The Problem of Institutional Controls*, 8 Race, Poverty and the Environment 15 (Winter 2001). Reprinted by permission of Race, Poverty and the Environment.

John A. Hird & Michael Reese, *The Distribution of Environmental Quality: An Empirical Analysis*, 79 Social Science Quarterly 693 (1998). Copyright 1997 by Social Science Quarterly and Blackwell Publishers. Reprinted by permission of Blackwell Publishers.

Dennis D. Hirsch, *Second Generation Policy and the New Economy*, 29 Capital University Law Review 1 (2001). Reprinted by permission of the Capital University Law Review.

Donald T. Hornstein, *Reclaiming Environmental Law: A Normative Critique of Comparative Risk Analysis*, 92 Columbia Law Review 562 (1992). Reprinted by permission of the Columbia Law Review.

Oliver A. Houck, *TMDLS IV: The Final Frontier*, 29 Environmental Law Reporter 10,469 (1999). Reprinted by permission of the Environmental Law Institute.

Stephen M. Johnson, *Economics vs. Equity: Do Market-Based Environmental Reforms Exacerbate Environmental Injustice?*, 56 Washington and Lee Law Review 111 (Winter 1999). Reprinted by permission of the Washington and Lee Law Review and the author.

Bradley C. Karkkainen, *Information as Environmental Regulation: TRI and Performance Benchmarking, Precursor to a New Paradigm?*, 89 Georgetown Law Journal 57 (2001). Reprinted with permission of the publisher, Georgetown Law Journal. Copyright 2001.

Alice Kaswan, *Environmental Laws: Grist for the Equal Protection Mill*, 70 University of Colorado Law Review 387 (1999). Reprinted by permission of the University of Colorado Law Review.

Robert Kuehn, *Remedying the Unequal Enforcement of Environmental Laws*, 9 St. John's Journal of Legal Commentary 625 (1994). Reprinted by permission of the St. John's Journal of Legal Commentary.

Robert Kuehn, *The Environmental Justice Implications of Quantitative Risk Assessment*, 1996 University of Illinois Law Review 103. Copyright 1996 by the Board of Trustees of the University of Illinois. Reprinted by permission of the University of Illinois Law Review.

Robert Kuehn, *A Taxonomy of Environmental Justice*, 30 Environmental Law Reporter 10,681 (2000). Reprinted by permission of the Environmental Law Institute.

Charles R. Lawrence III, *The Id, the Ego, and Equal Protection: Reckoning with Unconscious Racism*, 39 Stanford Law Review 317 (1987). Copyright 1987 by Stanford Law Review. Reproduced with permission of the Stanford Law Review via the Copyright Clearance Center.

Richard J. Lazarus, *The Tragedy of Distrust in the Implementation of Federal Environmental Law*, 54 Law & Contemporary Problems 311 (1991). Reprinted by permission of the Journal of Law and Contemporary Problems and the author.

Richard Lazarus, *Pursuing "Environmental Justice": The Distributional Effects of Environmental Protection*, 87 Northwestern University Law Review 787 (1993). Reprinted by special permission of Northwestern University School of Law, Law Review.

Richard J. Lazarus & Stephanie Tai, *Integrating Environmental Justice Into EPA Permitting Authority*, 26 Ecology Law Quarterly 617 (1999). Copyright 1999 by the Regents of the University of California. Reprinted by permission of the University of California, Berkeley.

Bradford C. Mank, *Environmental Justice and Title VI: Making Recipient Agencies Justify their Siting Decisions*, 73 Tulane Law Review 787 (1999). Copyright 1999 by Tulane Law Review Association. Reprinted by permission.

Bradford C. Mank, *Using § 1983 to Enforce Title VI's Section 602 Regulations*, 49 University of Kansas Law Review 321 (2001). Reprinted by permission of the University of Kansas Law Review.

Paul Mohai & Bunyan Bryant, *Environmental Racism: Reviewing the Evidence*, in Race and the Incidence of Environmental Hazards: A Time for Disclosure 163 (Bunyan Bryant and Paul Mohai eds., 1992). Copyright 1992 by Westview Press, Inc. Reprinted by permission of Westview Press, a member of Perseus Books, L.L.C.

Rachel Morello-Frosch, et al., *Environmental Justice and Southern California's Riskscape: The Distribution of Air Toxics Exposure and Health Risks Among Diverse Communities*, 36 Urban Affairs Review 551 (2001). Copyright 2001 by Sage Publications, Inc. Reprinted by permission of Sage Publications.

Mary O'Brien, Making Better Environmental Decisions: An Alternative to Risk Assessment (2000). Copyright 2000 by MIT Press. Reprinted by permission.

Catherine O'Neill, *Variable Justice: Environmental Standards, Contaminated Fish, and "Acceptable" Risk to Native Peoples*, 19 Stanford Environmental Law Journal 3 (2000). Reprinted by permission of the Stanford Environmental Law Journal.

Yale Rabin, *Expulsive Zoning: The Inequitable Legacy of Euclid,* in Zoning and the American Dream 101 (Charles M. Haar & Jerold S. Kayden eds., 1989). Reprinted by permission from Zoning and the American Dream. Copyright 1989 by the American Planning Association, Suite 1600, 122 S. Michigan Ave., Chicago, IL 60603-6107.

Clifford Rechtschaffen, *The Warning Game: Evaluating Warnings Under California's Proposition 65,* 23 Ecology Law Quarterly 303 (1996). Copyright 1996 by the Regents of the University of California. Reprinted by permission of the University of California, Berkeley.

Clifford Rechtschaffen, *Competing Visions: EPA and the States' Battle for the Future of Environmental Enforcement,* 30 Environmental Law Reporter 10,803 (2000). Reprinted by permission of the Environmental Law Institute.

Evan J. Ringquist, *Equity and the Distribution of Environmental Risk: The Case of TRI Facilities,* 78 Social Science Quarterly 811 (1997). Copyright 1997 by Social Science Quarterly and Blackwell Publishers. Reprinted by permission of Blackwell Publishers.

Robin Saha & Paul Mohai, "Explaining Race and Income Disparities in the Location of Locally Unwanted Land Uses: A Conceptual Framework," Paper presented at the 1997 Annual Meeting of the Rural Sociological Society (Toronto, August 1997). Reprinted by permission of the authors.

Paul Smith, *Lost in America,* Border/Lines (Winter 1991/1992). Reprinted by permission of the author.

Rena Steinzor, *Regulatory Reinvention and Project XL: Does the Emperor Have Any Clothes?,* 26 Environmental Law Reporter 10,527 (1996). Reprinted by permission of the Environmental Law Institute.

Rena Steinzor, *Devolution and the Public Health,* 24 Harvard Environmental Law Review 351 (2000). Copyright 2000 by the President and Fellows of Harvard College and the Harvard Environmental Law Review. Reprinted by permission.

Dean B. Suagee, *Symposium: Environmental Justice: Mobilizing for the 21st Century: The Indian Country Environmental Justice Clinic: From Vision to Reality,* 23 Vermont Law Review. 567 (1999). Copyright 1999 by Vermont Law Review. Reprinted by permission of the Vermont Law Review and the author.

Samara F. Swanston, *Environmental Justice: Mobilization for the 21st Century: Environmental Justice and Environmental Quality Benefits: The Oldest, Most Pernicious Struggle and Hope for Burdened Communities,* 23 Vermont Law Review 545 (1999). Copyright 1999 by Vermont Law Review. Reprinted by permission of the Vermont Law Review and the author.

Rebecca Tsosie, *Tribal Environmental Policy in an Era of Self-Determination: The Role of Ethics, Economics, and Traditional Ecological Knowledge,* 21 Vermont Law Review 225 (1996). Copyright 1996 by Vermont Law Review. Reprinted by permission of the Vermont Law Review and the author.

*Environmental Law Clinic Raises Environmental Justice and a Hostile Reaction From the Governor and the Louisiana Supreme Court,* Tulane Environmental Law News (Winter 1999). Reprinted by permission of Tulane Environmental Law News.

Robert Williams, *Large Binocular Telescopes, Red Squirrel Pinata, and Apache Sacred Mountains: Decolonizing Environmental Law in a Multi cultural World,* 96 West Virginia Law Review 1133 (1994). Reprinted by permission of the author.

Eric K. Yamamoto & Jen-L. W. Lyman, *Racializing Environmental Justice,* 72 University of Colorado Law Review 311 (2001). Reprinted by permission of the University of Colorado Law Review and Eric Yamamoto.

# Environmental Justice

# Chapter I

# Overview of the Environmental Justice Movement

## A. Introduction

### 1. AN INTRODUCTORY NOTE ON THE HISTORY OF THE MOVEMENT

In the 1980s, communities of color alarmed conventional environmental organizations, regulators and industry stakeholders with allegations of "environmental racism." These charges reflected long-standing frustration on the part of such communities, and their view that people of color systematically receive disproportionately greater environmental risk while white communities systematically receive better environmental protection. Across the country, communities of color began to challenge the siting of hazardous waste facilities, landfills, industrial activities and other risk-producing land practices within their community. These efforts at the grassroots level soon coalesced into a national campaign called the environmental justice movement. The roots of the movement lie in diverse political projects—the civil rights movement, the grass roots anti-toxics movement of the 1980s, organizing efforts of Native Americans and labor, and, to a lesser extent, the traditional environmental movement. *See generally,* LUKE COLE & SHEILA FOSTER, FROM THE GROUND UP: ENVIRONMENTAL RACISM AND THE RISE OF THE ENVIRONMENTAL JUSTICE MOVEMENT (2001)

"Environmental Justice" soon came to mean more than skewed distributional consequences of environmental burdens to communities of color. Becoming multi-issue and multi-racial in scope, the movement began to address disparities borne by the poor as well as people of color, acknowledging the substantial overlap between the two demographic categories. Concerns about regulatory processes surfaced as well. Often, the communities most impacted by environmentally risky activities had been excluded from important decisionmaking proceedings, sometimes intentionally so and sometimes because of a lack of resources, specialized knowledge, and other structural impediments. Initially, environmental justice activists used direct action such as demonstrations as the primary means to raise public awareness of the issue.

Largely in response to this early activism, several investigations and studies were undertaken which lent support to charges of environmental injustice. For example, a 1983 report by the U.S. General Accounting Office found that in the Environmental Protection Agency's (EPA's) Region IV, three of four major offsite hazardous waste facilities were located in predominantly African American communities; in 1987, a national study by the United Church of Christ Commission for Racial Justice found a positive correlation between racial minorities and proximity to commercial hazardous waste facilities and uncontrolled waste sites. Significantly, the study found that race was a more statistically significant variable than income. This early activism also culminated in an extraordinary gathering of grassroots activists at the First National People of Color Environmental Leadership Summit in Washington, D.C. on October 24–27, 1991, where the principles of environmental justice were adopted.

In 1992, a National Law Journal investigation found that EPA enforcement under various federal statutes and cleanup under the Superfund law was inequitable by race and, to a less pronounced degree, income. Other national and regional studies, including a review of the evidence by an EPA-established workgroup, began to find the same patterns of disproportionate siting, exposure to contaminants and adverse health effects in poor areas and in communities of color, further galvanizing the movement. Some researchers criticized the methodology of the early studies, and questioned the extent of disparities and whether they existed at the time of the initial siting of polluting facilities, thus leading to a round of subsequent studies. The later, more sophisticated studies confirmed several findings of the earlier studies, but not all of them. Debates on methodology and inconsistent findings continue to the present.

In response to the earlier studies and to continuing pressure from communities of color, former President Clinton in 1994 signed an Executive Order on Environmental Justice requiring all federal agencies to make environmental justice part of their mission. (The Order is reproduced in Chapter XV.) In 1992 the EPA established what ultimately came to be called the Office of Environmental Justice. The EPA also established the National Environmental Justice Advisory Committee (NEJAC), a diverse stakeholder group charged with making recommendations to the Agency concerning a broad range of environmental justice matters. An interagency working group on environmental justice was established under the direction of the Executive Order on Environmental Justice. The EPA began to take steps to include environmental justice organizations and community residents in a variety of agency projects, such as the EPA-sponsored "Brownfield" initiatives, which involves the re-use of idle industrial sites that are contaminated or underutilized because they are perceived to be contaminated. Similar initiatives are now occurring in some states. These actions mark a new course for environmental regulation, as environmental regulators did not traditionally consider demographics and social context in the course of their regulatory activities.

At the same time, heavily impacted communities continued to organize and began undertaking legal efforts to redress the inequitable environmental burdens that were apparent across the country. As explored in detail later in this book, legal challenges have met with mixed success. Claims alleging violations of the equal protection clause of the U.S. Constitution have failed because of the difficulty of proving intentional discrimination. Other claims using traditional environmental law theories, sometimes applied with an "environmental justice twist," have been somewhat more successful. Luke W. Cole, *Environmental Justice Litigation: Another Stone in David's Sling*, 21 FORDHAM URB. L. J. 523 (1994). Community groups have also filed numerous administrative complaints with EPA against state and regional environmental agencies alleging violations of Title VI of the Civil Rights Act of 1964. Title VI, which prohibits discrimination in programs or activities that receive federal financial assistance, has historically been applied in the education and employment context but not in the environmental context until relatively recently.

EPA was slow to develop a framework for investigating and deciding the Title VI cases, issuing Interim Guidance in 1998 and an expanded Draft Guidance in 2000. But the Agency was even slower in taking any specific action on the complaints; since 1993, it has decided only one case on the merits, while numerous Title VI matters have yet to be investigated.

As discussed, environmental disparities have been found in the siting, compliance and cleanup contexts. However, it also appears that environmental inequities can be caused in part because of the failure to consider environmental justice when regulatory standards are set and programs are designed. Accordingly, it is clear that environmental justice issues must be considered at the earliest stages of regulatory activity, not only at the permitting and enforcement stages, but particularly during the formation of policy, including the design of new programs.

Unfortunately, integrating environmental justice into environmental regulation in a manner that meaningfully responds to both the distributional and process issues has proven to be exceptionally complex. Environmental regulators are concerned with the scope of their authority to consider environmental justice under environmental statutes, to what extent they may have a legal duty to do so under the civil rights laws, as well as the uncertainty and complexity such an undertaking might add to their regulatory programs. The regulated community is concerned about the potential for increased delay and cost. Environmental justice advocates continue to attempt to address concerns and participate in various proceedings under severe resource constraints, and in some areas still confront considerable hostility and resistance by government officials. In addition, participation by environmental justice advocates is hampered by the tendency among other stakeholders and governmental agencies to view environmental justice as a "special interest." Yet, environmental justice advocates stress that the relevant issues are not demands for special treatment, but are grounded upon precepts of basic fairness and equal treatment: that there should be a level playing field for all stakeholders and that environmental burdens and benefits should not fall in disproportionate patterns by race and income.

The thrust of this book is therefore twofold, first to examine the complexities presented by environmental inequity; and second, to explore the potential that exists within the current system to move environmental regulation forward in a responsible manner that makes good on a promise of a more just society and, ultimately, an ecologically sustainable environment.

## *Pathfinder on Environmental Justice Generally*

Among the numerous books and articles about environmental justice are RACE AND THE INCIDENCE OF ENVIRONMENTAL HAZARDS: A TIME FOR DISCOURSE (Paul Mohai & Bunyan Bryant, eds. 1992); CONFRONTING ENVIRONMENTAL RACISM: VOICES FROM THE GRASSROOTS (Robert D. Bullard, ed. 1993) and UNEQUAL PROTECTION: ENVIRONMENTAL JUSTICE AND COMMUNITIES OF COLOR (Robert D. Bullard, ed. 1994); BUNYAN BRYANT, ENVIRONMENTAL JUSTICE: ISSUES, POLICIES AND SOLUTIONS (1995); CHRISTOPHER FOREMAN, THE PROMISE AND PERIL OF ENVIRONMENTAL JUSTICE (1998), THE LAW OF ENVIRONMENTAL JUSTICE: THEORIES AND PROCEDURES TO ADDRESS DISPROPORTIONATE RISKS (Michael B. Gerrard, ed. 1999); and LUKE COLE & SHEILA FOSTER, FROM THE GROUND UP: ENVIRONMENTAL RACISM AND THE RISE OF THE ENVIRONMENTAL JUSTICE MOVEMENT (2001).

The Center for Race, Poverty & the Environment and Urban Habitat publish a (usually semi-annual) newsletter entitled *Race, Poverty & the Environment* that focuses in depth on particular environmental justice issues. EPA's Office of Environmental Justice has a very useful web page: http://es.epa.gov/oeca/main/ej/index.html. Other very useful resources can be found on the web page of the Environmental Justice Resource Center at Clark Atlanta University, http://www.ejrc.cau.edu/. The Resource Center has published THE PEOPLE OF COLOR ENVIRONMENTAL GROUPS DIRECTORY 2000, which lists more than 400 people-of-color groups working on environmental justice. Another useful resource is the GUILD LAW CENTER FOR ECONOMIC AND SOCIAL JUSTICE, ENVIRONMENTAL JUSTICE AND THE COMMUNITY: AN ORGANIZING AND RESOURCE HANDBOOK. An overview for researching environmental justice issues is provided in Carita Shanklin, *Pathfinder: Environmental Justice*, 24 ECOL. L. Q. 333 (1997). Professor Denis Binder has collected environmental justice cases in two articles, *Index of Environmental Justice Cases*, 27 URB. LAW. 163 (1995) and *Environmental Justice Index II*, 3 CHAPMAN L. REV. 309 (2000).

# B. Fairness and Justice Considered

The fundamental question that presents itself when considering environmental justice is the working definition of "fairness" and "justice." Consider the views of these prominent environmental justice scholars. In the first excerpt, Professor Robert Kuehn explains that underlying the environmental justice movement are four concepts of justice: distributive, procedural, corrective and social justice.

## Robert R. Kuehn,
## A Taxonomy of Environmental Justice
### 30 Environmental Law Reporter 10,681 (2000)

Efforts to understand environmental justice are [ ] complicated by the term's international, national, and local scope; by its broad definition of the environment—where one lives, works, plays, and goes to school; and by its broad range of concerns—such as public health, natural resource conservation, and worker safety in both urban and rural environs. Disputes at the international level include allegations that governments and multinational corporations are exploiting indigenous peoples and the impoverished conditions of developing nations. At the national level, although an overwhelming number of studies show differences by race and income in exposures to environmental hazards, debate continues about the strength of that evidence and the appropriate political and legal response to such disparities. At the local level, many people of color and lower income communities believe that they have not been treated fairly regarding the distribution of the environmental benefits and burdens....

*Shifting Perspectives and Uses of Terms*

The U.S. Environmental Protection Agency (EPA) initially used the term "environmental equity," defined as the equitable distribution of environmental risks across population groups, to refer to the environmental justice phenomenon. Because this term implies the redistribution of risk across racial and economic groups rather than risk reduction and avoidance, it is no longer used by EPA, though it is still used by some states.

In some instances, the phrase "environmental racism," defined as "any policy, practice or directive that differentially affects or disadvantages (whether intended or unintended) individuals, groups, or communities based on race or color," is used to explain the differential treatment of populations on environmental issues. Commentators disagree over the proper usage of this term, particularly over whether an action having an unequal distributive outcome across racial groups would in itself be a sufficient basis to label an action environmental racism or whether the action must be the result of intentional racial animus. Today, many environmental justice advocates and scholars avoid the term "environmental racism," though the phrase continues to be employed and is useful in identifying the institutional causes of some environmental injustices. This shift is attributable to a desire to focus on solutions rather than mere identification of problems, as well as a desire to encompass class concerns and not to be limited by issues of intentional conduct....

In 1994, President Clinton issued Executive Order No. 12898...and adopted the phrase "environmental justice" to refer to "disproportionately high and adverse human health or environmental effects...on minority populations and low-income populations."...The Executive Order's use of the term "environmental justice" is significant in at least three respects. First, the Executive Order focuses not only on the disproportionate burdens addressed by the term environmental equity, but also on issues of enforcement of environmental laws and opportunities for public participation. Second, the Executive Order identifies not just minorities but also low-income populations as the groups who have been subject to, and entitled to relief from, unfair or unequal treatment. Finally, the Executive Order, and in particular the accompanying memorandum, refers to environmental justice as a goal or aspiration to be achieved, rather than as a problem or cause.

In 1998, EPA's Office of Environmental Justice set forth the Agency's "standard definition" of environmental justice:

> The fair treatment of people of all races, cultures, incomes, and educational levels with respect to the development and enforcement of environmental laws, regulations, and policies. Fair treatment implies that no population should be forced to shoulder a disproportionate share of exposure to the negative effects of pollution due to lack of political or economic strength.

Going beyond the issues of disproportionate exposures and participation in the development and enforcement of laws and policies, EPA further elaborated that environmental justice:

> is based on the premise that: 1) it is a basic right of all Americans to live and work in "safe, healthful, productive, and aesthetically and culturally pleasing surroundings;" 2) it is not only an environmental issue but a public health issue; 3) it is forward-looking and goal-oriented; and 4) it is also inclusive since it is based on the concept of fundamental fairness, which includes the concept of economic prejudices as well as racial prejudices.

Professor Bunyan Bryant defines environmental justice as referring "to those cultural norms and values, rules, regulations, behaviors, policies, and decisions to support sustainable communities, where people can interact with confidence that their environment is safe, nurturing, and protective." Some critics of environmental justice contend that these definitions of environmental justice by government agencies and environmental justice advocates are so broad and aspirational as not to state clearly the ends of environmental justice.

An alternative approach to defining environmental justice that does state its desired ends, albeit very ambitious ones, was developed by environmental justice leaders during the 1991 First People of Color Environmental Leadership Summit. Its "Principles of Environmental Justice" sets forth a 17-point paradigm [excerpted below]....

Dr. Robert Bullard has distilled the principles of environmental justice into a framework of five basic characteristics: (1) protect all persons from environmental degradation; (2) adopt a public health prevention of harm approach; (3) place the burden of proof on those who seek to pollute; (4) obviate the requirement to prove intent to discriminate; and (5) redress existing inequities by targeting action and resources. In his view, environmental justice seeks to make environmental protection more democratic and asks the fundamental ethical and political questions of "who gets what, why and how much."...

Students and lawyers are often left without an understanding of unifying themes or common political, legal, or economic approaches to addressing allegations of injustice. The classification method set forth in this Article seeks to overcome this shortcoming and to advance the understanding of environmental justice by disassembling the term into the four traditional notions of "justice" that are implicated by allegations of environmental injustice....

### Environmental Justice as Distributive Justice

...Distributive justice has been defined as "the right to equal treatment, that is, to the same distribution of goods and opportunities as anyone else has or is given." Aristotle is often credited with the first articulation of the concept and explained it as involving "the distribution of honour, wealth, and the other divisible assets of the community, which may be allotted among its members." The focus of this aspect of justice is on fairly distributed outcomes, rather than on the process for arriving at such outcomes.

In an environmental context, distributive justice involves the equitable distribution of the burdens resulting from environmentally threatening activities or of the environmental benefits of government and private-sector programs. More specifically, in an environmental justice context, distributive justice most commonly involves addressing the disproportionate public health and environmental risks borne by people of color and lower incomes....

Distributive justice in an environmental justice context does not mean redistributing pollution or risk. Instead, environmental justice advocates argue that it means equal protection for all and the elimination of environmental hazards and the need to place hazardous activities in any community. In other words, distributive justice is achieved through a lowering of risks, not a shifting or equalizing of existing risks.

With such a strong focus on the inequitable distribution by race and income of environmental hazards, an often overlooked aspect of distributive justice is that it also involves the distribution of the benefits of environmental programs and policies, such as parks and beaches, public transportation, safe drinking water, and sewerage and drainage....

### Environmental Justice as Procedural Justice

Claims of procedural injustice also are common in environmental justice disputes, and it is not usual for people of color and low-income communities to complain about both the distributive and procedural aspects of an environmental policy or decision. Indeed, in many situations, a community's judgment about whether or not an outcome was distributively just will be significantly determined by the perceived fairness of the procedures leading to the outcome.

Procedural justice has been defined as "the right to treatment as an equal. That is the right, not to an equal distribution of some good or opportunity, but to equal concern and respect in the political decision about how these goods and opportunities are to be distributed." Aristotle referred to this as a status in which individuals have an "equal share in ruling and being ruled." It involves justice as a function of the manner in which a decision is made, and it requires a focus on the fairness of the decision-making process, rather than on its outcome....

The Executive Order on environmental justice has a strong focus on procedural justice, directing agencies to ensure greater public participation and access to information for minority and low-income populations. The Principles of Environmental Justice demand that public policy be based on mutual respect and justice for all peoples and free from bias or discrimination, affirm the fundamental right to self-determination, and insist on the right to participate as equal partners at every level of decision-making.

Environmental justice complaints raise both *ex ante* and *ex post* considerations of procedural fairness. Looking at the process in advance of its use (*ex ante*), they question whether the decision-making and public participation procedures are fair to all concerned or whether they favor one side over the other. Also, looking back (*ex post*), the complaints question whether the completed decision-making process did, in fact, treat all with equal concern and respect.

One way to judge procedural justice *ex ante* is to determine if those to be affected by the decision agree in advance on the process for making the decision. Thus, procedural justice requires looking not just to participation in a process but to whether the process is designed in a way to lead to a fair outcome. In this respect, environmental decision-making processes have been roundly criticized by commentators who have examined issues of environmental justice and public participation. One common observation is that the predominant expertise-oriented, interest-group model of environmental decision-making favors those with resources and political power over people of color and low-income communities. Even the [civic] republican process, which outwardly seeks to advance community interests over private interests, may obscure the true private interests at issue and the continuing disparities in resources, power, and influence. In general, to achieve procedural justice, observers advocate developing more deliberative models of decision-making, providing disadvantaged groups with greater legal and technical resources, and ensuring equal access to decision-makers and the decision-making process....

An unresolved aspect of procedural justice is whether a fair process can negate a claim that a disproportionate outcome is unjust. Some argue that if the decision-maker has given impartial attention to and consideration of competing claims to different benefits, an outcome would not be unjust even if the result were to subordinate one group to another....

While environmental justice requires, at a minimum, a procedurally just process, the emphasis on disparate effects, rather than discriminatory intent, in the Executive Order, Principles of Environmental Justice, and Title VI's implementing regulations indicates that a fair process alone will not negate claims of distributive injustice....

Although there has been a great deal of discussion about the need to reform existing public participation models and although many government agencies now recognize their failure to ensure meaningful participation by disadvantaged populations, EPA's refusal to require that waste facilities and permitting agencies "make all reasonable efforts to ensure equal opportunity for the public to participate in the permitting process" [in EPA's Resource Conservation and Recovery Act's public participation regulations], the antagonistic attitudes of some state officials toward allegations of environmental justice, the hostility of environmental justice critics toward government grants to community groups for environmental education and outreach efforts, and the assertions by some regulated entities that increased public participation is not appropriate do not bode well for finding consensus on the format of a fair decision-making process or for avoiding future allegations of procedural injustice....

### Environmental Justice as Corrective Justice

The third aspect of justice encompassed by the term environmental justice is "corrective justice," a notion of justice that is sometimes referred to by other names and may be subsumed within claims for distributive or procedural justice....

"Corrective justice" involves fairness in the way punishments for lawbreaking are assigned and damages inflicted on individuals and communities are addressed.... Corrective justice involves not only the just administration of punishment to those who break the law, but also a duty to repair the losses for which one is responsible....

Therefore, as reflected in claims made in the environmental justice context, corrective justice encompasses many aspects of wrongdoing and injury and includes the concepts of "retributive justice," "compensatory justice," "restorative justice," and "commutative justice." I adopt the term corrective justice here because environmental justice seeks more than just retribution or punishment of those who violate legal rules of conduct. Corrective justice is also preferred over the phrase compensatory justice because the latter term may imply that, provided compensation is paid, an otherwise unjust action is acceptable. It is also important to note that although some concepts of corrective justice view fault or wrongful gain as a necessary condition for liability, environmental justice principles impose responsibility for damages regardless of fault (e.g., the polluter-pays principle). Corrective justice, therefore, is not used in the narrow Aristotelian rectificatory sense but instead in a broader, applied sense that violators be caught and punished and not reap benefits for disregarding legal standards and that injuries caused by the acts of another, whether a violation of law or not, be remedied....

### Environmental Justice as Social Justice

The fourth and final aspect of justice implicated by the term environmental justice is "social justice," a far-reaching, and some say nebulous, goal of the environmental justice movement....

Social justice is "that branch of the virtue of justice that moves us to use our best efforts to bring about a more just ordering of society—one in which people's needs are more fully met." "The demands of social justice are...first, that the members of every class have enough resources and enough power to live as befits human beings, and second, that the privileged classes, whoever they are, be accountable to the wider society for the way they use their advantages."

Environmental justice has been described as a "marriage of the movement for social justice with environmentalism" integrating environmental concerns into a broader agenda that emphasizes social, racial, and economic justice. Dr. Bullard refers to this as-

pect of environmental justice as "social equity:... an assessment of the role of sociological factors (race, ethnicity, class, culture, lifestyles, political power, and so forth) in environmental decision-making."

Professor Sheila Foster has argued that a narrow focus on issues of distributive justice
neglects the search for social structures and agents that are causing the environmental
problems. A social justice perspective presents environmental justice as part of larger
problems of racial, social, and economic justice and helps illustrate the influence of politics, race, and class on an area's quality of life. This broader social perspective contrasts
with traditional environmentalism and its narrower focus on wilderness preservation
and the technological aspects of environmental regulation.

Environmental justice's focus on social justice reflects reality. As one community organizer explained, oppressed people do not have compartmentalized problems — they
do not separate the hazardous waste incinerator from the fact that their schools are underfunded, that they have no day care, no sidewalks or streetlights, or no jobs. The reason disadvantaged communities do not separate these problems is that their quality of
life as a whole is suffering and the political, economic, and racial causes are likely interrelated....

Social justice influences can work in two ways. The same underlying racial, economic, and political factors that are responsible for the environmental threats to the
community also likely play a significant role in why the area may suffer from other
problems like inadequate housing, a lack of employment opportunities, poor schools,
etc. In turn, the presence of undesirable land uses that threaten the health and well-
being of local residents and provide few direct economic benefits negatively influences
the quality of life, development potential, and attitudes of the community and may lead
to further social and economic degradation.

Government officials are often hesitant to embrace the social justice aspects of environmental justice, reflecting a reluctance to take on the broader systemic causes of
environmental injustice or to consider issues outside the narrow technical focus of the
agency. Nonetheless, the President's Executive Order acknowledges the significance of
social justice by directing each federal agency to consider the economic and social implications of an agency's environmental justice activities, and the memorandum accompanying the Executive Order requires analysis of the economic and social, not
just environmental, effects of federal actions on minority and low-income communities....

[C]riticism of environmental justice as too myopic and a diversion of scarce resources away from other more important social and public health problems is not well-
founded. Most often, environmental justice efforts do not wastefully divert a community's attention but instead bring residents together to focus on a broad array of social
justice problems.... [G]overnment officials and firms seeking community acceptance
for environmentally risky projects must as a practical, if not also moral, matter consider
whether social justice is served by their projects. For if the environmental and other social burdens of a proposed project are imposed on the local community while the economic and other benefits flow elsewhere, "community opposition will be fierce and the
chances for success lessened."...

* * *

The following article presents various models of fairness in one important area of
environmental justice, the siting of local unwanted land uses [LULUs].

# Vicki Been,
# What's Fairness Got to Do With It? Environmental Justice and the Siting of Locally Undesirable Land Uses
### 78 Cornell Law Review 1001 (1993)

The various legislative solutions to the problem of disproportionate siting reflect different conceptions about why disproportionate siting is wrong, and about what would constitute "fair" siting. The differences are not surprising. Calls for environmental justice are essentially calls for "equality" and, as Peter Westen has noted, "equality in the end is a rhetorical device that tends to persuade precisely by virtue of 'cloak[ing] strongly divergent ideas over which people do in fact disagree.'" Advocates of environmental justice have wisely chosen to advance general concepts of equality, rather than endanger their coalition by attempting to specify the precise content of "justice," "equity" or "fairness."...

### Fairness in the Pattern of Distribution

A broad conception of fairness in siting would require that a LULU's burdens be spread on a per capita or proportional basis over society as a whole....

There are strong and weak versions of the equal division conception of fairness. Under the strong version, fairness demands a proportional distribution of benefits....

A weaker version of the theory asserts that fairness requires a proportional distribution of burdens, even if benefits are not allocated proportionally. The United States embraces this view regarding societal burdens, such as jury duty and military service under a draft. This version of the theory assumes that an objective distinction can be drawn between burdens and the absence of benefits, and that the distinction mandates an equal division of burdens regardless of the distribution of benefits....

Several means of distribution are plausible under the proportional distribution of burden theory. One scheme would impose a *physical* proportional distribution: LULUs themselves would be distributed equally among neighborhoods. This distribution could be either equal *ex post* or equal *ex ante*. In an *ex post* scheme, the facilities and the harms that they pose would be distributed proportionately among neighborhoods. For example, if New York City requires facilities for 10,000 homeless individuals and has 100 neighborhoods, all holding some land suitable for a facility, each neighborhood would receive one facility housing 100 individuals. In an *ex ante* scheme, each neighborhood has an equal chance of being selected for the site through a lottery process. For example, if New York City requires a sewage sludge treatment plant, each of the 100 neighborhoods would have a 1/100 chance of being selected for the site. The *ex ante* physical distribution scheme is particularly well-suited to situations in which there are economies of scale in building and operating fewer but larger LULUs. Some types of hazardous waste, for example, are stored most efficiently in large, centralized facilities....

Instead of either *ex ante* or *ex post* physical equality, a distribution might seek "compensated" equality. In this distribution scheme, all individuals or communities that gain a net benefit from a particular LULU must compensate those who suffer a net loss. For example, if a sludge treatment plant imposed costs upon a neighborhood, each of the neighborhoods that benefitted from the plant, but did not suffer the detriment of close proximity, would have to pay a proportionate share of the costs....

Both the *ex ante* and *ex post* mechanisms for physically distributing LULU burdens face significant problems of definition and measurement....

First, what criteria should be used to compare the burdens of the LULUs to be distributed? Depending upon the basis of comparison, even the same type of facility may impose different types or levels of burden upon various communities. Two neighborhoods hosting identical hazardous waste treatment plants, for example, might bear different burdens if the basis of comparison is health risk, because the geology or transportation networks or composition of the workforce of one area could make one plant somewhat riskier than the other. Some criteria, such as health risk or loss in property value, are obvious grounds for comparison. But others, such as psychological harms or interference with social networks, are controversial.

When the LULUs being compared are different, such as a prison and a sludge treatment plant, comparisons will require agreement on how different criteria are to be weighted or reduced to some common metric such as dollar loss. Whether and how to translate burdens such as health risks to monetary terms is also a controversial issue....

Although environmental justice advocates have not been specific about the grounds for their assertion that compensation schemes are immoral, several arguments could be offered. One argument against compensation schemes would focus on the immorality of commodifying certain matters involving life, health and safety, or human dignity....

An additional argument could assert that compensation schemes take unfair advantage of the existing unequal distribution of wealth....When a community suffers severe disadvantage from existing inequalities of wealth, the voluntariness of its agreement to host the LULU is questionable....

Compensatory schemes face a variety of pragmatic hurdles. The most important hurdle is the difficulty of translating the risks of a LULU into monetary terms. As a first step, the proponents of the facility, regulators, and those affected by the facility must reach some consensus about the probability and expected consequences of the hazards posed by the facility....

Compensation mechanisms also raise difficult questions about who should receive compensation: residents, property owners, the neighborhood itself, or some combination of the three. Residents would claim that they bear the most immediate risk and injury. Landlords, however, would assert that they absorb at least some, if not all, of the tenants' damages through lower rents. Moreover, if residents received compensation, the rights of future residents would have to be considered because they undoubtedly would bear part of the risks. For residents who benefit from the LULU (by obtaining employment at the facility, for example) difficult questions will arise about whether those benefits sufficiently offset any damages that those residents also incur. Additionally, compensation paid to the neighborhood itself would raise questions about how to define the affected neighborhood and whether to spend the money to mitigate the harms caused to individual residents....

One could argue that a fair distribution of LULUs would require advantaged neighborhoods to bear more of the burden that LULUs impose than poor and minority neighborhoods. Such a distribution could involve either a physical siting scheme in which advantaged neighborhoods receive a disproportionately greater number of LULUs or a compensated siting scheme in which advantaged neighborhoods pay a greater share of the cost of LULUs. One rationale for such "progressive" siting would be compensatory justice: advantaged neighborhoods should bear more of the LULU burden in order to redress or remedy past discrimination against poor and minority neighborhoods....

*Fairness As Cost-Internalization*

Many environmental justice advocates argue that fairness requires those who benefit from LULUs to bear the cost of the LULUs. Forcing the internalization of costs leads to greater fairness in two ways. First, it is fairer to hold individuals responsible for their actions than to let costs fall on innocent bystanders. Second, forcing the internalization of costs results in greater efficiency, and greater efficiency is likely to mean fewer LULUs. Purchasers of products that generate waste will reduce consumption once the prices of the products reflect the true cost of waste facilities. In turn, producers will develop more efficient means of production, given the cost of disposing the waste generated. The number of LULUs will thereby decrease to the socially optimal level—the level at which the marginal utility of the product necessitating the LULU equals its costs.

Such a "user pays" approach is not always possible because it requires a precise matching of benefit and burden. Additionally, some LULUs, such as homeless shelters, result more directly from political decisions about how to allocate society's resources than from personal consumption choices. In those circumstances, fairness as cost-internalization requires that the burdens be spread throughout society, so that all are forced to confront the costs of society's choices and to make better decisions....

The practical problems of calculating the full costs of a LULU and determining who should receive compensation also remain. The problem of ensuring that all costs are accounted for is especially troubling. Compensation set at a negotiated level, for example, would undermine the goal of full internalization unless negotiations were carefully structured to ensure that the community did not settle for insufficient compensation.... [T]he process by which the community negotiates a compensation package may undervalue the interests of a particular subgroup within the community. Protecting against such bargaining failures would be costly and difficult....

*Fairness as Process*

Rather than focusing on the distribution of burdens to determine whether the siting process is equitable, the fairness as process theory focuses on the procedures by which the burden is distributed. The most obvious theory of fairness as process would assert that a distribution is fair as long as it results from a process that was agreed upon in advance by all those potentially affected. Although there are examples of interstate siting compacts and regional intrastate siting agreements, in which all participants voluntarily agree to a particular siting process, most LULUs are sited in communities that had no opportunity to remove themselves from the selection process. Therefore, this Section focuses on theories of fairness as process that do not rest upon voluntary agreement for their legitimacy....

A siting decision motivated by hostility toward people of a particular race is unfair under almost any theory of justice, and would not be considered fair under the Constitution. Under the intentional discrimination theory, fairness requires that a decision to site a LULU be made without any intent to disadvantage people of color.

The first problem with an intentional discrimination theory is the difficulty of proving intent. Many in the environmental justice movement charge that developers and siting officials "deliberate[ly] target[] people of color communities for toxic waste facilities." Siting opponents have yet to prove that charge to the satisfaction of a court. Their efforts have been stymied, in part, by the general difficulty of proving the intent of a legislative or administrative body. That difficulty is compounded in the siting context because siting choices tend to involve a series of decisions by a variety of multi-member entities....

Even if discrimination is unintentional or based upon characteristics that do not trigger strict scrutiny under the Equal Protection Clause, disproportionate siting arguably would be inappropriate if it stemmed from a siting process that failed to treat people with "equal concern and respect," instead valuing certain people less than others. Under this theory, if a siting process is more attentive to the interests of wealthier or white neighborhoods than to the interests of poor or minority neighborhoods, that process illegitimately treats the poor and people of color as unequal. . . .

The notion that fair siting requires treating all potential host communities as equals is extremely difficult to implement on a practical level. The most plausible way to ensure that decision makers accord equal concern to all communities is through an "impact statement" requirement. This would require decision makers to consider all of the effects that a siting might have on a neighborhood, including its impact on health, the environment, and the neighborhood's quality of life. Theoretically, by forcing decision makers to examine the possible effects of a siting, the process would ensure that the decision reflects equal consideration for both communities. In reality, impact statements may give only the illusion of neutrality in their analysis of a facility's potential effects. Further, decisionmakers required to think about such effects may give only the illusion of consideration. . . .

Like several other theories of fairness, the treatment as equals theory rests on the problematic premise that the costs and benefits that a LULU imposes upon communities are measurable, and that different costs and benefits can be reduced to a common metric. Even if that premise were true, impact statements detailing the potential effects of a siting still would not necessarily show equal concern for the interests of the poor and minorities. . . .

* * *

## Notes and Questions

1. The different models of fairness outlined by Professor Been can be summarized as follows: (1) even apportionment of LULUs among all neighborhoods; (2) compensation of communities hosting LULUS by other communities; (3) progressive siting—wealthier neighborhoods receive more LULUs; (4) cost internalization—those who benefit bear the cost; (5) the siting process involves no intentional discrimination; (6) the siting process shows "equal concern and respect" for all neighborhoods and (7) [not included in the above excerpt] all communities receive an equal number of vetoes that can be used to exclude a LULU. What model of "fairness" do you favor?

In the following excerpt, Christopher Foreman critiques the environmental justice movement. In his remarks, does he reveal a preference for any particular conception of justice?

# Christopher H. Foreman, Jr.,
# The Promise and Peril of Environmental Justice
### 64–67, 115–121 (1998)

Reducing and avoiding threats to health is a major, but often unproductive, theme of environmental justice advocacy. When activists call attention to alleged unfair environmental burdens, surreptitious mass poisoning is a primary (if sometimes implicit) fear. After all, why care about an inequity unless it makes a difference? And isn't the difference between life and death the biggest difference of all? Given the vehemently articulated community health anxieties evident in countless public forums, including the National Environmental Justice Advisory Council (NEJAC), one might mistakenly conclude that health is the main, or even sole, focus of environmental justice activism.

[P]olicymakers and activists alike have tended to concentrate on questions and mechanisms of community involvement, not community health. This is not surprising. One reason for this focus is that activists and policymakers alike possess a far better understanding of procedural inclusion, and of the tools that seem useful for producing it, than they do of ways to reduce risk and enhance health.... For activists, involvement offers outlets for advocacy, opportunities for dialogue and the casting of blame, and the promise of institutional accountability. Resourceful and well-timed advocacy may even lead to significant material benefits for a community. On the other hand, involvement mechanisms allow policymakers to exhibit responsiveness and deflect criticism. By comparison, channeling health anxieties effectively toward risk reductions and improved health prospects among low-income and minority persons is far more difficult.

It is not hard to understand why activists are inclined to think that what they do generally promotes healthy communities. An ability to exercise power, as when a neighborhood effectively mobilizes to block visible sources of perceived additional risk, strongly implies a protective capacity. People commonly attribute harm to things they intensely dislike or fear, such as dumps and pollution. While both can certainly cause harm, so can many other things not nearly so fearsome. Moreover, fighting polluters clearly requires collective action or governmental intervention; rugged individualism cannot suffice.... Finally, health, wealth, and political efficacy are clearly correlated; no one would deny that wealthy persons extract better health care, healthier surroundings, and greater overall solicitude from politicians than poor persons.

For these reasons it may appear obvious that successfully exercising power over environmental questions where health concerns have been raised is in fact to protect health.... But the victory may actually be hollow or insignificant, for the connection between successful activism and the advancement of public health is much less straightforward than it might appear. In fact environmental justice advocacy and policymaking might subtly impede efforts to improve and protect health among precisely those persons or advocates and policymakers desire to help. This can occur if mechanisms of mobilization and involvement draw citizen concern and protective effort away from important sources of risk (to less important sources) and away from preventable adverse effects (to unpreventable or unsubstantiated ones). Citizen energies thus displaced may complicate the task policymakers must face in allocating scarce resources to their most productive use....

The [environmental justice] movement's obsession with disproportionate adverse impact may obscure more important questions relating to the absolute size, scope and source of such impacts. Second, environmental justice proponents generally eschew personal behavior (and necessary changes in it) as a primary variable in the health of low-income and minority communities. Third, from among the vast array of issues raised to date under the environmental justice rubric, adherents have been incapable of fashioning a coherent agenda of substantive public health priorities. Instead the movement is drawn to an overall procedural priority of citizen involvement, an orientation that unrealistically envisions every issue as a substantive priority.

These limitations exist largely because environmental justice is not mainly a public health movement. It is instead a loose coalition of citizens and groups advocating greater grassroots democracy, usually with an eye fixed on broader social justice goals. Because its primary political aims are to bind residents together, to raise their collective profile in policy debates and decision-making, and to reallocate society's resources, environmental justice activism can ill afford an agenda driven solely by health impacts....

Hazards perceived to be imposed on residents by firms-especially by ones viewed as community intruders-or by governmental actors suspected of being distant, unaccountable, or racist are more suitable for this purpose. Under such circumstances, anger and suspicion easily overwhelm risk and health as driving forces. Hazards linked strongly to individual behavior (such as smoking and excessive alcohol consumption) generally have far larger implications for personal and collective health but do not easily resonate politically.... [R]eminding residents that they consume too many calories, or the wrong kinds of food, is likely to appear intrusive, insensitive, or simply beside the point.

Once their underlying democratizing aims are clearly understood it is not hard to make sense of the insistent emphasis by environmental justice activists and by grassroots environmentalists generally on relatively unlikely or weakly documented—but nevertheless profoundly fear-inducing—hazards, such as dioxin and Superfund sites. This democratizing imperative accounts for the deference regularly accorded intuitive (as opposed to scientific) perceptions of risk, as illustrated by the enduring folk myth of a so-called cancer alley in Louisiana.... Anemic mobilizing capacity (that is, low usefulness for generating collective outrage) helps explain why many well-established health hazards, including tobacco use, find no place in the litany of environmental justice concerns.

The political imperatives of the movement also explain why environmental justice lacks substantive health priorities. Real priorities would mean downgrading the concerns of at least some movement constituents, creating the great likelihood of conflict.... [Thus, environmental justice advocates] primarily advance general concepts of equality, not wishing to endanger their coalition by specifying the precise methods of achieving "justice," "fairness," or "equity." The egalitarian position that everyone should be heard and that no one should suffer maintains movement harmony, but at the cost of focus....

### Conceptual Drawbacks of Environmental Justice

From a rationalizing perspective, a major problem with the environmental justice version of the democratizing critique is that, like ecopopulism more generally, it threatens to worsen the problem of environmental policy's mission priorities. As Walter Rosenbaum elaborates:

> Like the man who mounted his horse and galloped off in all directions, the EPA has no constant course. With responsibility for administering nine separate statutes and parts of four others, the EPA has no clearly mandated priorities, no way of allocating scarce resources among different statutes or among programs within a single law....

Environmental justice inevitably enlarges this challenge of missing priorities, and for similar reasons. As noted earlier, the movement is a delicate coalition of local and ethnic concerns unable to narrow its grievances for fear of a similar "political bloodletting."... Real priority-setting runs contrary to radical egalitarian value premises and no one (perhaps least of all a strong democratizer) wants to be deemed a victimizer.

Therefore movement rhetoric argues that *no* community should be harmed and that *all* community concerns and grievances deserve redress. Scholar-activist Robert Bullard proposes that "the solution to unequal protection lies in the realm of environmental justice for all Americans. No community, rich or poor, black or white, should be allowed to become a 'sacrifice zone.'" When pressed about the need for environmental risk priorities, and about how to incorporate environmental justice into priority setting, Bullard's answer is a vague plea for nondiscrimination, along with a barely more specific call for a "federal 'fair environmental protection act'" that would transform "protection from a privilege to a right."

Bullard's position is fanciful and self-contradictory, but extremely telling. He argues essentially that the way to establish environmental priorities is precisely by guaranteeing that such priorities are impossible to implement. This is symptomatic of a movement for which untrammeled citizen voice and overall social equity are cardinal values. Bullard's position also epitomizes the desire of movement intellectuals to avoid speaking difficult truths (at least in public) to their allies and constituents.

Ironically, in matters of health and risk, environmental justice poses a potentially serious, if generally unrecognized, danger to the minority and low-income communities it aspires to help. By discouraging citizens from thinking in terms of health and risk priorities... environmental justice can deflect attention from serious hazards to less serious or perhaps trivial ones....

From a health perspective, the [environmental justice] model's most serious drawback may be subtle opportunity costs. If one accepts that citizens inherently have limited time and energy to devote to their health, attention to distant or relatively minor health risks—however politically compelling—very likely means less attention for some more substantive health problems. And if one accepts that low-income citizens, in particular, have even fewer resources, and greater vulnerabilities, than more affluent citizens, then a focus on relatively low or unlikely risks could have a particularly insidious effect.

More frequent resort to a rationalizing, if not solely economic, perspective would encourage minority and low-income citizens and community leaders to think more carefully about priority-setting and myriad tradeoffs. Might widespread successes of NIMBY (not in my back yard) initiatives keep older and dirtier pollution sources active *longer* and thus adversely affect minority and low-income persons living adjacent to those sources? By the same token, does local insistence on full treatment at some Superfund sites (that is, the obsession with [Justice Stephen] Breyer's "last ten percent" [raised in his 1993 book, The Vicious Circle: Toward Effective Risk Regulation] mean that risks elsewhere might have been addressed under a more limited or flexible regime will not get attended to at all?...

If conventional environmental justice advocacy cannot confront risk magnitudes honestly, it cannot help much in the assessment and management of tradeoffs, either of the risk/risk or risk/benefit varieties. The notion that attacking some risks may create others is largely foreign to environmental justice—beyond a fear that attacking the risk of poverty with industrial jobs may expose workers to hazardous conditions. A focus on community inclusion, although necessary to the ultimate acceptability of decisions, offers no automatic or painless way to sort through tradeoffs.

When confronted with choices posing both risks and benefits—such as a proposed hazardous waste treatment facility that would create jobs, and impose relatively low risks, in a needy area—environmental justice offers, along with disgust that such horrendous choices exist, mainly community engagement and participation. But because such situations tend to stimulate multiple (and often harshly raised) local voices on *both* sides of the issue, activists are at pains to decide where (besides additional participation and deliberation) the community's interest lies. Because an activist group will be in close touch with both the fear of toxics and the hunger for economic opportunity, the organization itself may be torn. The locally one-sided issue presents far preferable terrain for activists. It should surprise no one that activists are anxious to deemphasize community-level disagreement of this sort. Nor is it surprising to learn from the head of a prominent environmental justice organization that her group tries to avoid situations that pose precisely these locally polarizing tradeoffs....

A further problem pervading environmental justice discourse is that some analysts insist on viewing the issue primarily through the prism of race, as environmental *racism*, and this is probably a misplaced focus. Although Clinton's Executive Order 12898 presents environmental justice in terms of both race and class, many movement partisans unhesitatingly assign race a dominant causal role leading to unfair outcomes. Environmental historian Martin Melosi explains this insistence on a starkly racial analysis:

> The core view that race is at the heart of environmental injustice is borne of an intellectual and emotional attachment to the civil rights heritage of the past several decades. Few would deny—including the EPA—that poor people of color are *often* disproportionately impacted by *some* forms of pollution. But the qualifiers are significant. Outside the movement, there has been serious questioning: Is the issue really environmental racism or just poverty? Even within the movement there are those who cannot cleanly separate race and class in all cases.

One additional, and especially disturbing, potential pitfall stems from an unwarranted focus on race as a dominant cause. Such analyses may encourage the dishearteningly alienated frame of mind that leads substantial numbers of African Americans to embrace racial conspiracy explanations. If people of color have been deliberately targeted for environmental poisons, then it stands to reason that they were "set up" for AIDS and crack cocaine and other evils as well. Conversely, this conspiracy mindset doubtless contributes to the grassroots appeal of environmental racism rhetoric. America's legacy of slavery, segregation, and racism (epitomized in the health arena by the infamous Tuskegee syphilis study) has nurtured an understandable inclination among many African Americans to believe the worst of the system....

* * *

## Notes and Questions

1. As Professor Kuehn noted, a prominent criticism of the environmental justice movement is that the terms "justice" and "fairness" are too vague to translate into coherent environmental policy. Do you agree? Can you think of other instances in environmental regulation where broad, aspirational concepts generate regulatory and legislative initiatives? In your view, what would be the best way to incorporate environmental justice goals into environmental policy and implementation?

2. From a taxonomic perspective, how would you categorize each of the principles of environmental justice that are set forth in the next section? Does it matter whether any given claim is based upon distributive, procedural, corrective or social justice? Do some categories of justice naturally lend themselves to more successful regulatory reform efforts? If so, why? Given the principle that impacted communities should speak for themselves, is it appropriate for academics to attempt to situate environmental justice claims within broader theoretical frameworks? Why or why not?

3. The criticisms made by Foreman are premised upon three main assertions: (a) environmental justice advocates focus too much on involuntary (public) risks and not enough on voluntary (behavioral) risks; (b) environmental justice advocates refuse to prioritize risks; (c) environmental justice advocates focus too much on procedural reforms. How would you evaluate the criticisms made by Foreman? Are his criticisms premised upon a lack of theoretical consistency or political viability? Does it matter? If premised upon political viability—and assuming Foreman's empirical observations are correct—might there be good strategic reasons why advocates focus on public risks and procedural reforms while refusing to engage in a debate about priorities and tradeoffs? How would you evaluate the "opportunity costs" born by adopting environmental justice strategies as described by Foreman? In other words, if environmental justice advocates were to change their focus in response to Foreman's criticisms, how would you predict their chances of success?

Just as Foreman criticized the work of various scholars and researchers, Foreman has been subsequently criticized for his failure to acknowledge studies with better methodology that supported the (criticized) seminal studies of environmental inequities, his failure to acknowledge the work of environmental justice scholars who advocate reform (rather than abolition) of risk assessment, and his "indulging in a superficial psychological deconstruction of the movement." Alan Ramo, *Book Review, The Promise and Peril of Environmental Justice*, 40 Santa Clara L. Rev. 941, 942 (2000). *See also* David Lewis Feldman, L. & Pol. Book Rev. 2, 66–69 (Feb. 1999) (acknowledging Foreman's contribution but questioning his reliance on risk-based studies that are inconclusive and also noting that use of the emotion-packed rhetoric with which activists have been attributed is commonly heard among a wide range of stakeholders).

4. In thinking about the work of the writers excerpted in this introductory chapter, do you believe in the possibility of an "objective," "neutral" or "value-free" analyses of environmental justice, or are all analyses necessarily colored by the ideological perspective of the author?

5. As you proceed to consider the various environmental justice campaigns that are described throughout this book and the writings on various subjects, bear in mind the fundamental theoretical questions posed by the foregoing discussion of what it means, within the context of environmental protection, to be "fair and just."

# C. "We Speak for Ourselves"

Environmental justice advocates have long observed that environmental laws have not prevented disproportionate environmental harms from occurring. The reasons for this are examined in Chapter II. With few exceptions, environmental regulation focuses on improving overall ambient environmental conditions, and does not consider the distributional consequences of where pollution is occurring. Therefore, the relationship between environmental justice activists and conventional environmental organizations, industry and government stakeholders has been influenced both by suspicion as well as the pragmatic need to work collaboratively to address serious problems. The wariness felt by environmental justice leaders toward environmental regulators, environmental law and mainstream environmental organizations is reflected in a 1990 letter sent by environmental justice activists to the leaders of the ten largest environmental organizations. In addition, many activists were concerned that business interests, academics and others were misinterpreting their positions. Thus, in 1991 environmental justice activists gathered in a historic summit and proposed a set of principles to guide their efforts and clearly state their positions. A decade later, a group of activists again sent a letter, this time to President George W. Bush. These writings reflect the strongly held view by many activists, a view that people living in heavily impacted communities, who are on the forefront of political campaigns, "speak for themselves."

# Letter, Circa Earth Day 1990

March 16, 1990

Addressed individually to Jay Hair, National Wildlife Federation; Michael Fisher and others from the Sierra Club; Federick Sutherland, Sierra Club Legal Defense Fund; Peter Berle and others from the National Audubon Society; Federick Krupp, Environmental Defense Fund; Mike Clark, Environmental Policy Institute/Friends of the Earth; Lack Lorenz and others, Izaak Walton League; George Frampton and others from the Wilderness Society; Paul Pritchard, National Parks and Conservation Association; John Adams, Natural Resources Defense Council:

Dear [Representative]:

We are writing this letter in the belief that through dialogue and mutual strategizing we can create a global environmental movement that protects us all.

We are artists, writers, academics, students, activists, representatives of churches, unions, and community organizations writing you to express our concerns about the role of your organization and other national environmental groups in communities of people of color in the Southwest.

For centuries, people of color in our region have been subjected to racist and genocidal practices including the theft of lands and water, the murder of innocent people, and degradation of our environment. Mining companies extract minerals leaving economically depressed communities and poisoned soil and water. The U.S. military takes lands for weapons production, testing and storage, contaminating surrounding communities and placing minority workers in the most highly radioactive and toxic worksites. Industrial and municipal dumps are intentionally placed in communities of color, disrupting our cultural lifestyle and threatening our communities' futures. Workers in the fields are dying and babies are born disfigured as a result of pesticide spraying.

Although environmental organizations calling themselves the "Group of Ten" often claim to represent our interests, in observing your activities it has become clear to us that your organizations play an equal role in the disruption of our communities. There is a clear lack of accountability by the Group of Ten environmental organizations towards Third World communities in the Southwest, in the United States as a whole, and internationally.

Your organizations continue to support and promote policies which emphasize the clean-up and preservation of the environment on the backs of working people in general and people of color in particular. In the name of eliminating environmental hazards at any cost, across the country industrial and other economic activities which employ us are being shut down, curtailed or prevented while our survival needs and cultures are ignored. We suffer from the end results of these actions, but are never full participants in the decision-making which leads to them.

[Selected examples from the letter follow. Eds]:

- Organizations such as the National Wildlife Federation have been involved in exchanges where Third World countries will sign over lands (debt-for-nature swaps) to conservation groups in exchange for creditors agreeing to erase a portion of that country's debt. In other cases the debt is purchased at reduced rates; the creditors can then write it off. This not only raises the specter of conservation groups now being "creditors" to Third World countries, but legitimizes the debt itself through the further expropriation of Third World resources. The question arises whether such deals are in the long term economic interests of both the countries involved and of the people living on the land.

- The lack of people of color in decision-making positions in your organizations such as executive staff and board positions is also reflective of your histories of racist and exclusionary practices. Racism is a root cause of your inaction around addressing environmental problems in our communities.

- Group of Ten organizations are being supported by corporations such as ARCO, British Petroleum, Chemical Bank, GTE, General Electric, Dupont, Dow Chemical, Exxon, IBM, Coca Cola, and Waste Management, Incorporated. Several of these companies are known polluters whose disregard for the safety and well-being of workers has resulted in the deaths of many people of color. It is impossible for you to represent us in issues of our own survival when you are accountable to these interests. Such accountability leads you to pursue a corporate strategy towards the resolution of the environmental crisis, when what is needed is a *people's strategy* which fully involves those who have historically been without power in this society.

Comments have been made by representatives of major national environmental organizations to the effect that only in the recent past have people of color begun to realize the impacts of environmental contamination. We have been involved in environmental struggles for many years and we have not needed the Group of Ten environmental organizations to tell us that these problems have existed.

We again call upon you to cease operations in communities of color within 60 days, until you have hired leaders from those communities to the extent that they make up between 35–40 percent of your entire staff. We are asking that Third World leaders be hired at all levels of your operations....

Sincerely,

/S/ 117 signatures of organizations and individuals.

\* \* \*

# Principles of Environmental Justice, Proceedings, The First National People of Color Environmental Leadership Summit
### xiii (October 24–27, 1992)

WE THE PEOPLE OF COLOR, gathered together at this multinational *People of Color Environmental Leadership Summit*, to begin to build a national and international movement of all peoples of color to fight the destruction and taking of our lands and communities, do hereby re-establish our spiritual interdependence to the sacredness of our Mother Earth; to respect and celebrate each of our cultures, languages and beliefs about the natural world and our roles in healing ourselves; to insure environmental justice; to promote economic alternatives which would contribute to the development of environmentally safe livelihoods; and, to secure our political, economic and cultural liberation that has been denied for over 500 years of colonization and oppression, resulting in the poisoning of our communities and land and the genocide of our peoples, do affirm and adopt these Principles of Environmental Justice:

1. Environmental justice affirms the sacredness of Mother Earth, ecological unity and the interdependence of all species, and the right to be free from ecological destruction.

2. Environmental justice demands that public policy be based on mutual respect and justice for all peoples, free from any form of discrimination or bias.

3. Environmental justice mandates the right to ethical, balanced and responsible uses of land and renewable resources in the interest of a sustainable planet for humans and other living things.

4. Environmental justice calls for universal protection from nuclear testing, extraction, production and disposal of toxic/hazardous wastes and poisons and nuclear testing that threaten the fundamental right to clean air, land, water and food.

5. Environmental justice affirms the fundamental right to political, economic, cultural and environmental self-determination of all peoples.

6. Environmental justice demands the cessation of the production of all toxins, hazardous wastes, and radioactive materials, and that all past and current producers be held strictly accountable to the people for detoxification and the containment at the point of production.

7. Environmental justice demands the right to participate as equal partners at every level of decision-making including needs assessment, planning, implementation, enforcement and evaluation.

8. Environmental justice affirms the right of all workers to a safe and healthy work environment, without being forced to choose between an unsafe livelihood and unemployment. It also affirms the right of those who work at home to be free from environmental hazards.

9. Environmental justice protects the right of victims of environmental injustice to receive full compensation and reparations for damages as well as quality health care.

10. Environmental justice considers governmental acts of environmental injustice a violation of international law, the Universal Declaration On Human Rights, and the United Nations Convention on Genocide.

11. Environmental justice must recognize a special legal and natural relationship of Native Peoples to the U.S. government through treaties, agreements, compacts, and covenants affirming sovereignty and self-determination.

12. Environmental justice affirms the need for urban and rural ecological policies to clean up and rebuild our cities and rural areas in balance with nature, honoring the cultural integrity of all our communities, and providing fair access for all to the full range of resources.

13. Environmental justice calls for the strict enforcement of principles of informed consent, and a halt to the testing of experimental reproductive and medical procedures and vaccinations on people of color.

14. Environmental justice opposes the destructive operations of multinational corporations.

15. Environmental justice opposes military occupation, repression and exploitation of lands, peoples and cultures, and other life forms.

16. Environmental justice calls for the education of present and future generations which emphasizes social and environmental issues, based on our experience and an appreciation of our diverse cultural perspectives.

17. Environmental justice requires that we, as individuals, make personal and consumer choices to consume as little of Mother Earth's resources and to produce as little waste as possible; and make the conscious decision to challenge and reprioritize our lifestyles to insure the health of the natural world for present and future generations.

Adopted today, October 24, 1991, in Washington, D.C.

\* \* \*

# Letter, Circa Earth Day 2001

April 19, 2001

George W. Bush
President of the United States of America
The White House
1600 Pennsylvania Avenue NW
Washington, DC 20500
USA

Dear Mr. President,

We are writing you today to express our profound concern with your new climate change policies with respect to their impacts on poor people and people of color in the United States and around the world.

It is our firmly held belief that climate change is not only an ecological, economic or political question, but it is a moral issue with profound ramifications for all of the inhabitants of this planet Earth. It is a question of environmental justice and human rights. It is also an issue of equity between nations.

Particularly hard hit will be low-lying countries like Bangladesh and small island states whose very existence is threatened. The poor here in the United States—especially poor people of color—will also bear the brunt of climate change. Your policies will only intensify those impacts.

Given its potentially profound ramifications, climate change must be tackled with serious and vigorous leadership and international cooperation rather than a misguided isolationist approach that protects a handful of powerful fossil fuel corporations.

The United States, whose four percent of the world's population generates one-quarter of all man made carbon dioxide—the leading global warming gas—must take the lead in reversing its role as the main contributor to this looming global crisis.

Certainly, your predecessor's climate change policies came up well short of the measures we believe are necessary to address the problem. But your administration's response so far—your failure to follow through on campaign promises to reduce carbon dioxide emissions and your abandonment of the Kyoto Protocol—borders on nothing short of gross global negligence.

Your negation of the increasingly irrefutable scientific evidence on climate change is distressing. It is no longer a question of whether sea levels will rise, but rather of how many coastlines, people, communities, and entire island nations will be submerged.

Global warming is starting to make itself felt. The 1990s was the warmest decade and 1998 was the warmest year on record. The icecap atop Mount Kilimanjaro in Africa is melting away and will completely disappear in less than 15 years. It is an abuse of power to turn your back on this, the most serious environmental issue ever to confront humanity.

If it is not halted, climate change will probably result in increased frequency and severity of storms, floods and drought. And it will cause the spread of diseases, such as malaria. It will increase hunger and bring about displacement and mass migrations of people with ensuing social conflict.

Mr. President, you claim that you don't want to harm the American consumer, yet you're setting us all up to pay a huge price in the future. This is especially true for the poor. Earlier this year, the United Nations Intergovernmental Panel on Climate Change (IPCC) concluded that the impacts of global warming "are expected to fall disproportionately on the poor."

People who are highly dependent on farming, fishing or forestry, especially indigenous people, are most likely to see their livelihoods destroyed by climate change. Meanwhile, the urban poor—mostly people of color in the U.S.—will be most vulnerable to climate change-related heat waves, diseases and respiratory ailments.

Many of us come from or work with communities that are already directly affected by the oil industry. These are communities and workers that are suffering the social and environmental effects of oil exploration, production, transportation, refining, distribution and combustion. These communities are also some of those who will be hardest hit by climate change—whether they are in Nigeria's Niger Delta, in Arctic Village Alaska, or in Louisiana's "cancer alley." These communities face a "double whammy" suffering oil's acute toxic impacts first and then its long-term effects in the form of the harsh hand of global warming.

Rather than cater to the socially and ecologically destructive oil industry, Mr. President, you should severely curb U.S. carbon emissions and support the Kyoto Protocol. At home you should also support a just transition for fossil fuel industry workers and fenceline communities while investing the United States' resources in energy efficiency and renewable energy resources, such as solar, wind and biomass.

Mr. President, we urge you to reconsider your position on climate change before the United States becomes universally known as an environmental rogue state, and you go down in history as G.W. Bush, the Global Warming President.

Sincerely,

/S/ Nnimmo Bassey, Oilwatch Africa; Ricardo Carrere, World Rainforest Movement, Uruguay; Chee Yoke Ling, Third World Network, Malaysia; Oronto Douglas, Environmental Rights Action/Friends of the Earth, Nigeria; Tom Goldtooth, Indigenous Environmental Network, U.S.; Sarah James, Gwich'in Steering Committee, U.S.; Esperanza Martinez, Oilwatch International, Ecuador; Richard Moore, Southwest Network for Environmental and Economic Justice, U.S.; Ricardo Navarro, CESTA/Friends of the Earth, El Salvador; S. Bobby Peek, GroundWork, South Africa; Amit Srivastava/Joshua Karliner, CorpWatch, U.S.; Connie Tucker, Southern Organizing Committee for Economic and Social Justice, U.S.; Dr. Owens Wiwa, African Environmental and Human Development Agency, Nigeria

Cc: Christie Todd Whitman, Administrator, U.S. Environmental Protection Agency

Endorsed by: /S/ Tom Athanasiou, EcoEquity, U.S.; Dr. Lilian Corra, Asociacion Argentina de Medicos por el Medio Ambiente, Argentina; John Harrington, Harrington Investments, Inc., U.S.; Allan Hunt-Badiner, Rainforest Action Network, U.S.; Daniel Kammen, University of California, Berkeley, U.S.; Ansje Miller, Redefining Progress, U.S.; Aaron Rappaport, Ph.D., American Lands Alliance, U.S.; Satinath Sarangi, Bhopal Group for Information and Action, India; Karla Schoeters, Climate Network Europe, Belgium; Richard Sherman, Earthlife Africa, South Africa; Jon Sohn, Friends of the Earth, U.S.

\* \* \*

## Notes and Questions

1. The writing of environmental justice activists is both aspirational and hard-hitting. To many, it strikes a dissonant chord with the brand of technical jargon used both by regulators and academics, perhaps intentionally so. What are the implications of a "bottom up" perspective for addressing environmental problems in fora that is dominated by formal professionalization? As you consider the various strategies—legal and technical—to reduce environmental disparities, consider which of them are better equipped to work with and utilize a grassroots perspective. Also consider which strategies are likely to build capacity within impacted communities to continue to ward off environmental assaults after the campaign at issue has concluded.

2. Some people believe that environmental policies to protect communities of color and low income communities from environmental hazards are needed, but many environmental justice advocates resist top-down government approaches, noting that the decisions of scientists, bureaucrats, lawyers, and judges are often paternalistic and disempower them. Is there an inherent tension between the movement's process-oriented goals of having greater voice and power, and the movement's morality-based goals of eliminating risk of environmental harm altogether? In other words, is it possible that greater participation would not lead to the policies environmental justice activists desire, and that the adoption of regulatory policies that environmental justice advocates desire would not lead to improved empowerment of these communities?

# Chapter II

# Theories of Causation

## A. Introduction

What is responsible for the disproportionate distribution of environmental burdens and amenities that has been documented by researchers and that is discussed in detail in Chapter III? Explanatory theories offered are numerous and varied, drawing from economics, political science, urban planning, history, sociology, and other disciplines. Clearly, there are multiple, sometimes overlapping factors at work. Clearly, also, this area has been and likely will remain quite controversial, because so much rides on what the answers are. This chapter outlines some of the major theories that have been advanced to explain the prevalence of environmental inequities.

## B. Land Use Practices

In part, the current distribution of environmental hazards is the result of land use and zoning practices that started over one hundred years ago. Restrictive racial covenants, exclusionary zoning practices like density and use restrictions, urban renewal policies that displaced thousands of residents, and other land use mechanisms all contributed to residential segregation and the prevalence of unwanted land uses in low income communities and communities of color. In the following excerpt, Professor Yale Rabin describes one such long-standing zoning practice.

### Yale Rabin,
### Expulsive Zoning: The Inequitable Legacy of *Euclid*,
### *in* Zoning and the American Dream 101
#### (Charles M. Haar & Jerold S. Kayden eds., 1989)

What follows sets forth the hypothesis that zoning, in addition to its well-recognized use as an exclusionary mechanism, also has been frequently employed in ways that have undermined the character, quality, and stability of black residential areas; that zoning not only has been used to erect barriers to escape from the concentrated confinement of the inner city, it has been used to permit—even promote—the intrusion into black neighborhoods of disruptive incompatible uses that have diminished the quality and undermined the stability of those neighborhoods. For reasons explained later, I refer to this practice as *expulsive zoning....*

[T]here is evidence to suggest that expulsive zoning practices have been relatively commonplace in black residential areas. The record, while admittedly fragmentary, indicates that in the years following the [Supreme] Court's rejection of racial zoning in 1917 and continuing through the thirties, and perhaps much later, a number of cities—mainly, but not exclusively, in the South—zoned some low-income residential areas occupied mainly, but not exclusively, by blacks for industrial or commercial use. These practices were sometimes carried out even in neighborhoods of single-family detached houses, thus undermining the quality of the very types of neighborhood housing which zoning ostensibly was intended to protect. To the extent that these practices were effective—that is, to the extent that residential uses were replaced by industrial or commercial uses, residents were displaced. Therefore, the term *expulsive zoning.* Because it appears that such areas were mainly black, and because whites who may have been similarly displaced were not subject to racially determined limitations in seeking alternative housing, the adverse impacts of expulsive zoning on blacks were far more severe and included, in addition to accelerated blight, increases in overcrowding and racial segregation....

[T]hese expulsive zoning practices are entirely consistent with the more general findings of my studies: that the land-use-related policies and practices of government at all levels, but particularly the decisions and initiatives of local government, have been and continue to be instrumental influences on both the creation and perpetuation of racial segregation. Expulsive zoning, as one of these practices, does not occur as an isolated or independent action, but as one element in a web-like pattern of interacting public practices that serve to reproduce and reinforce the disadvantages of blacks. Urban renewal, public housing site selection, and code enforcement are a few of the other frequently encountered cords in the web....

### Jackson, Tennessee

The most extensive and blighting effects of expulsive zoning that I have encountered have been in Jackson, Tennessee. Here expulsive zoning has been and continues to be a fundamental influence on other land-use-related policies and actions of the city which adversely affect the welfare of black residents....

South Jackson, a section of the city which until the mid-1960s housed approximately half of the city's black population, had been zoned industrial since the city first adopted zoning in 1928. The other half of the city's black population lived in northeast Jackson, in an area surrounding all-black Lane College area. That area had been and continues to be zoned residential. Housing in the Lane College area, while modest, is, with the exception of a few scattered pockets of slum housing, sound and well maintained.

Although south Jackson is bounded along its southern edge by a number of labor-intensive, forestry and agriculture-related industries, the area itself always has been overwhelming residential. The area's residents have been the city's lowest income blacks, the housing they occupied was of poor quality and what remains has become severely blighted as a direct consequence of city policies and actions.

Since the early 1960s the city has repeatedly and publicly made clear its intentions to redevelop much of south Jackson for industrial and commercial use and since that time has halted all code enforcement and municipal improvement in the area. At the time of my first visit in 1978, two urban renewal projects were underway. One, at the southwestern edge of the city, was to provide land for industrial development, and in the other, in the center of south Jackson and adjacent to the central business district, a civic center was already under construction. By the city's own estimates, these two projects involved the displacement of approximately 940 black families including more than 2,600 people—about one-fifth of the city's black population. Between the two projects there remained an all-black-occupied public housing project and nearly 20 city blocks of black-occupied slum housing and unpaved streets....

By failing to require even minimal maintenance of housing and withholding maintenance of infrastructure, the city accelerated the deterioration of the housing in south Jackson and reduced the costs to the city of subsequent property acquisition. By failing to provide relocation resources they caused an increase in the level of racial segregation and overcrowding in the city, and prolonged the time during which south Jackson residents were subject to that area's deplorable living conditions....

*Summary and Conditions*

The adverse impacts evident in these 12 cases of expulsive zoning vary widely. They include environmentally blighting nuisances, displacement, and life threatening hazards.... [T]he evidence to date does appear to support three significant generalizations. First, illustrated most vividly by the case of Detroit, the magnitude and severity of adverse impacts are not necessarily proportional to the scale of intrusion or the extent of displacement. A single intrusive use can sometimes have disastrous effects. Second, the blighting and disruptive effects of expulsive zoning grow, rather than diminish, with the passage of time. Finally, expulsive zoning is not merely an historical remnant of a racially unenlightened past, but a current practice that continues to threaten, degrade, and destabilize black and other minority neighborhoods.

\* \* \*

# Robert Collin,
## Environmental Equity: A Law and Planning Approach to Environmental Racism
### 11 Virginia Environmental Law Journal 495 (1992)\*

Zoning is the regulation of land use to control growth and development for the health, safety and welfare of the community.... Although approaches to land use control by zoning differ greatly by state and community, in general practice, the land use control framework determines where unwanted land uses are permitted.

Many early land use practices systematically excluded people on the basis of race, though today such an exclusionary practice is illegal.... Race-based exclusionary practices, however, can take forms other than official zoning laws. For example, the enforcement of racially restrictive covenants, racially discriminatory site selection, tenant distribution procedures in public housing and the enactment of many urban renewal policies have also effectively excluded certain people from living in certain areas.

Zoning can be more than exclusionary; it can be expulsive. Expulsive zoning often designates black residential areas for industrial or commercial uses, a practice which results in the eventual displacement of blacks from these areas.... Expulsive zoning may

---

\* Reprinted by permission of the Virginia Environmental Law Journal.

have provided the original mechanism in land use law that has led to the current racially disproportionate distribution of environmentally hazardous land uses. It is possible that the roots of environmental inequity lie partially in these traditional race-based zoning practices. Before environmental regulation, many industrial and commercial facilities located in minority communities on account of zoning and may have disposed of waste either on-site or nearby because of the lower cost of doing so.

Many communities have excluded locally unwanted land uses (LULUs) from their neighborhoods by means of a well-documented process and philosophy that has been characterized as the "not-in-my-backyard" (NIMBY) syndrome. As a general proposition, a landfill is one of the most unwanted land uses, especially if that landfill will contain toxic and hazardous waste. Professor [Robert] Bullard maintains that these unwanted land uses are sited in politically and economically disenfranchised neighborhoods in a process he calls "PIBBY" or "place-in-blacks'-backyards."

As the need for new landfill sites increases, and as communities become aware of the potential hazards of landfills, the siting process becomes a decisive battleground. In general, the greater the known or suspected physical effects of an unwanted land use are, the greater the residential resistance will be. The concern over possible property devaluation deepens in communities with a higher ratio of homeowners to renters....

*Hazardous Waste Site Selection: State Supervision, Local Resistance and Private Enterprise*

Because the states are responsible for implementing the Resource Conservation and Recovery Act (RCRA) and other EPA regulations, they effectively control the siting of toxic and hazardous waste landfills. Unfortunately, state control of the siting process has not diminished the NIMBY problem. States generally take one of three broad approaches to site selection: super review; site designation; or local control.

Under the super review approach, the developer of the hazardous waste facility selects a possible site and applies for a land use permit from the state authorizing agency. The agency then reviews the application and evaluates the environmental impact. If the state decides to issue the permit, it then appoints a special administrative body to allow the public to participate in the site selection. These administrative bodies encourage public participation in order to decrease community resistance and to "minimize the issue of political expediency and emphasize environmental safety." All of the states that use this approach have preemption clauses that permit the siting despite community resistance.

Because private developers initiate the site selection process, the costs of acquiring the land and assembling the site influence decisions in the early phases of site selection. Unfortunately, low land cost and easy site assembly do not necessarily lead to the best site for waste transfer or disposal. Low-income and racial minority communities are often in areas with lower land values. With relatively few sites chosen in the initial phase of site selection, subsequent phases often place a final site in a minority neighborhood, due in large part to the lower community resistance that often accompanies minority sitings. The super review approach, then, probably does not alleviate inequitable distribution of waste disposal sites.

Under the site designation approach, the state, not a private developer, creates an inventory of possible sites. Techniques for developing the inventory vary from state to state. Because this approach lessens the cost incentive in site selection, it may lead to a more equitable distribution of waste sites. Furthermore, it provides the state with a statewide data gathering mechanism that can inform environmental decision-making in the future.

The third approach basically defers to local land use control. Here, the state does not exercise its right to preempt the authority of the locality to regulate toxic or hazardous wastes. This approach allows those communities that do not want a toxic or hazardous waste facility to simply prohibit that type of land use. As such, it does little but facilitate the NIMBY practice.

It is very difficult for any of these state siting approaches to overcome entrenched, well-funded community resistance. In wealthier communities, this resistance can take the form of protracted litigation. In site selection approaches that are developer-driven, the threat and reality of a lawsuit can increase the cost of the site and the site preparation process. Therefore, communities that cannot afford to litigate will be more vulnerable to site selection. Wealthier communities may also have better access to informal networks in the state government....

In addition to statutory site selection procedures, other environmental regulations governing land use, recycling and waste toxicity have made waste disposal sites more difficult to acquire and thus more likely to locate in minority communities....

*  *  *

## Craig Anthony Arnold, Planning Milagros: Environmental Justice and Land Use Regulation
### 76 Denver University Law Review 1 (1998)

The use of zoning and other land use regulatory mechanisms—requirements of large lots, minimum floor space, and significant setbacks; low-density zoning; and restrictions on multi-family housing—to exclude low-income people who cannot afford large single-family homes on large lots (exclusionary zoning) has been well documented. Exclusionary zoning has had the effect of contributing to and perpetuating residential segregation not only by class but also by race. In addition, Yale Rabin has focused scholarly attention on expulsive zoning, the practice of local governments rezoning neighborhoods of color to allow incompatible and noxious land uses.... However, Rabin's study did not attempt to quantify the distribution of zoning patterns in low-income neighborhoods of color and compare those distributions with zoning patterns of high-income white neighborhoods in the same cities. The distributional studies that have emerged in the environmental justice literature have focused on specific LULUs, not on land use regulatory patterns. This article documents land use regulatory patterns—the percentages of area designated for different land uses—in thirty-one census tracts in seven cities nationwide. Low-income, minority communities have a greater share not only of LULUs, but also of industrial and commercial zoning, than do high-income white communities.

### Methodology

The study measures the percentages of area in census tracts that local zoning ordinances have designated for each type of land use. It contains data from thirty-one census tracts in seven cities: Anaheim, California; Costa Mesa, California; Orange, California; Pittsburgh, Pennsylvania; San Antonio, Texas; Santa Ana, California; and Wichita, Kansas....

### Data and Analysis

The data shows that low-income, high-minority neighborhoods in the cities studied are subjects of more intensive zoning, on the whole, than high-income, low-minority neighborhoods. This conclusion is supported by data from across the various types of cities studied, regardless of the cites' geographic features, spatial development, population, political characteristics, and the like. With respect to industrial zoning—the most intensive land use—thirteen out of nineteen low-income, high-minority census tracts had at least some industrial zoning, and in seven of those census tracts, the city had zoned more than 20% of the tract for industrial uses. In contrast, only one of the twelve high-income, low-minority census tracts contained any industrial zoning at all, only 2.84% of the tract....

The zoning of low-income neighborhoods of color for industrial uses places highly intensive activities near local residents' homes, creating the very sort of incompatibility of uses that zoning is designed to prevent. For example, among the "as of right" permitted uses in Pittsburgh tract #2808 are ammonia and chlorine manufacturing, automobile wrecking, blast furnace or coke oven, chemical manufacturing, iron and steel manufacturing and processing, airplane factory or hangar, brewery, poultry slaughter, and machine shop, and among the conditional uses are atomic reactors, garbage and dead animal reduction, rubbish incineration, radio and television transmission and receiving towers, and storage of explosives and inflammables....

Commercial uses are also located in greater concentrations in low-income, high-minority neighborhoods than in high-income, low-minority neighborhoods. In ten out of the nineteen low-income, high-minority census tracts, at least 10% of the area is zoned for commercial use, and in seven of those tracts, at least 20% of the area is zoned for commercial use. In contrast, only two of the twelve high-income, low-minority census tracts had at least 10% of the area zoned for commercial use, and none had more than 20% commercial zoning.

Although the term "commercial" conjures up images of office buildings and retail stores which may create parking and scale/shadow impacts on neighboring residences but generally do not pose health hazards, the cities studied allow in their various commercial districts uses that are far more intensive than offices and stores.... In about 30% of San Antonio tract #1307.85, permitted uses include electro-plating, brewery, chicken hatcheries, poultry slaughter and storage, machine shop, and certain kinds of manufacturing, such as ice cream, ice, brooms, mattresses, paper boxes, candy, cigars, and refrigeration....

Over 75% of the area in each of six high-income, low-income tracts studied is zoned for single-family residences. If open space, a country club, and a private university (with significant open space) are included with single-family residential zoning, eleven of the twelve high-income, low-minority tracts have more than 75% of their respective areas zoned for these low-intensity land uses....

In contrast, the only low-income, high-minority census tract with more than 75% of the area zoned for single-family residential or open space uses is Pittsburgh census tract #2609.98—one tract out of nineteen. Although zoning for single-family residences or open space may preclude affordable housing needed by low-income people, the contrast in zoning patterns highlights the disparate impact of zoning designations on low-income people of color....

*Caveats and the Call for Further Studies*

[T]his study does not establish a national pattern....Perhaps most importantly, national trends are only marginally relevant to addressing overly intensive zoning (or expulsive zoning) of low-income communities of color. Instead, the existing patterns and the neighbors' concerns and land use goals are inherently local (indeed, specific to the neighborhood in question) and the regulatory authority is local. Changes will occur locality by locality, neighborhood by neighborhood, and not at a national level....

* * *

## Notes and Questions

1. Professor Arnold advocates greater use of land use planning tools to protect against disproportionate environmental sitings. Some of his suggestions are discussed in Chapter XII(B).

2. Practices such as expulsive zoning and exclusionary zoning can have profound impacts on the character of communities and the land uses that are sited there. Another potential threat to neighborhood stability in many urban areas is gentrification, a phenomenon that grew substantially throughout the 1990's. In response to skyrocketing housing costs, the high market demand for land, the growth in information technology-based companies, and other factors, urban neighborhoods, including low-income communities or communities of color that had long received little development attention, became much more attractive to investors. While increased economic development can bring important benefits to these areas, it also can make neighborhoods unaffordable and displace long time residents. San Francisco's Mission District, for example, long an enclave for working class and recent immigrant Latino families, was targeted for development by many investors, particularly "dot com" and other internet firms. This has had the result of "squeezing out longtime tenants, small mom-and-pop stores, non-profits, artists and working class people of all colors." Such displacement is particularly devastating in San Francisco, where rental vacancies are scarce and 40% of renters pay more than a third of their incomes for housing. ANTONIO DIAZ, PEOPLE ORGANIZING TO DEMAND ENVIRONMENTAL & ECONOMIC RIGHTS (PODER), RACE & SPACE: DOT-COLONIZATION, DISLOCATION AND RESISTANCE EN LA MISÍON DE SAN FRANCISCO (2001). Should environmental or land use policy in any fashion attempt to address the displacement of people of color by destabilizing demographic shifts? In this regard, consider research by Professor Manuel Pastor and his colleagues (discussed in Chapter III) finding that whether an area is undergoing ethnic transition was a significant predictor of the likelihood of a hazardous waste facility being sited there. The authors of the study posit that these ethnic shifts result in relatively weaker social bonds that may preclude successful opposition to the siting of LULUs.

3. Given the intensely local nature of gentrification and expulsive zoning, and the absence of a systematic national pattern of zoning practices, would federal or state preemption of local zoning matters be justified? If not, how should these causes of environmental injustice be remedied?

# C. The Market

Many critics who challenge the salience of race and/or ethnicity in explaining environmental disparities argue that market forces best account for these differences. This section considers two types of "market force" explanations—the first focusing on market forces in the site selection process, the second examining market-driven changes that occur after siting decisions are made.

## 1.  MARKET FORCES IN SITE SELECTION

# Robin Saha & Paul Mohai, Explaining Racial and Socioeconomic Disparities in the Location of Locally Unwanted Land Uses: A Conceptual Framework (1997)

The economic explanation of disproportionate siting relies on classic economic theory and focuses on industry's site selection rationale, reducing it down to strictly economic criteria....In calculating the feasibility of a particular location, a company evaluates the transaction costs associated with the siting process and anticipated operating costs which affect the competitiveness and profitability of the service that can be offered at a particular location...The transaction costs are associated with site selection, design, permitting, and construction. These costs can be quite high, especially if public opposition results in long delays, court costs, large financial compensation package, or other exactions....

It has been argued that disproportionate conditions arise coincidentally out of private site selection decisions concerning the transaction costs of acquiring land for proposed facilities. The sole purported basis of these decisions is to minimize property values costs. Disproportionate siting is said to occur because cost-efficient industrial areas with low property values are also likely to be nearby areas with low residential property values. These areas, in turn, typically suffer from depressed economic conditions relative to other areas. Thus, the reasonable presumption that areas with low property values coincide with areas with high proportions of persons of low socioeconomic status (SES) is used to explain disproportionate siting with respect to SES. In addition, the interaction between low SES and race has been used to explain racial siting disparities.

Another aspect of the economic explanation holds that the calculation of transaction costs stemming from potential public opposition may result in disproportionate siting. According to [Professor James] Hamilton:

> A firm's anticipation of the price of public opposition from a given area can thus be thought of as an aggregation of the costs imposed on the firm by residents: the costs of participating in extensive regulatory proceedings and court battles . . . and direct payments to the community in terms of corporate donations and taxes....

A rejected proposal is a costly matter for a sponsoring firm. Numerous activities are involved with putting forward a siting proposal such as securing finances and guarantees, conducting site assessments (e.g. geotechnical testing), developing business plans, negotiating and letting design contracts, and filing permit applications. These efforts represent "sunk costs" and are largely unrecoverable, since these investments of time, personnel, and money do not simply transfer to another proposal but must be carried out anew if a different location must be selected....

[I]t has been suggested that industry considers the potential costs of public opposition and selects a location where the probability of incurring such costs are minimized....One way of avoiding the high costs of siting delays or defeats is to select communities where the likelihood of public opposition is reduced....Evidence exists to support the claim that middle-income, affluent, and better educated communities are better equipped to wage effective opposition campaigns....

[A]s part of their transaction and operating costs firms are likely to consider the compensation costs that might be demanded in order for a community to accept a proposal....Studies on class differences in the value placed on environmental quality suggest that communities with relatively well-educated and affluent residents are willing to pay more to preserve environmental amenities than communities with less educated and low-income residents. Even though these findings may reflect differences in ability to pay, they suggest that communities of lower SES would accept relatively smaller compensation packages in order to accept new facilities (disamenities)....More importantly, it appears that anticipated class differences in levels of acceptable compensation could be a factor firms consider, which, in turn, may contribute to disproportionate siting....

* * *

Luke Cole and Sheila Foster question the assumption that race neutral "market" forces are what drive siting decisions.

## Luke Cole & Sheila Foster,<br>From the Ground Up: Environmental Racism and the Rise<br>of the Environmental Justice Movement 70–74 (2000)

*Social Structure and the Siting Process*

Conventional industry wisdom counsels private companies to target sites that are in neighborhoods "least likely to express opposition"—those with poorly educated residents of low socioeconomic status. Not surprisingly, many communities that host toxic waste sites possess these characteristics. State permitting laws remain neutral, or blind, toward these inequalities; they therefore perpetuate, and indeed exacerbate, distributional inequalities.

In most states, the hazardous wastes siting process begins when the private sector chooses a site for the location of a proposed facility. Because the proposed location of a hazardous waste facility near, particularly, a neighborhood of white people of high socioeconomic status often faces strong public opposition, there is a limited supply of land on which to site such facilities. Inevitably, the siting process focuses on industrial, or rural, communities, many of which are populated predominantly by people of color. Because land values are lower in heavily industrial and rural communities than in white suburbs, these areas are attractive to industries that are seeking to reduce the cost of doing business. Furthermore, these communities are presumed to pose little threat of political resistance because of their subordinate socioeconomic, and often racial, status.

Rarely does a "smoking gun"—explicit racial criteria or motivation—exist behind the decision to locate a toxic waste facility in a community of color. The reasons frequently given by companies for siting facilities are that such communities have low-cost land, sparse populations, and desirable geological attributes. Notably, however, there is evidence that portions of the waste industry target neighborhoods that possess the attributes of many poor communities of color, using "race-neutral criteria." In 1984, the California Waste Management Board commissioned a study on how to site waste incinerators. The report, written by the political consulting firm Cerrell Associates of Los Angeles and entitled *Political Difficulties Facing Waste-to-Energy Conversion Plant Siting* (popularly known as the Cerrell Report), set out "to assist in selecting a site that offers the least potential of generating public opposition." The report acknowledged that "since the 1970s, political criteria have become every bit as important in determining the outcome of a project as engineering factors." The Cerrell Report suggests that companies target small, rural communities whose residents are low income, older people, or people with a high school education or less; communities with a high proportion of Catholic residents; and communities whose residents are engaged in resource extractive industries such as agriculture, mining, and forestry. Ideally, the report states, "officials and companies should look for lower socioeconomic neighborhoods that are also in a heavy industrial area with little, if any, commercial activity."...

Likewise, even the "race-neutral" criteria used by government and industry for siting waste facilities—such as the presence of cheap land values, appropriate zoning, low population densities, proximity to transportation routes, and the absence of proximity to institutions such as hospitals and schools—turn out not to be "race neutral" after all, when seen in their social and historical context. Race potentially plays a factor in almost every "neutral" siting criterion used. "Cheap land values" is, understandably, a key siting criteria for the waste industry and other developers. However, because of historical segregation and racism, land values in the United States are integrally tied to race. In urban areas across the United States, this is starkly clear: an acre of land in the San Fernando Valley of Los Angeles has roughly the same physical characteristics as an acre of land in South Central Los Angeles, but people are willing to pay a premium to live in all-white neighborhoods. In rural areas, the pattern is similar: low land values tend to be found in poor areas, and people of color are over represented among the rural poverty population.

The land value cycle is vicious, too: once a neighborhood becomes host to industry, land values typically fall or do not increase as quickly as those in purely residential neighborhoods. Thus, a community that initially has low land values because it is home to people of color becomes a community that has low land values because it has a preponderance of industry, which in turn attracts more industry, creating a cumulative effect on land values.... [C]alling these changes "market driven" naturalizes the underlying racism in the valuation of the land....

Zoning is inextricably linked with race, as well.... Yale Rabin's studies of historical zoning decisions have documented numerous instances where stable African American residential communities were "down-zoned" to industrial status by biased decision makers.... [Such "expulsive zoning"] permanently alters the character of a neighborhood, often depressing property values and causing community blight. The lower property values and the zoning status are then easily invoked as "neutral" criteria upon which siting decisions are made....

Proximity to major transportation routes may also skew the siting process toward communities of color, as freeways appear to be disproportionately sited in such communities. Similarly, locational criteria—prohibitions against the siting of waste facilities near neighborhood amenities like hospitals and schools—skew the process toward underdeveloped communities of color, since such communities are less likely to have hospitals and schools. Hence, siting criteria that prohibit the siting of waste facilities close to such facilities perpetuate the historical lack of such amenities in these communities.

The sociologist Robert Bullard documented this underlying racial discrimination in an otherwise "neutral" siting process. Bullard's documentation was recognized in a 1997 decision by the Nuclear Regulatory Commission's Atomic Safety and Licensing Board, which overturned a facility's permit.... The race-neutral siting criteria—including the criteria of low population and the need to site the facility five miles from institutions such as schools, hospitals, and nursing homes—operated in conjunction with the current racial segregation and the resulting inferior infrastructure (e.g., lack of adequate schools, road paving, water supply) to ensure that the location selected would be a poor community of color. [This case, *In the Matter of Louisiana Energy Services, L.P.*, is discussed in Chapter XII (C). Eds.]

\* \* \*

## Notes and Questions

1. The excerpts above indicate how difficult it can be to distinguish and categorize different factors underlying siting decisions with precision. How would you classify, for instance, a decision by a company to favor siting in areas with less-educated and lower-income residents because of a perception that these residents will accept smaller compensation packages in order to accept a new LULU?

2. Businesses were quick to disavow use of the 1984 Cerrell Report, referenced above. What role do you think factors like those discussed in the report actually play in siting decisions?

3. As Cole and Foster point out, rarely does a "smoking gun" document exist in which companies explicitly target low-income communities or communities of color for siting unwanted land use facilities. Another example of such a document from the international context is a 1991 internal memo authored by Lawrence Summers (then chief economist of the World Bank, later U.S. Treasury Secretary, and currently President of Harvard University) that advocated siting toxic waste facilities in the world's poorest countries because workers there had lower earnings. Summers queried: "Shouldn't the World Bank be encouraging more migration of the dirty industries to LDCs [Less Developed Countries]?" In his view, such targeting was appropriate because:

> [t]he measurement of the costs of health impairing pollution depends upon the foregone earnings from increased morbidity and mortality. From this point of view a given amount of health impairing pollution should be done in the country with the lowest cost, which will be the country with the lowest wages. I think the economic logic behind dumping a load of toxic waste in the lowest wage country is impeccable and we should face up to that.

(Quoted in Robert Bullard, *Anatomy of Environmental Racism and the Environmental Justice Movement*, in Confronting Environmental Racism: Voices from the Grassroots 19–20 (Robert Bullard ed. 1993)). Summers also noted that there was likely to be less demand in developing countries for a clean and healthy environment. *Id.* When the memorandum was publicized, Summers issued a statement claiming that his remarks were intended as a "sardonic counter-point, an effort to sharpen the analysis." *World Bank Dumps on Third World Again*, Race, Poverty & the Env't 12 (Fall 1991/Winter 1992). The response is strikingly similar to the response of decisionmakers in the wake of the Cerrell report. In both instances, policymakers or decisionmakers stress that the proffered advice to prefer impoverished areas over areas with wealthier populations for the distribution of environmentally risky activities was in fact not acted upon. Implicit in these subsequent positions is that the "economic logic" was in fact ignored, presumably because of overriding ethical considerations. Should additional safeguards be put into place to guard against these economic impulses? If so, what safe-guards would be appropriate?

4. If market forces are in fact primarily responsible for the current distribution of en-vironmental "bads," does this make the distribution less unfair and more acceptable? This issue is explored in the excerpt below.

# Lynn E. Blais,
# Environmental Racism Reconsidered
### 75 North Carolina Law Review 75 (1996)

Although the environmental racism movement conveys a simple story of discrimi-nation, the reality of the siting of environmentally sensitive land uses is much more complex. At some point, and at some level, representatives of host communities make political and market-based determinations to permit the challenged sitings. In addi-tion, the residents of these communities have made decisions either to remain in the community after the challenged use was sited, or, in many cases, to migrate to a com-munity playing host to such a land use. In such circumstances, it is not clear why these preferences are more suspect than the myriad of others that emerge from the political and market system. Indeed, it is quite plausible that the communities and residents are better off, given the constrained positions from which they enter the market and/or the political process, with the challenged uses than they were without them....

That more recent empirical evidence indicating that class influences (such as job sta-tus and income level) are more significant in the distribution of environmentally sensi-tive land uses than are racial factors should not be surprising. The market allocates ac-cording to ability to pay: the more money one has, the more of any particular good—including a clean environment—one can afford to purchase. Moreover, people tend to live near their jobs, those that depend on public transportation even more so than oth-ers. Thus, people employed in environmentally sensitive industries will be more likely to live in or near a community that hosts such industries. Finally, the political process responds to people who have the time, money, education, and inclination to partici-pate. The more one has of any or all of these, the more likely one is to have an effective voice in policy-making or enforcement decisions. Accordingly, we should ask ourselves the very difficult question whether the current distribution of environmentally sensitive land uses represents simply the revealed preferences of a society characterized by sub-stantial and growing disparities in income and opportunities. As part of this new focus, we must be mindful that, in our society, class and race continue to interact in many dis-turbing ways. Thus, while the cries of environmental "racism" may be exaggerated, the plaint of inequity may not be. It may just be misdirected.

### Private Preferences, Collective Judgments, and Choices

Our society relies on markets and the political process to allocate and distribute a vast array of society's goods and services, including many that are essential to health, welfare, and prosperity, and many that are risky or hazardous. In general, the market measures individual (or private) preferences through the very rough proxy of market choices and translates those preferences (choices) into allocative and distributive deci-sions. The political process responds to the community's preferences, or, if you will, its collective judgments. Measures designed to interfere with the preferences revealed through these institutions generally demand substantial justification....

In a very limited set of circumstances, society has determined that particular decisions should be removed from the political process or the market system altogether. More commonly, we may consign the allocation and distribution of particular resources to these spheres, while at the same time adjusting those processes, or the preferences expressed through them, when demonstrated process failures undermine our confidence in the accuracy of the preferences they reveal. Additionally, society may reject even accurately measured private preferences. This generally occurs when society concludes that certain preferences are illegitimate or unacceptably harmful to self or others.... The task facing the environmental justice movement is to demonstrate that decisions resulting in the current distribution of environmentally sensitive land uses implicate one or more of the generally accepted justifications for rejecting choices expressed in the market or political arena.

Before we undertake that task, however, it seems that we should at least explore the possibility that these processes have functioned well, and that the distribution of environmentally sensitive land uses reflects the accurately measured, unobjectionable preferences of host and non-host communities.

### Risk, Rewards, and Rational Preferences in the Siting on Environmentally Sensitive Land Uses

It is not difficult to construct a theoretical framework in which the choice to live in a community that hosts an environmentally sensitive land use is neither irrational nor otherwise objectionable.... Whether evaluated by a policy-making body or by individual residents of a proposed host community, the risk posed by a particular environmentally sensitive land use necessarily will fall along a continuum: At one end will be those environmentally sensitive land uses that have a low probability of a relatively minor adverse effect, at the other end will be those facilities that have a high probability of a catastrophic outcome. In between will be the entire range of facilities that have a measurable risk of some level of harm.

In contrast to the possible harms associated with residential proximity to environmentally sensitive land uses, many such uses offer benefits to residents of the host community. Such benefits may include increased job opportunities, increased property tax revenues, sharing of user fees, infusion of money into the local economy through increased demand for services, the building and maintenance of infrastructure, and even the environmental benefits of shifting from older to newer technology for industrial production or waste disposal....

### Rational Preferences Revisited: Winners, Losers and Race

Citizens of affluent states and communities regularly exchange tax concessions and other benefits to serve as the location of new facilities for major enterprises, expecting to recoup their concessions through increased employment and tax revenues. For example, Austin and other central Texas communities routinely offer tax incentives to high-tech industrial enterprises to entice them to locate production facilities in central Texas instead of Silicon Valley.... For predominantly poor and/or minority communities, there may be no excess revenue to accommodate offers of tax breaks, or any other carrots to dangle before the desired industry. These communities can trade only what they have, and many have offered the willingness to accept risk. To be persuasive in their claims of inequity, environmental racism scholars must demonstrate why we should permit (and perhaps even encourage) the former exchange and prohibit the latter....

*Siting Decisions in the Past: Sumter County Alabama*

A facility often held up as the leading example of discriminatory siting or environmental racism is Chemical Waste Management Corporation's Emelle hazardous waste treatment, storage, and land disposal facility in Sumter County, Alabama. African-Americans account for 69% of the residents of Sumter County, and for 90% of the residents who live in poverty. Environmental racism scholars allege that the facility was "foisted on the Emelle community without their input" because "no blacks held public office or sat on governing bodies, including the state legislature, county commission, or industrial development board (an agency that promotes industrial operation in the county) from predominantly black Sumter County."...

However, the story of Sumter County and Chemical Waste Management is much more complex. Formerly a rich farming and cotton-producing region (its heritage from the plantation system of slavery), for decades before the Emelle plant was built in 1978, Sumter County struggled against the decline of its agricultural economic base....Between 1940 and 1980, the population of Sumter County declined more than 40%. Its remaining residents faced an extremely high incidence of poverty, alarming rates of illiteracy, and infant mortality rates that were among the highest in the state. With no hope that the agricultural economy could be revitalized, the opportunity to host an industry that would bring jobs and tax revenues may well have looked attractive to Sumter County residents....

[I]t is unlikely that Sumter County was chosen as the location for the Emelle plant because its residents were poor and black. Prior to Chemical Waste Management's decision to purchase the Emelle site, the Environmental Protection Agency had identified it as one of the ten most protective sites in the nation for disposal of hazardous waste. The site's suitability was based on such factors as rural location and access to appropriate transportation systems. More important, the geologic conditions of Sumter county make it ideally suitable to the land disposal of hazardous wastes....

Moreover, it is not at all clear that the presence of the Emelle facility has been burdensome to its host community. While it may be true, as Professor Bullard claims, that "the Emelle hazardous-waste site has not brought about an economic renaissance to this poor blackbelt community," the benefits are tangible. The facility employs over 400 people, 60% of whom live in Sumter County, and has an annual payroll of $10 million. State law provides that a portion of the hazardous waste excise tax collected at the Emelle facility be committed to Sumter County, with a minimum annual guarantee of $4.2 million. Since the landfill was opened in 1977, this increased tax revenue has been used to build infrastructure, enhance educational opportunities for the children of the county, and improve the deliverance of health care services. These services have reversed the percentages of illiteracy and infant mortality....

The economic transformation of Sumter County, from a declining agricultural community to a more stable industrial one, indicates that land uses which may be considered undesirable by some communities may in fact provide benefits to the host communities which outweigh their burdens. These benefits may be particularly attractive to those without jobs, social services, or adequate educational opportunities for their children....

* * *

## Notes and Questions

1. Professor Blais assumes that most community residents have made a voluntary choice to live near LULUs. Is this a reasonable assumption? What form should evidence

of such a choice take? Is the eventual siting evidence that such a choice had been made, or should the choice be put to a vote or referendum? More broadly, to what extent are the preferences of individuals as revealed in the market or political process themselves shaped by non-market forces and social institutions, such as racial discrimination in housing and employment?

2. Are rich people always more likely to live in cleaner, less polluting areas? Is it fair to characterize Professor Blais' position in this way? Can you think of situations in which this is not the case? Does an inequitable distribution of LULUs caused by the market justify government intervention to correct?

3. Professor Blais argues that siting prohibitions will harm poor and minority communities by preventing them from accepting facilities that will result in jobs and other net benefits. Many environmental justice activists dispute the claim that LULUs bring significant economic benefits to local residents in their communities. Professor Robert Kuehn gives the following examples:

> In the Shintech case [a proposed polyvinyl chloride plant in Convent, Louisiana], Louisiana offered Shintech, which was already realizing an annual $750,000 per-employee after-tax profit at its comparable PCV plant in Texas, a taxpayer-financed subsidy of almost $800,000 for each permanent job created.... [B]ecause of Shintech's need for employees with computer knowledge and the low educational level of most Convent residents, the staff director of the state agency promoting the plant admitted that "very few" of the permanent jobs created by the company would go to local residents.... Similarly, residents of West Harlem complain that although they are saddled with a disproportionate number of New York's sewage treatment plants, no minority contractors were hired to construct the most recent $1.1 billion plant; the few local minorities that were hired as plant workers were all gone within a year. In the Genesee Power Station case [in Genesee, Michigan], no minorities from the majority African-American area were hired to construct or were working at the $80 million plant, and the owners all resided outside the community. The judge found these facts "to be appalling" and opined that, in permitting industrial facilities, society ought to take into consideration that the people living in the polluted surrounding communities get no job benefits from the plants. Robbins, Illinois, stands as an example of a town that thought its support of a new waste incinerator would bring jobs and economic development but finds itself "arguably worse off than before" as the economic benefits never materialized and the town is now "saddled with a soaring, smoke-belching trash burner that shoos away commercial investment like a scarecrow guarding a cornfield."

Robert Kuehn, *A Taxonomy of Environmental Justice,* 30 ENVTL. L. REP. 10,681, 10,701 (2000). Which strikes you as the more correct view—that of Professor Blais or Professor Kuehn. Why? To what extent should demonstrated, tangible benefits to a host community be required to justify a siting?

## 2.  POST SITING CHANGES

One of the more provocative arguments in environmental justice scholarship is that the prevalence of LULUs in low-income communities and communities of color results from market-driven changes that occur in neighborhoods after an unwanted land use is located there. This thesis has been prominently developed by Professor Vicki Been.

## Vicki Been, Locally Undesirable Land Uses in Minority Neighborhoods: Disproportionate Siting or Market Dynamics?
### 103 Yale Law Journal 1383 (1994)

The environmental justice movement contends that people of color and the poor are exposed to greater environmental risks than are whites and wealthier individuals.... [R]esearch does not, however, establish that [communities hosting LULUs] were disproportionately minority or poor at the time the sites were selected. Most of the studies compare the *current* socioeconomic characteristics of communities that host various LULUs to those of communities that do not host such LULUs. This approach leaves open the possibility that the sites for LULUs were chosen fairly, but that subsequent events produced the current disproportion in the distribution of LULUs. In other words, the research fails to prove environmental justice advocates' claim that the disproportionate burden poor and minority communities now bear in hosting LULUs is the result of racism and classism in the *siting process* itself.

In addition, the research fails to explore an alternative or additional explanation for the proven correlation between the current demographics of communities and the likelihood that they host LULUs. Regardless of whether the LULUs originally were sited fairly, it could well be that neighborhoods surrounding LULUs became poorer and became home to a greater percentage of people of color over the years following the sitings. Such factors as poverty, housing discrimination, and the location of jobs, transportation, and other public services may have led the poor and racial minorities to "come to the nuisance"—to move to neighborhoods that host LULUs—because those neighborhoods offered the cheapest available housing....

### Market Dynamics and the Distribution of LULUs

The residential housing market in the United States is extremely dynamic. Every year, approximately 17% to 20% of U.S. households move to a new home. Some of those people stay within the same neighborhood, but many move to different neighborhoods in the same city, or to different cities. Some people decide to move, at least in part, because they are dissatisfied with the quality of their current neighborhoods. Once a household decides to move, its choice of a new neighborhood usually depends somewhat on the cost of housing and the characteristics of the neighborhood. Those two factors are interrelated because the quality of the neighborhood affects the price of housing.

The siting of a LULU can influence the characteristics of the surrounding neighborhood in two ways. First, an undesirable land use may cause those who can afford to move to become dissatisfied and leave the neighborhood. Second, by making the neighborhood less desirable, the LULU may decrease the value of the neighborhood's property, making the housing more available to lower income households and less attractive to higher income households. The end result of both influences is likely to be that the neighborhood becomes poorer than it was before the siting of the LULU.

The neighborhood also is likely to become home to more people of color. Racial discrimination in the sale and rental of housing relegates people of color (especially African-Americans) to the least desirable neighborhoods, regardless of their income level. Moreover, once a neighborhood becomes a community of color, racial discrimination in the promulgation and enforcement of zoning and environmental protection laws, the provision of municipal services, and the lending practices of banks may cause neighborhood quality to decline further. That additional decline, in turn, will induce those who can leave the neighborhood—the least poor and those least subject to discrimination—to do so.

The dynamics of the housing market therefore are likely to cause the poor and people of color to move to or remain in the neighborhoods in which LULUs are located, regardless of the demographics of the communities when the LULUs were first sited....

If the siting process is primarily responsible for the correlation between the location of LULUs and the demographics of host neighborhoods, the process may be unjust under current constitutional doctrine, at least as to people of color....

On the other hand, if the disproportionate distribution of LULUs results from market forces which drive the poor, regardless of their race, to live in neighborhoods that offer cheaper housing because they host LULUs, then the fairness of the distribution becomes a question about the fairness of our market economy. Some might argue that the disproportionate burden is part and parcel of a free market economy that is, overall, fairer than alternative schemes, and that the costs of regulating the market to reduce the disproportionate burden outweigh the benefits of doing so. Others might argue that those moving to a host neighborhood are compensated through the market for the disproportionate burden they bear by lower housing costs, and therefore that the situation is just. Similarly, some might contend that while the poor suffer lower quality neighborhoods, they also suffer lower quality food, housing, and medical care, and that the systemic problem of poverty is better addressed through income redistribution programs than through changes in siting processes.

Even if decisionmakers were to agree that it is unfair to allow post-siting market dynamics to create disproportionate environmental risk for the poor or minorities, the remedy for that injustice would have to be much more fundamental than the remedy for unjust siting *decisions*. Indeed, if market forces are the primary cause of the correlation between the presence of LULUs and the current socioeconomic characteristics of a neighborhood, even a siting process radically revised to ensure that LULUs are distributed equally among all neighborhoods may have only a short-term effect. The areas surrounding LULUs distributed equitably will become less desirable neighborhoods, and thus may soon be left to people of color or the poor, recreating the pattern of inequitable siting....

### The Evidence of Disproportionate Siting

Several recent studies have attempted to assess whether locally undesirable land uses are disproportionately located in neighborhoods that are populated by more people of color or are more poor than is normal. [One of the] most frequently cited of those studies, which is often credited for first giving the issue of environmental justice visibility, was conducted by the United States General Accounting Office (GAO). [The GAO found that in three of the four communities where hazardous waste landfills were sited in eight southeastern states, the population was disproportionately African-American and poor.] Another frequently cited local study was conducted by sociologist Robert Bullard and formed important parts of his books, *Invisible Houston* and *Dumping in Dixie*. Professor Bullard found that although African-Americans made up only 28% of the Houston population in 1980, six of Houston's eight incinerators and mini-incinerators and fifteen of seventeen landfills were located in predominantly African-American neighborhoods.

[Professor Been then re-analyzed the GAO study and the Bullard study, looking at demographic characteristics of the host communities at the time of siting decisions and tracing subsequent changes in the demographics of these communities. She found mixed support for her thesis: of the four communities reviewed by the GAO, all were disproportionately African American at the siting, and in each case the percentage of African Americans decreased after siting decisions were made. For ten communities studied by Professor Bullard, she found 50% were sited in predominantly African American communities, and that the percentage of African Americans in all neighborhoods surrounding the landfills subsequently increased (as did the percentage of the population with incomes below the poverty level in all but two host neighborhoods.) The literature on disproportionate siting is examined in Chapter III. Eds.]

\* \* \*

## Notes and Questions

1. A subsequent and far more comprehensive study by Professor Been and her colleague Francis Gupta produced different results that undermine the market dynamics theory. That study found that areas where hazardous waste facilities were sited are disproportionately Hispanic, and that neighborhoods did not become poorer or more heavily minority after hazardous waste facilities were sited there. This study is excerpted in Chapter III(B).

2. Scholars have criticized the fact that while Professor Been identifies racial discrimination in housing as a factor in post-siting demographic change, she nonetheless includes this under the rubric of market forces. "Housing choices among whites may be determined by the market, what is available and affordable, individual preferences (of which the neighborhood racial mix may be one), and utility functions. In contrast, choices among minorities may be severely limited by various forms of institutionalized discrimination altogether separate from ability and willingness to pay. Been recognizes that market processes may result in a gradual downgrading in the economic status of residents of a host neighborhood and that housing discrimination may have a separate effect of concentrating minorities. Yet in combining both factors under the label of market dynamics, Been seems to negate the fact that demographic change due to housing discrimination is a fundamentally different process." Saha & Mohai, *supra*, at 19.

3. How does Professor Been's market dynamics theory square with Professor Rabin's and Professor Arnold's findings documenting expulsive zoning practices in communities of color? Is expulsive zoning an indication of a well-functioning market allocating risks and amenities efficiently, i.e., to those willing to pay the most for the resource in question (either an environmental good or the absence of an environmental risk)? Or, alternatively, is expulsive zoning evidence of a poorly functioning market?

4. While public opinion polls and research on risk perception and environmental attitudes support the notion that LULUs render host areas less desirable places to live, Saha and Mohai caution that a mix of factors influences the decision of residents to leave a neighborhood. For example, they argue, a neighborhood's pre-existing level of

stability or change may be equally or more important than the impact of the LULU itself. Saha & Mohai, *supra*, at 21.

# D. Politics

Sociopolitical factors also help explain the current distribution of environmental harms and benefits. As described above, companies may chose to site noxious facilities in low income communities or communities of color because this represents the path of least political resistance. Minority and poor residents often have less political power than wealthier white communities, for a variety of reasons: lack of access to elected officials, lack of awareness of the appropriate officials to contact, and under-representation in local government. They are "likely to lack the know-how, the administrative, legal, and scientific expertise to participate effectively in administrative process of siting decisions." Saha & Mohai, *supra*, at 9, 11–13.

Other political explanations focus on the structure of environmental law and environmental policymaking (This includes land use practices, discussed above). The following two excerpts explore this issue in greater detail.

## Luke Cole, Empowerment as the Key to Environmental Protection: The Need for Environmental Poverty Law

19 Ecology Law Quarterly 619 (1992)

### Environmental Law as the Problem, Not the Solution

Environmental laws are not designed by or for poor people. The theory and ideology behind environmental laws ignores the systemic genesis of pollution. Environmental statutes actually legitimate the pollution of low-income neighborhoods. Further, those with political and economic power have used environmental laws in ways which have resulted in poor people bearing a disproportionate share of environmental hazards.

### Two Views of the Political Economy of Pollution

Mainstream and grassroots environmentalists generally have different views of the causes of pollution, and thus offer different solutions to the problem of pollution. The legal-scientific movement's law and policy in the past twenty-five years has largely been based on a "single bad actor" understanding of the causes of pollution. This "bad actor" theory holds that pollution occurs when a particular actor (such as a polluting corporation) acts outside societal norms; laws are thus written to punish particular violators of pollution standards....

[Grassroots activists] have acquired an "institutional" understanding of the political economy of pollution, which stands in contrast to the single bad actor theory. The institutional theory posits that the *normal operations* of some institutions (such as U.S. corporations) generate environmental hazards. People living in or near industrial communities know that law-abiding companies and law-breaking companies differ in degree only: both put pollutants out the smokestack, and both thus poison nearby communities. In contrast to the single bad actor model, which seeks to identify and punish indi-

vidual bad actors, the institutional model identifies individual polluters "not as explanations themselves," but merely as part of an overall system centered on maximizing
profit.

Mainstream environmentalists see pollution as the *failure* of government and industry—if the environmentalists could only shape up the few bad apples, our environment
would be protected. But grassroots activists come to view pollution as the *success* of
government and industry, success at industry's primary objective: maximizing profits
by externalizing environmental costs. Pollution of our air, land, and water that is liter-
ally killing people is often not in violation of environmental laws. Grassroots environmentalists, realizing this, have a far more radical and systemic view of the changes
needed to eliminate pollution....

### Control v. Pollution

Because environmental laws were designed around the single bad actor model, they
have failed to serve low-income communities. Traditional environmental law has focused on pollution *control:* on technologies to be placed on the end of the pipe to control or clean up the poisons coming out. This concept is the foundation for the complex regulatory scheme designed and honed by the mainstream environmental
movement.

In contrast, grassroots activists have a different understanding and approach....
[They] are pressing for the elimination of the chemicals themselves and arguing for a
change in the processes that produce these chemicals in the first place....

Grassroots activists around the country, by stopping the siting of toxic waste disposal
facilities in their communities, have begun to force industry to move from pollution
*control* to pollution *prevention.* Put simply, because so few waste disposal sites exist, and
because it is so difficult to establish new sites, the price of toxic waste disposal has risen
to the point where companies are seriously working to replace toxic inputs to their
manufacturing processes in order to minimize the production of toxic waste. By forcing
companies to pay a cost closer to the true societal cost of toxic waste, grassroots activists
have forced companies to begin to reduce toxic waste production.

### NIMBY Works

...Environmental laws, and the siting of polluting facilities, are products of a political process which has historically excluded poor people, and in which poor people remain grossly under-represented. The importance of the political process is heightened
by the procedural emphasis of many environmental laws. Lacking substantive standards, such statutes depend on the vigor of the political process for achieving environmental goals. In the end, it is those with political clout who win in the administrative
process or siting decision. Because siting decisions are political decisions, the
outcome—more facilities in poor communities—is neither surprising nor unpre-
dictable. Thus, the decisions to place unwanted facilities in low-income neighborhoods
are made not *in spite* of our system of laws, but *because* of our system of laws.

When middle-class neighborhoods say NIMBY (Not in My Back Yard) and use environmental laws to defeat proposed locally unwanted land uses (LULU's), such as toxic
waste dumps or polluting industry, the developers usually go to a different neighborhood, where opposition is less organized and powerful. Thus, LULU's end up in poor
neighborhoods and in communities of color. It is *because* the law works for white middle-class communities that it does not work for the poor, or for people of color....

* * *

## Richard J. Lazarus, Pursuing "Environmental Justice": The Distributional Effects of Environmental Protection

87 Northwestern University Law Review 787 (1993)

*Exacerbating Causes: The Structure of Environmental Policymaking*

[T]here exist...factors more endemic to environmental law itself that may exacerbate distributional inequities likely present in the context of any public welfare law. These factors suggest more than the disturbing, yet somewhat irresistible thesis, that the distributional dimension of environmental protection policy likely suffers from the same inequities that persist generally in society. They suggest the far more troubling, and even less appealing, proposition that the problems of distributional inequity may in fact be more pervasive in the environmental protection arena than they are in other areas of traditional concern to civil rights organizations, such as education, employment, and housing.

Indeed, it is the absence of that minority involvement so prevalent in the more classic areas of civil rights concern that may render the distributional problem worse for environmental protection. Minority interests have traditionally had little voice in the various points of influence that strike the distributional balances necessary to get environmental protection laws enacted, regulations promulgated, and enforcement actions initiated. The interest groups historically active in the environmental protection area include a variety of mainstream environmental organizations representing a spectrum of interests (conservation, recreation, hunting, wildlife protection, resource protection, human health), as well as a variety of commercial and industrial concerns. Until very recently, if at all, the implications for racial minorities of environmental protection laws have not been a focal point of concern for any of these organizations.

Much of environmental protection lawmaking has also been highly centralized, with the geographic focus in Washington, D.C. The enactment of environmental statutes within that geo-political setting has required the expenditure of considerable political resources. As evidenced by the thirteen years required to amend the Clean Air Act, it is no easy task to obtain the attention of the numerous congressional committees, and to form the coalitions between competing interest groups, so necessary to secure a bill's passage.

Environmental legislation has ultimately been produced through intense and lengthy horse-trading among interest groups, a process necessary to secure a particular environmental law's passage. This process has often depended upon the forging of alliances between diverse interests both within the environmental public interest community and within government bureaucracy. Often, these unions have included so-called "unholy alliances" between environmentalists and commercial and industrial interests, where the latter have perceived an economic advantage to be gained (or disadvantage to be minimized) by their supporting an environmental protection law that allocates the benefits and burdens of environmental protection in a particular fashion....

It is not surprising, therefore, that those environmental laws enacted by Congress typically address some, but hardly all, environmental pollution problems. And, even with regard to those problems that are explicitly addressed, there are usually discrepancies and gaps within the statutory scheme. Which problems are confronted, and where the discrepancies and gaps occur, is quite naturally an expression of the priorities of those participants who wield the greatest influence and resources in the political process.

For this reason, much environmental legislation may not have focused on those pollution problems that are of greatest concern to many minority communities. For instance, air pollution control efforts typically have focused on general ambient air quality concerns for an entire metropolitan region rather than on toxic hot spots in any one particular area. Accordingly, while there has been much progress made in improving air quality as measured by a handful of national ambient air quality standards, there has been relatively less progress achieved over the last twenty years in the reduction of those toxic air emissions which tend to be of greater concern to persons, disproportionately minorities, who live in the immediate geographic vicinity of the toxic polluting source....Likewise, and at the behest of mainstream environmental groups, substantial resources have also been directed to improving air and water quality in nonurban areas. Programs for the prevention of significant deteriorations in air quality, the reduction of "acid rain," and the protection of visibility in national parks and wilderness areas, all require significant financial expenditures. Substantial resources have similarly been expended on improving the quality of water resources that are not as readily accessible to many minorities because of their historical exclusion. Without meaning to suggest that these programs lack merit on their own terms (for the simple reason that they possess great merit), their return in terms of overall public health may be less than pollution control programs directed at improving the environmental quality of urban America's poorer neighborhoods, including many minority communities....

[R]acial minorities have had little influence on either the lawmaking or priority-setting processes at any of the legislative, regulatory, or local enforcement levels. They have not been well represented among the interest groups lobbying and litigating before governmental authorities on environmental protection issues. Nor have they been well represented, especially at the national level, within those governmental organizations actively involved in the relevant environmental processes. Their voices have not been heard in the mainstream environmental public interest organizations that participate in the policymaking debates and that, in the absence of governmental enforcement, are behind citizen suits filling the void. Traditional civil rights organizations have historically had little interest in, and have infrequently become involved with, environmental issues. At the same time, mainstream environmental organizations have historically included few minorities in policymaking positions. In 1990, this fact prompted several members of various civil rights organizations and minority groups to send a widely publicized letter to the national environmental public interest organizations charging them with being isolated from minority communities.... [The letter is excerpted in Chapter I(C). Eds.]

* * *

## Notes and Questions

1. If environmental burdens are disproportionately distributed in society, why haven't environmental laws remedied the problem? Does the current pattern of environmental inequities represent a failure of our environmental protection laws, or the *success* of these laws, as Luke Cole argues? Why haven't mainstream environmental groups traditionally been more concerned with environmental justice issues?

2. Given the decentralized nature of the environmental justice movement, and the limited resources available, what would be the most potentially useful points of inter-

vention? Direct action (e.g., demonstrations), litigation (court access), collaborative projects, legislative lobbying, pressure upon agencies? Can you think of other means? In which venues would lawyers likely be the most helpful?

# E. Racial Discrimination

Another set of explanations for disproportionate environmental burdens and benefits involves racial discrimination. In part this refers to intentional racism, i.e. targeting communities of color based on pure racial prejudice. In today's society, such conduct is far less frequent than in the past, and given the prevailing societal opprobrium toward overt discrimination, far less likely to occur in the open. Communities of color may also be targeted for unwanted land uses by those who believe they will be less likely to organize effective opposition than white communities or more willing to trade off health risks for possible economic benefits. A broader view of discrimination encompasses actions that are not intentionally racist but because of the structure or workings of social and political institutions, have discriminatory effects. For example, an all white zoning board may render decisions with discriminatory effects because of unconscious racial prejudices, or because minority citizens, who do not live in the same neighborhoods and are not part of the same social networks as the board members, have less access to them, or because the white board members do not live in the area impacted by a proposed LULU, or because the decision makers are less interested in the fate of minority residents for political reasons. In some respects, all of the above authors' insights point to specific mechanisms by which a form of "structural" or "institutional" racism works. For example, as elaborated in the excerpt by Cole and Foster, see Section C above, employing seemingly technical criteria—such as that a facility should not be sited in proximity to schools, hospitals, or other sensitive institutions—can discriminate against minority residents who because of past and present housing discrimination disproportionately live in areas without such facilities. In the following article, Professor Lawrence adds to the general theory of structural racism. By using psychological concepts, he articulates a theory for why racial discrimination may be far more prevalent than appears on the surface.

## Charles R. Lawrence III, The Id, the Ego, and Equal Protection: Reckoning with Unconscious Racism
### 39 Stanford Law Review 317 (1987)

Americans share a common historical and cultural heritage in which racism has played and still plays a dominant role. Because of this shared experience, we also inevitably share many ideas, attitudes, and beliefs that attach significance to an individual's race and induce negative feelings and opinions about nonwhites. To the extent that this cultural belief system has influenced all of us, we are all racists. At the same time, most of us are unaware of our racism. We do not recognize the ways in which our cultural experience has influenced our beliefs about race or the occasions on which those beliefs affect our actions. In other words, a large part of the behavior that produces racial discrimination is influenced by unconscious racial motivation....

*Racism: A Public Health Problem*

Not every student of the human mind has agreed with Sigmund Freud's description of the unconscious, but few today would quarrel with the assertion that there is an unconscious—that there are mental processes of which we have no awareness that affect our actions and the ideas of which we are aware. There is a considerable, and by now well respected, body of knowledge and empirical research concerning the workings of the human psyche and the unconscious. Common sense tells us that we all act unwittingly on occasion. We have experienced slips of the tongue and said things we fully intended not to say, and we have had dreams in which we experienced such feelings as fear, desire, and anger that we did not know we had....

Racism is in large part a product of the unconscious. It is a set of beliefs whereby we irrationally attach significance to something called race. I do not mean to imply that racism does not have its origins in the rational and premeditated acts of those who sought and seek property and power. But racism in America is much more complex than either the conscious conspiracy of a power elite or the simple delusion of a few ignorant bigots. It is a part of our common historical experience and, therefore, a part of our culture. It arises from the assumptions we have learned to make about the world, ourselves, and others as well as from the patterns of our fundamental social activities....

[H]ow is the unconscious involved when racial prejudice is less apparent—when racial bias is hidden from the prejudiced individual as well as from others? Increasingly, as our culture has rejected racism as immoral and unproductive, this hidden prejudice has become the more prevalent form of racism. The individual's Ego must adapt to a cultural order that views overly racist attitudes and behavior as unsophisticated, uninformed, and immoral. It must repress or disguise racist ideas when they seek expression.

Joel Kovel refers to the resulting personality type as the "aversive racist" and contrasts this type with the "dominative racist," the true bigot who openly seeks to keep blacks in a subordinate position and will resort to force to do so. The aversive racist believes in white superiority, but her conscience seeks to repudiate this belief, or, at least, to prevent her from acting on it. She often resolves this inner conflict by not acting at all. She tries to avoid the issue by ignoring the existence of blacks, avoiding contact with them, or at most being polite, correct, and cold whenever she must deal with them. Aversive racists range from individuals who lapse into demonstrative racism when threatened—as when blacks get "too close"—to those who consider themselves liberals and, despite their sense of aversion to blacks (of which they are often unaware), do their best within the confines of the existing societal structure to ameliorate blacks' condition....

*A Cognitive Approach to Unconscious Racism*

Cognitive psychologists offer a contrasting model for understanding the origin and unconscious nature of racial prejudice.... [T]hey view human behavior, including racial prejudice, as growing out of the individual's attempt to understand his relationship with the world (in this case, relations between groups) while at the same time preserving his personal integrity. But while the ultimate goal of the cognitive process is understanding or rationality, many of the critical elements of the process occur outside of the individual's awareness....

Cognitivists see the process of "categorization" as one common source of racial and other stereotypes. All humans tend to categorize in order to make sense of experience.

Too many events occur daily for us to deal successfully with each one on an individual basis; we must categorize in order to cope. When a category—for example, the category of black person or white person—correlates with a continuous dimension—for example, the range of human intelligence or the propensity to violence—there is a tendency to exaggerate the differences between categories on that dimension and to minimize the differences within each category....

The content of the social categories to which people are assigned is generated over a long period of time within a culture and transmitted to individual members of society by a process cognitivists call "assimilation." Assimilation entails learning and internalizing preferences and evaluations. Individuals learn cultural attitudes and beliefs about race very early in life, at a time when it is difficult to separate the perceptions of one's teacher (usually a parent) from one's own. In other words, one learns about race at a time when one is highly sensitive to the social contexts in which one lives....

Furthermore, because children learn lessons about race at this early stage, most of the lessons are tacit rather than explicit. Children learn not so much through an intellectual understanding of what their parents tell them about race as through an emotional identification with who their parents are and what they see and feel their parents do. Small children will adopt their parents' beliefs because they experience them as their own. If we do learn lessons about race in this way, we are not likely to be aware that the lessons have even taken place. If we are unaware that we have been taught to be afraid of blacks or to think of them as lazy or stupid, then we may not be conscious of our internalization of those feelings and beliefs....

Case studies have demonstrated that an individual who holds stereotyped beliefs about a "target" will remember and interpret past events in the target's life history in ways that bolster and support his stereotyped beliefs and will perceive the target's actual behavior as reconfirming and validating the stereotyped beliefs. While the individual may be aware of the selectively perceived facts that support his categorization or simplified understanding, he will not be aware of the process that has caused him to deselect the facts that do not conform with his rationalization. Thus, racially prejudiced behavior that is actually the product of learned cultural preferences is experienced as a reflection of rational deduction from objective observation, which is nonprejudicial behavior. The decisionmaker who is unaware of the selective perception that has produced her stereotype will not view it as a stereotype. She will believe that her actions are motivated not by racial prejudice but by her attraction or aversion to the attributes she has "observed" in the groups she has favored or disfavored.

### Unconscious Racism in Everyday Life

Whatever our preferred theoretical analysis, there is considerable commonsense evidence from our everyday experience to confirm that we all harbor prejudiced attitudes that are kept from our consciousness.

When, for example, a well-known sports broadcaster is carried away by the excitement of a brilliant play by an Afro-American professional football player and refers to the player as a "little monkey" during a nationally televised broadcast, we have witnessed the prototypical parapraxes, or unintentional slip of the tongue. This sportscaster views himself as progressive on issues of race. Many of his most important professional associates are black, and he would do doubt profess that more than a few are close friends. After the incident, he initially claimed no memory of it and then, when confronted with videotaped evidence, apologized and said that no racial slur was intended. There is no reason to doubt the sincerity of his assertion. Why would he intentionally risk antagonizing his audience and damaging his reputation and career? But his inadvertent slip of the tongue was not random. It is evidence of the continuing presence of a derogatory racial stereotype that he has repressed from consciousness and that has momentarily slipped past his Ego's censors. Likewise, when Nancy Reagan appeared before a public gathering of then-presidential-candidate Ronald Reagan's political supporters and said that she wished he could be there to "see all these beautiful white people," one can hardly imagine that it was her self-conscious intent to proclaim publicly her preference for the company of Caucasians.

Incidents of this kind are not uncommon, even if only the miscues of the powerful and famous are likely to come to the attention of the press. But because the unconscious also influences selective perceptions, whites are unlikely to hear many of the inadvertent racial slights that are made daily in their presence....

* * *

## Notes and Questions

1. Under current jurisprudence, only acts of intentional discrimination are unconstitutional. Professor Lawrence argues that this view is unduly narrow and that "the law should be equally concerned when the mind's censor successfully disguises a socially repugnant wish like racism if that motive produces behavior that has a discriminatory result as injurious as if it flowed from a consciously held motive." *Id.* at 344. These issues are discussed more in Chapter XIII.

2. How might unconscious racism play a role in a decision to site a hazardous waste facility or other wanted land use? In Bean v. Southwestern Waste Management Corp., 482 F. Supp. 673 (S.D. Texas 1979), *aff'd without op.,* 782 F.2d 1038 (5th Cir. 1986), a case discussed in more detail in Chapter XIII, plaintiffs alleged that the siting of a solid waste facility in a minority community in Houston was part of a pattern of racially discriminatory sitings by the Texas Department of Health (TDH). In rejecting plaintiffs' request for an injunction, the trial court noted:

> If this Court were TDH, it might very well have denied this permit. It simply does not make sense to put a solid waste site so close to a high school, particularly one with no air conditioning. Nor does it make sense to put the land site so close to a residential neighborhood. But I am not TDH and for all I know, TDH may regularly approve of solid waste sites located near schools and residential areas, as illogical as that may seem....
>
> At this juncture, the decision of TDH seems to have been insensitive and illogical. Sitting as the hearing examiner for TDH, based upon the evidence adduced, this Court would have denied the permit. But this Court has a different role to play, and that is to determine whether the plaintiffs have established a substantial likelihood of proving that TDH's decision to issue the permit was motivated by purposeful discrimination in violation of 42 U.S.C. § 1983 as construed by superior courts. [The Court found plaintiffs had not made this showing.]

*Id.* at 679–681. Do you think that TDH's decision, described by the judge as "insensitive and illogical," might have resulted from unconscious racism? Would it be appropriate for a judge to somehow take into consideration the phenomenon of unconscious racism?

3. Race and class are at times viewed as competing, rather than complimentary, theories for disparity in environmental risk and burdens. What do you think the relative role of each is as a causative factor? How does your conclusion inform the choice of remedies to address environmental disparities?

4. One of the more highly charged issues surrounding the environmental justice movement is the claim that environmental racism underlies disproportionate environmental outcomes. The term environmental racism reportedly was coined by Rev. Dr. Benjamin Chavis in 1987, as he was preparing to publicly present the findings of the United Church of Christ study on toxic waste sites and race (discussed in Chapter III(B)). Should the term be used to describe practices that unintentionally disadvantage groups based on race? Professor Richard Lazarus notes that Chavis' statement deliberately eschews the more neutral rhetoric of equity in favor of the far more volatile claim of racism, and that as a result "has had a transforming effect on environmental law. If environmental justice had not been so cast in terms of race, it is quite doubtful that the movement would have enjoyed such a strong political half-life." Richard J. Lazarus, "*Environmental Racism! That's What It Is.*," 2000 U. ILL. L. REV. 255, 259 (2000). Do you agree?

# Chapter III

# The Evidence

## A. Introduction

A central building block of the environmental justice movement is empirical evidence about the unequal distribution of environmental benefits and burdens. Such evidence has played a key role in galvanizing public attention to the issue of environmental justice and helped inform what the appropriate legal responses should be. Conversely, those who challenge the existence of environmental discrimination and the breadth of environmental justice claims have questioned how solid the evidence of environmental inequities is and whether seeming disparities are better explained by other demographic factors. This chapter examines some of the most important evidence on this critical issue.

There long has been widespread anecdotal evidence that communities of color and low income communities suffer disproportionate environmental burdens. This includes the alarming rates of lead poisoning among minority children, the high rates of pesticide-related illness among farm workers, a predominantly Latino work force, the high rates of Native Americans who mined uranium ore and suffer lung cancer, the growing rates of childhood asthma in inner-city areas, and the proximity of communities of color to hazardous waste sites and polluting facilities in areas throughout the country. Charles Lee, Environmental Justice: Creating a Vision For Achieving Healthy and Sustainable Communities 8–9 (1996) (unpublished manuscript). Over the past decade, however, especially since publication in 1987 of the United Church of Christ's study of the siting of toxic waste facilities (see below), academics and others have more systematically evaluated the distribution of environmental harms and benefits.

Some of the most well publicized research concerns the location of hazardous waste facilities. Numerous studies document that these facilities are concentrated in communities of color and low income communities, although there are a few that reach contrary results. In part the conflict in the evidence results from differences in the methodological design of the various studies. Section B examines some of the most important of these studies.

There also is a substantial body of research documenting that low income communities and communities of color are disproportionately exposed to a wide range of other environmental harms. Some of the studies analyze distributions dating back to the early 1970's. Section C looks at some of these studies, including recent studies that respond to criticisms about the design of earlier studies.

Researchers also have increasingly focused on how environmental benefits are distributed. Sections D & E examine studies about environmental enforcement and the distribution of environmental amenities, such as transportation funding, open space, and access to the waterfront.

### Pathfinder on Race and Income Disparities

An annotated bibliography of studies about racial and income disparities in environmental harms can be found in LUKE COLE & SHEILA FOSTER, FROM THE GROUND UP: ENVIRONMENTAL RACISM AND THE RISE OF THE ENVIRONMENTAL JUSTICE MOVEMENT (2000). Three surveys of the empirical literature are Paul Mohai & Bunyan Bryant, *Environmental Racism: Reviewing the Evidence, in* RACE AND THE INCIDENCE OF ENVIRONMENTAL HAZARDS: A TIME FOR DISCOURSE (Bunyan Bryant & Paul Mohai eds., 1992); BENJAMIN GOLDMAN, NOT JUST PROSPERITY: ACHIEVING SUSTAINABILITY WITH ENVIRONMENTAL JUSTICE (1994); and Andrew Szasz & Michael Meuser, *Environmental Inequalities: Literature Review and Proposals for New Directions in Research and Theory*, 45 CURRENT SOCIOLOGY 99 (July 1997). Some research on the siting of waste and hazardous waste facilities is summarized in U.S. GENERAL ACCOUNTING OFFICE, 10 STUDIES ON DEMOGRAPHICS NEAR WASTE FACILITIES, GAO/RCED-95-158R (1995).

A number of articles discuss methodological issues involved in environmental justice research. These include Christopher Boerner & Thomas Lambert, *Environmental Injustice*, 118 PUB. INT. 61 (Winter 1995); Paul Mohai, *The Demographics of Dumping Revisited: Examining the Impact of Alternate Methodologies in Environmental Justice Research*, 14 VA. ENVTL L.J. 615 (1995); Vicki Been & Francis Gupta, *Coming to the Nuisance or Going to the Barrios? A Longitudinal Analysis of Environmental Justice Claims*, 24 ECOLOGY L.Q. 1 (1997); Robert Bullard, *Environmental Justice: It's More Than Waste Facility Siting*, 77 SOC. SCI. Q. 493 (1997); Liam Downey, *Environmental Injustice: Is Race or Income a Better Predictor?*, 79 SOC. SCI. Q. 766 (1998); and Laura Pulido, *A Critical Review of Methodology of Environmental Racism Research*, 28 ANTIPODE 142 (1996).

# B. Hazardous Waste Facilities

## 1.   AN INTRODUCTORY NOTE ON WASTE FACILITY SITING

One of the seminal events in the environmental justice movement occurred in 1982, when the siting of a polychlorinated biphenyl (PCB) landfill in predominately African American Warren County, North Carolina sparked nonviolent demonstrations resulting in over 500 arrests. Against a well-publicized charge that the community was targeted for siting because the residents were predominantly African American, the General Accounting Office (GAO) undertook an investigation in the southern region (EPA Region IV) and found that three of the four major offsite hazardous waste facilities were in fact located in predominantly African American communities, even though African Americans comprised only about one-fifth of the region's population. U.S. GEN. ACCOUNTING OFFICE, SITING OF HAZARDOUS WASTE LANDFILLS AND THEIR CORRELATION WITH RACIAL AND ECONOMIC STATUS OF SURROUNDING COMMUNITIES, GAO/RCED 83–168 (1983). Other early research was conducted by Professor Robert Bullard, who found that the 21 of Houston's 25 solid waste facilities were located in predominantly

African American neighborhoods, even though African Americans made up only 28% of the Houston population in 1980. Robert Bullard, *Solid Waste Sites and the Black Houston Community*, 53 Soc. Inquiry 273, 275, 278–283 (1983).

In 1987, the United Church of Christ's Commission for Racial Justice (CRJ) released an influential national study that documented a significant relationship between the location of commercial hazardous waste facilities (often referred to as Treatment, Storage and Disposal Facilities, or TSDFs) and uncontrolled toxic waste sites and race. The study was based on a comparison of such facilities and demographics in zip codes throughout the country. The CRJ reported the following conclusions:

*Race proved to be the most significant among variables tested in association with the location of commercial hazardous waste facilities. This represented a consistent national pattern.

*Communities with the greatest number of commercial hazardous waste facilities had the highest composition of racial and ethnic residents. In communities with two or more facilities or one of the nation's five largest landfills, the average minority percentage of the population was more than three times that of communities without facilities (38% vs. 12%).

*In communities with one commercial hazardous waste facility, the average minority percentage of the population was twice the average minority percentage of the population in communities without such facilities (24% vs. 12%).

*Although socio-economic status appeared to play an important role in the location of commercial hazardous waste facilities, race still proved to be more significant. This remained true after the study controlled for urbanization and regional differences. Incomes and home values were substantially lower when communities with commercial facilities were compared to communities in the surrounding counties without facilities.

The report also found that three out of every five blacks and Hispanics, and approximately half of all Asian/Pacific Islanders and American Indians lived in communities with uncontrolled toxic waste sites. Commission for Racial Justice, United Church of Christ, Toxic Wastes and Race in the United States: A National Report on Racial and Socio-Economic Characteristics of Communities with Hazardous Waste Sites (1987).

In 1994, researchers updated the CRJ study (using 1990 census data as opposed to 1980 data) and confirmed that zip codes hosting one facility had more than twice the percentage of minorities as zip codes with no facilities. The study also found that the concentration of people of color living in zip codes with commercial hazardous waste facilities actually increased between 1980 and 1993. Benjamin Goldman & Laura Fitton, Toxics Wastes and Race Revisited: An Update of the 1987 Report on the Racial and Socioeconomic Characteristics of Communities with Hazardous Waste Sites (1994).

Also in 1994, researchers at the Social and Demographic Research Institute [SADRI] of the University of Massachusetts released a study at odds with the conclusions of the CRJ report. They found that based on 1980 census data there was no statistically significant difference in the percentages of the population that were African American or Hispanic in census tracts hosting commercial hazardous waste facilities as opposed to non-host tracts. An excerpt from this report follows.

# Douglas Anderton, Andy B. Anderson, Peter H. Rossi, John Michael Oakes, Michael R. Fraser, Eleanor W. Weber, & Edward J. Calabrese, Environmental Equity: The Demographics of Dumping

### 31 Demography 229 (May 1994)

[This article reports] the results from a national analysis of the distribution of commercial hazardous waste facilities.... This analysis is based on population data characterizing census tracts, areal units which are smaller and more refined than zip code areas.... Generally a census tract is a small statistical subdivision of a county with clearly identifiable boundaries and a relatively homogeneous population of about 4,000 persons. Tracts are the most commonly used geographic regions of analysis; as an additional advantage, they are delimited by local persons and thus "reflect the structure of the metropolis as viewed by those most familiar with it."...It seems appropriate to make a locally delimited area the basis for our analysis....

Our initial concern in this analysis is to determine how census tracts with TSDFs [Treatment, Storage and Disposal Facilities] differ from those without TSDFs. We compared the tracts containing [TSDFs] to the tracts without TSDFs but within SMSAs [Standard Metropolitan Statistical Areas] that contain at least one facility inside their borders.

[The results show that] the percentage of black persons in census tracts with TSDFs is approximately the same (14.54%) as in tracts without TSDFs (15.2%).... [W]e found no significant difference in the median percentage Hispanic [in tracts with TSDFs, and] we found no significant difference in the mean percentage of families below the poverty line or of households receiving public assistance.... Both the mean and the median percentage of males in the civilian labor force who are employed are lower in tracts with TSDFs than in tracts without. In what are the most dramatic differences, both the mean and the median percentages of the population employed in precision manufacturing occupations are substantially greater in tracts containing TSDFs than in other tracts....

These findings based on census tracts differ substantially from prior studies based on zip code areas, which are larger....

[An] analysis of [areas surrounding a TSDF] suggests how [census] tract-level results may be reconciled with previous studies by using larger geographic units of analysis such as zip code areas. TSDFs appear to be located in census tracts characterized by industrial activities. Also, the tracts surrounding these industrialized areas appear to contain higher concentrations of minority and economically disadvantaged residents. If it is a general feature of the social character and structure of cities that such groups are more likely to live near industrial centers, then the use of larger geographic areas in an analysis might obscure local neighborhood differences and indicate (correctly) that this larger geographic unit contains both industrial enterprises, such as TSDFs, and a higher average percentage of minority and disadvantaged persons.... [When] TSDF tracts are combined with their surrounding-area tracts for comparison with the remaining tracts of the SMSAs [the] larger unit of comparison...produces findings more similar to prior studies based on larger geographic units of analysis....

[The results of regression analysis in which the authors controlled for the effects of various demographic factors confirmed that manufacturing employment and the apparent industrial nature of areas were important factors in determining the location of TSDFs, and that racial characteristics of an area were not.]

[W]hen the areal unit of analysis is the metropolitan census tract, we find almost no support for the general claim of environmental inequity.... [O]ne variable is conspicuous for its strong, consistent association with TSDF location. The concentration of persons in manufacturing occupations is consistently higher in TSDF tracts for the nation as a whole and in nine of the 10 EPA regions....

\* \* \*

## Note and Questions

1. The above article reports findings based on 1980 census tract data. The same research team reported similar results based on their study of 1990 census tract data, although in the latter study they also found that a significantly higher percentage of low income families and families receiving public assistance lived in tracts where TSDFs are located. Andy B. Anderson et al., *Environmental Equity: Evaluating TSDF Siting Over the Past Two Decades*, 25 WASTE AGE 83, 84 (July 1994).

2. Differences between the CRJ and SADRI studies appear to stem from differences in the methodological designs of the studies. First, the SADRI study did not use the entire U.S. as its comparison group, but only metropolitan areas with commercial waste sites on the theory that areas without currently operating waste facilities are not feasible for TSDFs. Professor Paul Mohai criticizes this approach, arguing that being rural (or a metropolitan area without an existing waste site) does not necessarily disqualify an area from being considered for waste siting, and in fact the largest commercial hazardous waste landfill in the country, with 23% of the nation's hazardous waste landfill capacity, is located in the rural (predominantly African American) community of Emelle, Alabama. The effect of using the narrower control group is to increase significantly the percent of people of color in the control areas, which reduces the likelihood of finding racial disparities. Mohai argues:

> In effect, the UCC [CRJ] study addresses the question of where hazardous waste facilities are most likely to be located, regardless of whether these areas are urban or rural. The UMass [SADRI] study, on the other hand, addresses the question of where within metropolitan areas currently containing a facility such facilities are likely to be located. Unlike the UCC study, the UMass study treats as unimportant the fact that metropolitan areas currently hosting hazardous waste facilities are places with simultaneously high concentrations of people of color.

Paul Mohai, *The Demographics of Dumping Revisited: Examining the Impact of Alternate Methodologies in Environmental Justice Research*, 14 VA. ENVTL L. J. 615, 648 (1995). Second, the SADRI study did not examine disparities for all people of color as a group, but rather only separately for blacks and Hispanics, which leaves out eleven percent of the people of color population in the U.S. Third, the SADRI study uses census tracts rather than zip codes as its geographic unit of analysis. When the SADRI researchers combined census tracts to create larger local areas, they also found racial disparities. Benjamin Goldman and Laura Fitton note that these results "suggest that there may be a complex pattern of white enclaves within black areas with waste facilities. Since [the researchers] also found that white enclaves had higher levels of industrial employment, their findings suggest that there may be an imbalance between the distribution of beneficial employment effects (only in the white enclaves) and potentially adverse environmental effects (in both the white enclaves and surrounding black areas) of commercial hazardous waste sites and associated industries." Goldman & Fitton, *supra*, at 15.

Professor Vicki Been and Frances Gupta subsequently conducted a national study to (a) examine where TSDFs are sited, and (b) test Been's "market dynamics" theory that areas hosting polluting facilities become more minority after the facilities are sited there (see Chapter II for excerpt of article elaborating that theory).

## Vicki Been & Francis Gupta,
## Coming to the Nuisance or Going to the Barrios? A Longitudinal Analysis of Environmental Justice Claims
### 24 Ecology Law Quarterly 1 (1997)

[[E]nvironmental justice advocates point to a score of studies that analyze the correlation between the location of LULUs [locally unwanted land uses] and the demographics of the neighborhoods....I cautioned against making policy changes based on this evidence in early 1994, arguing that the research failed to examine whether the host communities were disproportionately poor or minority at the time the sites were selected, or whether they became so following the siting....Instead, the research left open the possibility that the sites for the facilities originally were chosen in a manner that was neither intentionally discriminatory nor discriminatory in effect, but that market responses to the facilities led the host neighborhoods to become disproportionately populated by the poor, and by racial and ethnic minorities....

Determining whether siting processes, market dynamics, or some combination of the two were responsible for the disproportionate burden revealed by [prior studies] required an analysis of the demographics of host communities at the time their facilities were sited, and of subsequent changes in the demographics of those communities....

[M]y research team conducted a nationwide study of the demographics of the 544 communities that in 1994 hosted active commercial hazardous waste treatment storage and disposal facilities....Our research focused on the same types of facilities that the CRJ and SADRI studied—commercial hazardous waste treatment storage and disposal facilities (TSDFs)....

*The Geographic Area Analyzed*

There is a great deal of controversy about whether census tracts, smaller census units like block groups, larger zip code areas, or concentric circles of various radii are the preferred unit of analysis for environmental justice studies. For our longitudinal analysis, census tracts were the only option....Census tracts are preferable to zip codes for several other reasons as well. Census tracts are drawn up by local committees, and are intended to reflect the community's view of where one neighborhood ends and another begins. Zip codes are drawn to enhance the efficiency of mail delivery; they are not intended to reflect neighborhoods. Concentric circles are unlikely to bear much relationship to the community's views of its borders, which often are linked to natural or physical boundaries such as waterways, highways, or major roads....

We compared the demographics of host tracts to those of all non-host tracts [as opposed to comparing host tracts to just non-host tracts in metropolitan areas that contained at least one TSDF. Eds.]....

*Were Host Communities Disproportionately Composed of Minorities or the Poor at the Time the Facility Was Sited?*

...[W]e examined whether the areas selected to host facilities were disproportionately populated by minorities at the time the siting decisions were made....

[C]omparisons of the means and comparisons of the distributions of host and non-host tracts provide little evidence that between 1970 and 1990 TSDFs were sited in communities that had disproportionately high percentages of African Americans at the time of the siting. Both types of tests provide evidence, however, that at least those facilities sited in the 1970s were placed in communities that had higher than average percentages of Hispanics.

Both the comparisons of means and distributions focus only on one dimension of a neighborhood's demographic profile at a time. They leave open the possibility that although the mean percentage of African Americans is not significantly different in host and non-host tracts, other variables that are closely correlated with the percentage African Americans, such as mean family income, are hiding some of the relationship between race and the probability of a siting. To isolate the influence of each demographic variable if all other variables are held constant, multivariate techniques are necessary....

[Multivariate analysis] of the demographic characteristics of those tracts chosen to host facilities since 1970, as of the census conducted immediately before the site was selected, reveals scant evidence that the siting process has a disproportionate effect on African Americans.... The analysis also provides no support for the notion that neighborhoods with high percentages of poor are disproportionately chosen as sites. Indeed, in 1980, the percentage of poor in a tract was a negative and significant predictor of which tracts would be selected as hosts.

The analysis does support the claim that the siting process was affected, either intentionally or unintentionally, by the percentage of Hispanics in potential host communities. The comparison of means in 1970 reveals a significantly higher percentage of Hispanics in host tracts than in non-host tracts, and the [results of the multivariate analysis] for both 1970 and 1980 show that the percentage of Hispanics is positively and significantly correlated, at the ninety-nine percent confidence level, with the probability that a tract hosts a facility....

*Did the Demographics of Host Tracts Change Significantly Following the Siting of a Facility?*

The primary competing explanation of why facilities might be located in areas that are now disproportionately composed of African Americans and Hispanics blames the residential housing market for the problem. Under this theory, the presence of a TSDF makes the host neighborhood less desirable because of the nuisance and risks the facility poses. Property values therefore fall, and those who move into the neighborhood are likely to be less wealthy and have fewer housing choices than those who leave the neighborhood. The siting of the facility results, then, in a neighborhood with lower housing values, lower incomes, and higher percentages of those who face discrimination in the housing market—primarily racial and ethnic minorities—than the neighborhood had before the siting.

To test [the] market dynamics theory, we compared the demographic characteristics of host and non-host neighborhoods as of the decennial census before the siting and as of the 1990 census.... [T]he study does not support the argument that market dynamics following the siting of a TSDF change the racial, ethnic, or socioeconomic characteristics of host neighborhoods. The analysis suggests that the areas surrounding TSDFs sited in the 1970s and 1980s are growth areas: in host areas, the number of vacant housing units was lower than in sample areas, and the percentage of housing built in the prior decade was higher. Such growth suggests that the market for land in the host areas is active and should respond to any nuisance created by the TSDFs. It also may suggest that the burdens of the TSDF are being off-set by the benefits, such as increased employment opportunities....

### The Current Demographics of Host Neighborhoods

We compared the means of various demographic variables for the 544 tracts hosting active TSDFs in 1994 to those of the approximately 60,000 non-host tracts, as of the 1990 census.... As the claims of the environmental justice movement suggest, the percentages of African Americans and Hispanics both are significant positive predictors of the presence of a facility. Contrary to the claim that host neighborhoods currently are disproportionately poor, the percentage of individuals with incomes below the poverty line is a significant but negative predictor: the higher the percentage of the poor, the lower the likelihood that the tract hosts a facility. Also contrary to expectations, median family income is positive and significant, and median housing value is positive, although not significant....

\* \* \*

## Notes and Questions

1. Been & Gupta conclude that the poorest neighborhoods appear to repel, rather than attract, facilities, and that working class or lower middle class neighborhoods bear a disproportionate share of TSDFs facilities. What factors might account for this? A recent study of the distribution of TSDFs in Los Angeles County also found that rising income has a positive, then negative effect on the probability of TSDF location. The study concludes that "some areas are too poor to have any economic activity, even a TSDF, while others are wealthy enough to resist TSDFs being sited nearby. In short, the most "at-risk" and impacted communities are working class, heavily minority neighborhoods located near industrial activity." J. Tom Boer et al., *Is There Environmental Racism? The Demographics of Hazardous Waste in Los Angeles County*, 78 Soc. Sci. Q. 793, 795 (1997).

2. Been & Gupta report a seeming inconsistency: even though they found that the percentage of African Americans in a tract at the start of 1970 or 1980 did not lead to a greater likelihood that the tract would be selected to host a facility sometime in that decade, and even though they found no support for the thesis that host tracts become more heavily African American after a facility is sited there, as of 1990, there existed a positive correlation between the percentage of African Americans in a community and the likelihood that a TSDF was present there. They attribute this ongoing disparity in large part to the disproportionate siting of facilities in African American areas prior to 1970. *See* Been and Gupta, *supra*, at 32.

3. In an earlier article reporting on the results of her study, Been concludes that "[i]n total, the analysis [reveals] that environmental injustice is not a simplistic PIBBY — "put it in Black's backyards." It suggests, instead, a much more ambiguous and complicated entanglement of class, race, educational attainment, occupational patterns, relationships between the metropolitan areas and rural or non-metropolitan cities, and possibly market dynamics." Vicki Been, *Analyzing Evidence of Environmental Justice*, 11

J. LAND USE & ENVTL L. 1, 21 (1995). What implications do the conclusions of the Been and Gupta study have for policymakers attempting to craft solutions to disproportionate siting of unwanted facilities?

4. Another nationwide study found that having a TSDF facility sited in a community did not lead to significant increases in the percentage of African American or Hispanic residents living there. Rather, demographic shifts in these communities are better explained by general population trends. John Michael Oakes et al., *A Longitudinal Analysis of Environmental Equity in Communities with Hazardous Waste Facilities*, 25 Soc. Sci. Res. 125, 147 (1996). A recent study of high-capacity TSDFs in Los Angeles County likewise found little support for the market dynamics theory, concluding that areas that attracted TSDFs were disproportionately minority, but that siting of TSDFs did not encourage minority move-in. Interestingly, that study also found that whether an area was undergoing ethnic transition also was a significant predictor of siting. The authors posit that "such ethnic transitions may weaken the usual social bonds constituted by race and make an area more susceptible to siting." Manuel Pastor et al., *Which Came First? Toxic Facilities, Minority Move-In, and Environmental Justice*, 23 J. URBAN AFFAIRS 1 (2001).

5. As noted above, the choice of the appropriate geographic unit of analysis—zip codes, census tracts, or other units, such as an area that approximates the geographic impacts from a facility—can significantly affect the outcome of siting studies. Been and Gupta used census tracts in the above study. Professor Mohai notes some of the limitations of census tracts:

> First, there is a lack of consistency in the size and shape of such units. Furthermore, hazardous waste facilities and other locally unwanted land uses may be located anywhere within them—in the center, off-center, or near a boundary. Although results of statistical analyses implicitly assume that all parts of the unit are equally affected and that the impacts stop at the boundaries, this is not likely the case. Some parts of the unit may be more greatly affected than others, and it is possible that neighboring units may be as heavily impacted, if not more so, than the host unit.
>
> [Some researchers] note that census tracts may be better than larger units, such as zip code areas, because they are not as subject to "aggregation errors" or "ecological fallacies" and because they can be used as "building blocks." However, just as there are potential pitfalls from using units that are too big, there are also dangers in using units that are too small.
>
> If units are too big, then it is difficult to know whether people within the unit are close to potential sources of pollution and unwanted land uses within the unit. If units are too small, the area that is adversely impacted may extend well beyond the boundaries of the unit. Lumping the adversely impacted neighboring units with the control population will likely dilute any differences between the populations being compared. This risk is particularly likely for inner city census tracts, which tend to be especially small. [Depending on the urban area, the radius of a census tract could be as small as one-quarter mile or less.] Unfortunately, this is where both people of color and pollution tend to be concentrated.

Mohai, *The Demographics of Dumping Revisited, supra*, at 649–650.

6. A 1995 study by the General Accounting Office found that persons of color and low-income residents were not disproportionately located in a one-mile radius sur-

rounding most solid waste (nonhazardous) municipal landfills. U.S. GEN. ACCOUNTING OFFICE, HAZARDOUS AND NONHAZARDOUS WASTE: DEMOGRAPHICS OF PEOPLE LIVING NEAR WASTE FACILITIES GAO/RCED-95-84 3(1995). Some other studies have reached contradictory results.

7. The evidence supports the view that sites listed on EPA's National Priority List (NPL) under Superfund are more likely to be located in predominantly nonwhite areas, but not in areas that are less wealthy. *See, e.g.,* John A. Hird, *Environmental Policy and Equity: The Case of Superfund,* 12 J. POL'Y ANALYSIS & MGMT. 323 (1993). As Professors Hird and Reese note, however, NPL sites do not represent a random sample of all hazardous waste sites. "Indeed, one could argue that inclusion on the list — which is a precondition to federal cleanup support — is itself a function of political influence or greater wealth on the part of a particular community." John A. Hird & Michael Reese, *The Distribution of Environmental Quality: An Empirical Analysis,* 79 SOC. SCI. Q. 693, 697 (1998). Contaminated sites are examined in Chapter IX.

# C. Other Industrial Activities and Environmental Harms

While some of the most highly publicized research about environmental justice concerns hazardous waste facilities, there is a substantial body of evidence about the distribution of a broad range of other environmental hazards. This section looks at some of this research.

## 1. EARLY STUDIES

The following excerpt summarizes the major studies about disparate environmental harms that had been done as of 1992, including studies dating back to the 1970's.

### Paul Mohai & Bunyan Bryant, Environmental Racism: Reviewing the Evidence, *in* Race and the Incidence of Environmental Hazards: A Time for Discourse 163
(Bunyan Bryant & Paul Mohai eds., 1992)

Table 1 contains a summary of 15 studies which provide systematic information about the social distribution of environmental hazards. In assessing the distribution of these hazards by income, the typical approach has been to correlate the average or median household or family income of the community (usually approximated by U.S. Census tracts or zip code areas) with the degree of exposure to the hazard. In assessing the distribution of environmental hazards by race, the minority percentage of the community has been typically employed....

A number of interesting and important facts emerge from an examination of Table 1....Rather than being a recent discovery, documentation of environmental

## Table 1
### Studies Providing Systematic Empirical Evidence Regarding the Burden of Environmental Hazards by Income and Race

| Study | Hazard | Focus of Study | Distribution Inequitable by Income | Distribution Inequitable by Race | Income or Race More Important? |
|---|---|---|---|---|---|
| CEQ. (1971) | Air Poll. | Urban Area | Yes | NA* | NA |
| Freeman (1972) | Air Poll. | Urban Areas | Yes | Yes | Race |
| Harrison (1975) | Air Poll. | Urban Areas | Yes | NA | NA |
| | Air Poll. | Nation | No | NA | NA |
| Kruvant (1975) | Air Poll. | Urban Area | Yes | Yes | Income |
| Zupan (1975) | Air Poll. | Urban Area | Yes | NA | NA |
| Burch (1976) | Air Poll. | Urban Area | Yes | No | Income |
| Berry et al. (1977) | Air Poll. | Urban Areas | Yes | Yes | NA |
| | Solid Waste | Urban Areas | Yes | Yes | NA |
| | Noise | Urban Areas | Yes | Yes | NA |
| | Pesticide Poisoning | Urban Areas | Yes | Yes | NA |
| | Rat Bite Risk | Urban Areas | Yes | Yes | NA |
| Handy (1977) | Air Poll. | Urban Area | Yes | NA | NA |
| Asch & Seneca (1978) | Air Poll. | Urban Areas | Yes | Yes | Income |
| Gianessi et al. (1979) | Air Poll. | Nation | No | Yes | Race |
| Bullard (1983) | Solid Waste | Urban Area | NA | Yes | NA |
| US GAO (1983) | Haz. Waste | Southern Region | Yes | Yes | NA |
| United Church of Christ (1987) | Haz. Waste | Nation | Yes | Yes | Race |
| Gelobter (1987;1992) | Air Poll. | Urban Areas | Yes | Yes | Race |
| | Air Poll. | Nation | No | Yes | Race |
| West et al. (1992) | Toxic Fish Consumption | State | No | Yes | Race |

*NA = Not Applicable.

injustices stretches back two decades, almost to Earth Day—an event viewed by many as a major turning point in public awareness about environmental issues.... Also worth noting is that [some of] these studies have focused on single urban areas, such as Washington, DC, or Houston, others have focused on a collection of urban areas, while still others have been national in scope. This observation is important in that it reveals that the pattern of findings is not simply an artifact of the samples used....

It is clear from examining the results in Table 1 that, regardless of the environmental hazard and regardless of the scope of the study, in nearly every case the distribution of pollution has been found to be inequitable by income. And with only one exception, the distribution of pollution has been found to be inequitable by race. Where the distribution of pollution has been analyzed by both income and race (and where it was possible to weigh the relative importance of each), in most cases race has been found to be more strongly related to the incidence of pollution....

* * *

## Notes and Questions

1. Mohai and Bryant's excerpt demonstrates that information about environmental inequities has been available for some time. Why has it taken a considerable time for public awareness to catch up with this empirical evidence?

2. Based on its own review of the literature, in 1992, EPA concluded that racial minority and low income populations experience higher than average exposures to certain air pollutants, hazardous waste facilities (and by implication, hazardous waste), contaminated fish, and agricultural pesticides. EPA further concluded, however, that there was insufficient data to determine whether these populations also suffer disparate health effects. The one exception was childhood lead poisoning. ENVTL. PROTECTION AGENCY, ENVIRONMENTAL EQUITY: REDUCING RISK FOR ALL COMMUNITIES, VOL. 2: SUPPORTING DOCUMENT 7–15 (June 1992). Indeed, there is unambiguous evidence that childhood lead poisoning—widely recognized as the most serious environmental health hazard facing young children—disproportionately affects low-income children and children of color. While blood lead levels of all children have been dropping nationwide, children from poor families are eight times more likely to be poisoned than those from higher income families, and African-American children are five times more likely to be poisoned than white children. 46 MORBIDITY AND MORTALITY WKLY. REP. 141 (1997).

In 1994, Benjamin Goldman reviewed 64 empirical studies examining a wide range of environmental hazards, and reported that all but one found disparities by either race or income. When race and income were compared for significance, race proved more important in three-quarters of the tests (22 out of 30 studies). BENJAMIN GOLDMAN, NOT JUST PROSPERITY: ACHIEVING SUSTAINABILITY WITH ENVIRONMENTAL JUSTICE (1994).

* * *

Two of the specific areas in which both EPA and Professors Mohai and Bryant found disparities are exposure to agricultural pesticides and contaminated fish. The next two articles explore these issues.

## 2. Farmworker Exposure to Pesticides

# Ivette Perfecto & Baldemar Velásquez,
# Farm Workers: Among the Least Protected
### 18 EPA Journal 13 (March/April 1992)

The United States is the largest single user of pesticides in the world. By EPA's own estimate, each year U.S. farmers use about 1.2 billion pounds of pesticides at an expenditure of $4.6 billion. More than 600 active ingredients are combined with other ingredients to form approximately 35,000 different commercial formulations. Yet, full evaluation of their hazards lags far behind the development of new products....

Those who suffer most directly from the chemical dependency of U.S. agriculture are farm workers, who are working in the fields while some of the most toxic substances known to humans are sprayed. The World Resources Institute has estimated that as many as 313,000 farm workers in the United States may suffer from pesticide-related illnesses each year. Another source estimates that 800 to 1,000 farm workers die each year as a direct consequence of pesticide exposure.

Ninety percent of the approximately two million hired farm workers in the United States are people of color: The majority are Chicanos, followed by Puerto Ricans, Caribbean blacks, and African Americans. This primarily minority population has among the least protected jobs of all workers. Farm workers are intentionally excluded from the Occupational Safety and Health Act (OSHA), which governs health and safety standards in the workplace; from the Fair Labor Standards Act, which governs minimum wages and child labor; and most importantly, from the National Labor Relations Act, which guarantees the right to join a union and bargain collectively.

The exclusion of farm workers from OSHA regulations has particular relevance to the pesticide issue. Under OSHA's principles of environmental hygiene, when workers are exposed to a toxic substance in the workplace the priority course of action is to eliminate the substance from the workplace altogether or to replace it with a nontoxic or less toxic substitute. If this is impossible, the option next in priority is to separate the workers from the toxic substance. The last option usually involves provisioning workers with some protective measures (e.g., protective clothing, masks, glasses, etc.)

Not being covered by OSHA, and therefore not able to legally petition the Occupational Safety and Health Administration, farm workers are forced to petition EPA, which is the agency in charge of regulating pesticides. But such petitioning offers few formal legal remedies, leaving farm workers virtually unprotected against pesticide hazards....

Furthermore, evidence indicates that for some acutely toxic pesticides, extant protective measures are ineffective. A case in point is the deadly pesticide ethyl parathion, a leading cause of farm worker poisoning in the United States and worldwide....

Parathion is only one of many acutely toxic pesticides belonging to the organophosphate family. These pesticides came into wide use approximately 20 years ago, when environmental awareness called for limitations on persistent pesticides that were contaminating the environment and damaging wildlife. Many of the persistent pesticides belong to the organochloride family and have been associated with chronic health effects.... The organophosphates, on the other hand, degrade much faster and therefore reduced the risk for wildlife and for consumers.

However, for farm workers the switch from organochlorines to organophosphates meant exposure to more acutely toxic pesticides, since many of these rapidly degradable pesticides (parathion is one of them) are characterized by acute toxicity, which can cause dizziness; vomiting; irritation of the eye, upper respiratory tract, and skin; and death. There is an irony here that has not escaped the attention of farm workers: The new wave of environmental consciousness, which forced welcome changes in production technologies, may have actually made things more precarious for farm workers, substituting acute symptoms for chronic ones....

*  *  *

## Notes and Questions

1. Does racism explain the legal system's treatment of farmworkers, who face some of the greatest occupational risks from environmental hazards?

2. Outside the farmworker context, a number of studies show that workers of color and low-wage workers are more likely than the rest of the population to work in jobs with higher exposures to toxic chemicals and other hazardous conditions, and that they experience greater risks of occupational disease and injury. Some of these studies are discussed in George Friedman-Jiménez, M.D., *Achieving Environmental Justice: The Role of Occupational Health,* 21 FORDHAM URB. L.J. 604, 610–613 (1994). For example, Asian workers are disproportionately exposed to hazards in the high-tech industry, including exposure to solvents that cause reproductive harm and other chronic illnesses, and repetitive motion injuries. Employee exposures to toxics are typically far higher than those experienced by community residents surrounding industrial facilities. In its 1990 comparative risk project, for example, EPA ranked occupational exposures as among the risks deserving greatest regulatory attention. Dr. Friedman-Jiménez notes that occupational diseases caused by exposure to toxic substances or hazardous conditions in the workplace are widespread: "The best available evidence indicates that 350,000 workers develop new onset occupational diseases and 50,000–70,000 active, disabled, or retired workers die of occupational diseases each year in the United States." *Id.* at 606. Why do you think workplace risks have received comparatively little attention from environmental groups in the past?

3. Social and economic factors add to the workplace risks faced by low-wage workers and workers of color. Because these employees are the most economically vulnerable, they may be less able than the general population to refuse or leave hazardous jobs, or to complain about unhealthy conditions. Recent immigrant workers fear retaliation not only in terms of potential job loss but also their immigration status. Moreover, "[l]imited English skills prevent them from grasping the scanty information on health hazards that is available. Many times, as new immigrants unfamiliar with the American system, they are afraid and unaccustomed to speaking out, challenging their employer, and complaining about their illnesses and work environment." Flora Chu, *Asian Workers at Risk ,* 3 RACE, POVERTY & ENV'T 10, 12 (Spring 1992).

## 3. EXPOSURE TO CONTAMINATED FISH

## Patrick West, Health Concerns for Fish-Eating Tribes?
### 18 EPA Journal 15 (March/April 1992)

There is concern that Native Americans may consume much greater amounts of Great Lakes fish than the general population and hence be at greater risk for dietary exposure to toxic chemicals.

To date, most studies of fish consumption have looked at licensed sport fishermen; they inadvertently exclude reservation-based Indian subsistence fishermen, who by treaty rights, are not required to obtain state fishing licenses. The few studies that have been completed so far provide only indirect evidence that Michigan Great Lakes reservation Indians may have disproportionally high fish consumption levels. . . .

The Michigan Great Lakes tribes of the Bay Mills, Grand Traverse, and Sault Ste. Marie bands of Chippewa all have a long and well documented fishing culture. When they ceded the lands of Michigan in the Treaty of 1836, they carefully reserved their most important resource, the Great Lakes fishery. (These rights were recently upheld by the courts.)

With this resource so highly valued both culturally and economically by these tribes, we would expect to find high levels of fish consumption—especially on the Bay Mills reservation, where high levels of poverty prevail and subsistence small-skiff fishermen are common. . . .

In addition to these historical and cultural indicators, we have evidence that off-reservation Native Americans in Michigan consume more than whites or than other minorities. Off-reservation Indians do need state fishing licenses, and in our recent statewide survey of consumption by Michigan sport fishermen, we picked up a significant subsample of off-reservation Native Americans. . . .

The current State of Michigan standard used to regulate point [source] discharge of toxic chemicals into surface waters (Michigan Rule 1057) assumes a fish consumption rate of 6.5 grams/person/day. The formula is very complex. However, the important thing to emphasize here is that the greater the fish consumption assumed in the formula, the tighter the standard becomes—in other words, the lower the levels are set for toxics permitted to be discharged by industrial and municipal drain pipes. If assumed consumption is too low, toxic emissions may be permitted that are a danger to public health.

In our study, the average consumption for the full sample was 18.3 grams/person/day, quite a bit higher than the 6.5 gram assumption currently used in Rule 1057. Further, when the sample was broken down by ethnic groups, non-reservation Native Americans consumed 24.3 grams/person/day compared to 20.3 grams/person/day for other minorities, and 17.9 grams/person/day for whites. In an analysis involving multiple variables, we found that middle-age Native Americans had the highest rates of consumption of all Native Americans, or 30.6 grams/person/day.

We would expect on-reservation subsistence fish consumption to be even higher than these levels, especially on poorer reservations, such as Bay Mills, where poverty dictates subsistence fishing as a protein source that is also sanctioned by traditional culture. For all Great Lakes tribes with high fish consumption levels, there is strong reason for concern for the public health of the reservation. By way of illustration, studies have found a high correlation between high levels of consumption of Great Lakes fish and high levels of PCBs in the blood of consumers....

\* \* \*

## Notes and Questions

1. West's findings have been replicated in other areas. For example, several recent studies rates document that fish consumption rates for Native American subpopulations in the Pacific Northwest are significantly greater, in some cases three to four times greater, than comparable rates for the general population in Washington and in the United States. These studies are summarized in Catherine O'Neill, *Variable Justice: Environmental Standards, Contaminated Fish, and "Acceptable" Risk to Native Peoples*, 19 STAN. ENVTL. L.J. 3, 51–54 (2000), discussed in Chapter VI.

2. If Native Americans consume three or four times the amount of fish assumed by water quality standards, should the standards be changed to take into account these higher rates of consumption? This issue is explored in Chapter VI.

## 4.   A NOTE ON METHODOLOGICAL CRITICISMS

As noted in some of the excerpts above, differences in methodological questions such as the appropriate geographic unit of analysis and the appropriate comparison population can significantly influence the results of environmental justice research. Critics have challenged the research documenting disproportionate environmental hazards on other methodological grounds as well. Some argue that early studies were inconclusive because they failed to clarify the independent effects of race, income, population density, and other demographic factors, or were limited in geographic scope. Others contend that the studies have only evaluated proximity to polluting facilities, which does not equate with elevated risk levels. For example, Christopher Boerner and Thomas Lambert maintain that:

> [A] flaw in the existing environmental-justice studies is that they imply rather than explicitly state the actual risk presented by commercial TSDFs. While the research attempts to disclose the prevalence of commercial-waste plants in poor and minority communities, there is no corresponding information about the dangers associated with living near such facilities. The regulatory requirements regarding the building and operation of industrial and waste facilities in the United States are among the most stringent of any industrialized country in the world. These requirements, along with the voluntary efforts of industry, significantly reduce the noxious emissions of commercial-waste plants and other facilities. Moreover, health risks are a function of actual exposure, not simply proximity to a waste facility. The environmental-justice advocates' claims of negative health effects are not substantiated by scientific studies.

Christopher Boerner & Thomas Lambert, *Environmental Injustice*, 118 THE PUBLIC INTEREST 61, 67 (Winter 1995).

More recent studies have attempted to address these and other perceived methodological shortcomings in the empirical literature.

## 5. MORE RECENT STUDIES

### a. CROSS-CUTTING ENVIRONMENTAL HARMS

# John A. Hird & Michael Reese,
# The Distribution of Environmental
# Quality: An Empirical Analysis

### 79 Social Science Quarterly 693 (1998)

[This paper examines the relationship between demographic characteristics and the distribution of twenty-nine indicators of environmental quality throughout the nation, including industrial air emissions, industrial water discharges, water quality, air quality, and proximity to hazardous wastes. The results are reported as follows]:

*Income.* Somewhat surprisingly, in [thirteen] of twenty-nine cases, income is positively and significantly related to pollution levels, and in only four cases...is higher income associated with less pollution at a statistically significant level. Therefore, the interpretation of the income variables is mixed....

*Poverty/Unemployment.* [W]hile there appears to be a strong positive relationship between the location of unemployed residents and increased pollution levels, the relationship is frequently negative between poverty rates and pollution levels. These confounding results do not allow us to confidently assert any clear relationship between pollution levels and counties with a large percentage of residents either unemployed or in poverty.

*Race/Ethnicity.* Even when numerous other potentially relevant variables are included in the analysis, race and ethnicity remain strongly associated with environmental quality, with both nonwhite and Hispanic populations experiencing disproportionately high pollution levels....

*Political Mobilization.* There is a strong and generally consistent association in the analysis between the level of potential political mobilization and pollution levels. For many pollutants examined, a higher level of actual or potential political mobilization is associated with lower pollution levels. For owner-occupied housing [one of the factors used to measure levels of political mobilization], the relationship is particularly strong....

*Manufacturing.* As expected, the level of manufacturing activity, measured as the number of manufacturing establishments per square mile, is positively related to most pollution level indicators....

*Population Density.* One of the strongest empirical relationships is, not surprisingly, between population density and a wide variety of pollutants. Urban areas are subjected to far greater pollution than their rural counterparts, even accounting for differences in manufacturing, income, poverty, and unemployment....

The results of this study suggest that environmental quality is unevenly distributed, that nonwhites and Hispanics are significantly affected by that uneven distribution, and that this uneven distribution is a national rather than a regional phenomenon. Pollutants tend to be distributed in a way that disproportionately affects people of color, even across different model specifications, different pollutants, and when many other confounding characteristics are taken into account. This conclusion is all the more powerful because plausible alternative political and economic explanations are here modeled explicitly (e.g., the influences of income, urban locations, manufacturing activity). At the same time, the results show that a variety of other demographic variables play an important role in explaining the uneven distribution of environmental quality throughout the United States. For example, the negative relationship between indicators of political mobilization and pollution is one of the strongest, and the positive relationship between income and pollution appears to be an important factor explaining the distribution of some indicators of environmental quality, as does population density and manufacturing activity....

\* \* \*

## Notes and Questions

1. What factors might explain the somewhat surprising findings of the above study that for a number of environmental indicators, income is positively related to pollution levels, and poverty rates are negatively related?

### b. TRI FACILITIES

# Evan J. Ringquist, Equity and the Distribution of Environmental Risk: The Case of TRI Facilities

### 78 Social Science Quarterly 811 (1997)

Are racial minorities and the poor exposed to greater environmental risks? [This study analyzes factors] accounting for the locational patterns of three underexamined elements of environmental risk; the distribution of Toxic Release Inventory (TRI) facilities, the density of TRI facilities, and the concentration of TRI pollutants....

Since 1987, the Environmental Protection Agency (EPA) has required over 75,000 industrial facilities to report their releases of some 200 toxic chemicals. [The number of chemicals subject to TRI reporting is now 654. Eds.] Together, this information makes up the Toxics Release Inventory (TRI)....

[The results of this study are as follows]: First, race clearly matters with respect to the distribution of TRI facilities.... TRI facilities are significantly more likely to be found in ZIP codes with large numbers of African American and Hispanic residents.... Second, class characteristics are associated with the distribution of TRI facilities.... [T]he probability that a residential area hosts a TRI facility is negatively associated with median household income. However, the probability that a residential ZIP code contains a TRI facility is also negatively associated with poverty rates and the percentage of adults who do not have a high school diploma. Thus, while TRI facilities are not prevalent in wealthy areas, neither are they disproportionately present in "underclass" neighborhoods. This suggests that these facilities, perhaps predictably, are located in working class residential areas....

[T]he factors explaining the [density] of TRI facilities in a residential area are very similar to the factors explaining the probability that any residential area will have a TRI facility....

Proximity to these facilities, however, may not substantially increase one's exposure to environmental risk.... In order to do away with the assumption that proximity is a good proxy for risk, I obtained data on the total weight of TRI pollutants released in each residential ZIP code.... [The] results paint a picture of TRI pollutants being concentrated in urban working class neighborhoods.... However, once again race matters.

All other things equal, residential areas with large concentrations of African Americans and Hispanics are exposed to substantially higher levels of TRI pollutants....

These results suggest three general conclusions regarding the distribution of risk from TRI facilities. First, there are racial biases in the distribution and density of TRI facilities and the concentration of TRI pollutants. Even when controlling for other factors, African American and Hispanic residential areas are more likely to be exposed to higher levels of these environmental risks. Second, certain class attributes also affect the likelihood that a residential area will host TRI facilities and high concentrations of TRI pollutants. The class results, however, are less predictable and consistent than many members of the environmental justice community might expect.... Finally, while racial and class biases in environmental risk should not be discounted, we have to remember that the general background characteristics of residential areas best account for the distribution of environmental risks from TRI facilities....

* * *

## Notes and Questions

1. As Professor Ringquist notes, while most environmental justice research examines the characteristics of hazardous waste facilities, sources with TRI emissions are much more prevalent, outnumbering hazardous waste facilities by almost 40 to 1. *Id.* at 813.

2. Professor Ringquist argues that proximity to a TRI facility may not necessarily translate into heightened environmental risk. Should the adverse impacts of a facility on neighboring residents be defined only by reference to the volume and toxicity of the facility's emissions? What other considerations might be relevant?

3. Another study using TRI generated for each zip code in the U.S. an air toxics exposure index, based on the volume of TRI emissions, their relative toxicity, and the distance of exposed persons from emission sources. The study found that communities with higher proportions of African Americans face greater exposures to air toxics, even after controlling for a variety of economic and political variables, compared to communities with lower educational attainment, high poverty levels, and higher renter occupied housing. Nancy Brooks & Rajiv Sethi, *The Distribution of Pollution: Community Characteristics and Exposure to Air Toxics*, 32 J. ENVT. ECON. & MGMT. 233, 243–246 (1997).

### c. AIR TOXICS EXPOSURES

## Rachel Morello-Frosch, Manuel Pastor, Jr., & James Saad, Environmental Justice and Southern California's Riskscape: The Distribution of Air Toxics Exposures and Health Risks Among Diverse Communities

36 URBAN AFFAIRS REVIEW 551 (2001)

[Environmental justice researchers] have largely limited their inquiries to evaluating differences in the location of pollution sources between population groups, while placing less emphasis on evaluating the distribution of exposures or, more important, potential health risks. Of special concern has been the need to move beyond substance-by-substance analysis toward a cumulative exposure approach that accounts for the exposure realities of diverse populations....

This paper tackles this challenge.... We specifically study air pollution in the Southern California Air Basin looking at 148 air toxics, also known as hazardous air pollutants (HAPs) listed under the 1990 Clean Air Act Amendments. By combining modeled concentration estimates with cancer toxicity information, we derive estimates of lifetime cancer risks and examine their distribution among diverse communities in the region....

[The study shows that] [e]stimated lifetime cancer risks associated with outdoor air toxics exposures in the South Coast Air Basin are ubiquitously high, with a mean and median of 59 per 100,000, and a range from 6.8 to 591 per 100,000. Overall, cancer risks exceed the Clean Air Act Goal of 1 in a million by between one and three orders of magnitude....

[To explore the correlation between race/ethnicity and lifetime cancer risks associated with outdoor air toxics exposures], we calculated population risk indices (PRIs) for each racial and ethnic group. Results in Table 2 show that estimated lifetime cancer risks on average are high for each group, exceeding the Clean Air Act goal of one in one million by two orders of magnitude. Moreover, estimated cancer risks for people of color are higher than for Anglos and exceed the average PRI for all groups in the region, with Latinos experiencing the highest risk levels.

| Table 2: Average Personal Risk Index (Excess Lifetime Cancer Risk) by Race/Ethnicity for the South Coast Air Basin | |
| --- | --- |
| **Racial/Ethnic Group** | **PRI for Estimated Individual Lifetime Cancer Risk** |
| African American | 63/100,000 |
| Latino | 65/100,000 |
| Asian American | 63/100,000 |
| Anglos | 49/100,000 |
| People of Color | 64/100,000 |
| Average Across all Groups | 57/100,000 |

[These] racial/ethnic disparities in estimated cancer risks persist across household income strata....

[The] results suggest persistent racial differences in estimated cancer risks associated with ambient HAP exposures.... [T]he probability of a person of color in southern California living in a high cancer risk neighborhood is nearly one in three, while the probability for an Anglo resident is about one in seven....

[The results hold true] after controlling for well-known causes of pollution such as population density, income, land use, and a proxy for political power and assets (home ownership)....

\* \* \*

## Notes and Questions

1. Recall the criticism voiced above by Boerner and Lambert that environmental justice studies do not demonstrate that poor and minority communities face disproportionate environmental *risks*, as opposed to simply being in proximity to polluting facilities. Do the more recent studies adequately address this criticism?

2. As noted by Professor Morello-Frosch and her colleagues, an analysis of the cumulative risks reveals a much more comprehensive picture than risks posed by individual substances in isolation, or risks posed by one source in isolation (a facility risk analysis, for example). Relatively few studies have examined the distribution of cumulative risks, in part because of the lack of data about ambient environmental conditions in the U.S. (Indeed, some activists argue that historically fewer air monitoring stations have been placed in environmental justice communities.) EPA has undertaken a project to begin addressing the information gap that hinders cumulative risk analysis, the Cumulative Exposure Project discussed in Chapter IV.

3. Another largely unexplored area of research is synergistic risks, the chemical interaction of particular substances to create a new and additional risk, rather than the additive effects of several substances. Beyond suspecting that certain chemicals tend to have a strong synergistic effect upon other chemicals, how should we account for the limited state of scientific knowledge about synergistic effects in quantifying risks? This issue also is explored in Chapter IV.

4. One of the perhaps surprising results of the Morello-Frosch study is that the concentration of hazardous air pollutants and their associated health risks in communities of color results mostly from smaller area and mobile sources, as opposed to large industrial facilities. As the authors of the study note, these sources are smaller, more widely dispersed and diverse in terms of their emissions and production characteristics than larger stationary sources, and have been subject to fewer regulatory controls. What special challenges do controlling such sources pose for policymakers? Does it suggest a greater need for examining land use and transportation policies?

5. Most decisions to site or permit polluting facilities are made at the local, regional or state level, by land use planning boards or state environmental agencies. In light of this, how relevant are national-level analyses of the distribution of environmental harms? Are regional studies, such as the one by Professor Morello-Frosch, et al., more useful for environmental decision makers?

6. In 1999, the Institute of Medicine's Committee on Environmental Justice reviewed the available scientific literature and concluded "that there are identifiable communities of concern that experience a certain type of double jeopardy in the sense that they (1) experience higher levels of exposure to environmental stressors in terms of both frequency and magnitude and (2) are less able to deal with these hazards as a result of limited knowledge of exposures and disenfranchisement from the political process. Moreover, factors directly related to their socioeconomic status, such as poor nutrition and stress, can make people in these communities more susceptible to the adverse health effects of these environmental hazards and less able to manage them by obtaining adequate health care...." COMMITTEE ON ENVTL. JUST., INST. OF MEDICINE, TOWARD ENVIRONMENTAL JUSTICE RESEARCH, EDUCATION, AND HEALTH POLICY NEEDS 6 (1999). A contrary view is offered by Christopher Foreman, who concludes that "even a reasonably generous reading of the foundational empirical research alleging environmental inequity along racial lines must leave room for profound skepticism regarding the re-

ported results." CHRISTOPHER FOREMAN, THE PROMISE AND PERIL OF ENVIRONMENTAL JUSTICE 27 (1998).

7. Professor Laura Pulido offers a different critique of environmental justice scholarship. She argues that the central questions pursued by environmental justice researchers reflect incomplete understandings about the nature of societal racism: the effort to determine by regression analysis whether race or income better explains disparate environmental harms assumes that racism is a specific thing whose affects can be neatly isolated, while the question of which came first, minority residents or the polluting facility, presupposes that racism is a specific, conscious act of discrimination. She further argues that the focus on these questions is due to the underlying political agendas (referred to as "racial projects") of two opposing groups. The first group of researchers, which seeks to refute the existence of environmental racism, views racism as an abnormality rather than a structural feature of U.S. society, and therefore aims to restrict any claims on government by nonwhites. The second group, which seeks to prove the existence of environmental racism and the primacy of racism as a cause, wishes to adopt an agenda in which race-based policies are pursued, thereby allowing more resources, consideration and authority to flow to nonwhites. Laura Pulido, *A Critical Review of Methodology of Environmental Racism Research*, 28 ANTIPODE 142 (1996). Do you find Professor Pulido's argument persuasive? Do you think that the competing ideologies have framed environmental justice research questions too narrowly?

# D. Disparities in Enforcement and Cleanup

In 1992, the National Law Journal ("NLJ") published a report analyzing whether EPA's enforcement of environmental laws was discriminatory. *See* Marianne Lavelle & Marcia Coyle, *Unequal Protection: The Racial Divide in Environmental Law*, NAT'L L. J., Sept. 21, 1992, at S1 to S12. The report reviewed all civil judicial enforcement cases resolved by EPA from 1985 to 1991 (with minor exceptions). It also looked at EPA responses to abandoned toxic waste sites under the Superfund program (the Comprehensive Environmental Response, Compensation, and Liability Act, or CERCLA), specifically examining all sites listed on EPA's National Priority List (NPL) from 1980 to 1992 (again with minor exceptions). The study classified zip codes around the facilities or waste sites into four quartiles, ranging from those with the highest white population and highest income to those with the lowest white population and income. It then compared the quartile with the highest white population (which it termed the "white community") with the quartile with the lowest population (referred to as the "minority community") and the quartile with the highest median income ("high income") with the lowest median income ("low income").

The study found that penalties for violations of federal environmental laws were substantially lower in minority communities than in white communities. Specifically, average penalties imposed under the federal hazardous waste management law, the Resource Conservation & Recovery Act (RCRA) were 500% lower; under the Clean Water Act, 28% lower, the Clean Air Act, 8% lower, the Safe Drinking Water Act (SDWA), 15% lower, and in multi-media actions involving enforcement of several statutes, 306% lower. The overall average penalty for all environmental statutes was 46% lower in minority communities than white communities ($153,067 vs. $105,028).

With respect to the effect of a community's income on penalties, the picture was less clear. The report found that the average penalty for all violations was significantly lower in poor communities than in wealthy areas—$95,664 per case compared to $146,993. But this result varied considerably by individual statute. Penalties under four statutes—the Clean Air Act, SDWA, Superfund, and RCRA—were higher in poor areas, ranging from three percent (RCRA) to 63% (SDWA) greater than in wealthy areas. On the other hand, in Clean Water Act cases average penalties in low income communities were 91% lower than in upper income areas, and in multi-media cases, the average fine in high income areas was $315,000 compared to $18,000 in low income communities. The study concluded that the pattern of penalties varied so markedly depending upon the particular law involved that income was not a reliable predictor of the size of penalties.

The study also found racial disparities in EPA's response to contaminated waste sites. In particular, it found that abandoned hazardous waste sites in minority areas take 20 percent longer to be placed on the national priority action list than those in white areas (5.6 years from the date of discovery until its listing on the NPL vs. 4.7 years). The report found that by the time cleanup commenced, this gap had narrowed and minority sites were only 4% behind white sites (10.4 years vs. 9.9 years), although in half of the EPA regions this difference was 12% to 42%. The study also found that EPA chose less protective cleanup remedies at minority sites, opting for "containment" (the capping or walling off of a waste site) 7% more frequently than permanent treatment methods that reduce or eliminate the volume or toxicity of hazardous substances. (EPA is required by section 121(a) of CERCLA to give preference to such permanent remedies.) At white sites, the EPA ordered treatment 22% more often than containment.

Finally, the study found gaps between poor and wealthy communities in responses to waste sites, although less pronounced than that between white and minority areas. Sites took 10% longer to be listed on the NPL in poorer communities; moreover, EPA chose containment 18% more often than permanent treatment methods in low income areas, and 35% more frequently in rich neighborhoods.

The National Law Journal study has been criticized on a number of methodological grounds. Critics have argued that the study's use of quartiles to divide cases into white and minority areas resulted in areas being classified as "minority" even though they were not in fact predominantly minority; that the disparities reported were not statistically significant; and that the NLJ failed to control for other variables that might affect penalties.

Two subsequent studies of the cases reviewed by the NLJ have questioned its conclusions. Professor Evan Ringquist found that the results varied depending on how one grouped the historical data. He first confirmed the study's findings that penalties from 1985–1991 were higher in white areas, but also found that penalties were higher in poor communities. Ringquist also examined civil judicial enforcement actions filed by EPA dating back to 1974, and concluded that from 1974 to 1985, penalties were higher in minority and poor communities, and that during the entire period from 1974 to 1991, there was little difference in average fines between white and minority areas (and that penalties were higher in poor areas). After controlling for other factors that could influence penalties, Ringquist concluded that "minorities are not disadvantaged by case outcomes in environmental protection, and the case for class bias in these outcomes is weak." Evan J. Ringquist, *A Question of Justice: Equity in Environmental Litigation, 1974–1991*, 60 J. POL. 1148, 1162 (1998).

More recently, Professor Mark Atlas also reevaluated the cases analyzed by NLJ using some different methodologies, such as geographic concentric rings around facility locations as the units of analysis (rather than facility zip codes), and correcting for mistakes in EPA's original enforcement database. Atlas found that the income level of an area had no meaningful effect on penalties, and that while a community's race affected penalties, it was in the opposite direction of what the NLJ found, i.e. penalties *increased* as the proportion of minorities in an area increased. Atlas also concluded that factors that influenced penalties the most were the specific characteristics of the case, such as the types of violations, whether more than one facility location was involved in the violation, and how recently the case was resolved (also noting that many other factors likely to influence penalties, such as severity of the offense, past violations, recalcitrance by the defendant, etc. were not available in the database and could not be measured). Mark Atlas, Rush to Judgment: An Empirical Analysis of Environmental Equity in U.S. Environmental Protection Agency Enforcement Actions (unpublished manuscript).

As summarized by Professor Robert Kuehn, there also have been a number of additional studies examining bias in EPA's responses under Superfund, with mixed results:

> Professors Hamilton and Viscusi [concluded] that EPA Superfund cleanups were less stringent for sites in communities with a higher percentage of minorities, finding that while there was not much difference in the pace of cleanup, regulators did treat sites differently in terms of the cleanup remedies selected and the cost expended per cancer case averted based on the racial characteristics of the community exposed. Other published studies of EPA's enforcement of the Superfund program have found that: eligible rural poor sites were placed on the Superfund NPL at half the rate of sites in other areas, but they were receiving the same level of EPA attention for site inspections and emergency removal actions; the higher the percentage of black population around a Superfund site, the less likely it is that EPA has yet issued a record of decision; the pace of cleanup depended not on socioeconomic factors but mostly on the site's potential hazard; and neither the level of contamination deemed to require cleanup nor the level of permanence in the remedies chosen by EPA was related to the racial composition or median income of the communities surrounding Superfund wood preservation sites.

Robert Kuehn, *A Taxonomy of Environmental Justice*, 30 ENVTL. L. REP. 10,681, 10,695 (2000).

## Notes and Questions

1. What factors other than bias might explain unequal penalties in EPA's enforcement cases? Enforcement issues are discussed in greater detail in Chapter XI.

# E. Disparities in Other Environmental Amenities

Although less systematically than with respect to environmental hazards, researchers have begun to assess the inequitable distribution of environmental goods or benefits. The first two excerpts below look at the distribution of transportation funding, which raises important issues of social and economic, as well as environmental, inequality. The third excerpt considers open space and access to the waterfront.

## 1. TRANSPORTATION BENEFITS

# Robert Bullard, Glenn Johnson, & Angel Torres, The Routes of American Apartheid

15 Forum for Applied Resources & Public Policy 66 (Sept. 22, 2000)

The modern civil rights movement has its roots in transportation. In 1953, over half a century after Plessy vs. Ferguson relegated blacks to the back of the bus, African Americans in Baton Rouge, Louisiana, staged the nation's first successful bus boycott. Two years later, on December 1, 1955, Rosa Parks refused to give up her seat at the front of a Montgomery, Alabama, city bus to a white man. In so doing, Parks ignited the modern civil rights movement. By the early 1960s, young "freedom riders" risked death by riding Greyhound buses into the deep South. This was their way of fighting transportation apartheid and segregation in interstate travel.

Today, despite those heroic efforts, transportation remains a civil-rights and quality-of-life issue. All communities are still not created equal. Indeed, some communities accrue benefits from transportation development projects, while others bear a disproportionate burden in paying the costs. Generally, benefits are more widely dispersed among the many travelers who use new roads, while costs or burdens are more localized. Having a seven-lane freeway next door, for instance, is not a benefit to someone who does not own a car.

Lest anyone dismiss transportation as a tangential racial issue, consider that Americans spend more on transportation than any other household expense except housing. The average American household spends a fifth of its income—or about $6,000 a year—for each car it owns and operates. Americans also spend more than 2 billion hours a year in their cars. According to the latest figures published in the Federal Highway Administration's Highway Statistics, total vehicle miles traveled in the United States increased by 59 percent from 1980 to 1995.

Federal tax dollars subsidized many of the roads, freeways, and public transit systems in our nation. Many of these transportation projects had the unintended consequences of dividing, isolating, and disrupting some communities while imposing inequitable economic, environmental, and health burdens on them....

### Old War, New Battles

...Currently, only about 5.3 percent of all Americans use public transit to get to work. Most American workers opt for private automobiles, which provide speed and convenience, and most of them forgo car pooling. Indeed, nationally, 79.6 percent of commuters drive alone to work. Generally, people who commute using public transit spend twice as much time traveling as those who travel by car. Consider, for instance, that the average commute takes about 20 minutes in a car, 38 minutes on a bus, and 45 minutes on a train. People of color are twice as likely as their white counterparts to use non-auto modes of travel—public transit, walking, bicycles—to get to work....

[I]n Macon, Georgia, a city whose population is evenly divided between blacks and whites, [over] 90 percent of the bus riders in Macon are African Americans, and more than 28 percent of Macon's African Americans do not own cars, compared with only 6 percent of the city's whites.

A disproportionate share of transportation dollars in Macon and Bibb County, however, have gone to road construction and maintenance at the expense of the bus system. In 1993, Macon and Bibb County devoted more than $33 million of federal, state, and local funds for roads, streets, and highways, of which some $10 million came from federal funds. During the same year, local officials accepted no federal funds for the Macon-Bibb County Transit Authority and budgeted only $1.4 million for public transportation. Overall, the bulk of federal transportation monies received by Macon and Bibb County have been accepted to support road construction....

[R]ace is at the heart of Atlanta's regional transportation dilemma....The 10-county Atlanta metropolitan area has a regional public transit system only in name. In the 1960s, the Metropolitan Atlanta Rapid Transit Authority [MARTA] was hailed as the solution to the region's growing traffic and pollution problems; but today, MARTA serves just two counties, Fulton and DeKalb....

Between 1990 and 1997, Atlanta's northern suburbs reaped the lion's share of new jobs and economic development. During that period, Atlanta's northern suburbs added 273,000 jobs. This accounted for 78.4 percent of all jobs added in the region. Another 70,500 jobs or 20.3 percent were added in the southern part of the region. Only 4,500 jobs were added in the region's central core of Atlanta, representing only 1.3 percent of all jobs created during the height of the region's booming economy.

Clearly, Atlanta's people of color and the poor could benefit by having public transit extended into the job-rich suburbs. Public transit, however, does not go where most of the region's jobs are located....

* * *

## Robert Garcia, Mean Streets

15 Forum for Applied Resources & Public Policy 75 (September 22, 2000)

Martin Luther King Jr. recognized that urban transit systems in most American cities are a genuine civil rights issue. Today, close to half a century later, urban transit systems remain largely untouched by the reforms of the civil rights movement....

Consider the case of Kyle, a 26-year-old single Latina mother of two and a bus rider in Los Angeles. She works at a drug prevention program after having come off of welfare, which she describes as hell. Now she faces the new hell of her daily commute.

At 6 a.m. Kyle is at the bus stop with her children. Fourteen-month-old Ishmael is asleep on her shoulder; five-year-old Mustafa holds her hand. Two buses later she drops off Mustafa at school in Inglewood. Then she rides two more buses to get Ishmael to his baby sitter in Watts. From there it is half an hour to work. Kyle arrives about 9 a.m., three hours and six buses after starting. "The boys [sic] and Tread. We play games, we talk to other people, we spend the time however we can," she said. "In L.A. County, it's very difficult to live without a car."

Kyle's story is all too common. It illustrates the need for a national transportation equity agenda — one that provides choices to people who currently lack them.

The typical bus rider in Los Angeles is a Latina woman in her 20s with two children. Among riders, 69 percent have an annual household income of $15,000 — which is below the federal poverty line — and no access to a car; 40 percent have household incomes under $7,500. Elsewhere in the United States, the statistics may change but the stories are similar....

Ruthie Walls, a single mother looking for affordable housing for her children, bought a house in Atlanta surrounded by freeways on three sides. Cleaner cars have not stopped the harm she and her neighbors still suffer from the air, water, and noise pollution of increased traffic congestion. Their children play in toxic brake and tire dust collected in the creek that often floods their homes with runoff from the roads. They breathe the diesel exhaust from dirty buses. But they pay higher taxes for storm water cleanup caused by roads that serve suburban commuters and truck drivers....

### Equity into Action

...The historic 1996 case Labor/Community Strategy Center v. Los Angeles County Metropolitan Transportation Authority, filed on behalf of low-income and minority bus riders [showed the following]:

* Racial disparities. While 80 percent of the people riding MTA's bus and rail lines were minorities, most of the minorities rode only buses. On the other hand, only 28 percent of riders on Metrolink—MTA's commuter rail line—were minorities. Thus, the percentage of minorities riding Metrolink varied by 173 standard deviations from the expected 80 percent. The likelihood that such a substantial departure from the expected value would occur by chance is infinitesimal.

* Subsidy disparities. While 94 percent of MTA's riders rode buses, MTA customarily spent 70 percent of its budget on rail. Data in 1992 revealed a $1.17 subsidy per boarding for an MTA bus rider. The subsidy for a Metrolink commuter rail rider was 18 times higher, however, or $21.02. For a suburban light-rail streetcar passenger, the subsidy was more than nine times higher, or $11.34; and for a subway passenger, it was two-and-a-half times higher, or $2.92.

*For three years during the mid-1980s, MTA reduced the bus fare from 85 cents to 50 cents. Ridership increased 40 percent during the period, making this the most successful mass transit experiment in the post-war era. Despite this increase in demand, MTA subsequently raised bus fares and reduced its peak-hour bus fleet from 2,200 to 1,750 buses.

* Security disparities. While MTA spent only three cents for the security of each bus passenger in fiscal year 1993, it spent 43 times as much, or $1.29, for the security of each passenger on the Metrolink commuter rail and the light rail, and 19 times as much, or 57 cents, for each passenger on the subway.

* Crowding disparities. MTA customarily tolerated overcrowding levels of 140 percent of capacity on its buses. In contrast, there was no overcrowding for riders on Metrolink and MTA-operated rail lines. Metrolink was designed to have three passengers for every four seats so that passengers could ride comfortably and use the empty seat for their briefcases or laptop computers....

* * *

## Notes and Questions

1. The lawsuit described in the article, which alleged that MTA's operations of its transit system violated Title VI of the Civil Rights Act, was settled, with MTA agreeing to invest over a billion dollars to improve its bus system. What other measures would you recommend to redress some of the transportation-related inequities detailed in the Bullard and Garcia articles? In 1998, the Southern California Association of Govern-

ments adopted a regional transportation plan that explicitly analyzes the impact of transportation proposals on low income communities and communities of color.

## 2.  OPEN SPACE AND ACCESS TO THE WATERFRONT

### Samara F. Swanston,
### Environmental Justice: Mobilizing for the 21st Century: Environmental Justice and Environmental Quality Benefits: The Oldest, Most Pernicious Struggle and Hope for Burdened Communities
23 Vermont Law Review 545 (1999)

In urban areas particularly, trees promote environmental health. A recent study found that hospital patients recover from surgery faster if they can see trees from their rooms and that the sight of trees can quickly lower blood pressure and relax muscle tension. Another study found that people whose housing units were surrounded by trees got along better with their families and their neighbors.... Trees also remove soot and dust particles from the air, pervasive components of urban air pollution.... Trees improve property value....

[The] lack of open space is an important environmental justice issue for urban communities of color. The State of New York examined the benefits of open space and prepared a state-wide Open Space Conservation Plan at the direction of the legislature. That plan, which is revised and updated every three years, studies the open space needs of the state's residents and identifies which open space areas and historic sites should be preserved for future generations of New Yorkers. The 1994 Open Space Plan states that a vacant lot or a small marsh can be open space in an urban area. The Open Space Plan includes a Statewide Comprehensive Outdoor Recreation Plan ("SCORP") funded by the Federal Land and Water Conservation Fund. The SCORP evaluates the status of the state's recreational resources and their uses and forecasts demand over a fifteen to twenty year period. Each year that the SCORP has been prepared, only nine counties out of the sixty in the state have been found to be near or at their resource use limits or underserved by open space. Those counties naturally include the five counties in New York City, the counties adjoining New York City, and Erie County, where the city of Buffalo is located. New York City has the lowest open space standards for its citizens of any metropolitan area in the country—only 2.5 acres of open space per 1000 residents. Despite that low standard, two thirds of the community planning districts (primarily communities of color) do not meet that standard. The Open Space Plan identifies substantial social benefits from open space and land, including escape and relaxation, particularly for lower income citizens, for whom outdoor recreation may be the only affordable form of relaxation.... [It states] that open space in urban areas is as significant to the environmental health of city residents as areas in pristine condition are to people in rural areas....

[Another important environmental benefit] is access to the waterfront. It is undeniable that racism has played an historical role in limiting access to the waterfront and waterfront amenities for people of color in this country. New York City has had nonsegregated public beaches for decades, but its 578 miles of coastal waterfront are managed in a discriminatory manner. Seven years ago, New York City issued the first and most comprehensive analysis of its waterfront, prepared pursuant to the federal Coastal Zone

Management Act. That document identified coastal wetlands, fish and wildlife habitat designations, water quality goals, the location of sewage treatment plants, areas in need of combined sewer overflow abatement, areas of existing and proposed public water-front access, areas of existing and proposed greenways, and it made recommendations for future management and development along the waterfront. While the coastal zone is in all five boroughs, the only Significant Fish and Wildlife Habitat designations are in white communities. Surface water quality goals change dramatically according to the ethnicity and income of the adjoining community. The lowest water quality goals are found in the poorest and most diverse communities. For example, in the East River to the Throgs Neck Bridge, the water quality goal for the next century is "fishing" and fish consumption (since fishable waters means that it is safe to eat the fish), but as if an imaginary line was drawn directly through the water east of the Throgs Neck bridge, where the adjoining communities are all white and wealthy, the water quality goal is, amazingly, "bathing." In some areas designated "Special Natural Waterfront Area[s]," where public land acquisitions are planned or have taken place, legal public access is difficult or unavailable. There are also fewer public access points and amenities such as marinas and greenways, existing or planned, in communities of color. In fact, all of the industrially zoned waterfront ("Working Waterfront") is located in communities of color, and there are no residentially zoned or commercially zoned districts or approved redevelopment projects in communities of color. New York City has recently revised its Waterfront Revitalization Plan.... It proposes, in violation of the goals of the Coastal Zone Management Act, to limit or prohibit access to the waterfront in industrially zoned areas....

Disparities also exist in New York City in the location of trees and greening, the environmental quality benefit mentioned in the beginning of this Essay. Communities of color in New York City also have the lowest percentages of tree canopy. This means that in the areas that have some of the highest rates of asthma morbidity and mortality in the nation, such as Community Boards 1 and 2 in the Bronx, the City is missing the opportunity to improve environmental quality and environmental health by planting trees.

Some of the biggest disparities in environmental quality benefits New York City residents have seen in recent years are disparities in "green debts." The first and most striking example of this overt inequity and environmental injustice is Governor Pataki's [$1.7 billion] 1996 Clean Water/Clean Air Bond Act.... Of the $150 million set aside for open space acquisition, so far New York has acquired more than 178,000 acres of open space, primarily in communities overserved by open space upstate. Not one square inch of the acquisitions has been in underserved communities of color in New York City....

* * *

## Notes and Questions

1. Swanston, an attorney and adjunct law professor, notes that "environmental justice activists have been known to criticize national environmental groups for caring more about trees than people." *Id.* at 548. In light of the arguments she raises in her article, is this a fair criticism?

2. Attorney Robert Garcia reports similar disparities in access to parks and recreation in Los Angeles:

> Los Angeles is park poor. Los Angeles has fewer acres of parks per 1,000 residents compared to any major city in the country. Los Angeles has less than an

acre of park per thousand residents, compared to the ten acres that is the National Recreation and Park Association standard.

There are also vast disparities in access to parks and recreation. In the inner
city where low income communities of color live, there are .3 acres of parks per
thousand residents, compared to 1.7 acres in disproportionately white and relatively wealthy parts of Los Angeles. The paucity of park land is matched by
the lack of recreational facilities. Within a five mile radius of [a] planned Bald-
win Hills state park, for example, in the historical heart of African-American
Los Angeles, there is one picnic table for every 10,000 people, one playground
for 23,000 children, one soccer field for 30,000 people and one basketball court
for 36,000 people. These figures do not take into account the privatization of
public space. More affluent white communities have back yards and swimming
pools and basketball hoops over the garage and access to country clubs and
private beaches that low income communities of color do not have. The children in these neighborhoods lack adequate access to cars or to a decent transit
system to reach parks in other neighborhoods.

Robert Garcia, Building Community: Lessons From The Urban Parks Movement in Los
Angeles (unpublished manuscript).

3. Poor people and people of color have long faced barriers gaining access to public
beaches. A classic example occurred in New York City in the 1930's and 1940's when
master urban planner Robert Moses designed access roads to the city's suburban
beaches with overpasses too low to accommodate buses with poorer city residents. The
story of how localities in Connecticut and New Jersey excluded poor people and people
of color from their beaches in the 1970's is told in Marc R. Poirier, *Environmental Justice
and the Beach Access Movements of the 1970s in Connecticut and New Jersey: Stories of
Property and Civil Rights*, 28 CONN. L. REV. 719, 742–744(1996):

In the late 1960s and early 1970s, the public use of beaches became a highly
contested issue. Ocean beaches were more and more congested, due to increased
recreational use and the enclosure of portions of beaches in connection with new
housing developments, highrises, and industrial development.... [W]here
beaches were municipally owned, as in parts of Connecticut and New Jersey, the
shore municipalities often limited beach use to a town's residents, or put beach
fees or other barriers in the way of nonresidents' use of town beaches. Tactics of
indirect exclusion included charging much more for nonresident beach passes,
making cheap seasonal passes difficult or impossible for nonresidents to get, limiting parking near the beach and/or banning on-street parking altogether, making
beach access contingent on membership in a beach club which, in turn, would be
available only to residents of the community, barring disrobing and wearing
swimwear on the streets (which effectively meant one had to belong to a beach
club), and banning eating on the beach (which discouraged day trippers with pic-
nics). Such private and municipal actions limiting access to a beach often were
motivated not just by a desire to prevent overcrowding or to preserve privacy, but
were undertaken to keep out "those people"—that is, people of color, the poor,
people from the inner cities, hippies, and so on. Thus, restrictions on beach access, particularly through governmentally imposed policies that favored residents
only, sometimes took on the dimensions of a type of exclusionary zoning.

4. As seen in more detail in Chapter II, the "market dynamics" theory is offered to
explain the presently existing disparate distribution of environmental harms. According

to this theory, industrial facilities seek to locate in low-income neighborhoods because of economically rational factors such as the costs of land, favorable transportation infrastructure (such as nearby railroads), and a good local labor pool, not because the residents are low income or minority and have lack the political resources to resist the siting. In addition, according to the theory, the initial siting may occur in white, wealthier communities but the racial and income characteristics may change post-siting as residents with more resources may move out, resulting in a present racial or income inequity despite an initial nondiscriminatory siting. However, does the fact that environmental benefits seem to be inequitably distributed as well undermine this theory? There are no apparent cost justifications for providing more benefits in wealthier communities; in fact, according to the market dynamics theory, the opposite would occur. Since land for open space is cheaper in poorer communities, one would expect municipalities to site city parks in lower income neighborhoods.

# Chapter IV

# Risk Assessment

## A. Introduction

One of the most important issues of law and science is the use of risk assessment as the basis for environmental decisions. Regulatory agencies began relying on risk assessments with some frequency during the early 1980's, and since then, despite criticism on all sides, its use has greatly increased. Risk assessment's role could become even more prominent if various regulatory reform proposals that Congress has considered from 1994 to the present are enacted into law.

### Pathfinder on Risk Assessment

An excellent source about the risk assessment process is the National Research Council, Risk Assessment in the Federal Government (1983). Two more recent national reports are National Academy of Sciences, Issues in Risk Assessment (1993) and National Research Council, Science and Judgment in Risk Assessment (1994). In addition to the article excerpted by Professor Robert Kuehn in the text, articles that examine risk assessment and environmental justice include Brian Israel, *An Environmental Justice Critique of Risk Assessment*, 3 N.Y.U. Envtl. L. J. 469 (1995); Carl F. Cranor, *Risk Assessment, Susceptible Subpopulations, and Environmental Justice, in* The Law of Environmental Justice: Theories and Procedures to Address Disproportionate Risk 308 (Michael Gerrard ed., 1999); and Ashley C. Schannauer, *Science and Policy in Risk Assessments: The Need for Effective Public Participation*, 24 V. L. Rev. 31 (1999). Comparative risk assessment is advocated in Stephen Breyer, Breaking the Vicious Circle: Toward Effective Risk Regulation (1993) and John D. Graham & James K. Hammitt, *Refining the Comparative Risk Framework, in* Comparing Environmental Risks 93 (J. Clarence Davies. ed., 1996). In addition to the article by Professor Donald Hornstein and the book by Mary O'Brien excerpted below, comparative risk assessment is critiqued in Carl F. Cranor, *The Use of Comparative Risk Judgments in Risk Management, in* Toxicology and Risk Assessment: Principles, Methods, and Applications 817 (Anna Fan & Louis Chang eds., 1996) and Ellen Silbergeld, *The Risks of Comparing Risks*, 3 N.Y.U. Envt. L. J 405 (1995).

# B. Quantitative Risk Assessment

## 1. AN INTRODUCTORY NOTE ON QUANTITATIVE RISK ASSESSMENT

Quantitative risk assessments, the type most often used by environmental agencies, attempt to quantify the probability of an adverse effect occurring because of exposure to a given hazard (for instance, the likelihood of residents adjacent to a factory emitting benzene, contracting cancer). The process consists of four principal steps: (1) Hazard identification: determining whether the item under study (e.g. a chemical substance) causes an adverse health effect; (2) Dose-response assessment: determining the relationship between a given dose of the hazard and the probability of the health effect occurring; (3) Exposure Assessment: determining the extent of human exposure to the hazard in the environment; and (4) Risk Characterization: describing the nature and magnitude of the risk associated with exposure to the hazard. (For carcinogens, this is usually expressed as the additional number of deaths or diseases that will occur in the exposed population; for example, a 1 in one million risk means that one additional person per 1 million persons exposed will contract cancer).

Although the process seems to convey scientific precision, risk assessment is filled with substantial data gaps and scientific uncertainties. For example, estimating human risks based on laboratory animal testing—which is what most dose-response assessments entail—involves extrapolating from the effects at high doses of substances fed to rodents (to have large enough effects in the small samples of animals to produce statistically significant results) to low dose-effects in them and then extrapolating from rodents to humans. A variety of mathematical or other models can be used to make these extrapolations, often leading to very different results. Cranor, *Risk Assessment, supra,* at 325. Likewise, there is often limited data on actual human exposure to chemicals, and estimating exposures frequently requires crude assumptions about the fate and transport of chemicals in the environment. The National Research Council has identified 50 quantitative risk assessment "components," each with "inference options," requiring the risk assessor to select between different plausible scientific judgments about uncertain data or theoretical connections. At each point, the consequences of selecting one assumption over another are substantial. NATIONAL RESEARCH COUNCIL, RISK ASSESSMENT IN THE FEDERAL GOVERNMENT: MANAGING THE PROCESS 28–33 (1983).

*Risk management* refers to policy decisions about how to manage risks determined by risk assessments or through other processes—i.e., what level of risk is acceptable, and what steps society will take to control unacceptable risks. For instance, some statutes require that EPA protect the public against "significant risks," some mandate that standards be set at a level that is "requisite to protect the public health," allowing for an adequate margin of safety, while others require EPA to protect against "unreasonable risks," based on a balancing of costs and benefits. EPA and other federal and state environmental agencies use risk assessments to inform a variety of regulatory decisions. Perhaps the most common and controversial use of quantitative risk assessment is to decide if actions or chemicals are "safe" or if the risk presented by a chemical or activity is "acceptable" or "significant." Risk assessments are used in setting ambient environmental health exposures, in the registration of pesticides, in permitting the manufacture of new products that use toxic substances, and in governing the reduction or concentration levels of such substances. They also have a role in site specific decisions, such as deciding whether to permit new facilities, and guiding cleanup levels for contaminated waste sites and environmental assessments of brownfield sites. They also are used in tort liability cases to determine whether persons exposed to toxic substances have been harmed by the exposure. Cranor, *Risk Assessment, supra,* at 308.

The following readings explore some of the tensions between risk assessment and the tenets of environmental justice.

# Robert R. Kuehn,
# The Environmental Justice Implications
# of Quantitative Risk Assessment
### 1996 University of Illinois Law Review 103

*Methodological Limitations of Quantitative Risk Assessment and Their Impact on Environmental Justice*

Quantitative risk assessment is frequently described as merely a tool to aid decision makers, not a process that dictates certain risk management results. The methodology, however, raises serious environmental justice concerns, because the results of risk assessments often are not representative of the risks borne by all segments of the population and the aspects of risk that risk assessment seeks to measure do not capture the concerns of all members of the public.

*1 + 1 Does Not Always Equal 2*

On a daily basis, people are exposed to numerous pollutants from a variety of different sources. The National Academy of Sciences estimated in 1984 that there were more than 64,000 different chemicals currently produced, with over 12,000 manufactured in substantial amounts. In 1989 alone, almost six trillion pounds of chemicals were produced in the United States.... The effects of such multiple exposures and mixing, however, are a matter of dispute and a problem for risk assessment.

Quantitative risk assessment has problems addressing the aggregation of risks, which include multiple exposure, cumulative exposures, and existing exposures. Multiple exposures occur when a person is exposed to a combination of two or more different chemicals or pollutants, while cumulative exposures result when an individual is exposed to one or more chemicals or pollutants from different media or over time. Existing or "background" exposures or risks are those exposures that a person presently experiences, before the addition of any new exposures or risks. Risk assessments generally address the risks posed by one chemical or one source, and a regulatory decision of what is an "acceptable" risk customarily focuses on the risk posed by that single chemical or source. The total risk that a person faces, however, is an aggregate of these many, many risks, each of which individually may be deemed acceptable but in the aggregate may be quite substantial. If a person already has a significant level of existing or background exposure or risk, then the addition of even a small exposure or risk may have a greater effect on that person than on another person who is not already above or near some threshold of safety.... Because minorities and low-income communities face greater exposures to environmental contaminants, it is reasonable to conclude that the failure of risk assessment to account for multiple and cumulative exposures impacts these subpopulations more adversely than other population groups....

Synergistic effects among pollutants that mix also pose a methodological problem for quantitative risk assessment. Possible effects when pollutants mix include "additivity," "synergism," and "antagonism." "Additivity," the simplest effect, occurs when chemicals or pollutants mix and result in an exact combination of all the individual effects. "Synergists" are chemicals or pollutants that, when combined, result in a greater than additive effect. "Antagonism" occurs when the mixture results in diminished toxicity....

The phenomenon of synergism may be widespread among pollutants. Approximately 5% of chemicals exhibit effects that are more or less than additive. Although this percentage may seem relatively small, because there are so many chemicals, synergistic possibilities are huge. For example, if there were 12,000 chemicals in commerce today, and 2.5% reacted synergistically, almost 1.8 million pairs of chemicals would act synergistically.

Despite the propensity for chemicals to react synergistically and increase in toxicity, risk assessments rarely take synergism into account....

### A 70 kg, White Male Complex

...There is a high degree of variability in the response of humans to different levels of pollution. Age, lifestyle, genetic background, sex, ethnicity, and race may all play an important role in enhancing the susceptibility of persons to environmentally related disease. Studies have shown human variability of more than 1000-fold in drug metabolism and between 3 and 150-fold in the carcinogenic metabolism of various chemicals.

Variability in susceptibility may not only be large, but also wide-spread. Five percent of humans may be as much as twenty-five times less or more susceptible to cancer than the average person; one percent may be more than 100 times more susceptible....

The National Academy of Sciences found that interindividual variability is not generally considered in the EPA's cancer risk assessment....The default assumption usually employed in a risk assessment is that humans on average have the same susceptibility as persons in epidemiologic studies or as the most sensitive of the few animal species tested. Most epidemiology studies used in risk assessments are based on studies of healthy white male workers....[C]ertain genetic traits that increase susceptibility to environmental pollutants are more prevalent in racial minorities. In addition, biological differences may make certain diseases such as hypertension, chronic liver disease, chronic respiratory disease, and sickle-cell anemia more prevalent among minority populations and increase their risk of adverse outcomes to environmental exposures.

Lifestyle and socio-demographic factors also place minority populations at higher risk. Alcohol, tobacco, and drug use are more frequent in minority populations and result in impaired respiratory, cardiovascular, and metabolic processes, and in reduced ability to metabolize or eliminate toxic substances. Most minority populations also have a higher proportion of young persons and women of childbearing age. Because fetuses, neonates, infants, children, and pregnant women are more susceptible to the adverse effects of pollution, minority groups are more severely impacted by pollution because a higher proportion of these susceptible individuals are found in minority populations. Inadequate diets due to poverty and high risk diets due to cultural or historical reasons also may be more prevalent in minority communities and increase susceptibility; lack of access to health care or poorer quality care may increase the adverse effects of environmental exposures on poorer minority and ethnic communities....

[R]isk assessment most accurately portrays the risks of a particular subgroup—the healthy, seventy-kilogram, white male. Risk assessments use a seventy-kilogram male with the general biology of a Caucasian, as a so-called reference man, in developing dose-response predictions and assume that this reference man is an appropriate surrogate for minorities, as well as women and children. In addition, the dose-response models used to extrapolate from high-dose animal studies to lower-dose human exposures are based on the assumption that the exposed population is of uniform susceptibility. The result of relying on this reference man is a risk assessment characterization that fits far less than half the nation's population, because the majority are women, children, the elderly, sick, or people of color. . . .

### Just the Probabilities and Nothing but the Probabilities

. . . Risk assessment also tends to avoid certain aspects of environmental harm. Although nothing in the methodology limits its use to cancer effects, risk assessment, as presently practiced, usually limits itself to an examination of the risks of developing cancer, apparently viewing cancer as a proxy for all risks posed by an environmental agent or source. Noncancer health effects, such as respiratory, neurologic, reproductive, psychologic, liver damage, birth defects, cardiovascular, and hormonal or immune deficiencies, as well as effects on ecology, welfare, and quality of life, are often overlooked in the risk characterization. . . .

The distribution of risks has not been a focus of risk assessment, at least to date. The social aspects of risk, which concern not only environmental justice advocates but also the public in general, are simply not part of the risk assessment calculus. In addition, the almost obsessive nature of risk discussions that revolve around the difference between risks of one in 100,000 and two in 100,000 undoubtedly ignore equally important questions such as who are these persons who are at risk; what benefits will those who must bear the risk receive from this increased risk; what benefits will those who produce the risk enjoy; and is it really necessary to impose the risks on these or any other people. . . .

### The Effect of Quantitative Risk Assessment on the Democratic Principles of Environmental Justice

. . . Environmental justice is not just about distributional equity; it is also about procedural equity. . . . Under an ideal democratic model, citizens would participate fully and equally in the risk assessment process, along with agency officials and representatives of those who create environmental risks. Quantitative risk assessment, however, is a highly specialized decision-making tool that few can use or fully understand. To prepare, or even critique, a risk assessment takes a sophisticated understanding of complex issues of animal and human toxicology and physiology, mathematical modeling, and exposure measurements and predictions. . . .

Risk assessment is also information intensive. Toxicological data must be generated through studies or tests, or, at the very least, such data must be located and interpreted, and information on exposure must be gathered or predicted. Thus, preparing, critiquing, or even understanding a risk assessment requires substantial expertise and resources. Few people possess such expertise; only a few organizations have the resources to hire such expertise and to gather or generate needed information. Given their resource limitations, people of color and lower-income communities rarely, if ever, are in a position to participate meaningfully in the risk assessment process. . . .

Thus, quantitative risk assessment appears to reinforce, if not enhance, the special access and influence that powerful interest groups have on environmental agency decision making....

Quantitative risk assessment is extraordinarily information and resource intensive. Often little is known about how chemicals react in test animals and humans, or about the fate and transport of pollutants and the amounts that actually get to a target organ.... The cost of obtaining this necessary data is substantial. More than $1 million may be needed for an assessment of a single chemical.... Reliance on risk assessment not only results in fewer environmental hazards being addressed, but where regulatory action is taken, it is often subject to interminable delays....

*Putting Quantitative Risk Assessment in Its Proper Place*

Quantitative risk assessment provides the justification for a risk management paradigm that is hard to reconcile with the principles of environmental justice. Environmental justice is not about probabilities, statistical lives, acceptable levels of exposure to cancer-causing chemicals, substituting science for democratic decision making, or putting the opinions of experts before the wants and needs of citizens. "It is not about tinkering with risk analysis, risk assessment, risk management. It is about a new paradigm shift that emphasizes prevention and intervention." [Quoting Professor Robert Bullard. Eds.] Instead of measuring and defining an acceptable level of risk from a hazard, environmental justice adopts the public health approach of seeking to prevent the threat before it occurs and of remedying problems that already exist. In addition, the distribution of societal benefits and burdens and the justifications for actions that result in harm are as important as the science-based characterizations of environmental hazards....

\* \* \*

## Notes and Questions

1. Professor Kuehn, noting that "some form of risk assessment is not just here to stay, but given the current political climate, is likely to increase in use," advances numerous suggestions for reforming the risk assessment process. For example, he proposes that distributional information (the demographic characteristics of the populations at risk) and information on multiple and cumulative exposures be included in all risk assessments. Another suggestion is to provide for meaningful public participation at all stages of the risk assessment process, including its design, data collection, and analysis. He also recommends that risk assessment should inform the public about the pervasive uncertainties underlying the risk assessment process, suggesting that "[w]hen these unknown factors and assumptions are revealed, the public may see the lack of confidence in the estimates and may well question the reliability and relevance of risk assessment in resolving questions about environmental exposures." *Id.* at 150–153, 158-166. The latter suggestion is essentially a call for greater transparency in the risk assessment enterprise. How do you think industry stakeholders and government regulators are likely to react to these proposals?

2. Can you think of strategies for including the public in the design of risk assessments, as well as the subsequent data collection and analysis? How might research become more community-based as well as community-friendly?

3. Professor Robert Verchick argues that basing decisions about human suspectibility to hazards on healthy white males is illustrative of numerous gender biases in the risk

assessment process. Another is the usual choice of risk assessments to focus on the risks of cancer deaths, as opposed to the risks of miscarriages or birth defects. He also notes numerous differences in the way that men and women perceive risk, a point further discussed in the section following Professor Hornstein's article. *See* Robert R. M. Verchick, *In A Greener Voice: Feminist Theory and Environmental Justice*, 19 HARV. WOMEN'S L. J. 23, 62–87 (1996).

4. Because of the many uncertainties and data gaps in the risk assessment process, the outcome reflects discretionary decisions by risk assessors. Mary O'Brien argues that the economic interests of risk-producing entities inevitably influence how these subjective decisions are made:

> [M]ost risk assessments are prepared when permission is sought by a business, an agency, or a corporation to initiate or continue a hazardous activity or to use a poison. That is, a risk-management decision that will have consequences for a business or an agency is already on the horizon. The risk assessor is generally hired by private industry or by the government to do a risk assessment of a value-laden and sometimes highly controversial situation. Most risk assessors do not stay clear of risk-management considerations during the process of estimating risk. Since there is a wide choice of which numbers will be plugged into a risk assessment, and since no one usually knows for sure what is the "right" number to use, the pressure on a risk assessor to use numbers that will fulfill the wishes of the company or agency by which she or he is employed becomes tremendous. The bottom line in most (if not all) risk assessments is that if someone wants to continue some activity or to get a permit or approval for some activity, and if the outcome of the risk assessment will get in the way of that activity, there will be pressure to use optimistic numbers in the risk assessment.... An industry or an agency wanting to defend its activities would be more likely to hire a risk assessor known for seeing "less" risk rather than "more" risk in various activities.

Mary O'Brien, Making Better Environmental Decisions: An Alternative to Risk Assessment 27, 37 (2000). She offers one example of how the varying assumptions and biases of risk assessors can lead to widely varying results:

> As of 1993, the Intel Corporation had sold about $1.8 billion worth of Pentium computer chips (at the time, Intel's most powerful chip). This chip served as the brain of approximately 6 million desktop computers. But the Pentium could not do arithmetic correctly. For instance, the Pentium would get a wrong answer if you asked it to divide 4,195,835 by 3,145,727.
>
> Some IBM personal computers were built around the Pentium chip, but IBM in 1993 was planning to market its own microprocessor, called the Power PC, to compete with the Pentium.
>
> On November 24, 1994, the *New York Times* broke the story that the Pentium chip made mistakes when it did mathematics. A week later, Intel published results of an internal risk assessment saying that "average" computer users would get a wrong answer only once per 27,000 years of computer use. A "heavy user" might see an error once per 270 years, according to Intel's risk assessment.
>
> On December 13, 1994, IBM announced it was halting sales of IBM personal computers that depended on the Pentium chip. IBM's risk assessment

had determined that the Pentium chip could cause an error once per 24 days for average users, and a large company running 500 Pentium-based computers might produce 20 errors per day.

On December 13, the *Times* noted that the two different risk assessments might be colored by financial interests: "But some analysts said yesterday that IBM might have mixed motives in criticizing the Pentium. They noted that IBM was developing its own chip to rival Intel's. In other words, Intel stood to benefit from a risk-assessment conclusion that the Pentium chip was "safe," while IBM stood to benefit from a risk-assessment conclusion that the Pentium chip was "unsafe" (i.e. inaccurate).

If the Pentium chip caused an error once per 27,000 years (Intel's risk assessment conclusion), maybe Intel wouldn't have to buy back $1.8 billion worth of their Pentium chips. If it caused an error once per 24 days (IBM's risk-assessment conclusion), maybe IBM would have captured a chunk of the desktop-computer market for its Power PC chips.

*Id.* at 35–36. Is there a solution to the problem O'Brien identifies? Is there any way to prevent risk assessors from being influenced by the financial stakes at issue for their employers?

5. Some commentators argue that greater reliance on risk assessment in the environmental decision making process will benefit low-income communities and communities of color. They suggest that risk assessments will help identify the greater risks to which these communities are exposed, and thus result in more resources being directed toward these risks. Do you agree? One supportive example is that risk assessments showing harms to children and others from lead exposure played a major role in EPA's decision in 1985 to order the rapid phase out of lead additives in gasoline. The resulting reductions in childhood blood lead levels have been especially beneficial to low income children and children of color, who disproportionately suffer from lead poisoning. Conversely, other scholars point out that some of the disparate environmental harms discussed in Chapter III have occurred in areas regulated by statutory schemes like RCRA, Superfund and FIFRA that rely extensively on risk assessment.

6. Other critics of risk assessment, typically industry stakeholders and some from the scientific community, charge that the process as practiced by regulators relies on unduly conservative (protective) methods and assumptions, therefore overstating the risks posed by various activities. For instance, some criticize the practice of exposing laboratory animals to their maximum tolerated dose (MTD) of a suspected carcinogen, on the grounds that this causes abnormally high rates of cell division that make cells more susceptible to cancer. Others charge that the assumption employed in risk assessment that residential exposures will continue for 70 years is unrealistic in light of the frequency with which people move. A report by the National Research Council in 1994, however, concluded that the risk assessment methodology used by EPA was fundamentally sound. NATIONAL RESEARCH COUNCIL, SCIENCE AND JUDGMENT IN RISK ASSESSMENT (1994). Others contend that it is prudent to continue to use conservative assumptions given the fact that historically some toxic substances turned out to be much more harmful than once believed. For example, the recognized level for lead toxicity in the U.S. has been lowered dramatically over the past 30 years, from 60 to 10 micrograms of lead per deciliter of blood (Some recent studies found children with blood lead levels as low as 5 micrograms experience learning problems, and many experts believe there is

no safe level of lead exposure). What are the pros and cons of using conservative assumptions in the risk assessment process?

7. Risk assessment practice is starting to change to take into account the disproportionate risks faced by children. Children are especially vulnerable to environmental hazards because their systems are still developing, because they eat proportionately more food, drink more fluids, and breathe more air than adults, and because their behavior patterns, such as playing close to the ground and hand-to-mouth activity, increases their exposure to hazards. In 1995, EPA adopted a policy requiring that the environmental health risks of children be explicitly evaluated in risk assessments. EPA also pledged that it would set new regulatory standards at levels protective enough to address the potentially heightened risks faced by children and that it would re-evaluate a number of existing regulations to see if they met this standard. *See* <http://www.epa.gov/children/whowe/leadership.htm>. In 1997, President Clinton issued an executive order requiring that each agency make it a high priority to identify and assess environmental health risks and safety risks that may disproportionately affect children, and ensuring that its actions address these disproportionate risks. Protection of Children from Environmental Health Risks and Safety Risks, Exec. Order No. 13,045, 62 Fed. Reg. 19,885 (1997). The 1996 Food Quality Protection Act also explicitly requires EPA to address the special risks to infants and children when setting pesticide tolerances, the levels of chemical pesticide residues permissible on foods. If EPA does not have complete or reliable data to assess risks to children or infants, it can require an additional tenfold safety factor. 21 U.S.C. 346a(b)(2)(C).

# C. Comparative Risk Assessment

A second type of risk assessment, known as comparative risk assessment, is used to rank environmental problems by their seriousness or relative risk (as opposed to quantitative risk assessment, an enterprise that merely quantifies any given risk). Advocates of comparative risk assessment believe that it can be the basis for redirecting regulatory efforts toward the most serious environmental risks. Prominent proponents include John Graham, director of the Office of Information & Regulatory Affairs in the White House Office of Management and Budget, and Supreme Court Justice Stephen Breyer. Justice Breyer, for example, has argued that EPA and other federal agencies spend too much time and resources regulating small risks and that there are "many concrete possibilities for obtaining increased health, safety, and environmental benefits through reallocation of regulatory resources." STEPHEN BREYER, BREAKING THE VICIOUS CIRCLE: TOWARD EFFECTIVE RISK REGULATION 23 (1993). Two well publicized comparative risk reports by EPA likewise concluded that the agency's regulatory efforts were not targeted toward the environmental risks that experts believed were the most serious (and that they were instead more closely aligned with the public's ranking of risks). U.S. ENVTL. PROTECTION AGENCY, UNFINISHED BUSINESS: A COMPARATIVE ASSESSMENT OF ENVIRONMENTAL PROBLEMS (1987); SCIENCE ADVISORY BD., U.S. ENVTL. PROTECTION AGENCY, REDUCING RISK: SETTING PRIORITIES AND STRATEGIES FOR ENVIRONMENTAL PROTECTION (1990). In the excerpt below, however, Professor Hornstein questions the current methodology for ranking risks. He advocates greater—not less—deference to public risk preferences. As you read the excerpt, consider the environmental justice implications of the debate concerning the use of comparative risk analysis.

# Donald T. Hornstein,
# Reclaiming Environmental Law: A Normative
# Critique of Comparative Risk Analysis
## 92 Columbia Law Review 562 (1992)

To support *comparative* risk analysis, its proponents invoke the allure of rationality, of an analytic enterprise that can employ a common metric—risk—to separate those risks worth society's attention from those risks that are not. The impulse toward making choices according to a common metric is predominantly a utilitarian one, owing much of its contemporary force to the regulatory babble that can arise in an agency that must administer statutes which follow different, and in many ways conflicting, policy paradigms and to a political system in which the orderly administration of programs sometimes can disintegrate into a regulatory bazaar, with legislators and administrative managers responding to whichever combinations of political, beneficiary-group, and media pressures make the most noise. The resulting policy outcomes often seem to strain at the gnat while ignoring the camel, a state of affairs that comparative risk analysts find quintessentially irrational. . . .

### Expected Utility Theory and the Problem of Equity: The Failure of Comparative Risk Analysis to Accommodate Equitable Considerations

Much of environmental law addresses public health risks carried through environmental media, such as the risks posed to human populations by air pollution and groundwater contamination. Typically, comparative risk analysts evaluate these risks according to their expected losses across populations (generally referred to as "population effects" or "population risk"). But in doing so, comparative risk analysts tend to emphasize aggregate effects and to downplay how public health risks are distributed. For example, if the widespread use of chlorine in public drinking water systems causes each year an estimated 400 excess cancers nationwide, an evaluation based on population effects would rank it as a worse cancer risk than that posed by active hazardous waste sites regulated under the Resource Conservation and Recovery Act (RCRA) if air and water pollution from such sites cause no more than 100 excess cancers annually. For the "hard" comparative risk analyst, the evaluation of these risks is simple arithmetic: 400 cancers are worse than 100. This section argues that the full evaluation of these two risks is not so simple.

A system of environmental law must account for equities and inequities in risk-bearing if it is even to purport to incorporate one of the principal goals of any system of justice. Yet, after incorporating considerations of equity, a perfectly plausible case can be made that the risks posed by RCRA sites are "worse" than the risks posed by chlorine by-products in public drinking water: the ex ante chances of developing cancer from RCRA sites are concentrated on relatively few individuals rather than widely shared over the general population; the ex post distribution of actual cancers from RCRA sites is similarly concentrated, and unlike the case of low-level chlorine use, includes the heightened risk of destroying whole families or neighborhoods; and the cancer risks from RCRA sites are disproportionate in relation to the (indirect) benefits from hazardous chemical use enjoyed by the few risk-bearers.

That decisionmakers *might* plausibly reach different evaluations of environmental risks raises what I take to be an important attribute of environmental law: it must be able to reflect and define our values, and not simply count how many of us will suffer. . . .

## The Role of Equity in the Utilities of Public Risk

...Imagine an island community of one million people that must choose between three sources of electricity: a nuclear reactor, a biomass converter (which burns agricultural waste), and a coal-fired power plant. Assume further that (1) the nuclear reactor's *only* risk is a one-in-one-million chance of a meltdown which would kill everyone on the island, (2) the *only* risk from the biomass converter is its emission of small amounts of dioxin, which presents a one-in-one-million chance of causing cancer, and (3) the *only* risk from the coal-fired plant is its emission of sulphur dioxide, which presents a one-in-ten-thousand chance of causing death among the island's subpopulation of 10,000 asthmatics. To a comparative risk analyst interested only in the number of fatalities, the risks of the three electricity options are identical because each can be measured as posing the risk of a single expected fatality. Such a comparative risk analyst therefore concludes that the island community should be indifferent among the options.

Yet surely an evaluation of the risks, and the texture of the public debate, should be richer than comparative risk analysis suggests. The coal-fired plant, for example, is unfair in both the ex ante and ex post senses. It distributes the chances of becoming a fatality only among asthmatics (ex ante inequity) and will concentrate actual fatalities only on one subgroup of the population (ex post inequity). Although the nuclear reactor and biomass converter spread the chances of becoming a fatality equally among the island's entire population (and thus are fair in the ex ante sense), they surely differ as to ex post equity. Only the nuclear reactor assures that everyone on the island is "in it together" and will share a common fate. This hardly means that the nuclear reactor will be, or should be, chosen. There will undoubtedly be different, strongly held viewpoints about the reactor's risk-distribution profile. Some people may be attracted to its common-fate quality and to the fact that it offers by far the greatest chance of producing electricity without *any* fatalities. Others will be horrified by the worst case prospect of a meltdown....

The electricity-on-the-island hypothetical provides an opportunity to introduce a third type of equity, benefits-related equity. Assume that our island community chooses the biomass converter and then discovers it actually has two siting options: it can put the converter on either the leeward or windward side of the island. If placed on the windward side (from which the prevailing winds blow), the converter's dioxin emissions will drift onto the island's population. But if placed on the leeward side, the dioxin emissions will be blown over and settle onto Next Island and its population of 500,000. A fatality-oriented analysis of comparative risk may well favor the leeward site, after all it offers a significant reduction in expected fatalities (from 1 expected cancer to 0.5 expected cancers). Yet considerable empirical evidence suggests that most people would find the risks from a leeward site objectionable because these risks would be imposed upon a population (on Next Island) that doesn't share in the converter's benefits. All else held constant, benefits-related equity prefers an even distribution of risks and benefits.

## The Implications of Equity for Comparative Risk Analysis

That equity can affect the meaning of risk raises several theoretical difficulties for comparative risk analysis. The first, and most obvious, is that the comparative risk analyst's typical preoccupation with expected losses, especially "total" or "aggregate" risk levels, may not yield normatively defensible policy.... [Another theoretical difficulty] stems from the impossibility of ever trying completely to "model" equity. Environmental equity is a large concept, involving far more depth than is captured by the three "types" of equity that economists have abstracted for formal consideration. Society, for example, may find it particularly inequitable to impose environmental risks on the poor, on children, on the elderly, on fetuses, on future generations, or on racial minorities. Equity also involves process and participatory values, by which the ability of risk-bearers to share power in decision-making is independently valued....

### Expected Utility Theory and "Cognitive Error": The Failure of Comparative Risk Analysis to Accommodate Legitimate Public Valuations of Risk

The attitude of comparative risk analysts toward public participation in policy decisions is mixed at best. "Hard" comparative risk analysts scoff openly at the public's irrationality toward risk, noting with irony that the technologies which have propelled the country to such a high standard of living have also transformed it into a nation of worry-warts. Repeatedly, public rankings of risk are ridiculed when compared to those of experts....

### The Argument from Cognitive Error Theory: Misperception of Risk

...The core insight of cognitive error theory is that individuals often reach inconsistent conclusions about risky options solely as a function of the way these options are framed. As psychologists Amos Tversky and Daniel Kahneman stated in an important summary, "[b]ecause of imperfections of human perception and decision, however, *changes of perspective* often reverse the relative apparent size of objects and the relative desirability of options." Cognitive error theorists trace mental distortions of risk to a variety of "heuristics" (rules of thumb) and mental "biases" that people tend to use in lieu of expected-utility-type calculations in approaching risk.... Some of the heuristics that have been identified by cognitive psychologists suggest that the lay public tends to err in its assessment of the probabilities of public risks....

[It] is not clear, even with heuristics and framing effects, that public decisionmaking about environmental risks is substantively poor....

Consider, for example, that the availability heuristic may reflect a sensible way for the public to evaluate the *quality* of much statistical information about risk. [The availability heuristic describes the tendency of people to weight the probability of an event by the ease with which some relevant information comes to mind; other information, although relevant, is ignored simply because it does not come to mind so quickly.] Sociologist Charles Perrow notes that when a nuclear reactor suffers a major mishap, it is viewed by the risk analyst as "merely the occurrence of a rare event, that would be expected to occur, say, once in three hundred years for that reactor." But the public, when it responds with concern to the available information about this single mishap, may not necessarily be committing the fallacy of extrapolating from a single datum point a higher risk curve for nuclear reactors. Instead, the public may legitimately be concerned that there was *no* reliable risk curve for reactors in the first place.... To the extent the availability heuristic reflects public concern that formal projections of risk may themselves be conjectural, it can hardly be characterized as irrational. Even those committed to the hardest of versions of comparative risk analysis will concede that formal risk assessments are often "speculative" and "elusive."...

Even more importantly, public intuitions about risk can often be unpacked to reveal concern about a whole set of values that rational people may legitimately consider, values which are captured only dimly (if at all) in the technical risk estimates used by comparative risk analysts. Psychologist Paul Slovic, for example, has isolated "dread risk" as a decisionmaking factor (heuristic, if you like) that explains better than any other the difference between public and expert appraisals of risk. Dread risk is associated with the public's concern with lack of control over an activity, high catastrophic potential for fatalities, inequitable distribution of risks and benefits (including the transfer of risks to future generations), and the way in which fatalities may occur (for example death by radiation, death by cancer). These are hardly inconsequential values that should clearly be ignored in any rational calculation of a risk's social utility....

### The Failure of Comparative Risk Analysis to Frame Environmental Alternatives

... By tending to compare environmental risks with each other, rather than to alternative possibilities, comparative risk analysis emphasizes the wrong risk baseline, one that fails to capture the law's moral direction (as well as its abhorrence of market externalities). The result is an ideological scheme, based on an inward-looking set of comparisons, that is decidedly biased toward the status quo....

### The Baseline Problem: Bias Against Fundamental Reform

Comparative risk analysts inevitably fall back onto the importance of opportunity costs to justify the logic of using other risks as the proper baseline. The argument is that marginal analysis can be penny wise but pound foolish if it fails to consider among the "costs" of groundwater protection and other low-risk-oriented efforts (such as oil-spill prevention), the foregone benefits of progress that *could have been made* against global warming, stratospheric ozone depletion, indoor radon exposure, and other particularly high-risk problems....

[T]he wisdom of parsing environmental problems into discrete risks *among* which to force trade-offs, is heavily dependent on the basic assumption that environmental risks (and environmental-risk-reducing dollars) should only be traded off against each other. Certainly one can imagine emergency circumstances—where environmental problems plainly swamp identifiable, available resources—in which this form of triage makes sense as a reactive decisionmaking strategy. But in a country of considerable resources, can it really be said with confidence that the proper trade-off is between groundwater pollution and global warming, rather than between groundwater pollution and the $35 billion consumers spend annually for soft drinks? Only a system that fully values the damage done by groundwater pollution (through prices, taxes or regulatory standards) can force society to contemplate the opportunity costs of, say, the $78.7 million spent to watch *Teenage Mutant Ninja Turtles*....

\* \* \*

## Notes and Questions

1. As Professor Hornstein explains, a major criticism of risk assessment and comparative risk assessment is that they present risk as a single numeric estimate—the number of expected deaths or diseases in a given population. The public, however, evaluates risk based on a range of social, psychological, moral and emotional factors other than the probability of a hazard occurring. These include whether the risks are involuntary, familiar, preventable, evoke dreaded consequences, are within a person's control, impact children or future generations, and whether those at risk from an activity are those that gain its benefits. *See, e.g.* Vincent T. Covello, *Communicating Right-to-Know Information on Chemical Risks*, 23 Envtl. Sci. & Tech. 1444 (1989). Professor Covello notes that "people perceive many types of risk in an absolute sense. An involuntary exposure that increases the risk of cancer or birth defects is perceived as a physical and moral insult regardless of whether the increase is small or whether the increase is smaller than risks

from other exposures." *Id.* at 1448. Moreover, perceptions of risk tend to differ by gender and race. One survey, for example, found that nonwhites perceived greater risks from most hazards than whites did, and that women perceived greater risks from most hazards than men did. When race and gender were considered together, white males as a group differed from everyone else, perceiving risks as much smaller and much more acceptable than did other people. James Flynn et al., *Gender, Race, and Perception of Environmental Health Risks*, 14 RISK ANALYSIS 1101, 1102–06 (1994). As Professor Kuehn notes, white males are "most likely to be the risk assessors, officials with companies who are risk producers, and government decision makers," Kuehn, *supra*, at 156.

2. Comparative risk assessment and cost benefit analysis based on risk assessments are politically attractive because they hold out the promise that the public will receive "more protection from the greatest dangers at less costs than is being provided today." John Graham, *Edging Toward Sanity on Regulatory Risk Reform*, ISSUES SCI. & TECH. 61, 61 (Summer 1995). Do you agree that some form of risk ranking of environmental hazards is desirable to promote a better use of governmental resources? If so, how should the ranking incorporate factors other than the strict probability of a hazard occurring?

3. As noted above, Justice Stephen Breyer has been highly critical of our current system of risk regulation, arguing that federal agencies do not rationally prioritize their regulatory agendas. He attributes this in considerable part to differences between how the public, as opposed to scientific experts, perceives risk (he argues that agency priorities more closely reflect public perceptions than agency perceptions). He also maintains that the numerous uncertainties in the risk assessment process can lead to random regulatory decisions. His proposed solution is to create a small, centralized politically insulated, "blue ribbon" committee of health and environmental experts (a sort of super civil service), charged with developing coherent risk priorities for various federal agencies that regulate risk, including EPA. The committee would have authority to reallocate resources among agencies (e.g., shifting money from cleaning up toxic waste sites to vaccination or prenatal care), decide on uniform assumptions to employ in the risk assessment process, and so forth. *See* Breyer, *supra*, at 55–81. Underlying Breyer's proposal is the belief that insulating risk decisions from the current political and regulatory processes will produce superior results. Do you agree? Assuming it will, is it worth the trade off in terms of reduced opportunities for public participation?

4. Proponents of regulatory reform often cite studies that compare the cost per life saved of various federal regulations and which suggest that environmental regulations are far more costly than safety regulations designed to prevent deaths from accidents. Professor Lisa Heinzerling criticizes these studies for employing a technique that has come to be known as "discounting lives."

> That is, they reduced the government's estimates of the number of lives that would actually be saved by a regulation in the future by a fixed percentage for every year expected to pass before the deaths would otherwise have occurred. Discounting future lives is, like discounting future money, often justified by the idea that a benefit received in the future is worth less than a benefit received today. The "discount rate" for human lives has typically been calculated the same way as the discount rate for money; that is, according to the prevailing rate of return on private investment.... For money, at least, the idea behind discounting is that the present value of a sum of money to be received in the future depends on the rate at which the same amount of money, received today, could be invested to produce even more money in the future.

Discounting can have a profound effect on the perceived present-day benefits of actions whose purpose is to prevent future harm.... Because it is premised on the idea that a benefit received in the future is worth less than a benefit received today, discounting starts from the assumption that life-saving measures that produce immediate returns (such as measures to prevent auto accidents) are superior to life-saving measures that produce benefits over the long haul (such as measures to prevent diseases, like cancer, that develop over a long period).

Lisa Heinzerling, *The Perils of Precision*, ENVTL. F. 38, 39 (Sept/Oct. 1998). Do you agree that discounting is an appropriate technique for calculating the benefits of regulatory actions? Valuing life in this manner essentially means that a life saved ten years from now is worth less on a regulatory scale than a life saved today. Does this technique accurately reflect peoples' actual preferences for consuming sooner rather that later, and for living longer rather than shorter? Or do you think the public cares more about latent risks, and risks to future generations, than about immediate risks? Is discounting lives consistent with the Principles of Environmental Justice excerpted in Chapter I?

# D. An Alternative to Risk Assessment

Some scholars have raised a more fundamental challenge to risk assessment, arguing that it asks the wrong question: it starts from a premise that accepts the presence of risk as a given, rather than asking how to avoid the risk altogether. One such critic is Mary O'Brien. She argues that risk assessments should be replaced by alternatives assessments which consider a broad range of reasonable alternatives to environmentally damaging activities.

## Mary O'Brien,
## Making Better Environmental Decisions:
## An Alternative to Risk Assessment
### 3, 84, 113, 129, 135–36, 147, 171–172 (2000)

Imagine a woman standing by an icy mountain river, intending to cross to the other side. A team of four risk assessors stands behind her, reviewing her situation. The toxicologist says that she ought to wade across the river because it is not toxic, only cold. The cardiologist says she ought to wade across the river because she looks to be young and not already chilled. Her risks of cardiac arrest, therefore, are low. The hydrologist says she ought to wade across the river because she has seen other rivers like this and estimates that this one is not more than 4 feet deep and probably has no whirlpools at this location. Finally, the EPA policy specialist says that the woman ought to wade across the river because, compared to global warming, ozone depletion, and loss of species diversity, the risks of her crossing are trivial.

The woman refuses to wade across. "Why?" the risk assessors ask. They show her their calculations, condescendingly explaining to her that her risk of dying while wading across the river is one in 40 million.

Still, the woman refuses to wade across. "Why?" the risk assessors ask again, frustrated by this woman who clearly doesn't understand the nature of risks.

The woman points upstream, and says "Because there is a bridge."...

*Risk assessment obscures and removes the fundamental right to say "no" to unnecessary poisoning of one's body and environment.*

When citizens question hazardous activities on risk-assessment grounds, they are forced to operate on the playing field of formulas, models, quantification of data, hidden assumptions, biases, and selective use of information. If the citizens try to wade through this, they may forget that they have a right to deal with much more fundamental questions, such as the following:

Is this hazardous activity essential?

Do more sensible alternatives exist?

Should this community have a right to say no to being poisoned?

Does anyone have a right to take away something that belongs to us all (e.g., the Earth's ozone layer, the nation's public native grasslands, salmon species, migratory-bird flyways)?...

Prioritizing environmental problems using risk assessment implies that some are unimportant and can be ignored. A better way to approach our multitude of environmental problems would be to rank the most effective ways to give society the incentives and ability to prevent and solve all environmental problems.

In William Styron's 1979 novel *Sophie's Choice*, a mother is given a diabolical choice by Nazi bureaucrats. She is asked "Which child will you hand over to us: Your daughter or your son?" We all know that question should never have been asked.

When we, as a society, ask ourselves the comparative-risk-assessment question "Which environmental problems are of highest priority for our action?" we are asking a "Sophie's choice" question, because that question in essence also asks "Which environmental problems are of low priority for action?...

Alternatives assessment means looking at the pros and cons of a broad range of options....

Whenever an alternatives assessment is used to consider a broad range of reasonable options, two things are more likely to happen than when the risks of only one activity or a narrow range of options are examined:

Because the differing benefits of the various alternatives remind us of divergent considerations, it is likely that we will ask a broader range of questions about the alternatives. Some of these questions will relate to social, democratic, economic, and political issues. In contrast, a risk assessment tends to focus narrowly on biological questions (e.g., toxicity, disease, mortality).

The hazards of the more hazardous options are more likely to seem unacceptable, because those options seem more unnecessary when compared to reasonable alternatives that probably won't cause many hazards.

If you wanted to get approval to undertake a particular hazardous activity, would you want people asking big questions about the activity? Would you want people to think that the hazards or the potential risks were unnecessary? Alternatives assessment threatens the status quo. Alternatives assessment can make social change seem both desirable and possible....

Alternatives assessment can be installed as a sensible three-step public process for making decisions about all behaviors that affect the environment. The steps are these:

Consider a range of reasonable alternatives.

Discuss the potential environmental, public-health, and social benefits of each alternative.

Discuss the potential adverse environmental, public-health, and social impacts of each alternative....

Risk assessment of bad options is the main decision-making process in our society at the moment. Unfortunately, too many citizen groups think they have to cooperate with it, but they don't have to. When they do resist risk assessment, citizen groups employ two major strategies: saying "No" to unnecessary bad options or to risk assessment itself and advocating for "Yes" to better alternatives....The "Yes" strategy bypasses the question "How much damage shall we cause through X activity?" by saying "Here is a much better and yet feasible alternative activity." The more determined players of this strategy do not easily concede to charges of political infeasibility. They know that most significant environmental and public-health advances have been considered "politically infeasible" at one time or another. They likewise reason that if we can undertake the intense Manhattan Project to make nuclear bombs, or a space effort to transport humans to the moon, then we can institute alternatives to destroying the environment....

*   *   *

## Notes and Questions

1. Environmentalist Alon Tal argues that environmental groups make a strategic mistake by calling for the abolition of risk assessment only and not also seeking to reform the risk assessment process. He argues that "[r]isk assessment has been picking up steam as a practice for twenty years...[and] it may take twenty more years before an alternative process receives sufficient support to enhance or replace [it]." He contends that "[by] failing to solidify their position and actively enter the debate about QRA [Quantitative Risk Assessment]—which would mean accepting some degree of risk assessment in environmental and health and safety regulation—environmentalists opposed to, or a least wary of, its use have created a policy vacuum into which industry's position, which embraces QRA wholeheartedly, has flooded....By entering the technical [risk assessment] debate, environmentalists can keep risk assessments conservative and put a leash on the numbers, stopping them from taking on a 'life of their own.'" To do otherwise "is to abandon a substantial part of the playing field on which environmental health decisions are made." Alon Tal, *A Failure to Engage*, 14 Envt. F. 13, 13–14, 21 (Jan./Feb. 1997). Do you agree? For community groups opposed to the use of risk assessment, which is the better approach to effect change—that advocated by Alon Tal or Mary O'Brien? Which is more feasible for these groups?

# E. Cumulative and Synergistic Risks

As noted in Section B, risk assessments have traditionally evaluated the risks posed by a single pollutant, a single source or category of emissions, or a single environmental medium (such as air or water). In reality, people tend to be exposed through multiple pathways to numerous pollutants originating from a variety of sources. Moreover, risks from these various sources may be greater than just the sum of their parts. Agencies have resisted analyzing cumulative or synergistic risks because of scientific uncertainty about the nature of such risks, the lack of data about cumulative exposures, and other information gaps. They also have interpreted their regulatory mandates as not requiring such broader analysis (a topic discussed in more detail in Chapter VIII). The environmental justice movement, however, has brought these issues to the fore, and agencies are now starting to more seriously grapple with them.

Some agency policies have been changed to reflect concerns about cumulative risks. For instance, new guidance for federal agencies carrying out the National Environmental Policy Act recommends that they consider cumulative impacts in low income communities and communities of color. (See Chapter XII (C)(2)). EPA's new Urban Air Toxics Strategy is an attempt to deal with cumulative risks from air toxics in urban areas. Environmental justice activists have prompted the Air Quality Management District in southern California (the South Coast Air Quality Management District, or SCAQMD) to focus greater attention on cumulative risks. Concerned by evidence that cumulative risks from air toxics in the region are as high as 1,500 in 1 million, SCAQMD has required across the board reductions in emissions from existing facilities and begun to regulate diesel emissions from trucks and other sources. As a result of the Food Quality Protection Act, in setting pesticide tolerances EPA must consider aggregate exposure to the pesticide from all dietary, drinking water, and other sources (except for occupational sources). 21 U.S.C. §§346a(b)(2)(A)(ii); 346a(b)(2)(D).

In 1997, EPA adopted a significant guidance document requiring broader use of cumulative risk assessments. The policy notes that "[f]or most of our history, EPA has assessed risks and made environmental protection decisions based on individual contaminants—such as lead, chlordane, and DDT—with risk assessments for these chemicals often focused on one source, pathway or adverse effect. Today, better methods and data often allow us to describe and quantify the risks that Americans face from many sources of pollution, rather than by one pollutant at a time." The guidance directs each office to take into account cumulative risk issues in scoping and planning major risk assessments and to consider a broader scope that integrates multiple sources, effects, pathways, stressors and populations for cumulative risk analyses in all cases for which relevant data are available. It also requires risk assessors to consider risks faced by sensitive subgroups or individuals. The guidance acknowledges that social, economic, behavioral or psychological factors, such as existing health conditions, anxiety, nutritional status, crime, and congestion, can contribute to cumulative risks faced by individuals, but concludes that measuring these impacts is too difficult at present. U.S. Envtl. Protection Agency, *Guidance on Cumulative Risk Assessment—Phase I Planning and Scoping*, <http://www.epa.gov/ORD/spc/cumulrsk.htm> and <http://www.epa.gov/ORD/spc/cumrisk2.htm>.

EPA is also starting to address the information gap that hinders cumulative risk analysis. In 1994 it initiated a Cumulative Exposure Project designed to estimate cumulative public exposures to toxic contaminants in air, food, and drinking water. The air portion looks at the concentrations of 148 hazardous air pollutants in each census tract in the U.S.; the food component estimates exposures to 37 contaminants in 34 foods for 110 subpopulations, and the drinking water component estimates national exposure levels for 23 chemical contaminants found in public and private drinking water supplies. The project also includes a community-specific study in the Greenpoint/Williamsburg area of Brooklyn, New York that tests methodologies for conducting community-specific cumulative exposure analyses. *See* U.S. Envtl. Protection Agency, *Cumulative Exposure Project,* <http:www.epa.gov/cumulativeexposure/index.htm>.

Less regulatory attention has been paid to synergistic environmental risk. Scientific understanding of chemical synergy has been accelerating in recent years, and a number of studies document potent impacts of chemical combinations. One of the most prominent examined pesticides that cause mild hormone-disrupting effects in isolation. The study found that combinations of two or three of these pesticides at low levels that might be found in the environment are up to 1600 times as powerful as any of the individual pesticides by themselves. One chemical, chlordane, which does not disrupt hormones individually, greatly magnifies the ability of other chemicals to do so. Steve F. Arnold et al., *Synergistic Activation of Estrogen Receptor with Combinations of Environmental Chemicals,* 272 SCIENCE 1489 (1996). Despite these studies, enormous data gaps exist with respect to synergistic risks. As one commentor notes:

> [T]here are now 70,000 chemicals currently in commercial use, with about 1000 new ones added each year. [Of these only a small fraction have been tested]. The prospect of testing the toxicity of this number of chemicals, even one at a time, is daunting.... If scientists have to study combinations of chemicals, their job is vastly increased. For example, to test just the commonest 1000 toxic chemicals in unique combinations of 3 would require at least 166 million different experiments (and this disregards the need to study varying doses). Even if each experiment took just one hour to complete and 100 laboratories worked round the clock seven days a week, testing all possible unique 3-way combinations of 1000 chemicals would still take over 180 years to complete.

Rachel's Environment & Health News, *Dangers of Chemical Combinations* (June 13, 1996), <http://www.rachel.org/bulletin/idex.cfm?Issue_ID=625&bulletin_ID=48>.

## Notes and Questions

1. Most risk assessments deal with chemical combinations by simply adding up the individual toxicities of the chemicals to which persons are exposed. Does this mean that risk assessments routinely underestimate the risks of such combinations? In the face of uncertainty about the nature of synergistic risks, what is the appropriate response for agencies?

# Chapter V

# The Dynamics of Federal Environmental Regulation

## A. The Political Context

Recall that the environmental justice movement first gained national recognition in the late 1980's. Environmental justice entered the regulatory scene at a time of instability and ultimately, significant transformation of regulatory decisionmaking at the EPA. Considering the special challenges facing the EPA at that time helps to explain the ensuing tensions between environmental justice activists and other stakeholders in the 1990s. In 1990, on the eve of EPA's 20th birthday, Professor Richard Lazarus eloquently described the circumstances that led to this instability and what he described as a pathological cycle of distrust and agency failure. These circumstances helped set the stage for EPA's movement away from traditional "command and control" regulation in favor of more flexible, market oriented approaches to pollution control and other forms of regulatory innovation, greater autonomy for states and a more accommodating federal presence, and an effort to shift agency decisionmaking more toward negotiation and consensus. These shifting regulatory approaches (termed "reinvention" under the Clinton Administration and "second-generation initiatives" more generically) have significant environmental justice consequences.

In the first section of this chapter, we consider various approaches to implementing legislative mandates. We then examine different modes of agency decisionmaking, including newer forms of collaboration and consensus. We conclude with a discussion of the structure of EPA/state relations and the move to devolve greater authority to the states. EPA's market oriented approaches and other innovations are discussed in greater detail in Chapter VII.

## Richard J. Lazarus, The Tragedy of Distrust in the Implementation of Federal Environmental Law

### 54 Law and Contemporary Problems 311 (1991)

*In the dream, it works something like this: The huge hall of Environmental Control is lit from above. Operators below press controls and the translucent dome glows with the streams slashing the Upper Atmosphere, shaping the world's weather. Other controls are pressed and the flow changes color. Now it illuminates the Middle Atmosphere over America, showing regional smog-bearing inversions that may lock over cities within hours. In and out of walls glide panels on which river basins shine with flood-crest warnings or change hue to show rise and fall of pollution.... Nearby, in the Surveillance Center of Environmental Health Services, pesticides, oxides, nitrates, adulterants, all 30,000 chemicals used by industry or everyday life are indexed, cross-referenced, computerized for interaction and contaminations.*

Author Theodore White offered this fantastical description of a federal environmental agency just two weeks before President Nixon transmitted to Congress on July 9, 1970 his long-awaited executive order proposing the creation of the United States Environmental Protection Agency ("EPA"). Were EPA's performance now to be measured, more than twenty years later, against that of the mythical agency in White's dream, many would consider EPA a colossal failure. Surely, however, no one would use such a yardstick to judge EPA. White's portrait was not intended to reflect reality.

Imagine nonetheless that Congress had rejected the President's proposal back in 1970 and enacted in its place enabling legislation creating an EPA more akin to that fantasized by White. Also imagine that the statute mandated that the new EPA achieve that level and type of environmental control within six months.

Faced with an impossible task, EPA might have adopted a "loose" construction of the law under which it could reject such an approach based on the law's impracticability. A court, however, would likely have overturned the agency's construction, thereby compelling EPA to spend substantial resources in making a good faith, albeit futile, effort to comply with the congressional mandate. Significant institutional obstacles would then have quickly arisen. The Office of Management and Budget ("OMB") would invariably have opposed such a wasteful expenditure of monies. Heads of other federal agencies would have likely expressed opposition based on the program's potential interference with the operation of their own programs. State government officials would have been concerned with its federalism implications. The congressional appropriations committees, feeling the pressure to fund other programs competing for scarce federal dollars, would likely have provided EPA with only limited funds to develop an environmental control command center of such dubious efficacy. Those on the appropriations committees concerned about the impact on free market forces, other federal programs, or federalism, might have also placed riders on EPA's appropriations, limiting the agency's ability to spend funds on certain aspects of the program.

When EPA failed to meet the statutory deadline, the congressional subcommittees that drafted the agency's enabling law would have condemned the agency at oversight hearings. Those subcommittees would also have secured passage of legislation imposing additional deadlines on the agency and eliminating the agency's substantive discretion to ensure future agency compliance.

At EPA, the resulting crisis atmosphere would have stifled pollution control efforts. Agency resources would have been spent preparing for litigation, testifying before oversight hearings, placating state officials, and justifying agency expenditures on the program to skeptical OMB and White House officials. EPA officials would have created numerous working groups to consider how, in the absence of any foundation in science or technology, they might have created the type of highly centralized system of command and control envisioned by Congress. Because of the pending litigation, the agency's lawyers would have displaced other agency professionals (scientists, engineers, and economists) in developing the agency's response. OMB would have sought to delay any implementation of the plan. When the program was finally promulgated, affected industries would have promptly sought a federal court injunction barring any effort by EPA to implement a program disruptive of industry's vested economic interests. Based on the program's severe economic impact and the thinness of its scientific support, the court would have likely granted the injunction and remanded to EPA for further administrative proceedings.

Within EPA, the congressional, judicial, and public demand for immediate results would have discouraged long-term planning. The pall of suspicion cast upon the agency's motives by repeated failures would have likewise deterred innovation. The agency's inevitable loss of credibility before Congress, the courts, and the public would have decreased its influence in those forums. As a result, the agency's own perception of national environmental priorities would have increasingly diverged from that of the public and its elected representatives, leading to increasingly inflexible programs mandated by Congress. Because most of the agency professionals were attracted to EPA by a strong sense of its mission rather than by hope of significant monetary reward, their consequent demoralization would have prompted quick turnover and the loss of sustained agency expertise. Needless and irreversible degradation of the natural environment would have continued.

The imagined scenario should seem highly improbable, if not absurd. Congress would never mandate that an agency perform the impossible, decline to appropriate the funds necessary for a good faith effort in the mandated direction, and then condemn the agency publicly for trying and failing. Nor would any such philosophical schism concerning environmental protection policy persist between the executive and legislative branches, thus placing a federal agency charged with the policy's implementation in an untenable position. After all, both the president and Congress are responsive to the same electorate. Finally, there should be no reason to believe that courts would order EPA to take certain action, only subsequently to impede the agency's specific efforts at achieving the judicial mandate.... A review of EPA's last twenty years, however, suggests otherwise....

Congress has repeatedly demanded that the agency perform impossible tasks under unrealistic deadlines. Courts have rejected many of the agency's efforts to provide itself with more leeway in their implementation, while the White House, OMB, and congressional appropriation committees have simultaneously resisted subsequent agency efforts to comply with strict judicial mandates. The agency spends much of its limited resources defending its decisions in court, negotiating with OMB and the White House, and justifying its decisions to multiple congressional committees. A virtual state of siege and a crisis mentality have persisted at the agency for much of its existence as Congress has responded to each EPA failure by passing even more restrictive deadline legislation that the agency again fails to meet.

In short, a pathological cycle has emerged: agency distrust has begotten failure, breeding further distrust and further failure....

The cycle results from the way in which our governmental institutions have responded to persistent public schizophrenia concerning environmental protection policy. Public aspirations for environmental quality are relatively uniform and strongly held. But those aspirations contrast sharply with the public's understanding of their implications and its demonstrated unwillingness to take the steps necessary to have those aspirations realized. There is an appearance of harmony underlain by much actual disharmony....

*The Origins of EPA and Its Early Years: Agency Capture and the Seeds of Distrust*

... [T]hree variants of agency capture theory have predominated and strongly influenced EPA's institutional development. The first hypothesis, identified with the works of

Professor Marver Bernstein, concerns the tendency of administrative agencies to ally themselves, over time, with the community they regulate. At the time of EPA's creation, Ralph Nader's organization had published a series of books, relying on Bernstein's thesis, that accused various federal agencies (including the Department of Agriculture's pesticides program) of being in a state of agency capture.

The second thesis, most thoughtfully articulated by Professor Joseph Sax, concerns the tendency of agency personnel to bargain away environmental values as part of the political process. According to Sax, agency officials are simply incapable of providing natural resources with long-term protection from persistent and influential economic interests. The constant demands on the bureaucracy for compromise are too great.

Finally, there are those who fear the agency's capture by its own bureaucracy. Unlike the other two theories, the primary proponents of this view are concerned with the agency paying too little attention to the needs of the regulated. The theory is premised on the reputedly liberal, proregulatory bias of the federal bureaucracy, particularly that in an agency rearrangement such as EPA with a social mission.

EPA's creation and the manner in which it was initially received within the executive branch, by Congress, and the courts can largely be traced to these three different capture theories....

### The Collision of Institutional Forces: The Breeding of Regulatory Failure and Controversy

The tug-of-war in which EPA found itself might have turned out to be nothing more than a benign, even healthy, application of the checks and balances necessary to realize this country's commitment to the separation of powers. After all, where important regulatory authority is at stake, the various branches will invariably vie for influence in fashioning national policy. It should be no great surprise, moreover, that those institutions should do so at the behest of an interest group seeking to avoid the domination of the regulatory process by an adverse and competing interest.

In the case of EPA, however, the effect has been neither benign nor healthy. The institutional forces set into motion by the various capture theories have repeatedly collided, breeding conflict, controversy, and ultimately a destructive pattern of regulatory failure. No one individual or institution is to blame for this phenomenon. Indeed, "blame" is an inappropriate characterization. Many of the problems that have arisen in the implementation of environmental law were likely the inevitable result of such a dramatic infusion of new values and priorities into the nation's laws....

Most simply put, the forces designed to prevent EPA's capture became pathologically destructive because the country's spiritual environmental awakening in the 1970s occurred without much of an intellectual understanding of its implications. A strong national consensus in favor of environmental protection prompted the President to create EPA, Congress to pass sweeping environmental laws, and courts to open their doors to environmental plaintiffs. But both the public and those institutions were remarkably unsophisticated about the demands that they were placing upon themselves.

There was little, if any, sense of the huge short-term costs associated with treating pollution as a cost of doing business. Nor was there much awareness of the degree to which settled expectations and lifestyles could be disrupted if the natural environment were to be treated as more than an economic commodity. The public and governmental institutions likewise did not truly appreciate the incalculable nature of the benefits of environmental protection, including the scientific uncertainty associated with the measurement of those benefits and the long term intergenerational nature of their realization. There was especially little apprehension of how those characteristics would challenge the patience of both those sympathetic to, and those skeptical of, the new federal programs....

### The Breeding of Regulatory Failure

Congress responded to the perception of a national consensus in environmental protection by passing a series of laws in the 1970s that set the stage for institutional conflict and agency failure. Congress lacked the incentive to address or emphasize the pitfalls and chose instead to join the chorus in favor of immediate and fundamental change. The congressional votes in favor of the new laws were accordingly overwhelmingly favorable. The average vote in favor of major federal environmental legislation during the 1970s was seventy-six to five in the Senate and 331 to thirty in the House. As one legislator put it in describing his reluctant vote in favor of safe drinking water legislation in 1974, " after all, if one votes against safe drinking water, it is like voting against home and mother."

### From Public Aspiration to Statutory Mandate

The federal environmental statutes of the early 1970s were dramatic, sweeping, and uncompromising, consistent with the nation's spiritual and moral resolution of the issue.... The statutes imposed hundreds of stringent deadlines on the agency and removed much of the agency's substantive discretion in accomplishing them. One-third of the deadlines were for six months or less. Sixty percent were for one year or less. According to EPA's current administrator, William Reilly, Congress and the courts had imposed 800 deadlines on the agency through 1989....

The result was a seemingly never-ending onslaught of impossible agency tasks. Eighty-six percent of the statutory deadlines applied specifically to EPA. EPA was "told to eliminate water pollution, and all risk from air pollution, prevent hazardous waste from reaching ground water, establish standards for all toxic drinking water contaminants, and register all pesticides." To date, EPA has met only about 14 percent of the congressional deadlines imposed and has had 80 to 85 percent of its major regulations challenged in court....

### The Coalition for Failure

These series of impossible tasks did more than guarantee repeated agency failure; they triggered a chain of events that profoundly influenced EPA's institutional development and the evolution of federal environmental law. Those who supported these statutory mandates sought judicial review and enlisted some in Congress to oversee EPA's implementation. Their aim was to guard against EPA's abdication of its statutory responsibilities. At the same time, those who were opposed to the statutory mandates but who were unable to muster the political capital to defeat their passage, were nonetheless quite successful in enlisting others in Congress, the executive branch, and some courts to impede EPA's implementation of the mandates.

### Agency Funding

Forces within Congress were able to secure passage of various environmental statutes that reflected the nation's aspirations for environmental quality, but a very different set of institutional forces was responsible for appropriating funds for the implementation of those laws. Members of the appropriations committees typically did not share the environmental zeal of those on the committees who drafted the laws. Indeed, some were quite skeptical of the efficacy of those laws. The skeptics may have been reluctant to voice publicly their opposition to passage of the statutes—because of the popular appeal of environmental protection—but they felt far more secure in undermining the statutory mandates in a less visible way through the appropriation process. Such congressional skeptics were joined in their efforts by those in the executive branch, especially in the White House and OMB, who shared their policy outlook and who, accordingly, routinely requested less funding for EPA than Congress ultimately provided. This coalition for modest EPA funding proved virtually unbeatable....

Of course, during this same period, Congress dramatically increased the scope of EPA's statutory responsibilities....EPA consequently has had far fewer lawyers per significant regulation and fewer dollars for evaluation than other federal agencies....

Hence, Congress has spoken with two different voices to EPA. Each voice reflected the distinct legislative path followed by the authorization and appropriation processes within Congress. Legislators demanded immediate action requiring a massive agency undertaking. At the same time, however, they never provided a remotely commensurate level of agency funding. Ironically, therefore, while Congress was willing to ask American business and the public to curtail pollution, regardless of the cost, in order to ensure public health, Congress itself refused to fund the level of agency activity necessary for even a good faith effort to implement such an ambitious program....

*Executive Branch Oversight*

...Of even greater historical significance was the substantive role [the Office of Management and Budget (OMB)] defined for itself in reviewing proposed EPA regulations to influence their final content. Both the White House and OMB were motivated at least in part by fear of possible "capture" of agency political appointees by career staff....

The review process reached its zenith under President Reagan and his first OMB director, David Stockman.....

During 1985, 1986, and 1987, EPA revised 74.5, 66.2, and 66.2 percent, respectively, of agency rules reviewed by OMB. When disagreements between EPA and OMB have arisen, OMB has invariably won. OMB continues to "hold" EPA rules for months and years based on OMB concerns with the cost of compliance with a rule....

*Judicial Oversight*

Partly to prevent agency capture, Congress encouraged judicial oversight of EPA by including citizen suit and judicial review provisions in each of the environmental statutes and by requiring EPA to follow decision making procedures more rigorous than those normally employed in informal notice and comment rulemaking....The deadlines and mandatory duties contained in the various federal laws, along with their carefully crafted legislative histories, provided environmentalists with enormous leverage over EPA through litigation, which they used as their dominant tool to influence agency decisions. Whenever EPA failed to meet a deadline, or otherwise to satisfy a statutory obligation, which was inevitably often, environmentalists used litigation to compel EPA to negotiate with them in drafting a consent decree. Environmentalists utilized the consent decree and the threat of contempt sanctions to control the agency's future actions. The filing of lawsuits also provided environmentalists with media events that provided publicity for their cause and incidentally aided fundraising efforts. The media was naturally receptive to accusations of agency malfeasance, and the result was a steady stream of negative articles about EPA in the national press....

Especially during EPA's early years, courts of appeals frequently rejected the agency's efforts to relax the statutory mandates through "loose" construction of their terms. The courts also often remanded agency rulemaking for further proceedings based on perceived inadequacies in the rulemaking record. Environmentalists benefitted from many of the courts' more expansive constructions of the federal environmental laws. Industry, however, benefitted from many of the judicial remands of agency rules. The deadlines compelled agency decisions within exceedingly short time frames, and, due to the scientific complexity of the mechanics of environmental pollution and the associated scientific uncertainty, the scientific bases for agency rulings were often quite sparse and subject to effective criticism....

### Congressional Oversight

Perhaps the most important (and most often overlooked) of the institutional forces that have buffeted EPA has been the operation of congressional oversight, long referred to as Congress's "neglected" function....

Much of the oversight has been driven by a desire to prevent EPA's capture by industry and by those in the White House and OMB who are perceived (accurately) as unsympathetic to the statutory policies of the laws within EPA's jurisdiction. Others within Congress, however, have been more concerned about the possibility of bureaucratic or environmentalist capture and have used the same oversight tools to counsel EPA against strict application of those laws. Because the statutes demand the impossible of EPA and require EPA to demand the impossible, or at least very painful, from others, there has historically been plenty to fuel criticism from both constituencies within Congress. "EPA bashing" has been commonplace on Capitol Hill as legislators from both sides of the aisle have perceived its political advantages....

Oversight of EPA ultimately spread to both chambers and to authorization, government operations, and appropriations committees. The expansion roughly coincided with a general increase in congressional appreciation of the political advantages of "subcommittee government" and "fire alarm" oversight, which in turn spurred a dramatic increase in committee staff and oversight during the last few decades. When EPA failed to meet statutory deadlines, members of Congress held hearings in which they chastised the agency for neglecting the public trust. Conversely, when EPA made politically unpopular decisions in an effort to comply with its statutory mandates, other members of Congress promptly joined in the public denunciation (including some who originally sponsored the strict environmental laws)....

### Congressional Prescription

Congress has not confined itself to overseeing EPA's work. In the aftermath of repeated regulatory failures, Congress has favored passing increasingly detailed environmental statutes to guard against agency dereliction in the first instance. Oversight therefore has been supplemented with prescription....

The likelihood that EPA will again fail to meet Congress's mandates seems great. When EPA does fail, environmentalists and legislators will likely once again widely denounce EPA in the news media. Each agency decision or "lapse" will prompt new litigation. Consent decrees will dictate agency behavior. At the behest of environmental or industry plaintiffs, courts will remand the agency's regulations for further proceedings based on the inadequacy of administrative records prepared under short deadlines. Oversight hearings and the news media will again recount the "administrative horror stories" that result from EPA's strict enforcement of the law. Appropriations riders will seek to prevent such strict application, while the committees from which the legislation originated will simultaneously draft even more restrictive legislation in response to EPA's "failure." The "spiral of unachievable standards, missed deadlines, resulting citizen suits, and even more prescriptive legislation by Congress continues."...

### Wasted Resources and Misdirected Priorities

...Indeed, congressional oversight of EPA has periodically been so intense that the agency has been effectively paralyzed as a result. Ironically, therefore, much of the delay about which Congress complains may be the product of its own oversight of the agency.

Another adverse effect of excessive oversight of EPA is that it has caused the agency to go "underground" in its lawmaking. To avoid overseers, EPA has increasingly resorted to less formal means of announcing agency policy determinations. Instead of promulgating rules pursuant to the Administrative Procedure Act, EPA now frequently issues guidance memoranda and directives. Also, many important agency rulings are not reflected in generic rulemaking, but in individual permit decisions. OMB oversight is thereby avoided, and judicial review of agency action is limited....

\* \* \*

## Notes and Questions

1. Assuming each variant of agency capture theory has some legitimacy, how could the state of capture affect the EPA and the states' abilities to respond to environmental justice concerns?

2. If, as Professor Lazarus suggests, the crisis in regulation occurred largely because we as a society were not prepared to pay the costs of our newly-found environmental sensitivity, what mechanisms did the regulatory apparatus come to use to attempt to resolve this inherent conflict? Is the existence of distributional inequity itself the inevitable outcome of such a conflict?

3. In the face of an impossible number of tasks and deadlines, how might the agency proceed to prioritize agency actions in a manner that responds both to legislative mandate and protects public health to the maximum extent possible? What strategy would you devise to deal with the inevitable budgetary cutbacks and congressional interference?

4. As an EPA official, what strategies would you devise to decrease negative media coverage? How would you alter administrative proceedings to increase the chances of success on appeal (having courts uphold agency decisions)? Is there a way that the agency can successfully respond to legislative oversight hearings and increasingly prescriptive environmental legislation?

5. Consider Professor Lazarus' generous interpretation of the same agency dynamics:

> EPA's dilemma could nonetheless be viewed positively as a small price to pay in the United States' first effort to reshape its relationship with its natural environment. Certainly this nation's accomplishments in seeking to produce a legal regime for environmental protection have been extraordinary. In relatively few years, the nation's laws have been dramatically rewritten. Viewed from this per-

spective, repeated regulatory failure could be seen as the necessary cost of our attempt to address pressing environmental problems in the face of scientific uncertainty. There was not sufficient time to delay governmental action until its environmental objectives could have been fairly and accurately defined....

There is also some advantage to the public in the way environmental laws have evolved in response to repeated agency failure. The statutes allow for less agency discretion while arguably reflecting greater congressional assumption of responsibility for making public policy. Congress was faulted for unfairly (and improperly) passing the buck to EPA in the environmental statutes of the 1970s. In the more prescriptive environmental statutes, Congress is now making many of the difficult policy determinations necessary to fashion environmental quality standards.

Finally, there is even a positive way to view public distrust of EPA. After all, "political distrust has been a recurrent and perhaps a permanent feature of the history of the republic." Effective democracy undoubtedly requires criticism of government based on mistrust of its institutions.

Lazarus, *supra,* at 348–49. Do you agree? Why or why not?

6. Does the answer to agency distrust and failure lie in an agency insulating itself from conflicting political pressures, or, alternatively, from encouraging participation by all stakeholders? Consider the approach the agency in fact opted for. As a response to unrealistic mandates and conflicting political pressures, the EPA increasingly resorted to regulation by guidance and customized permit decisions. While this state of affairs continued into the 1990's, the Congress was experiencing its own brand of paralysis in the environmental area, causing a simultaneous decrease in environmental legislation but at the same time leaving the EPA with prescriptive statutes that, some argue, are ill-suited to respond to persistent environmental problems. This set of circumstances sparked a regulatory movement to reform or "reinvent" environmental regulation, that is described in Chapter VII. But regulatory reform also sought in an indirect way to change the process of agency decisionmaking, effecting a shift in implementation of legislative mandate that relied more heavily upon stakeholder negotiation and consensus, a subject to which we now turn.

# B. Agency Decisionmaking

This section studies agency decisionmaking through the lens of federal regulatory processes. Although the dynamics may differ slightly, the same principles can be applied to states and local governments.

## Jody Freeman,
## Collaborative Governance in the Administrative State
### 45 University of California Los Angeles Law Review 1 (1997)

*Rule Making*

The focus in recent reform proposals on increasing or diversifying oversight mechanisms assumes that the central problem of [traditional] administrative law and process continues to be unconstrained agency discretion. These proposals seem unresponsive to a number of important arguments about other obstacles to sound governance. There are, in fact, a variety of reasons beyond broad delegations and a failure to use cost-benefit analysis why informal rule making is not conducive to producing effective, implementable, and legitimate rules.... One frequently noted complaint is that the indirect nature of rule making tends to undermine problem solving and reward adversarialism. Because the agency is the focal point of informal rule making, parties miss opportunities to engage constructively with each other in a sustained way. They often take extreme positions in notice and comment, preferring to posture in anticipation of litigation rather than focus on the regulatory problem posed by the agency. This encourages the agency to compromise or split the difference between competing positions, which can constrain the range of solutions to numeric limits or standards that fall somewhere between the poles represented by the parties. Notice and comment also undermines the implementation of rules by failing to encourage dialogue and deliberation among the parties most affected by them. This is one of the key criticisms that motivated proposals for stakeholder negotiation of rules....

Other problems receive relatively less academic attention, but nonetheless ought to be considered in any attempt at reform. For example, the notice and comment process often fails to make the best use of available data and information. This is in part a product of timing: only after the Notice of Proposed Rule Making (NPRM) do parties supply detailed arguments about the technical and practical difficulties of implementing a rule, instead of much earlier when the information might be more valuable to the agency in formulating the proposed rule. Also, because the agency must first actually propose a rule in order to invite comment, the definition of the regulatory problem can be frozen at the time of the NPRM, thus circumscribing at the outset which data and information will be relevant and which will be extraneous. As a result, an agency may frame regulatory problems at the early stages of a rule making in a way that limits rethinking at later junctures.

Moreover, informal rule making and implementation suffers from a conceptual divide between legitimate public and private roles in governance. Because private parties are viewed as purely self-interested and unaccountable, the agency alone promulgates, implements, and enforces regulations; the agency alone is responsible for protecting the public interest. In traditional rule making, interest groups, private parties, and local communities are experienced as a threat to the integrity and expertise of the agency. As a result, regulation overburdens agencies and undervalues the capacity of nongovernmental groups to participate in governance....

Rules produced through notice and comment are also resistant to revision and adaptation. This resistance may stem from four factors. First, a rule may be viewed as a discrete event—a transaction rather than a process. Second, the enormous resources required to successfully promulgate a rule under current conditions can create disincentives to reconsider it. Third, frequent revision is viewed as creating uncertainty for parties that must make decisions based on their expectations of the rule. Finally, a rule is usually intended to be universally applied, not tailor-made to specific contexts or parties....

*Implementation and Enforcement*

...Industrial plants that emit air and water pollutants must apply for and obtain permits that implement, through the imposition of controls, the regulatory standards and rules promulgated under federal environmental statutes. Negotiating permits with state agencies, to which authority is usually delegated by the EPA, can be an excruciatingly costly and time-consuming process. The slow pace of permitting makes it particularly burdensome to industries in which production processes change rapidly and require modified or new permits. Because facilities must obtain separate permits for the different media into which they emit pollution (for example, air and water), and because a facility may require individual permits for a number of different sources (for example, smokestacks or pipes), a single facility may need multiple, single-media permits. For firms with numerous permits expiring on different dates, the application and renewal process is continual, causing companies to incur considerable fees for consultants, engineers, and lawyers.

The traditional permitting process has been criticized as highly adversarial and rule-bounded. The agency and applicant typically adopt an adversarial posture toward each other. For example, when denying a permit, agency officials often decline to suggest process or management changes that might satisfy the permit requirements, causing the company to engage in a guessing game to determine how to amend the application. Even when firms and agency officials negotiate the contents of permits, negotiations can be adversarial, time-consuming, and expensive.

The application process is not only burdensome, but it can also undermine the goal of environmental protection. Applications demand a great deal of information from firms, but the information may or may not be relevant to diagnosing how processes or practices might be altered to improve environmental performance. In other words, permitting is not treated as an open-ended inquiry into ways of achieving compliance. As a result, important data concerning how production processes work and how they could be improved is lost or ignored. In addition, as drafted by the EPA, permits are primarily legal documents—they can dictate extremely technical and detailed effluent and emission limits, as well as design and technology standards. These permits are often incomprehensible to workers who must comply with them.

In addition, public participation in the permitting process is relatively limited. Most environmental statutes (or agency regulations pursuant to the statutes) contain public notice requirements and provide for public hearings in limited circumstances. In addition, aside from providing written and sometimes oral testimony (and unless they mount a legal challenge), parties other than the agency and the applicant are not directly involved at either the drafting or implementation stage. As with rule making then, much of the debate and discussion over permits takes the form of paper exchanges between the applicant, the agency, and any interested parties.

Enforcement is no less problematic. It is enormously difficult for the EPA to monitor compliance with the hundreds of thousands of permits issued under the multitude of regulatory statutes over which it has jurisdiction, even though most of the administration is performed by the states. Administrators and academics complain that the agency is neither adequately funded nor sufficiently staffed to meet its enforcement responsibilities. In addition, regional EPA offices perform inspections inconsistently, and penalties are not well targeted to punish the worst offenders or prioritize among different harms.

This frequent arbitrariness is the product of institutional incentives. EPA employees have traditionally received the most rewards and recognition for successful enforcement actions. The agency's method of evaluating enforcement is based on a numerical count of its own administrative enforcement actions and its referrals of civil and criminal enforcement matters to the Department of Justice. With the priority on meeting referral targets and collecting fines, enforcement officials forego opportunities to assist in diagnosing and solving the technical or production problems that can lead to noncompliance. This approach to enforcement robs the regulatory process of important feedback concerning how well the rules work. Thus, because agencies do not track rule implementation in a systematic way, and because the numerical "bean-counting" approach to enforcement fails to provide information about the reasons for noncompliance, it is difficult to learn how rules might be improved. Even if one could collect such information, there is no systematic way to have it inform the decision-making process....

### Interest Representation

...While the theory of interest representation first articulated by Richard Stewart... might explain a great deal of interest-group behavior, failure to question its assumptions makes it difficult to imagine an alternative regulatory process built upon a different view of the parties' relationships and responsibilities. The assumptions of interest representation that often go unquestioned can be summarized in the following way:

1. Agency discretion should be constrained. Excessive and unchecked agency discretion creates a crisis of legitimacy in the administrative state. The best way to constrain discretion is to encourage competition among interest groups in rule making. Judicial review is critical to this regime: courts ensure that the relevant parties are represented in the rule making process by requiring agencies to take the parties' views into account in reasoned decision making. Through the threat of legal challenge, then, parties derive indirect bargaining rights.

2. Rules are bargains. Rules are transactions that require bargaining. Interest representation is motivated by a pluralist theory of politics.

3. Agency officials are insiders, whereas stakeholders are outsiders. Interested parties compete to influence agency decisions and have the right to challenge agency decisions in court, but they have no direct responsibility for devising or implementing solutions to regulatory problems.

4. Relationships are adversarial. Adversarialism drives interest representation. The goal for stakeholders is to maximize their interests by winning on important issues.

5. The agency is neutral and reactive. The agency is a neutral arbiter among stakeholders. It takes the relative power of interest groups as it finds it, and it seeks compromise in response to pressure from outsiders....

### A Normative Model of Collaboration

...Collaborative governance seeks to respond to the litany of criticisms about the quality, implementability, and legitimacy of rule making by reorienting the regulatory enterprise around joint problem solving and away from controlling discretion. Collaborative governance is characterized by the following features.

1. A problem-solving orientation. The focus is on solving regulatory problems. This requires information sharing and deliberation among parties with the knowledge most relevant to devising and implementing creative solutions.

2. Participation by interested and affected parties in all stages of the decision-making process. Broad participation has an independent democratic value and may facilitate effective problem solving. It may take different forms in different contexts.

3. Provisional solutions. Rules are viewed as temporary and subject to revision. This requires a willingness to move forward under conditions of uncertainty. It also demands a willingness to devise solutions to regulatory problems without foreclosing a re-

thinking of both solutions and goals. To this end, continuous monitoring and evaluation are crucial.

4. Accountability that transcends traditional public and private roles in governance. Parties are interdependent and accountable to each other. New arrangements, networks, institutions, or allocations of authority may replace or supplement traditional oversight mechanisms. These might include self-monitoring and disclosure, community oversight, and third-party certification. In these arrangements, traditional roles and functions are open to question.

5. A flexible, engaged agency. The agency is a convenor and facilitator of multi-stakeholder negotiations. It provides incentives for broader participation, information sharing, and deliberation. It acts as a capacity builder of parties and institutions by providing technical resources, funding, and organizational support when needed. While the agency may set floors and ceilings and act as the ultimate decisionmaker, it views regulatory success as contingent on the contributions of other participants....

The collaborative claim that problem solving tends to produce higher-quality rules rests upon the belief that unanticipated or novel solutions are likely to emerge from face-to-face deliberative engagement among knowledgeable parties who would never otherwise share information or devise solutions together. A process conducive to the disclosure and debate of data is more likely to make better use of available information and expose information gaps than one that promotes secrecy and indirect communication. Moreover, parties have a difficult time insisting on arbitrary or indefensible positions when they are confronted with data or arguments that undermine their view. Problem-oriented deliberation is widely thought to be more conducive to creativity and innovation than either positional bargaining or indirect communication through a paper record....

The central claim supporting a commitment to provisionalism in a collaborative governance regime is that a flexible, adaptive system capable of responding to advances in science, technology, knowledge, and shifting human judgments will produce better rules that are more likely to accomplish legislative goals. When solutions are provisional, rules are shaped by, and responsive to, the particular contexts in which they are deployed. A system based on these understandings requires feedback mechanisms through which information can be processed and made operational. Provisionalism requires learning. In this sense, it is pragmatic. Provisionalism requires parties to agree about regulatory goals and standards, devise mechanisms to achieve them, and create a system for evaluating and reassessing those agreements on a regular basis. Monitoring and information exchange are crucial to an effective implementation and compliance regime, as is the capacity to measure compliance. Rules are not one-time transactions, but rather, they are building blocks in a process, alternative hypotheses to be deployed and revised in light of experience....

Far from undermining the agency's authority, facilitating broad participation depends upon an agency's ultimate authority to impose its own solutions. The state must be strong in order to engage in collaboration. Agency officials need not be agnostic about outcomes. They may limit the universe of subjects open to negotiation by establishing, for example, a health-based standard as the minimal floor, while leaving to a consensus-based process how high above that minimum the standard should ultimately be set in light of feasibility, cost effectiveness, and community priorities. In order to prevent well-resourced groups from dominating deliberative processes, the agency may provide technical assistance grants or other needed support to consumer or community groups. When collective action problems or differential power make balanced representation within a negotiating group impossible, the government itself will need to self-consciously represent the concerns of unrepresented interests. The critical difference here is the agency's posture toward outside groups: in traditional rule making, the agency reacts when groups exert pressure, as they are primarily viewed as a threat. In a collaborative model, the agency cultivates participation as part of its mission because outside groups are potential contributors....

The idea that good negotiation consists of problem solving is not new. A prominent school of alternative dispute resolution espouses just this view. Even proponents of negotiation through problem solving, however, view negotiations as discrete events that conclude a problem "once and for all." One can see how this is reinforced in the reg-neg process: a negotiating committee officially disbands once it achieves consensus. Recent empirical evidence suggests that in the period between committee consensus and rule promulgation, parties retreat to their traditional adversarial roles and may attempt to influence and undo agreements made during negotiations. Such behavior is only encouraged when the group's responsibility for the rule effectively ends once they sign the consensus document....

At the same time, public interest groups continue to follow the litigation strategy that has served them so well throughout the first twenty-five years of environmental regulation. Indeed, the institutional incentives in public interest groups no more facilitate collaboration than do the incentives in government bureaucracies. Lawyers in these organizations have powerful identities as litigators. Staking out tough positions and launching lawsuits attracts media coverage, public attention, and financial support. While some environmental organizations seem interested in using ADR methods in some contexts, the groups are generally wary of them. Uttering the words, "collaboration" or "reinvention" in the presence of lawyers for the major environmental groups can be like waving a red flag; they are suspicious of "informality" because it has historically worked against their interests....

*The Limits of the New Processes*

*Lack of Institutional Incentives for Experimentation*

...Even if they wished to embrace collaboration, however, chronically understaffed public interest groups cannot afford to participate in multiple negotiations over multiple policy issues and at the same time continue to fight their traditional battles in courts and legislatures. Consensus-based processes, especially those that envision continued engagement and responsibility for oversight, require a tremendous commitment of resources. Public interest groups would also need to diversify their skill base to engage effectively in deliberation. Very few organizations, and almost no community groups, have the requisite scientific and technical knowledge, as well as legal expertise. Even for those groups that can claim sufficient expertise, such as the [Natural Resources Defense Council], representatives resist sharing oversight responsibilities with the government. Rather, they view enforcement and oversight as the government's responsibility. As it turns out, then, public interest groups are as deeply committed to the public-private divide as any institution.

By contrast, industry groups suffer no lack of resources or technical knowledge. They may also have the strongest incentive to collaborate, given the possibility of reducing the expense, delay, and frustration associated with adversarial regulation. Still, front-end negotiations are very costly, forcing industry to underwrite much of the expense. The pressure to show short-term profit discourages executives from making large investments of company time and resources in uncertain processes that cannot guarantee results. It may be less costly, at least in the short term, to pursue a strategy of trench warfare. Indeed, it may not be in the industry's interest to collaborate when it can "win" battles over rules and permits in other fora. Industry groups have proven adept at exerting influence in legislatures and courts: they have successfully resisted enforcement of environmental regulation even when they could not defeat the legislation or persuade the agencies to weaken the rules. Fines are rarely so high that they cannot be efficiently internalized. Both corporate executives and their lawyers are skilled at adversarialism; indeed, the lawyers have a financial stake in it. . . .

### Limited Participation by Public Interest and Community Groups

. . . The least represented groups across EPA negotiations appear to be environmental organizations, particularly smaller, community-based environmental groups. While there is no empirical evidence suggesting that agencies attempt to "stack the deck" with parties that can be relied upon to achieve a predetermined result, there remains a danger that convenors will manipulate the convening process. One would expect, however, that such a practice would quickly and permanently undermine negotiated rule making. All the evidence suggests that convenors take considerable care in selecting parties so that a balance of interests is represented. Still, they appear to do so primarily to insulate the consensus rule from later challenge. . . .

Given the substantial obstacles to broad participation and the degree to which it can delay and complicate already difficult negotiations, many would argue that, while desirable, broad participation should not be viewed as a necessary feature of collaborative governance. Indeed, some would argue that the degree of public participation in these processes already exceeds that which outsider groups currently enjoy in the traditional rule-making and permitting process. While reforms like reg-neg are imperfect, they would say, informal notice and comment hardly functions as an ideal vehicle for broad participation.

Still, the absence of employee, public interest, and community group representatives threatens to undermine the potential for achieving creative, implementable solutions that are widely viewed as legitimate. Public interest groups view this lack of participation as the weakest link in proposals like Project XL; for some, it thoroughly undermines the process. While the EPA has recently taken steps to strengthen stakeholder participation, the agency continues to hold the applicant company responsible for creating a stakeholder team. Forcing companies to shoulder this burden only exacerbates the problem of resource disparity.

Unless one imagines a collaborative model that includes only agencies and industry (a system that would doubtless revitalize capture theory), agencies must view building the institutional capacity of communities—that is, their technical and financial ability to participate in the regulatory process—as part of their mission. Such a shift would radically depart from the defensive stance many agencies have adopted in the notice and comment process. Cultivating participation requires more than providing resources for technical experts. Agencies could build institutional capacity by promoting connections between universities and community groups or by investing directly in community organizations. Even if such steps go beyond what agencies can afford, or are legally entitled to do, they could take smaller steps, such as appointing a staff advocate or ombudsman for underrepresented groups. . . .

In the end, despite their potential limitations and obvious shortcomings, initiatives such as negotiated rule making and Project XL provide glimmers of what a collaborative regime might look like. And yet, curiously, even the proponents of these new initiatives appear to minimize their potential to challenge the prevailing conceptual framework of administrative law.... [S]ome of the hesitancy to push these ideas further may be rooted in an unwillingness to grapple with the traditional model of the administrative process and the dominant conception of public and private roles in governance. Faced with having to envision a new decision-making regime, erect the legal structures necessary to support it, and defend its constitutionality, it is easier to insist that nothing really new is going on.

\* \* \*

# Eileen Gauna,
## The Environmental Justice Misfit: Public Participation and the Paradigm Paradox
### 17 Stanford Environmental Law Journal 3 (1998)

Scholars have proposed several different models to prescribe the way in which administrative decisions should be made and the public's role within each model. These scholars also describe how regulatory ideals operate with varying degrees of influence in the models. The expertise model, a decision-making structure heavily reliant upon the regulatory ideal of formal expertise, ultimately rests upon empiricism and faith in the ability of science and technology to solve environmental problems. The pluralist model, with predominant regulatory ideals of interest group inclusion and agency neutrality, rests on a foundation of utilitarianism. The recently proposed civic republican model rejects utilitarianism in favor of a belief in true civic virtue. Under this model, citizen inclusion is a regulatory ideal but is employed to achieve a form of deliberation focusing on true public good solutions rather than utility maximization. The form and efficacy of citizen participation may vary depending upon which model predominates in agency proceedings and the institutional mechanisms that might favor one approach over another.

### The Ideal of Expertise and the Traditional Administrative System

One could look at agency decision-making as requiring no public input. Agency officials could regulate according to clear legislative mandate; in absence of such clarity, officials could use their expertise to fill in the detail. An extreme form of this view, supported by a strong belief in the ideal of formal expertise, could justify the rejection of public participation entirely....

Under this traditional view, the primary inquiry posed by legislation is the permissible extent of governmental intrusion into the sphere of private autonomy; it is the private interests that are at risk, not the public interest. Accordingly, there is no role for the general public in agency proceedings. Despite a concern about agency discretion, the ideal of formal expertise appears to dominate this bipolar structure. The regulated community's participation is allowed only to keep agency expertise within the consensual boundary of the legislation in question.

### The Ideals of Pluralism and the Modern Administrative System

While agencies must be mindful of their non-representational footing and of their place in political theory, they also must perform their duties by implementing legislation. Viewed in this light, just as the regulated are protected from exuberant regulation, the public in general must be protected against inadequate regulation. The regulated community's entry into agency proceedings gave rise to a second concern: as they matured, regulatory agencies might develop a bias in favor of the organized interests of the regulated and might come to have a stake in the well-being of the industries they regulate. Consequently, agency officials might fail to discharge their respective mandates.

In order to protect against this new risk, the then-expertise-oriented traditional system had to change in order to accommodate interests other than the liberty and property interests of the regulated....

The interest representation model relies relatively less upon the regulatory ideal of expertise and more upon ideals associated with pluralism, although expertise is still important. This more recent view has been heavily influenced by the writings of theorists who posit that the behavior of regulators is influenced by inherent reward structures. Agency expertise alone is thus not likely to produce optimal regulation. A decision-making structure which accounts for and minimizes undue influence by the regulated is preferable....

The shift to a pluralist model was more than a corrective measure against the risk of bias; it signaled an ascendant belief in utilitarianism. Grounded in the belief that one group's vision of what is best is not inherently superior to another's, pluralism holds that all participants are equally qualified to participate in decisions. Accordingly, preferences of the participants stand on substantively equal footing. A strong pluralist conception blurs the distinction between private and public interests, as public interests become mere aggregated private preferences. The public interest in very clean air, for example, would simply reflect the aggregated preferences for clean air by most people, a preference not inherently superior to an alternative aggregated preference for unfettered automobile use and industrial activity resulting in severely polluted air....

To illustrate the utilitarian focus of the pluralist view in the environmental agency context, consider a legislative mandate to regulate toxic substances in a manner that is least burdensome but protects health and the environment against unreasonable risk. The "least burdensome" mandate is a signal for the agency to consider the economic interests of industries using toxic substances in their processes, while the "protects health and environment" mandate is a signal to protect the interests of the general public in health and a safe environment. The utility of toxic substance use must be weighed against the utility of health and a clean environment. Here, environmental values appear to be legislatively expressed as utilitarian. If health and a clean environment were viewed as a greater public good grounded in universal values, or as an ethical imperative, then the agency's authority to protect these values probably would not be curtailed by the prerequisite that the Administrator first find an "unreasonable risk" and the requirement to use only the "least burdensome" regulatory strategies. By force of logic, if only unreasonable risks are unacceptable, then reasonable risks to health and a safe environment become acceptable....

[A]n agency structure that accommodates pluralist ideals is one that is accessible to representatives of all legitimate interests and one that requires officials to maintain a relative neutrality towards the interest groups and legislatively expressed preferences. Under this conception, the agency is not a preference generator but a preference mediator. In the environmental context, the EPA's mission becomes less that of a "Protector of the Environment," and more a risk broker which manages risk within a legislatively expressed range of options....

This view supports the position that public participation in agency proceedings is necessary, not only to guard against agency bias toward the regulated, but also for the agency to get a clear grasp of the preferences of all interest groups and to successfully mediate among those preferences.....

The judicial role in this model differs from that incorporated in the traditional expertise-oriented system, which primarily consisted of containing agency discretion to properly legislated matters. In a pluralistic structure, the judicial role is essentially an examination to determine whether the surrogate political process is contaminated by exclusion or favoritism, resulting in a policy, rule, or decision corrupted by distorted preferences....

Although presently operating within a pluralistic paradigm, the environmental regulatory apparatus is not static.... The former view that environmental values were special has been replaced by the view that environmentalism is just another special interest. As environmental values are grounded in utility, environmental concerns are subsumed in an economic benefit-cost model on equal footing with other preferences. Finally, an earlier judicial enchantment with agency capture theories has been replaced by a confidence that agencies are competent to develop sound public policy....

The shift in judicial political assumptions thus identified has important implications for citizen participation at the agency level. Agencies expanded participation avenues in response to early judicial decisions that reflected a suspicion of unfettered agency discretion and agency bias. More recent decisions expressing strong judicial deference toward agencies might foreshadow agency retreat from a commitment to participation to a decision-making approach that enjoys greater reliance on agency expertise. Although many environmental statutes have formal rights of participation that cannot be ignored by the agency, agencies still retain wide discretion in implementing those formal rights. Informal avenues of participation are at the greatest risk. Conditions are therefore favorable not for another transformation, but for a retreat to the early traditional model.

### The Ideals of Modern Civic Republicanism and the Proposed Administrative System

...Neorepublicanism rejects the belief that the public interest is merely aggregated self-interested utility. Rather, the public interest is an expression of a common good grounded in values people pursue not as individuals but as a community. This common good is the product of the deliberative process, not its discovery. This deliberative process does not involve utility-maximizing but instead requires participants to exercise civic virtue by putting aside their self-interested preferences to focus upon the greater, common good. Belief in civic virtue necessitates a correlative belief that proper deliberation can yield agreement upon the common good and substantively correct outcomes.... The product of a well-functioning deliberative process is not a set of aggregated preferences without intrinsic superiority to any other possible outcome; rather, the product is a universal common good which is substantively superior....

Pluralists are skeptical of the participants' ability to set aside personal preferences. From the pluralist vantage point, deliberation appears to yield under the legitimizing label of the transcendental "public good," a consensus that reflects aggregated preferences at best and "parochial perspectives in the guise of neutrality" at worst....

In the agency context, pluralism and modern civic republicanism have been described as "theories of conflict resolution" rather than of political power. Alternatively, they can be conceptualized as decision-making modes characterized by particular foundational and regulatory ideals. Yet substantial problems arise when institutions rely too heavily upon unattainable ideals. Not surprisingly, reality falls short of all ideals. The conditions necessary to ensure that all models work perfectly do not exist. The impediments imposed upon conceptual models by a second-best reality may simply perplex academicians and provide for interesting observations. But the imposition of more idealistic decision-making approaches upon an imperfect society carries consequences of greater import....

\* \* \*

## Notes and Questions

1. Professor Freeman maintains that the adversariness and disincentive to share information is premised upon an interest representational model that is essentially pluralist. Because of this, Freeman believes that stakeholder participation would be curtailed under a civic republican approach because of the risk of faction, i.e., that participants would pursue self interest rather than public good. How do environmental justice advocates fit into this conceptual duality? Do they pursue utilitarian self interests or do they pursue a greater public good? How would they fare under a predominantly pluralist (utilitarian) approach to agency decisionmaking? How would they fare under a civic republican approach? According to one of the authors,

> Environmental justice illuminates the conundrum inherent in environmental decision-making. The expertise approach is helpful to address scientific and technical questions, but it is inappropriate to resolve conflicting preferences and distributional issues in particular. Because of its focus on the public good, a [civic republican] approach might be helpful in resolving ethical conflicts, but it is not well-suited to resolve technical issues and, by definition, would not address conflicting utilitarian preferences. The pluralist model does address competing preferences, but when it contemplates an optimal distribution of environmental benefits and burdens, it breaks down. This occurs regardless of what one concludes is an "optimal" distribution. A fair distribution is not only difficult to value in economic terms, it is hard to legitimate using a short-term economic conception of rationality. An unfair distribution, although optimal in terms of economic efficiency, is an unethical preference. As a result, utilitarianism is unable to address the ethical dimension of distributional issues. This explains why the present approach of environmental regulation, which leans heavily towards utilitarian pluralism, is marked by persistent resistance to environmental justice claims.

Gauna, *supra*, at 51. If the central problem lies in the fact that environmental decision-making entails decisions about a range of matters that cannot be completely addressed by any one decisionmaking approach (expertise oriented, pluralist oriented, or civic republican oriented approach), can you see other alternatives? For further exploration on this theme, *see e.g.,* Jonathan Poisner, *A Civic Republican Perspective on the National Environmental Policy Act's Process for Citizen Participation,* 26 ENV'T. L. 53, 57 (1996); Rena Steinzor, *The Corruption of Civic Environmentalism,* 30 ENVTL. L. REP. 10,909 (2000).

2. Freeman offers "collaborative governance" as a third alternative to escape the perversities of pluralism and the utopianism of civic republicanism. Under a collaborative approach, the agency is not the neutral umpire of pluralism nor the enlightened decisionmaker of civic republicanism, but rather is a facilitator and capacity builder. The success of this approach appears to depend upon the ability of the agency to define both the benefits and the measurement of those benefits, leaving to the stakeholders the task of deliberating about how to achieve them, presumably with an eye towards understanding the limitations and potential of various approaches. How does that differ from the present interest-representation (pluralist) model? Does the provisional nature of the enterprise, the fact that the participants must also devise a way to evaluate

and reassess the agreements they come to, mark the point of departure? Would this provisionality enure to the benefit of environmental justice adovcates? How?

3. Under Freeman's approach, the agency is not a neutral arbiter but rather self-consciously undertakes to make sure the playing field is level and undertakes to represent unrepresented interests. Is this going to require a significant change in agency culture? If so, what institutional mechanisms might facilitate this transformation?

4. Freeman proposes that the risk that well-financed industry stakeholders will dominate the process are reduced by public meeting requirements and the ability of the agency to reject the consensus recommendation. Are these safeguards adequate? Why or why not?

5. Freeman sees a much larger oversight role by private citizens in the collaborative regime, while acknowledging that very few public interest organizations have the expertise for (or interest in) such a role. How will this oversight role be financed? What mechanisms will be in place to keep the overseers accountable? Given our adversarial culture, is it unrealistic to propose that regulated entities will willingly accept citizen oversight? If so, how could such resistence be overcome?

If capacity building, collaboration, provisionalism and private oversight mark a fundamentally new direction for environmental regulation, could this new regime impede democratic values? If it is the legislative branch that is empowered to strike the ultimate bargain—be it a utilitarian preference or public good—how far should the agency venture from the realm of strict implementation of legislative mandate? Professor William Funk has a less optimistic view of the new environmental regulatory regime, specifically the practice of regulatory negotiation.

# William Funk,
# Bargaining Toward the New Millennium: Regulatory Negotiation and the Subversion of the Public Interest
### 46 Duke Law Journal 1351 (1997)

*Negotiated Rulemaking and the Perversion of the Administrative Process*

### The Rule of Law

First, consider the theory and principles of the [Administrative Procedure Act]. Implicit in the APA is the notion of the rule of law. Agencies exist to carry out the law. Their statutory directions may be specific or general, but the agencies' actions are justified and legitimized by their service to those direction.... The statute is not just a brake or anchor on agency autonomy; it is the source and reason for the agency's actions.

Now consider regulatory negotiation. The law still exists, but the law is now merely a limitation on the range of bargaining. The parties to the negotiation are not serving the law, and the outcome of the negotiation is not legitimized by its service to the law. The regulation that emerges from negotiated rulemaking is, as [Philip] Harter said, legitimized by the agreement of the parties. Accordingly, Harter argued, if the parties agree that a rule should contain a particular provision, the legality of that provision should not be determined by traditional methods. Instead, the courts should defer to an agreement of the parties that is not manifestly inconsistent with the purpose of the authorizing statute. Harter explains why:

The parties are typically better able [than courts] to determine "what works" within the theory of the statute and hence what is the best way of achieving its overall goal. Or, a provision may be included in a statute to benefit a particular interest. If that interest does not insist on its full exercise as part of the agreement,... [the fact] [t]hat they agreed indicates the interest achieved the protection sought in the statute.... In short, law becomes nothing more than the expression of private interests mediated through some governmental body....

### The Agency as Responsible Actor

A second principle central to the APA is the role of the agency as the responsible actor. The agency is not a broker or mediation service....Nor is the agency merely an enforcer of private agreements. Rather the agency is the authority responsible for and empowered to achieve the statutory design.

This is not, however, the role of the agency in regulatory negotiation....

[T]he formalities remain in place; the agency is titularly acting in a sovereign capacity. But the dynamics of the process all run in the opposite direction....If [the agency] rejects or blocks consensus by invoking its "authority," it engenders bad will among those it has induced to come to the table; it largely negates any benefit of the negotiation and may have wasted valuable time and resources on a futile endeavor; and it is back to "square one" with its rulemaking. In short, the dynamics of "getting to yes" pervert the role of the agency as sovereign....

### Rulemaking as an Undertaking of Instrumental Rationality

...As Harter wrote,

> Under the traditional hybrid process, the legitimacy of the rule rests on a resolution of complex factual materials and rational extrapolation from those facts, guided by the criteria of the statute. Under regulatory negotiation, however, the regulation's legitimacy would lie in the overall agreement of the parties. The logical consequence of this is that "[i]t would be inappropriate to require the negotiating group and the agency to conduct research similar to that required in the hybrid process." "The agency would not be required to prove either the existence of a problem or the feasibility of the proposed solution if those who would be affected agree on both issues." In short, the facts don't matter as long as everyone is happy.

### The Search for the Public Interest

...Many laws besides the Negotiated Rulemaking Act encourage and support methods to provide a voice for affected interests in developing rules that affect them. The APA's notice-and-comment requirement is an obvious beginning; the National Environmental Policy Act's notice-and-comment procedure for environmental impact statements is another. The various substantive statutes including hybrid rulemaking provisions are other examples....Nevertheless, an inspection of all these laws rebuts any suggestion that these enhanced public participation requirements substitute for the agency's responsibility to engage in reasoned decisionmaking in search of the public interest. For example, environmental impact statement requirements are consistently described as intended to improve the agency's decisionmaking....Thus, while modern rulemaking seeks full participation by interested persons, the agency still determines the public interest....

The effect on the culture and identification of the agency may outlive the particular negotiation. That is, when the negotiation is over, the consensus is obtained, and the rule is promulgated, where is the agency's interest in assuring compliance with the rule, in assuring that the rule continues to serve its purposes? The agency does not have the same sense of responsibility for the rule, because it does not reflect the agency's considered determination as serving the public interest; instead, it reflects the bargain of the parties. It is the parties' rule, not the agency's....

* * *

## Notes and Questions

1. Professor Funk questions the wisdom of allowing the agency to act as an equal participant in the negotiations while at the same time having ultimate veto authority as sovereign decisionmaker. Professor Freeman in turn envisions yet another role for the agency, one which self-consciously advocates for the interests of unrepresented or inadequately represented stakeholder groups. Each role varies in the degree of "neutrality" that agency officials can appropriately maintain. What are the potential environmental justice pitfalls of this tenuous position? For example, in the course of rulemaking, can the agency seek to protect the interests of disempowered communities potentially impacted by the proposed rule while pursuing its own interests as participant while maintaining the "neutrality" presumably necessary as ultimate arbiter of multiple conflicting interests?

2. Could Funk be overstating the potential divide between a rule that is the product of consensus and one that is the product of "instrumental rationality" or reasoned decisionmaking? After all, as Freeman points out, a collaborative, problem-solving process requires each participant to demonstrate why proposed solutions are sound or unsound, and to marshal the facts necessary to support its position. Wouldn't the same hold true for an interest representation process that relies upon consensus for its legitimacy?

3. All things considered, how would environmental justice advocates fare in an implementation process that leans toward the following:

a. An expertise-oriented approach where the agency officials makes a decision based upon the "best science" or technology with little or no prior stakeholder participation.

b. A pluralist (interest representation) approach where there is full stakeholder participation and the agency attempts in some fashion to make tradeoffs that accommodate the interests of all groups. This approach would rely heavily upon consensus.

c. A civic republican approach where the agency—with or without stakeholder participation—attempts to come to a decision that will capture the public interest or public good embodied in the environmental legislation.

d. A collaborative approach where the agency focuses upon building capacity of stakeholder groups and attempts to put mechanisms in place that continually reevaluate and refine the decision. This approach would also rely heavily upon consensus.

Which approach might work better in a difficult political context, one involving budgetary restraints, OMB oversight and congressional review? Which approach might work better in a context where there is substantial pressure to promote market and incentive regulatory tools and devolve authority to the local level?

# C. Devolution

Many of the major federal environmental laws, including the Clean Water Act, the Clean Air Act, and the Resource Conservation and Recovery Act (RCRA), reserve a significant implementation role for the states. These statutes require EPA to establish minimum national standards, while authorizing delegation of authority to implement the programs, including issuing permits, monitoring compliance, and taking enforcement action, to states that meet minimum federal requirements. (If a state chooses not to assume responsibility for administering a federal program, EPA operates and administers the program directly.) Once a state receives program authorization, EPA oversees the state's activities to ensure that they continue to meet federal standards. This relationship has come to be known as the "cooperative federalism" model. State agencies now administer over 75 percent of the major federal environmental programs that can be delegated to them. In recent years the states (and others) have advocated that they should be given greater autonomy in administering federal requirements, and should assume a more prominent role in environmental regulation, while federal involvement should be reduced. Some of the implications of devolving greater authority to the states are explored in the excerpt below (issues specifically relating to devolution and enforcement are examined in more detail in Chapter XI, and issues relating to devolution and collaboration are examined in Chapter XV).

## Rena I. Steinzor, Devolution and the Public Health
### 24 Harvard Environmental Law Review 351 (2000)

*Races-to-the-Bottom and the Realities of Interstate Commerce*

...If states are willing to sacrifice their authority to develop more stringent local laws, they are also more likely to weaken state regulation when federal standards are devolved. Unless the Federal government responds to such backtracking by withdrawing delegated authority, levels of protection could reach a bottom that is unacceptably low. Moreover, as mentioned earlier, EPA has never carried out a threat to withdraw a delegation, undermining its credibility as a referee of such races-to-the-bottom....

Applying public choice theory, [scholars] argue that moving decision-making authority to the level of government closest to the people ensures that democratic and economically efficient decisions are made about the level of protection people are willing to finance and the level of pollution they are willing to tolerate....

One response to such theories is that the economic inefficiency of reinventing scientific and technical knowledge at the state level more than counterbalances the supposed advantages of moving the standard-setting aspects of such decision-making closer to the people.

Another response is that the exercise of free public choice depends on good, readily accessible information about the implications of available alternatives. However, when people exercise public choice in this context, they do not understand the ramifications of a state hitting the bottom because information about the states' actual environmental performance is so poor.

Perhaps the most compelling evidence that races-to-the-bottom will produce unacceptably lax regulation is the business community's strong interest in avoiding a "patchwork" of state regulatory requirements. This concern was a major motivation for the enactment of federal environmental laws, with congressional proponents arguing that maintenance of the free floor of interstate commerce requires a consistent system of uniform regulatory requirements. Because a patchwork of aggressive state regulatory programs would prove anathema to large corporations, the only plausible explanation for industry's tolerance of devolution is the belief that state regulatory activism will be foreclosed, rolling back federal regulation without allowing newly strengthened state regulatory programs to take its place....

### Expired permits

Permits are the primary method used to achieve pollution control under the Clean Air and Clean Water Acts. Permits prescribe the efforts industrial facilities must make to control, reduce, and prevent pollution and serve as the vehicle for policing lapses in those efforts. Permit periods typically run for five years, with the clear expectation that the responsible federal or state agency will tighten their terms and conditions as necessary. If some states revise their permits and others do not, disparate levels of protection affect the communities near industrial facilities as well as the facilities' competitors.

Permit renewals are especially critical under the Clean Water Act because they are the opportunity to apply regulatory standards issued since the original permit was drafted. Because EPA's development of water quality standards has been so slow, lengthy delays in renewing permits written in the 1980s means that, as a practical matter, these new standards are never implemented....

[T]he senior officials responsible for permitting policy at EPA's headquarters admitted that the backlog of expired permits was increasing in twenty-five states. Only fifteen states would reduce their backlogs to ten percent by December 2001. The backlog had climbed to twenty-eight percent overall, with 26.2% of permits expired in state-run programs and forty-four percent in EPA-run programs. Nearly half of the facilities with expired permits discharge into waters classified as impaired under section 303(d) of the Clean Water Act.

This breakdown is significant because it suggests that the regulatory infrastructure is aging and weakened, a circumstance that does not bode well for unrestricted devolution. If EPA and the states lack the resources—or the willpower—to maintain the current regulatory foundation, unrestricted devolution could threaten the progress made in safeguarding public health without ever achieving the beneficial reforms that devolutionists have promised....

### State Water Quality Standards

In many ways, the Total Maximum Daily Load ("TMDL") standards for water quality that Congress authorized the states to write under section 303(d) are the ultimate answer to critiques of unduly rigid, one-size-fits-all, technology-based controls. To develop TMDLs, state regulators must analyze the actual condition of a specific water body, taking into account all the discharges that it receives. Working backwards, they must define the pollution load the water can tolerate and still be suitable for its designated use. State regulators must then adopt plans to implement these standards by incorporating new conditions into the permits for individual sources to ensure that discharges are controlled to the point that TMDLs are met in receiving waters. In sum, TMDLs are based on a consideration of cumulative risk in an actual water body. They require the states to develop standards that will limit pollution to a level that makes such resources sustainable....

To be sure, TMDLs are extremely difficult to write, and the states have encountered a series of economic, administrative, scientific, and political hurdles in performing the job they fought to obtain. Included in these difficulties is EPA's notable, and admitted, failure to provide adequate technical support. It may take as long as fifteen years for most states to write a workable set of TMDLs....

[Difficulties] that states have encountered in implementing the TMDL program are introduced here not to suggest that the states are slothful and that EPA is a paragon of regulatory virtue. Rather, the TMDL saga suggests that devolving additional standard-writing authority to states will only work if three conditions are met. First, the federal government must be prepared to offer clear and timely technical support. Second, the states themselves must either raise or receive the resources to undertake such demanding programs. Third, the law must provide an enforcement mechanism against states that are unable to meet their responsibilities.

If one-size-fits-all regulation is as abominable as its critics claim, devolution will prove a better alternative only if states have the resources necessary to do a complicated, demanding, and expensive job. The alternative is a regulatory system that is blind to the cumulative risks caused by pollution loading of environmental media from multiple sources, a phenomenon of overriding importance to the protection of public health. From a public health perspective, it is no exaggeration to suggest that the assessment and reduction of such cumulative risks are the single most important mission of EPA and the states for the foreseeable future....

*Indicia of Economic Health*

Finally, it is worth noting the paradox that states with large, low income populations and corresponding large social welfare "burdens" may have to spend more than comparatively wealthy states to achieve comparable levels of public health protection. Poor diet and lack of access to medical care can compound the harm caused by exposure to pollution because people in poorer condition physically are less likely to be able to resist adverse health effects....

There are troubling indications that [states] are falling behind in accomplishing the most basic functions, from writing permits to enforcing the law. Unable to keep pace with respect to traditional first-generation environmental problems [i.e., pollution caused by large identifiable point souces], many states are in no position to tackle second-generation problems [pollution from numerous diverse sources and land management practices] by innovative methods or otherwise.

The states appear to make decisions regarding the resources they commit to environmental protection for reasons unrelated to their environmental challenges. There are no obvious reasons to predict that more devolution of regulatory authority will result in improvement of this faltering performance. To truly stabilize environmental regulation in order to provide a baseline of protection for public health, devolution should proceed more slowly. States should have to demonstrate that they are prepared to manage additional responsibilities successfully....

\* \* \*

## Notes and Questions

1. Consider Professor Sheila Foster's views on devolution and its effect on environmental justice communities:

> There is, notably, a shift underway to decentralize environmental decision-making and devolve more degree of influence to the "community" or local

level. The shift is most discernable in a number of recent initiatives by EPA, particularly its Community-Based Environmental Protection (CBEP) initiative. If the last wave of environmental decisionmaking was marked by a "command-and-control" approach, the CBEP suggests that the next wave will be marked by the empowerment of those individuals who physically live in the communities most impacted by environmental decisions.

Community-based environmental decisionmaking promises, in theory, enhanced dialogue and shared power between governmental decisionmakers and ordinary citizens (public-private), as well as between citizens differently situated vis-a-vis particular environmental decisions (private-private). The promise of more egalitarian and meaningful public-private and private-private relations follows, in part, from the devolution of varying degrees of decisionmaking responsibility and influence to the local or "community" level. The CBEP recognizes, at least implicitly, that risk-bearing communities provide an important type of expertise in, and are more effectively able to bring forth public/community values into, the decisionmaking process.

How much the move toward community-based environmental decisionmaking will address the challenges of incorporating "justice" into environmental law remains to be seen. In many ways, such an approach mimics ongoing efforts to employ alternative dispute resolution processes in siting and other environmental decisions. Like those efforts, there may still be unresolved problems of representation, resource inequality (due to differences in education and training), and capture by more powerful interests in the deliberation process. Unfortunately, not enough research has been conducted on whether informal dispute resolution processes are necessarily the most appropriate or effective method of resolving conflicts with traditionally disempowered groups of people, such as racial minorities and the poor. Nevertheless, the movement toward more decentralized environmental decisionmaking is encouraging for its embrace of the importance of moving away from a narrow, technocratic decisionmaking and its effort to provide all communities with more meaningful participation with regard to the environmental and health risks they bear.

Sheila R. Foster, *Meeting the Environmental Justice Challenge: Evolving Norms in Environmental Decisionmaking*, 30 ENVTL. L. REP. 10,992, 11,005 (2000). From an environmental justice perspective, what are the benefits and risks of devolution to the states or to local authorities? What about devolution of authority over a particular resource to local groups? Is there a way to decentralize environmental decisionmaking while imposing safeguards for vulnerable communities? *See,* Sheila R. Foster, *Environmental Justice in an Era of Devolved Collaboration*, 26 HARV. ENVTL. L. REV. (2002) (see also Chapter XV).

# Chapter VI

# Standard Setting

## A. Legal Complexities

### 1. AN INTRODUCTORY NOTE ON THE TAXONOMY OF STANDARDS

Environmental standards are the foundation upon which all regulatory requirements rest. These standards have been described under the rubric of two intersecting categories. The first category differentiates between a "specification standard" and a "performance standard." A specification standard is more prescriptive, with the environmental agency telling the regulated entity how to achieve the desired result. A performance standard sets the goal and the regulated entity unilaterally picks the means to achieve the goal. For example, if an agency tells a power plant that it must use low sulfur coal to produce electricity, it has announced a specification standard. But if the agency tells a power plant that it cannot exceed emissions by X amount for each unit of electricity produced, it has announced a performance standard. Performance standards are sometimes called "end of the pipe" standards because the internal processes of the firm are not directly regulated. However, the power plant operator may decide to achieve the standard by using pollution control technology, or by voluntarily adjusting its internal production processes in any number of ways, for example, using low sulfur coal.

The second category of standards differentiates the reference point of the standards. Some standards are made by reference to what is a safe level for humans and the environment. These are called "health-based" or "risk-based" standards and are often expressed by the ambient amount of a pollutant that is safe. For example, if the agency announces that if the air contains over X amount of sulfur dioxide per cubic meter over a 8 hour period, the air is deemed unhealthy when the standard has been exceeded. If there are too many exceedances, then the air shed is deemed to be in "nonattainment" with the national ambient air quality standard ("NAAQS" or "NAAQ standard"). "Technology-based" standards, on the other hand, are made with reference to what is currently technologically possible to achieve, regardless of whether it results in a healthy environment or not. For example, the EPA may announce that new facilities emitting sulfur dioxide in nonattainment areas must control their emissions using the "lowest achievable emissions reductions" possible, and "LAER" becomes the standard. It may be that using LAER will still result in troubling ambient conditions. A third type of standard is termed "technology-forcing" because it is made by reference to technology not yet available, but it is intended to force the development of cleaner technologies. For example, the Congress or the EPA may announce that manufacturers of automobiles must find a way to reduce tail pipe emissions by 10% below 1990 emissions by a certain date, 2004 for example. The auto industry is then in a position of having to develop the technology to achieve the reductions (called "rollbacks") in order to have vehicles certified for sale by the year 2004.

These standards work in concert. Often, technology-based standards and technology-forcing standards are included in a variety of regulatory strategies designed to achieve the ambient, or health-based standards. For example, a state may wish to impose technology-based standards in addition to auto emission controls to reduce ambient concentrations of carbon dioxide in order to achieve compliance with the health-based carbon dioxide NAAQ standard. Permit conditions often contain requirements made with reference to technology-based standards, but these standards in turn depend upon the stringency of health-based standards the jurisdiction is attempting to achieve.

There is often confusion concerning terminology, with some suggesting that technology-based standards, such as "LAER," are uniformly specification standards, but this is not the case. Some, in fact many, technology-based standards are performance standards. For example, if EPA announces that "LAER" for a particular activity (coal fired power plants, for example), is a 95% reduction in sulfur dioxide, then that is a performance, not a specification, standard. However, if there is only one available technology and/or production process that can achieve a 95% reduction, it may be viewed as a de facto specification standard. As discussed in Chapter VII, reinvention proponents deride "command and control" standards, but there is some confusion in the literature as to whether they are speaking of specification standards (the most prescriptive of the standards) or more broadly about any standards, including performance standards, that restrict the range of options available to facility operators. Industry stakeholders often criticize the inefficiencies of technology based standards, arguing that uniform standards ignore cost differentials among firms and that it is irrational for firms to install expensive technologies to control emissions that will have no real effect on ambient conditions because the media (e.g., the air shed or water body) may be able to adequately absorb, filter and/or disperse the pollutants without harm to the resource.

The standards that appear to most concern environmental justice advocates are the health-based standards. Some claim that these standards are often insufficiently protective because they are made by reference to their effect upon healthy adult males. In addition, many such standards are made in isolation, a "chemical by chemical approach" that does not factor in the possibility that the exposed individual may use the resource more than the average citizen, may be subject to a range of other pollutants, may be vulnerable because of certain genetic predispositions or health conditions, or may have fewer preventative and health care resources available. Thus, they claim that ambient health-based standards should be tightened. This will have a direct effect upon other types of standards, which similarly would need to be tightened in order to achieve the ambient standards.

As in all matters, because environmental justice is not specifically identified in current federal environmental laws, more general sources of standard setting authority must be identified.

## 2.   LEGAL SOURCES OF AUTHORITY

# Richard J. Lazarus & Stephanie Tai,
## Integrating Environmental Justice
## Into EPA Permitting Authority
26 Ecology Law Quarterly 617 (1999)

*The Clean Air Act*

The Clean Air Act (CAA) presents EPA with more opportunities to integrate environmental justice concerns into the Act's substantive standards than the Agency has utilized. The national ambient air quality standards (NAAQS) that serve as the Act's cornerstone are illustrative. Pursuant to the CAA, EPA administrators must promulgate NAAQS to protect "public health" with an adequate margin of safety. It is well settled that Congress intended for EPA to consider especially sensitive subpopulations in determining what pollutant levels would meet the "public health" standard. Pollutant levels that pose no health hazard to average healthy individuals may nonetheless present significant hazards to some individuals who, because of preexisting physical conditions, have heightened vulnerabilities. The Act, accordingly, instructs EPA in developing the "air quality criteria" upon which the NAAQS are based to include information on "those variable factors...which of themselves or in combination with other factors may alter the effects on public health or welfare."...

EPA's statutory authority in this respect is also of a continuing nature. It does not end once a NAAQS is first promulgated. Pursuant to CAA Section 109(d), EPA is required to revise air quality criteria and standards at a minimum of every five years or as needed to ensure their adequacy in light of new information and changing circumstances. For example, the American Lung Association and the Environmental Defense Fund recently challenged EPA's refusal to issue a five-minute sulfur dioxide ($SO_2$) NAAQS, a standard that the organizations contended was especially necessary to address the health concerns of environmental justice communities vulnerable to short-term exposures to high levels of $SO_2$. Because EPA did not adequately explain its conclusion that such exposures did not lead to a public health problem, the U.S. Court of Appeals for the D.C. Circuit remanded back to EPA its order refusing to promulgate more stringent $SO_2$ NAAQS. The D.C. Circuit's ruling, therefore, suggests more than that EPA possesses statutory authority to consider the special sensitivities of environmental justice communities when establishing air quality standards under the CAA. The CAA may, in this respect, provide an instance in which the federal law mandates such consideration.

Section 112 [dealing with controls for hazardous air pollutants] also includes two other subsections relevant to environmental justice priorities. Section 112(c)(3) and Section 112(k) both authorize EPA to consider the aggregate effects of multiple sources of hazardous air pollutants, especially those emitted in urban areas....

*The Clean Water Act*

...The water quality standard provisions of the CWA offer another opportunity for EPA to exercise its authority to consider and address environmental justice concerns. Under the CWA, states must establish water quality standards applicable to waters within the states' borders. Unlike the CAA's NAAQS, which are nationally uniform, these state water quality standards may not only vary between states, but need not be uniformly applied to all water bodies within any one state. A state may legitimately apply different levels of water quality protection to different water bodies depending on the specific uses (for example, recreation, transportation, or industry) the state designates for each body of water. EPA oversees a state's promulgation of water quality standards primarily to ensure that the standards are consistent with the state's "designated uses" but also to ensure compliance with EPA's nondegradation policy, which guards against unwarranted degradation of existing uses of water and associated water quality. CWA permits must ensure compliance not only with the Act's various technology-based effluent limitations, but also with the state water quality standards. The latter aspect of the Act requires the federal (or state) agency responsible for permitting, first, to determine the total maximum daily loads (TMDLs) of pollutants consistent with the water quality standard applicable to each body of water and, second, to allocate those loads among all the sources contributing pollutants to the water body. Because of the practical and political obstacles in making each of these two determinations, EPA and the states have historically made little headway in their implementation until very recently.

The water quality program is especially relevant to environmental justice because it involves EPA and the states making a series of judgments with clearly distributional consequences. For instance, EPA's nondegradation policy, which protects "existing uses" of water, should provide protection to such existing uses by environmental justice communities, including those that are economically or culturally dependent on the subsistence use of water. TMDL planning, however, is even more relevant. EPA can ensure, through its oversight of state TMDL determinations, that the resulting allocations do not unfairly burden low-income communities or communities of color.... [See excerpt from Oliver Houck, subsection (B)(3) below. Eds.]

### Resource Conservation and Recovery Act

Many provisions of the Resource Conservation and Recovery Act (RCRA) [governing hazardous waste management] include broad wording that leaves EPA with substantial authority to take into account environmental justice concerns in the Agency's implementation of this Act. The touchstone for the Agency's promulgation of regulations under Sections 3002, 3003, and 3004 applicable to generators, transporters, and owners and operators of hazardous waste treatment, storage, and disposal facilities is the same: "as may be necessary to protect human health and the environment." One of the major lessons of environmental justice is that EPA's past failure to account for aggregation of risks and cumulative impacts has caused EPA's existing standards to fail to protect human health and the environment in certain communities. EPA's authority under RCRA to correct this problem cannot be gainsaid. The relevant statutory language specifically directs the Agency to accomplish an objective that can be achieved only by considering the actual (including aggregated) human health and environmental effects of hazardous waste management on disparately affected low-income communities or communities of color...

### Toxic Substances Control Act

...Like the other environmental laws, [the Toxic Substance Control Act's (TSCA)] substantive standards are susceptible to an agency interpretation that addresses environmental justice concerns. Particularly relevant is TSCA's instructing EPA to consider, among other factors, "cumulative or synergistic effects" in determining the regulatory border between reasonable and "unreasonable risk[s] to health or the environment." Such effects are precisely those that environmental justice advocates contend have been overlooked too often in considering the risks imposed by toxic substances on low-income communities and communities of color.

*The Federal Insecticide, Fungicide, and Rodenticide Act*

The Federal Insecticide, Fungicide, and Rodenticide Act (FIFRA) confers substantial authority on the EPA Administrator to address environmental justice concerns. EPA's principal responsibility in administering FIFRA is its registration of pesticides to guard against "unreasonable adverse effects on the environment." Environmental justice advocates are interested in FIFRA's administration for many reasons, one of which is the substantial threat to the health of farmworkers posed by the unreasonably dangerous use of pesticides. FIFRA provides EPA with significant authority to eliminate these unreasonable risks through tactics as varied as use restrictions, disposal restrictions, labeling requirements, registration denials, and conditional registrations. EPA's authority is broadly worded and turns on the "unreasonable adverse effects" touchstone, thereby leaving the Agency with significant discretionary authority to take into account wide ranging concerns when implementing FIFRA. Environmental justice concerns with risk accumulation, cumulative effects, and worker notice all fall easily within the core of the Agency's regulatory authority under FIFRA....

\* \* \*

## Notes and Questions

1. If the EPA's authority under the federal environmental statutes is as broad and discretionary as Lazarus and Tai suggest, why has the agency arguably failed to promulgate standards that are protective enough to address cumulative impacts and synergistic risks? Under the statutory authorities outlined above, is it possible to devise a standard for any particular pollutant that will account for multiple source impacts of the pollutant as well as its potential interaction with other pollutants?

2. Many environmental justice activists have long maintained that the lack of an adequate response to insufficiently protective standards does not stem from lack of legal authority, scientific understanding or engineering capability, but from lack of political will among regulators. In your opinion, how do each of these impediments factor into an overall lack of an adequately protective response?

3. A quick review of environmental cases can lead one to the conclusion that the EPA will get sued regardless of the standard promulgated, i.e., either the industrial stakeholders or environmental stakeholders will be dissatisfied, or possibly both. Those wishing to uphold the EPA's decision will point to case law affording the agency great deference in technical matters. Those wishing to defeat the agency's decision will use a variety of arguments generally premised upon the failure of the agency to follow the legislative mandate, thus acting outside of the statute's scope. It is likely that the ultimate success of these arguments will depend upon the inclination of the courts to be deferential to the EPA. In reviewing the note below, in addition to judicial deference, also consider the importance of the NAAQS from the standpoint of public health and how much is at stake with the establishment or revision of these standards.

## 3. JUDICIAL REVIEW—A NOTE ON THE NAAQS

As noted by Lazarus and Tai, two important standard setting provisions allowing for integration of environmental justice concerns are sections 108 and 109 of the Clean Air Act, under which EPA is authorized to establish and periodically revise NAAQS for certain air pollutants, called "criteria" pollutants. As stated above, ambient standards refer to the amount of pollutant in the environmental media (like an airshed or waterbody) over a period of time. Presently, only a handful of pollutants are regulated under this section, as opposed to an extensive list of hazardous air pollutants regulated under another section of the Clean Air Act (Section 112). Despite the relatively fewer number of NAAQS, regulation of these pollutants is the heart and soul of the Air Act because these pollutants are both serious in their health implications and are difficult to regulate because they come from numerous and diverse sources. NAAQS presently cover six pollutants—particulate matter, sulfur dioxide ($SO_2$), ozone, nitrogen oxides, carbon monoxide and lead. However, since ozone is a photochemical reaction in the air, pollutants that are precursors to ozone are directly regulated as surrogates; they include nitrogen oxides, volatile organic compounds, nonmethane organic gases and hydrocarbons. *See generally*, R. Percival, A. Miller, C. Schroeder and J. Leape, Environmental Regulation: Law, Science and Policy, 551–570 (3d 2000); Steven Ferry, Environmental Law: Examples and Explanations 156–160 (2d 2001).

One of the most controversial features of setting the NAAQS is that the endeavor is supposed to be entirely cost blind, meaning that the EPA cannot consider how costly it will be to achieve the national standards. Theoretically, NAAQS are supposed to reflect allowable concentrations of these pollutants in the outdoor air that are protective of health, even if achieving such levels will shut down entire industries and cause the national economy to crumble. These standards are not as draconian as they appear (even in theory), however, because economic considerations can play a significant role in how the standards are implemented. States have several opportunities to consider economics and costs in developing their state implementation plans (SIPs), which are plans submitted to the EPA for the regions (air sheds) in each individual state demonstrating how the state proposes to come into attainment with NAAQS in those regions within a given time frame.

Many regions in the U.S. do not meet NAAQS. This failure has significant health and environmental justice implications. Environmental attorney Curtis Moore explains some of the harmful health impacts of particulate matter and ozone, pollutants for which the NAAQS were recently tightened:

> A large body of compelling evidence demonstrates that particulate matter is associated with early and unnecessary deaths, aggravation of heart and lung diseases, reduction in the ability to breathe normally, and increases in respiratory illnesses, leading to school and work absences. As particulate levels rise, so do runny or stuffy noses, sinusitis, sore throat, wet cough, head colds, hayfever, burning or red eyes, wheezing, dry cough, phlegm, shortness of breath, and chest discomfort or pain, as well as hospital admissions for asthma and bronchitis. Studies have shown that chronic cough, asthma, and emphysema rise among nonsmoking Seventh-Day Adventists; bronchitis and chronic cough increase in school children as do emergency room and hospital admissions. In Utah, when particulate levels rose, hospital admissions of children for respiratory illnesses tripled. Acute respiratory symptoms and/or illness have also been associated with particulate air pollution in six eastern towns, in adults in 63 cities, and in two Swiss cities. In plain terms, at levels commonly encountered, particulate pollution kills and disables Americans, especially children, the elderly, and those who are ill....

> [I]t is clear that the impacts of ozone exposure are grave. The body of evidence that ozone causes chronic, pathologic lung damage is overwhelming. At levels routinely encountered in most American cities, ozone burns through cell

walls in lungs and airways, tissues redden and swell, cellular fluid seeps into the lungs, and over time their elasticity drops. Macrophage cells rush to the lung's defense, but they too are stunned by the ozone. Susceptibility to bacterial infections increases, possibly because ciliated cells that normally expel foreign particles and organisms have been killed and replaced by thicker, stiffer, nonciliated cells. Scars and lesions form in the airways. At ozone levels that prevail through much of the year in California and other warm-weather cities, healthy, nonsmoking young men who exercise can't breathe normally. Breathing is rapid, shallow, and painful.

As ozone levels rise, hospital admissions and emergency department visits do the same. In some laboratory animals, cancers appear. Children at summer camp lose the ability to breathe normally as ozone levels rise, even when the air is clean by reference to the former federal standard, and these losses continue for up to a week....

Curtis Moore, *The Impracticality and Immorality of Cost-Benefit Analysis in Setting Health-Related Standards*, 11 TULANE ENVTL. L. J. 187, 195–198 (1998). Sulfur dioxide also can present significant health effects. As noted in a widely-adopted environmental law casebook, "[s]tudies of asthmatics indicate that they experience measurable changes in respiratory functions when exposed to sulfur dioxide ($SO_2$) concentrations greater than 0.6 ppm [parts per million] for periods as brief as five minutes [i.e., $SO_2$ "spikes" or "peaks"]. These exposures can make it difficult for asthmatics to breathe...." PERCIVAL, *supra*, at 559 (citing EPA's Clean Air Science Advisory Committee report).

The health effects, in turn, appear to disproportionately affect people of color and the poor. As noted by Professor Craig Oren,

> [A]sthma is apparently becoming more common—even though air pollutant concentrations have been dropping—and appears to be concentrated among the poor and non-white. According to the Center for Disease Control in Atlanta, the incidence of acute asthma attacks among children has doubled in the past decade, even though highly effective medications have been developed. Asthma is the most common cause of hospitalization among children—five million hospitalizations each year—and deaths among children with asthma rose by 78 percent from 1980 to 1993. The disease in concentrated in heavily populated urban areas. A recent study in New York City shows that hospitalization rates for asthma are far higher in poorer, minority areas than in affluent areas....

Craig N. Oren, *Run Over by American Trucking Part I: Can EPA Revive Its Air Quality Standards?* 29 ENVTL L. REP. 10,653, 10,661 (1999).

Once the EPA Administrator determines that a pollutant may endanger public health and its presence in the ambient air comes from numerous or diverse mobile or stationary sources, it is required to promulgate air quality criteria and a NAAQS for the pollutant. However, because of the scientific uncertainty involved in determining a precise dose threshold that may trigger harmful health effects, the EPA has substantial discretion in applying this standard. In fact, lead is the only new criteria pollutant EPA has added to the initial statutory list, and it did so only because of a successful citizen suit under a previous iteration of Section 108.

Revising the existing NAAQS is also an area where the Administrator enjoys substantial discretion, but not without judicial scrutiny. EPA at various times declined to revise the existing NAAQS for $SO_2$, carbon monoxide, nitrogen oxides and particulate matter, despite new evidence indicating that levels of exposure below the standards might be harmful. As noted by Lazarus and Tai, moreover, EPA also declined to issue a new short term exposure NAAQS for $SO_2$ (even though the longer averaging times under the existing standard allow harmful $SO_2$ spikes to occur), a decision the D.C. Circuit Court of Appeals remanded because of the agency's failure to explain "[w]hy is the fact that thousands of asthmatics can be expected to suffer atypical physical effects from repeated five minute bursts of high-level sulfur dioxide not a public health problem?" American Lung Association v. EPA, 134 F.3d 388, 392 (D.C. Cir. 1998). But conversely, judicial scrutiny, or "hard look" review, has also been applied to EPA's decisions to revise and tighten certain NAAQS. In 1997, EPA lowered the ozone standard from 0.12 ppm over a one-hour average to 0.08 ppm over an eight hour average and added a new standard for particulate matter of 2.5 microns or less (in addition to the existing standard of more coarse particulate matter of 10 microns or less). These more stringent standards (in addition to saving thousands of lives) are anticipated to throw many more regions into nonattainment status and necessitate the revision of numerous state implementation plans, not to mention the direct affect upon the regulated community. In reviewing the standards, the D.C. Circuit again admonished the EPA, but this time by invoking the long-dormant "non-delegation" doctrine (a doctrine that prohibits unduly broad grants of authority from Congress to the Executive Branch), a legal rationale that provoked vigorous critique by academics. According to the D.C. Circuit, the EPA (instead of the Congress) violated the nondelegation doctrine by not articulating an intelligible principle upon which the standards were based. Ultimately, the U.S. Supreme Court rejected the view of the D.C. Circuit and upheld the revised standards, although the Supreme Court did remand to the EPA for a better interpretation of the nonattainment implementation provisions at issue for the ozone NAAQS. Whitman v. American Trucking Ass'ns, 121 S.Ct. 903, 149 L.Ed.2nd 1, 531 U.S. 457 (2001).

The saga of the particulate and ozone NAAQS revisions illustrates the scientific, economic and political difficulties in revising the standards despite evidence that existing standards are insufficiently protective. The history of NAAQS revisions also demonstrates the particular difficulties in achieving environmental justice through the standards. NAAQS are supposed to be designed and revised to protect individuals who are particularly sensitive to the pollutants and are also supposed to provide for an adequate margin of safety. Yet, EPA has a strong incentive not to tighten the standards to such a stringent degree because of the ripple effect that such a standard would have on the states, the regulated community and the economy in general. This leaves the EPA in the untenable position of at least pretending not to consider costs but nonetheless attempting to justify a standard that is not too strict or too lax.

## Notes and Questions

1. For each NAAQS, there is typically a range of potential standards that are plausibly protective given the scientific information available at the time the standard is being considered. For example, in *American Trucking*, the D.C. Circuit questioned why the EPA chose an 0.08 ppm level for ozone but not a level of 0.07 or 0.09, presumably standards that would have been sufficiently protective as well. How is the EPA supposed to choose which standard is best without considering costs? Should the distributional aspects of adverse health effects play a role in choosing among several plausible options? It seems that asthma sufferers are a particularly sensitive subpopulation and the EPA likely considered this group in arriving at various NAAQS in the past. Should EPA also consider that asthma is increasingly common among the poor

and non-white? If, for example, the EPA were to find that racial and ethnic minorities are disproportionately affected by its decision to set the ozone standard at 0.08 instead of 0.07 (a more stringent standard), should the agency reconsider its decision? Similarly, if the EPA were to find that the poor suffer disproportionately from $SO_2$ spikes, should it reconsider its decision not to issue a short term $SO_2$ NAAQS, especially because this group is less able to afford medications that can help prevent bronchoconstriction during peak episodes? What are the advantages and disadvantages to letting an environmental justice analysis help guide the agency to a more precise national standard?

# B. The Case of the Clean Water Act Standards

## 1. AN INTRODUCTORY NOTE ON THE ROLE OF STANDARDS UNDER THE CLEAN WATER ACT

The rest of this chapter will look at the environmental justice implications of standards primarily though the lens of the Clean Water Act where, like many of the environmental statutes, there is an interplay between health-based and technology-based standards. In this statute, the standards that have been most vigorously implemented are the technology based standards, generally under the National Pollutant Discharge Elimination System (NPDES) program. In this permitting program, a "point source" must acquire a permit before it discharges effluent that contains certain contaminants into a water body. State or tribal governments may obtain authority from the EPA to carry out the NPDES permit program (about three-quarters of the states have done so), but the EPA retains oversight authority, including the ability to veto state-issued permits. NPDES permits typically require the installation of technology based standards, such as "best available technology" (BAT) for dischargers of toxics, or "best conventional technology" for conventional pollutants such as biological oxygen demanding chemicals, fecal coliform, suspended solids and pH. BAT is promulgated by reference to industrial sectors under the assumption that the processes of all facilities that produce certain products, e.g., computer chips, are similar. Municipally owned waste water treatment facilities are also required to obtain NPDES permits and have their own sets of technology-based requirements. *See generally,* PERCIVAL, *supra*, at 637–42.

It may strike you that if there are too many point sources discharging pollutants into a small water body, the water resource may be severely degraded despite the installation of "BAT." This has in fact been the case in many instances. But the Clean Water Act has provisions designed to prevent this from occurring. The Act envisions a safety net of health-based standards, called water quality standards.

Ideally, a water quality standard should be designed so that, if the water body meets the standard, it should be safe for certain designated uses. The baseline use is determined by the EPA to be "fishable/swimable" waters. This means that for the majority of water bodies, water quality standards should be sufficient to protect persons who swim in and consume fish caught from the water body. If a water body does not meet the applicable water quality standards it may be categorized as "water quality limited" or "hot spot listed" and point source dischargers (typically industrial and publically owned treatment facilities) might have to undertake limitations to their processes above the normally required technology based standards.

Implementation of the safety net of health-based standards involves a difficult procedure. Agencies must determine how much of a pollutant loading the water body can take before it exceeds the applicable water quality standards. Once this is determined, a "total maximum daily load" (TMDL) plan is developed that will essentially ration the amount each contributor can discharge, resulting in the possibility that some point source dischargers will have their NPDES permits limited further with "waste load allocations." However, as noted by Lazarus and Tai in the excerpt above and by Professor Houck in the excerpt below, the section of the Clean Water Act that mandates such action has gone largely unimplemented until recent years, when citizen suits forced the issue. Now, state and local governments are in the process of designing TMDL plans.

Thus far, we have been discussing only point source dischargers, but runoff from streets, agricultural activities, logging and other "non-point" activities are, in fact, now the primary contributors to degraded water quality. These activities have gone largely unregulated. EPA has recently taken the position that TMDL plans should control non-point pollution as well, a controversial position that has been challenged.

From an environmental justice perspective, the present state of implementation of the Clean Water Act raises several important environmental justice issues. First, the promulgation of the default "fishable/swimable" water quality standards requires an estimate of how much fish people typically eat. As the first excerpt illustrates, the empirical assumptions supporting environmental standards can mean the difference between a standard that is uniformly protective and one that is likely to result in significant racial or income disparities. Secondly, since tribes may obtain authority to administer their own environmental programs, this raises jurisdictional conflicts, as well as an ironic twist when an environmental justice community itself becomes the regulator. The case following Professor O'Neill's article illustrates this conflict. (Native American issues are further discussed in Chapter XVI.) The third issue involves timing. Because the conceptual and legal groundwork for the TMDL program is presently being developed, this presents an opportunity for environmental justice protections to be programmatically developed at the front end of regulatory activity, instead of in a typically reactive fashion. The third excerpt explains the legal, scientific, economic and political conflicts surrounding this controversial endeavor, and allows us to pose the question of how environmental justice might fare during the process of program design.

## 2.  WATER QUALITY STANDARDS

# Catherine O'Neill,
# Variable Justice: Environmental Standards, Contaminated Fish, and "Acceptable" Risk to Native Peoples
### 19 Stanford Environmental Law Journal 3 (2000)

*Fish Consumption Rate*

...EPA currently assumes a fish consumption rate of 6.5 grams/day [when setting water quality standards]. This amounts to approximately one fish meal per month. The 6.5 grams/day value is derived from a diet recall study conducted in the mid-

1970s of the general population of the United States, fish consumers and non-consumers alike. Researchers from National Purchase Diary, Inc. used standardized questionnaires to conduct a market survey of 25,165 individuals about their consumption of marine, estuarine and freshwater fish. The resulting data set was interpreted by Javitz, et al. in 1980, who arrived at an arithmetic mean consumption rate of 14.3 grams/day for fish consumers in the general population. The EPA then corrected this number (1) to reinclude members of the general population who did not consume fish at all, and (2) to exclude marine species, arriving ultimately at a value of 6.5 grams/day. This standard assumption is used by EPA when it sets health-based environmental standards....

### Non-quantified Evidence of Fish Consumption

Abundant evidence exists that American Indian subpopulations consume greater quantities of fish than the general population....

Until quite recently, however, studies quantifying fish consumption of Native American subpopulations have been nonexistent. The lack of quantitative, as opposed to "anecdotal" or qualitative, evidence has meant that the higher fish consumption rates of these subpopulations have gone unaccounted for....

Most regulators have been reluctant to adjust standard assumptions about the FCR [Fish Consumption Rate] on the basis of "mere" anecdotal evidence, and courts have not required them to do so. Thus the Ninth Circuit in *Dioxin/Organochlorine Center v. Clarke* noted that the only available evidence of the Native Americans' higher fish consumption rates was anecdotal, which EPA was free to ignore in setting the total maximum daily load ("TMDL") for dioxin in the waters of the Columbia River basin under the Clean Water Act. The court therefore upheld EPA's recourse to its standard 6.5 grams/day fish consumption rate. EPA had acknowledged in its risk analysis document that "about 15,000" Native Americans (along with several hundred thousand Asian Americans and low-income individuals) "are much more likely to catch and consume fish that has been contaminated with dioxin from the effluent discharged from the [pulp and paper] mills than other populations in the area." The EPA had also acknowledged that these subpopulations consume "an average of between 100 and 150 grams of fish flesh each day over the course of the year." Yet the EPA argued to the court that "no definitive study has established the quantity and variety of contaminated fish consumed by these subpopulations."...

### Quantified Evidence of Fish Consumption: Puget Sound and the Columbia River Basin

Various studies of fish consumption rates in Puget Sound and the Columbia River Basin reveal that identifiable subpopulations such as recreational anglers and Native Americans are more highly exposed than the general population. Of particular note, these data indicate marked differences among Native American subpopulations and the general population.... These studies also show that the fish consumption rates for Native American subpopulations in the Pacific Northwest are greater even than for other identifiable higher-consuming subpopulations, such as recreational anglers....

According to a 1994 diet recall study conducted by and of the Nez Perce, Umatilla, Yakama, and Warm Springs tribes fishing along the Columbia River, the 50th percentile or median fish consumption rate for tribal members is between 29 and 32 grams per day; the arithmetic mean is 58.7 grams per day; the 90th percentile is between 97.2 and 130 grams per day; the 95th percentile is 170 grams per day; and the 99th percentile is 389 grams per day. The maximum consumption rate is 972 grams per day.

According to a 1981 creel study conducted by the Tacoma-Pierce County Health Department of recreational anglers in Commencement Bay of the Puget Sound, the 50th percentile or median fish consumption rate for these individuals is 23 grams/day; and the 90th percentile is 54 grams/day....

Of particular note is the difference between the fish consumption rates currently employed in various regulatory contexts and the fish consumption rates for Native Americans evidenced by the Toy et al. and [Columbia River Inter-Tribal Fish Commission] CRITFC studies. Compare the EPA's standard assumption of 6.5 grams per day, a number based on the mean value from the Javitz study, (corrected to exclude marine species, and adjusted to include fish non-consumers) with the arithmetic mean from Toy et al., at between 60.9 and 82.9 grams per day and with the arithmetic mean from CRITFC, at 58.7 grams per day....

Second, fish consumption rates within a subpopulation may also vary considerably. In the non-standard distribution that characterizes the Puget Sound tribal subpopulation, for example, individuals at the median consume between 35.6 and 48.7 grams per day, while individuals at the 95th percentile consume between 205.1 and 280.5 grams per day — roughly five times the median.

### "Lower Yet Adequate" Protection for Higher-Consuming Native American Subpopulations

In [the] *Dioxin/Organochlorine Center* [case], the EPA employed its default assumption for the FCR, 6.5 g/day. Relying on this standard assumption about exposure, EPA derived a water quality standard, the TMDL for dioxin, by solving the risk equation for concentration with cancer risk held at $1(10^{-6})$).* If a particular environmental standard is set, assuming the exposure of the "average American," to result in risk of no more than 1 in 1,000,000, that same standard will result in greater risk to a more highly exposed subpopulation. In *Dioxin/Organochlorine Center*, this greater risk was estimated to be 23 in 1,000,000 or 2.3 in 100,000.

The Ninth Circuit accepted the EPA's choice of an FCR of 6.5 g/day by asserting that the resulting standards would provide "lower yet adequate protection," the court held that even if these subpopulations consume 150 g/day of fish and would therefore be subject to excess risk of $1(10^{-5})$, "this level of risk protection is within levels historically approved by the EPA and upheld by courts." The court endorsed EPA's argument that "the one-in-a-million risk level mandated by the state water quality standards for the general population does not necessarily reflect state legislative intent to provide the highest level of protection for all subpopulations but could reasonably be construed to allow for lower yet adequate protection for specific subpopulations."

[M]ost egregious, the court accepted the EPA's argument that, so long as a subpopulation's risk level falls within the range generated by Ohio v. EPA,[where the court in a challenge to Superfund regulations upheld a risk range of 1 x $10^{-4}$ to 1 x $10^{-6}$] it is "adequate" and there is no harm even from the systematic provision of "lower yet adequate" protection to "specific subpopulations," even where the specific subpopulation harmed is Native American. The court was apparently untroubled by the discriminatory effect of its holding.

---

* [For carcinogens, risk is typically expressed as the increased probability that an individual will contract cancer; thus, at this risk level, there is expected to be one additional case of cancer per one million exposed individuals].

*EPA's Draft Water Quality Criteria Methodology Revisions*

[In 1998, EPA] issued Draft Revisions to the Methodology for Deriving Ambient Water Quality Criteria for the Protection of Human Health ("Draft AWQC Revisions") [the source of its 6.5 grams/day fish consumption rate. EPA is required periodically to revise its water quality criteria to ensure they are "accurately reflecting the latest scientific knowledge...on the kind and extent of all identifiable effects on health and welfare... which may be expected from the presence of pollutants in any body of water...."]

EPA proposes a new default fish consumption rate of 17.80 grams/day. This value is the 90th percentile value for consumption of freshwater and estuarine fish by the general population (fish consumers and fish nonconsumers)....EPA also proposes a new default fish consumption rate of 86.30 grams/day for "subsistence fishers/minority anglers." This value is the 99th percentile value for consumption of freshwater and estuarine fish by the general population (fish consumers and fish nonconsumers), also derived from the USDA's [Continuing Survey of Food Intake by Individuals (CSFII)] for the years 1989, 1990, and 1991....Significantly, EPA proposes to treat together what it terms "subsistence fishers/minority anglers." Although EPA nowhere makes clear precisely who it views to be included in this grouping or to which studies it refers for the "range of averages," it would appear that EPA's category includes various Native Americans, Asian-Americans, low-income individuals, and other individuals who simply eat a lot of fish....

In addition to the proposed changes to the default fish consumption rate, EPA proposes a new approach to acceptable risk levels....EPA recommends a range for risk level from $1(10^{-5})$ to $1(10^{-6})$ for the general population. While EPA adds that states and tribes are free to choose a more protective level, such as $1(10^{-7})$, it urges, "care should be taken however, in situations where the AWQC includes fish intake levels based on the general population to ensure that the risk to more highly exposed subgroups (sportfishers or subsistence fishers) does not exceed the $1(10^{-4})$ level. Thus, EPA's Draft AWQC Revisions introduces two tiers of permissible risk levels. While risk levels as protective as $1(10^{-6})$ (and even $1(10^{-7})$) are to be secured to members of the general population, risk levels as great as $1(10^{-4})$ are permissible for members of more highly exposed subpopulations, including subsistence fishers....

*Variability, Identifiability, and the Case for Differential Treatment of Highly Exposed Native American Subpopulations*

Large variability in fish consumption rates, and the location of identifiable subpopulations at the high end of the exposure distribution, raise implications for current agency risk assessment practice. As discussed above, the available fish consumption data (both anecdotal and quantified) paint a clear picture: variability is large and the distribution is skewed....

In the regulatory context, risk is generally expressed and considered in terms of incremental increases in the chance of some occurrence (e.g., developing cancer) in an individual's lifetime. The individual here is meant to be generic. A risk assessor's conclusion that a particular cleanup level for surface water will result in a lifetime increased cancer risk of $1[x](10^{-6})$ for those who eat fish from that water is meant to refer with equal likelihood to every individual who is an intended beneficiary of the cleanup action. How descriptive this estimate is of any one individual's risk, however, depends on how closely that individual's particular circumstances of susceptibility and exposure track the assumptions used by the risk assessor to arrive at her estimate of risk.

Some commentators have argued that if variability exists, but the identity of the individuals who will occupy a particular region of the distribution is not and cannot be known, agencies might legitimately ignore the variability. For example, some members of the National Research Council of the National Academy of Sciences have suggested that variability can be viewed as irrelevant "if the variation is and will remain unidentifiable."...

However, the necessary condition for this situation, that the variability is and will remain unidentifiable, is unlikely to exist in the context of exposure in health and environmental risk assessment....And, of course, Native Americans and other groups have identified themselves among the highly exposed and have begun to gather and quantify their observations.

The mere fact that highly exposed subgroups exist in a context where the stakes are high necessitates differential treatment by health and environmental agencies....The more significant the differences in the circumstances of exposure or susceptibility between the subpopulation and the general population, the more suspect an agency decision that fails to disaggregate these groups for differential treatment....

Differential treatment for Native American groups is necessary to protect their cultural integrity. Emerging norms in the United States and elsewhere value a diversity of cultures and support the protection of cultural integrity....Members of any cultural group — even a majority or dominant cultural group — have an equal claim to respect for cultural integrity. But because the integrity of cultural groups in the numerical minority, or otherwise in a nondominant position, are more likely to be vulnerable to breach than cultural groups in a majority or dominant position, a focus on the protection of minority cultural groups is justified....

* * *

## Notes and Questions

1. What is your view of the merits of the "lower but adequate protection" rationale relied on by the Ninth Circuit?

2. At what point (if any) should agencies be permitted to set standards that are protective of the majority of the population but not similarly protective of "outliers" — members of the population whose susceptibilities and circumstances of exposure place them at the extreme in a population distribution? What if it could be shown that it would be enormously costly to protect these highly susceptible or highly exposed individuals, and that they comprise only a small fraction of the population? How is your response affected if these individuals were revealed to be members of various groups (e.g., various indigenous peoples, various Asian American communities, African American communities), each of which might have quite different group-based environmental justice claims? Once the identity of the populations at greater risk is clearly known, is it unethical to ignore the heightened risks they face? What difficulties in accommodating the varied and complex histories of different groups might you imagine from the perspective of an environmental agency engaged in standard setting?

3. Given the substantial legal authorities to address environmental justice concerns when promulgating standards, including water quality standards, why would states and the EPA be hesitant to use this legal authority? The following case illustrates the political and legal difficulties involved when a Native American tribe took up the challenge to promulgate strict water quality standards.

# City of Albuquerque v. Browner

97 F. 3d 415 (10th Cir. 1996)

[In 1987, Congress amended the Clean Water Act to allow Indian tribes to receive authority from EPA to administer the Clean Water Act in lieu of EPA, authority comparable to that possessed by states. (This authority is contained in 33 U.S.C. § 1377.) Once a tribe has achieved such "treatment as state" status, it has authority to set water quality standards for waters within its reservations or that are held by the tribe or in trust for the tribe.]

*McKay, Circuit Judge:*

This case involves the first challenge to water quality standards adopted by an Indian tribe under the Clean Water Act amendment.

The Rio Grande River flows south through New Mexico before turning southeast to form the border between Texas and Mexico. Plaintiff City of Albuquerque operates a waste treatment facility which dumps into the river approximately five miles north of the Isleta Pueblo Indian Reservation. The EPA recognized Isleta Pueblo as a state for purposes of the Clean Water Act on October 12, 1992. The Isleta Pueblo adopted water quality standards for Rio Grande water flowing through the tribal reservation, which were approved by the EPA on December 24, 1992. The Isleta Pueblo's water quality standards are more stringent than the State of New Mexico's standards.

The Albuquerque waste treatment facility discharges into the Rio Grande under a National Pollution Discharge Elimination System [NPDES] permit issued by the EPA. The EPA sets permit discharge limits for waste treatment facilities so they meet state water quality standards. Albuquerque filed this action as the EPA was in the process of revising Albuquerque's NPDES permit to meet the Isleta Pueblo's water quality standards....

Albuquerque argues that § 1377 does not expressly permit Indian tribes to enforce effluent limitations or standards under § 1311 to upstream point source dischargers outside of tribal boundaries.... Under the statutory and regulatory scheme, tribes are not applying or enforcing their water quality standards beyond reservation boundaries. Instead, it is the EPA which is exercising its own authority in issuing NPDES permits in compliance with downstream state and tribal water quality standards. In regard to this question, therefore, the 1987 amendment to the Clean Water Act clearly and unambiguously provides tribes the authority to establish NPDES programs in conjunction with the EPA. Under §§ 1311, 1341, 1342 and 1377, the EPA has the authority to require upstream NPDES dischargers, such as Albuquerque, to comply with downstream tribal standards.

Albuquerque next claims that the EPA failed to comply with the procedural requirements of the Administrative Procedure Act [APA] in approving the Isleta Pueblo's water quality standards.... The intent of Congress expressed in the Clean Water Act, however, was to require states or tribes to provide for public participation in the adoption of water quality standards. Section 1313(c)(1) provides: The Governor of a State or the State water pollution control agency of such State shall from time to time (but at least once each three year period...) hold public hearings for the purpose of reviewing applicable water quality standards and, as appropriate, modifying and adopting standards. Results of such review shall be made available to the Administrator. Under the water quality standards provisions of the Clean Water Act, it is the states and tribes which conduct rulemaking proceedings. This is in accord with Congress's intent to preserve a primary role for the states and tribes in eliminating water pollution. The results of state and tribal rulemaking proceedings are then presented to the EPA for approval. The Fourth Circuit has explained the EPA's limited role in reviewing water quality standards proposed by states, stating:

> EPA sits in a reviewing capacity of the state-implemented standards, with approval and rejection powers only....
>
> [S]tates have the primary role, under § 303 of the CWA (33 U.S.C. § 1313), in establishing water quality standards. EPA's sole function, in this respect, is to review those standards for approval....

Albuquerque also claims that the EPA's approval of the Isleta Pueblo standards was unsupported by a rational basis on the record and was therefore arbitrary and capricious. Albuquerque argues that the EPA was required to reject the Isleta Pueblo's water quality standards unless the EPA had established its own record based on a sound scientific rationale for each particular provision.

The EPA, however, reviews proposed water quality standards only to determine whether they are stringent enough to comply with the EPA's recommended standards and criteria. If the proposed standards are more stringent than necessary to comply with the Clean Water Act's requirements, the EPA may approve the standards without reviewing the scientific support for the standards. Whether the more stringent standard is attainable is a matter for the EPA to consider in its discretion; sections 1341 and 1342 of the Clean Water Act permit the EPA and states to force technological advancement to attain higher water quality. The EPA's letter approving the Isleta Pueblo standards explains that it is approving the standards, despite their departure from the EPA's guidelines, based on the Tribe's authority to adopt standards more stringent than the minimum requirements of the Clean Water Act.

The EPA considered Isleta Pueblo's rationale for each of the standards challenged by Albuquerque, and the tribe's record contains detailed responses to all of the criticisms expressed by the EPA and Albuquerque. The record contains a detailed explanation of the Isleta Pueblo's scientific, technical, and policy reasons for choosing to establish more stringent standards. For example, the Isleta Pueblo stated that stringent standards are justified because of prevailing drought conditions and the need to protect sensitive subpopulations. The EPA concluded that the standards were consistent with the Clean Water Act's requirements and should therefore be approved. The arbitrary and capricious review standard is very deferential; "an agency ruling is 'arbitrary and capricious if the agency has...entirely failed to consider an important aspect of the problem.'" Albuquerque has not shown that the EPA failed to consider an important aspect of the Isleta Pueblo's water quality standards....

In its next claim, Albuquerque argues that the Isleta Pueblo criteria approved by the EPA are not stringent enough to protect the Tribe's designated use standard described as primary contact ceremonial use. The Tribe describes primary contact ceremonial use as involving the "immersion and intentional or incidental ingestion of water." Albuquerque argues that this requires the river water quality to meet the standards of the Safe Drinking Water Act, 42 U.S.C. § 300f, and the Isleta Pueblo's water quality criteria approved by the EPA fail to protect water used under the ceremonial use standard.

As the district court stated:

This argument seems far-fetched. The primary contact ceremonial use appears to resemble a fishable/swimmable standard, which assumes the ingestion of some water, more than it resembles a safe drinking water standard, which assumes the ingestion of a volume of water daily.

Albuquerque, 865 F.Supp. at 740. The federal drinking water standards apply only to a "public water system," which is defined as a system supplying piped water for human consumption serving at least twenty-five persons or having at least fifteen service connections. 42 U.S.C. § 300f(4). The Isleta Pueblo's ceremonial use standard does not convert the Rio Grande River into a public water system. The EPA considered and approved this aspect of the Isleta Pueblo water quality standards. We decline to second-guess the EPA's technical determination, which is entitled to substantial deference, that the Isleta Pueblo's water quality criteria adequately protect its ceremonial designated use standard....

Albuquerque next claims that the EPA's approval of the Pueblo's ceremonial use designation offends the Establishment Clause of the First Amendment. The First Amendment provides in relevant part: "Congress shall make no law respecting an establishment of religion...." U.S. Const. amend. I. Government action does not violate the Establishment Clause if "[t]he challenged governmental action has a secular purpose, does not have the principal or primary effect of advancing or inhibiting religion, and does not foster an excessive entanglement with religion."

The EPA approved Isleta Pueblo's promulgation of "Primary Contact Ceremonial Use" as a designated use of the Rio Grande River within the boundaries of the Indian reservation. The tribe defines "Primary Contact Ceremonial Use" as "the use of a stream, reach, lake, or impoundment for religious or traditional purposes by members of the PUEBLO OF ISLETA; such use involves immersion and intentional or incidental ingestion of water." Albuquerque argues that the EPA's approval of this standard violates all three aspects of the Establishment Clause under Lemon [v. Kurtzman, 403 U.S. 602 (1971)].

First, Albuquerque argues that the reason for the designated use is explicitly sectarian. The secular purpose requirement does not mean that a law's purpose must be unrelated to religion because that would require " 'that the government show a callous indifference to religious groups,'...and the Establishment Clause has never been so interpreted." The EPA's approval of the primary contact ceremonial use designation serves a clear secular purpose: promotion of the goals of the Clean Water Act. The EPA's purpose in approving the designated use is unrelated to the Isleta Pueblo's religious reason for establishing it. The Isleta Pueblo's designation of a ceremonial use does not invalidate the EPA's overall secular goal.

Second, Albuquerque claims that the EPA's action has a primary effect of advancing religion. We disagree. The EPA is not advancing religion through its own actions, and it is not promoting the Isleta Pueblo's religion. The primary effect of the EPA's action is to advance the goals of the Clean Water Act.

Third, Albuquerque asserts the designated use results in excessive governmental entanglement with religion because the Pueblo and the EPA must inquire on an ongoing basis whether the standards adequately protect religious uses of the river water. This argument is meritless. "There is no genuine nexus between" the EPA's approval of the ceremonial use standard "and establishment of religion,"...and the EPA's approval of the standard provides only an incidental benefit to religion. The EPA's approval of the ceremonial use standard does not require any governmental involvement in the Isleta

Pueblo's religious practices. Excessive governmental entanglement will not result when the EPA incorporates the Isleta Pueblo's water quality standards in issuing future NPDES permits....

* * *

## Notes and Questions

1. As this case illustrates, the designated use of the water body had a direct bearing upon the applicable water quality standard, which in turn had a direct effect upon the permit of an upstream discharger (in this case, the City of Albuquerque's waste treatment facility). The waste treatment facility is an activity undertaken for the environmental benefit of the public at large. Should it matter that a discharger is itself engaging in environmentally beneficial activities?

2. Professor Denise Fort published an article on the dispute shortly before the above opinion was issued. In the article, she discusses a variety of important factual questions that this controversy raised:

> ...[I]n any dispute over water quality standards, the underlying factual questions are likely to be persuasive in how one views the merits of the dispute. For example, are tribal standards unreasonably strict, or are the state's unreasonably lax? How expensive will it be for upstream dischargers to comply with the standards? Should a tribe be allowed to continue its historic use of a river for ceremonial purposes, involving drinking from the river, when alternative water supplies are available, and if the answer is affirmative, should upstream taxpayers bear the cost of making a river safe for those practices? Should upstream polluters be allowed to endanger those who depend on a river, and, is it relevant that those uses predate the upstream discharge? One's views of the legal merits may vary with the answers to these questions. It is noteworthy that a state's standards provide the lens through which these questions are viewed; if tribes were to adopt standards identical to those of the surrounding states, dischargers would have no grounds to object. The Pueblo of Isleta's standards were at issue in the Browner case, not the standards set by the State of New Mexico.

Denise D. Fort, *State and Tribal Water Quality Standards Under the Clean Water Act: A Case Study*, 35 NAT. RESOURCES J. 771, 775–76 (1995). As with the issues concerning water quality standards and fish consumption discussed above, the legal issues in this dispute were framed with reference to the dominant population. Does framing environmental justice issues as deviations from an existing norm affect the analysis? If so, why did the tribe prevail in this case? In what ways is the case helpful to resolving environmental justice disputes outside the context of tribal sovereignty? For a detailed discussion of tribal implementation of the water quality standards programs under the CWA, see Dean Suagee & James H. Havard, *Tribal Governments and the Protection of Watersheds and Wetlands in Indian Country*, 13 ST. THOMAS L. REV. 35 (2000); see also, *Wisconsin v. E.P.A.*, 266 F.3d 741, 748 (7th Cir. 2001) (upholding, over challenge by Wisconsin, EPA's decision to grant Sokaogon Chippewa Community "treatment as state" status for purpose of adopting water quality standards, and noting that once a tribe is given such status, "it has the power to require upstream off-reservation dischargers...to make sure that their activities do not result in contamination of the downstream on-reservation waters.")

* * *

## 3. New Program Possibilities

# Oliver A. Houck,
# TMDLS IV: The Final Frontier

29 Environmental Law Reporter 10,469 (1999)

At the mouth of the Mississippi River and spreading west to Texas, the Gulf currently experiences a "dead zone" of hypoxic water, water with less than 2 percent concentration of oxygen, extending up to 16,000–18,000 square kilometers. Sea life is eliminated. Bottom-dwellers die, menhaden and shrimp move out, and with them go the rest of the food chain up to and including humans. The dieoff is from nutrients, loaded into the Mississippi River from distances and with consequences unimaginable at an earlier time and denied by some yet today. Nearly 90 percent of these nutrients originate from farms: fertilizer runoff and animal wastes. Nearly three-quarters originate from lands above the confluence of the Ohio and Mississippi Rivers, more than 975 river miles away.

This is not an isolated story. Every state and every major watershed in America is experiencing similar problems from similar sources. The waters of northern Wisconsin are polluted by dairy farms, in North Carolina by hogs, in Maryland by chickens, in south Florida by sugar, in Wyoming by beef cattle, in Oregon by clearcuts, in Maine by logging roads, in California by irrigation return flows, and across suburban America by an expanding and irreversible crop of tract housing and subdivisions, all of which have several characteristics in common. Individually small, it is their cumulative impacts that are the problem, and we have not yet found the way to convince people to fix problems for which they are only a contributing factor. Furthermore, although individually small, these sources are supported by industries with a political lock on state legislatures and, in some cases, on the U.S. Congress as well. Most importantly, they are by nature diffuse, not outfalls from pipes, and therefore long considered to be beyond those regulatory requirements of the Clean Water Act that have led to its success.

Which would end the story, but for the remarkable resurrection of a long-dormant provision of the Clean Water Act, §303(d), now taking the field and forcing a showdown on the last water quality frontier, nonpoint source pollution....

The task ahead for §303(d) is to address nonpoint source pollution, and it is doubly daunting because the approach of §303(d)—ambient-based regulation—has never really worked in pollution control, and because no approach under other sections of the Clean Water Act has been remotely effective in reversing the nonpoint tide....

*Reviewing the Bidding*

...As of this writing, EPA was on the verge of proposing new regulations for the implementation of §303(d). These regulations promise to be as contentious as any in environmental law and, with others also in the works, will raise many of the unresolved issues that have surrounded water pollution control since 1948. Two issues stand head and shoulders above the crowd, however. The first is whether §303(d) covers nonpoint source pollution at all, and agribusiness interests (supported by the U.S. Forest Service) have already filed litigation asserting the contrary. The second is whether a TMDL is simply an arithmetic calculation that states are then free to incorporate in subsequent "planning," or whether the TMDL is itself both a calculation and a plan. The outcome of these issues will be huge, indeed dispositive, on the effect of §303(d) and its contri-

bution to the Clean Water Act. If nonpoint sources are held to be beyond the mandatory provisions of this section, they will be relegated to the essentially ineffectual planning exercises that have characterized the last 25 years in nonpoint source control. And
if TMDLs, even if they include nonpoint sources, are deferred to the never-never land
of state water quality management planning, they will disappear down the same sink-
hole with hardly a trace behind....

All of which brings us to the major issue of today. If the Clean Water Act is going to
move forward on its last great frontier, nonpoint source pollution, through the vehicle
of TMDLs, is there any reason to think that an ambient water quality-based approach
will work any better this time than it has in the past? This approach failed in the 1950s
and 1960s for basically the same reasons that it went dormant in the 1970s and 1980s
and is proving so difficult to effectuate today. We are short on science. And we are very
short on political will.

### TMDLs and the Limits of Science

—Inside EPA Weekly Report:

> ...The requirements of science also make ambient-based systems far more
> resource intensive than their proponents are willing to acknowledge. Working
> systems require constant and large infusions of money for training, monitor-
> ing, modeling, site assessments, surveillance, and enforcement. Precisely be-
> cause "one size does not fit all"—as states and industry are quick to claim—
> every size, every water body, is a separate control system and one that is always,
> further, subject to change. Whatever data it produces, moreover, science is
> never satisfied. Scientists are not trained to be satisfied, or to project their
> opinions, or to predict; they are trained to question even the most obvious
> conclusion until all reasonable hypotheses have been disproved. And if the sci-
> entists are not satisfied—if they are not conclusive in their data and results—
> the regulated community will never be satisfied and will have a ready reason to
> resist abatement costs. Ambient-based regulation is truly a system that never
> rests, and that never stops asking for money....

—[In 1987,] an Office of Technology Assessment study concluded:

> Only limited data are available on ambient pollutant concentrations in re-
> ceiving waters, variability in these concentrations, and the fate of these pollu-
> tants and their impacts on indigenous organisms. In addition, our ability to
> monitor water quality in relation to potential environmental or human im-
> pacts is relatively primitive.

Despite occasional EPA assertions, and repeated state assertions, to the contrary,
these conditions have not much changed....[For example a 1998 Federal Advisory
Committee Act (FACA)] committee on TMDLs noted that, even at this late date, only
19 percent of the nation's waters were monitored for pollution, and that the states were
in need of every manner of technical assistance from monitoring to assessment to enforcement in order to meet the demands of §303(d)....

The states and TMDL-implicated communities, meanwhile, are alert to these weak-
nesses in monitoring and assessment and have already signaled their willingness to ex-
ploit them. The first counterattack has come on the required biennial submissions of
polluted waters under §303(d). Opposing listings as based on inadequate science
("drive-by listings," in the words of one agriculture industry attorney—a characterization that in some cases may not be far from the truth), farm and other nonpoint inter-

ests have persuaded states to reduce their submissions on impaired waters to the absolutely proven, with significant results. Incongruous as it may seem in the face of new EPA listing criteria designed to be all-inclusive, to err on the side of listing, and to facilitate the use of "all relevant data," many states have actually cut their §303(d) lists in half since 1996, relegating hundreds of waters to such categories as "further study," "insufficient information," and only "moderately impaired." The state of Wyoming, for example, reduced its list of over 400 waters to 61 identified as polluted and 315 as needing "further monitoring." Perhaps coincidentally—but only perhaps—275 of the 315 waters deferred for "further monitoring" were contaminated by nonpoint sources, primarily cattle grazing....

This said, identifying polluted waters is, from the point of view of the science involved, the easy step. The next is to identify the causes of impairment and to allocate their loads. Here is where lines get drawn deep in the sand....

EPA now finds itself with its TMDL program in the position of a home renovator who, having furbished an elegant new structure, needs to deal with the foundation. The situation is even more dicey because states and their industry supporters have been complaining for years that the existing [Water Quality Standards] WQS regulations are, conversely, too rigid and inflexible, insensitive to cost-benefit analysis and insufficiently responsive to local conditions. While this perspective and rhetoric have been around since at least the [Water Quality Act of 1965] WQA, they led a strong and nearly successful attack on the federal program in 1982 during the Reagan Administration, another in 1996 with the Contract With America Congress, and are now ready to use this opportunity to try again. On July 7, 1998, EPA opened up the whole ball of wax with an advance notice of proposed rulemaking, inviting comment on every aspect of its water quality program, including use designations, attainability, downgrading, aquatic criteria, antidegradation, mixing zones, and application factors. This rulemaking will be a donnybrook among environmental interests, states, and the discharge industries, reminiscent of the legislative arguments that have marked the CWA over the years, and no more likely to put them to rest....

We have now slid back into the maw of a program that Congress all but rejected in 1972 for, among other things, its uncertain science and elaborate indirection. The program was retained because states and industry lobbied to retain it with claims that they had this technology on hand and could do this drill, claims that they have repeated to Congress nearly every year since. In the light of the obvious shortcomings of this technology and the equally obvious shortage of resources devoted to it, these claims must seem odd, until one realizes that they are not made in the abstract but as arguments to reassert state primacy over water pollution control. Pollution control is turf control, and this is where the success of the TMDL program is most in doubt. With enough commitment of resources—and it will take another order of magnitude beyond anything yet committed under the Act—adequate science to deal with the aquatic impacts of nonpoint sources is within the realm of the possible. Adequate political will is a different story.

### TMDLs and the Limits of Will

...Perhaps some states were defeated by the science and monitoring required, but all states? Certainly every state had adequate data on at least a few of its waterways and, as certainly every state was aware, many of these waterways were highly degraded. Indeed, for years they had been reporting these waters as degraded under the non-action-forcing provisions of §305(b).

Perhaps TMDLs were deflected by the absence of state laws supporting those measures that TMDLs would impose, particularly on forestry and agriculture. Legislation in some states does in fact place these sources on a pedestal beyond the reach of environmental controls—in itself a statement about state commitment to clean water. But as a recent Environmental Law Institute study documents, many other states do not, and all states retain the residual authority in their water quality programs to move on some nonpoint sources, and in some states, on all sources.

Perhaps the states were daunted by the apparent lack of ready abatement measures to incorporate into TMDL measures which could have appeared too ill defined, inchoate, or expensive. But the truth of TMDLs is that the remedial measures are usually obvious. And low-tech. And cheap. Imagine what it might take to reduce fertilizer runoff from a corn field, and streamside setbacks come to mind. For other crops and animal husbandry we have such options as winter cover, retention ponds, shelterbelts, and caps on fertilizers in amounts that the soil will retain and the crops will use. Many farms practice these measures as a matter of sound economics and conservation....

And so, we run out of excuses. TMDLs did not vaporize from the restrictions of science or technology or state law. They vaporized on the will to do a very hard thing, to make demands on large, local industries without the backing of explicit federal standards and permits and the threat of federal enforcement. No state employee in his or her right mind would volunteer to take on the Florida sugar industry. Even the subsidy-eliminating national farm bill of 1996 tried that and failed. No Idaho water quality official rises in the morning eagerly anticipating a confrontation with Boise Cascade over logging roads. The cattle industry is no easier a customer in, say, Catron County, New Mexico, where "custom and culture" ordinances have attempted to outlaw all federal environmental requirements, or in Nevada where federal land management offices are occasionally bombed. We are all human, and the path of least resistance toward nonpoint sources for the life of the Clean Water Act has been the happy land of planning, for which there was a steady (if thin) stream of federal funding and nothing was enforceable: a states-rights dream.

Until the TMDL litigation shattered the dream. The state and industry reactions that followed have shown the classic symptoms of psychological trauma from shock to denial, anger, and grief. It is too soon to know whether we will get to Stage Five, reconciliation, and the point where states will take hold of this exercise, make it their own, and implement it with effective, enforceable plans. The early returns are at best mixed.

On the bright side, the state of Missouri is reported to have put $1.8 million into its state budget to fund additional water pollution control staff. New York claims to have put $14.2 million over the past five years toward nonpoint source management. Additional TMDL funding has been reported in Virginia and—to illustrate just how far this issue travels—even Louisiana. Oregon has authorized its Department of Agriculture to implement and enforce TMDLs on private agricultural lands. Tennessee is said to be restricting, and even denying, new permits for impaired waters, pending the development of TMDLs.... North Carolina took on its hog farmers, imposed a moratorium and subsequently pollution control requirements, and survived. It can be done.

These bright spots noted, they are not the norm. Some states remain in denial. Faced with the enormity of the Midwest's contribution to the Gulf of Mexico's dead zone, the President of the Iowa Corn Growers Association, still in Stage Two, contended, "It doesn't jive. Two and two isn't making four.... Agriculture is being hung with the blame and we don't think it can be substantiated." West Virginia has reportedly allocated no monies toward TMDLs and defaulted the process to EPA. Nebraska has stated that it has sufficient resources to complete no more than one TMDL per year. Kansas has reportedly backed off monitoring for suspended solids and diluted its water quality criteria for chlorides, in anticipation of having otherwise to develop TMDLs....Beyond the rhetoric, state §303(d) lists of impaired waters submitted last year reflected a marked tendency to minimize water quality problems and deflect data to the contrary, limiting the scope of work to come. The TMDLs themselves are no better. A study completed last year of 55 TMDLs approved by EPA showed little quantification of pollution loadings, less identification of nonpoint sources, and a near-total avoidance of implementation measures.

The news is not a great deal more encouraging on the political front, where in August 1998 the National Governors' Association proposed a substitute for TMDLs based on state programs that EPA would be compelled to approve unless the Agency found "no reasonable likelihood" of the attainment of water quality standards within the next 15 years....

In February 1999, the governors took their case to Congress, where they met a warm reception as warriors "on the front line of the clean water battlefield."...

As we come into the endgame of EPA's new regulatory framework for TMDLs and its many efforts to jawbone, woo, cajole, and near-bribe the states and user groups toward getting with the program, it will all come down to the will of a majority of states to do hard things that they have never been willing to do before, that will alienate powerful constituencies, and that will require in some cases changing state laws through legislatures long captured by forest, farm, and construction industries and in no mood to change. Against these odds, TMDLs are not fertile soil for those prophets of a "New Environmentalism" that go "Beyond Regulation" to a happy world of stakeholder consensus and cooperation. Ambient-based water quality management has tested this utopia many times before, indeed continuously through one program or another since the 1960s, without measurable cooperation, consensus, or result. The reason TMDLs have emerged as the force they are, bringing poultry and other industries to offers of "voluntary" abatement, jolting the national governors, convening the western governors forums, stimulating honest, on-the-ground review of what condition our waters are actually in, and extracting new revenue measures for nonpoint source abatement from states with no appetite for expenditures and with little more for environmental protection, is that TMDLs are different from voluntary, consensus-based exercises. They require more.

### Concluding Thoughts

...Which leaves us with the ultimate question: Are TMDLs worth it? The jury has gone out on this question, once again. For all the reasons described in this Article and others, ambient-based controls have met with little success in environmental law. All the money and effort spent in calibrating loads and "proving" impacts could be better spent developing explicit technology-based best management practices, sweetening them through financial incentives, and enforcing them through the same permit mechanisms that have proven so successful in the CWA and other laws. Their consumption of resources aside, TMDLs also contain the threat of eroding the significant gains made in CWA point source controls by trading the certainty of point source permit emission limits for the amorphous and unenforceable content of state water quality and nonpoint source plans. This risk is real, and rising.

All of this said, TMDLs retain the upside potential for significant nonpoint source pollution control because they sound logical, they remain flexible, they defer largely to state prerogatives, and, most importantly, they, too, are enforceable. The logic is political. As imperfect as their assessments may be—and all environmental assessments are imperfect—TMDLs provide both a bottom line and their own reason to get there, a reason that everybody can understand. The costs and difficulties of ambient standards are the price of political buy-in for parties that neither Congress nor state legislatures are otherwise willing to touch. They are a means for previously unregulated sources to have their say, and for leveraging them to get beyond it. We are not "treating for treatment sake," as advocates of ambient approaches are quick to say; we are treating for something tangible that we all drink, fish, swim in, and simply look at with the pleasure of knowing that it is alive and well.

TMDLs, further, carry their own flexibility, with full potential for pollution trading and more cost-effective abatement, once all parties are firmly and inescapably (if unhappily) at the table. Positive effects from this leverage are beginning to surface in several states, with financial assistance from municipalities—which would otherwise incur significant treatment costs—for less expensive and more proactive land use controls upstream.

Moreover, the states are indispensable players in an effort of this magnitude and TMDLs respect state primacy for ambient-based water pollution control....

In the end, however, TMDLs are worth the effort because they, and they alone, have brought the same driving force into nonpoint source pollution that drove the CWA point source program toward meeting its own deadlines, promulgating its standards, issuing its permits, enforcing their provisions and reducing pollution discharges: people who care about clean water. There are a great many of them, as Congress in this decade learned. There is a watchdog group in nearly every major watershed in the country, and there are many more formed around small streams and tributaries like the Hoosik River of New York and the Tangipahoa River of Louisiana that are not well known to the nation but that are cared for and defended as conscientiously as the borders of the United States. It was these people whose lawsuits brought the TMDL program out of its 20-year slumber, and these same people are collecting samples on their waterways, reviewing the state data, and commenting on inventories. They are ready and poised to do the same for TMDLs.

These people will not be convenient for states, industry, or EPA. Some states, perhaps many states, will twist in several directions to minimize their TMDL responsibilities, reduce their listed waters, propose as few tangible solutions as possible, and defer implementation to the far horizon. Few TMDLs to date do otherwise. No EPA in the most willing of Administrations can bird-dog them all, and a willing Administration is never a given; it has never even been a fact. At the baseline, every day, it is the Hudson Riverkeeper and SAILORS Inc. and volunteer groups like them that, in the best tradition of participatory democracy, advance the goals of law through the use of law, and no better illustration of the need for these groups exists than in the history of TMDLs.

For these reasons, TMDLs hold the best prospect of those now available for coming to grips with the last major, unregulated sources of water pollution in this country. They are not perfect mechanisms. They will require money, significantly more than we have committed to date, but if America can't afford these resources while it is running its largest budget surplus of the century—as are many states, as well—then it is hard to imagine when America can. They will require acknowledgment from nonpoint industries that they are the problem, cooperation from the states, staying power from the Administration, patience from Congress, and reinforcement by the courts, but if ever there were a program that fit the year 2000 rhetoric of "stakeholder decisionmaking," this is the one. And if ever there were a stakeholder program likely to produce more results than bologna, it is §303(d). Because it has numerical targets and prescribed steps to achieve them, and because it empowers people with the energy and the ability in law to see that they take place.

* * *

## Notes and Questions

1. Professor Houck appears to have little faith that voluntary collaborative processes will result in the types of changes in land practices needed to control nonpoint runoff. How does this skepticism square with his vision of a TMDL program driven by participatory democracy? How does the role of the public differ under each scheme?

2. Does a TMDL/water quality based strategy better address disproportionate environmental risks than a technology-based approach, which has been the centerpiece of regulation under the Clean Water Act? What role do you see for environmental justice advocates in formulation of a TMDL plan? What are the potential pitfalls to advocacy in this context?

3. Professor Houck notes that TMDL plans have inherent flexibility, including the potential for using market regimes to control nonpoint runoff. Issues surrounding trading pollution credits in the point source context are discussed in Chapter VII.

# Chapter VII

# Program Design and Regulatory Innovation

## A. Introduction

Just as inequities can result from regulatory functions such as standard setting, permitting, enforcement, and cleanup, the way that programs are designed can also generate inequities. This potential is increasingly evident in the newer, innovative regulatory programs that EPA and state regulatory agencies have undertaken in recent years in their attempt to replace more traditional forms of environmental regulation. Under the traditional regulatory approach (often referred to as "command and control" regulation), the government establishes uniform pollution limits and controls that all regulated entities must comply with. Regulated industries have long expressed frustration with such regulation, claiming that these requirements cost too much and forestall more efficient approaches to controlling pollution. In the late 1990s, these critiques jelled into a campaign to "reinvent" environmental regulation, also known as the effort to formulate "second generation" environmental policy. These approaches—which substitute self-regulation, increased use of performance-based standards and market-based trading systems for requirements that plants install pollution control technology or cut down their air emissions or water discharges—have gained considerable momentum. While they have the potential to exacerbate environmental conditions in poor or minority neighborhoods, members of those communities have rarely participated in the processes that establish such programs.

This chapter first examines some of the broader implications of reinvention as it has been practiced to date, such as how they fit into a practice that Professor Daniel Farber generically terms "slippage." Next, this chapter examines how the goal of many regulatory innovations is to give regulated companies more flexibility in their operations, but such flexibility may prove problematic to host communities. Some of the most popular and widespread reinvention approaches include the use of "caps" or "bubbles" that allow regulated sources to exchange emission "credits" or "allowances" within a facility. More complex approaches allow facilities to trade pollution credits to other regulated sources within a given geographic region,. This chapter concludes with an examination of these and other economic incentive programs.

The excerpt below describes in general fashion the development of "second generation" regulatory tools.

# Dennis D. Hirsch,
# Second Generation Policy and the New Economy

29 Capital University Law Review 1 (2001)

*The Call for a Second Generation of Environmental Policy*

…During the past quarter century, this "first generation" of environmental regulation has brought us significant environmental protection….

This period has also seen the rise of an intellectual critique of "command-and-control" regulation, as some call the first generation policy because of its mandating of pollution control requirements….Professor [Richard] Stewart has pointed out that nationally uniform technology standards, by their very nature, cannot take into account the fact that the effects of pollution and the costs of controlling it vary widely among facilities within a given industrial category. This means that almost any nationally uniform regulation, no matter how well drafted, will result in great inefficiencies as applied to at least some regulated facilities. This is an inherent problem in any "one-size-fits-all" pollution control standard….If all that is required is compliance with best available technology, there is no reward for going further, and hence no incentive to do so. Indeed, there is a disincentive to disclosing new technologies that might have the result of making BAT [Best Available Technology—a common pollution-control standard] more stringent….

According to this view, the gains we have made in the past twenty-five years have largely come by achieving reductions at the most accessible pollution points, such as previously unregulated smokestacks. In order to continue to improve our environment today we need to control the harder to reach, more costly increments of pollution, such as the remaining ten percent of pollution emitted by an already regulated smokestack. We will only be able to afford to do this by making our regulatory methods more efficient.

Those who share this view call for a *second* generation of environmental regulation: a more effective set of regulatory instruments that will allow us to reach our pollution reduction goals….[T]he 1990s have seen a flowering of innovative approaches that attempt to respond to the shortcomings of the first generation approach….

*Second Generation Initiatives*

…American businesses create all manner of new products and technologies. If this tremendous capacity for innovation were turned towards environmental performance it could yield more effective and more protective approaches. In contrast to first generation regulation, which largely dampens creative energies of this type, second generation policy seeks to unleash them. One of the ways in which it does this is through the use of market-based incentives….

Many of the first generation environmental statutes focus on controlling pollution as it is being released into the environment. They shy away from regulating the manufacturing process itself for fear of interfering with important production decisions. Unfortunately, this "end-of-pipe" approach overlooks important opportunities to alter the production process in ways that will benefit the environment (such as substituting different raw materials, or redesigning processes). These "upstream" pollution prevention strategies are often far more cost effective than end-of-pipe controls.

Second generation environmental policy seeks to encourage businesses to think creatively about pollution prevention as a means of achieving environmental goals. Mind-

ful of the need to respect industry discretion over the production process, it seeks to involve the regulated businesses themselves in the development of pollution prevention
strategies for their facilities....

Second generation policy seeks to make environmental regulation more flexible. One
of the tools employed for this purpose is "environmental contracting," a method that
lies at the core of one of EPA's most significant second generation initiatives, Project XL.

Launched in 1995, Project XL gives a limited number of regulated parties the opportunity to demonstrate "eXcellence and Leadership" by developing an innovative approach to pollution control at their facility. Where the facility can demonstrate that the
new approach will protect the environment better than the existing regulations would
have, and can show that it consulted with and received support from a diverse group of
"stakeholders," EPA agrees to lift the traditional rules and replace them with the alternative strategy (the Agency refers to this as "regulatory flexibility"). EPA and the project
sponsor then enter into an agreement—the "environmental contract"—in which the
project sponsor promises to achieve superior environmental performance and EPA
agrees to provide the regulatory flexibility that will make the new approach possible....

Project XL's promise of regulatory flexibility raises some obvious questions about accountability. One can easily imagine a scenario in which EPA, under pressure from a
regulated industry, might try to abuse the power to substitute a more tailored approach
in place of existing requirements that have been vetted through notice-and-comment
rulemaking.

One answer to this problem is to deny EPA the power to grant regulatory flexibility.
While this would help to ensure accountability, it would also prevent EPA from addressing the problems (outlined above) caused by "one-size-fits-all" regulation. Second generation policy takes another approach. Rather than denying EPA the opportunity to
make regulation more flexible, it seeks to expand the public's ability to monitor EPA
and make sure that the Agency exercises its discretion responsibly....

One way to encourage businesses to generate innovative pollution control ideas is to
get them to integrate the search for such improvements into their normal management
practices. For years companies have carefully managed and evaluated the "business" side
of their enterprises so as to identify possible improvements, but it is not until recently
that they have begun to apply the same approach to the environmental dimension of
their business. Today, increasing numbers of private companies are adopting "environmental management systems" (EMS) for just this purpose. While EMS can vary in their
composition, a standard EMS consists of a process by which corporate managers set
ambitious environmental goals, generate innovative ideas for ways to achieve those targets, conduct rigorous monitoring of the company's progress towards the objectives and
of its compliance with existing regulatory requirements, and commit to continuous improvement in environmental performance and compliance. Because the core function of
EMS is to get a company to reflect on and analyze its own environmental performance,
some refer to those policies that promote EMS as "reflexive regulation."

The reflexive approach can yield important environmental benefits. The process of
setting ambitious environmental goals and figuring out how best to achieve them can
generate useful pollution prevention and other "upstream" design ideas. In addition,
the periodic and systemic review of the company's environmental compliance status can
lead to the self-detection of violations that government inspectors may not have identified until many years later. This allows these compliance issues to be addressed much
more quickly than they otherwise would have....

Second generation policy uses the "stick" of punishment but supplements it with "carrots" intended to motivate businesses to utilize their talents and resources in the service of environmental protection.... [See discussion in Chapter XI(B). Eds.]

EPA hopes that the program incentives, coupled with the ambitious criteria for obtaining them (which include adoption of an EMS), will motivate companies to put their energies towards achieving environmental excellence rather than towards resisting regulatory requirements.... The Clinton Administration claims that these programs provide better environmental protection, for less cost, without sacrificing accountability. Or, as the President has often said, they are "cheaper, cleaner and smarter."

Do the programs really live up to this billing? We now have a sufficient track record to begin to ask the hard questions about these initiatives. Do these programs really address the critique of command and control? Do they regulate more efficiently? Do they promote innovation in pollution control methods? Are they truly more protective of the environment? In fact, are they even as protective as first generation controls? Are they able to assure accountability, or does the flexibility and collaboration that is integral to these projects open the door to abuse?

### Second Generation Policy and the New Economy

... The critique of first generation regulation has been with us for a while. Why are we beginning to see a policy response now?

The common answer is that the Clinton Administration's "environmental regulatory reinvention" efforts arose out of a pragmatic response to the 1994 Republican ascendancy in the Congress....

I would suggest that there is another factor at work that, even if not the main cause of these policy developments, at the very least helps us to see their significance for the twenty-first century. This is the connection between second generation environmental policy and the "new economy." ...

This new "digital and global" economy differs from the old "smokestack" economy in a number of important ways. First, in a global economy, American companies are subject to increasingly fierce competition from all corners of the planet. For example, in 1965 IBM faced 2,500 competitors for all of its markets; by 1992, it faced 50,000. The share of the U.S. economy subject to foreign competition rose by 50% between 1985 and 1994.

Second, in order to deal with global competition, companies must move faster to introduce new and better products and respond to changing market conditions. Today it is the fast, nimble, and creative companies that succeed; not the tradition-bound and institutional....

If our system of environmental regulation were beginning to adapt to these fundamental economic transformations, what would we expect the adjustment to look like? We would expect the system to become more cost effective so as not to harm the competitiveness of American businesses trying to survive in a global market. Given the constant innovation in production, we would expect the system to seek to respond more quickly to changing business products and processes. On the one hand, this might mean faster governmental action, such as permitting decisions on new constructions or modifications. On the other, this might mean faster identification of new risks and environmental damage caused by new products or processes.

Along with faster response time, we would expect it to be more flexible in its regulatory requirements so as to make them adaptable to continuously and rapidly changing business behavior. Given that the system was going to provide more flexibility, we would also expect it to seek to produce more accountability and transparency to ensure that environmental values are not compromised....

Finally, we would expect it to reign in the increasing capacity to damage the environment that comes with increasing amounts of globally accumulated capital that can be directed at developing natural resources....We would expect the regulatory system to respond to this by making environmental protection more a part of the global regulatory structure....

[P]ressures on the international front, and the push for second generation environmental policy at home, may be linked. Both can be understood in part as responses to the increasing globalization and digitization of the economy. That is, if first generation environmental policy was "smokestack" environmentalism designed for a manufacturing economy, then second generation policy may be "micro-chip" environmentalism designed for a high-tech, knowledge-based, globalized economy. This, perhaps, is why it has come to the fore in the late 1980s and 1990s—almost exactly contemporaneous with the economic transformations described above....

\* \* \*

### Notes and Questions

1. How does environmental contracting, which affords firms more flexibility in controlling their emissions, lead to a greater ability to compete in the global market?

2. Given the pressures to compete against other economies that may not have comparably stringent environmental laws, how does domestic environmental regulation afford regulatory flexibility but still ensure that environmental values are not compromised? Is Hirsch overly optimistic in this regard, or can you see a way to accomplish both goals?

3. Some commentors note that a legislative revision of environmental laws was and is not politically feasible for a variety of reasons. In your view, what might some of those reasons be? Assuming this assumption is correct, how should regulation proceed in the face of existing, highly prescriptive laws? Is there leeway to deviate from requirements? Consider the following excerpt, in which Professor Daniel Farber discusses deviation from statutory mandates at work, not only in flexible permits, but in other regulatory functions such as standard-setting, rule promulgation and enforcement.

# B. "Reinventing" Environmental Statutes (Informally) Through Program Implementation

## Daniel A. Farber,
### Taking Slippage Seriously: Noncompliance and Creative Compliance in Environmental Law
23 Harvard Environmental Law Review 297 (1999)

There is many a slip 'twixt the cup and the lip." Nowhere is this more true than in environmental law. In all areas of law, there are gaps between the "law on the books" and the "law in action," but in environmental law the gap is sometimes a chasm....

*The Anatomy of Slippage*

...Slippage between regulatory standards and the actual conduct of regulated parties is far from being a peripheral element of the legal regime. What environmental lawyers do much of the time could be considered "slippage management." It could almost be said—admittedly, with some exaggeration—that what the standard description characterizes as slippage is actually the primary feature of the system: the so-called standards are important only because they help channel the informal interactions between agencies and regulated parties....

"Negative" slippage is a feature of environmental law so ubiquitous that we take it for granted: something that is legally mandated simply fails to happen. Deadlines are missed, standards are ignored or fudged, enforcement misfires. This is such a commonplace phenomenon that it becomes almost invisible; naturally, we are more likely to focus our attention on what *is* happening than on what isn't. We also fail to notice the processes that take the place of the mandated standards, such as ad hoc permitting: *something* is being done, even if it is not what Congress planned.

"Affirmative" slippage is more interesting: the required standards are renegotiated rather than ignored, resulting in a regulatory regime that may bear little resemblance to the "law on the books." A current example is given by the Clinton Administration's revamping of the Endangered Species Act ("ESA"), reading an obscure escape clause (permits for incidental takes) so broadly that it now threatens to eclipse the rest of the statute. Often, as in the ESA example, these creative revisions involve intense negotiation between stakeholders rather than the execution of conventional regulatory mandates. Affirmative slippage seemingly is becoming more common, as the renegotiation process has become an increasingly attractive alternative to conventional standard-setting. Prominent examples exist as early as the mid-1970s....

Slippage also has implications for policy debates over environmental standards. If standards are not automatically translated into compliance, our understanding of their costs and benefits may shift. [W]e seriously misunderstand the regulatory system if we ignore the pervasive effect of compliance issues on the system as a whole. The problem of obtaining compliance—and sometimes, even knowing what "compliance" means—is pervasive. Regulatory slippage...deserves much more attention than it has received....In environmental law, however, shortfalls are widespread at all levels of the system, for reasons that cannot simply be attributed to antisocial or deviant conduct....

For instance, under § 304(b) of the Clean Water Act, passed in 1972, EPA was required to issue effluent guidelines no later than October 18, 1973. These guidelines were to form the basis for effluent limitations under § 301, which in turn had deadlines as early as 1977, with a 1983 deadline for stricter standards. But the task proved to be far beyond EPA's capabilities, and the agency fell far behind schedule....As a result of such delays, many permits were issued in the meantime without the benefit of the mandated EPA regulations. Under the statute, until these regulations are in place, permits are to be issued under "such conditions as the Administrator determines are necessary to carry out the provisions of this chapter." The result was, in practice, the imposition of pollution requirements largely unrelated to the apparent demands of the statute....Thus, many control measures imposed in the permits bore little resemblance to the technology-based requirements mandated by the statute.

This situation did not come to an end when the § 301 standards were finally forthcoming. Even today, according to a recent General Accounting Office ("GAO") report, "there is no real consistency in how pollutant levels are set in...permits."

Similar stories can be told about other environmental statutes. EPA has apparently sometimes found it preferable to leave certain mandates unimplemented....

Environmental statutes often call for states to assume enforcement authority, subject to federal supervision. In reality, the supervision is often lax, and states often are able to deviate openly from statutory requirements. The "threat of EPA withdrawing approval for any state enforcement programs and having the federal government assume primary responsibility" is "hollow due to a lack of federal resources and an expanding number of regulated entities."

...Although it has as much legal authority as it needs, the federal government cannot implement its air pollution program without the substantial resources, expertise, information, and political support of state and local officials. Congress and EPA can quell minor revolts among state agencies, but widespread dissatisfaction—manifested in the time-honored "go-slow" approach—will bring EPA and even Congress to the bargaining table.

As a result, [Professor John] Dwyer says, "the states have been able to work compromises with EPA rather than be slavishly subject to federal dictates."

Similarly, under the Clean Water Act, states have found it possible to dodge or disobey federal mandates outright. As the GAO found, one state refused to apply new federal standards simply because it found them to be too strict, but "EPA did not withdraw the program because it was 'an unrealistic option.'"...

It would be a travesty to say that the federal environmental statutes are a dead letter. But it is equally obvious that translating legal mandates into actual compliance is far from automatic....

EPA's Inspector General documented widespread breakdowns in enforcement, even by the agency itself. For instance, in two states, federal authorities "had not issued or renewed hundreds of permits required for factories and waste water treatment plants, often for as long as ten years." In recent years, EPA's Seattle office had written thirty-three permits, but there was a backlog of a thousand applications, most of them over four years old. Compliance by state agencies was also spotty....

Rather than slipping "behind," implementation can instead slip "sideways" or sometimes even "forward" *vis a vis* the formal standards. We will discuss three scenarios. In the first, the result of slippage is a de facto (and sometimes ultimately de jure) modification in the regulatory standards themselves. That is, the agency follows the normal procedures for setting standards, but the substance of the decision diverges from statutory requirements. In the second, the standard setting process itself is displaced by some kind of negotiated agreement, sometimes encompassing federal and state regulators as well as regulated parties. In the third scenario, the slippage occurs during the enforcement stage, when individual sources are faced with sanctions of some sort....

### Morphing Standards

A classic example of the first scenario is provided by the history of toxics regulation under the Clean Water Act. As enacted in 1972, the statute required EPA to promulgate standards providing an "ample margin of safety" for all toxic water pollutants. This section was never implemented as written, in part because it would have resulted in widespread plant closings. EPA was sued for its failure to implement the toxics program, and entered into a settlement. But the consent decree did not call for regulation under the "ample margin" standard mandated by the statute. Instead of basing regulations purely on risk levels, as the statute required, the consent decree required EPA to issue regulations based on the best available technology for various industries. Thus, risk-based standards were replaced, via the consent decree, with technology-based standards. This was a somewhat startling rewrite of the statutory standards by way of litigation, but received Congress's approval a few years later when the statute was amended to incorporate the main provisions of the consent decree. . . .

### Renegotiating Regulations

. . . The best known example is Project XL, in which the agency attempted to negotiate with individual sources to reduce their net environmental impact below what could be achieved by full compliance with existing regulatory standards. [See excerpt above. Eds.]

### Creative Enforcement Measures

The environmental statutes provide a battery of enforcement measures including injunctions, civil penalties, and criminal sanctions. EPA has created another enforcement measure, the Supplemental Environmental Project ("SEP"). A SEP is an environmentally desirable measure that a violator agrees to implement in place of some of the penalty which it would otherwise be legally required to pay. From 1992 to 1994, EPA negotiated more than 700 SEPs, with an estimated cost exceeding $190 million. A case study of ten SEPs found some significant pollution prevention efforts. . . .

It is particularly significant that here, as in some of the examples discussed earlier, what appeared to be slippage was later partially ratified by Congress. This phenomenon helps account for the ambiguous legitimacy of slippage: even conduct that seems dubious at the time in formal terms, may be "baptized" after the fact. . . .

### The Implications of Slippage

. . . Thus, rather than focusing on regulatory standards in isolation, we need to see them as part of a larger process of negotiation between government actors, industry, and environmentalists. Thus, we don't need to "reinvent regulation"—in some sense, what we would now regard as the "reinvented version" has been around us all along, for better or worse. . . .

### Reevaluating the Standards Debate

[S]tandards may commonly function as starting points in the lengthy interactions between agencies and regulated parties, rather than as end points of compliance. Often, so-called standards may serve as threat points in negotiation or as penalty defaults that force information disclosure. The optimum "standards" for these purposes may well be quite different from (and often harsher than) the ultimate performance level that we wish to attain.

To the extent this situation holds true—to the extent, that is, that slippage is widespread—it is far from clear that the standards themselves should reflect an optimum balance of compliance costs and environmental benefits. The fact that the standards are sometimes too harsh—that they have compliance costs that are too high compared with benefits—may be perfectly reasonable. In effect, the standards may merely be the government's opening demand in negotiations, and the final bargain is likely to be more favorable to the other side. If the government began the negotiations with an "optimal" regulatory demand (optimal in the sense that implementation would maximize net social benefits), the ultimate bargain would probably be too favorable to the regulated party. Thus, the criticism that regulatory standards are too harsh loses some of its force, once it is recognized that the standards are often only partially implemented.

Similarly, attacks on the "one size fits all" nature of regulation also lose some of their force once slippage is taken into account....Consequently, we might expect that enforcement (and thus the ultimate outcome) will be strictest for sources with low compliance costs and high environmental impacts, and weakest for sources with high costs and low impacts. As a result, the costs and benefits of pollution control will be roughly matched, rather than making the level of pollution control independent of individual circumstances....

So the practical issue is not whether to have complete national uniformity, which is a chimera, but whether the constraining effect of the national standards on local variation is useful. It is quite possible that full implementation of uniform national standards would be undesirable, but that partial implementation is useful as a safeguard against local regulatory breakdowns....

The argument here is not that a recognition of slippage necessarily reverses the conclusions one would reach about regulatory standards and how they should be issued. Slippage is only part of the story, and in some settings it may be more important than in others. But in at least some settings, it might significantly undermine the standard economic critiques of federal "command and control" regulation. The reason is simple: in those settings, command and control regulation does not really exist in the first place. Instead, what looks like a regulatory command is only one stage in a larger and more flexible process.

*Reinventing Reinvention*

...First, if there is already slippage between supposedly clear regulatory standards and actual conduct, we must wonder how much additional slippage might occur between the reinvented regulatory regime and actual compliance. That is, will we have slippage (from the reinvented regulations to actual compliance) on top of slippage (from original standards to reinvented regulation)? Currently, the informal and partially illicit nature of creative compliance measures is a disincentive for sources to enter into those bargains with EPA that informally modify compliance requirements. But it is also a strong incentive to keep those bargains, once made, because a breach of the bargain can easily lead the regulator to revert to the formally binding regulatory standards. Thus, the source may have some reluctance to initiate a second round of negotiation over how fully to implement the bargain resulting from the first round. But when the bargain itself is given full formal recognition, it may become the starting point for yet another round of negotiation, leading to further slippage. If we cannot count on full compliance with supposedly clear-cut national standards, we might also be unwise to assume that deals with individual sources will be a firmer basis for further enforcement efforts. Indeed, monitoring and enforcement problems might be even greater with more flexible, result oriented requirements for sources than with simpler, technology-based standards.

Second, slippage raises substantial problems of transparency and accountability....[T]he regulatory process has often deviated from the public, formally binding standards supposedly required by law. Much important policy is made through regulatory inaction, settlement of litigation, and other techniques that operate outside of full public view. Moreover, these techniques do not contain the usual opportunities for public input or the normal mandates for deliberative decision making. They take place, in other words, very much in the shadow of the law, not in the light of public deliberation....

Reinvention is close to the idea of affirmative slippage discussed previously in this Article. The risk, however, is that frameworks designed to foster affirmative slippage will instead provide fertile ground for negative slippage—in other words, a reversion to the environmental evils that the regulatory system was designed to thwart in the first place....

*Conclusion*

Slippage happens....

The hardest question of all, however, is whether slippage is good or bad. Given its often unrealistic demands, it is hard to see how the system could operate without at least some degree of slippage—recall that Congress mandated an end to all water pollution by 1985, a quixotic demand that is still part of the statute today. Without some escape hatch, industry might be overwhelmed by unrealistic regulatory burdens. Besides ameliorating the sometimes impractical demands found in the statutes, slippage has also provided an opportunity for some important innovations in environmental regulation.

But slippage also has an inevitable cost in terms of damage to our concept of the rule of law. Widespread noncompliance with formally binding requirements undermines the concept that good citizens—and even more so, governmental officials—obey the law. For this reason, as much as it engages our interest, and as much as it may be in some respects socially beneficial, slippage must also remain a troubling concept.

\* \* \*

## Notes and Questions

1. If existing standards do not reflect reality, but are merely a starting place in negotiations among the regulators, the regulated, and conventional environmental groups, should this change the way that environmental justice claims are evaluated? Should it matter whether the standards are violated due to negative (behind) slippage, or affirmative (forward or sideways) slippage? Why? In evaluating distributional claims, does "slippage matter" or does one just compare the community of concern against an appropriate comparison population?

2. How should combinations of slippage be evaluated in overburdened communities? Should negotiated, site-specific standards (affirmative slippage) be allowed in areas where noncompliance (negative slippage) is a problem? If not, does that unfairly punish a project sponsor that needs a flexible permit in order to respond to rapidly changing market conditions? What if the project sponsor negotiates a level of control that will theoretically result in a superior level of performance over the existing standards?

3. Can overburdened communities do anything about affirmative slippage? Consider that "slippage" is essentially noncompliance with existing legal requirements. In such a context, how do you evaluate the potential success of a citizen suit action against the facility operator for failure to comply with statutory requirements?

4. As noted, at times the Congress has subsequently ratified EPA's substitution of technology-based standards for risk-based standards. As noted in Chapter VI, technology-based standards are often insufficient when there are multiple source impacts in an area. In view of that, is "morphing" or substituting technology based standards an appropriate regulatory response?

5. Professor Farber speculates that national standards may be beneficial, not necessarily to achieve a uniform level of control, but as a constraining effect and a safeguard

against local regulatory failure. In his analysis, does Farber account for variations in political power that might affect the implementation process? Similarly, doesn't his speculation that enforcement will be strict for firms that have low compliance costs and high impacts assume that enforcement actors (regulatory officials and private citizens using citizen suits) are cognizant and sensitive to a firm's compliance costs? What factors might affect the validity of this assumption?

6. Farber argues that firm standards are necessary as a final stick by the regulatory agency. If flexibility becomes the norm rather than a point of departure from firm standards, this may result in a chain reaction of increasingly lax standards. Do you agree? Can you think of a concrete example where a flexibility that currently departs from regular standards, if it becomes itself a standard, will encourage more slippage? What effect would this have on an overburdened host community? Does the tendency of slippage to occur "in the shadow of the law" create additional difficulties? How?

7. Do Farber's thoughts on slippage undermine the force of Professor Hirsch's optimistic view of second generation initiatives? Hirsch assumes that such initiatives can be implemented with adequate transparency, public accountability and enforceable safeguards. If you represented a community-based organization in permit proceedings for a project XL facility, what assurances would you request?

8. Does slippage really do violence to the notion of the rule of law, as Farber suggests, or alternatively, does affirmative slippage really signal the development of a more collaborative form of governance, as suggested by Professor Freeman in Chapter V? Before it began utilizing "environmental contracting" or facility-specific negotiated permits, the EPA had experimented with negotiated rulemaking proceedings as an alternative to traditional "notice and comment" rulemaking. Under negotiated rulemaking, the EPA convenes a diverse stakeholder group to discuss the merits of the agency's tentative proposals prior to proposing the rule. Ultimately, the agency attempts to design a rule that either reflects the consensus of the stakeholder group or the EPA proposes tradeoffs that the agency anticipates will be acceptable to the majority of diverse stakeholders. The EPA believes this approach to be more efficient in the long run because it reduces the likelihood that the rule will be legally challenged. Thus, in the context of designing regulatory programs, there are at least two distinct issues raised by the interplay between negotiated rulemaking and regulatory innovation. The first is the extent to which a multistakeholder process—whether characterized as negotiated or collaborative—has advantages or disadvantages to impacted communities. The second issue is whether the substantive move away from "command and control" regulation—as envisioned by the statutes—towards a more "reflexive" or flexible approach advocated by market proponents has positive or negative environmental justice implications. The excerpt below examines EPA's issuance of a draft guidance document on permitting that seems to have been intended to replace (at least in part) a proposed rule that was derived largely through input from a multistakeholder federal advisory group, a distinctly collaborative process. As you read this excerpt consider the process implications, i.e., whether impacted communities would fare better under a process of program design that is unilaterally imposed by an agency or one derived through a multistakeholder process, or does it matter? In terms of substance, as you read the excerpt, bear in mind Professor Farber's observations about regulatory "slippage." In light of the potential environmental justice consequences of the proposed guidance, also consider whether a more flexible approach to permitting appears more or less environmentally protective than a "command and control" approach.

# C. Facility Specific Approaches — Operational Flexibility

## Eileen Gauna,
## EPA at Thirty: Fairness in Environmental Protection
### 31 Environmental Law Reporter 10,528 (2001)

*Environmental Justice and Reinvention*

...Perhaps more than any other venue, the reinvention enterprise is at its most aggressive in the area of permitting emissions of criteria air pollutants—usually by large industrial facilities—via a preconstruction permitting program termed "new source review" (NSR)....To magnify the difficulty of this [potential] conflict, the preconstruction air permitting program under the federal Clean Air Act is extraordinarily complex, with separate statutory requirements for permitting major sources of criteria pollutants in attainment areas (termed PSD review) and nonattainment areas (termed nonattainment NSR). Joining these preconstruction permitting programs is the umbrella operating permit program under Title V of the 1990 Amendments....

Since 1993, EPA has been engaged in ongoing dialogues with various stakeholders to reform NSR. The most recent product of this effort is a Draft Guidance on Design of Flexible Air Permits (*Draft Flexibility Guidance*), also known as "White Paper Number 3," which partly draws upon alternative permitting approaches proposed but never formally adopted by final rule....White Paper Number 3 is interesting in several respects. First, although not finalized, the proposed guidance reveals current Agency thinking on potential alternative permitting strategies under consideration, at least in some quarters of the Agency. However, the proposal contains flexibilities which may be problematic to communities impacted by these large facilities....White Paper Number 3 was issued as proposed guidance, a move that departed from the Agency's seven-year effort to accomplish reform of new source review and its eight-year effort to revise the operating permit program regulations by rule. Indeed, the expressed mid-stream change of position—that the changes contemplated by the proposed guidance were authorized by the current regulations all along—provoked a particularly sharp comment by the [Natural Resources Defense Council, or NRDC], an environmental organization that had significantly and consistently participated in the ongoing rulemaking process....

One of the central strategies to provide flexibility is the use of a bubble (plant-wide or partial) to avoid applicability of new permit proceedings when changes are made subsequent to the initial permit. A plantwide applicability limit (PAL) allows units to be added and modified, and emissions increased within the PAL level without triggering new source review or without the type of state agency review and approval that is usually required in connection with the [equipment] change. Although PALS have been allowed, typically they have been granted in connection with a permit pilot project, with the Agency promising to evaluate claims of superior environmental performance and the practical enforceability of the experimental approach before adoption by rule....

Although PALS may eliminate major NSR/PSD applicability, the addition of new equipment under the PAL might trigger minor source review and Title V requirements. Therefore, the *Draft Flexibility Guidance* contains another strategy that will allow the source to avoid these subsequent permit proceedings as well. This flexibility tool—also asserted to exist under current law—is the advance approval. Under this concept, if the permit applicant anticipates a need to add or modify processing equipment or pollution control devices in the future, the applicant can request advance approval of those changes in the application for the initial flexibility permit. Advance approval can even be obtained when the precise changes are not specifically known at the time of the initial permit application. Under the *Draft Flexibility Guidance*, the family of advance approvals can apply to "a potentially wide spectrum of changes, including the addition of specific new process units, modifications to existing units, or even for the addition or modification of units which are not known but which are within a described category of changes." Advance approvals may also be used in connection with PALs and other strategies that are designed to allow the source to avoid triggering new source review. Conceding that the number of different operating scenarios could be extensive, EPA advised that where it was impractical to describe the operating scenarios in detail, they could be described as a category of advance approved changes.

To assure permit authorities that the future changes will comply with legal requirements, the facility operator could state in advance a menu of "replicable operating procedures"(ROPs), mechanical procedures that do not require judgment and would yield identical results regardless of the operator. Anticipating that compliance requirements would necessarily change with a change in operations and equipment, the guidance provides for streamlining compliance requirements as well. The source operator can approve significant changes in advance by [using] a menu of compliance requirements (such as monitoring, recordkeeping and reporting) with a protocol for choosing the appropriate compliance approach. When minor compliance details are missing, it is possible for the source to add the details later through the Title V minor permit modification process, a process that does not require advance notice to the public or public hearing opportunities.

The aggressive use of bubbles, a menu approach (of advance approved changes and compliance requirements) and the Title V minor permit modification process results in significant obstacles to effective public participation. As the Agency acknowledged, advance approved changes can be incorporated into the Title V permit without public review unless the proposed advanced change itself would constitute a major modification. However, since advance approved changes are generally designed to keep the source from subsequently undergoing the type of modifications that trigger Title V proceedings, as a practical matter, all that EPA can do is encourage (but not require) the permitting authority to provide notification to the public at the time of the change. Even for advance approvals of "non-Title V requirements," EPA announced its intent to grant deference to the states in interpreting their own rules and SIPs, thus signaling its endorsement of [a more aggressive use of flexible permits by the states].

The upshot is that new facilities acquiring a flexible permit can avoid the potential applicability of major NSR or PSD, minor NSR and Title V, and can make any subsequent changes through the minor Title V modification process and avoiding public participation requirements. To be sure, there is public review of the initial flexible permit. At that point, however, any concerned member of the public can expect to encounter a dizzying menu of operating procedures, materials, equipment, and compliance protocols designed to cover an array of choices the facility operator may or may not make during the term of the permit. Citizens or community-based organizations on a limited budget might want to forego technical review of all of the proposed advance approvals and turn instead to the compliance provisions, reasoning perhaps that they may obtain adequate assurances if they can effectively monitor compliance of emission limits during the term of the permit (regardless of the operations employed under the PAL or partial cap). In this respect, reports obtained from instrumental continuous emissions monitoring equipment (CEMs) may be the best information available. Unfortunately, however, the *Draft Flexibility Guidance* allows non-instrumental "CEMs-equivalent" monitoring methods, such as "equations for mass balance or stoichiometric calculations or records of fuel or raw material purchases or usage," an approach which can be confounded by technical problems. Thus, technical review of a menu of these types of proposed compliance methods is likely to be beyond the resource capabilities of ordinary citizen groups. Another potential problem is that, due to strong industry pressure, the use of CEMs-equivalent monitoring may be applied in practice so liberally as to yield little, if any, verification of compliance. In short, Clean Air Act permits are notoriously complex to begin with, and the *Draft Flexibility Guidance* promises to increase that complexity by orders of magnitude without assurances that compliance can be adequately verified.

The flexibilities advanced by this guidance pose additional impediments to environmental justice communities that host the facility.... [For example,] the community is now in the position of having to raise money to obtain the technical expertise to independently evaluate a permit application that has an assemblage of advance approvals and compliance protocols instead of one set of requirements. As noted by NRDC and others, EPA is "condensing all of the public's opportunities to participate in permitting through minor NSR, PSD, major NSR, and Title V into one fleeting 30-day period every five years." Even an association of air pollution control officials—who strongly support the concept of operational flexibility—expressed concern about the increased complexity and resource burdens that would be required to process flexible permits.

Assuming that these obstacles are overcome, however, others remain. An advance approved change may subsequently occur without anyone considering socioeconomic factors and health indicators at the time of the change. For example, if recent studies document an abnormally high rate of respiratory illnesses or elevated blood lead levels, an emissions increase can occur without notifying the community about the increase, much less giving the community an opportunity to bring the health-related information before the permitting authority. Even though the increases [associated with the advance-approved change] may be considered under the cap (or partial cap) or *de minimis* for regulatory purposes, the emission increases still may present problems to a vulnerable community when combined with other sources of pollutants. At a time when environmental justice advocates and others are encouraging the Agency to bring the public into the permitting and pre-permitting process as early as possible in order to resolve potential problems, the *Draft Flexibility Guidance* substantially weakens public participation opportunities....

Another problem is that the ability of the facility owner to change processes, equipment and compliance protocols at any time without public notice will impede the ability of the community to monitor operations and use private citizen suit enforcement rights to keep the facility in compliance. The community is in the difficult position of having to discern which sets of processes, equipment, materials, and compliance protocols pertain within any given time frame to determine if suspected violations have in fact occurred or are occurring. In particular, correlating and interpreting data to evaluate whether a violation has occurred when non-instrumental compliance protocols are allowed may again lie beyond the resource capabilities of a community-based group.... All of this contradicts EPA's expressed desire to promote private enforcement capacity within environmental justice communities. Indeed, for many of these communities, public enforcement even under a more prescriptive, and, therefore, more enforceable regime has proven inadequate. Thus, the *Draft Flexibility Guidance* may well promote an unintended perverse incentive; it appears to benefit well-resourced industries that anticipate compliance problems by allowing them to obtain a flexible permit and locate in a community that is lacking private enforcement capacity due to [its] inability to obtain expensive technical advice.

[T]he *Draft Flexibility Guidance* similarly neglects to mention environmental justice and procedural and distributional issues are not addressed. This may not be surprising, considering that the seven-year intensive stakeholder process through the NSR FACA committee [New Source Review Federal Advisory Committee] did not appear to have an environmental justice representative. Instead, the Agency gave an information briefing session on this complicated guidance to the [National Environmental Justice Advisory Council] NEJAC Air and Water Subcommittee during a monthly telephone conference shortly before publication of the document. Subsequently, many environmental justice organizations were unable to prepare their own comment letter but opted to co-sign the comment [letter] by NRDC and others that opposed the adoption of the *Draft Flexibility Guidance* on a variety of grounds. Ultimately, this may be a case where, because of the daunting complexity of the permitting program coupled with the relative lack of stakeholder involvement by environmental justice advocates, the full environmental justice implications of this proposal and similar broad-based reinvention initiatives may never be analyzed and voiced prior to ultimate adoption and implementation. This is a serious obstacle considering that [this and similar] initiatives represent a fundamental shift from a permitting regime founded upon public participation and contemporaneous review to one that, while affording flexibility, also reduces public participation and is heavily dependent upon source-conducted after-the-fact verification. This effectively negates the one limited remedy that the Agency has indicated its willingness to adopt in response to environmental justice claims, i.e., enhanced public participation opportunities....

At the rulemaking or guidance-making level, the regulatory dynamics that impede fairness-oriented reform are even more troubling [and] environmental justice is rendered invisible by its absence in major rules and guidance documents [pertaining to permitting]. During the critical stakeholder intensive processes that informed attempts to develop efficiency-oriented reform of air permitting programs, environmental justice representatives were absent. In contrast, industry stakeholders, conventional environmental groups, state and local regulatory agencies and even federal land managers for years engaged in extensive discussions about the technicalities of air permitting in an attempt to understand the constraints of each group and to work out acceptable tradeoffs. This put environmental justice advocates in the unfortunately reactive position of attempting to understand the dauntingly complex proposals and address the environmental justice implications within a hopelessly short time frame. When environmental justice concerns become unavoidable at the rulemaking level, the Agency responded not by integrating more protective strategies within the framework of the permitting process, but by a combination of assuming away the problem, further study, separate after-the-fact stakeholder processes, or [...by committing itself] to address the problem on a case-by-case basis....

\* \* \*

## *Notes and Questions*

1. The flexible permit envisioned by White Paper 3 is essentially a form of "environmental contracting" as described by Professor Hirsch, above. The ability to get advance approvals to shift among different operational states at a facility is essentially an application of what Professor Hirsch terms "reflexive" regulation, i.e., regulation that allows a regulated entity to respond quickly to changing market conditions and control technologies without having to undergo lengthy permit revision proceedings. Are there environmental justice consequences to allowing individual facility owners to contractually negotiate their own customized permit requirements? Is this more "reflexive" approach potentially beneficial to environmental justice communities that host the facility? How does a community assess whether a customized permit results in greater pollution control?

2. If EPA alters its permitting approach to allow the widespread use of plantwide emission caps and/or a menu of advance approved changes, can you think of any environmental protection safeguards that can be designed into such a permitting regime?

3. Postscript: as of December, 1, 2001, the EPA had not finalized either the *Draft Flexibility Guidance* or the earlier proposed rule on NSR. In May of 2001, the National Energy Policy Development Group recommended that the EPA Administrator Christine Whitman examine NSR regulations and report to President Bush, within 90-days, on the impact of NSR on investment in new utility and refinery generation capacity, energy efficiency and environmental protection. The EPA subsequently issued a background report, *see* Environmental Protection Agency, NSR 90 Day Review Background Paper (June 22, 2001), Docket A-2001-19, Document II-A-01, but as of February 1, 2002, had not issued its report on the NSR 90-Day Review. The Agency's Background Report was criticized by the Clean Air Task force of the National Campaign Against Dirty Power. *See* Clean Air Task Force, Power to Kill: Death and Disease from Power Plants Charged with Violating the Clean Air Act (July 2001), available at <http://www.cleartheair.org>. Thus, how the statutory requirements of this major permitting regime will be implemented remains an open issue.

4. Note that with the "plantwide applicability limit" or PAL, the facility operator can increase emissions by adding new equipment as long as there are emission decreases in other parts of the facility. This is in essence a type of internal trade, very much consistent with the new market-oriented approach to environmental regulation, discussed in greater detail below.

# D. Other Economic Incentive Programs

As noted by Professor Hirsch in the excerpt at the start of this chapter, critics have charged that command and control regulation is inefficient in a number of respects, most prominently because it normally requires all polluters to comply with the same pollution limits even though their costs of compliance may vary considerably. As a result, economists and other critics have called for greater reliance on economic incentives, or market-based tools, to achieve environmental objectives. Economic incentives are a range of tools that rely on the economic self-interest of businesses, rather than direct regulation, to reduce pollution and that therefore allow businesses to reduce their pollution in a more cost-effective manner. Market-based tools can take numerous forms: pollution charges, which impose a fixed dollar amount for each unit of pollution emitted or disposed; deposit refund systems (such as bottle bills) in which purchasers receive a refund when an article is properly returned or disposed of; government subsidies or tax breaks for certain environmental behavior; or plantwide caps, in which the total emissions for a given facility are capped at some amount, and the facility is given flexibility to trade among different sources within the facility to achieve the cap (such as the PAL discussed in Section C above). Broader "cap and trade" or market programs allow trading of emissions among facility owners and other sources within a particular region or even across the United States or internationally.

## Pathfinder on Economic Incentives

For general background about market-based approaches programs, see Robert Stavins, *In the Toolkit, Economic Incentives*, 18 EPA J. 21 (May/June 1992); Daniel Dudek & John Palmisano, *Emissions Trading: Why is this Thoroughbred Hobbled?*, 13 COLUM. J. ENVTL L. 217 (1988); Bruce Ackerman & Richard Stewart, *Reforming Environmental Law*, 37 STANFORD L. REV. 1333 (1985). For a more critical view of market-based programs, see David Driesen, *Is Emissions Trading an Economic Incentive Program?: Replacing the Command and Control/Economic Incentive Dichotomy*, 55 WASH & LEE L. REV. 289 (1998). In addition to the articles excerpted in the text, other articles exploring the environmental justice implications of market approaches include Lily N. Chinn, Comment, *Can The Market Be Fair And Efficient? An Environmental Justice Critique of Emissions Trading*, 26 ECOLOGY L.Q. 80 (1999); Thomas Lambert, Christopher Boerner, *Environmental Inequity: Economic Causes, Economic Solutions*, 14 YALE J. ON REGULATION 195 (1997); Lorna Jaynes, Comment, *Emissions Trading: Pollution Panacea or Environmental Injustice?*, 39 SANTA CLARA L. REV. 207 (1998); and Dawn Somerville Zalfa, *Air Pollution Trading Programs Under the Clean Air Act: Compliance or Civil Rights Contravention?*, 20 WHITTIER L. REV. 485 (1998).

Some of the most widely used market-based tools and some of their environmental justice implications are discussed in the excerpt below.

# Stephen M. Johnson,
# Economics vs. Equity: Do Market-Based Environmental Reforms Exacerbate Environmental Injustice?
### 56 Washington and Lee Law Review 111 (1999)

*The Shift from Command and Control Regulation to Market-Based Reforms*

[T]he federal government and state governments are increasingly implementing market-based approaches to address environmental problems. The Clinton Administration has suggested that "[m]arket incentives should be used to achieve environmental goals, whenever appropriate," and a recent report by the Environmental Law Institute estimates that governments are using over one hundred different economic incentive mechanisms to address environmental problems in the United States....

*Inevitable Inequities in Market-Based Reforms*

...Although the traditional [regulatory] approach clearly has not adequately addressed distributional inequities, market-based approaches will inevitably exacerbate those inequities. While the traditional command and control environmental laws and regulations do not explicitly require the government to avoid actions that disparately impact low-income or minority communities, those laws also do not affirmatively encourage unequal distribution of pollution. By contrast, as explained below, many market-based approaches to environmental protection affirmatively encourage polluters to shift pollution to lower-income communities....

Classical economic theory institutionalizes and exacerbates existing social disparities that are based on unequal distributions of income. As Judge Richard Posner suggested, in a free market economy, in which voluntary exchange is permitted, "resources are shifted to those uses in which the value to consumers, as measured by their willingness to pay, is highest. When resources are being used where their value is highest, we may say that they are being employed efficiently." Although Judge Posner defined "value" in terms of "willingness to pay," on closer reflection it is clear that Judge Posner and other economists incorporated "ability to pay" into the concept of "willingness to pay." Thus, under traditional economic theory, a pollutant trading program, tax program, or similar market-based reform that shifts pollution to low-income communities is operating efficiently and, therefore, desirably because resources, such as clean air and clean water, are shifted to the uses in which the value to consumers, as measured by their willingness (and ability) to pay, is highest. Because wealthy communities are "willing to pay" more for clean air and water than low-income communities, the market operates efficiently when it funnels those resources to those communities rather than to low-income communities. In a free market, low-income communities will never have sufficient financial resources to buy clean air, clean water, and similar environmental and public health resources from wealthy communities or polluters....

[E]conomists admit that economic theory does not make value judgments regarding the distribution of resources or regarding the moral or social implications of "efficient" allocations of resources. Economists admit that economic theory does not address the important underlying question regarding whether an efficient allocation of resources is socially or ethically desirable....

However, environmental law developed and flourished precisely because economic theory, and the free market, did not address those social concerns.... While environmental laws should weigh economic issues, the laws should not substitute economic considerations for the important social considerations that motivated legislators to enact the laws in the first place....

### Market-Based Environmental Programs and Potential Disparate Impacts
### Pollutant Trading Systems and Potential Disparate Impacts

Most of the pollutant trading programs that have been implemented in the United States have focused on reducing air pollution.... [T]he EPA began experimenting with pollutant trading under the Clean Air Act in the 1970s. Those early experiments matured into EPA's 1986 Clean Air Act emissions trading policy for "criteria" pollutants, including sulfur dioxide, nitrogen dioxide, particulates, carbon monoxide, lead, and ozone. Under the policy, companies are allowed to build new major air pollution sources or make major modifications to major air pollution sources in areas of the country where national air pollution standards are not being met if the companies build the source to meet certain technology-based standards and enter into an agreement with an existing air pollution source in the area whereby the existing source reduces its pollution output by at least as much pollution as the new or modified source plans to discharge. The policy refers to the reductions as "emission reduction credits," which can be used to "offset" proposed pollution increases. Companies can obtain offsets by entering into agreements with other companies or by reducing the output of pollution from another source that they own in the polluted area where the new or modified source will be sited....

While EPA's emission trading policy was the agency's first major foray into pollutant trading, the sulfur dioxide emission trading program created by the 1990 Clean Air Act Amendments often is cited as a model for future pollutant trading programs at the federal and state levels. The trading program is designed to reduce by half sulfur dioxide emissions from coal-fired electric power plants by early in the next century. During Phase I of the program, which began in 1995 and ends in 2000, 111 of the dirtiest power plants were given annual "allowances" to emit 2.5 pounds of sulfur dioxide for every million Btu consumed by the plant. During Phase II, which begins in 2000, all power plants that produce more than 25 megawatts will be given "allowances" to emit 1.2 pounds of sulfur dioxide for every million Btu consumed by the plant. Total emissions from all of the plants are capped at 8.90 million tons of sulfur dioxide at the end of the program....

States have also implemented pollutant trading programs, primarily to address air pollution problems. Regulators in Los Angeles have implemented the Regional Clean Air Incentives Market (RECLAIM) to reduce emissions of sulfur dioxide and nitrogen oxides.... [RECLAIM mandates annual emission reductions of nitrogen oxides and sulfur dioxide emissions from regulated entities but provides industry with the flexibility to achieve these reductions by either reducing their own pollution or purchasing emission reduction credits from other sources. It is discussed further, below. Eds.]

While the state and federal pollutant trading programs promise to reduce pollution in a "cost-effective" manner, these programs could disparately impact low-income communities. First, while some trading programs limit trading to a specific air quality control region, many trading programs do not include any geographic limits on trades. As a result, while trading programs may decrease overall pollution levels, they may increase pollution in certain areas and create "toxic hot spots." Older, heavily polluting industries may find that it is more cost-effective to continue polluting and to buy pollution rights than to install new technologies to reduce pollution. Thus, communities surrounding those industries will be exposed to higher levels of pollution than other communities. Geographic limits on trades will not eliminate the "toxic hot spot" problem, especially if the geographic area in which trades are authorized is fairly large, but the limits could, at least, reduce the potential volume of pollution that will be imparted into a toxic hot spot....

If the trading programs will create toxic hot spots, economic theory suggests that the hot spots will most likely occur in low-income communities. Low-income communities are disproportionately impacted by air pollution, the siting of locally unwanted land uses (LULUs), and the siting of heavily polluting industries. This trend will likely continue as pollution trading programs expand for several reasons that are grounded in economic theory. First, heavily polluting industrial facilities (the facilities that may purchase pollution credits) will more likely be sited in low-income, urban areas than in middle-to upper-income, suburban areas. Second, low-income communities may be less likely than affluent communities to urge an outdated, heavily polluting industry to implement new pollution controls instead of buying pollution rights. Low-income communities may fear that if they urge the industry to adopt new pollution controls, then the industry will close, depriving the community of essential jobs and tax revenue. Finally, low-income communities often lack the political power to influence industries to adopt new pollution controls instead of buying pollution rights.

As trading programs have proliferated, examples of the disparate impacts of such programs have begun to proliferate as well....

Eleven northeastern states and the District of Columbia have agreed to implement a pollutant trading program, beginning in 1999, to reduce emissions of nitrogen oxides from utilities and industrial boilers. EPA is developing a rule that would establish a similar cap and trade program to reduce nitrogen oxide emissions in the thirty-seven states that are located east of the Mississippi River. Both proposals include an overall cap on emissions but neither imposes any geographic limit on pollutant trades within the areas covered by the program. Accordingly, both programs have the potential to create pollution hot spots.

When the federal and state governments complete the ongoing restructuring of electric power transmission regulation, heavily polluting, outdated power plants may have additional incentives to continue operating and creating toxic hot spots. In 1996, the Federal Energy Regulatory Commission (FERC) began a process that will require utilities to provide open access, non-discriminatory transmission services over their power lines. This will allow utilities to deliver power to a wider distribution area and, presumably, lead to more cost-efficient energy production. EPA and public interest groups criticized the proposal because it could increase the market for older, heavily polluting power plants and could encourage utilities to continue operating those plants. Accordingly, the proposal could lead to the creation of toxic hot spots of pollution around the power plants and downwind from the plants....

### Pollution Taxes, Fees, and Charges and their Potential Disparate Impacts

Pollution taxes, fees, and charges promise to reduce pollution in cost-effective ways similar to pollutant trading programs....The federal government has used pollution taxes to phase out the production of various chlorofluorocarbons and to encourage auto makers to manufacture fuel-efficient cars....Several states impose variable fees on polluters for water pollution permits or air pollution permits based on the volume or toxicity of the pollution authorized by the permit.... [M]any municipalities are implementing variable waste disposal fees...[where] residents pay variable waste disposal fees, which depend on the amount of waste that they dispose, instead of paying uniform fees....

[P]ollution taxes, fees, and charges...can also perpetuate environmental injustices. First, if governments impose uniform tax rates on pollution discharges based on the volume or toxicity of the discharge without regard to the location of the discharge, pollution taxes could create toxic hot spots in the same manner as pollutant trading systems. It may be more cost-effective for old, heavily polluting industries to pay pollution taxes than to reduce their pollution discharges, especially when the taxes are not set at rates that force polluters to reduce pollution. Unless governments tax pollution in heavily polluted areas at a higher rate than pollution in other areas, only newer, cleaner industries will have any incentive to reduce their pollution.

More significantly, though, pollution taxes could have regressive effects on low-income communities. For instance, low-income households would feel the impacts of an energy tax much more keenly than high-income households because low-income households spend a greater proportion of their income on heat, electricity, and gasoline than high-income households. Similarly, variable-rate waste disposal fees impose more significant financial burdens on low-income residents than high-income residents....

### Addressing Environmental Justice in Market-Based Reforms

...Because Congress and EPA will continue to implement market-based environmental reforms, this Part examines some of the ways that laws could be reformed to empower low-income communities to participate more fully in the markets for environmental or public health benefits....

*Information and the Market*

Theoretically, markets operate "efficiently" if consumers have perfect information. In practice, consumers almost never have perfect information. As a result, in the environmental arena, a community may be unaware that a particular action could adversely affect the health or the environment of the community, and the community may, therefore, fail to bargain with the actors to prevent the action. If the community had more information, it might bargain with the actor to prevent the harm. In such a situation, the market allocates resources inefficiently because consumers have imperfect information.

One obvious way to address this market failure and to foster environmental justice is to improve consumers' access to information. Market-based reforms could include provisions that require participants or the government to provide detailed information to communities about the potential environmental and public health impacts of pollution trades, waivers, or modifications of regulatory requirements or similar market-based initiatives. Existing "information disclosure" laws should also be expanded and improved. Those information disclosure requirements would reduce, but not eliminate, the likelihood that the market would allocate resources inefficiently....

Accordingly, legislators and regulators should take several steps to incorporate information disclosure requirements into market-based reforms and to expand and to improve the information disclosure requirements in existing laws (like EPCRA) to provide more complete and more accurate information.

*Grants, Loans, and Economic Assistance for Market Participation*

[T]o facilitate the participation of low-income communities in the market-based decisionmaking process...technical assistance grants to review trades, waivers, and other market-based actions could be expanded and simplified and targeted at low-income communities or communities that have been disparately impacted by pollution....

*Public Participation*

While technical assistance grants and loans may increase the likelihood that a community can afford to participate in environmental decisionmaking in market-based programs, other obstacles have limited public participation by low-income and minority communities in environmental decisionmaking in the past....

Accordingly, broad and flexible public participation procedures should be included in all pollutant trading, regulatory waiver or variance programs, and other market-based environmental protection programs that enable low-income communities, and all citizens, to participate in the market for health and environmental amenities. In addition, broad and flexible public participation procedures should be incorporated into traditional command and control programs to ensure that baseline pollution levels in low-income communities are not disproportionately high before trading or other market-based programs are implemented....

\* \* \*

## Notes and Questions

1. Professor Johnson argues that providing environmental justice communities with more information about the environmental and public health impacts of pollu-

tion trades, and providing them with technical assistance grants to review market-based actions, will help them more effectively participate in market-based environmental programs. Do you agree that this is an effective approach? What limits are there to relying on information disclosure as a strategy for communities to safeguard their interests? Consider that information about environmental risks may be confusing, technical, and difficult to process for most individuals. Are these insurmountable obstacles?

2. Professor Johnson uses an illuminating example to identify what may be a fundamental theoretical problem with an efficiency oriented approach. In a footnote, he explains that :

> Judge Posner relates the following story to explain the economist's definition of "value":
>
>> Suppose that pituitary extract is in very scarce supply relative to the demand and is therefore very expensive. A poor family has a child who will be a dwarf if he does not get some of the extract, but the family cannot afford the price.... A rich family has a child who will grow to normal height, but the extract will add a few inches more, and his parents decide to buy it for him. In the sense of value used in this book, the pituitary extract is more valuable to the rich than to the poor family, because value is measured by willingness to pay....
>
> Richard A. Posner, Economic Analysis of Law § 1.1, (4th ed. 1992), at 13. While Posner suggests that the rich family is more "willing to pay" for the extract than the poor family, it seems that the rich family is more "able to pay" than the poor family, rather than more "willing to pay." Posner's definition of willingness to pay, therefore, seems to incorporate ability to pay.

Johnson, *supra*, at 118, n. 43. If willingness to pay is heavily dependent upon our ability to pay, then this fundamental economic metric does not accurately reflect true preferences. It would be hard to imagine that heavily impacted communities near refineries and other large facilities "value" clean air less than the rest of society. Thus, carried to its logical extreme, is such a metric tantamount to a position that the preferences and values of the poor simply do not count? If so, is the movement to market-based environmental protection inconsistent with democratic values, including pluralistic ideals discussed in Chapter V?

3. Are some market regimes inconsistent with efficiency principles themselves? In the acid rain trading program described by Professor Johnson, anyone can purchase pollution credits. In fact, law students at the University of Maryland regularly hold a fundraiser to purchase and retire sulfur dioxide emissions, credits that are put up for auction by the Chicago Board of Trade. Under this conception, the resource (ability to pollute sulfur dioxide) gets efficiently shifted to the entity who values it most in the economic sense (the one most willing—and presumably able—to pay the most). However, some trading regimes do not advertise the sale of pollution credits on the open market and credits are in fact bought and sold among a small groups of industrial polluters. Is this efficient in the economic sense? In short, aren't economic incentive programs designed more for *cost effectiveness* for industry stakeholders rather than *efficiency* for society at large?

4. During the 1990s, the most advanced local air pollution trading program in the country was established in the Los Angeles region. The program has been looked to as a test case for evaluating the effectiveness of emission trading strategies. The following ex-

cerpt critiques a central component of this program that allowed stationary sources to satisfy their pollution control obligations by purchasing credits from mobile sources.

# Richard Toshiyuki Drury, Michael E. Belliveau, J. Scott Kuhn & Shipra Bansal, Pollution Trading and Environmental Injustice: Los Angeles' Failed Experiment in Air Quality Policy

9 Duke Environmental Law and Policy Forum 231 (Spring 1999)

*Los Angeles: A Test Market for Air Pollution Trading*

The Los Angeles, California, region provides an ideal testing ground for environmental policies. Los Angeles' environmental problems are severe, its regulatory agencies are sophisticated, its resources are relatively ample, and the region's population is multiracial and economically diverse.... The South Coast Air Basin, which includes the metropolitan Los Angeles area, suffers the worst air quality in the nation. For example, nearly 6,000 premature deaths caused by particulate air pollution occur in the Los Angeles area each year, representing about a tenth of such fatalities nationwide. Additionally, millions of residents of the region are exposed to unhealthy levels of ground level ozone, which causes aching lungs, wheezing, coughing, headache and permanent lung tissue scarring. Levels of toxic chemicals in the air pose significant risks for causing cancer and other chronic diseases.... A richly diverse, multi-racial and multi-ethnic population lives, works, and plays in the Los Angeles region, raising the environmental justice concern that people of color and poor people are unfairly exposed to more air pollution than others. Therefore, air pollution reduction strategies, including pollution trading programs, should be evaluated not only for their efficacy in reducing air pollution, but also for their effect on achieving environmental justice....

*Pollution Trading Comes of Age in Los Angeles: From Rule 1610 to RECLAIM and Beyond*

...In 1993, SCAQMD [the South Coast Air Quality Management District] approved the first old vehicle pollution trading program in the country, known as Rule 1610 or the "car scrapping program." Rule 1610 allows stationary source polluters (such as factories and refineries) to avoid installing expensive pollution control equipment if they purchase pollution credits generated by destroying old, high-polluting cars. Ideally, an equal or greater amount of pollution can be reduced at a much lower cost by purchasing and destroying old cars than by forcing stationary sources to install expensive pollution control equipment.

Under Rule 1610, "licensed car scrappers" can purchase and destroy old cars. SCAQMD then grants the scrapper emissions credits based on the projected emissions of the car had it not been destroyed, which may then be sold to stationary source polluters (e.g. factories). The stationary sources use the pollution credits to avoid on-site emission reductions that would be required under the technology-based regulatory regime. Rule 1610 requires polluters to purchase credits representing twenty percent more emission reductions than would be achieved through compliance with technology-based regulations for their plant. Although industrial plants avoid emission reductions, the scrapping of older, high polluting cars should result in greater air quality improvements at a lower cost than regulatory mandates....

*Toxic Hot-Spots and Environmental Injustice: The Mad Science of Pollution Trading*

... SCAQMD's pollution trading programs have resulted in the creation of toxic hot-spots by concentrating pollution in communities surrounding major sources of pollution. Rule 1610 provides the clearest example. SCAQMD studies indicate that cars destroyed through the Rule 1610 program were registered throughout the air quality management district, a four-county region. Air pollution from these automobiles would have also been distributed throughout this region. By contrast, stationary sources in Los Angeles are densely clustered in only a few communities in this four-county region. As a result of these distribution patterns, Rule 1610 effectively takes pollution formerly distributed throughout the region by automobiles, and concentrates that pollution in the communities surrounding stationary sources.

Most of the emissions credits purchased to avoid stationary source controls have been purchased by four oil companies: Unocal, Chevron, Ultramar and GATX. Of these four companies, three are located close together in the communities of Wilmington and San Pedro; the fourth facility, Chevron, is located nearby in El Segundo. These companies have used pollution credits to avoid installing pollution control equipment that captures toxic gases released during oil tanker loading at their marine terminals. When loading oil tankers, toxic gases are forced out of the tanker and into the air, exposing workers and nearby residents to toxic vapors, including benzene, a known human carcinogen. Thus, by using pollution credits, these companies are allowed to avoid reducing local emissions of hazardous chemicals in exchange for reducing regional auto emissions. As a result of Rule 1610, the four oil companies created a toxic chemical hot-spot around their marine terminals, exposing workers and nearby residents to elevated health risks.

Exposure to the emissions from loading marine vessels poses a cancer risk greater than 150 in 1 million for the maximum exposed individual. By comparison, the typical significant risk threshold for cancer risk ranges from one to one hundred in 1 million. Neither of these risk estimates considers the cumulative impact of marine terminal emissions in combination with all the other sources of toxic air contaminants to which people in the region are exposed....

To add insult to injury, the public health risks from the extra pollution concentrated in these neighborhoods constitutes a case of environmental injustice. The demographics of this hot-spot area starkly contrast with that of the metropolitan Los Angeles region. The residents living in San Pedro and Wilmington, which host a majority of the oil companies emitting hazardous toxic chemicals, are overwhelmingly Latino. Furthermore, the racial composition of communities living near three of the marine terminals ranges from 75 to 90 percent people of color, while the entire South Coast Air Basin has a population of only 36 percent people of color....

The hazards of trading extend beyond the shifting of pollution from a dispersed region to more concentrated localized areas; inter-pollutant trading can also create toxic hot-spots. Many trading programs allow facilities to trade pollution credits generated through reductions in a large variety of chemicals. For example, the Rule 1610 program allows pollution credits to be generated through reductions in VOCs [Volatile Organic Compounds]. VOCs are a family of over 600 chemical compounds, some of which have high toxicity and some of which have low toxicity. VOC trading raises concerns about the difference in toxicity of VOC emissions from marine terminals compared to VOCs from automobiles. For example, benzene levels may be higher in VOC emissions from marine terminals than from cars, which leads to greater exposure and risks concentrated in the communities around the marine terminals.... Therefore, the Rule 1610 program may allow continued release of highly toxic chemicals into certain communities in exchange for small area-wide reductions in much less toxic chemicals. Yet, no source testing has been required by SCAQMD to accurately characterize the differences in chemical composition and toxicity among VOC emissions subject to trading.

In addition to concerns about variable toxicity, VOCs also exhibit different degrees of reactivity related to their ability to form photochemical smog. These differences in photochemical reactivity have long been recognized in air pollution regulation and have guided priority setting in the control of VOC sources for smog control. In pollution trading programs, however, if highly reactive VOCs are emitted by purchasing credits earned for reducing low reactivity VOCs, then downwind ozone (smog) formation may be increased rather than reduced. This represents another inter-pollutant trading flaw in pollution trading programs that include VOCs.

The complex chemistry of air pollution leads to further problems with pollution trading. Emissions are composed of complex mixtures of chemicals, not the single pollutants often targeted for regulation or trading. We use the term "co-pollutants" to describe the secondary pollutants that inextricably accompany the emission of primary targeted pollutants. Further, air pollutants can later undergo chemical changes into more hazardous pollutants downwind. The initially emitted chemicals are commonly referred to as "precursors" to the hazardous pollutants formed later. Since pollution trading enables polluters to avoid emission reductions, or even increase emissions, at one location by purchasing credits earned elsewhere, the co-pollutants associated with that emission source may also persist and concentrate around that polluter. Likewise, if emissions contain precursors, then greater exposure to the pollutants formed later may occur downwind when credits are purchased to maintain or increase emissions at a facility....

*Public Participation Suffers Under a Pollution Trading Regime*

...Most states have permitting procedures through which affected community members can advocate for pollution control requirements on facilities. However, pollution trading allows facilities to avoid those permit requirements—usually without the knowledge or involvement of the affected community. Pollution trades made pursuant to Rule 1610 and RECLAIM are not subject to public review or comment. In fact, the public faces numerous difficulties finding out what companies are trading to avoid compliance with pollution control standards. For instance, RECLAIM credits can be purchased from independent brokers, without any environmental agency or public oversight. A company wishing to increase or continue its pollution need only purchase the required credits on the open market, without any public review or comment. In this way, the democratic will, as represented in permit and regulatory requirements imposed after full public review and comment, can be reversed by a simple economic transaction....

* * *

## Notes and Questions

1. In addition to the points raised in the excerpt above, environmental attorney Richard Drury and his colleagues also pointed out that the car scrapping program had a substantial number of design flaws that potentially worsened the situation:

> Pollution trading programs primarily rely on industry self-reporting of emission reductions and increases. Based on these self-reports, regulatory agencies must allocate air pollution credits. In Los Angeles, widespread under-

reporting, inaccurate modeling, and potential financial windfalls for polluters plague the pollution trading program.

In the Rule 1610 program, for example, oil companies purchase pollution credits from the scrapping of old cars to offset their VOC emissions. In order to determine the number of emission reduction credits that oil companies need to purchase from car scrappers, SCAQMD relies on industry self-reporting of emissions. The program creates an incentive to under-report actual emissions. By under-reporting their air pollution, the companies can reduce their purchase of emission reduction credits.

Rather than measure actual emissions released, companies estimate emissions using emission factors developed by the Western States Petroleum Association. Emissions factors are surrogate estimates of emissions based on activity level....Emissions factors are poor surrogates for actual measurements. With margins of error ranging from fifty percent to one hundred percent, emissions factors are highly uncertain, making claimed emission reduction difficult to verify....

Information recently obtained through the Freedom of Information Act reveals that the oil companies did, in fact, measure their emissions. When the actual measurements were compared to reported emissions based on industry emissions factors, striking differences were revealed. Oil companies under-reported their oil tanker emissions by factors between 10 and 1000. As a result, the oil companies purchased between 10 and 1000 times too few credits from scrapping old, high-polluting cars to offset their tanker pollution. This persistent problem was completely overlooked by SCAQMD and was only detected through a time-consuming investigation by Communities for a Better Environment. However, despite this under-reporting, SCAQMD continues to allow the use of emissions factors to underestimate emissions.

Exacerbating the huge gap between actual emissions and credits purchased by polluters, credit generators—the car scrappers—have abused the system. Many of the cars allegedly destroyed through the Rule 1610 program were not, in fact, destroyed, according to Bruce Lohmann, SCAQMD's Chief Inspector for the Rule 1610 program. While the car bodies were crushed, many of the engines which produce the pollution were not. Instead, many of those engines were sold for re-use, despite the fact that pollution credits for destroying the car had been granted by SCAQMD. EPA has refused to approve the Rule 1610 program precisely because car engines are not always destroyed.

Several assumptions underlying the Rule 1610 program are also dubious. In order to quantify the credits generated by scrapping a vehicle, SCAQMD assumes that the old cars would have been driven approximately 4,000 to 5,000 miles annually for an additional three years and that the owner of the car would replace it with a "fleet average" automobile. Although these assumptions were based on studies of old car driving patterns, they have not been borne out in reality.

According to Inspector Lohmann and an audit conducted by SCAQMD, many of the cars scrapped through the Rule 1610 program were at the end of their useful life, and would have been destroyed through natural attrition. Each year, between 100,000 to 200,000 old vehicles are naturally scrapped or abandoned without the intervention of the Rule 1610 trading programs. No "surplus" credits should be counted from scrapping one of those thousands of cars, since those reductions would have naturally occurred. Since less than 23,000 cars have been destroyed through the Rule 1610 program in its five-year life, most of these cars are probably among those that would have been destroyed even without the program.

Drury, et al., *supra*, at 259–262. Can these design flaws be overcome or are flaws of this nature endemic to a market program? For example, in designing market programs, should reductions that would have occurred anyway, such as those that occur when a facility shuts down for economic reasons, count as offsets? Should emission reductions that occurred in years past be used for offsets years later? Why or why not? In switching from a traditional system to a market system, how should emission credits be allocated among facilities initially?

2. EPA's most recent guidance for states seeking to incorporate economic incentive programs (EIPs) in their State Implementation Plans (SIPs) under the Clean Air Act recognizes that market-based programs may raise environmental justice concerns. The guidance requires that EIPs must meet an equity principle, consisting of a "general equity" and an "environmental justice" element. The general equity element requires that "no segment of the population receive a disproportionate share of a program's disbenefits," while the environmental justice element requires EIPs to address the potential for disproportionate impacts to low income and or minority communities from incentive programs. Of particular concern to EPA is the possibility that trading programs may lead to hot spots of toxic air emissions in low income and minority communities caused by VOC emissions. To prevent such toxic hot spots from occurring, EPA's guidance suggests a number of provisions that could be included in EIPs such as establishing "no-trade" zones, restricting increases in toxic emissions beyond a certain threshold or requiring compensating offsets for any increases, requiring a site-specific analysis for each prospective activity, and requiring a certain level of emission controls (known as Reasonably Available Control Technology or "RACT") for all sources in environmental justice communities, regardless of the possibility to trade. The guidance also mandates that states make extra efforts to encourage public participation in the design, implementation, and evaluation of their EIPs. *See* U.S. EPA, Draft Economic Incentive Guidance, §§ 5.2, 17.2. EPA's Guidance on Economic Incentive Plans can be found at http://www.epa.gov/ttn/oarpg/t1/memoranda/eip9-2.pdf.

3. Drury and his colleagues call for even broader reforms in trading programs, including prohibitions on the trading of any toxic substances, trading between mobile and stationary sources, and "cross-polluant" trading (trading for credits generated by reduced emissions of less hazardous pollutants). They also argue that a demographic analysis of affected communities should be required before any trading program is approved, and that affected communities should be given the right to review and comment on any proposed trade that would increase or continue the release of toxic emissions in a given community. Agencies should retain the discretion to reject or amend the proposed trade based on community comments. Drury, *supra*, at 283–286.

4. Proponents of trading programs argue that the concern about air toxic hot spots occurring from trading programs is overstated. First, they contend that trading occurs within the limits established by federal and state air toxic regulations (such as section 112 of the Clean Air Act) that are designed to reduce risks from toxic air emissions to a level of insignificance. Second, they question the premise that there are existing toxic hot spots caused by stationary sources. For example, in 2000, the South Coast Air Quality Management District completed a monitoring study of toxic emissions across the

South Coast Air Basin (which covers Los Angeles, Orange & Riverside counties), known as the MATES II study, that concluded that the level of toxic air contaminants associated with stationary source emissions was reasonably uniform across regions. The study concluded that the ambient risk from air toxics was much more dramatically influenced by mobile sources (such as diesel particulate emissions) than stationary sources. *See* Michael Carroll, Environmental Justice: Update on Federal and State Law and Market Trading, Remarks at Environmental Law Conference at Yosemite (Oct. 14, 2000).

5. Reforms that place geographic limits on trading or that increase the government's role in reviewing trades can be considered command and control "safety nets." While designed to protect vulnerable communities, they also interfere with the unfettered functioning of the market and in part undermine the efficiency rationale of market-based tools. Professor Johnson notes, for example, that determining whether trades or other actions in market-based programs disparately impact certain communities may require the government to gather large amounts of data regarding community demographics and the cumulative and synergistic impacts of pollution on a community, a potentially time-consuming and expensive task. Likewise, advocates of tradable permits oppose giving the public notice and the right to comment on proposed trades, arguing that this would delay or chill trades. To what extent are limitations that undermine the efficient functioning of market-based reforms — that may make businesses less likely to utilize market-based tools — justified?

# Chapter VIII

# Facility Permitting

## A. Introduction

Although disparities in environmental protection have occurred in enforcement, cleanup and standard-setting endeavors, most environmental justice challenges appear in the permitting context. There are good reasons why this occurs. First, consider the immediacy of the adverse impacts on a local level that not only affect health but significantly impair an already tenuous quality of life, such as toxic air emissions, chemicals that are discharged into waterways that residents may use for fishing and water supplies, dust that aggravates respiratory vulnerabilities, increased truck traffic through neighborhood streets, noise, odor, and perhaps increased vermin and rodents. Thus, residents in overburdened communities often view a new facility or a facility expansion as the proverbial straw that breaks the camel's back. Also consider that it is difficult for community-based groups to fully participate in state and national rulemaking proceedings where the standards that ultimately end up as permit conditions are first promulgated. Therefore, even if the facility operator remains in perfect compliance with the permit conditions, the community may still sustain unwanted impacts because of the inadequacy of the associated standards that support typical permit conditions, as illustrated in Chapter VI. But beyond this, permit proceedings also raise concerns about whether the facility operator will comply with the permit terms, raising as issues subsequent enforcement and potential contamination. Therefore, the permit is in a sense the gateway to environmental inequity caused by inadequacies that may exist in enforcement, cleanup and standard-setting.

More often than not, community groups are first made aware of matters when public notice requirements of permit proceedings are triggered. At that point, the community is placed in a reactive position, often attempting in some fashion to challenge the siting of the facility or attempting to make sure the permit terms are as protective as possible. This mission often pits community groups against the facility sponsor and permitting officials as well, at times unfairly causing community groups to be characterized as anti-development or "NIMBY" [Not In My BackYard].

This section explores both the legal authority under environmental statutes to impose additional permit conditions as well as the difficulties encountered in attempting to change the permitting status quo to better respond to environmental inequities. The focus is mainly on federal statutes and federal permitting decisions. But to set the context for these issues, we first examine a state case involving an air permit (which involves both federal and state law issues).

# B. A State Law Perspective

## NAACP—Flint Chapter v. Engler

Genessee (Michigan) County Circuit Court
(Transcript of Ruling, May 29, 1997)

*Hayman, Circuit Judge:*

[The case arose out of the Michigan Department of Environmental Quality's (DEQ's) decision to approve an application of the Genesee Power Station Unlimited Partnership for a permit to operate a wood waste incinerator in Genesee Township in 1992. The permit allowed the incinerator to emit lead in the amount of 2.2 tons per year, or 65 tons over its life-span, which had the potential to increase the concentration of lead in the soil by ten to fifteen percent. The incinerator was located immediately adjacent to a predominantly African American (and heavily polluted) neighborhood near Flint. After the permit was unsuccessfully appealed to EPA's Environmental Appeals Board, the incinerator began operation in 1995. Plaintiffs then filed suit in state court alleging violations of federal and state civil rights and environmental statutes.

The trial judge found that the cumulative impact of multiple sources emitting multiple pollutants imposed a significant burden on the area near the facility, that soil in the area contained levels of lead substantially above statewide background levels, and that at least 50 percent of the children in the northern sector of Genesee County exceeded the maximum level of lead exposure as defined by the health community.]

In analyzing this case the Court would first note that under Article IV, Section 51 of the Michigan Constitution, it provides: "The public health and general welfare of the people of the State are hereby declared to be matters of primary public concern. The Legislature shall pass suitable laws for protection and promotion of the public health."

Here the Constitution of Michigan has given the representatives of the people of Michigan the authority to pass laws for the protection and promotion of the public health and welfare.

Defendants contend that the Clean Air Act requires them to grant permits when zoning has been approved and the permit meets the [National Ambient Air Quality] NAAQ Standards [commonly referred to as NAAQS]. They argue that they have no authority to deny permits which meet the above stated standards.

This Court disagrees with Defendant's position on this issue. The Clean Air Act and its amendments to same recognize the states' ability to regulate emissions. The act encourages the enactment of uniform State and local laws relating to the prevention and control of air pollution on an interstate level. The act gives primary responsibility for implementation of these interstate standards to State governments, not to the Federal Government. The Federal domain in matters covered by the Clean Air Act has been held not to be exclusive or preemptive of State legislation....

Further, a state may impose pollution control requirements which are more strict than those specified by the Federal plan....

Under the facts of this case, the Court holds that the policies and regulations that are enforced by the State do not go far enough to carry out the duty the State has under Constitution to protect the health, safety and welfare of its citizens, regardless of their race.

There are some facts in this case that need noting at this point. First, the plant that is at issue in this case was sited in Mt. Morris Township, right at the northeast border of Flint. The relevance of this fact to the decision in this case is that the zoning decision for this plant was made by Mt. Morris Township's local governmental authorities. The significant impacts of pollution fallout will be felt in the City of Flint, by approximately 3,000 white residents to the southeast of the plant and by as many as 50,000 or more African-Americans to the south of the plant. The Plaintiffs are all residents of the City of Flint. Therefore, they had little, if any, standing or political influence to prohibit the zoning approval for the plant in Mt. Morris Township. The elected officials in Mt. Morris did not represent, nor were they elected by City of Flint residents.

Second, the communities in Flint that will be hit by the two tons per year of increased pollution during the estimated 35 years span of this plant already suffer from significant pollution in the environment. Many of the major polluting facilities are located on the north side of Flint and have been there for many years polluting the environment. The soil in this area of Genesee County has an extremely high lead content. The housing stock is old and many have lead based paint, a major source of lead pollution in the environment. The experts have testified that as many as 50 percent of the children in these communities have lead levels that exceed the national maximum exposure to lead. This causes significant problems for developing children.

Third, since the State has taken the position that they are only concerned with meeting the NAAQS, there was no Risk Assessment Study required to determine the impact of introducing this additional two tons of pollution into an environment that already is beyond being safe due to pollution sources.

This Court also finds that Defendant violated the Michigan Air Act by failing to perform a Risk Assessment Analysis in this case. The Michigan Clean Air Act states in Section B: "The Michigan Department of Environmental Quality [M.D.E.Q.] may deny or revoke a permit if installation of the source presents or may present an imminent and substantial endangerment to human health, safety, or welfare, or the environment."

Unless the M.D.E.Q. performs a Risk Assessment to determine the impact of the plant in the surrounding area, at least within a five-mile radius, it cannot conclude that the plant does not violate this provision and must therefore refuse to grant a permit....

Another problem that exists in this case is with the Defendant's failure to provide a meaningful avenue for cities and other governmental units, who are in the situation that Flint is in this case, to have a meaningful and knowledgeable opportunity to have it's [sic] concerns and those of its residents considered in the siting process involving plants that are located in another jurisdiction, but which pollute adjoining governmental units.

And I think that's a big problem in this case. The Department of Environmental Quality is saying, look, we have no authority to decide where the plants are going to be sited. That's a local issue. But in this particular case, you have a local governmental authority deciding to site a plant and it's polluting another community that has no authority to stop that local community from zoning that plant. And there has to be a procedure in place to give those communities an opportunity to be heard.

The State's position that zoning is a local issue is harmful to the health, safety and welfare of citizens who are situated like Flint who do not have a voice at zoning board meetings that are held outside of their communities. In these situations the State must have in place a procedure that gives adjoining communities a fair opportunity to be notified and heard concerning the siting of pollution facilities near their borders that pollute their communities.

There is little or no incentive for Mt. Morris Township to deny zoning to a facility that will pollute an adjoining community. Mt. Morris gets an increased tax base and the residents of the City of Flint will get pollution.

The Defendants have argued that the City of Flint will benefit from siting of this plant because it will provide employment opportunities to minorities in the area. The evidence presented in this case refutes that claim. The plant was constructed at a cost of at least eighty million dollars and there's no evidence that one minority was employed in its construction. There are 30 permanent jobs in this plant and out of this only one minority, at most, was hired to work there. The evidence shows that the minority hired was hired at minimum wage.

To sum up, the people who will benefit from the profits of the plant do not reside in the neighborhood. However, those who will bear the brunt of the pollution cannot even obtain employment in the plant.

Given that this Court has concluded that the State has violated its constitutional duty to protect the health, safety and welfare of its citizens by failing to enact policies that protect cities like Flint and its residents and gives them a fair opportunity to be heard in a meaningful way, this Court concludes that there is no remedy at law and therefore it is appropriate to exercise its equitable power and to grant an injunction against the Michigan Department of Environmental Quality preventing it from granting permits to major pollution sources—and I use the term major pollution sources—until a Risk Assessment is performed and those interested parties and governmental units that will be impacted based upon the Risk Assessment Study are notified and given an opportunity to be heard before the Michigan Department of Environmental Quality....

And it has to also give interested parties and governmental units that that study shows will be impacted by the pollution an opportunity to be heard and an opportunity, a meaningful opportunity, not just an opportunity to come in front of the Commission and air their voices, but something meaningful, before zoning is granted for major polluting facilities and permits are granted....

\* \* \*

## Notes and Questions

1. The trial judge found DEQ's actions inadequate because the agency failed to consider the cumulative risks of lead exposures from various sources facing community residents. He noted that the DEQ did not normally consider background risks in deciding whether to issue permits. Bear in mind how this holding might differ from the decisions of the Environmental Appeals Board discussed in detail below.

2. The trial court was troubled by the fact that the economic benefits of the plant flowed to persons who lived outside the neighborhood, while residents of the impacted area were unable to obtain jobs from the plant. What is the legal relevance of this finding? The court also found problematic the fact that the impacts of the projects would be felt largely by persons outside the permitting agency's jurisdiction, in the next town. If this is an inevitable consequence of the local nature of most permitting decisions, how should the permitting agency account for this complication? Are there mitigation requirements that it should consider, or should it deny the permit altogether if the impacts reach a particular magnitude?

3. Postscript: on appeal, the court of appeals in an unpublished decision, reversed, ruling that the trial judge had improperly granted relief based on claims that plaintiffs had not pleaded or raised at trial. *NAACP—Flint Chapter v. Engler*, No. 205264 (Mich. Ct. Appeals, Nov. 24, 1998).

# C. Statutory Sources of Authority to Address Environmental Justice

The excerpt below discusses the extent to which federal environmental statutes give agencies the discretion to address the type of cumulative environmental harms at issue in the *Engler* case above.

## Richard J. Lazarus & Stephanie Tai, Integrating Environmental Justice Into EPA Permitting Authority
### 26 Ecology Law Quarterly 617 (1999)

*Background: The Meaning of "Environmental Justice" in the EPA Permitting Context*

... In the context of an EPA permitting decision, the core expression of environmental justice is that EPA should take into account the racial and/or socioeconomic makeup of the community most likely to be affected adversely by the environmental risks of a proposed activity. This involves two steps: the identification of the environmental justice community and the incorporation of that community's concerns into the permitting process. Taking into account the makeup of the community does not mean that EPA must automatically deny a permit solely because the affected area is a community of color or low-income. The Agency's inquiry into these characteristics of the community is, however, necessary to allow the Agency to make an informed permitting decision regarding the actual environmental and health effects of a permit applicant's proposed activity....

Some of the environmental justice concerns that can be addressed through permit conditions are discussed below. They include the enhancement of a community's capacity to participate in environmental enforcement and compliance assurance, assessment of risk aggregation or cumulative risk, and identification of disproportionality in risk imposition. The relevance of each of these concerns to the permitting process is fairly clear. What is less clear to those officials responsible for issuing the permits is whether they have the necessary authority to consider such concerns and to take actions, including the imposition of permit conditions, based upon those concerns....

*Community Participation*

... [T]he permitting process could promote environmental justice if permitting authorities possessed the authority to impose upon permittees conditions providing affected communities with greater capacity to oversee and ensure permit compliance. An effective permit condition might seek to redress the resource deficiencies of environmental justice communities by making monitoring reports more readily available to the community. Or such conditions could reach further by giving the community access to the facility for inspection, funding a community oversight operation, or providing legal assistance to the community....

### Risk Aggregation

...As with community participation, cumulative effects could in theory be addressed through the permitting process in a variety of ways. In extreme circumstances, the permitting authority might have to deny the permit altogether. In other cases, the risks authorized by the permit might need to be reduced in light of the risks the community already faces. Finally, the permitting authority might create a host of permit conditions designed to guard against unacceptably high cumulative risk, including conducting studies and possibly imposing further permit restrictions based upon the results of such studies....

### Risk Disproportionality

A third distinct inquiry relates to the Agency's authority to consider disproportionality or equity concerns. This third aspect of environmental justice is related to the unacceptably high aggregation (or cumulative impact) issue, as aggregation is the fundamental cause of disproportionality. Furthermore, in many circumstances aggregation and disproportionality occur simultaneously; in such instances, accounting for aggregation may make it possible for the Agency to realize that one community is exposed to unacceptably high levels of risk while another community is not.

But for many, equity is a legitimate consideration, independent of whether aggregation of risk violates EPA's established environmental or human health norms for acceptable risk. They would like to see EPA deny or condition a permit based on whether the affected community would otherwise be subject to a disproportionate share of environmental risk. Thus, proof of disproportionality alone would be sufficient. There would be no additional need to establish that the level of risk was otherwise unacceptably high from either a health or environmental perspective. In short, disproportionality itself would be presumptively unreasonable or perhaps even *per se* unreasonable, absent mitigating permit conditions....

### Survey of Federal Statutory Provisions Authorizing Permit Conditions or Denials Based on Environmental Justice

The history of environmental law is replete with instances when broadly worded statutory language or regulations have been successfully enlisted in support of arguments that the federal government has authority or obligations beyond those initially contemplated by the regulated entities, environmentalists, affected communities, or even the government itself....

The [Clean Air] Act's nonattainment provisions provide [] potential environmental justice opportunities. Section 173 describes the requirements for a nonattainment permit. An explicit permit requirement in the Act mandates that [a permit cannot be granted unless] "an analysis of alternative sites, sizes, production processes, and environmental control techniques for such proposed source demonstrates that benefits of the proposed source significantly outweigh the environmental and social costs imposed as a result of its location, construction, or modification." The references to both "social costs" and "location" serve as strong bases for EPA's assertion of statutory authority to take environmental justice concerns into account in evaluating the "location" of a facility seeking a nonattainment permit....

In the context of permitting, the CAA provisions of greatest interest are those that may allow EPA (or a state permitting authority that has assumed permitting responsibility pursuant to CAA Section 502) greater discretion in using the permitting process to increase community participation and build community enforcement capacity. Section 504 would seem to confer on EPA just such authority. Subsection (a) provides that "[e]ach permit issued under this subchapter shall include...such other conditions as are necessary to assure compliance with applicable requirements of this chapter...." A major component for achieving compliance assurance under the CAA is the citizen suit provision of that statute.... Without that provision acting as a credible enforcement threat, there is no assurance of compliance. Therefore, Section 504(a) may authorize EPA to impose upon those receiving CAA permits the condition that they take certain steps to enhance the affected community's ability to ensure that the permitted facility complies with applicable environmental protection laws. Such conditions could range from simply providing more ready access to the information necessary to overseeing the permitted facility's operation and compliance to working to increase the resources of citizen groups participating in environmental oversight and compliance assurance.

To that same effect, Section 504(b) authorizes EPA to prescribe "procedures and methods for determining compliance," and Section 504(c) requires that each permit "set forth inspection, entry, monitoring, compliance certification, and reporting requirements to assure compliance with the permit terms and conditions." There is nothing on the face of the statute to preclude either Section 504(b)'s "procedures and methods" or Section 504(c)'s "requirements to assure compliance" from extending to permit conditions that enhance the community's own capacity to oversee the permitted facility's compliance.

Finally, Section 128 of the CAA may provide the Administrator with the authority to ensure that state permitting boards and pollution control enforcement authorities are sensitive to environmental justice concerns. Section 128 mandates that [State Implementation Plans] require that "any board or body which approves permits or enforcement orders under this chapter shall have at least a majority of members who represent the public interest." The "public interest" standard may allow the Administrator to require that persons concerned with environmental justice issues or representatives of environmental justice communities be included on state boards or bodies with permitting or enforcement authority....

Section 402 of the [Clean Water Act]...is likely the most significant potential source of permit conditioning authority [under that statute]. Section 402 provides that the Administrator may issue a permit for the discharge of any pollutant: "upon condition that such discharge will meet either (A) all applicable requirements under [various sections of the CWA], or (B) prior to the taking of necessary implementing actions relating to all such requirements, such conditions as the Administrator determines are necessary to carry out the provisions of this chapter." A broad construction of clause (B) could confer on the Administrator wide ranging authority to impose permit conditions promoting environmental justice....

With regard to permit conditions [under the Resource Conservation and Recovery Act], EPA may have substantial authority to consider environmental justice in deciding to grant, conditionally grant, or deny a permit by considering the possibility that a particular community is subject to disparate environmental risks. [See discussion of *In re Chemical Waste Management, Inc.*, in Lazarus & Tai excerpt below.]

[A]lthough the [Safe Drinking Water Act] permits a state with primary enforcement to grant variances from national primary drinking water regulations to public water systems, the statute further provides that any such variance "shall be conditioned on such monitoring and other requirements as the Administrator may prescribe." Here, too, the Administrator could strive to fashion conditions that reflect the noncompliance risks faced especially by many environmental justice communities....

* * *

## Notes and Questions

1. In late 2000, EPA's General Counsel issued a memo that similarly found significant authority under numerous statutory provisions for addressing environmental justice issues in the permitting process, including some not discussed by Lazarus and Tai. *See* Memorandum dated December 1, 2000 from Gary Guzy, General Counsel to the assistant administrators of various program offices within the EPA. One interesting additional source is the "public interest review" mandated under section 404 of the Clean Water Act before the Army Corps of Engineers can issue a permit to fill wetlands. The relevant regulations authorize the Corps to consider, among other things, aesthetics, general environmental concerns, safety, and the needs and welfare of the people. 33 CFR § 320.4(a). However, in the memo, the General Counsel cautioned that "[a]lthough the memorandum presents interpretations of EPA's statutory authority and regulations that we believe are legally permissible, it does not suggest that such actions would be uniformly practical or feasible given policy or resource considerations or that there are not important considerations of legal risk that would need to be evaluated." Why would the General Counsel specifically decline to endorse the use of legal authority as a matter of policy?

The OGC memo was not the first memorandum of this sort. An internal memo drafted by EPA's General Counsel in 1994 outlined authorities for incorporating environmental justice into a broad range of EPA activities other than permitting, including enforcement, standard-setting, cleanup actions, pesticide registration, authorization of state delegated programs, grants, procurement, and audits by EPA's Inspector General. This broader memo was never finalized, however, apparently because it was too politically controversial. *See* John Stanton, *Special Report, EPA 'Buried' 1994 Plans for Major Environmental Justice Roadmap.* INSIDE EPA, 1–2, 24 (March 3, 2000).

# D. The Environmental Appeals Board Decisions

Although it appears that broadly worded clauses in federal environmental statutes grant authority to condition or deny permits on environmental justice grounds, the willingness of permitting authorities to use these authorities—either at the local, state or EPA regional level—will be critically important in years to come. In order to prompt federal agencies to take more aggressive action to address environmental inequities, in 1994 then President Clinton issued Executive Order 12898, requiring federal agencies to "make achieving environmental justice part of [the agency's] mission by identifying and addressing, as appropriate, disproportionately high and adverse human health or environmental effects of its programs, policies and activities...." (See Chapter XV). Ideally, this message from the highest levels of the federal executive branch should prompt permitting authorities to further test the potential of existing sources of authority. However, if permitting officials decline to do so, the role of reviewing bodies becomes key to the longer-range goal of a protective permitting system. Administrative judges and courts will be increasingly called upon to support these efforts in two respects. The first is to recognize the authorities in omnibus clauses. Beyond that, however, reviewing bodies may prompt the development of substantive environmental justice criteria to be applied to permitting. As you read the following section, consider how the cases decided by the Environmental Appeals Board either support the permitting status quo or encourage the development of more protective permitting approaches. In this respect, also consider the additional views of the authors of the immediately preceding article.

## Richard J. Lazarus & Stephanie Tai, Integrating Environmental Justice Into EPA Permitting Authority
### 26 Ecology Law Quarterly 617 (1999)

The evolving perspective of the Environmental Appeals Board [EAB] on EPA's authority to base permits on environmental justice grounds can be seen in a series of decisions beginning in September 1993 and continuing to the present. Although the Executive Order on Environmental Justice expressly did not enlarge any agency's permitting power, the Order has had a marked effect on the Board's interpretation of the scope of authority available to permitting agencies. Prior to the Order, the Board rejected an environmental justice community's claim that environmental justice concerns should be considered in an air quality permitting process. The Board held instead that permitting agencies lacked environmental justice authority because they were limited to considering whether a facility would meet federal air quality requirements.

After the Order was issued, the Board seemed to accord increasingly more acceptance to the contention that permitting agencies were able to condition permits on environmental justice grounds. Although none of these decisions required agencies to interject environmental justice considerations into their permitting processes, the opinions focused less on whether complainants were able to claim that agencies failed to consider environmental justice concerns and more on whether those agencies adequately considered environmental justice concerns. The net effect of the Order may have been to draw attention to existing areas of authority that the Board had previously overlooked so that agencies had the means to actually comply with the Order....

*Increasing Willingness to Find Discretionary Authority*

...The shift [in the Board's] willingness to find authority is evident in the opinions of three substantial Board decisions....

In [the 1995 decision of] *In re Chemical Waste Management, Inc.*, local citizens challenged on environmental justice grounds EPA Region V's decision to grant a permit to a landfill pursuant to RCRA Section 3005. The Region held an informational meeting with concerned citizens and industry representatives to discuss, among other items, environmental justice issues. The Region also prepared a demographic study based on a one-mile radius around the facility.

The citizens' challenge included several arguments based explicitly on environmental justice concerns. The citizens claimed that the Region had acted in a clearly erroneous fashion and had abused its discretion in seeking to implement Executive Order 12,898 in the absence of the Agency's promulgation of a national environmental justice strategy. They also contended that the demographic study was clearly erroneous because of its restricted one-mile radius scope and because the Region had ignored evidence regarding the impacts of the permitted facility and the racial and socioeconomic composition of the affected area.

The Board rejected both contentions. It concluded that Executive Order 12,898 "does not purport to, and does not have the effect of, changing the substantive requirements for issuance of a permit under RCRA and its implementing regulations." The Board further concluded that "if a permit applicant meets the requirements of RCRA and its implementing regulations, the Agency must issue the permit, regardless of the racial or socio-economic composition of the surrounding community and regardless of the economic effect of the facility on the surrounding community." ...

The more significant part of the opinion, however, is that portion in which the Board goes beyond procedural requirements to consider the possible substantive significance to environmental justice under the omnibus clause in RCRA Section 3005(c)(3): "[e]ach permit issued under this section shall contain such terms and conditions as the Administrator (or the State) determines necessary to protect human health and the environment." The Board agreed that this clause requires the Agency to condition, and if necessary, to deny a permit "if the operation of a facility would have an adverse impact on the health or environment of the surrounding community" as necessary to prevent such impacts. The Board concluded that EPA had the authority under RCRA to take "a more refined look at its health and environmental impacts assessment" in response to environmental justice claims. The Board specifically acknowledged that an assessment looking only at "a broad analysis might mask the effects of the facility on a disparately affected minority or low-income segment of the community." Accordingly, the Board held that: "when a commenter submits at least a superficially plausible claim that operation of the facility will have a disproportionate impact on a minority or low-income segment of the affected community, the Region should, as a matter of policy, exercise its discretion under Section 3005(c)(3) to include within its health and environmental impacts assessment an analysis focusing particularly on the minority or low-income community whose health or environment is alleged to be threatened by the facility."

Finally, the Board stressed that the omnibus clause in Section 3005(c)(3) could not be used as a statutory basis for injecting into the analysis factors other than "ensuring the protection of the health or environment or low-income populations. The Region would not have discretion to redress impacts unrelated or only tenuously related to human health and the environment, such as disproportionate impacts on the economic well-being of a minority or low-income community."

Notwithstanding the stark terms of the Board's threshold suggestion that "the racial or socio-economic composition of the surrounding community" is irrelevant to the permitting authority under RCRA, the Board's opinion leaves substantial room for EPA to exercise its authority to promote environmental justice when exercising its permitting authority under RCRA. The opinion allows the Agency to engage in the kind of risk aggregation analysis upon which environmental justice claims are frequently grounded.

This includes a closer examination of both the cumulative impacts of various risk producing facilities affecting an environmental justice community as well as the possibility that certain subpopulations may be differentially susceptible to harm from environmental pollutants. The Board also suggested a potentially low threshold trigger for the preparation of such analysis: "a superficially plausible claim [of]...disproportionate impact on a minority or low-income segment of the affected community."...

In [the 1995 decision of] *In re Puerto Rico Electric Power Authority*, a citizen group in Puerto Rico sought review of EPA Region II's issuance of a PSD permit to the Puerto Rico Electric Power Authority (PREPA). The group claimed, among other things, that PREPA and Puerto Rico should have prepared an epidemiological study of the area surrounding the proposed facility and that their failure to do so violated Executive Order 12,898 and the United States Constitution. The Board rejected the claim, relying on Region II's explanation that it had fully responded to environmental justice issues raised during the comment period, including the preparation of a demographic analysis of the affected area. The Region concluded that the facility "would cause no disproportionate adverse health impacts to lower-income populations." Finally, the Board likewise rejected the citizen group's contentions that the Region had relied on flawed meteorological data and had failed to consider adequately PREPA's "history of violations."

The precedential significance of this decision is fairly limited because the citizen group's petition for review appears to have been too cursory to be persuasive. The matter is nonetheless significant because it underscores both the limited resources available to most community-based environmental justice organizations and the importance of EPA's adoption of a more proactive view of its affirmative ability to promote environmental justice in the permitting context. It is no great surprise that when, as in this case, an EPA region declines to actively pursue the environmental justice concerns of an affected community, the Board will almost always affirm that ruling. Unless the local community group has managed to obtain substantial legal expertise and resources, the group is unlikely to be able to articulate their concerns in a manner likely to prompt the Appeals Board to second-guess the Region. As the Board emphasized, it will not grant a petition for review "unless the decision is based on either a clearly erroneous finding of fact or conclusion of law, or involves an important matter of policy or exercise of discretion that warrants review."...

In [the 1996 decision of] *In re Envotech, L.P.*, local residents and nearby municipalities challenged EPA Region V's decision to grant two underground injection control (UIC) permits under the Safe Drinking Water Act [SDWA]. The permits authorized Envotech to drill, construct, test, and operate two hazardous waste injection wells in Washtenaw County, Michigan. The local opposition raised many objections, including Envotech's poor history of environmental compliance, the unsafe and unproven nature of underground injection, the absence of necessary state and local governmental approvals, flawed geological assessments, errors in characterizations of the hazardous wastes to be received by the facility, and failure to provide required waste minimization certification. The residents also raised distinct environmental justice claims alleging that the permits should be denied because the area already hosted many undesirable land uses.

The Board rejected all of the claims raised by the local groups except for the claim that a waste minimization certification was required....

The Board, however, used the matter as another opportunity to state its views on the significance of environmental justice in the permitting context. Citing its earlier ruling in *Chemical Waste Management*, the Board stated that, as with RCRA permitting under

Section 3005, "if a UIC permit applicant meets the requirements of the SDWA and UIC regulations, the 'Agency must issue the permit, regardless of the racial or socio-economic composition of the surrounding community and regardless of the economic effect of the facility on the surrounding community.'" But, as in *Chemical Waste Management*, the Board went on to identify "two areas in the UIC permitting scheme in which the Region has the necessary discretion to implement the mandates of the Executive Order."

The "two areas" described by the Board as existing within the Safe Drinking Water Act UIC program are virtually the same as those described by the Board in *Chemical Waste Management* as existing within RCRA. The first area is the right to public participation, allowing the Region to "exercise its discretion to assure early and ongoing opportunities for public involvement in the permitting process." The second area is the discretionary authority the Board derived from the "regulatory 'omnibus authority' contained in 40 C.F.R. § 144.52(a)(9)," which authorizes "permit conditions 'necessary to prevent the migration of fluids into underground sources of drinking water.'" The Board reasoned that "there is nothing in the omnibus authority that prevents a Region from performing a disparate impact analysis when there is an allegation that the drinking water of minority or low-income communities may be particularly threatened by a proposed underground injection well." Finally, the Board concluded that in order to implement Executive Order 12,898, the Region should exercise its discretionary authority to undertake such an analysis "when a commenter submits at least a superficially plausible claim that a proposed underground injection well will disproportionately impact the drinking water of a minority or low-income segment of the community in which the well is located." This creates a low threshold to initiate a disparate impact analysis and shifts the burden to the Region to respond by examining the environmental justice concerns raised by the proposed injection well....

The Appeals Board's ruling is favorable to environmental justice advocates to the extent that it demonstrates the Board's willingness to find that the Agency can ground discretionary authority to promote environmental justice in the Agency's regulations. Therefore, presumably the Board does not need to rely on statutory language in the first instance. In *Chemical Waste Management*, the omnibus authority was contained in statutory language. Second, the omnibus language upon which the Board relied on in *Envotech* was less obviously expansive than that construed in *Chemical Waste Management*. The Board's willingness to find such broad-based authority in the regulatory language "necessary to prevent migration of fluids" increases the possibility that similar omnibus authority can be found in other environmental statutes and regulations. As the Board explained in a footnote, the Board had already indicated that "necessary" could "arguably extend to imposition of more-stringent financial responsibility requirements than are generally prescribed for UIC permittees." If so, "necessary" might likewise extend to more stringent monitoring and reporting requirements, or even enhancement of community enforcement capacity, for those facilities located where there is reason to believe that absent such a condition, oversight necessary for compliance assurance will be lacking....

A clear pattern emerges from the past ten years of Appeals Board rulings. The Board is no longer reflexively skeptical of the merits of environmental justice claims and has begun to consider the claims more carefully. Now, when the Board rejects environmental justice claims, it centers its rejections less on deference to regional office discretion and more on factual challenges within the scope of the environmental justice determinations already made by the regional office permitting authorities. When it has determined that available facts are inadequate, the Board has remanded the issue for further documentation and public comment. In all of these decisions, the Board recognized regional office authority to rely on informal environmental justice guidelines. Therefore, expected challenges to citizen groups wanting to appeal permitting decisions on environmental justice grounds will revolve more around rallying the necessary expertise to identify factual areas of contention within regional office environmental justice determinations. Such a challenge will likely prove difficult because courts have long given deference to agencies' technical determinations. The expected challenge to EPA will be to develop guidelines in which these environmental justice concerns can be adequately addressed and in which reasoned individualized determinations exist to provide factual responses to reply to any environmental justice disputes that may arise....

* * *

## Notes and Questions

1. Note on Clean Air Act Permitting. Air emissions from industrial facilities are problematic for environmental justice communities, particularly in combination with air pollution from motor vehicles, construction and other land use practices. By its very nature, air pollution cannot be contained on site. Under the federal Clean Air Act, when a major source of air pollution is undergoing a modification which will result in a significant net increase in air emissions, or is being newly built, it must first obtain a preconstruction permit. A "modification" entails a change in operations and usually the addition of equipment that increases the facility's capacity to produce, and correspondingly, its potential to emit additional air pollutants. The process of obtaining this preconstruction permit is termed "new source review." Thereafter, periodically (usually every five years), the facility must obtain renewal of an "operating" permit. As will become apparent, however, the preconstruction permit proceeding phase is a critically important point of intervention for environmental justice communities, either to challenge the siting altogether or to make sure that sufficient mitigation measures are taken at the design and construction phase, measures that will be in place for the life of the facility.

As discussed in Chapter VI, air sheds are classified as "attainment" or "nonattainment," depending upon whether they meet the NAAQS for several criteria pollutants. This classification is critical for purposes of preconstruction permitting. If the major source is located or being sited in a nonattainment area, the new source review (NSR) requirements are far more stringent. Generally, the source must control its air emissions using the "lowest achievable emissions reduction" (LAER) possible, often the most advanced and very expensive technology. Further, the source must obtain emission "offsets," which are proven reductions in air emissions from other sources within the air shed in order to compensate for the new emissions it will introduce into the air shed. To obtain these offsets, the source can curtail emissions in other facilities it owns, purchase surplus reductions from other firms who are able to control their emissions beyond requirements, or obtain offsets from an "emissions bank" if the jurisdiction has in fact established one. These are the two requirements of most concern to facility sponsors. There are additional statutory requirements that appear to be enforced to a lesser degree, but that may be potentially beneficial to environmental justice communities. These are requirements that (a) the facility sponsor certify that any other major sources it owns in the state are in compliance; (b) the state implementation plan (a plan that each state must submit to the EPA that demonstrates how it is achieving or maintaining the NAAQS) is being adequately implemented; and (c) a requirement that the applicant has conducted an analysis of alternative sites, sizes, production processes and environmental control techniques that demonstrates that the facility's benefits outweigh the environmental and social costs it imposes. The potential of this latter "social cost" criterion is discussed in greater depth in a note below. Because nonattainment NSR is stringent, *existing* sources often try to avoid application of NSR by reducing enough emissions elsewhere within the facility so that overall facility emissions after the modified processes do not result in a "significant" increase. This is called "netting out" of new source review. For an elaboration of nonattainment NSR requirements, *see, e.g.,* Eileen Gauna, *Major Sources of Criteria Pollutants in Nonattainment Areas: Balancing the Goals of Clean Air, Environmental Justice, and Industrial Development,* 3 HASTINGS W.-N.W. J. ENVTL. L. & POL'Y 379 (1996); *see also* STEVEN FERRY, ENVIRONMENTAL LAW: EXAMPLES AND EXPLANATIONS, 168–169 (2d 2001).

If the major source is located in an area that is in attainment with the NAAQS, it must undergo a different type of preconstruction new source review. In these areas, the goal is not to achieve healthy air, but to prevent healthy air from becoming unhealthy. Therefore, these areas are subject to a regulatory program called "prevention of significant deterioration," or PSD, and the major source preconstruction permitting program is often called "PSD review" (as opposed to nonattainment NSR). Under this program, the new or modified major source must demonstrate that its emissions are within an established increment that is determined to be protective of the air resource. In other words, the new or additional emissions from the source have to be below an amount that will keep the air shed from experiencing a significant deterioration in air quality from current levels. There is a lesser amount of "degradation" allowed if the area is near a national park or national scenic area, particularly for pollutants that impair visibility. The new or modified source must also use pollution control that is the "best available control technology" (BACT) which is often less stringent than LAER but is nonetheless expensive. As discussed below, requirements for determining the appropriate BACT may provide additional authority to consider environmental justice. For further elaboration of the PSD program, *see* Craig N. Oren, *Prevention of Significant Deterioration: Control Compelling Versus Site-Shifting,* 74 Iowa L. Rev. 1 (1988); *see also* FERRY, *supra,* at 170–172.

2. When broadly worded omnibus clauses—the statutory clauses that provide general authority for agencies to take environmentally protective measures[1]—are used to support an environmental justice claim, permitting authorities have tended to be fairly conservative in abiding by constraints plausibly inherent in the language of the clause. Accordingly, what remains unclear from the EAB decisions is the outer bounds of regulatory discretion to condition or deny a permit based upon environmental justice considerations. The cases to date generally involve challenges by environmental justice advocates who claim that the permitting agency did not exercise its discretion in a sufficiently protective manner, instead of permit applicants claiming that the permit conditions were too onerous. In all instances, the Regions ultimately concluded that there was no disproportionate adverse impact on the basis of race or income, either due to the results of a demographic analysis or an impact analysis, although in two cases additional conditions appear to have been placed on the permit in response to concerns of the affected communities. The methodology the Regional officials used in the environmental justice analysis appear to follow a basic approach that uses (1) 1990 census data to determine demographics (mean income or ethnic minority), and (2) a one or two

---

1. An example of such an omnibus clause is RCRA's provision that each permit shall contain "such terms and conditions" that EPA "determines necessary to protect human health and the environment."

mile radius to determine the area of maximum impact. The methodology for identifying a potential environmental justice community and determining disparity is particularly difficult and vulnerable to complicating factors, and is continually changing and evolving. What is the role of an administrative law judge or court in reviewing this critical threshold question?

3. A note on Air Permitting in Nonattainment Regions. The statutory provisions under the Clean Air Act for permitting major sources of criteria pollutants in nonattainment areas have omnibus authority that is particularly broad. This authority has yet to be explored for its potential to address environmental justice. The nonattainment New Source Review (NSR) provisions are set forth generally at §§ 172 (c)(5) and 173. As noted by Lazarus and Tai, these statutory provisions specifically require a showing that "an analysis of alternative sites, sizes, production processes, and environmental control techniques for such proposed source demonstrates that benefits of the proposed source significantly outweigh the environmental and social costs imposed as a result of its location, construction, or modification." § 173 (a)(5). The reference to alternative sites and production process give agencies the authority to condition or deny permits altogether if the chosen site is inappropriate. The reference to social costs could support consideration of a broad range of contemporary issues, bringing into permit proceedings diverse problems such as species loss, natural resource depletion and abandoned brownfields, at least to the extent these considerations bear upon the location and design of the facility. Adverse impacts that fall disproportionately upon the poor and communities of color is also an unacceptable social cost in a society committed to environmental protection for all and thus falls within the wording and spirit of the omnibus authority.

In two EAB cases, the alternative and social cost criteria of the nonattainment provisions was not explicitly tied to an environmental justice challenge, although one case involved a Native American tribe and the other involved a low income people of color community. In *In Re Campo Landfill Project, Campo Band Indian Reservation*, 6 E.A.D. 505 (June 19, 1996, NSR Appeal 95-1), the petitioner claimed that an alternative site should have been chosen because the site of a proposed landfill was situated over a sole-source aquifer of a Native American reservation. The EAB noted that there were appropriate control measures to reduce the risk to insignificant levels, and that because part of the reason for the project was to develop and diversify the economic base of the tribe, use of nontribal land was not a viable alternative. In *In the Matter of Operating Permit Formaldehyde Plant Borden Chemical, Inc.* (December 22, 2000, Petition No. 6-01-1, Permit No. 2631-VO), the petitioner contended that the alternatives/social cost analysis was insufficient because the environmental impacts outweighed the "social and economic benefit" of the facility, not because of any disparate impacts on the community. The Administrator reasoned that the process and control equipment met and at times exceeded applicable requirements and impacts were minimized or avoided as much as possible. As in the *Campo* decision, the Administrator used the socioeconomic profile of the community to support the site, noting that the area was a designated enterprise zone and construction and operation would increase employment and tax revenue. Although speculative at this point, the analysis might have differed if the petitioner had argued that a disparate adverse impact (assuming one existed) was itself a social cost to be weighed against the granting of a permit. What are the pros and cons of incorporating a disparate impact analysis into a nonattainment NSR proceeding via the social cost criterion? For a discussion of how complicated measuring a disparate impact can become, see Chapter XIV.

4. Six of the EAB appeals involved PSD permitting. The PSD statutory provisions for permitting do not have a counterpart to the references to "alternatives" and "social cost"

in nonattainment area requirements. However, there are other statutory grants of omnibus authority that are likely to support an environmental justice analysis. For example, a BACT analysis requires a case by case determination that takes into account "energy, environmental and economic impacts and other costs." § 169 (3). The reference to "other costs" may be read broadly to account for the social costs of risk and undesirable impact distributed disproportionately by race, ethnicity or income. In addition, one of the purposes of Part C is to assure that "any decision to permit increased air pollution [in an attainment or unclassifiable region] is made only after careful evaluation of all the consequences of such a decision and after adequate procedural opportunities for informed public participation in the decisionmaking process." § 160 (5). The reference to "careful evaluation of all the consequences" should include causing or exacerbating environmental inequities.

The PSD cases brought before the EAB, however, do not specifically rest their challenges upon the sources of authority described above, but instead upon the permitting official's general scope of discretion. In addition, these cases illustrate an interesting progression in the EAB's approach to environmental justice issues, from initial skepticism of environmental justice claims to a requirement of an administrative record sufficient for the EAB to evaluate the permitting official's responses to the environmental justice claims (as discussed more generally by Lazarus and Tai above). In the case below, consider how closely the EAB reviewed the administrative record and whether the degree of deference it granted the permitting agency was appropriate.

This case is particularly technical, and may be difficult to follow, but as you read and consider it, think about how this level of technicality may affect the ability of a community group to participate in the permitting process.

# In Re: AES Puerto Rico, L.P.
## 1999 EPA App. LEXIS 17

*Ronald L. McCallum, Edward E. Reich, and Kathie A. Stein, Environmental Appeals Judges:*

### Background

The proposed AES facility [AES Puerto Rico, L.P.] would be the first coal-fired power plant in Puerto Rico. The facility is designed with two circulating fluidized bed ("CFB") boilers with a combined maximum heat input rate of 4,922.7 million British Thermal Units per hour ("MMBTU/hr"). The plant will produce both electricity to be sold to Puerto Rico's electric utility and steam to be used by local industries. The proposed facility is subject to PSD [Prevention of Significant Deterioration] review because it is a major new stationary source of pollutants including nitrogen oxides ("$NO_x$"), $SO_2$, carbon monoxide ("CO"), and fine particulate matter ("$PM_{10}$")....

PSD review is a preconstruction permitting program for major stationary sources located in areas where ambient air quality meets or exceeds national ambient air quality standards ("NAAQS")....Puerto Rico is considered to be in attainment for $SO_2$... [t]herefore, a PSD permit is required before a facility such as the proposed AES facility may be constructed. Two of the most critical elements of the PSD permit process are: 1) the requirement that emissions of certain pollutants be controlled by "best available control technology" ("BACT") and 2) that an air quality analysis be conducted to determine whether a proposed project would cause or contribute to exceedances of NAAQS or PSD increments.... The PSD permit issued to AES by the Region contains BACT limits on $SO_2$ emissions by requiring a combination of three control strategies: 1) CFB boilers with limestone injection, 2) low sulfur coal (maximum sulfur content of 1.0%), and 3) an add-on dry scrubber....

The petitioners' primary focus is on the air quality analyses conducted during the permitting process for $SO_2$....

The third item at issue in this case is an environmental justice challenge contained in SURCCo's petition claiming that Region II's permit decision for this facility does not meet the standards of the Executive Order on environmental justice. The proposed facility is to be located in an industrial area of Guayama, a city on the south coast of Puerto Rico. According to the petitioners, Guayama is a low-income community and home to several pharmaceutical and petrochemical plants....

*Standard of Review*

The Board is guided by language in the preamble to section 124.19 [40 C.F.R. § 124.19, a section in the Code of Federal Regulations authorizing review by the Environmental Appeals Board] that states the "power of review should be only sparingly exercised," and "most permit conditions should be finally determined at the Regional level." The petitioners bear the burden of establishing that review is warranted....

*Issues Pertaining to Sulfur Dioxides ($SO_2$) Emissions and Air Quality Analysis*

The petitions for review are largely focused on the potential impacts of $SO_2$ emissions from the proposed AES facility. The PSD regulations require that an air quality analysis be performed for each regulated pollutant that a new source has the potential to emit in significant amounts. The significance level for $SO_2$ is 40 tons/year. The AES facility has a potential to emit 453 tons/year of $SO_2$. Thus, AES prepared an $SO_2$ air quality analysis....

An air quality analysis generally proceeds in stages. EPA has issued a guidance document that outlines various elements of the PSD review process, including the air quality analysis. The air quality analysis typically begins with a preliminary analysis that uses modeling to predict air quality impacts based solely on the proposed facility's emissions. The preliminary analysis does not take into account existing ambient air quality or emissions from other sources. The results are used to determine whether additional analyses are necessary and to define the scope of any additional analyses. The results of the preliminary analysis are compared to a set of values often referred to as "monitoring de minimis levels" because they are used to determine whether a permit applicant may be exempted from the requirement to obtain preconstruction ambient air monitoring data. The PSD regulations contain a list of the monitoring de minimis levels and provide that a permit applicant may be exempted from preconstruction monitoring requirements if air quality impacts from the proposed source are less than the de minimis levels.... AES qualifies for the exemption from preconstruction ambient air monitoring for $SO_2$. AES requested such an exemption from Region II and the Region determined that an exemption was appropriate....

As can be seen from the table [Table I], the modeled $SO_2$ impacts from the proposed AES facility are all less than corresponding SILs.[significant impact levels]. Thus, the Region did not require, and AES did not conduct, a full impact analysis for the proposed facility.

| Table 1 SO$_2$ Air Quality Impacts from AES | | |
|---|---|---|
| **Averaging Time** | **AES Modeling Results (in [micrograms]µg/m3)** | **Significant Impact Level (in [micrograms]µg/m3)** |
| Annual | 0.55 | 1 |
| 24-hour | 4.97 | 5 |
| 3-hour | 20.0 | 25 |

Petitioners do not dispute that PSD regulations and guidance authorize the Region's decisions to exempt AES from preconstruction monitoring and to accept the preliminary air quality analysis in lieu of a full impact analysis. However, the petitioners argue that the Region should have used its discretion to require preconstruction monitoring and a full impact analysis in light of a variety of factors that, in petitioners' opinion, warrant these studies....

In the course of assessing options for control of SO$_2$ from the boilers, the Region determined that a combination of three controls would constitute the best available control technology ("BACT") for this facility.... The resulting emission limit... was used to determine SO$_2$ impacts from the proposed facility for purposes of the preliminary air quality analysis. Petitioners do not believe that it is appropriate to presume that AES's emissions will meet the emission limit specified in the permit in light of the fact that the three required SO$_2$ controls have not previously been used in combination....

The Region claims that the emission limit... is technically feasible even if it is lower than the emission limits at previously permitted facilities....

The petitioners contend that the only reason AES proposed this combination of SO$_2$ controls was to avoid the obligation to prepare a full impact air quality analysis. The controls reduce the maximum permitted SO$_2$ emissions from the proposed facility to the point where SO$_2$ impacts attributable to the facility are at levels below the SILs....

We do not disagree with the Region's assessment on this issue. This permit requires a level of SO$_2$ control that appears to be unprecedented for this type of facility. Consequently, the Region's decision breaks new ground on potentially available control options for similar facilities and may be replicated, yielding beneficial decreases in SO$_2$ emissions at other facilities. In this respect, the BACT determination is to be commended. In addition, the emission limit is an enforceable standard....

The Gonzalez petition raises several technical challenges to the SO$_2$ modeling conducted by AES....

In his petition for review, Dr. Gonzalez states that he performed a "sensitivity analysis" on the [the air quality model] used by AES. Dr. Gonzalez challenges the [model's] results because the model inputs used an SO$_2$ emission rate equal to the rate specified by the permitted emission limit. Dr. Gonzalez calculated potential SO$_2$ impacts for emission rates higher than the permitted rate. He notes that "when the SO$_2$ base emission rate... is exceeded, significant levels [SILs] are exceeded." The SO$_2$ emission rate is dependent upon the sulfur content of the coal and the efficiency of the sulfur removal technology. Dr. Gonzalez believes that it is unlikely that AES will be able to effectively control these two factors and therefore concludes that AES's SO$_2$ emissions will have a significant impact on the surrounding area.

The scenarios modeled by Dr. Gonzalez presume that AES will not operate within the established permit limits. As such, this argument is similar to the issue addressed… regarding the achievability of the BACT limit for $SO_2$. While Dr. Gonzalez may be correct that AES does not have much room for error in controlling the sulfur content of the coal and the operation of the sulfur removal equipment, the $SO_2$ permit limit requires AES to avoid errors that would result in a permit violation. If AES operates the facility in accordance with the permit requirements, the $SO_2$ impacts are predicted to be less than the $SO_2$ SILs. Because AES is expected and required to operate the facility in such a fashion, it is appropriate to rely upon modeling results that presume compliance.…

Petitioners argue that the Region should have used its discretion to require AES to conduct a multi-source air quality analysis, i.e., a full impact analysis, for $SO_2$ [an analysis that also considers the emissions from other stationary sources in the surrounding vicinity]. Petitioners point out that AES's modeling results indicate $SO_2$ impacts that are "minutely below" the SILs. They are particularly concerned about the predicted 24-hour $SO_2$ impacts, estimated at 4.97 [micrograms] µg/m3. The 24-hour SIL for $SO_2$ is 5.0 [micrograms] µg/m3.

The SILs are a tool used by EPA to screen emissions for projects such as the proposed AES facility. Instead of requiring every PSD applicant to perform costly and time-consuming full impact air quality analyses, the SILs allow EPA to readily identify those projects whose air quality impacts will be less than significant. In this case, the modeled $SO_2$ impacts from the proposed AES facility are less than significant, using the SILs as the basis for that determination. If predicted air quality impacts are less than significant, EPA guidance allows a permit applicant to forego the full impact air quality analysis, including multi-source modeling.

We acknowledge petitioners' concern that the predicted 24-hour $SO_2$ impact from the proposed facility is very close to the corresponding SIL. It may seem that a difference of only 0.03 [micrograms] µg/m3 between AES's predicted impact and the SIL is an insufficient basis upon which to decide that AES need not conduct multi-source modeling. Notably, the PSD regulations do not specifically mandate multi-source modeling. Rather, the regulations contain a general requirement that permit applicants demonstrate that a proposed source will not cause or contribute to a violation of the NAAQS or a PSD increment. The "requirement" for multi-source modeling comes from EPA guidance, and a permitting authority may insist on such modeling as a matter of discretion. In exercising that discretion, it is reasonable for the permitting authority to be guided by generally applicable thresholds in determining how detailed an air quality analysis needs to be. In this case, the Region's decision to abide by the SIL threshold is also supported by the quality of the modeling that produced the 4.97 [micrograms] µg/m3 estimate.…

In addition to concerns about the accuracy of the $SO_2$ modeling for the proposed facility, petitioners raise questions about the $SO_2$ attainment status of Guayama. Petitioners believe that their concerns and a general dearth of data about current ambient air quality in Guayama should have caused the Region to require preconstruction monitoring from AES. Petitioners acknowledge that AES's predicted $SO_2$ impacts are below the de minimis monitoring levels but believe that the Region should have used its discretion to nonetheless require preconstruction monitoring.

The Region points out that a 1983 study of Puerto Rico air quality, performed in conjunction with Puerto Rico's State Implementation Plan ("SIP"), determined that Guayama was in attainment of the $SO_2$ NAAQS. The Region believes that the 1983 attainment demonstration is still valid for Guayama because there has been no major source construction in Guayama since that date. The Region further states that there are "no data to suggest that there is an existing exceedance of any of the NAAQS." During this permit process, the Region obtained an estimate of $SO_2$ concentrations in ambient air by examining data from a monitoring facility at Cerro Modesto, located approximately seventeen kilometers from the proposed site. The Cerro Modesto data showed $SO_2$ concentrations well below the NAAQS. Although the Region concedes that conditions at Cerro Modesto may not be identical to Guayama, it believes that the data are useful for estimating background conditions. Thus, the Region has offered several rationales for concluding that Guayama's $SO_2$ attainment status is valid. However, in the interest of verifying ambient air conditions in Guayama, the Region has required AES, as a condition of its permit, to perform ambient air monitoring for $SO_2$ after the facility commences operations.

Petitioners are skeptical of the Region's position regarding ambient $SO_2$ levels in Guayama. They believe that a variety of other factors militate in favor of requiring preconstruction monitoring. Petitioners first point out that the 1983 SIP attainment demonstration was based on modeling, not actual ambient air quality data, and that little ambient air quality data have been collected in the interim. Petitioners also counter the Region's assertion that no data suggest an existing exceedance of the NAAQS. Petitioners offer the results of $SO_2$ modeling performed by the Puerto Rico Environmental Quality Board ("PREQB") in 1990. According to [petitioner] SURCCo, the PREQB modeling predicts $SO_2$ concentrations in the Guayama area that exceed the NAAQS. Third, petitioners question the representativeness of the Cerro Modesto data. Finally, petitioners claim that existing sources already emit large quantities of $SO_2$ and that certain sources may be violating the terms of their permits, thus compounding problems with $SO_2$ air quality....

Legally, the $SO_2$ attainment designation for Puerto Rico is still in effect, even if the underlying study in support of that designation dates from 1983. That designation may not be challenged in this proceeding. Because Guayama is officially an $SO_2$ attainment area, the PSD regulations govern the preconstruction permitting process. Thus, the PSD regulation providing for an exemption to preconstruction monitoring may be validly applied in this case. The Region has established that such an exemption was justified in this case because the predicted $SO_2$ impacts from the proposed facility are lower than the de minimis monitoring levels. Moreover, a showing that the predicted impacts are also below the SILs generally constitutes an acceptable demonstration of compliance with the NAAQS. If a proposed facility has modeled impacts that are below the SILs, that facility is not considered to cause or contribute to a violation of an air quality standard. The Agency has made a judgment that, as a general matter, proposed facilities with insignificant air quality impacts (i.e., impacts below the SILs) do not cause or contribute to air quality violations. Thus, even if SURCCo's information conclusively supported a finding that there are current NAAQS violations in Guayama, the AES facility as proposed would not be considered a cause of or contributor to such violations. AES could still therefore obtain a PSD permit.

### Environmental Justice

Petitioners' final basis for Appeal of the Region's PSD permit decision for AES invokes President Clinton's Executive Order on environmental justice. Petitioners' environmental justice arguments rest in large part on their technical arguments, but with a slightly different emphasis. Petitioners state that the proposed location for the AES facility is a low-income community and therefore the Region should have taken additional safeguards to protect this community on the basis of environmental justice. Petitioners believe that the Region should not have strictly adhered to its "significant impact" levels, should have required additional air monitoring and modeling prior to permit issuance, and should not have relied on the 1983 attainment demonstration. In addition, petitioners claim that the Region did not consider public comment and testimony regarding health problems in the Guayama area. They also suggest that the Region could have done more to enhance public participation and comment....

The Region's environmental justice analysis begins by analyzing income levels in the areas of maximum potential impact from AES emissions. The Region concluded that these areas are low-income and therefore proceeded to assess whether the proposed AES project would result in a disproportionately high and adverse effect on human health or the environment in these areas. The Region prepared a thorough assessment of the potential impacts of air emissions from the proposed AES facility. The Region looked at maximum short and long-term impacts of carbon monoxide, sulfur dioxide, nitrogen dioxide, and fine particulate matter. Not only were all maximum predicted concentrations of these pollutants below the corresponding NAAQS, the maximum predicted concentrations of carbon monoxide, sulfur dioxide, and nitrogen dioxide were all below the SILs as well. The Region pointed out that NAAQS are health based standards, designed to protect public health with an adequate margin of safety, including sensitive populations such as children, the elderly, and asthmatics.

In support of environmental justice for this community, the Region took steps to require that many elements of the air quality analyses performed during the permit process be reconfirmed after the permit is issued. As conditions of the permit, AES is required to conduct ambient $SO_2$ monitoring and to perform a multi-source air quality analysis for $SO_2$. These permit conditions are a testament to the role of public participation in the permit process. Because of the concerns raised during the public comment period, this permit contains additional conditions that are not mandated by the PSD regulations but are within the Region's discretion to require. The Region incorporated the conditions into the permit as a tangible response to the community's concerns about air quality and to fulfill the goals of the Executive Order.

The Region also addressed information submitted during the public comment period regarding adverse health impacts and studies of health impacts that were previously conducted in the community. The Region further analyzed the distribution of Toxic Release Inventory ("TRI") facilities on the island of Puerto Rico and the quantity of toxic chemical releases reported by those facilities. The information from the health studies and the TRI analysis pertains primarily to toxic chemicals rather than criteria pollutants (which are the focus of the PSD program), but the Region's effort to provide meaningful responses on these issues contributes to environmental justice for the Guayama community.

Finally, with regard to opportunities for the public to participate and provide comments on the AES permit decision, the Region points out that it provided expanded public comment opportunities and engaged in extensive correspondence with petitioner SURCCo over the course of the permit process. The Region also took several steps to ensure that comments could be received in either English or Spanish and all comments were granted equal consideration. In light of the Region's thorough environmental justice analysis and incorporation of environmental justice elements into the permit decision, we find that petitioners have not demonstrated that the Region committed clear error on issues of environmental justice....

\* \* \*

## Notes and Questions

1. The AES Puerto Rico case is one of the few EAB decisions where the permitting officials clearly found a vulnerable community, in this case based upon income rather than race. That fact would appear to raise a central question of what are appropriate measures for a permitting official to undertake in those circumstances. Are traditional regulatory benchmarks and standards sufficient or should permitting officials use more stringent criteria where there is little margin for error in light of troubling ambient conditions? Professor Sheila Foster notes that the EAB in the permit decisions is attempting to mediate between what she characterizes as "utilitarian/efficiency norms" and "equity/justice norms" by tempering utilitarian impulses with equity considerations. Sheila R. Foster, *Meeting the Environmental Justice Challenge: Evolving Norms in Environmental Decisionmaking*, 30 ENVTL. L. REP. 10,992 (2000). To what extent does the opinion excerpted above reflect a tempering process by permitting officials? Conversely, to what extent did EPA Region II officials adhere to a more traditional model of risk assessment and determination? In your view, does the permitting process need to go further in protecting fenceline communities? If so, what strategies would better accomplish this goal?

2. Is the refusal of the EAB to order a multi-source air quality analysis in AES consistent with the judge's opinion in the *Engler* case to require a risk assessment to evaluate cumulative risks from the proposed incinerator? How do you explain the different outcomes?

3. How would you evaluate the approach to judicial review that the EAB exercised in the *AES Puerto Rico* case in light of the cases discussed previously? How did the administrative law judge evaluate the exercise of authority by permitting officials? Is this consistent with the Board's earlier position that discretion should be exercised in a manner consistent with the goals of the Executive Order on Environmental Justice?

4. Did the community have a meaningful role in the process of assessing and managing the risk posed by the AES facility? As affected stakeholders, did they occupy a similar status and have comparable resources to the permit applicant? Should this matter, or should we assume that permitting officials are adequately representing the interests of the public? Assume that you are an administrative law judge deciding this case and you are inclined to rule in favor of the petitioners. How would you support a decision in their favor based upon the EAB cases discussed above?

5. Postscript: the Petitioners in *AES Puerto Rico* sought judicial review of the Board's decision in the First Circuit. Among other claims, petitioners were concerned that there would be no opportunity to review and comment upon post-construction ambient monitoring and the post-construction multi-source modeling analysis. The First Circuit rejected petitioner's claim, noting that although there was no legal requirement for public comment of post-construction permit analysis, the analysis would be conducted in accordance with EPA models and protocols. The remainder of the petitioner's challenges were similarly rejected. *See* Sur Contra La Contaminacion v. EPA, 202 F.3d 443 (1st Cir. 2000).

# E. The Permit Applicant's Perspective

Given the broad grants of authority under environmental laws and the legal activity under Title VI of the Civil Rights Act, consider the following comments and observations of Terry Bossert, who represents permit applicants and who also served for four years as Chief General Counsel to the Pennsylvania Department of Environmental Protection.

## Terry R. Bossert, The Permit Applicant's Perspective
18 Temple Environmental Law and Technology Journal 135 (2000)

Let me start by answering the question that I posed in the title of my talk, "what does environmental justice mean to the permit applicant?" As we stand here today, what it means to the permit applicant is uncertainty, confusion, and delay with regard to your permit application. Which is not to say there is anything wrong with the environmental justice movement or the issues that are being raised. I am simply saying that things are in such a state of uncertainty that it is difficult for a businessperson who says "I want to create a facility and I want to get a permit."...

In fairness, [state environmental regulators] tend to look at technical and scientific solutions; they don't tend to look at social issues. Compound this with the fact that they have been told repeatedly by the court, by the legislatures, by their own lawyers, over the years, that they must act within the confines of the authority given to them by the Legislature.

What does that mean in the permitting context? That means that you get a permit application as the permit reviewer and you think it is a lousy permit, location, or facility, you think the owner is a lousy person, too bad. If they meet the laws, they get the permit. The other thing they have been told, in Pennsylvania particularly, land use and zoning belongs to the local municipality. Even though there are 2300 local municipalities, and trying to make any of their zoning laws match up and make any sense is difficult, it is their business. Years ago when DEP [Pennsylvania Department of Environmental Protection] tried to venture into that area and make decisions based on what they thought was wise land use, they were slapped down rather significantly by the Commonwealth Court....

Now, what happens next? Guess who brings the environmental justice issue to them? Their favorite agency in the federal government, the EPA. EPA says, "remember those [Title VI] regulations we have had around for all of those years that we never talked about and remember every year when we would give you those millions of dollars in your grant and you sign off on the form and say you are going to comply with those regulations, well, by the way, those regulations that we never mentioned and you never read and we never enforced, we just realized, that we should have been paying attention to those and you guys have to start paying attention to those too."...

What does that mean more realistically? Well, what it means is if I am thinking about raising an environmental justice claim, I am not going to go to EPA where there has been one environmental justice decision and it appears to say something environmental justice advocates do not like. I am going to go to court and seek my relief there.

So where does that all leave the permit applicant? You might understandably think that they are confused. Are you going to file an application and are you going to run the risk of making the state make a decision which will get it accused of being discriminatory or get it pressured by EPA and face a threat of loss of funds? Maybe...you are going to get sued by citizens who are opposed to the facility. All right, that is one side. What is the other side of the equation. What is the state's authority to deny my permit on environmental justice grounds? I don't know. It has not been decided, there is nothing out there. You can't go to the DEP's regulations and find the environmental justice section. Okay, you want to do the right thing. What are the standards? How do you satisfy environmental justice concerns? Don't know the answer to that either. There aren't any standards. There is no guidance. There is EPA internal guidance, which may give you some help but a limited amount.

So, what do you do? What you do has been the biggest success to date of the environmental justice movement[.] That is that if you are a savvy applicant you recognize that all of these uncertainties make it difficult for the agency to act and your job is to make it easier for the agency to act. And how do you do that? You have more, not less, public outreach, public visibility, involvement with the community. You show up at DEP public meetings. You explain your application and your facility, not in acronyms and formulas and coefficients and calculations, but in ways that people can understand. You try to find out what are the real concerns of the community. Maybe their real concern is that they hate your facility and you are not going to be able to do anything about that. But maybe their real concern is that you are going to bring twenty trucks a day through their neighborhood and they don't like that. Maybe you have the ability to build another road a different way to get into your facility. Maybe their concerns are just more quality of life concerns and you have some ability to make some contribution to the community. Those aren't legal requirements, those aren't guidelines or rules, but they are a way to get around the uncertainty to try to get your permit to move forward....

What else are you seeing? Well, states are recognizing, as I indicated, that public participation has to be improved. Agencies, like DEP, have looked at public notice and public involvement very mechanistically and very rigidly. I used to say when I was at DEP that we could hold a public hearing, get three inflatable dolls, put them behind a podium, and the hearing could go on anyway because we never responded to everything. People got up and they railed about everything under the sun and we never said anything except for 'thank you for your comments.' It was the stupidest way to have a public hearing that there ever was. The region that Stanley Sneath is in [Southeast Regional Office of DEP] has pioneered efforts to have open house type public meetings where people can come and actually get answers and actually find out information and actually understand what these projects are all about. Again, the states are going to do that, the states are going to make applicants do that, applicants that have a brain are going to do it themselves....

I want to end on what I see as kind of the most significant potential impact down the road for the environmental justice movement, at least as it is played out in Pennsylvania. That is, I think, when the dust clears we are going to see that this was not a civil rights movement at all but an environmental movement. And the reason that I say that is because, and again at least as it is played out in Pennsylvania, environmental justice has focused on where facilities are located, how many of them are located there, what sorts of fringe environmental impacts have they had. If you applied the Select Steel logic [a Title VI administrative complaint rejected by EPA because the proposed new facility would not cause a violation of the Clean Air Act's health-based standards, see Chapter XIV. Eds. ] to the facilities in Chester [Pennsylvania, a community with a disproportionate concentration of polluting facilities], they would all pass. But the facilities in Chester had impacts on traffic, noise, light pollution, odors, stigma, quality of life issues. The question is, is that something that an environmental agency should look at?

Frankly, DEP's authority and their enthusiasm for regulating nuisance type impacts is questionable. If you looked at some regional enforcement statistics, you would find that malodors are the biggest complaints that the agency responds to. Again, a nuisance type impact. What is possible is that this whole movement will cause a refocusing and a reexamination of how environmental controls and traditional land use controls should work together and what an environmental agencies roles should be. Now, DEP is never going to get the authority to say "you have to put the facility right here." But maybe they will get the authority to say, maybe they already have the authority to say, "you can't put this facility here even though it complies with local zoning because it is going to have an inappropriate impact on the community." A lot of people talk about cumulative impacts. When they talk about that, they talk about air emissions, cancer risks and all that stuff we haven't gotten there yet scientifically. But how about cumulative nuisance impacts? They are a lot easier to analyze. Maybe more subjective but a lot easier to analyze....

\* \* \*

## Notes and Questions

1. Bossert's article describes responses that are often voiced by state permitting agencies to environmental justice issues—that siting decisions are local land use and zoning matters, and that cumulative impacts and non-environmental impacts are problems beyond their authority to address. What do you think of Bossert's advice to permitting applicants and permitting agencies? Does it make sense from a business perspective? Another perspective from a developer's lawyer is offered by Michael Gerrard in Chapter X.

2. The Environmental Appeals Board permitting cases illustrate the tension, on appeal, between the principal of deference to agencies embodied in an abuse of discretion standard on review, and the counter-balancing principal recognized by the EAB that discretion should be exercised in a more protective manner where impacts affect vulnerable communities. The EAB's recent approach has been to resolve this tension by a more probing review of procedural matters, requiring a detailed environmental justice analysis and good evidentiary support for a claim of disparate impact. However, at this point, the EAB will not look too closely into how discretion was in fact exercised by the permitting official. This may be due in part because this is an area of law that has yet to be developed. However, as methodologies advance and more specific criteria is developed, reviewing bodies may have a better basis to evaluate the adequacy of a permitting authority's response to environmental justice concerns. Given the need to substantially improve conditions in overburdened communities, while at the same time affording permit applicants fairness and certainty in the permitting process, how would you devise a more protective permitting scheme that accomplishes these goals? Consider, as one example, a framework analogous to that used by the Army Corps of Engineers for protecting wetlands. Under the Clean Water Act, the permitting authority determines if there is a practicable alternative to placing fill material in a wetland. If an alternative site is available, the permit is denied without further inquiry into the suitability of the proposed site. See 40 C.F.R. § 230.10. What do you think of this approach? Also keep in mind that a permitting scheme must be workable against the backdrop of the push for devolution of authority to local levels, regulatory reinvention, and Title VI complaints, discussed in Chapters V, VII and XIV, respectively, and explored briefly below.

# F. Environmental Justice in a Reinvention Context

Facility permitting cases—as interesting as they are—are even more intriguing when considered in a broader regulatory context. In addition to traditional regulatory actions, environmental justice challenges often encounter resistence because they are thought to interfere with alternative forms of regulation that have emerged in recent years. In addition to "market based" regimes, the EPA has undertaken to change environmental regulation from a more prescriptive "command and control" system to a system that expedites permit proceedings, provides greater operational flexibility to facility operators and gives greater authority and deference to state and local permitting officials. (See Chapters V and VII). Both the regulated community and regulators worry that environmental justice challenges could disrupt or derail important experiments with alternative regulatory approaches. To explore this potential conflict in the context of facility permitting, this section examines permitting issues posed by one of EPA's flagship reforms, Project XL. As you read the following excerpt, consider the potential impact of experimental approaches on heavily impacted host communities.

## Rena I. Steinzor,
## Regulatory Reinvention and Project XL:
## Does the Emperor Have Any Clothes?
26 Environmental Law Reporter 10,527 (1996)

*The Rationale for Project XL*

Project XL offers companies the opportunity to seek waivers from existing regulatory requirements in exchange for their commitment to achieve improvements in environmental quality through innovative changes in their manufacturing processes or practices. From industry's perspective, the Project provides three major benefits: saving money on compliance with existing regulation, achieving rapid review of alternative compliance plans, and winning freedom from constant reevaluation of pollution control strategies so that companies can respond to competitive challenges in national and international markets.

As implemented to date, a central theme of Project XL is the replacement of "command-and-control" requirements that limit emissions to specific media (air, water, and land) with facility-wide "bubbles" and "caps" that allow companies to trade emissions among pollutants and among media. For example, a company might propose increasing its total emissions of volatile organic compounds above the levels allowed in existing permits in exchange for reductions in emissions of sulfur dioxide or nitrogen oxide below permit limits. Or it might propose trading air emissions of a class of chemicals for water emissions of the same or a different class.

EPA made a determination at the outset of the Project not to establish any firm standards, baselines, or limits on either the substance or the process for developing XL proposals. Review by federal and state regulators familiar with the manufacturing practices, available technologies, and permit conditions at issue in the proposals has been erratic, and conducted in an atmosphere of significant political pressure to "fast-track" project approvals. In theory, Project XL requires a site-specific process for building consensus among affected stakeholders. But EPA has delegated responsibility for this process to project proponents without suggesting any guidelines for how to conduct it, with the result that in most cases public participation has been cursory and ineffective....

The issues raised by Project XL fall into three distinct but related categories: (1) the substance of individual proposals; (2) the process for public participation; and (3) the legal issues raised by EPA efforts to implement the program. Both the problems and recommendations for reform in each area are profoundly affected by what is done in the others. The absence of uniform substantive standards for judging the merits of projects places extreme pressure on the public process for evaluating them....

*The Problems*

As with so many EPA programs, to understand the rationale—and the resulting flaws—of Project XL, it is necessary to get a clear picture of its institutional genesis. The Project was designed and is being implemented by EPA staff assigned to the Office of Policy, Planning, and Evaluation (OPPE). The decision to confer this responsibility on a staff steeped in the abstract theory and rhetoric of reinvention, but lacking any independent regulatory authority of its own, was undoubtedly intended to protect the Project from being sandbagged by turf-conscious, career program and enforcement staff.... The Project XL staff has a demonstrable commitment to innovation and experimentation, but it lacks the technical expertise and experience necessary to foresee the substantive problems posed by industry proposals. Its performance is measured by how fast it gets projects up and running. Judging from lengthy delays in the project approval process, the Project staff is having increasing difficulty in obtaining approval from the EPA program staff and state and tribal regulators it must coordinate....

These difficulties are compounded by EPA's decision to foster industrial creativity by refraining from establishing any firm guidelines regarding the content of project proposals beyond the deceptively simple formulation that projects must "achieve environmental performance that is superior to what would be achieved through compliance with current and reasonably anticipated future regulation." The Federal Register notice launching the facilities XL establishes only the most general criteria for evaluating project proposals, including such unassailable but vague goals as achieving better environmental results; reducing costs and paperwork; and developing "new," "innovative," and "transferable" pollution prevention and control strategies....

The predictable result is that Project XL has become a regulatory free-for-all, with companies requesting lengthy lists of unrelated exemptions in exchange for environmental "improvements."...

[A] major problem is that Project XL proposals frequently define environmental "improvement" as cross-pollutant trades within a facility-wide—or even broader—emissions "cap." Rather than comparing before and after emissions of the same pollutants, the proposals require EPA, state and tribal regulators, and public interest stakeholders to evaluate the implications of trading decreased emissions of one aggregate class of pollutants (e.g., volatile organic compounds) for increased emissions of another class of pollutants (e.g., sulfur dioxide and nitrogen oxide). Not only is it difficult to qualitatively evaluate such exchanges, but by aggregating pollutants into classes, the proposals allow the companies to change the composition of those classes over time, increasing the amount of the most toxic individual chemicals in relation to more benign substances. Other proposals require evaluation of emissions trades between media, achieving lower air emissions in exchange for higher releases into surface water or land.

In most cases, overall emissions are traded rather than substantially reduced, and the claim that the proposal represents an improvement depends on the far from self-evident conclusion that decreasing emissions in one chemical category or one medium will produce a sufficient benefit to justify increasing emissions in another category or medium.

[T]he issue at the heart of Project XL's substantive failures is EPA's ambivalence about defining the baseline for measuring environmental improvement. In the absence of an EPA standard—or even a range of acceptable options—companies may define baselines as improvements over actual emissions, improvements over allowable emissions, or improvements over expected future emissions if a plant expands. Each approach poses distinct problems for the environment.

While a decrease in actual emissions appears on its face to be the most straightforward and fair approach, this approach could allow some serious abuses if a facility is very old, does not use state-of-the-art pollution control technology, and is producing pollutants that EPA is on the verge of controlling more stringently. Measuring improvement as a decrease in the emissions that are allowable under existing permits poses similar but even more severe problems. Such permits may have been written permissively years ago, may no longer represent the average performance within an industry, and may be about to expire, requiring the application of updated and more stringent regulatory requirements. Finally, a baseline that allows a company to measure improvement against anticipated emissions when a facility expands would authorize increased pollution without the compensating benefits of expanded industrial production if the expansion does not materialize.

The failure to define "baseline" is especially dangerous in the context of cross-media and cross-pollutant trading, given the dearth of reliable science regarding the long-term implications of such exchanges....

From the outset, EPA has maintained that it will consider "the extent to which project proponents have sought and achieved the support of parties that have a stake in the environmental impacts of the project" as an "important factor" in the decision to approve projects. It has defined "local" stakeholders ambiguously to include "communities near the project, local or state governments, businesses, environmental and other public interest groups, or other similar entities."

EPA requires public participation in Project XL for practical, legal, and principled reasons. An open process, if well-run, would protect both EPA and the company's reputations, forestalling charges that a secret sweetheart deal with "polluters" has been negotiated. Further,... unless legislation is enacted authorizing Project XL experimentation, the projects are vulnerable to citizen suits charging that they allow ongoing violations of existing regulatory standards. By establishing a stable, broad-based consensus with public interest representatives, EPA and the companies may be able to prevent such challenges. Lastly, EPA's leadership is committed—at least theoretically—to the principled notion that the participation of public interest stakeholders will produce a better result.

Despite EPA's avowed commitment to stakeholder involvement, EPA's staff has been equally adamant that running the process remains the exclusive responsibility of the company submitting a proposal. In effect, then, EPA has charged the companies with responsibility for involving local stakeholders without clearly defining who those stakeholders might be or establishing basic guidelines for accomplishing meaningful participation as proposals are developed....

There are four fundamental and closely related problems with EPA's approach. First, because EPA has not established substantive standards for judging the environmental improvements that will be achieved by proposals and has not set limits on the regulatory exemptions that may be requested, Project XL places much of the onus on "stakeholder involvement" to ensure that the public interest is protected....

Second, EPA has not required companies to disclose a standardized set of comprehensive—and comprehensible—information about their projects and the proposals typically omit information essential to allow regulators and the public to evaluate their merits, especially data on their likely effect on the environment and public health.

Third, in the absence of ground rules for facilitating and mediating public participation, many proposals omit a meaningful process entirely....

Finally, EPA does not commit its own resources, and does not require industry to commit resources, to providing independent technical assistance to public interest stakeholders so that they can meaningfully participate in the debate over the highly technical issues involved in determining which regulatory exemptions to grant, evaluating what environmental benefits will be achieved, and predicting what adverse effects might be condoned in the project. Without adequate technical support, most local community representatives have great difficulty evaluating the long-term implications of a proposal, and are certainly not equipped to play the role traditionally played by government regulators when industry-wide standards are drafted....

The true source of Project XL's multiple legal problems is not, as many people contend, the absence of legislation giving EPA the authority to approve site-specific agreements, although legislation might overcome these problems, at least temporarily. Rather, Project XL is vulnerable as a legal matter because of its dual commitment to fostering site-specific experimentation and developing "transferable" models for regulatory change. When combined with a weak public participation process and the absence of standards for evaluating the substance of proposals, the possibility that the precedents set in individual projects will be applied industry-wide raises very high stakes for regulators, environmentalists, and citizen groups....

\* \* \*

## Notes and Questions

1. Project XL is a prominent example of EPA's willingess to stretch the bounds of its regulatory authority to promote flexible reinvention proposals. Professor Steinzor quotes an internal EPA motto to the effect that "If it ain't illegal, it ain't XL." How does this attitude contrast with EPA's reluctance to push the boundaries of its permitting authority to address environmental justice issues?

2. Professor Steinzor notes several obstacles to community groups effectively participating in debates over specific XL projects, obstacles that may be particularly acute in environmental justice communities (for instance the lack of technical resources to review projects). In addition, Project XL does not require the consensus of all stakeholders before a project can go forward. Should environmental justice groups be given a disproportionate vote or even a veto power over XL projects in their communities?

# Chapter IX

# Contaminated Properties

## A. Cercla Cleanups — An Introduction

While the 1976 Resource Conservation and Recovery Act (RCRA) regulates the management of hazardous waste, including hazardous waste treatment, storage and disposal facilities (TSDFs), the Comprehensive Environmental Response, Compensation and Liability Act (CERCLA), enacted in 1980, focuses on the remediation of spills or releases of hazardous substances onto the land. A large part of CERCLA, its implementing regulations and its case law, concerns the questions of who is potentially liable for cleaning up existing contamination and the extent of liability. However, this chapter foregoes these liability issues and will instead focus upon the issues involved in the cleanup of contaminated sites. CERCLA also provides funds to cleanup abandoned contaminated sites. Thus, CERCLA is often called "Superfund" which is somewhat of a misnomer because statutorily responsible parties are also called upon to financially contribute to site cleanups, either directly or by reimbursing the "Superfund" for monies expended by government agencies. Private parties and potentially responsible parties (PRPs) who incur cleanup costs also can seek reimbursement from other PRPs. The "Superfund" is but one part of the much broader CERCLA statute.

There are hundreds of thousands of contaminated sites where releases of hazardous substances occurred or are occurring. Some of these sites remain undiscovered, many are less serious and receive attention by state and local authorities, and some of the more seriously contaminated sites trigger response activities under CERCLA. The cleanup process is distinctively linear. First, when a site is identified, the EPA has the authority to undertake a short term removal action or emergency response if the release or threatened release constitutes a public health or environmental emergency. The National Contingency Plan (NCP), adopted by EPA, sets forth guidelines and procedures to determine the appropriate extent of a removal or more long-term remedial measures. After the site has been identified, EPA undertakes a preliminary assessment, placing the data in a CERCLA information system called CERCLIS, a database of all hazardous substance release sites. It then quantifies the potential risks considering such factors as toxicity, quantity and concentration of wastes, giving the site a numerical score under the Hazard Ranking System (HRS). The higher scoring sites are placed on the National Priorities List (NPL). Priority for determining the order of cleanup is based upon factors such as the population at risk, the hazard potential, and the potential for contamination of water supplies, ecosystem destruction, public contact, and damage to natural resources that might affect the human food chain.

After any short term emergency responses are conducted, the EPA undertakes a remedial investigation and feasibility study (RI/FS) to evaluate a range of remedial options. Several factors are considered and balanced. In choosing an appropriate level of cleanup, CERCLA statutorily establishes a preference for remedial actions that permanently and significantly reduce the volume, toxicity or mobility of the hazardous substances. CERCLA also requires the selection of a remedy that is protective of health and the environment, that is cost effective, and one that uses permanent solutions to the maximum extent practicable. The statute also mandates that remedial actions must provide a level of cleanup equivalent to that required by any legally applicable or relevant and appropriate federal or state standard (such standards are known as ARARs). The ARARs are confusing and controversial, and entail the exercise of considerable discretion. For example, an ARAR might be to clean contaminated groundwater to "potable water" standards under the Safe Drinking Water Act because of the presence of nearby drinking water wells, or to standards that would apply to industrial uses because the contaminated property is an industrial site. The difference in cost may be considerable.

As you might imagine, the laundry list of factors gives environmental agencies wide latitude in choosing a cleanup remedy from among a set of plausible options. As noted in Chapter III, some activists question whether agencies routinely choose less protective cleanups for poor and minority communities, and note that such sites generally take longer to achieve NPL listing. Another commentator, through a case study, questions whether in fact cost has as limited a role as CERCLA anticipates, arguing that "EPA has . . . failed to develop a rule that will prevent the ad hoc decision-making on cleanup standards for which EPA has been so frequently criticized in the past." Donald A. Brown, *EPA's Resolution of the Conflict Between Cleanup Costs and the Law in Setting Cleanup Standards Under Superfund*, 15 COLUM. J. ENVTL. L . 241, 258 (1990). Notably, under CERCLA citizens cannot initiate an enforcement action against potentially responsible parties to compel the cleanup of a contaminated site, and cannot challenge cleanup remedies selected by the government before they are completed.

In addition, the "how clean is sufficiently clean" question is compounded by the economic reality that the marginal costs of cleanup are extraordinary. The "last ten percent" of cleanup on any particular site may mean that fewer funds will be available to clean up equally problematic sites on the NPL. The complicating factor is that many contaminated sites are in areas that allow both industrial and residential uses. The difficult question that arises is whether the site should be cleaned up to costly residential standards or to less expensive "industrial use" cleanup standards. If the less expensive "industrial use" standards are used, then the agencies involved and the communities affected must decide whether relocation is feasible. The remainder of this chapter addresses the redevelopment of such properties for industrial use (often called "brownfield redevelopment") and the difficult tradeoffs that face residents in nearby communities.

A brief trip through the principal provisions of CERCLA can be found in R. PERCIVAL, A. MILLER, C. SCHROEDER AND J. LEAPE, ENVIRONMENTAL REGULATION: LAW, SCIENCE AND POLICY 263–269, 318–325 (3d 2000) and STEVEN FERRY, ENVIRONMENTAL LAW: EXAMPLES AND EXPLANATIONS 340–344 (2d 2001).

# B. Brownfields

From an environmental justice perspective, brownfield redevelopment leads to the potential for both good and bad consequences. On the positive side, brownfield redevelopment may result in more clean urban environments and economic development. The industrial abandoned sites called "brownfields" contribute to urban blight, at times become a magnet for drug activity, may contain unremediated contamination, and generally become a source of community demoralization. From that grim baseline, any degree of cleanup and added employment opportunities is attractive, especially if the redevelopment project involves light industrial use or a non-polluting business. On the negative side, the less stringent use-based cleanup standards are problematic when considering the existing aggregate pollutants impacting many host communities. Because firms often purchase these sites with plans to return the site to heavy industrial use, brownfield redevelopment has the effect of locking in the legacy of past industrial development.

The issues involved in brownfield redevelopment are complicated and interrelated. The first issue is a familiar empirical issue of causation: what causes sites to remain undeveloped and unutilized? Although fear of liability is often touted as the primary disincentive, other reasons for the proliferation of these sites are apparent, making it questionable whether reducing liability and lowering cleanup standards will result in successful redevelopment projects. In addition to the optimal mix of incentives that may be necessary, the host community's role is controversial. Some argue that public participation is indispensable while others are concerned that too much participation may be the kiss of death for a project. Brownfields, being both an intensely local issue and a significant national concern, also raise issues about the respective roles of state and federal governments. In the excerpts provided below, thoughtful commentators examine these issues in greater detail.

## Pathfinder on Brownfields and Environmental Justice

For those wishing to research this area further, in addition to the articles excerpted here, see Gabriel A. Espinosa, *Building on Brownfields: A Catalyst For Neighborhood Revitalization*, 11 VILL. ENVTL. L.J. 1 (2000); Bradford C. Mank, *Reforming State Brownfield Programs to Comply with Title VI*, 24 HARV. ENVTL. L. REV. 115 (2000); Samara Swanston, *Brownfields Cleanup Standards: Consistency with the Principles of Environmental Justice Can Result in Clean Cleanups and Economic Development Too*, 11 FORDHAM ENVTL. L.J. 857 (2000); Lincoln L. Davies, *Working Toward a Common Goal? Three Case Studies of Brownfields Redevelopment in Environmental Justice Communities*, 18 STAN. L. J. 285 (1999); Joel B. Eisen, *Brownfields Policies for Sustainable Cities*, 9 DUKE ENVTL. L. & POL'Y F. 187 (1999); E. Lynn Grayson, *An Alliance of Necessity: Envirojustice and Brownfields*, 14 NO. 6 ENVTL. COMPLIANCE & LITIG. STRATEGY 4 (1998); Paul Stanton Kibel, *The Urban Nexus: Open Space, Brownfields, And Justice*, 25 B.C. ENVTL. AFF. L. REV. 589 (1998); John S. Applegate, *Risk Assessment, Redevelopment, and Environmental Justice: Evaluating the Brownfields Bargain*, 13 J. NAT. RESOURCES & ENVTL. L. 243 (1997–1998); Stephen M. Johnson, *The Brownfields Action Agenda: A Model for Future Federal/State Cooperation in the Quest for Environmental Justice?*, 37 SANTA CLARA L. REV. 85 (1996); Georgette C. Poindexter, *Separate and Unequal; A Comment on the Urban Development Aspect of Brownfields Programs*, 24 FORDHAM URB. L. J. 1 (1996); Douglas A. McWilliams, *Environmental Justice and Industrial Redevelopment: Economics and Equality in Urban Revitalization*, 21 ECOLOGY L.Q. 705 (1994).

# Joel B. Eisen,
# Brownfields of Dreams?: Challenges and Limits
# of Voluntary Cleanup Programs and Incentives

1996 University of Illinois Law Review 883

*The Challenge of Brownfield Redevelopment*

A "brownfield" is best defined as "abandoned or underutilized urban land and/or infrastructure where expansion or redevelopment is complicated, in part, because of known or potential environmental contamination." Brownfield sites include abandoned industrial facilities, warehouses, and other commercial properties such as former gas stations and dry cleaning establishments. Although brownfields exist in many areas, they are concentrated in aging, predominantly minority and lower-income neighborhoods of "Rust Belt" cities such as Newark and Chicago. For decades, manufacturers have been fleeing these cities and moving to "greenfields" locations in the suburbs. The abandonment of inner-city sites has left a 'witch's brew of contamination' at abandoned brownfield sites.

The number of brownfield sites, and the magnitude of contamination at them, is not known. Despite this uncertainty, brownfield sites have significant potential for redevelopment. Developers propose projects that range from industrial uses to retail uses, technology and office centers, airports, and even sports stadiums.

Although the costs of continued inactivity at brownfield sites are potentially immense, they are not well quantified. The types of costs, however, are well understood. Inner-city neighborhoods fail to benefit from jobs that redevelopment might provide. Cities receive lower property tax revenues from brownfield sites, which weakens their ability to provide basic services such as education. Brownfields are unsightly and threaten to contaminate drinking water and cause neighborhood health problems. Vacant properties contribute to high crime rates and deterioration of urban neighborhoods. They encourage further environmental abuse, such as "midnight dumping." Finally, brownfields are conspicuous symbols of the decline of lower-income and minority neighborhoods in which they are overwhelmingly located. They discourage urban investment and contribute to a pervasive sense of poverty and hopelessness.

Moreover, there are substantial environmental costs to locating new commercial or industrial activities at a greenfield site instead of a brownfield site. Greenfield development often devours previously unspoiled land. Development in suburbs and exurbs exacerbates their growing pollution problems. These developments will have adverse impacts for many years to come, even long after their useful lives have ended. Stormwater, groundwater, and air pollution from additional traffic will increase. Suburban and exurban jurisdictions will have to build or expand existing infrastructures such as highways and public water and sewer systems to serve new development. Officials in these jurisdictions are concerned about the financial burden this imposes on them, a burden that is often alleviated to some extent by wasteful subsidies (in the form of grants and other funding) from the federal and state governments.

By contrast, brownfield redevelopment can take advantage of existing urban infrastructures. A brownfield site often features excellent water and sewer systems, and rail and highway access to the metropolitan area, the region, and outlying areas. Densely concentrated urban areas offer better accessibility to workers and other advantages. Other potential benefits include aesthetic qualities such as waterfront access and views, proximity to downtown business districts, public tax and financing initiatives to support development, access to major universities and medical centers, and ancillary benefits of spending by rejuvenated industries and their workers on local goods and services.

### The Fear of Environmental Liability

Despite these potential advantages, brownfields remain abandoned or underutilized. In the eyes of many, this is due to widespread fears of brownfield developers that they will face liability under the environmental laws and that the cost of cleaning brownfield sites to meet government standards is both so uncertain and so high that it might outweigh the sites' market value. The literature is replete with anecdotes about developers who shunned brownfield sites "due to" the fear of environmental liability. Developers, it is said, demand the lower and more predictable cost of building new facilities in greenfield locations. From a developer's perspective, the list of obstacles to brownfield redevelopment starts with the threat of liability under CERCLA. This is widely perceived as the most serious barrier to redevelopment, outweighing all benefits. A developer must also be concerned about the uncertainties caused by state hazardous waste cleanup programs, because it cannot predict at the outset whether it will be subjected to state or federal regulation. The states have primary responsibility for sites that do not rise to the threshold for federal action and for sites that states have decided to regulate in the absence of federal requirements....

### Uncertainty for Developers

...This uncertainty [concerning potential CERCLA liability] is attributable in part to the considerable vagueness and uncertainty associated with applicable cleanup standards. For example, it is nearly impossible to determine in advance the required level or cost of a cleanup under CERCLA. The cleanup standard embodied in Section 121 of CERCLA forces a detailed inquiry to be undertaken at each site. Establishing the appropriate level of cleanup requires a wealth of information about the remedies that might work at each site. This information is generated in a lengthy, multistep process that is expensive and has been called a "slow-motion Kabuki." Cleanups also must comply with the standards of other federal and state laws that are "applicable or relevant and appropriate" which introduces a maddening complexity to the process. Furthermore, there is no ability to learn from past experiences and develop predictability: under the statute, each site must be analyzed individually.

Proponents advance several justifications for promoting certainty in cleanup standards. First, they argue that predetermining (i.e., standardizing) the level of cleanup required can help make project decisions more efficient. Standardizing cleanup standards allows project developers to internalize project costs and, therefore, helps to ensure that only those projects that are efficient will be built. Owners and prospective investors presumably will be more motivated to invest in brownfield redevelopment if they can determine in advance whether they will recoup their expenditures on cleanups. Lenders, once wary of any involvement at brownfield sites, will open the money tap and provide the indispensable funding for brownfields. Insurers can even underwrite the cost of remediation, so that there will be a 'cap' on financial responsibility. Finally, the pace of cleanups can be more rapid with pre-set standards.

Brownfield redevelopment advocates also say Superfund's cleanup standards are too strict. They believe that cleanup standards are based on inaccurate and unrealistic assumptions about the risks posed by hazardous waste that overestimate the true risks posed by Superfund sites and produce overly stringent cleanups, particularly because cleanups are required to meet residential standards at all sites. If this view is correct, standards could be relaxed without increasing the actual threat to human health and the environment. This is particularly true in the brownfield context, many say, given the intended use of most property for industrial or commercial purposes....

### Uncertainty for Lending Institutions

Perhaps even more important than the disincentives for developers is the perception of lenders that they face risks for lending on contaminated property. As "the traditional sources of capital for factory rehabilitation and renovation for start-up companies," their participation at brownfield sites is crucial to the success of most projects. However, lenders often practice "greenlining," routinely refusing to extend loans to brownfield redevelopers....

There are other considerations besides liability. Lenders fear that the discovery of contamination at the site will decrease the market value of their collateral or compel borrowers to spend large sums on cleanups, forcing them to default on loans....

### The Call for Reform

[However, w]e should be cautious about making generalizations about the impact of developers' fears of environmental laws and, for that matter, any other assertion that environmental laws prevent activity that would otherwise take place. The flight of businesses to greenfield sites began long before CERCLA's enactment in 1980. Researchers have yet to establish a causal link between businesses' location decisions and perceived environmental costs. Moreover, fear of environmental liability is not the only problem with brownfield sites. A recent study by the nonprofit group Resources for the Future concluded that there are many other reasons besides fear of environmental liability why brownfield sites remain undeveloped. High urban crime rates, obsolescence of existing infrastructures and manufacturing facilities at brownfield sites, and access from greenfield sites to amenities and recreation are frequently cited as reasons for developers' flight to greenfield sites....

### Features of Voluntary Cleanup Statutes

[The design and details of brownfield programs vary by state.] Most states require a developer to submit a work plan for cleanup actions that is typically accompanied by the site investigation report and other supporting documents. This plan may be part of, or submitted pursuant to, an agreement with the state to remediate the site. Indiana, for example, requires a developer to enter into a "voluntary remediation agreement" that sets forth the terms and conditions of a "work plan" for the site. In some states, the plan may be part of a consent decree entered in judgment to memorialize the agreement between the state and a developer who is a responsible party at the site. Under some approaches, the plan may provide for a partial cleanup either of certain contaminants or of a portion of the site....

Although some state programs do not change existing cleanup standards, many attempt to implement modified, risk-based standards as an incentive to developers. The Office of Technology Assessment has termed modifications to cleanup standards "perhaps the most significant feature in many voluntary programs." Most states aim to spur redevelopment by redefining cleanup standards in terms of actual risks posed to human health and the environment. There is widespread variation in the states' approaches to developing cleanup standards due to differing assumptions about the risk associated with contamination (e.g., toxicity, exposure pathways, and other factors), the importance of considering the proposed use of the site, and other considerations such as the effectiveness of engineering controls....

States are developing two general types of cleanup standards: (1) standardized state-approved generic statewide cleanup standards, based on assumptions about exposure to contamination; and (2) site-specific standards, requiring a risk assessment to be performed at every site, but often incorporating consideration of the future use of the site (i.e., industrial, commercial, or residential) and allowing some cleanups that result in a public health risk higher than that currently allowed under CERCLA....

The site-specific approach holds considerable promise for developers. A number of states provide explicitly for standards allowing levels of health risk higher than those permitted under CERCLA. The allowable level of risk for carcinogens can be higher than a 1 in 1 million ($1 \times 10^{-6}$) lifetime upper bound risk; as high as 1 in 10,000 ($1 \times 10^{-4}$) in some instances. Site-specific standards, like generic standards, also consider factors such as the intended use of the property. A number of states provide explicitly that the cleanup required at a site must be based on the public health risk that is expected in light of the site's proposed or reasonably anticipated future use....

Some states modify or reverse the usual statutory preference for permanent remedies such as destruction of hazardous substances. The preference for engineering controls (measures designed to entomb the contamination at the site, such as placement of a parking lot over contaminated soil) or institutional controls (managerial controls such as fences and warning signs, and land use restrictions), which reduce cleanup costs significantly, is perhaps the "ultimate relaxation of cleanup standards." States incorporate a variety of provisions regarding engineering or institutional controls....

A number of states do not mandate public participation in their voluntary cleanup programs. The reason for this is readily apparent: public involvement is often viewed as a "deterrent to undertaking a voluntary cleanup."...

In states that require public participation at each site, some require that the affected community be notified of proposed cleanup activities. The most typical form of public participation is a brief notice and comment period (often less than thirty days) on the proposed remedial action plan. The form of notice to be used varies, with few states requiring direct notice to residents in the affected community. A minority of states provide for more participation than a notice and comment process allows by requiring that a public hearing be held on the remedial action plan; the hearing, however, is often available only upon a written request....

### The EPA's Brownfields Action Agenda

While the states have taken the lead in promoting voluntary cleanups at brownfield sites, the EPA has also been active. In 1995, it launched a "Brownfields Economic Redevelopment Initiative" with an "Action Agenda" consisting of several projects designed to spur brownfield redevelopment. The EPA announced its intent to remove sites from the CERCLIS database, expand an existing grant program for local brownfield pilot projects, clarify liability issues under CERCLA (particularly for prospective purchasers, municipalities, and lenders), and work with states implementing voluntary cleanup programs....

The EPA is funding a number of brownfield "pilot projects" to develop strategies for redeveloping brownfield sites, with individual grants of up to $200,000. This seed money may not be used for actual cleanups. Instead, it is intended to achieve three purposes: testing of redevelopment strategies and models; promoting cooperative efforts to bring together the stakeholders involved in brownfield policy; and forcing 'jump start' assessment and evaluation activities at individual sites....

### Comparing Voluntary Cleanup Statutes and Negotiated Compensation Statutes

...One possible means of soliciting additional community input in brownfield redevelopment projects is to allow the community to prepare a statement of a project's environmental impacts. This "community impact statement"(CIS) would be similar in purpose to the environmental impact statement of the National Environmental Policy Act (NEPA) and its state analogues. That is, it would seek to force state regulators and developers to consider environmental impacts of their project decisions, such as the community's perception of added health risk stemming from the proposed project....

Environmental impact statements, however, have proven to be largely unhelpful in changing agency decisions. As Professor [Vicki] Been and a number of others have indicated, experience to date with NEPA and the state "little NEPAs" engenders "great dissatisfaction with the impact statement as a tool for 'making bureaucracies think.'" A community impact statement would therefore be unsuccessful in prompting regulators and developers to consider the consequences of their actions and act accordingly. Another problem is that impact statements create only a procedural mandate and confer no rights of review of their substance....

[An] intriguing option is available to communities. They could conceivably use their zoning power to displace a generic cleanup standard. Unlike the negotiated compensation statutes, which prevent localities from adopting zoning provisions that would defeat proposed facilities, voluntary cleanup statutes contain no preemption provisions....

The rise of the voluntary cleanup statutes is consistent with the trend of devolving responsibility for environmental protection to the states. The states are bearing an increased share of the environmental protection burden, and some states are moving forward aggressively with environmental protection programs. However, there is reason for concern. The federal environmental laws were developed in large part because the states' environmental protection efforts were viewed as dismal failures, and concern about state regulatory efforts has not abated. States may be inclined to approve less stringent cleanups at brownfield sites because they want to attract businesses and the tax revenues and jobs they provide. State involvement in both the negotiated compensation and voluntary cleanup contexts invites two specific forms of criticism: regulators are captured by pro-development interests or are otherwise unaccountable to the public....

There are additional moral hazards in the brownfield context. The reduced likelihood of enforcement actions guarantees that the primary responsibility for ensuring cleanups' efficacy rests with the developers. The "reopener" provisions in many statutes that allow the state to sue the developer if it violates the terms of its agreement may not be invoked or may come into play too late to stop irreversible damage.

The states therefore place a premium on trusting developers to be "good actors," that is, entities with good environmental records. But, as in the negotiated compensation context, there are reasons to be wary of developers' honesty. The expense of site assessment may limit participation in the process to large corporations with suspect environmental records because "they alone have the funds to invest in site assessment and cleanup." Because developers voluntarily provide information to regulatory agencies that might later use it against them in enforcement actions, the potential exists for deceitful behavior. Developers can obscure the real nature of contamination at a brownfield site in a number of ways. They can build a structure or other improvement that makes discovery and cleanup of contamination more difficult. In addition, because they are assessing and remediating the preexisting level of contamination, developers are not guaranteeing that they will not cause pollution in the future....

The incentives for brownfield redevelopment are based on a "Brownfields of Dreams" premise: "if you provide the appropriate climate, they [developers] will clean and invest."...The transition away from the rigorous cleanup standards of the regulatory regime, however, is prompting the states to move too far to relax cleanup standards and requirements for contaminated sites, jeopardizing public health and safety....

The states must provide for meaningful opportunities for community input in the process, both in the planning stage and during the cleanup process. The suspect legitimacy of the states' decision making under voluntary cleanup statutes should be addressed by increased public participation in statewide decision-making bodies. The moral hazards should be addressed by amendments requiring effective risk communication and disqualifying prospective developers who are not "good actors." Finally, the EPA should be given authority to disapprove of a state's program if it does not impose protective cleanup standards or provide for effective community input. Then, and only then, will the voluntary cleanup programs begin to fulfill their tremendous promise.

* * *

## Notes and Questions

1. When the brownfield agenda first surfaced in the mid-1990s, environmental justice advocates quickly recognized that the discussion was too narrowly focused upon removing barriers to real estate transactions. In response, the Waste and Facility Siting Subcommittee of the National Environmental Justice Advisory Council (NEJAC) began a series of public dialogues to allow residents of impacted communities and environmental justice advocates to systematically contribute to the public policy debate. Environmental justice advocates argued that potential liability was a relatively minor impediment to brownfield redevelopment. Redlining by investment and insurance companies, lack of training, and the poor quality of education, public safety, housing and transportation all led to deindustrialization of urban areas, along with the contribution of indirect subsidies for suburban development. Activists promoted the concept of "urban revitalization," a community-based approach focused upon building capacity and mobilizing resources, as opposed to "urban redevelopment," a gentrification driven policy that displaces existing communities. If multiple factors result in abandoned and contaminated properties, what revitalization strategies would be necessary to provide the necessary incentives for private sector investment and insure meaningful community input?

2. Building upon the ambivalency concerning brownfields development, Professor Kirsten Engel observes that the negative view stems from a right-based perspective while the more positive view stems from a market perspective. In the article excerpted below, she promotes a third "pragmatic" approach as a means to resolve the tensions in brownfield redevelopment.

# Kirsten H. Engel,
## Brownfield Initiatives and Environmental Justice:
## Second-Class Cleanups or Market-based Equity?

13 Journal of Natural Resources and Environmental Law 317 (1998)

*State Voluntary Cleanup Laws*

...Regulations implementing CERCLA, as well as state Superfund laws, limit CERCLA-quality cleanup and liability to only the most hazardous sites presenting the most extreme threats to human health and the environment. Thus, the theoretical eligibility of the site for CERCLA cleanup is irrelevant; the reality is that if not addressed under the brownfields program, such sites will probably never be cleaned up at all. Focusing on this real life constraint, however, obscures the equity issues underlying the unavailability of CERCLA-quality remedies at brownfield sites. Most importantly, it obscures the fact that the unavailability of CERCLA-quality remedies at brownfield sites is a policy choice by agency officials, and not a requirement of CERCLA itself....

*The "Rights-Based" Critique of Brownfields Programs*

The dominant thrust of environmental justice is that all persons and communities, without regard to race or socio-economic status, are entitled to equal treatment under the law concerning the distribution of the environmental benefits and burdens of modern society. The violation of this rights-based norm is the basis for the environmental justice movement which has galvanized around empirical studies demonstrating that minority and low-income communities are disproportionately exposed to environmental hazards, such as hazardous waste landfills. The rights-based approach demands that state and local government agencies alter their siting and other environmental policies so as to achieve substantive equity in the distribution of environmental hazards by race and class and procedural equity in environmental decision-making so as to include traditionally disenfranchised groups such as minorities and the poor.

According to the rights-based conception of environmental justice, brownfield programs that contemplate reduced cleanup standards and less comprehensive liability by affected parties are antithetical to the goal of substantive and procedural equality in the distribution of environmental hazards across the lines of race, class, and ethnicity. Under the rights-based conception, state voluntary cleanup programs force the victims of environmental discrimination to bear the costs of that discrimination. Due to the low land values prevailing in their communities together with their relative political powerlessness, poor and minority communities have been targeted historically as the sites for heavy industrial development and, as a result, are subject to a disproportionate share of the environmental hazards that frequently accompany such development. Rather than reverse this legacy, brownfield cleanups could actually perpetuate it. If, for example, the cleanup of a brownfield site is sufficient only for future industrial uses, the community will never escape this industrial legacy but will continue to be located near potentially environmentally hazardous industrial development. In this manner, the rights-based conception of environmental justice could see brownfield initiatives as betraying the promise of Superfund legislation which, at least for the sites that qualify for Superfund remedies, would normally require more expensive cleanups consistent with future residential and recreational uses of the property.

The benefits touted by brownfield initiatives would likely be discounted by the rights-based environmental justice approach. The increased economic opportunities that are to accompany brownfield initiatives might be considered a "bribe" that asks residents to trade health for dollars....

### The "Market-Based" Approach to Achieving Environmental Justice

...According to the market-based approach to environmental justice, the pattern of disproportionate exposure to environmental hazards by poor minority and urban communities will only be broken when either the residents of such communities obtain the economic resources to leave contaminated urban neighborhoods or a rise in the value of urban land begins to attract less polluting businesses. The market-based approach holds that neither of these can take place, so long as urban neighborhoods are riddled with abandoned contaminated sites that operate as a net drag upon the already scarce resources of the community. Reforms of government industrial facility siting procedures, so as to prevent sitings that result in disproportionate impacts upon poor and minority communities, cannot achieve lasting gains in environmental equity unless the communities possess the infrastructure, skills, and political organization necessary to attract more desirable development. Given the economic and political empowerment of disadvantaged communities, the market-based view holds that environmental inequities will eventually disappear.

In contrast to the rights-based approach, the market-based approach to achieving environmental justice generally supports current state brownfield laws. To the extent compromises can be made concerning cleanup and environmental liability in exchange for the cleanup and redevelopment of such abandoned sites, the community will be better off. With increased economic resources, the community will gradually break the pattern of disproportionate exposure to environmental hazards.

### Finding a Middle Ground Between the Rights-Based and Market-Based Conceptions of Environmental Justice

...[A] third approach, labeled here as the "pragmatic" approach, supports departures from a strict rights-based approach to environmental justice where the probability of environmental harm is minimal and the potential economic benefits are large. Such departures, however, are only justifiable if mechanisms are in place to ensure that departures from the rights-based approach will result in concrete economic gains for disadvantaged communities. The pragmatic approach to environmental justice, in the context of brownfield programs, is suggested as a recommended approach to achieving environmental justice goals in the context of brownfield programs, and not as a replacement for either the rights-based or market-based approaches in other contexts where they may be more suitable to the achievement of environmental justice goals.

In the context of brownfields, the pragmatic approach would likely support the use of less extensive liability and use-based cleanup standards at contaminated urban sites because such departures from the CERCLA model may be necessary in order to attract new business opportunities and to obtain some remedial action at these sites. However, the pragmatic approach would insist that the government take more pro-active measures to ensure that brownfield redevelopment actually results in such opportunities. Accordingly, it is possible to sketch the requirements that might be necessary for brownfield-related laws and projects to meet the demands of a pragmatic approach to environmental justice: (1) completion of government or independent research studies demonstrating that environmental liability is responsible in substantial measure for the lack of development of brownfield sites; (2) that the local community be fully involved in all decisions made regarding brownfield redevelopment; and (3) that the local community be afforded real economic opportunities—jobs, job training, and opportunities for new or spin-off business start-ups—as part of any redevelopment proposal that reduces cleanup standards or immunizes any potentially responsible parties....

* * *

## Notes and Questions

1. Does looking at the potential conflicts surrounding brownfield redevelopment from a rights-based vs. market-based perspective help to understand the tensions involved? Notice that Professor Engel's "pragmatic" approach addresses causation, as well as public participation and incentive questions. What might be the potential problems involved in implementing her approach? For instance, what does it mean for the local community to be "fully involved" in all decisions regarding brownfield development? Should such decisions require a community consensus?

2. EPA-sponsored brownfield pilot projects may differ from some state initiatives in the degree to which public participation is required. The EPA reportedly revised its criteria for projects that it funds to require that community input be solicited and verified. *See* NATIONAL ENVTL. JUST. ADVISORY COUNCIL, WASTE AND FACILITY SITING SUBCOMMITTEE, ENVIRONMENTAL JUSTICE, URBAN REVITALIZATION, AND BROWNFIELDS: THE SEARCH FOR AUTHENTIC SIGNS OF HOPE, EPA 500-R-96-002 (December 1996). Local officials were concerned that extensive public involvement would be a disincentive for industry stakeholders, and were also concerned that Title VI civil rights claims, based upon disparate impact, would hinder brownfield redevelopment. In early 1999, in response to these concerns, the EPA conducted a study of seven EPA Assessment Pilot Projects. ENVIRONMENTAL PROTECTION AGENCY, BROWNFIELDS TITLE VI CASE STUDIES: SUMMARY REPORT, EPA 500-R-99-003 (June 1999). As expected, the case study disclosed that community residents were concerned about cleanup and reuse. However, community residents were generally supportive when the redevelopment was perceived to be an improvement over the existing blight and the project sponsor was willing to promote job creation for local residents. A more surprising finding of the case study is that typical redevelopment activities did not ultimately include pollution-heavy projects—a finding that may be generalized to a fair number of the EPA-sponsored pilots. Of the three pilots that involved heavy industrial use, an important component of reducing conflict was that "involving the community allowed potential problems to be identified and solved from the beginning when stakes were lower and design changes could more easily be made." For example, in a cement processing operation in Miami, a neutral toxicologist was hired to explain the emissions, and in Camden, the developer described the new, cleaner process and agreed to the community's request that an independent engineering firm conduct on-site monitoring.

Another important finding was that projects that provided tangible benefits for the community had greater community support. For example, a stamping press manufacturer in Chicago created 100 new jobs for local residents and a plastic rack manufacturer in Detroit created 30 new jobs with a potential for 70 more. As the case study report noted, what is striking is that the "community define[d] the problem [i.e., the abandoned site] from the vantage point of their aspirations," thus injecting more positive elements into an economic transaction formerly devoid of social responsibility or civic possibility. In the Chicago Pilot, for example, stakeholders built upon the brownfield-inspired relationship between the City and local communities to subsequently institute a cooperative enforcement program that included brochures in several languages, a hotline for citizens to report illegal dumping in their communities, and heavier penalties for violators.

The case studies indicate that use-based cleanup standards and new industrial activity can be acceptable to the community if there is early and meaningful public input, independent technical review, a genuine attempt to mitigate the facility's adverse impacts on health, safety and quality of life in the host community, and tangible benefits to the host community. These projects reflect a more comprehensive strategy of addressing brownfields in its complex social context.

3. As noted, many local officials have argued that potential Title VI claims will interfere with brownfields development. The EPA Case Studies Report, however, found that developers and investors do not perceive Title VI complaints to be a major barrier. In fact, no Title VI challenges have yet been filed to brownfields development projects as of the end of 2001(see Chapter XIV).

4. Many states have been hesitant to provide robust public participation opportunities in their voluntary cleanup programs because of concern about public opposition. However, as noted in NEJAC's Authentic Signs of Hope report, "[t]hose who claim that the community will always require the maximum level of cleanup, ignore the fact that far better than anyone else, the community recognizes the dangers of losing any cleanup by demanding a full cleanup." *See* NEJAC, *supra,* at 41. Moreover, other studies confirm the value of public participation. As one author notes, "In almost every case study analyzed, carefully orchestrated public outreach and involvement plans were implemented from the outset. Without this critical community buy-in, many project participants note, their efforts could easily have fallen apart." *See* Edith M. Pepper, Lessons from the Field: Unlocking Economic Potential with an Environmental Key 18 (1997). As noted in 1999, "[t]here is still a lag between reality and law, however, in that most state statutes still require little more than nominal public participation, and most public outreach efforts are done through ad hoc groups or task forces convened for particular projects. Where developers undertake public outreach efforts without a framework to constrain their activities, one person's 'carefully orchestrated' outreach can easily become another's 'illegitimate process.'" Joel B. Eisen, *Brownfields Policies for Sustainable Cities*, 9 Duke Envtl. L. & Pol'y F. 187, 224 (1999).

5. Given that there is the potential for significant positive gain from brownfield redevelopment, how might you devise a framework that would give firms the incentive to invest in brownfields that provide substantial benefits to local communities, while at the same time minimizing the risk of inadequate cleanups and potential recontamination? As in regulation generally, the devil is in the details. Consider the following admonitions about a primary brownfield strategy.

# Robert Hersh & Kris Wernstedt,
# Out of Site, Out of Mind: The
# Problem of Institutional Controls

8 Race Poverty & the Environment 15 (Winter 2001)

State voluntary cleanup programs are increasingly taking "risk-based" or "land-use based" approaches to brownfields redevelopment. The terms are shorthand for a decision-making process wherein—at least ideally—regulators, developers, site owners, and the local community determine a cleanup level in accordance with the site's probable future use. The premise is straightforward: instead of cleaning up a contaminated site to background levels for unrestricted use, prospective developers or site owners may be permitted to leave residual contamination on the site if its future use will be restricted to commercial or industrial activities. This requirement for less stringent cleanups may lead to less expensive remedies for developers, promote economic development in urban areas and improve public involvement in cleanup and reuse deliberations.

The decision to base cleanup levels on restricted land uses typically requires the establishment of institutional controls to ensure that the use of a site remains consistent with its level of cleanup. For example, a site remediated to an industrial standard would be precluded from residential development. These controls, primarily legal restrictions placed on land and groundwater use, can include zoning restrictions, permits to limit public access to contaminated groundwater, public advisory notices, and private property use restrictions. In essence, they aim to control exposure to hazards left on a site, rather than reducing the hazards themselves.

Institutional controls often are described rather bloodlessly as legal mechanisms, but they are better understood as a part of the political economy of brownfields. If institutional controls were to fail—exposing persons to hazardous chemicals, for example—one could argue that the benefits accruing to the brownfields developers and site operators from the less costly clean up has been borne by the local community in increased health risks, and that the municipality and regulatory agencies involved should shoulder the financial and administrative costs.

A number of factors limit the effectiveness of institutional controls. First, to be effective, institutional controls that rest on private property restrictions—such as easement—must bind both current and future users of the site. Although an easement between a site owner and a regulatory agency might bind the current owner to the stipulated restrictions, it is unclear to what extent subsequent owners will be bound by the agreement. The ability of third parties, such as community groups or local residents, to enforce a restriction at a site if the property owner fails to comply, and the holder of the easement fails to act promptly, is also uncertain.

Second, the efficacy of institutional controls based on zoning ordinances relies on the consistent application of those ordinances. Yet in no other area of American law are such frequent requests made for amendments to the law (i.e., requests for rezoning) or so many minor revisions made to the law under the guise of an administrative action (i.e., variances and special exemptions).

The most profound limitation to the reliability of institutional controls may be the incapacity of local government to track and enforce them. According to recent surveys of state and local administrators, budget cuts are eroding the capacity of local government to put inspectors in the field and coordinate data exchange among building, engineering, and public works departments. Perhaps even more disturbing, the results of a survey of members of the International City/Council Management Association suggest that only 26 percent of local government respondents have experience implementing and enforcing institutional controls at hazardous waste sites. The survey results also indicate that citizen complaints and property sales, rather than regular inspections, are more likely to prompt enforcement of institutional controls. A survey of state hazardous waste officials conducted by the Association of State and Territorial Solid Waste Management Officials reinforces those findings, concluding, "The lack of funding and lack of authority, along with unclear jurisdictional issues," are the main obstacles to the effective implementation of institutional controls.

Clearly, additional funding for monitoring and enforcement and more effective coordination between government agencies is necessary. But the larger concern is to consider what kinds of institutional arrangements are needed to design and enforce land use restrictions in a regulatory context in which cleanups increasingly are initiated and implemented by the private sector, and in which voluntary cleanup provisions provide few entrance points for public input. A first step, running somewhat counter to the prevailing trend, would be to include members of the local community in the design, implementation, and enforcement of institutional controls. While the participation of the local community would not be sufficient to ensure the integrity of institutional controls, it is a necessary and badly needed safeguard.

\* \* \*

## Notes and Questions

1. Given these considerations, can you think of a way to devise a system of institutional controls that would better protect host communities?

2. Some have argued that the parcel by parcel approach to brownfield redevelopment fails to account for the potential cumulative and synergistic effects of several sites located close together in an inner-city neighborhood, a concern that arises in permitting generally (see Chapter VIII). To better protect against this risk, some commentators advocate a city-wide approach to evaluating impacts and the use of traditional zoning classifications to create adequate buffer zones and other safeguards. Others have advanced the idea of a state certification program for brownfield redevelopment, with states reserving the authority to withdraw certification upon a failure of institutional controls or discovery of additional contamination. *See* Final Draft Guidance for Developing Superfund Memoranda of Agreement (SMOA) Language Concerning State Voluntary Cleanup Programs, 62 Fed. Reg. 47,495 (1997).

3. Another potential problem that may arise in brownfield projects that involve new industrial activity is recontamination. In the typical release of liability, the EPA may insert a "reopener clause" that provides that the EPA may revisit the issue of liability upon certain circumstances such as the subsequent discovery that past contamination is more extensive than previously thought, requiring additional cleanup. Would a reopener clause be triggered if post-cleanup industrial processes resulted in contamination? If the new industrial activity is similar to past activity, how will the EPA or its state counterpart distinguish between pre- and post-development contamination for purposes of using the reopener clause to finance additional cleanup?

4. Based upon the foregoing considerations, what types of requirements would you add to an ideal framework for brownfield redevelopment in the following areas:

1. cleanup (including engineering and institutional controls)

2. public participation

3. release of liability for past or future contamination.

5. Professor Eisen and others argue that the federal government must maintain a strong role in brownfield redevelopment because of the lax oversight and lack of robust public participation that some state programs have exhibited. This raises a complicated federalism issue. By way of background to discussing this issue, Professor Buzbee in the excerpt below notes three approaches to federalism that come into play. There is "constitutional federalism" that, as the name implies, largely concerns constitutional limits to federal authority. There is also "normative federalism," a preference for the primacy of state authority and limited federal control, partly rooted in constitutional structure and theory of government. There is also "instrumental federalism," which is concerned primarily with the issue of comparative institutional competence and the optimal roles of the dual sovereigns in light of that competence. Is there a way for the federal government to assure adequate protection for brownfield communities, while simultaneously allowing states to experiment with redevelopment approaches and respond to local political and economic complexities? Looking primarily through the lens of instrumental federalism, Professor Buzbee contemplates the question in greater detail.

# William W. Buzbee,
# Brownfields, Environmental Federalism,
# and Institutional Determinism
21 William and Mary Environmental Law and Policy Review 1 (1997)

*The First-Mover Phenomenon and Its Environmental Regulatory Parallels*

...From the time of its creation in 1970, EPA was an agency with concentrated authority and expertise, as well as an institutional stake in retaining or expanding its role as chief environmental enforcer. Consistent with the first-mover literature, EPA gained expertise and that expertise in turn built on itself as EPA attracted a substantial number of highly qualified and dedicated employees. Furthermore, once federal jurisdiction over environmental problems was established, the federal government, if it wanted to, could have chosen to rely upon the constitutional Supremacy Clause to preempt or dictate the content of state environmental regulation. Thus, the federal government, as the environmental first-mover, had a far stronger position than would two entities or jurisdictions of equal but competing power. Generally, however, federal environmental schemes left EPA with a potential oversight role, but with substantial involvement by the states in implementing federal goals. States also had ongoing state court jurisdiction over state common law environmental claims and explicit authority to provide greater environmental protections than under federal law. Some reliance on state implementation was inevitable, given the breadth of tasks assigned to EPA....

[States] began to build up their own institutional competence and attract high quality employees. Federal data-gathering and investigation into pollution control strategies resulted in widespread dissemination to the states of substantial pollution control information. As states built up their environmental regulatory apparatus, regulated entities invested in an ongoing state enforcement role. Furthermore, state efforts came both later in time than most federal initiatives and exhibited greater sensitivity to local desires and concerns, particularly the concerns of those bearing the burdens of regulation.

The idea that second and third generation "movers" will show greater flexibility than the first-mover and adjust to newly developed needs of the consumers of the relevant product is also a basic tenet of first-mover phenomena....

### State Stringency or a Preference for Local Enforcement?

...[An] observation can be drawn from state voluntary cleanup and mini-CERCLA enactments. While new state environmental laws and regulations add a new layer of law for industry to heed, they may paradoxically be intended to reduce or displace enforcement threats posed by federal regulators. These enactments do not legally preclude ongoing parallel federal enforcement. As a practical matter, however, they have an additional impact of substantially reducing the likelihood of unsought federal intervention at sites of concern. As discussed above, states have explicitly sought federal commitment to forbear any ability to revisit state-supervised voluntary cleanups. Notions of comity, coupled with limited federal dollars and excessive legal burdens on EPA, make federal activism substantially less likely once states enact parallel regulatory schemes and act at sites that would otherwise be of possible federal concern.

State parallel activity here therefore may be explainable in part by the following dynamic. Once industry confronts the inevitability of environmental regulation, state regulators offer several advantages; key among them is a greater sensitivity to local industry's needs. Concern with capital exit might lead state regulators to go easier on liable parties than would federal regulators, particularly in states where enforcement officials are not insulated from political pressure. Furthermore, any explicit or *de facto* delegation of authority to an agent (here the states), allows for some "slippage" or "drift" from the principal's ideal goal. In the context of Brownfields efforts, regulation of contaminated sites, and voluntary cleanup schemes, the federal government seldom has delegated authority to the states, but state activity as a practical matter has displaced most potential federal activity, even if a state's decisions might be different from what federal officials would make on their own....

To put the previous paragraphs' points differently, states' activism and increased competence in the environmental area are largely traceable to the federal first-mover and the benefits of vertical federal-state competition for political credit. States benefitted from copying (with some variation) federal schemes, and passed their own first-mover innovation of voluntary cleanup schemes, in part to reduce uncertainty and liability fears resulting from federal law. States also increased in competence and expertise due to delegated federal programs and access to federal databases about pollution control strategies. Thus, state activity is at least partially the result of preceding federal initiatives. If, as posited above, state environmental activity is in part intended to create a *de facto* displacement of federal enforcement, or at least to reduce the likelihood of federal intervention, then these state laws cannot be assumed to reflect independent or durable state commitment to environmental protection.

Nevertheless, retained spheres of state sovereignty, or at least areas of state implementation discretion, still provide regulatory benefits. As others have predicted about the dynamics of federalism...once one state created a legal innovation attractive to industry interested in investing in Brownfield sites, other states passed similar measures. Without retained state authority to create innovative strategies, states would not have created these schemes reducing incentives to abandon Brownfield sites.

Given substantial state interest in attracting or retaining industry, one would expect even facially stringent state laws to provide some room for state officials involved with the implementation or enforcement process to respond to industry concerns. A provocative United States General Accounting Office Study supports the soundness of such an expectation. This study reviewed how states establish and apply environmental standards in cleaning up contaminated sites, with a particular focus on states with more protective standards than under federal law. Greater stringency was found under portions of several states' laws, but under most more protective soil cleanliness requirements, state authorities linked that stringency with flexibility to modify obligations in the process of implementing those standards. Similarly, after the first wave of mini-CERCLAs, states cut back on the stringency of those laws by adding provisions responsive to industry concerns. Analogous sensitivity to industry concerns is found in the funding sources for most states' mini-CERCLAs; such state laws draw on a larger number of funding sources than their federal CERCLA counterpart, which is funded primarily by taxes on the most polluting industries. These observations are consistent with the thesis that states will enact environmental laws either in response to democratic pressure or to take electoral credit, but also seek through the implementation process or an amendment process to show sensitivity to industry concerns....

[In contexts] such as negotiations over cleanup obligations at a particular site, state officials would again face strong incentives to retain or attract industry, but would face a lower likelihood of public scrutiny or a negative electoral reaction. At times, zealous local interest in a particular site would reduce the odds of capitulation, but state officials would still be more vulnerable to industrial migration threats than would be federal officials. This likely difference in concern about industry threats is an immutable characteristic of state and federal governments under our Constitution. Even without the benefits of alternating innovations in a federalist scheme, some federal oversight role would reduce the likelihood of state or local surrender to industry demands....

### Assessing the Brownfields Policy Options

...On balance, federal subsidization of Brownfields rehabilitation efforts, coordinated principally by state and local governments, is appropriate. State and local governments have much greater familiarity with local market and political dynamics and a higher proportionate stake in the success of Brownfields rehabilitation than do federal authorities. Federal subsidies are "harnessing" natural political incentives of state and local governments to further ends shared by federal and state officials. In addition, because federal dollars are spent on Brownfields initiatives, it is less likely that the federal government would take any enforcement steps that could stigmatize a contaminated site and thereby jeopardize the benefits sought in federal monetary support. In effect, federal Brownfields grants further move hazardous waste law toward a *de facto* cooperative federalism scheme, reducing the degree of liability uncertainties. Given concerns about risks of agency capture and even government corruption at all levels, however, dollar grants or subsidies should be accompanied by oversight and post-expenditure review. The many failures of past and current urban renewal efforts following federal grants support the need for the tracking of any grant dollars....

### A Note on Institutional Determinism

...All institutions now appear eager to develop Brownfields initiatives. How politically durable that eagerness will be is questionable. If states develop a successful track record and vigorously protect the environment while returning such sites to reuse, a fairly stable cooperative federalism approach may result. If, however, states tend to sacrifice cleanup protectiveness to attract industry, a wholly different dynamic shifting enforcement authority back to the federal government may follow. Such a shift back to greater federal authority would be especially likely if environmental justice advocates' concerns were ignored by states. Were federal officials to conclude (in my view erroneously) that overlapping federal authority was no longer necessary in light of state environmental activity, the contextual dynamics of environmental federalism would lead one to predict a reduction in the stringency of state environmental enforcement....

\* \* \*

## Notes and Questions

1. In an earlier note, there was a reference to the EPA's guidance to states on brownfield redevelopment. In light of Professor Buzbee's insights on the appropriate role of federal and state governments, how would you analyze the following bit of regulatory history on the EPA guidance:

In September 1997, the EPA promulgated a draft guidance document specifying conditions under which it would enter into an amended "Superfund Memorandum of Agreement" ("SMOA") beyond those already in place with eleven states. A SMOA delineates the nature of federal-state relations with respect to cleanups of sites on the National Priorities List ("NPL"). In SMOA amendments, the EPA provides protection against federal liability for VCP [Voluntary Cleanup Programs] participants by agreeing to refrain from pursuing enforcement actions at certain brownfields sites successfully addressed in VCPs.

The EPA received 78 comments on the draft, many calling for its withdrawal. One former state official stated bluntly, "if the bureaucrats in EPA have a lick of common sense they will rescind this guidance." He was not alone. Other commenters termed the draft guidance a "disastrous mistake" that would do "severe damage to state brownfield initiatives" and "create further obstacles to achieving brownfields redevelopment."

The first area of controversy was the EPA proposal to limit its approval to lower-risk brownfields sites. The guidance featured a multi-step "screening process" for states to use to distinguish between higher-risk "Tier I" sites and lower-risk "Tier II" sites; only the latter would be eligible for liability protection. The EPA also stated, "if the EPA subsequently determines that a site was improperly classified as 'Tier II', the [liability protection] does not apply." This proposal drew strong criticism from many commenters who feared it would empower the EPA to substitute its judgments about environmental costs and benefits for those of the states. The EPA proposed to make its judgments in a manner consistent with its CERCLA mandate, intending to differentiate sites with "greater potential to require long-term or emergency cleanup work under the Federal Superfund program" from those earning its sign-off. This is an important analysis that would have allowed for consideration of all environmental impacts of brownfields projects.

Recognizing the extensive differences in VCPs, the EPA had also agreed to sign off only on sites remediated in approved programs which contained six specified features. This drew heavy fire from commenters, one of whom observed that the federal baseline would "give [ ] EPA veto power over state laws." The EPA planned to approve a VCP only if it "provided opportunities for meaningful community involvement... responsive to the risk posed by the site contamination and the level of public interest," including notice and other requirements. The EPA's proposal recognized that many VCPs require notice or a brief notice-and-comment period, while others require no public outreach efforts whatsoever. Thus decisions on site uses and cleanup standards are often precluded from community scrutiny, the first issue having been decided by developers and the second often determined by a generic cleanup standard. The EPA's attempt to bring community members into the process was overwhelmingly rejected as tending to "indirectly impose cost and procedural impediments on brownfields developers."

Other criteria called on states to "provide adequate oversight to ensure that voluntary response actions...are conducted in such a manner to assure protection of human health, welfare and the environment..." by, among other means, incorporating the CERCLA preference for permanent cleanups, and including "a requirement that the State program receives progress reports on site conditions, or [reserves] the State program's right to conduct site inspections." The states rejected these proposals. Once again, they resisted any EPA role in deciding whether a brownfields cleanup protects human health and the environment.... [T]he EPA proposal responded to an important procedural shortcoming of state programs, namely, the lack of consistent and effective means to guarantee that cleanups remain protective over time.

Bowing to the inevitable, the EPA withdrew the draft in January 1998.

Eisen, *Brownfields Policies for Sustainable Cities, supra,* at 208–213. Was the oversight role proposed by EPA optimal in terms of institutional competence and necessary to safeguard against undue pressure at the state level? Why or why not?

# C. Relocation

In addition to brownfield redevelopment, remediation of contaminated sites may be so problematic and fraught with uncertainties that the surrounding community wants to relocate. However, this presents the difficulty of balancing objectively quantifiable risks about the protectiveness of the proposed cleanup (and the scientific uncertainty endemic to such an endeavor) and more qualitative factors such as the community's perception of risk, and its effect upon quality of life and property values. The following report was prepared for a Relocation Roundtable meeting of the Pensacola (Florida) Relocation Pilot Project. In light of the limitations of science, as well as the economic, political and social complexities involved, what options appear to be most advantageous?

### Escambia Treating Company Case Study
### for the Relocation Roundtable Meeting[1]

The Escambia Treating Company (ETC) site is a former wood treatment facility located in the north central portion of Pensacola, Escambia County, Florida. The site is

---

1. This was prepared while relocation was under consideration by the EPA. Relocation was later approved by Record of Decision dated Feb 12, 1997.

currently abandoned, occupying 26 acres in a mixed industrial and residential area on Palafox Street between Fairfield Drive and Brent Lane.

The land use in the immediate vicinity of the site consists of single family homes, an apartment complex, an industrial park, various commercial facilities, and industrial manufacturing businesses. According to 1990 data from EPA, the population is 52% African-American, 47% white, and 1% other races within one-half mile of the ETC site. Most people own their own homes (63%), and the estimated median household income is approximately $13,500. Residents and businesses in the area are connected to city water supplies.

Treatment operations at the ETC site began in 1942 and continued through 1982. The facility used creosote and pentachlorophenol (PCP) to treat utility poles. Facility operations resulted in extensive creosote and PCP contamination in the soil and groundwater. Site soils also are contaminated with high levels of dioxin, which is a common impurity in commercial grade PCP.

In October 1982, ETC stopped wood treatment operations at the site, and for nearly a decade following the plant's closing, EPA and State regulators worked successfully with the site owners to secure proper closure and cleanup of the site under the Resource Conservation and Recovery Act (RCRA).

### Removal Action

After the site owners abandoned the property through bankruptcy proceedings in February, 1991, preliminary site assessment activities began. EPA's Emergency Response and Removal Branch initiated a removal action in October, 1991, to address the immediate threat posed by the site. According to EPA literature, removal activities were designed to stabilize the site while EPA evaluated long-term cleanup solutions for site contamination. After installing a security fence to restrict unauthorized access, EPA excavated approximately 255,000 cubic yards of contaminated soil and stockpiled these materials under a cover to prevent further migration of contaminants into the groundwater. As a result there are two large holes, each over 40 feet deep and about the size of two football fields. A drainage system was installed to prevent contaminated stormwater from migrating offsite. Extensive air monitoring was conducted during the removal. Removal activities were completed late in 1992.

Citizens living near the site became concerned during the removal action. In interviews with EPA personnel in April 1992, they expressed concerns over health (including asthma, itching eyes, skin rashes, and outbreaks of cancers in the neighborhood), disposal of the excavated soil, [and] relocation concerns (residents wanted to know if EPA would move them to hotels during cleanup, due to strong odors resulting from the excavation). Around this time, the Citizens Against Toxic Exposure (CATE) group was formed, and there was some talk of permanent relocation as an option.

EPA proposed the site for inclusion on the National Priorities List (NPL) in August 1994. After a 60-day public comment period, the site's listing on the NPL was finalized in December 1994. In January, 1995, EPA awarded a Technical Assistance Grant (TAG) to CATE to enable the community to hire experts to help interpret EPA findings and requirements and to provide input to EPA.

### Relocation Evaluation Pilot Status

...EPA collected soil samples in July 1995 from residential areas near the Escambia site to determine whether contaminants from the site had migrated off-site. According to a CATE publication, the sampling showed high levels of contamination in some residential areas surrounding the site. Neighborhoods sampled included Rosewood Terrace, Oak Park, Escambia Arms, and Goulding....

### Remedial Investigation Underway

In November 1995, EPA began the Remedial Investigation (RI) Phase of the cleanup at Escambia. The purpose of the RI is to collect and analyze samples from the soil, water, air and other materials to determine the type and amount of contamination on and around the site. Sampling for Phase I of the RI (soil and air samples) was scheduled to be completed in March 1996. During recent severe weather in Pensacola, erosion occurred in the excavated areas on-site, and part of the fence was damaged. According to EPA, the Florida Department of Environmental Protection has repaired the fence, and EPA has addressed the erosion damage....

### Case Study Interviews

To develop a case study, a questionnaire was developed to obtain information and get reactions related to the relocation of residents living near the Escambia site. Six people were interviewed for the site: four community members, the State Project Manager for the site and EPA's Remedial Project Manager for the site.... The following are some of the comments received from these interviews. [Selected questions and answers follow. Eds]

*How has the community been involved in the decision-making process for considering relocation of residents living near the Escambia site?*

Residents:

R1: We haven't been making the decisions, EPA is doing that.

R2: We became organized in early 1992 through the Citizens Against Toxic Exposure (or CATE). I feel we have been somewhat successful.

R3: Not as much as we would like. They came out and didn't tell us much. When I asked, they said "We've got it under control." We would have liked to have been told the truth in the first place, when they first started digging.

R4: Community residents living at the site wanted relocation right at the start—as soon as excavation began and they learned they couldn't stop it. The next best thing was to get away. People were having serious problems as a result of fumes and dust from the excavation. Symptoms included respiratory problems, skin rashes, eye irritation, and other more serious problems indicating permanent damage. They gained support from the wider community, working with CATE. Ms. [Margaret ] Williams has been an excellent leader.

State Project Manager: The community has been involved through public meetings and hearings. State representatives have attended several of these, and EPA has done a lot of community involvement work.

Remedial Project Manager: The community has been involved largely through the CATE group, which is also a [TAG grant] recipient.... EPA sent the draft and final sampling plans for review and comment. Residential sampling was postponed to work out differences between EPA and the group's Technical Advisor.... In December 1995, EPA briefed CATE on the status of the decision-making process.

*How was your community's quality of life affected by the contamination in your neighborhood? For example, has the pride in the community diminished after the community became aware of contamination problems? Did you see a change in the number or quality of community-sponsored events or in the recreational or commercial use of land or water in or near the community (e.g., boating, fishing, swimming)?*

Residents:

R1: We used to have gardens and cookouts, but we can't do that any more. We have to be careful with letting the children play outside.

R2: Quality of life has been completely affected. Especially since we found out how high the level of contamination is. The citizens' group has grown tremendously since people learned how bad the problem is.

R3: Pride in the community has greatly diminished. After we learned that the houses and yards are affected, residents became very angry.

R4: Community residents are experiencing health problems and symptoms of worse problems to come as a result of exposure. During the excavation, people couldn't go out of their homes. There are photos of children playing in the yards 15 feet away from cleanup workers in moon suits. The residents were outraged that a government agency had so little concern for their welfare and their health. But they also took a lot of pride in their ability to organize to fight this.

Remedial Project Manager: The community has coalesced around the fight for relocation. This has increased their community identity; however, pride in the community has been adversely affected. Contamination off-site is of concern, but limited. The citizens' conclusion that health effects are related to site contamination has not been documented. The lack of a consensus on this issue has been a serious detriment to working with them in finding solutions.

*How were real estate values affected? Was the availability of mortgages and other home loans affected?*

Residents:

R1: There was a drop in the value of homes in the community because of concern over contamination. I haven't tried to sell my house. I wouldn't feel right doing so.

R2: I moved out a year ago because of my health, but haven't tried to sell. I knew of one family where the residents died and their son tried to sell the house. But he got no takers.

R3: No one is going to buy it, people are aware of the contamination. People couldn't get a loan to fix up their homes, and they can't get out.

R4: I don't actually know. I have heard from residents that homes are virtually worthless and that tax assessments are dropping compared to the rest of Pensacola.

Remedial Project Manager: Not sure. I have seen only one house for sale in the past two years.

*Were there any apparent health effects that you feel may have been either directly or indirectly caused by the contamination at the site? Please explain.*

Residents:

R1: Since 1991 when EPA started digging, we have had 37 deaths, mostly from cancer, as well as respiratory problems, rashes, and generally bad feelings knowing that [you're] living on contaminated land.

R2: I've had thyroid trouble and upper respiratory problems. They've gotten better since I moved out of the neighborhood.

R3: I've noticed in myself that the chemicals have caused a cough, sinus and respiratory problems, and skin rashes. I cover up when I go out and wash when I come in. Many people in the neighborhood have died. I believe it was related to the chemicals, whether it was cancer or something else. I have a neighbor next door who has really gone down in the past year, she's not aware of what's causing it. I really can't say, but it must be these toxic chemicals that are causing it. The EPA made us aware of this. They took the tests and samples, and they themselves are the ones that told us how dangerous it was. That's what upset me. We need this relocation for health reasons. Whatever number of days we have left, let us live it normally. That's all I ask.

R4: Residents have acute symptoms, but I suspect they're signs of more serious disorders. These include respiratory problems, persistent strange rashes, eye problems. Things that the doctors were baffled with. More chronic effects are there too: many types of cancers, immune system damage, birth defects and other reproductive problems, cardiac and circulatory diseases, liver and thyroid and chronic respiratory diseases—things like chronic bronchitis and emphysema.

State Project Manager: I am aware that health effects are an issue at the site.

Remedial Project Manager: In my personal opinion, I do not believe that the health effects residents have identified (e.g., cancer and respiratory problems) are attributable to the site. The contaminants have been enclosed, and monitoring showed no evidence of exposure. There is no plausible exposure pathway. ATSDR [The Agency for Toxic Substances Disease Registry] attempted to do a health study for the site, but CATE [the community group] refused to agree to the testing, even after four different plans were proposed. The community group insisted that none of the proposals would result in valid findings.

*Was there any apparent exodus of community residents once contamination problems became known? If so, were these primarily renters, home owners, or both?*

Residents:

R1: Ninety percent of the community is now retirement age. We bought here intending to stay. Some renters have left but not many others.

R2: Just a few have already left. Most of the community is made up of retired homeowners, they don't want to go into debt at this time in their lives. They're waiting on EPA to make a decision.

R3: There are boarded up houses that have just gone down since no one is living there. The whole area is just becoming a slum. Hobos from the train yard are living in abandoned buildings. Most of the homeowners that haven't left are like me. I've been here 37 years. The ones that have left, their children have it now. The homes may have rented out or been left vacant.

R4: Most homeowners didn't have the capability to move. Most are retired, they spent all their lives building what they thought was equity in their homes.

It's a kind of economic entrapment. People who had worked the hardest on maintaining their homes were trapped. I think it's tragic. Renters could leave, and there was some exodus of homeowners because of health effects and the fear of greater health problems if they stayed.

Remedial Project Manager: I know that Mr. Stallworth and one other person have moved.

*What are the primary reasons or issues why relocation is being considered at the Escambia site?*

Residents:

R1: The main reason is the high level of contamination in the neighborhood. We live next to Mount Dioxin, a huge amount of contaminated soil that the EPA dug up and left there. And this site is supposed to be a pilot project on relocation.

R2: The primary reason is health problems from living on contaminated soil. The contamination can affect us by entering through pores, and we breathe the dust.

R3: Health of the residents. EPA is aware of the problems. We've gotten a runaround from Region 4, but have had some responsiveness from EPA headquarters. CATE has repeatedly let them know how serious the problem is. The government usually responds immediately if a community's health is in danger, but not for us. I think it is because we are the minority.

R4: The best reason is protection of human health. As we progressed we found that pressure was needed to get EPA to take us seriously. As we progressed, we learned. We got a TAG [Technical Assistance Grant] and a Technical Advisor. I think the TAG program is incredibly helpful. I wish it were easier to come by and that it allowed for independent testing. We found support from other community groups.

State Project Manager: Health-based issues. EPA has determined contaminants are there in the neighborhood. Dioxins are present. With dioxin, EPA has historically used 1 ppb [part per billion] as a threshold. If they consider this as the reason for relocation, it will not hold up because levels are lower than that. The community is alleging that the emergency removal response caused the problem. I do believe there are sociopolitical reasons for relocation. When the neighborhood was first developed, African Americans were forced to move there, because that's where they could buy a home. Now they are trapped.

Remedial Project Manger: To address community concerns, and because of the potential cost benefits it might contribute. For example, it might be cheaper to conduct the cleanup without the people there.

*How has the community reacted during the time relocation was first suggested as a possibility to the present time?*

Residents:

R1: We've had mixed emotions. Once we got started talking with EPA, we thought something positive would happen. But the community got upset because of EPA's decision making process. Each new proposal just seemed like another stalling tactic.

R2: Starting off, some said they didn't want to go anywhere. But at last count, during the last four years, 48 people had died in that area, a number of them from cancer. A lot of people felt that the toxics were causing that, they've now come around and joined us in the fight to relocate.

R4: There have been times of exasperation, anger, and apprehension, but on the whole people have been determined. They have been hopeful and they've been united. I think this may be the most important thing they could have accomplished in terms of getting something done....

* * *

## Notes and Questions

1. Some of the resident interviewees expressed ethical concerns over whether to sell their homes in light of the discovery of nearby contamination. Assume for a moment a different scenario, that no off site contamination has been detected. Should relocation proceed if residents are nonetheless hesitant to sell their homes because they fear that there might be undetected contamination? In this instance, many in the community were concerned because the excavation resulted in PCB-laden dust that could be inhaled or absorbed through the skin. Does this put the EPA in a "catch 22" position? If the EPA elects to cap the site, it would be accused of discriminating by instituting a less protective cleanup (containment rather than treatment), but by excavating the soil to treat it, it might be causing more exposure. If you were charged with the decision, what would you do?

2. Who should decide whether or to what extent the residents' concerns are irrational? Should it matter whether the independently-hired technical advisor concurs in the government's assessment of the risks involved?

3. In the Record of Decision, dated February 12, 1997, the EPA concluded that relocation would be the best option because of the health risks due to the presence of dioxin and BaP [benzo(a)pyrene] in portions of the relocation area. Although stressing that no one factor was determinative, the EPA listed as factors adverse impacts on residents from fear stemming from uncertainty about health impacts, loss of property values and psychological stress arising, in part, from the visibility of an extremely large stockpile of highly contaminated soil. It also listed as factors, anticipated impacts from "operational issues such as truck traffic, noise, dust, [and] equipment staging." The benefits of relocation included providing EPA with greater flexibility for a remedy selection enhanced by obviating the need to remediate soil in residential areas to residential risk levels and being able to use the relocation area as industrial property. *See* U.S. Envtl. Protection Agency, Region IV, Record of Decision, Interim Remedial Action and National Relocation Pilot Project: Escambia Treating Company Site, Pensacola, Escambia County, Florida (February 12, 1997). A preliminary evaluation indicated that some levels of BaP and dioxin exceeded the $1 \times 10^{-4}$ risk level. *Id.* at 12. At the time, the cost of the relocation was estimated to be $23,577,101. *Id.* at 13.

4. Subsequently, the extended remarks of CATE's relocation TAG advisor Michael J. Lythcott, who presented testimony at a NEJAC meeting on December 1, 1999, revealed several problems that arose while implementing the relocation. A selection of his comments began with this prelude:

It is important to CATE that this finding be stated first, that it be stated clearly and that it be understood completely. In the remainder of these comments we will focus on the many serious problems, issues and concerns regarding the *implementation* of the Relocation Program. As serious as those implementation problems are, however, you must not let them overshadow this first, glorious, successful finding. Many of you in this room and many others not here made this relocation happen....The affected families in Pensacola told me to say "thank you."...

The remarks continued, with particular focus upon EPA's decision to use the Uniform Relocation Assistance Act (URAA) as a Superfund relocation policy and to use the U.S. Army Corps of Engineers (USACE) to conduct the relocation:

...The vast majority of residents that responded to a recent CATE Poll were dissatisfied with how they are being treated by USACE Personnel. Residents site rudeness, unhelpfulness, unresponsiveness and too frequently passing-the-buck to EPA in Atlanta as their chief complaints. It would not be fair to say that USACE has no customer-focus because they do. Unfortunately they see EPA as their customer and not the residents that are trying to make some of the toughest and most critical decisions of their lives.

USACE uses out-of-state appraisers (Alabama, Arkansas, etc.) to conduct the property appraisals in Pensacola. They have no idea of what the neighborhoods looked like before they started their contamination-related decline and therefore cannot comply with instructions to: "appraise the properties as if they were not next to a Superfund site." The USACE office has been instructed not to let homeowners see the appraisals that determine their purchase offer. Residents who feel that they have been seriously "low-balled" (which is what all of the local real estate experts say) have no basis to make an appeal because they are forbidden to see their appraisals.

USACE Policy dictates that the properties be appraised and valued at the Highest and Best Use of "Residential"—even though it is clear *and certifiable* that the Highest and Best Use of the properties is "Commercial/Industrial."...

The City and County have announced "The Palifox Corridor Redevelopment Plan" [sic] it is a plan that will greatly increase land values in this infrastructure-rich and very desirable part of Pensacola. That redevelopment plan will undoubtedly be partially financed with federal monies. So what we are looking at here is a kind of "Robin Hood-in-Reverse" scenario. Government taking from the poor and give to the rich. Just run this scenario through your head:

You own a tract of vacant land in the affected area. You *must* sell that land to the Federal Government at a price that the government sets. If you refuse the government's offer they will condemn the land, take it by force and put that amount in an escrow account with your name on it. The government agency that bought your property (and your neighbor's properties) has now assembled a huge parcel of very desirable land which it turns over to another government agency that cleans up the contamination. That agency turns the land over to the State and County governments who then turn it over to developers. If you are lucky, wealthy and politically connected you might now be able to get your vacant land back. The only problem is that it will cost you four to five times what the government paid you for it. More likely though, you will now only be able to drive by the luxury condos and shops that sit on the land and try to remember exactly where it was that you and your grandfather planted that pecan tree.

If this mental exercise has stirred any feelings in you, just imagine what the property owners in Pensacola must be feeling.

Based on public records that I have researched, there are significant and disturbing disparities between the dollar amounts that some owners are being paid for their land and what other residents are being paid for identical lots in the same subdivision....

While we are still analyzing the comparative data for trends, there is some preliminary indication that in some cases, the higher and lower prices paid, track right along with the race of the recipients of the money....If something is wrong, it needs to be fixed right away....

Michael J. Lythcott, Relocation TAG Advisor For Citizens Against Toxic Exposure, Remarks at the NEJAC Meeting to Discuss the Pensacola Relocation Pilot Project and Escambia-Agrico Superfund Sites (Dec. 1, 1999) (transcript of extended remarks available from Citizens Against Toxic Exposure). How would you evaluate the merits of the community's concerns? What process could be put into place to afford residents a reasonable degree of comfort that they would receive fair market value for residential purposes absent the contamination? Should they receive the higher "industrial/commercial" use value? Does this higher value depend in part upon the desirability of the land as a large parcel, a feature that individual private sales could not have accomplished without great difficulty? Does the higher value take into account a degree of subsequent cleanup? On the other hand, doesn't the government essentially benefit from relocation because it does not have to clean up the contamination to residential use standards? Who should reap the benefit of this windfall?

# Chapter X

# Litigation as a Response

## A. The Role of the Lawyer

Environmental justice activists have an ambivalent relationship with the legal system and with lawyers. On the one hand, legal representatives can play a powerful and essential role in advocating on behalf of communities. In addition, lawyers working with community groups are often activists in their own right and deeply committed to the principles of environmental justice and its goals. On the other hand, many other activists and community residents are distrustful of lawyers and the legal process. In their view, past reliance on legal processes and procedures has resulted in the historic inequitable distribution of environmental harms. Lawyers can take over disputes from community leaders, and frame issues in narrow legal terms. Moreover, communities will rarely, if ever, be able to match the legal resources of the government or private entities. These tensions are reflected in some of the excerpts that follow.

### 1. ENVIRONMENTAL JUSTICE LAWYERING

The following article was written by Francis Calpotura, a long-time organizer with the Center for Third World Organizing in Oakland, California.

### Francis Calpotura, Why the Law?
#### Third Force (May/June 1994)

I was once told by an organizer friend of mine that lawsuits are a tactic to be used during a fight when you want to (a) end the campaign and move on to another issue, (b) inspire your members by showing that you are not afraid to take on these bastards, or (c) force the hand of your opposition to react to your initiative during a stalemate.

In none of these instances, I remember, is a lawsuit a strategy for winning a fight. It is always a tactical move. So where does this penchant for legal strategies come from? Indigenous community organizations normally don't have lawyers (some don't even have paid staff) on their payroll; environmental organizations do. I would argue that the alliance of community organizations with the proliferating Environmental Law Centers around the country has resulted in legal strategies for winning environmental justice fights, to the detriment of direct-action, community-oriented strategies.

245

The political implications are serious. A legal strategy affects how the issues that confront a community are understood. For example, the fight by [activists in the Georgia Sea Islands against development] was framed as a "preservation" issue in order to employ a variety of zoning and endangered species laws to delay development. This cut on the issue fails to show the racial and class character of the developer's strategy, something organizing for community control and equitable development would do to a much greater extent.

In addition, a legal strategy takes the fight away from arenas in which people can have some direct influence — their politicians, local development company offices, residences of the CEO, bank offices, etc. — to a place where they don't, i.e. in some chamber controlled by a judge where only the lawyers are allowed to speak (and only in English). This strategy does not facilitate the building of a cohesive, imaginative and militant base of people willing to employ various tactics on the opposition. This has great implications on how deep our organizational base is, and how leaders get developed....

* * *

## Notes and Questions

1. Do you agree with Calpotura's misgivings about relying on legal strategies? From the perspective of community groups, is it true that a lawsuit is never a strategy for winning a fight but is always a tactical move?

2. What role should be played by lawyers who represent communities in environmental justice controversies? What about lawyers who represent developers or public agencies? Does attorney/activist Luke Cole adhere to a different view of the role that a lawyer can take in an environmental justice situation than Francis Calpotura? Consider these questions as you read the following excerpts.

# Luke Cole,
# Empowerment as the Key to Environmental Protection:
# The Need for Environmental Poverty Law
### 19 Ecology Law Quarterly 619 (1992)

*Client Empowerment*

"Client empowerment" occurs when a lawyer's practice helps clients realize and assert greater control over decisions which affect their lives. Empowerment is also a process which enables individuals to participate effectively in collective efforts to solve common problems....Client empowerment is about creating in the client community the dynamics of democratic decision making, accountability, and self-determination — ideals which one would like to create in society.

In the environmental poverty law context, empowerment means enabling those who will have to live with the results of environmental decisions to be those who actually make the decisions. "Community-based" and "community-led" are key descriptive and prescriptive phrases for the environmental poverty lawyer, who should seek to decentralize power away from herself and to her clients. The client empowerment model is thus the reverse of the legal-scientific mode of lawyering used by mainstream environmental groups. Rather than solving a problem *for* a community, the empowerment model calls upon attorneys to help community members solve their own problems.

"Empowerment law" is more a *method* than a *product*, a practice through which the lawyer helps the group learn empowering methods of operation. Empowerment of clients is the answer to the political organizers' eternal question: "What happens when we go away?" By helping people take control over the decisions which affect their lives, an attorney leaves the community stronger than when she arrived....

### Law as a Means, Not an End

While our first instinct as lawyers might be to use legal tactics, they may not achieve the results our clients desire. Other tactics may be more useful in generating public pressure on an unresponsive bureaucracy or polluting corporation: tactics such as community organizing, administrative advocacy, or media pressure. Because environmental problems are political problems—some government official is allowing one actor to pollute the neighborhood of another—non-legal tactics often offer the best approach. As is so often the case, there may not even *be* a legal solution to the problem faced by the community. Or, the legal approach may radically disempower a client community and thus should be avoided. Translating a community's problems into legal language may render them meaningless.... Finally, lawsuits take fights into the arena most controlled by the adversary and least controlled by the community....

### Three Questions for Effective Advocacy

Activists for social change have long relied on three questions in evaluating prospective strategies and tactics. These three questions parallel the three tenets of environmental poverty law:

1. Will it educate people?

2. Will it build the movement?

3. Will it address the root of the problem, rather than merely a symptom?

*Will the strategy educate people?* This broad question fits the empowerment model of legal services because education is a key to empowerment. Environmental poverty lawyers must broadly construe their concept of "education"—it should encompass education of a client or client group by the lawyer, education of policymakers or decisionmakers, and education of the public. Further, the educational process should be two-way: a lawyer must not only educate her clients, but also be educated by them. By increasing the community's knowledge, and others' knowledge of the community's problems, the community's persuasive power is necessarily strengthened.

*Will it build the movement?* Group representation is a self-conscious strategy to build local movements by developing local community groups. Community groups and their lawyers should look for tactics that draw new members into a group, rather than alienate potential supporters. An environmental poverty law model which is based on community education and empowerment will necessarily "build the movement," while a narrow legal approach will almost certainly fail to build anything.

*Does the strategy address the cause rather than the symptoms of a problem?* Environmental issues—like most legal services issues such as housing, health care access and (un)employment—are systemic. The disproportionate burden borne by poor people is a direct result of the system of economic organization in the United States and the corresponding inequities in the distribution of political power. Legal solutions to the environmental problems faced by poor people most often treat only the symptom, the environmental hazard itself. Embracing non-legal approaches, and legal approaches which treat the law as a means rather than an end, can help environmental poverty lawyers attack the root cause of the environmental problems faced by their clients, political and economic powerlessness....

*What Does it Look Like?*
*Public Participation in Kettleman City*

*Background.* Kettleman City is a small, farmworker community located in California's San Joaquin Valley. The community is ninety-five percent Latino, and seventy percent of its 1,100 residents speak Spanish in the home. Most residents work in the agricultural fields that stretch out in three directions from the town. Many of Kettleman City's residents have lived there for years and own their own homes, purchased with low-interest loans from the Farmers Home Administration.

Kettleman City also hosts the largest toxic waste dump west of Louisiana. Established without the community's knowledge or consent in the late 1970's, Chemical Waste Management's (CWM) Kettleman Hills Facility is a Class I toxic waste landfill. Just four miles from town, it may legally accept just about any toxic substance produced.

In 1988, CWM proposed to build a toxic waste incinerator at the dump. A Greenpeace organizer tipped off the Kettleman City community about the proposal and gave residents information on toxic waste incinerators. Feeling that the incinerator would threaten their health, homes, and livelihoods, Kettleman City residents organized a community group, *El Pueblo para el Aire y Agua Limpio* (People for Clean Air and Water), held demonstrations, and pressured their local officials. In 1989, they also secured the legal representation of the California Rural Legal Assistance Foundation (CRLAF).

The young lawyer handling the case—his first—was faced with a dilemma [the lawyer was in fact the author, Luke Cole. Eds.]. The Kings County Planning Department, the local agency responsible for granting permits for the project, had issued a dense, tedious, more than 1,000-page Environmental Impact Report (EIR) on the proposed incinerator. The County had refused to translate the EIR into Spanish, despite repeated requests from Kettleman City residents. Kettleman City residents wanted to take part in the EIR process. The lawyer needed comment on the EIR, so that the administrative record would reflect the deficiencies of the document and the process. The lawyer faced a choice: the traditional mode of environmental lawyering or a new environmental poverty law approach.

*Traditional approach.* In the traditional model of environmental advocacy, the lawyer reads and analyzes the EIR document, shares parts of it with selected experts, and then writes extensive, technical comments on the EIR on behalf of a client group. These comments are submitted to the agency and form the basis of later lawsuits if the agency does not respond adequately.

*Lawyering for social change model.* The lawyer attempts to involve and educate the community while addressing the root of the problem: that the County is ignoring and dismissing the needs of Kettleman City residents without fear of repercussions because the residents are not organized.

*Environmental poverty law in Kettleman City: How it worked.* The lawyer chose the latter strategy. Working with several key leaders in the community, he and a CRLAF community worker held an initial series of three house meetings in Kettleman City. Each meeting was held in a different home, and all were held on the same day.

At a typical meeting, the community leaders would explain the incinerator proposal to eight to ten residents. The lawyer would then describe parts of the EIR and the County's response to the community's requests. The residents would ask questions, which the leaders and the attorney would answer to the best of their abilities. Discussions among the residents would ensue about the incinerator and why it was to be located in Kettleman City. The conversations were not limited simply to the incinerator, however. Residents would tell stories of health symptoms they had experienced (which they blamed on the existing toxic waste dump), of past dealings with County officials, and of other incidents they felt were important. Since the meetings involved almost entirely monolingual Spanish-speakers, the meetings were held in Spanish, with the community worker translating for the lawyer.

At the end of each meeting, the leaders and the attorney would ask each person present to write a letter of comment on the EIR to the Planning Commission. The letters—almost all in Spanish—questioned the Planning Commission about the incinerator, and also asked to have the EIR documents translated so that Kettleman residents could take part in the process. The meetings were as inclusive as possible: if a person was not literate, he or she would dictate a letter to a more educated Kettleman resident; children were encouraged to write as well. Out of the first three meetings, the community group generated twenty-five letters of comment on the EIR.

At the first meetings, people were asked to hold future meetings in their own homes, with five to eight of their neighbors. The community worker followed up with community leaders to ensure that the meetings continued. Over the course of the following three weeks more house meetings were held, and many more letters were written. When the EIR's public comment period closed, the record contained 162 comments from individuals—126 of them from Kettleman City residents. More importantly, 119 of the comments—seventy-five percent of all comments by individuals on the EIR—were in Spanish.

Although the results of such organizing are difficult to quantify—except, of course, for the large volume of letters—the letter-writing campaign served several important purposes. It brought Kettleman City residents together to learn about and discuss the incinerator. It allowed community leaders to bring Kettleman City residents up to date on the project. It informed the community of upcoming opportunities for participation, including a hearing before the Planning Commission. It encouraged individuals to take action—writing a letter—and to express themselves both in the house meetings and on paper. It validated residents' experiences with and concerns about the incinerator and the siting process by creating an opportunity to discuss and affirm them. People could collectively share other individual problems, tell their stories, and, through that process, see the commonality of their experiences. Lastly, the letter-writing campaign allowed residents to tell their stories to the Planning Commission, to act as "experts" in their own case.

Rather than gathering the residents' stories and translating them into narrow legal points (or even into English), the lawyer sought to facilitate the people of Kettleman City speaking for themselves. By asking others to hold meetings in their homes, the attorney and the community leaders fostered a sense of ownership of the campaign among members of the community. And finally, the letters created a stunning administrative record. The County could no longer claim that Kettleman residents and Spanish-speakers were not interested in the project: more than ten percent of the community had written letters to the Planning Commission. The attorney had helped create what he needed—the administrative record—in a way which fostered community action rather than shifting it.

The letter-writing campaign was an instance of empowering the client using group representation and non-litigation avenues. Ironically, by using tactics other than litigation, the campaign facilitated the litigation that ultimately resulted. The Kings County Board of Supervisors ultimately approved the incinerator proposal, and the environmental poverty lawyer was forced to take the County to Court. The Court overturned the County's approval, in part because of the County's exclusion of Spanish-speakers. [This case is discussed in Chapter XII(C). Eds.]

The letter-writing campaign also provided solid answers to the three questions environmental poverty lawyers must ask themselves. It educated people both in the community and in the County government. The campaign built the movement by bringing house meetings into new homes and involving residents who had not participated in the group to that point. Finally, it addressed the root of the problem, by using the EIR public comment process as an organizing focus and forcing the County decision makers to listen to the people of Kettleman City.

By contrast, a traditional approach would have educated Kettleman City residents that they were not intelligent or able enough to take part in the process. It would have reinforced, rather than challenged, what Joel Handler calls the "psychological adaptions of the powerless—fatalism, self-deprecation, apathy, and the internalization of dominant values and beliefs." The traditional approach would not have built the movement and would have perpetuated, rather than confronted, the problem of the people of Kettleman City not being heard. A traditional approach would not have highlighted the need for Spanish translation of the EIR, which was so apparent after the campaign. As Señor Auscencio Avila wrote, in Spanish, demanding a Spanish translation of the EIR, "To not do this is to keep the community ignorant of what is going to happen, and to keep the community without any political power, and to suppose that we do not have the mental ability to deal with our own problems...."

\* \* \*

## Notes and Questions

1. Should empowerment of communities be the primary goal of attorneys? Or is this a task better performed by community organizers, activists, and others? What happens when a specific dispute is resolved and the lawyer's involvement with the community ends?

2. Lawyers engaged in community activism must keep in mind the roles they are playing and be cognizant about issues of legal ethics. For instance, before an attorney has been retained by a community group, does the duty of confidentiality apply? Suppose the lawyer is privy to discussions about a planned illegal protest outside a facility? Likewise, could a lawyer who goes door to door organizing neighbors to oppose a power plant be accused of improperly soliciting clients? In short, how does a lawyer separate her role as an activist from her role as an "officer of the court?" For more discussion of these issues, see Irma Russell, *Issues of Legal Ethics in Environmental Justice Matters, in* THE LAW OF ENVIRONMENTAL JUSTICE: THEORIES AND PROCEDURES TO ADDRESS DISPROPORTIONATE RISKS 429 (Michael Gerrard ed., 1999).

3. Environmental justice activist Pat Bryant has stated that "lawyers should be on tap, not on top." In practical terms, what does this mean for lawyers representing community groups? Does this mean that an activist who undertakes legal representation of a community group can never have a role in strategizing or decisionmaking?

## Richard Toshiyuki Drury & Flora Chu, From White Knight Lawyers to Community Organizing: Citizens for a Better Environment-California
### 5 Race, Poverty & the Environment 52 (Fall/Winter 1995)

The recent attention to "environmental justice" has brought support from mainstream environmental organizations and the broader legal community, with dozens of lawsuits filed on behalf of community groups in the last five years. However, not all of this attention has been welcomed by the environmental justice community. Many longtime activists believe that litigation is a disempowering tool that transfers power from community members who are directly affected by pollution to a handful of lawyers speaking for the community. Many highly mobilized community groups have withered as they pumped all of their resources into protracted litigation. Environmental justice activists have railed against "white knight" lawyers who move active community struggles into the courtroom where the community is no longer able to direct or even participate in the battle.

This article outlines a community-based environmental justice strategy pursued by the West County Toxics Coalition (WCTC) in Richmond, California, with legal and technical support from Citizens for a Better Environment (CBE) and other Bay Area groups. After taking part in, and analyzing, the campaign, we conclude that while existing legal strategies for environmental justice are inadequate at best, lawyers can best use their skills by helping to open channels for community action. Lawyers are often most effective not when they attempt to solve the problems of the community through litigation, lobbying or advocacy, but rather, when they work together with affected community groups to help them identify effective ways to solve their own problems through community organizing. This role will usually not involve litigation....

### The West County Toxics Coalition Struggle

Chevron USA, Inc. is the nation's most profitable oil company. The Chevron refinery is the largest industrial complex in the City of Richmond, currently processing 245,000 barrels of oil per day. The refinery is also Richmond's largest polluter, releasing 68,000 pounds of air pollutants *each day*, including numerous highly toxic and carcinogenic chemicals. The Chevron refinery has a long history of serious accidental and ongoing chemical releases, which have had a disastrous effect on the neighboring community of North Richmond. In response to the toxic threat, for the past decade North Richmond residents have organized to combat Chevron and other polluters, forming the West County Toxics Coalition.

In mid-1993, Chevron quietly unveiled its "Clean Fuels" project. Research by staff scientists at CBE revealed that the so-called "Clean Fuels" project was actually "green" cover for a massive refinery expansion. The result would be hundreds of tons of additional pollution in the Richmond skies and entirely new accident risks for the low-income, African American fenceline communities. While the project would produce cleaner burning fuels for the rest of California, it would also mean more pollution and accident risks for local residents—once again transferring pollution from across California into the already overburdened City of Richmond.

In a series of meetings at the WCTC office in Richmond, CBE's scientists and lawyers discussed this information with active community members. The community leadership was clearly concerned about the project's local health and safety impacts—but the concern was far deeper than that. Community members saw this project as being only one in a long line of similar projects that had the cumulative impact of bringing upon Richmond an ever worsening spiral of urban blight, toxic health risks, residential flight, and declining property values.

The CBE staff discussed with community members various approaches to address the problems identified. The attorneys examined legal avenues, the scientists technical approaches, and the community members community organizing strategies. In the end, we settled on a hybrid strategy that incorporated all three of these approaches—law, science, and community organizing....

[The community members drafted a detailed plan for the project, including state-of-the-art pollution control and safety equipment, as well a package of far-reaching community mitigation measures, and organized support for this proposal from other community organizations. CBE scientists identified technologies to make the refinery cleaner and safer.]

Our primary legal vehicle was the California Environmental Quality Act (CEQA).... CEQA requires that prior to granting a permit for a proposed project a governmental agency must issue an Environmental Impact Report (EIR) analyzing the project's adverse impacts, and discussing ways to minimize those impacts. The agency must circulate the EIR for public comment, and must consider and respond to public comments, usually through a public hearing process....CEQA was an ideal statute for our campaign because it created a public forum for decisions that would otherwise have been made behind closed doors between government and industry. Each of the public hearings held on the Chevron project were opportunities for community organizing....

[After the city planning commission adopted the community package, the City Council, under intense pressure from Chevron, approved a scaled-down mitigation package that was not adequate for community groups.]

Our strategy up to this point had been to select fora that were open to the public, allowing community members to speak for themselves, and emphasizing our strengths in community organizing and mobilization. After the city council decision to accept Chevron's compromise package, the obvious choice would have been to file a CEQA lawsuit alleging deficiencies in the city's environmental impact report for the project and a failure to require Chevron to adequately mitigate the project's impacts. But a CEQA lawsuit would shift the focus from community members to lawyers. Once in court our legal team would take center stage, filing motions, pleadings, and making oral arguments on behalf of the community. Such a litigation strategy ran directly counter to our goal of having the community speak for itself. It also played to Chevron's strengths since Chevron had a law firm of over 400 lawyers and a substantial in-house legal team that would almost certainly attempt to "paper" us into submission. Our strengths on the other hand were in organizing and mobilizing people outside of the courtroom....

Instead, the community opted to move the battle to an obscure and little used forum that had been identified by a member of the legal team. The attorney noted that Chevron still needed to obtain a permit for the project from the Bay Area Air Quality

Management District (BAAQMD). While this process was usually uneventful, the attorney discovered a citizen appeal process that had not been invoked for nearly a decade. Crucial to our strategy, the process was completely open to the public. Any interested member of the public was allowed to testify on the project, making this another excellent forum to continue the community organizing campaign.

The law students of Boalt Hall's Environmental Law Community Clinic and Golden Gate Law School's Environmental Law and Justice Clinic worked with CBE's scientists to develop a strong legal case based on the federal Clean Air Act. The students filed a 70-page appeal with the Air District arguing that the Chevron project failed to incorporate best available control technology (BACT), in violation of the Clean Air Act. Chevron, believing that we had given up our fight when we decided not to file a CEQA lawsuit, was taken completely by surprise. We had successfully caught Chevron off guard and moved the battle once again into a participatory public forum. Finally, Chevron agreed to come to the negotiating table with the community leadership.

In a series of marathon sessions, Chevron's Richmond plant management met with WCTC's Henry Clark, other community leaders, and CBE's refinery experts—without attorneys. Rather than filtering all negotiations through the lawyers, we cut the lawyers completely out of the process, forcing the Chevron management to meet face-to-face with the community leadership. The direct negotiations generated a landmark agreement only minutes before the Air District hearing was to commence. Valued at over ten million dollars together with the earlier city council compromise agreement, the package included five million dollars in corporate giving to programs designed to benefit the low-income neighborhoods near the refinery, $2.1 million for a community health clinic, $400,000 to the Richmond schools, a job training and local hiring commitment for residents of the "fenceline" communities, restoration of natural areas near the refinery, installation of advanced pollution control technology to reduce toxic chemical emissions, and numerous other provisions.

The agreement was monumental not just for its pollution control and safety elements, but especially for its inclusion of community development elements like the jobs program, school funding and health care clinic. While the substance of the agreement was impressive, the process used to arrive at the agreement was at least as significant. Throughout the campaign, community organizing played the central role and was our primary leverage. The scientists and lawyers served as resources for the community members, rather than leaders of the campaign. Perhaps the single most important role played by the lawyers was in identifying public fora, decision makers, and pressure points around which the community could organize....

* * *

## Notes and Questions

1. What do you think of the strategy followed by CBE and the West County Toxics Coalition to negotiate a settlement agreement with Chevron without lawyers for either side present? Is it feasible only where litigation has been already initiated or is threatened?

2. Should a lawyer always recommend that the community group forego a legal strategy that does not have a component of public involvement (e.g., an appeal)? If not, under what circumstances might such a strictly legal strategy be beneficial?

3. In 1993, the American Bar Association passed a resolution calling for the additional training of environmental lawyers to "recognize, address and redress incidences

of environmental inequity" and for the expansion of law school curricula and clinical programs to deal with these problems. Community activists have mixed feelings about such efforts, as reflected in an open letter sent by San Francisco Bay Area environmental justice activists to Boalt Hall Law School, Golden Gate Law School, and Stanford Law School, all of whom were initiating clinics in late 1993. The activists noted that their excitement at the swell of interest in environmental justice clinical programs was mixed with trepidation:

> All of us have had many experiences with outside institutions which, with the best of intentions, have come to "save" or "rescue" our communities—often without our communities' knowledge or consent.... Legal clinics, like any well-intentioned social program, can foster a "dependence mentality"—as opposed to an empowering one—in its clients. Extreme caution must be taken to avoid the creation of clinical programs which emphasize communities' deficiencies as a means of creating a role for themselves.... The clinics should be as open and clear as possible about the limitations of the work they will be able to undertake in communities, so as not to build up false or unrealistic expectations on the part of community groups and residents.

*See* An Open Letter Sent by San Francisco Bay Area Environmental Justice Activists to Environmental Law Clinic Proponents at Boalt Hall Law School, Golden Gate Law School, and Stanford Law School (Dec. 1993), *reprinted in* 5 RACE, POVERTY & THE ENV'T 55 (Fall 1994/Winter 1995). What steps could a law clinic take to respond to these community concerns?

* * *

Another perspective about the role lawyers can play comes from an attorney who has represented developers in siting industrial facilities.

## Michael B. Gerrard, Building Environmentally Just Projects: Perspective of a Developers' Lawyer
### 5 Environmental Law News
### (Environmental Law Section, State Bar of California) 33 (1996)

The traditional method for picking sites for controversial construction projects has been called "decide/announce/defend." The developer selects the location; tells the world; and hopes to withstand the political and legal arrows that follow.

This method has proven self-defeating. Modern environmental law has evolved a series of sequential veto points. Today, if enough people are sufficiently unhappy about a project, they can often find at least one fatal flaw that will allow them to sink it. For example, in the last 20 years not a single new hazardous or radioactive waste landfill has opened in a community in the United States where there was sustained opposition consistently backed by the local government.

The environmental justice movement has expanded and strengthened the forces of project opponents. In addition to the usual objections over endangered species habitat, regulated wetlands, contaminated soils and the like, opponents can now look to the demographics of the nearby community as another basis for resistance.

More is at stake here than builders' profits. If many low-income communities are to lift themselves out of poverty, they must support the construction of job creating projects. Moreover, many of our environmental goals can be realized only through construction projects. Recycling plants, sewage treatment plants, sewage sludge treatment units, facilities to dispose of asbestos and lead from remediated buildings, mass transit facilities, and many others are, ironically, environmentally both necessary and controversial. It is past time to abandon the reflexive notion that every major construction is an evil that must be fought.

Project developers must learn to navigate in this treacherous ocean. Regardless of whether they are personally sympathetic to it, they must recognize the reality that the environmental justice movement, in conjunction with more conventional environmentalism, can be fatal to their plans. This article attempts to provide some navigational guidance, from the perspective of an environmental lawyer who has represented numerous developers on such journeys.

### Site Selection

A central, though hotly contested, argument of many in the environmental justice movement is that communities of color have been intentionally targeted for hazardous facilities. Without entering into that debate, it goes without saying that, if such a practice ever took place, it should no more. To take it a step further, facility siting should not attempt to target white communities, either, in an attempt to redress perceived past inequities. Use of any kind of racial or demographic criteria in facility siting is likely, once discovered, to be suicidal, because the targeted group—whatever it is—will be justifiably outraged.

Instead, siting should be resolutely colorblind. The standard considerations in site selection are always appropriate—e.g., proximity to raw materials and markets; sufficiency and cost of water, energy, and other infrastructure; land availability and price; labor supply. Ample environmental due diligence is also advisable before proceeding very far with a candidate site. But theorizing that the neighbors will be more amenable if they are white, black or green is both politically and empirically suspect.

It is certainly true that different communities will regard a given proposal in much different lights. Various people and groups of people perceive risk in diverse ways, largely as a matter of local culture. Waste disposal facilities, for example, are reviled by most communities, even though they tend to be much less polluting than many kinds of factories that some people willingly accept—such as fossil fuel power plants or steel mills. Places with one of those kinds of units, or with a military installation, especially one that is closing, are often willing to accept a waste disposal facility.

Numerous psychological studies have shown that people will accept voluntary risks that are several orders of magnitude greater than involuntary risks. People will parachute out an airplane or race a car, but they don't want to live ten miles from a secure landfill. By attempting to ram a facility down the throats of an unwilling community, the physical risks involved—even if objectively small—become involuntary and therefore magnified a hundredfold in the minds of the neighbors. It becomes a war—and a war that the facility advocates cannot win.

Local variations in risk perception, and the resistance to involuntary risks, combine to suggest that a voluntary approach to site selection can be successful for projects that are not by their nature pinned to a particular location. If a company announces publicly that it wants to build such-and-such a facility; that x hundred jobs will be created; that its site must meet certain specified physical characteristics; and that it is seeking invitations from interested communities, it is likely to find a line at the door.

A voluntary approach has worked in Canada. The provinces of Alberta and Manitoba both successfully sited hazardous waste disposal complexes by calling for volunteers; both were besieged with offers. Similar results were obtained when the U.S. government wanted to build the superconducting supercollider, and when certain automakers sought to build new assembly plants.

When a community invites in a developer, the political and psychological dynamics change entirely. Communities whose dominant culture of risk perception is to accept such a facility will select themselves and volunteer, without any demographic targeting. The project proponent is an invited guest rather than a resented intruder.

### Permitting Strategy

Once a site is tentatively selected, the developer's lawyer is (or at least should be) called upon to help devise a strategy for securing the necessary governmental approvals. For controversial projects, the motto should be: avoid shortcuts. The environmental impact review process, in particular, provides an invaluable opportunity to demonstrate, with some scientific rigor, that the project will not have the dire effects that opponents may suggest. Finding ways to sidestep this and other approval processes will raise public suspicions that the developers have something to hide. Sometimes market demands or other considerations will not allow the full, lengthy process to be played out, but attempts to shortcircuit the process should be treated very gingerly.

Despite frequent calls for one-stop-shopping laws that would preempt the layers of permits and reviews and ram through a project despite legal challenges, there appears to have been only one such statute in recent decades, at least at the federal level. It was a rider to an appropriations bill that directed the Tennessee Valley Authority to build the Tellico Dam, all legal challenges nothwithstanding.... All other attempts to enact such ramrod laws seem to have failed to meet their objective.... Efforts to use the legislative ramrod allow opponents to paint themselves as martyrs of due process. If, nonetheless, the shortcircuiting statute is somehow enacted, the opposition tends to pop up again in some effective political or technical forum. Especially if a plausible environmental justice argument can be raised against a project, then the fact that standard procedures were bypassed can become a powerful rallying cry. Opponents will demand studies of the project's perceived health threats and other feared impacts, and ultimately some official body is likely to grant this request, thereby robbing the developer of the time advantage.

Developers' counsel sometimes devote all their attention to the substance of the review process—for example, making sure that the traffic and air quality modeling are performed properly—while giving less scrutiny to the procedural details. This is a serious mistake, because the courts tend to be far more deferential to administrative agencies about the technical aspects of environmental reviews than about the procedural requirements. Forgetting to send out a particular public notice can be much more dangerous than using a disputed variable in a computer model.

### Political Strategy

The political strategy is closely linked to the permitting strategy, because (among other reasons) the attitudes of the regulatory agencies can often be heavily influenced by those of the elected officials. Politician's views are, in turn, often shaped by community leaders.

If "avoid shortcuts" is the motto of the permitting strategy, "meet early and often" is the motto of the political strategy. Building mutual trust and respect with the numerous relevant groups and individuals is very time intensive. This is not a business for those who hope to have dinner at home with their families most evenings.

During these numerous meetings, it is important to be as open and straightforward as possible. Relevant information that is concealed or colored will invariably come to light and become an open wound.

Depending on the nature of the project, it is worth considering making an offer to establish a community review team for the facility once it is operating. The team members would be able to inspect the facility and its records to assure themselves that it is operating properly. Public opinion polls have shown that this degree of local oversight can go a long way in assuaging public fears.

Offers of compensation to the community must be treated very carefully. If the community fears that the project will be harmful to public health, and particularly to the health of children, compensation may be viewed as a bribe and lead to more rather than less opposition; the idea of accepting money in exchange for endangering the health of one's child is horrific, and one who makes such an offer will be branded as a monster. However, compensation may well be viewed as appropriate if the concerns are for property values, demand on public services, traffic congestion, and other impacts that can be reduced to dollars without giving offense.

It is also important to emphasize the need for the project. Where a compelling case can be made that a project is required to meet fundamental human needs, or to serve important societal values, a project proponent can overcome much legal and neighborhood resistance. Homeless shelters, drug treatment centers, low-income housing projects, group homes, and other social service facilities have typically prevailed in the face of legal challenges brought by unwelcoming neighbors. Many courts have found opposition to such uses to be based on irrational fears or on impermissible racial motivations.

It is much more difficult to make a similarly compelling moral case for waste disposal facilities, power plants, highways, and the like. These are seen as fulfilling economic goals rather than deeper human needs, and the courts are more likely to entertain challenges to their construction. However, a compelling case can be made for some of these projects as well. Often they are built to replace old substandard facilities (frequently in minority communities) that violate the environmental laws but are allowed to continue in operation because they enjoy grandfathered status. Or the project may be necessary to meet another important environmental objective, such as recycling waste rather than incinerating or landfilling it, or processing sewage sludge for agricultural use rather than dumping it in the ocean.

### Project Design

Reduction in the generation of pollution and hazardous waste is an important goal of the environmental justice movement, as well as of the conventional environmental movement. In a project that raises environmental justice concerns, it is especially important to be able to demonstrate that all reasonable steps have been taken to keep pollution and waste generation as low as possible.

This effort to minimize adverse environmental effects creates important opportunities for project sponsors. Since the dawn of modern environmental law a quarter century ago, there has never been greater governmental receptivity to flexibility in regulation. If a developer can demonstrate that its project can reduce its overall environmental impact by the use of unconventional methods, it may well be able to persuade the regulators to allow it to, for example, utilize a low cost, highly effective treatment process for one un-regulated waste stream in exchange for avoiding an expensive, marginally effective treat-ment process for a different, regulated waste stream.

Non-environmental ways to make a facility a more benevolent neighbor should also be explored. Offering on-site day care for the children of plant employees is one ex-ample.

### Set Realistic Expectations

Many of the expectations that the environmental justice movement may hold for new facilities—that they be developed in an open, honest manner, with community participation—can be fulfilled. However, at least three common demands may not be realized, and it is important to be frank about that from the start so as not to build up false expectations.

The first is that there be total community agreement on a project. Unanimous sup-port is a laudable goal, but it is unachievable for a controversial project. The expecta-tion should be for widespread but not total agreement. To demand otherwise is to en-sure paralysis.

The second is that the facility not generate any pollution or hazardous waste at all. Technology has not advanced to the point where most complex industrial processes can operate without becoming, at a minimum, small quantity generators of hazardous waste. (Indeed, most households generate hazardous waste.) The developer can promise to minimize what is generated, and to handle its hazardous waste in a lawful manner that protects workers and neighbors from harm.

The third possibly unachievable demand is that, if the selected site currently has some soil or groundwater contamination from prior uses, it will automatically be cleaned up to natural levels before construction begins. Preexisting contamination should be cleaned to meet applicable legal standards and to ensure that the project will not endanger workers or neighbors, but making the site utterly pristine can involve a very high expenditure with little or no benefit. In fact, it can hurt more people than it helps by exposing cleanup workers, and those who travel the highways used by the trucks that haul away the dirt, to unnecessary dangers. Digging up and hauling away massive amounts of dirt—often the only way to totally eliminate contamination—can also violate the principles of environmental justice by dumping waste in another (often minority) community that does not want it. . . .

\* \* \*

## Notes and Questions

1. What is the central advice conveyed by Gerrard? Does he implicitly endorse com-munity vetoes? If so, is it likely his colleagues would agree with his position? What role does he envision for developers' lawyers in development disputes? Will following his guidance lead to environmentally just projects, as the title of his article suggests? If total community support is unrealistic, what kind and how much support would justify going forward with the project?

2. Virtually all environmental laws provide the opportunity for public participation in the decision making process. In another article, Luke Cole describes two approaches that community groups can follow in utilizing these public participation provisions in

the context of a land use permitting decision. Under the first approach, which he terms the "participatory"model, groups take part in every stage of the administrative process that provides an opportunity for public input—commenting on draft documents, attending scoping meetings and public hearings, and so forth. The second or "power" model is premised on the assumption that participation by community groups in the administrative process almost never helps them change undesirable outcomes and that their sole focus should be on the decision point and in actively trying to reach the actual decision makers. Luke Cole, *Legal Services, Public Participation and Environmental Justice*, 29 CLEARINGHOUSE REV. 449 (Special Issue 1995). If you were representing a community group, which approach would you advise your client to follow? Are the two approaches mutually exclusive? Is participation in the administrative process largely a futile and co-optive exercise? Does it provide an opportunity for educating and organizing community groups? Or is it likely to lead to a slightly improved project that is more resistant to later legal challenge?

One distinct disadvantage of not participating in the administrative process is that it often will foreclose the right of a party to file a legal challenge to an agency decision, since the right to sue is usually premised on having exhausted administrative remedies. *See, e.g.*, CAL. PUB. RES. CODE § 21177 (California Environmental Quality Act).

## 2. A NOTE ON THE TULANE ENVIRONMENTAL LAW CLINIC

There are now close to thirty environmental law clinics at law schools throughout the country, and some of them have been at the forefront of representing community groups in environmental justice matters. Law students are permitted to practice law under attorney supervision prior to their admission to the bar under state student practice rules, established by state bar associations or, in some instances, by state supreme courts.

With aggressive advocacy on behalf of environmental justice clients, however, the clinics themselves also have come under attack. In Louisiana, complaints by business organizations and Louisiana Governor Mike Foster against the Tulane Environmental Law Clinic led the Louisiana Supreme Court to greatly restrict the state's student practice rules. (The business organizations charged, among other things, that "the individual faculty and students' legal views [at Tulane] are in direct conflict with business positions.") These complaints arose from the clinic's representation of citizens living in the low-income, 84% African American industrial corridor town of Convent, in St. James Parish, Louisiana. The residents opposed a plan by Shintech, a multinational petrochemical firm, to build a polyvinyl chloride plant that would result in emissions of over 3 million pounds of air pollutants per year, including close to 700,000 pounds of toxic air pollutants. The proposed project site is located in an area where toxic air emissions exceed 16 million tons annually and on a per square mile basis, are 129 times higher than the statewide average and 658 times higher than the national average. As a result of administrative appeals filed by the clinic, EPA vetoed the state's proposed air permit for the facility and accepted the citizens Title VI civil rights complaint for investigation. As the controversy over the plant grew, Shintech eventually dropped its plans to site the facility in St. James Parish and opted to build a smaller facility elsewhere in the state. *Environmental Law Clinic Raises Environmental Justice...And A Hostile Reaction From the Governor and The Louisiana Supreme Court*, TULANE ENVTL. L. NEWS 1 (Winter 1999).

The revised Louisiana student practice rules, adopted in final form in 1999, take direct aim at the representation provided by Tulane's clinic. The rules prohibit student clinicians from representing any group unless an organization certifies that at least 51% of its members are considered indigent under federal Legal Services Corporations guidelines, and prohibit clinicians from representing individuals or organizations if any supervising attorney or clinician contacted them for the purpose of representation. LA. SUP. CT. R. xx. The Louisiana student practice rules are the most restrictive in the country, and appear to have achieved their desired result. In the first eighteen months after the amendments went into effect, the Tulane clinic filed only one state court case or agency comment (in contrast to the 30 new cases it accepted annually before the rules were changed). The story of the attack on Tulane's clinic is vividly recounted in Robert Kuehn, *Denying Access to Legal Representation: The Attack on the Tulane Environmental Law Clinic*, 4 WASH. U. J.L. & POL'Y 33 (2000). Professor Kuehn's account is replete with details of conflicts of interest; corrupt political practices, Louisiana style; business intimidation; and unequal justice.

### Notes and Questions

1. Why, as a practical matter, did the new rules effectively preclude representation of virtually all of the community and environmental organizations served by the Tulane clinic in the prior 10 years? Note that in other states, eligibility for clinic representation is based on whether an organization itself can afford to hire an attorney. What concerns are raised by requiring members of organizations to disclose personal financial information?

2. After the rules were finalized in 1999, a coalition of environmental organizations, law professors and law students challenged them on various First Amendment and other grounds. The case was dismissed by a federal district court. Southern Christian Leadership Organization v. Supreme Court of Louisiana, 61 F. Supp. 2d 499 (E.D. La. 1999), *aff'd* 252 F.2d 781 (5th Cir.), *cert denied* 2001 U.S. LEXIS 10017 (2001).

# B. Alternative Litigation-Oriented Responses

## 1.   INTRODUCTION

For lawyers litigating environmental justice disputes, the "law" of environmental justice is young and still evolving. Lawyers have employed environmental, land use, civil rights, common law, and other authorities to try and stop siting decisions, clean up contaminated facilities, or seek redress for environmental harms. Few cases have resulted in published appellate court decisions. In most cases where community activists have been successful, they have relied on a combination of political, organizing, and legal strategies. An excellent, practical guide to various legal theories for addressing disproportionate environmental risks is THE LAW OF ENVIRONMENTAL JUSTICE: THEORIES AND PROCEDURES TO ADDRESS DISPROPORTIONATE RISKS (Michael Gerrard ed., 1999).

Luke Cole counsels that in siting disputes, environmental justice lawyers should follow a litigation hierarchy. At the top, lawyers should use environmental laws in a traditional manner: "[j]udges are familiar with such challenges and understand them; the law is fairly clear and generally supports credible challenges to improperly permitted facilities." The next tool is environmental laws, particularly those which mandate public participation, used with an environmental justice "twist." This means, for example, arguing that the public participation requirements of environmental review statutes requires translation of environmental documents into Spanish where a significant portion of the affected community is Latino and monolingual Spanish. The third level of the hierarchy is civil rights statutes. The likely success of such challenges remains an important and unresolved question. At the bottom level are constitutional challenges based on the equal protection clause, since these have invariably been rejected by the courts. Luke Cole, *Environmental Justice Litigation: Another Stone in David's Sling?* 21 FORDHAM U. L. J. 523 (1994). Chapters XI–XIV examine these various legal strategies in more detail. Before doing so, we turn to another potential recourse for private citizens seeking redress from environmental harm, toxic tort litigation.

## 2.   A NOTE ON TOXIC TORT LITIGATION

Toxic tort actions traditionally have not been the favored response to pollution problems. As toxic tort attorney Allan Kanner notes, "When public consciousness first began to focus on our toxic problems nationally, it was thought that traditional private law would prove ineffective to clean up and protect the environment and public health. As a result, Congress and the states passed many new environmental laws. However, lawyers and citizen groups have been successful in using private law remedies to protect and clean up the environment. Private law has been used with increasing frequency, although it often builds on public records and public investigations. Most significantly, private law courts have responded to the unique nature of toxic tort injuries by developing new remedies, such as medical monitoring." Theories available to address environmental harm include nuisance, trespass, strict liability for ultrahazardous activity, fraud, breach of implied warranty, and others. *See* Allan Kanner, *Assisting Injured Individuals, in* THE LAW OF ENVIRONMENTAL JUSTICE, *supra,* at 640.

As Kanner points out, plaintiffs have achieved some important successes in actions seeking damages from catastrophic spills or accidents. For example, a lawsuit for injuries resulting from a tank-car explosion in a minority neighborhood in New Orleans resulted in a punitive damages award of $850 million against the railroad company (because of the company's attitude toward the community before and after the explosion). As a result of an explosion in 1993 that produced a toxic cloud over Richmond, California, a heavily poor and African American area, General Chemical Company agreed to pay $180 million in damages to injured community members.

Tort actions alleging harm from routine, ongoing environmental releases, however, are much more difficult to win. Proving causation is a particularly difficult hurdle. A plaintiff must prove both general causation—that the chemical substance to which he was exposed is *capable* of causing the type of injuries alleged at the levels of exposure alleged, and specific causation—that the defendant's exposure *actually* caused the alleged injuries. The former often is difficult because there is limited data about the toxic effects of many chemical substances used in commerce. Proving specific causation is difficult because many illnesses have long latency periods and because, except in the unusual case of a toxic substance that leaves a unique "fingerprint," defendants can argue that numerous other factors are the source of plaintiff's injury—exposures to other chemical substances; exposures to the same substance emitted by another party; the background risk for a disease, and so forth.

Moreover, as Kanner explains,

> [T]he environmental justice plaintiff often must surmount more hurdles than the typical plaintiff. These hurdles include the added causation problems presented by multiple possible industrial sources ("Cancer Alley" or "Refinery Row"), a history of poor medical care and a lack of medical records, risks associated with more dangerous work and lifestyle factors, and circumstances of the poor that often present as alternative casual factors (for instance, bad diet, infrequent medical attention, smoking), along with the problem of jurors judging others by their different life experiences. These combine to make it more difficult for low-income minorities to prove to a middle-class jury that they have suffered harm as a result of their environmental victimization and thus to prevail in toxic tort litigation.

*See* Kanner, *supra*, at 620. In addition, harsh legal economics often will discourage private attorneys from taking toxic tort cases, because of the uncertainty that damages will be awarded and the low projected earnings of poor plaintiffs. Likewise, for a variety of reasons, tort litigation has provided compensation for only a very small percentage of children injured by lead-based paint. Suits against paint manufacturers, for example, have failed because of the difficulty of linking an individual's injuries to a specific company's paint and the reluctance of courts to apply theories of collective liability, such as enterprise liability or market share liability. *See* Clifford Rechtschaffen, *The Lead Poisoning Challenge: An Approach for California and Other States*, 21 Harv. Envtl L. Rev. 387, 416–417 (1997).

Some contend that conditions now are increasingly favorable to toxic tort cases. *See* Margaret Graham Tebo, *Fertile Waters*, A.B.A. J. 36 (Feb. 2001). In part this optimism stems from the increased data showing the effects of pollutants on human health, and in part it derives from the success that plaintiffs' attorneys enjoyed in their litigation against the tobacco companies. Attorneys have begun to borrow some of the successful tactics used in the tobacco litigation, such as suing entire industries (such as the manufacturers of the gasoline additive MTBE) for concealing the dangers of their products, and suing on behalf of municipalities to recover medical expenses. For example, a number of municipalities (and at least two states, Rhode Island and Wisconsin), have filed class action lawsuits against lead-paint manufacturers (and in some cases gasoline lead additive manufacturers) seeking to recover costs expended for medical care for lead poisoned residents. These actions largely have survived threshold challenges, and are proceeding forward.

Some environmental groups believe that tort actions have more deterrence value than civil enforcement cases. Saying that they were concerned about lax government enforcement of environmental requirements, in late 2000 a coalition of a half-dozen environmental groups and 15 law firms announced that they had joined forces to implement a strategy of filing large-scale common law actions against polluters. According to members of the coalition, "the tobacco wars and other legal battles have taught that the most effective lever against corporate misconduct is the threat of court-ordered damage awards only a mass tort case can bring." Douglas Jehl, *Fearing Bush Will Win, Groups Plan Pollution Suits*, N.Y. Times, Dec. 7, 2000, at A37.

## Notes and Questions

1. Do you agree with the approach of environmental groups to rely more on tort cases as opposed to citizen enforcement actions to deter corporate noncompliance?

(Chapter XI (C) discusses some of the substantial hurdles plaintiffs face in bringing citizen suits). Consider on the one hand that damages in large tort cases (both actual and punitive damages) often far exceed the penalties imposed (or even theoretically available) in enforcement actions. On the other hand, establishing liability in a citizen enforcement case is typically far easier, since it often requires showing only that a defendant violated a permit requirement, and avoids complex issues of causation.

2. Attorney Kanner cautions that "[l]awyers have to be honest with their clients about the realistic goals of toxic tort litigation and vigilant in pursuing a client's goal. While toxic tort litigation can provide important compensation to victims who have been damaged, it can rarely alter the political status quo that has allegedly produced and sustained the complained-of-injustice....In most cases, facilities will not be moved." *See* Kanner, *supra*, at 620.

# Chapter XI

# Enforcement of Environmental Pollution Laws as a Response

## A. Introduction

Enforcement is a sometimes overlooked aspect of environmental regulation, since it is carried out quietly by federal and state agencies, removed from the public spotlight. But adequate enforcement is critical to achieving the objectives of our environmental laws, particularly in environmental justice communities where so many polluting facilities are located. As noted by Professor Robert Kuehn in Chapter I, the theme of "corrective justice"—fairness in the way punishments for lawbreaking are assigned and damages inflicted on individuals and communities are addressed—is an important concept underlying the environmental justice movement. *See* Robert Kuehn, *A Taxonomy of Environmental Justice*, 30 ENVTL. L. REP. 10,681, 10,693 (2000).

As described more fully in Chapter III(D), a 1992 study by the National Law Journal (NLJ) found that penalties imposed by EPA for violations of federal environmental laws were substantially lower in minority communities than in white communities. The effect of a community's income on penalties was more ambiguous. The NLJ study also found racial disparities in EPA's response to contaminated waste sites—abandoned waste sites took longer to be placed on the national priorities list than those in white areas and EPA chose less protective cleanup remedies more often at minority sites. The study found similar, but less pronounced, gaps between poor and wealthy communities.

The NLJ study had a powerful impact in environmental justice communities, as well as with policymakers. First, it reinforced widespread anecdotal evidence of unequal enforcement: "Lax government enforcement of restrictions on leaking underground storage tanks, hazardous waste incineration, lead smelters, petro-chemical plant emissions, and the cleanup of the Anacostia River in Washington, D.C., have all been attributed to discriminatory practices and policies of environmental agencies. It has also been noted that EPA was quick to authorize governmental buyouts of the homes of residents living around the predominantly white Superfund sites at Love Canal and Times Beach, but has been unwilling to authorize a buyout in the African-American town of Triana, Alabama." *See* Robert Kuehn, *Remedying the Unequal Enforcement of Environmental Laws*, 9 ST. JOHN'S J. LEGAL. COMMENT. 625, 633–634 (1994). More fundamentally, the NLJ study resonated with deeply held beliefs in minority communities that laws are enforced unfairly against them, concerns highlighted by racial profiling, bias in the administration of the death penalty, and other law enforcement practices beyond the environmental law context. In response to the study, EPA, while disputing charges of discrimination and arguing that its enforcement decisions were based on neutral criteria, acknowledged that there was clearly a perception of agency bias that needed to be addressed. *See id.* at 630–31. Some specific responses that EPA has since implemented are discussed below in Section B(3)(d).

Even assuming enforcement decisions such as where to inspect, where to allocate resources, what level of fines to impose, and so forth are made based on "neutral criteria" applied in an even-handed manner, environmental justice communities are likely to bear greater burdens simply because more polluting facilities are located in their midst than elsewhere, which means they disproportionately experience the impacts of noncompliance. Considerable evidence exists showing that rates of noncompliance among regulated entities are quite substantial. For example, EPA estimated that in fiscal year 1998, the rates of *significant* noncompliance for major facilities were 20 percent under the Clean Water Act, 21 to 28 percent under RCRA and at least 7 percent (and probably higher) under the Clean Air Act. The overall noncompliance rate under the Clean Water Act for major facilities was 50 percent. A 1999 study by the Environmental Working Group likewise shows that more than 39 percent of all major facilities in five large industrial sectors violated the CAA in the two year period starting in January, 1997, and on average were out of compliance half the time during this period. *See* Clifford Rechtschaffen, *Competing Visions: EPA and the States Battle for the Future of Environmental Enforcement*, 30 ENVTL. L. REP. 10,803, 10,817 (2000).

# B. Enforcement by Government Agencies

## 1. SOURCES OF DISPARATE ENFORCEMENT

The excerpt below by Professor Kuehn examines some factors that may contribute to disparate enforcement by environmental agencies.

## Robert R. Kuehn,
## Remedying the Unequal Enforcement of Environmental Laws
### 9 St. John's Journal of Legal Commentary 625 (1994)

Noncompliance with environmental laws is widespread.... The effects of noncompliance can be serious. Unauthorized releases of toxic chemicals may pose acute health hazards to those living in the vicinity of the facility. Moreover, if permits and pollution standards are carefully set at levels that provide an adequate margin of safety, and if noncompliance results in greater amounts of pollution being emitted than calculated by the agency in making its determination, then the surrounding community may not, in fact, be provided the protection required by the law or assumed by the agency. In addition, the failure to enforce means that an accurate history of noncompliance, and an accurate portrayal of the status of the facility and its operator, will not be available to the agency or the public in subsequent permit or enforcement proceedings....

While nondiscrimination against minorities and low income persons in enforcement of laws is expected by citizens and mandated by the law, the published enforcement policies of EPA do not identify this as a goal of the agency. This silence stands in stark contrast to the agency's repeated concern for evenhanded treatment of regulated industries....

Even if the empirical data of unequal enforcement of environmental laws is scarce and open to criticism, the conditions that could give rise to discriminatory enforcement are present. The causes of unequal enforcement are likely to be the same structural causes that have been blamed for the general unequal distribution of environmental hazards among minorities and low income communities. Racist attitudes, lack of economic and political clout, and lack of participation in government decisionmaking all play a causal role. To be sure, poor minority communities face some fairly high barriers to effective mobilization against toxic threats, such as limited time and money; lack of access to technical, medical or legal expertise; relatively weak influence in political or media circles; and cultural and ideological indifference or hostility to environmental issues.

In fact, the conditions that give rise to the discriminatory impact of environmental hazards may be even greater when the government acts as enforcer, since few areas of the law invest more discretion in agency employees or are more hidden from the public's view and oversight than an agency's enforcement actions. The initial decision about which facilities to inspect and how often to check for violations is generally left to the discretion of the agency, although some statutes do provide for annual or biannual inspections. Once the agency gets notice of a violation, it can choose to take an informal response, such as a phone call, site visit, warning letter or notice of violations; an administrative remedy, such as an administrative penalty assessment or compliance order; a judicial action for penalties or injunctive relief; or a criminal prosecution. The process for cleaning up waste sites, and the decisions regarding which, when, and how, provide similar opportunities for the exercise of discretion.

While agencies often develop guidance documents to assist them in determining the acceptable response or size of any penalty, those guidance documents are not binding on the agency and are designed with sufficient flexibility to allow the decisions to be influenced, whether intentionally or not, by the nature of the community in the area where the violator operates....

* * *

## Notes and Questions

1. As Professor Kuehn notes, the enforcement process is filled with opportunities for discretionary decisions. EPA and the states lack sufficient staff to inspect more than a fraction of regulated facilities or the resources to pursue more than a small percentage of violations (By one 1996 estimate, at least 700,000 facilities are subject to one or more federal environmental laws, while government agencies combined conduct fewer than 100,000 inspections per year). Under many environmental laws, EPA and the states have great latitude in choosing whether to prosecute a violation administratively, civilly, or criminally, or not at all. The Supreme Court has ruled that agency decisions about whether to initiate enforcement actions are generally not subject to judicial review. Heckler v. Chaney, 470 U.S. 821 (1985). When determining penalties in the approxi-

mately 95 percent of civil and administrative cases that settle before trial, EPA staff are instructed to follow agency penalty policies, but these also leave substantial room for judgment calls, such as determining the potential harm from noncompliance, a company's good faith efforts to remediate the violation, a violator's culpability, and its ability to pay, and other mitigating circumstances. *See, e.g.,* U.S. ENVTL. PROTECTION AGENCY, *Policy on Civil Penalties*, 17 ENVTL. L. REP. 35,083 (1984).

2. According to EPA, the purposes of imposing penalties are to recover the economic benefit derived by noncompliance, to specifically deter the violator, and to generally deter the larger regulated community from future noncompliance. As Professor Kuehn points out, a stated goal of EPA's penalty policies is the fair and equitable treatment of regulated entities. Do you agree with him that EPA should also include as a goal that enforcement policies should not discriminate against any communities? If so, what are the practical impediments in implementing such a policy?

## 2.   THE STATE TREND AWAY FROM ENFORCEMENT

The National Law Journal study described above focused on enforcement actions carried out by EPA. The states, however, rather than EPA, administer 75% of major federal environmental programs, and carry out 80–90% of inspections and enforcement actions in the country. As the following excerpt explains, the states have significantly changed their enforcement philosophy and practices in recent years.

## Clifford Rechtschaffen,
## Competing Visions: EPA and the States Battle
## for the Future of Environmental Enforcement
### 30 Envtl. L. Rep. 10,803 (2000)

An important battle is currently taking place over the future direction of environmental enforcement in the United States. The conflict is in part between businesses and government; more fundamentally, however, it is between the U.S. Environmental Protection Agency (EPA) and the states. EPA's vision of effective enforcement is one grounded in deterrence, the theory that generally underlies societal efforts to control unlawful behavior. Many states, by contrast, have been shifting to a more conciliatory, cooperation-oriented approach. Since environmental law rests on a federalism model giving states authority to implement federal statutes but only under federal oversight, and since the states' brand of enforcement does not follow EPA's deterrence-based policies, the area is rife with tension....

Broadly speaking, there are two different philosophies that regulators can follow to achieve compliance. One is a deterrence-based approach strategy....The competing strategy is one based on cooperation, variously termed a "negotiated," "flexible," "compliance-based," or "conciliatory" approach. In shorthand, deterrence relies on sticks to achieve compliance, while cooperation emphasizes carrots....

*Deterrence-Based Enforcement*

Deterrence-based enforcement is the approach that Americans are most familiar with; it is the prevailing societal strategy for regulating unlawful conduct. The deterrence model is premised on the idea that regulated entities are rational economic actors that act to maximize profits. Decisions regarding compliance are based on self-interest; businesses comply where the costs of noncompliance outweigh the benefits of noncompliance. The benefits of noncompliance with environmental regulations consist of money saved by not purchasing pollution control equipment, training workers, abating contamination, or taking other required measures. The costs of noncompliance include the costs of coming into compliance once a violation is detected, plus any penalties imposed for being found in violation, multiplied (discounted) by the probability that the violations will be detected. These costs can also include damage to the business' reputation, potential tort liability, legal system expenses, and increased regulatory scrutiny.... Under a deterrence model, the essential task for enforcement agencies is to make penalties high enough and the probability of detection great enough that it becomes economically irrational for regulated entities to violate the law.... EPA's enforcement system traditionally has been grounded in deterrence theory (although as noted below in actual practice EPA enforcement has been closer to a hybrid of deterrence and cooperation)....

### Cooperation-Based Enforcement

A cooperation-based system of enforcement is premised on a different set of assumptions about why individuals and corporations comply with the law. It views corporations not as economic actors solely interested in maximizing profits, but as influenced by a mix of civic and social motives, and generally inclined to comply with the law. Therefore, if corporations are found in violation of regulatory requirements, they should be treated like partners, and they will respond positively to suggestions and advice about how to achieve compliance.... Generally speaking, a cooperation-based system emphasizes securing compliance rather than punishing wrongdoing. It disfavors legalistic responses.... Penalties are seen as threats rather than sanctions, and are typically withdrawn if compliance is achieved....

### The State Approach to Environmental Enforcement

While there are significant differences among individual states...[g]enerally speaking, the states advocate a more cooperation-based enforcement strategy.... Many states argue that the appropriate response to noncompliance in almost all cases is working with violators to achieve compliance, rather than initiating enforcement actions....

States start from the premise that education and technical assistance is the preferred tool for achieving compliance.... Thus, over the past 5 to10 years the states have sought to develop and expand compliance assistance programs, particularly programs aimed at small businesses. These include workshops, newsletters, fact sheets, web page information, technical assistance visits, and "plain-English" guides explaining regulatory requirements....

At the same time that states have expanded compliance assistance programs, they have cut back on the use of deterrence-based tools — traditional inspections, administrative and civil enforcement actions, and penalties.... Thus, for example, very rough EPA data shows that the number of Resource Conservation and Recovery Act (RCRA) inspections conducted by states declined by 50 percent from fiscal year 1996 to 1998, and that state inspections for all federal environmental programs declined about 12%. Likewise, a series of audits by EPA's Inspector General and the [General Accounting Office] in the late 1990's found that states were not carrying out the monitoring and inspection activities required by EPA policy.... Many states now greatly temper or forego entirely enforcement actions in response to violations. EPA reported a 50% decline in the number of the state enforcement actions initiated under RCRA between 1993 and 1997....Apart from foregoing actions, in many instances, actions taken by the states are not "timely and appropriate"—characteristics which, according to deterrence theory described above, are necessary to deter future violations.

Many states also have chosen to de-emphasize penalties as a means of securing compliance. Several have adopted amnesty programs that expressly prohibit sanctions for minor violations....Beyond these initiatives, many states have stopped imposing penalties on violators, including significant violators, or now impose only very limited fines. (Some states never assessed large penalties in the first place.)...When penalties are imposed, according to a host of studies, they frequently are inconsistent with EPA's penalty policies. Many states fail to recover economic benefit when assessing penalties—a core element of deterrence theory designed to ensure that companies do not gain from noncompliance and that there is a level playing field among regulated entities....

A central element of the states' enforcement approach is greater reliance on industry self-policing and self-regulation, particularly voluntary audits. An environmental audit is a systematic review of a facility's compliance with environmental requirements....As companies began auditing more regularly [in the 1980's], they began lobbying the states for audit privilege and immunity provisions, arguing that without such protections firms would forego audits because of fear that the information discovered would be used against them in enforcement actions or tort lawsuits....Twenty four states currently have audit privilege or immunity statutes....The privilege measures generally bar the use of audit documents as evidence in litigation over compliance with environmental laws, and otherwise allow them to be withheld from public or governmental disclosure....The immunity laws protect companies from sanctions for environmental violations if the violations are discovered pursuant to the audit, voluntarily reported, and corrected within a certain time....

### Research on Cooperative Strategies

...Despite the widespread calls for moving away from a deterrence-based enforcement, there is relatively little data to support the argument that cooperation works better to achieve compliance with environmental law....

A few studies indicate improvements in compliance rates after cooperative strategies were substituted for traditional practices....We are also starting to see some data analyzing the effectiveness of compliance assistance programs being implemented by the states and EPA. For instance, in a 1998 survey of state hazardous waste officials, several states reported demonstrable improvements from various compliance assistance or other alternative enforcement activities....

There are only a handful of studies directly comparing the effectiveness of deterrence and cooperative-oriented strategies. A study by Kathyrn Harrison of the pulp and paper industries in the United States and Canada, where enforcement has been more aligned with the cooperative school, found that rates of compliance with effluent limitations in Canada are significantly lower than in the United States....Raymond Burby has conducted two studies comparing enforcement approaches. In his review of the nonpoint source control programs in 20 states, he found that the degree of coercion that programs apply to the private sector and to local governments is the critical element in explaining the program's effectiveness....Cooperative approaches were less effective than deterrence, particularly those that relied on building capacity and public awareness without providing technical assistance to regulated entities....

We have considerably more research examining the impacts of traditional enforcement activities [although] this data is relatively limited.... Thus, a series of studies of the pulp and paper industry in both the United States and Canada show that increased levels of traditional enforcement activity—including inspections, the threat of inspections, timely and appropriate enforcement responses, or other enforcement actions—tends to increase the rate of industry compliance.... A number of studies in other contexts reach similar conclusions about deterrence-based measures.... [S]everal empirical studies have demonstrated that increased monitoring activities by the Coast Guard reduces both the frequency and size of oil spills from oil tankers and barges.... Conversely, we have considerable evidence showing that the absence of deterrence-based enforcement, that is, the absence of a threat of meaningful sanctions, often translates into noncompliance. Thus, EPA and the states proved singularly unsuccessful in bringing municipalities into compliance with [Safe Drinking Water Act] requirements and municipal-treatment plan violations using solely a compliance promotion approach....

### The Theoretical Bases for Rejecting Deterrence-Based Models

...Critics [of deterrence-based enforcement] dispute the view of corporations as driven only by economic factors, and contend that corporate actors are instead motivated by a variety of social, civic, and other considerations. Some argue that corporations conceive of themselves as political citizens, who are ordinarily inclined to comply with the law, partially because of their belief in the law, and partially as a matter of their long-term self-interest.

The critics of deterrence-based enforcement are correct to reject an economically deterministic model as the only explanation for voluntary compliance.... But bottom-line profitability still matters a great deal in industry choices about compliance, and often overcomes even good-faith efforts to comply...Likewise, a number of observers have noted that environmental programs often hit a "green wall," a point at which an organization refuses to move forward with its strategic environmental management program. The lack of progress results from an uneasy fit of environmental management with traditional business functions and traditional business culture. Environmental management programs still are largely judged on their ability to make money for the company rather than their intrinsic merits.

Moreover, many critics understate the role that ideological resistance to regulation plays in undermining compliance. Absent deterrence, corporate actors are far more likely to adhere to laws that in their eyes are legitimate, particularly when compliance is expensive.... There is no question that many businesses remain philosophically opposed to some substantial portion of the current regime of environmental regulation, and indeed, consider it illegitimate....

### Internal Regulatory Systems

Commentators also argue that traditional enforcement approaches should be modified because many corporations have adopted extensive internal regulatory programs and effectively police themselves. Self-regulation can take a number of forms, ranging from relatively simple procedures for regularly monitoring for compliance, to sophisticated internal programs [such as environmental management systems, or EMSs] or codes of conduct that some observers contend are more comprehensive and more effective than government enforcement efforts....

[T]here is little hard data demonstrating the degree to which these self-policing policies, in particular EMS and codes of conduct, have actually enhanced compliance....At least a couple of studies have found that use of an EMS does not necessarily lead to better environmental performance. Second, many firms—certainly the great majority of regulated entities—cannot afford environmental audits or management systems and do not have sophisticated internal regulatory programs....Finally, and perhaps most fundamentally, the growth in self-policing by companies is directly linked to strong governmental enforcement; without such enforcement, the incentives for companies to spend money on internal compliance programs is greatly reduced. Thus, EPA has concluded that its strong enforcement efforts has played a major role in the growth of environmental auditing in recent years....

* * *

## Notes and Questions

1. If you were a member of a low income community or community of color concerned about disparate environmental impacts in your neighborhood, would you prefer to have environmental agencies use a "carrots" or "sticks" approach to enforcement? Would you favor the use of sanctions in response to noncompliance or greater emphasis on counseling and providing technical assistance to facilities to achieve compliance?

2. As noted by Professor Rechtschaffen, most federal environmental statutes allow states to implement federal statutes under EPA oversight, and the states have now been delegated authority to implement most of the major statutory programs. Over the past decade, many states have been pushing for less stringent federal oversight in order to pursue their preferred approach to enforcement and other regulatory programs. States argue that, as compared with EPA, they are more flexible, more innovative, have more interaction with regulated entities, and are more responsive to local conditions and priorities. Environmental groups counter that states are more susceptible to industry capture and that absent federal controls states will engage in a "race to the bottom" to attract industry by lowering environmental standards. They also cite evidence in some states of significant rates of noncompliance with environmental requirements and cutbacks in state enforcement activity and spending. The Bush Administration has indicated that it will be receptive to state desires for added flexibility in enforcement. What degree of state autonomy/federal oversight is desirable? Are states more or less likely than EPA to deal with concerns about inequitable enforcement and disparate impacts in environmental justice communities? Do we need a federal enforcement "gorilla in the closet" to ensure adequate state enforcement?

3. Perhaps the clearest difference between EPA and state enforcement practices is the level of penalties obtained. In a recent empirical study, for example, Professor Mark Atlas found that state hazardous waste penalties were consistently lower than those imposed by the regional EPA office in which the state is located, and that controlling for various characteristics about the nature of enforcement actions, state penalties are about half of what EPA would impose in similar circumstances. Mark Atlas, Separate But Equal?: An Empirical Comparison of State Versus Federal Environmental Enforcement Stringency, Address Before the Association for Public Policy Analysis and Management Annual Research Conference (Nov. 2, 2000). Other studies have reached similar conclusions, and additionally found that penalties vary widely among states.

(Studies also have found wide variations in per capita spending by states on environmental protection.) Whether these differences are problematic and whether significant penalties are necessary to deter violations and promote compliance depends upon your perspective. Many states argue that significant penalties are unnecessary to prompt compliance by most businesses, which in their view are generally inclined to obey the law, while EPA maintains that adequate penalties play a key role in deterring violators. From the perspective of impacted communities, even more may be at stake from the penalty disparities. In recent years, environmental agencies increasingly have been willing to reduce penalties that they would otherwise assess in exchange for environmentally beneficial projects, including ones that decrease pollution and directly benefit impacted communities. (Such Supplemental Environmental Projects, or SEPS, are discussed in section (3)(c) below.) Thus, lower state penalty assessments may in the end mean less money funneled to local communities for mitigation, community education, and pollution prevention.

## 3. STRENGTHENING PUBLIC ENFORCEMENT IN ENVIRONMENTAL JUSTICE COMMUNITIES

How can government enforcement efforts better address issues of noncompliance in low income communities and communities of color? Consider the following suggestions:

### a. ENHANCED PENALTIES

Most environmental statutes provide that in determining penalties, a court or EPA shall consider, in addition to specific factors, "such other factors as justice may require." *See, e.g.* Clean Air Act, §113(e)(1). Should EPA and states seek enhanced penalties against facilities in environmental justice communities to deter future violations? Richard Lazarus and Stephanie Tai suggest that such higher penalties may be justified because of inadequate past government enforcement in these areas and the lack of community resources to oversee facilities' ongoing compliance. *See* Richard J. Lazarus and Stephanie Tai, *Integrating Environmental Justice Into EPA Permitting Authority* 26 ECOL. L. Q. 617, 637 (1999). In addition to historically inadequate enforcement, are higher penalties also justified because of the enhanced cumulative risks facing community residents? Or do such increased fines unfairly penalize individual facilities for a problem caused by multiple entities? How do you evaluate this suggestion in light of the debate about the relative effectiveness of deterrence-oriented vs. cooperation-oriented enforcement strategies discussed above?

In assessing penalties, should a judge or agency consider whether a facility owner has a history of siting facilities, or a history of chronic noncompliance, in poor and minority communities? Professor Gauna has argued that "[t]he possibility of higher penalties in poor communities and communities of color could have a deterrent effect that might offset the corresponding incentive to locate in [these] communities because of actual or perceived underenforcement." Eileen Gauna, *Federal Environmental Citizen Provisions: Obstacles and Incentives on the Road to Environmental Justice*, 22 ECOL. L. Q. 1, 83 (1995).

### b. TARGETING ENFORCEMENT RESOURCES

How should an agency's enforcement resources be targeted? Should agencies devote more resources to communities in which there is a disproportionate share of polluting facilities? Should community residents be given a role in suggesting sites or industries to target for inspection? One study found that the per-capita income of communities surrounding pulp and paper mills influenced the likelihood of an inspection, with plants in more affluent communities more likely to be inspected (The study also found that the level of pollution in the surrounding community, weighted by population, increased the probability of inspection). *See* Eric Helland, *The Enforcement of Pollution Control Laws: Inspections, Violations and Self-Reporting*, 80 REV. ECON. & STAT. 141, 152 (1998). Some scholars have suggested that facilities in heavily impacted areas should be targeted for regular inspections to counteract the tendency of some regulators to inspect in response to complaints from affected parties. Are there disadvantages to limiting the scope of agency discretion in selecting targets for inspections?

Concerned about the dangers of childhood lead poisoning, which disproportionately affect low income and minority children, in 2000, the Department of Justice, EPA, and the Department of Housing & Urban Development began a targeted effort to enforce federal lead-based paint disclosure requirements. *See generally* Dennis Binder et al., *A Survey of Federal Agency Response to President Clinton's Executive Order No. 12898 on Environmental Justice*, 31 ENVTL. L. REP. 11,133, 11,145, 11,147 (2001).

### c. GREATER USE OF SUPPLEMENTAL ENVIRONMENTAL PROJECTS

Unlike damages, penalties awarded under environmental statutes typically go into the U.S. Treasury or a state's general fund, not directly to individuals impacted by a facility's noncompliance. Environmental agencies could enhance the impact of their enforcement actions in environmental justice communities by making greater use of nonmonetary sanctions against violators. For example, EPA's Supplemental Environmental Projects ("SEP") Policy allows violators to reduce penalties in exchange for undertaking environmentally beneficial projects such as pollution prevention or pollution reduction projects or public health projects designed to remedy damage to human health caused by a violation. EPA's policy on SEPs specifically encourages SEPs in communities where environmental justice may be an issue: "Emphasizing SEPs in communities where environmental justice concerns are present helps ensure that persons who spend significant portions of their time in areas, or depend on food and water sources located near, where the violations occur would be protected." U.S. Envtl. Protection Agency, Final Supplemental Environmental Projects Policy, 63 Fed. Reg. 24,796, 24,797 (May 5, 1998). Such projects could include establishment of community health centers, monitoring of environmental or health conditions, establishment of alternative water supply systems, reduction of emissions beyond required levels, and so forth. Many states also have SEP policies. Is the SEP approach good or bad for environmental justice communities? Why? What would be some of the incentives and disincentives involved in pursuing SEPs for violations in heavily impacted communities?

### d. EPA's RESPONSE

As noted above, in response to the National Law Journal study, EPA acknowledged a perception of bias in agency enforcement practices that needed to be addressed. Moreover, Section 1-103 of the Executive Order on Environmental Justice requires agencies to adopt environmental justice strategies that address enforcement of health and environmental statutes in areas with minority and low income populations. (The Executive Order is reprinted in Chapter XV.) In its 1995 Environmental Justice Strategy, EPA promised to use its enforcement discretion to focus on environmental justice communities. *See* <http://www.epa.gov/docs/oejpubs/strategy/strategy.txt.html>. During the Clinton Administration, Sylvia Lowrance, deputy assistant administrator in the Office of Enforcement and Compliance Assurance, pledged that the agency and its regional offices would strengthen their enforcement efforts in areas with high levels of pollution. However, NEJAC's enforcement subcommittee has pointed out that there is no empirical evidence that EPA has actually done this in high pollution minority or low income areas.

Some of EPA's regional offices also have released policies that address enforcement issues. Consider the following policy, adopted in December 2000 by EPA's Region II (which covers New Jersey, New York, Puerto Rico and the U.S. Virgin Islands). *See* <http://www.epa.gov/r02earth/community/ej/poltoc.htm#pdf>.

# EPA Region II
### Interim Environmental Justice Policy

*Environmental Justice and Civil Enforcement Guidelines*

[E]J communities, by definition, bear an unfair burden due to pollution, and affected residents and children may experience disproportionately high and adverse health effects. Therefore, it is important to provide equitable inspection coverage in low-income and minority areas. It is always important to return violating facilities to compliance as quickly as possible.

The Region will continue to provide compliance and enforcement information to those communities located in low income and/or minority areas. In particular, the Region will coordinate on-site compliance visits and seminars to specifically address EJ concerns. Further, EJ concerns will be considered in targeting single and multimedia inspections. Notwithstanding, the Region will respond to complaints from potential EJ communities, as well as all segments of the population, with the appropriate inspection.

*Identifying Potential Environmental Justice Cases*

Enforcement matters, including those which arise in environmental justice communities often present unique challenges.... It is expected that by utilizing existing enforcement standard operating procedures and these guidelines, Regional enforcement staff should, if appropriate:

identify potential EJ communities and enforcement matters involving such EJ communities;

ensure that violations that involve identified EJ communities are handled in an expeditious and thorough manner;

keep the community informed of developments; and as appropriate, seek early community input regarding the resolution of such matters....

*Implementing Environmental Justice in the Enforcement Process*

Where one or more of the above criteria are met, enforcement personnel should consider enhanced public outreach throughout the three stages of the enforcement process as discussed below....

*Initiation of Enforcement Actions*

EPA often issues a press release to announce a major enforcement action. For EJ matters, the enforcement staff should consult with [the Communications Division] as to the appropriateness of providing additional information to local, affected communities, taking into account both the enforcement sensitivities related to the action and the level of community interest.... [E]nforcement staff should consider...whenever possible and appropriate, providing notice to individuals and groups who are expected to have an interest in the action....

*Processing of Enforcement Actions*

After enforcement actions have been initiated, the affected community and other interested persons or groups should be kept informed of the progress of an enforcement action, as appropriate and pursuant to the Communications Plan developed pursuant to Section 5.2 [Section 5.2 is not excerpted here. Eds.] For cases that reach a hearing (either administrative or judicial), the enforcement staff should, as appropriate, keep concerned citizens informed of significant milestones in the litigation process.

*Negotiation and Settlement of Enforcement Actions*

Settlement discussions are a particularly sensitive phase with respect to community outreach. The specific terms of settlement discussions are generally confidential and ordinarily should not be discussed with the general public. Community input will be solicited, as appropriate, in enforcement action resolutions as discussed below, particularly if major SEPs or compliance activities may be involved.

> *Penalties.* In calculating a penalty, enforcement should employ EPA recognized Enforcement Response Policies. Consistent with the relevant penalty policies, the enforcement team staff should ensure that the penalty amount reflects the seriousness of the violation given existing burdens in the community.

> *Injunctive Relief.* Where a facility cannot immediately come into compliance, the schedule for compliance may be a matter of intense public concern. Similarly, depending on the nature of the case, other aspects of injunctive relief may have an impact upon the community.

To the extent possible and appropriate in a given case, the enforcement staff should seek to include in the settlement of the action provisions benefitting the community, such as:

> to encourage the responsible party to agree to provide information or other outreach to the community;

> to facilitate citizen information committees for ongoing community involvement in longer-term remedies;

> to foster participation from the affected community in monitoring compliance at the facility; or

> to provide technical assistance to the community.

*Supplemental Environmental Projects (SEPs)*

The Agency's 1998 "Supplemental Environmental Projects Policy" actively encourages the use of creative settlement approaches in enforcement actions.... The enforcement staff should encourage, whenever appropriate in discussions with the violating facility, the development of SEPs. Where appropriate, the affected community should be involved in development of the SEPs....

* * *

## Notes and Questions

1. How far does the Region II policy go in incorporating the suggestions made above for enhancing enforcement in environmental justice communities? For example, how likely is it that the policy will result in larger penalties in communities with high levels of pollution? The policy encourages settlements that provide community members with technical assistance and ongoing monitoring and oversight responsibilities. What obstacles are there to obtaining such settlements?

2. Similar to Region II's policy, the Department of Justice (which represents EPA in all court proceedings) now instructs its attorneys to review each case to determine if it raises potential environmental justice issues. If the case does, attorneys are directed to consider alternative dispute resolution or remedial solutions intended to directly benefit affected communities, and also are encouraged to make special efforts to encourage public participation and solicit community input. *See* Binder, *supra*, at 11,146–11,147.

3. The decline in enforcement actions by state agencies arguably makes citizen enforcement by local communities even more important, a topic to which we now turn.

# C. Private Enforcement — Citizen Suits

In addition to enforcement by federal and state agencies, citizens are authorized by most federal environmental laws to bring enforcement actions Over the past twenty years, mainstream environmental organizations have effectively used citizen suits to supplement traditional enforcement when government agencies fail to act, either because of lack of resources or political will. Citizen suits can prod agencies to target resources or press for stronger sanctions against certain facilities. For example, the National Law Journal study discussed in Chapter III found that cases in which citizen groups were involved resulted in higher penalties (it is not clear from the study whether this refers to cases triggered by citizen suit notices or where citizens actually intervened in the case).

## 1.  A NOTE ON PROCEDURAL AND STANDING HURDLES

In order to bring a case alleging a violation of federal environmental law, plaintiffs must satisfy various threshold procedural requirements. This section discusses some of the most important of these requirements. For a more detailed discussion of these requirements, *see* Ellen Chapnick, *Access to the Courts, in* THE LAW OF ENVIRONMENTAL JUSTICE: THEORIES AND PROCEDURES TO ADDRESS DISPROPORTIONATE RISKS 357 (Michael Gerrard ed., 1999).

Plaintiffs must first demonstrate that they have a right to sue under the statute that they are seeking to enforce. Most federal environmental statutes contain citizen suit provisions (such provisions are far less common under state law) authorizing suits by "any person" (or "any citizen" in the case of the Clean Water Act) in two circumstances: against a regulated entity for a violation of any standard or requirement of the act's substantive provisions; and against an agency for failure to perform a nondiscretionary duty, such as meeting a statutory deadline ("action-forcing" suits). Before initiating an action, citizens must provide sixty-days notice of the alleged violation to the defendant and government enforcement agencies. In Hallstrom v. Tillamook County, 493 U.S. 20 (1989), the Court ruled that the 60-day notice provision in RCRA [the Resource Conservation and Recovery Act], comparable versions of which are found in virtually all other federal environmental citizen suit provisions, is a jurisdictional precondition that must be complied with on penalty of dismissal of the action. Suits are authorized after 60 days provided that no government agency has commenced and is diligently prosecuting a civil or criminal action for the same violation.

For those environmental laws, such as the National Environmental Policy Act (NEPA), that do not have citizen suit provisions, citizens may bring claims under the general review provision of the Administrative Procedure Act (APA), which authorizes suits for persons "adversely affected" by a final agency action. See 5 U.S.C. §§ 702–04. In the absence of a statutory authorization to sue for violations, plaintiffs also can argue that a private right of action is "implied" in the statute, although the Supreme Court has greatly constricted the circumstances under which implied rights of action will be found. (See, e.g. Alexander v. Sandoval, 532 U.S. 275 (2001), discussed in Chapter XIV).

The Supreme Court significantly limited the reach of citizen enforcement actions in Gwaltney of Smithfield Ltd. v. Chesapeake Bay Foundation, 484 U.S. 49 (1987), in which it held that citizens cannot sue defendants for wholly past violations of the Clean Water Act. Rather, plaintiffs must allege at the time a complaint is filed a "state of either continuous or intermittent violation—that is, a reasonable likelihood that a past polluter will continue to pollute in the future." The Court's decision was based on the meaning of section 505 of the Act, which authorizes citizen suits against any person "alleged to be in violation" of the statute. The Gwaltney decision had far-reaching implications because the great majority of environmental citizen suits are filed under the Clean Water Act, and because several other federal statutes have similarly worded citizen suit provisions. In addition, as a result of several recent Eleventh Amendment decisions, citizen suits against states for damages under environmental statutes are now barred. See Seminole Tribe v. Florida, 517 U.S. 44 (1996) (Congress lacks authority under Article I of the Constitution to abrogate states' Eleventh Amendment immunity from private suits in federal court); Alden v. Maine, 527 U.S. 706 (1999) (Congress lacks authority to abrogate states' immunity from private suits in state courts).

Apart from enforcement actions against violators and action-forcing suits, citizens can also challenge actions taken by administrative agencies, such as the adoption of regulations and the issuance of permits. Such actions are generally subject to judicial review provided certain preconditions are met:

> The major federal environmental statutes specifically authorize judicial review of agency action taken pursuant to them, and they also specify the procedures for obtaining judicial review. These statutes, coupled with the judicial review provisions of the [Administrative Procedures Act], 5 U.S.C. §§ 701–706, lay out the ground rules for challenging agency decisions in the federal courts. They generally permit suits challenging final agency action (as distinguished from "preliminary, procedural, or intermediate agency action," which may be reviewed only when the final agency action is taken, APA §704) as long as it is not "committed to agency discretion by law" (such as a decision whether or not to initiate enforcement action, Heckler v. Chaney, 470 U.S. 821 (1985)). §701(a)(2). Plaintiffs seeking judicial review also must have exhausted admin-

istrative remedies by raising objections in the rulemaking proceeding before the agency. The agency's action also must be deemed sufficiently "ripe for review" by courts, who seek to avoid premature adjudication of issues that have not crystallized to the point at which they are having more than a hypothetical impact on prospective litigants.

R. Percival, A. Miller, C. Schroeder and J. Leape, Environmental Regulation: Law, Science and Policy 183 (3d ed. 2000). In Ohio Forestry Ass'n v. Sierra Club, 523 U.S. 726 (1998), the Supreme Court ruled that challenges by environmental groups to final forest management plans prepared under the National Forest Management Act are not ripe for adjudication, and that plaintiffs instead have to file numerous site-specific challenges when the plans are actually implemented. *Ohio Forestry* highlights the difficulty plaintiffs face in challenging programmatic agency decisions.

In addition to establishing a statutory right to sue and meeting other procedural preconditions, plaintiffs suing in federal court must demonstrate constitutional standing to sue. Several Supreme Court decisions in the 1990's made it considerably more difficult for environmental plaintiffs to prove standing, although this trend has been at least temporarily halted with the Court's most recent decision in *Friends of the Earth v. Laidlaw*, excerpted below.

Standing addresses "whether a party has a sufficient stake in an otherwise justiciable controversy to obtain judicial resolution of that controversy." Warth v. Seldin, 422 U.S. 490 (1975). Standing derives from Article III, §2 of the Constitution, which limits the jurisdiction of federal courts to "cases" and "controversies." To establish constitutional standing, a plaintiff must prove (1) an injury in fact that is concrete, affecting plaintiff in a personal and individual way, and actual or imminent; (2) that the injury complained of is fairly traceable to the actions of the defendant (causation); and (3) that an order in plaintiff's favor will redress the injuries complained of (redressability). The Court has also imposed a "prudential limitation," one that can be altered by Congress, which is that plaintiffs's injury arguably falls within the zone of interests that the statute plaintiffs are enforcing is designed to protect. In Bennett v. Spear, 520 U.S. 154 (1997), the Supreme Court held that citizen suit provisions authorizing "any person" to sue—the language typically used in federal environmental statutes—establish the broadest possible zone of interests, authorizing any party with constitutional standing to sue. An association has standing to bring suit on behalf of its members when its members would otherwise have standing to sue in their own right, the interests at stake are germane to the organization's purpose, and neither the claim asserted nor the relief requested requires the participation of individual members in the lawsuit. *See* Hunt v. Washington State Apple Adver. Comm'n, 432 U.S. 333 (1977).

In the first major environmental standing decision of the 1990's, Lujan v. National Wildlife Federation, 497 U.S. 871 (1990), plaintiffs challenged a decision of the Bureau of Land Management to open 180 million acres of federal land to possible mining and oil and gas claims. Plaintiffs filed affidavits from two of its members alleging that they used and enjoyed federal lands in the vicinity of about 2 million acres, approximately 4,500 acres of which were impacted by the BLM's action. The Court held that these allegations were insufficient to establish injury and that to prove standing, plaintiffs had to demonstrate that they actually use or visited the specific parcels of land affected by the BLM decision. Two years later, the Court issued the following opinion.

# Lujan v. Defenders of Wildlife
## 504 U.S. 555 (1992)

*Justice Scalia delivered the opinion of the Court:*

[This case involves a challenge to a rule promulgated by the federal government interpreting § 7 of the Endangered Species Act (ESA). The ESA requires each federal agency to insure that any action authorized, funded, or carried out by such agency will not jeopardize the continued existence of any endangered species or threatened species or result in the destruction or adverse modification of habitat of such species. In 1986, the Interior Department promulgated a regulation stating that Section 7 is not applicable to actions taken in foreign nations. Respondents filed suit seeking to invalidate the regulation.]

The party invoking federal jurisdiction bears the burden of establishing [the elements necessary to demonstrate standing]....When the suit is one challenging the legality of government action or inaction, the nature and extent of facts that must be averred (at the summary judgment stage) or proved (at the trial stage) in order to establish standing depends considerably upon whether the plaintiff is himself an object of the action (or forgone action) at issue. If he is, there is ordinarily little question that the action or inaction has caused him injury, and that a judgment preventing or requiring the action will redress it. When, however, as in this case, a plaintiff's asserted injury arises from the government's allegedly unlawful regulation (or lack of regulation) of *someone else*, much more is needed. In that circumstance, causation and redressability ordinarily hinge on the response of the regulated (or regulable) third party to the government action or inaction—and perhaps on the response of others as well. The existence of one or more of the essential elements of standing "depends on the unfettered choices made by independent actors not before the courts and whose exercise of broad and legitimate discretion the courts cannot presume either to control or to predict," and it becomes the burden of the plaintiff to adduce facts showing that those choices have been or will be made in such manner as to produce causation and permit redressability of injury. Thus, when the plaintiff is not himself the object of the government action or inaction he challenges, standing is not precluded, but it is ordinarily "substantially more difficult" to establish....

Respondents' claim to injury is that the lack of consultation with respect to certain [federal agency] funded activities abroad "increas[es] the rate of extinction of endangered and threatened species." Of course, the desire to use or observe an animal species, even for purely esthetic purposes, is undeniably a cognizable interest for purpose of standing. See, *e. g.*, Sierra Club v. Morton, 405 U.S. [727], 734 [1972]. "But the 'injury in fact' test requires more than an injury to a cognizable interest. It requires that the party seeking review be himself among the injured." *Id.* at 734–735. To survive the Secretary's summary judgment motion, respondents had to submit affidavits or other evidence showing, through specific facts, not only that listed species were in fact being threatened by funded activities abroad, but also that one or more of respondents' members would thereby be "directly" affected apart from their "'special interest' in the subject." *Id.* at 735, 739.

With respect to this aspect of the case, the Court of Appeals focused on the affidavits of two Defenders' members—Joyce Kelly and Amy Skilbred. Ms. Kelly stated that she traveled to Egypt in 1986 and "observed the traditional habitat of the endangered nile crocodile there and intend[s] to do so again, and hope[s] to observe the crocodile directly," and that she "will suffer harm in fact as the result of [the] American . . . role . . . in overseeing the rehabilitation of the Aswan High Dam on the Nile . . . and [in] developing . . . Egypt's . . . Master Water Plan." Ms. Skilbred averred that she traveled to Sri Lanka in 1981 and "observed the habitat" of "endangered species such as the Asian elephant and the leopard" at what is now the site of the Mahaweli project funded by the Agency for International Development (AID), although she "was unable to see any of the endangered species"; "this development project," she continued, "will seriously reduce endangered, threatened, and endemic species habitat including areas that I visited . . . [, which] may severely shorten the future of these species"; that threat, she concluded, harmed her because she "intend[s] to return to Sri Lanka in the future and hope[s] to be more fortunate in spotting at least the endangered elephant and leopard." When Ms. Skilbred was asked at a subsequent deposition if and when she had any plans to return to Sri Lanka, she reiterated that "I intend to go back to Sri Lanka," but confessed that she had no current plans: "I don't know [when]. There is a civil war going on right now. I don't know. Not next year, I will say. In the future."

We shall assume for the sake of argument that these affidavits contain facts showing that certain agency-funded projects threaten listed species—though that is questionable. They plainly contain no facts, however, showing how damage to the species will produce "imminent" injury to Mses. Kelly and Skilbred. That the women "had visited" the areas of the projects before the projects commenced proves nothing. As we have said in a related context, " 'Past exposure to illegal conduct does not in itself show a present case or controversy regarding injunctive relief . . . if unaccompanied by any continuing, present adverse effects.' " And the affiants' profession of an "intent" to return to the places they had visited before—where they will presumably, this time, be deprived of the opportunity to observe animals of the endangered species—is simply not enough. Such "some day" intentions—without any description of concrete plans, or indeed even any specification of *when* the some day will be—do not support a finding of the "actual or imminent" injury that our cases require.

Besides relying upon the Kelly and Skilbred affidavits, respondents propose a series of novel standing theories. The first, inelegantly styled "ecosystem nexus," proposes that any person who uses *any part* of a "contiguous ecosystem" adversely affected by a funded activity has standing even if the activity is located a great distance away. This approach, as the Court of Appeals correctly observed, is inconsistent with our opinion in *Lujan v. National Wildlife Federation*, which held that a plaintiff claiming injury from environmental damage must use the area affected by the challenged activity and not an area roughly "in the vicinity" of it. 497 U.S. at 887–889. It makes no difference that the general-purpose section of the ESA states that the Act was intended in part "to provide a means whereby the ecosystems upon which endangered species and threatened species depend may be conserved," 16 U. S. C. § 1531(b). To say that the Act protects ecosystems is not to say that the Act creates (if it were possible) rights of action in persons who have not been injured in fact, that is, persons who use portions of an ecosystem not perceptibly affected by the unlawful action in question.

Respondents' other theories are called, alas, the "animal nexus" approach, whereby anyone who has an interest in studying or seeing the endangered animals anywhere on the globe has standing; and the "vocational nexus" approach, under which anyone with a professional interest in such animals can sue. Under these theories, anyone who goes to see Asian elephants in the Bronx Zoo, and anyone who is a keeper of Asian elephants in the Bronx Zoo, has standing to sue because the Director of the Agency for International Development (AID) did not consult with the Secretary regarding the AID-funded project in Sri Lanka. This is beyond all reason. Standing is not "an ingenious academic exercise in the conceivable," *United States v. Students Challenging Regulatory Agency Pro-*

*cedures,* 412 U.S. 669, 688, 37 L. Ed. 2d 254, 93 S. Ct. 2405 (1973), but as we have said requires, at the summary judgment stage, a factual showing of perceptible harm. It is clear that the person who observes or works with a particular animal threatened by a federal decision is facing perceptible harm, since the very subject of his interest will no longer exist. It is even plausible—though it goes to the outermost limit of plausibility—to think that a person who observes or works with animals of a particular species in the very area of the world where that species is threatened by a federal decision is facing such harm, since some animals that might have been the subject of his interest will no longer exist. See *Japan Whaling Assn. v. American Cetacean Society,* 478 U.S. 221, 231 n. 4, 92 L.Ed. 2d 166, 106 S.Ct. 2860 (1986). It goes beyond the limit, however, and into pure speculation and fantasy, to say that anyone who observes or works with an endangered species, anywhere in the world, is appreciably harmed by a single project affecting some portion of that species with which he has no more specific connection.

Besides failing to show injury, respondents failed to demonstrate redressability. Instead of attacking the separate decisions to fund particular projects allegedly causing them harm, respondents chose to challenge a more generalized level of Government action (rules regarding consultation), the invalidation of which would affect all overseas projects. This programmatic approach has obvious practical advantages, but also obvious difficulties insofar as proof of causation or redressability is concerned. As we have said in another context, "suits challenging, not specifically identifiable Government violations of law, but the particular programs agencies establish to carry out their legal obligations . . . [are], even when premised on allegations of several instances of violations of law, . . . rarely if ever appropriate for federal-court adjudication."

The most obvious problem in the present case is redressability. Since the agencies funding the projects were not parties to the case, the District Court could accord relief only against the [Secretary of Interior]: He could be ordered to revise his regulation to require consultation for foreign projects. But this would not remedy respondents' alleged injury unless the funding agencies were bound by the Secretary's regulation, which is very much an open question....

A further impediment to redressability is the fact that the [U.S. federal] agencies generally supply only a fraction of the funding for a foreign project. AID, for example, has provided less than 10% of the funding for the Mahaweli project. Respondents have produced nothing to indicate that the projects they have named will either be suspended, or do less harm to listed species, if that fraction is eliminated. As in Simon [v. Eastern Ky. Welfare Rights Organization], 426 U.S.[26], 43–44 [1976], it is entirely conjectural whether the non-agency activity that affects respondents will be altered or affected by the agency activity they seek to achieve....

The Court of Appeals found that respondents had standing for an additional reason: because they had suffered a "procedural injury." The so-called "citizen-suit" provision of the ESA provides, in pertinent part, that "any person may commence a civil suit on his own behalf (A) to enjoin any person, including the United States and any other governmental instrumentality or agency . . . who is alleged to be in violation of any provision of this chapter." 16 U. S. C. § 1540(g). The court held that, because § 7(a)(2) requires interagency consultation, the citizen-suit provision creates a "procedural right" to consultation in all "persons"—so that anyone can file suit in federal court to challenge the Secretary's (or presumably any other official's) failure to follow the assertedly correct consultative procedure, notwithstanding his or her inability to allege any discrete injury flowing from that failure. To understand the remarkable nature of this holding one must be clear about what it does *not* rest upon: This is not a case where plaintiffs are seeking to enforce a procedural requirement the disregard of which could impair a separate concrete interest of theirs (*e.g.*, the procedural requirement for a hearing prior to denial of their license application, or the procedural requirement for an environmental impact statement before a federal facility is constructed next door to them).[7] Nor is it simply a case where concrete injury has been suffered by many persons, as in mass fraud or mass tort situations. Nor, finally, is it the unusual case in which Congress has created a concrete private interest in the outcome of a suit against a private party for the Government's benefit, by providing a cash bounty for the victorious plaintiff. Rather, the court held that the injury-in-fact requirement had been satisfied by congressional conferral upon *all* persons of an abstract, self-contained, noninstrumental "right" to have the Executive observe the procedures required by law. We reject this view.

We have consistently held that a plaintiff raising only a generally available grievance about government — claiming only harm to his and every citizen's interest in proper application of the Constitution and laws, and seeking relief that no more directly and tangibly benefits him than it does the public at large — does not state an Article III case or controversy....

We hold that respondents lack standing to bring this action and that the Court of Appeals erred in denying the summary judgment motion filed by the United States....

* * *

## Notes and Questions

1. In a concurring opinion, Justice Kennedy suggested that Congress might be able to define the violation of a statute as creating an injury in fact sufficient for Constitutional standing. He wrote that "[a]s government programs and policies become more complex and far reaching, we must be sensitive to the articulation of new rights of action that do not have clear analogs in our common-law tradition.... In my view, Congress has the power to define injuries and articulate chains of causation that will give rise to a case or controversy where none existed before, and I do not read the Court's opinion to suggest a contrary view." *Id.* at 580.

2. Professor Ann Carlson has argued that the tighter standing requirements imposed by the Supreme Court actually may improve the effectiveness of litigation as a tool for environmental protection by forcing plaintiffs to demonstrate why an environmental resource matters to people. "By requiring plaintiffs to demonstrate more directly and

---

7. There is this much truth to the assertion that "procedural rights" are special: The person who has been accorded a procedural right to protect his concrete interests can assert that right without meeting all the normal standards for redressability and immediacy. Thus, under our case law, one living adjacent to the site for proposed construction of a federally licensed dam has standing to challenge the licensing agency's failure to prepare an environmental impact statement, even though he cannot establish with any certainty that the statement will cause the license to be withheld or altered, and even though the dam will not be completed for many years. (That is why we do not rely, in the present case, upon the Government's argument that, *even if* the other agencies were obliged to consult with the Secretary, they might not have followed his advice.) What respondents' "procedural rights" argument seeks, however, is quite different from this: standing for persons who have no concrete interests affected — persons who live (and propose to live) at the other end of the country from the dam.

concretely that they have been "injured in fact," the recently invigorated rules may force environmental lawyers to think more seriously about how environmental problems actually harm human beings. This more careful consideration could, in turn, significantly assist environmental plaintiffs in building and presenting compelling cases in court and could transform the approaches they take outside of court to solving environmental problems." Ann Carlson, *Standing for the Environment*, 45 UCLA L. Rev. 931, 932 (1998). Do you agree with Professor Carlson's critique? Do the benefits she articulates outweigh some of the concerns she also identifies—the time and resources it takes for understaffed environmental organizations to meet the standing burden and fight standing challenges, and the potential for losing close cases on standing grounds? Professor Carlson also suggests that meeting the injury in fact requirements could lead environmental organizations to reach out beyond their normal constituencies and make their organizations more inclusive, an important goal of environmental justice advocates.

3. In the third major standing case of the 1990's, Steel Company v. Citizens for a Better Environment, 523 U.S. 83 (1998), plaintiffs sued a manufacturing company for its failure to file reporting forms required under the federal right-to-know law (the Emergency Planning and Community Right-to-Know Act, or EPCRA) from 1988 to 1995. The defendant had filed the overdue forms after receiving plaintiff's 60-day notice of intent to sue and before the litigation was initiated. The Supreme Court ruled that where a defendant has come into compliance at the time the complaint is filed, plaintiffs lack standing to bring a claim for civil penalties, at least where the penalties are awarded to the federal treasury, because such penalties could not redress plaintiffs' injuries. The Court held that in these circumstances plaintiffs (even those directly injured by defendant's noncompliance) share only an "undifferentiated public interest" in seeing the law complied with. The Court held that the availability of declaratory relief, attorneys fees, and litigation costs in the event plaintiffs prevailed also were insufficient to redress the injuries alleged by plaintiffs.

In Friends of the Earth v. Laidlaw Environmental Services, 149 F.3d 303 (4th Cir. 1998), the Fourth Circuit decided an issue not addressed by *Steel Company*: if a defendant is in violation at the time a plaintiff files her complaint, but comes into compliance at some other point during the litigation, does the plaintiff still have standing to sue for penalties? In *Laidlaw*, environmental groups sued the operator of a hazardous waste incinerator for violating its Clean Water Act permit. The trial court found that Laidlaw had committed hundreds of violations, including 36 after plaintiffs filed their complaint, and imposed a penalty of over $400,000. The court also found that Laidlaw had been in substantial compliance with its permit for several years at the time of the final order in the case, and denied plaintiffs' request for injunctive relief. The Fourth Circuit, relying on *Steel Company*, held that plaintiffs lacked standing to proceed because their only remaining relief requested was civil penalties paid to the federal treasury, and such penalties could not redress any injuries that plaintiffs had suffered. The Supreme Court granted plaintiffs' petition for certiorari, and issued this opinion.

# Friends of the Earth v. Laidlaw Environmental Services
## 528 U.S. 167 (2000)

*Justice Ginsburg delivered the opinion of the Court:*

This case presents an important question concerning the operation of the citizen-suit provisions of the Clean Water Act. Congress authorized the federal district courts to entertain Clean Water Act suits initiated by "a person or persons having an interest which is or may be adversely affected." 33 U.S.C. §§ 1365(a), (g). To impel future compliance with the Act, a district court may prescribe injunctive relief in such a suit; additionally or alternatively, the court may impose civil penalties payable to the United States Treasury. § 1365(a)....

[The Act] provides for the issuance, by the Administrator of the Environmental Protection Agency (EPA) or by authorized States, of National Pollutant Discharge Elimination System (NPDES) permits. NPDES permits impose limitations on the discharge of pollutants, and establish related monitoring and reporting requirements, in order to improve the cleanliness and safety of the Nation's waters. Noncompliance with a permit constitutes a violation of the Act.

In 1986, defendant-respondent Laidlaw Environmental Services (TOC), Inc., bought a hazardous waste incinerator facility in Roebuck, South Carolina, that included a wastewater treatment plant.... Shortly after Laidlaw acquired the facility, the South Carolina Department of Health and Environmental Control (DHEC), acting under 33 U.S.C. § 1342(a)(1), granted Laidlaw an NPDES permit authorizing the company to discharge treated water into the North Tyger River. The permit, which became effective on January 1, 1987, placed limits on Laidlaw's discharge of several pollutants into the river, including—of particular relevance to this case—mercury, an extremely toxic pollutant.... Once it received its permit, Laidlaw began to discharge various pollutants into the waterway; repeatedly, Laidlaw's discharges exceeded the limits set by the permit.... The District Court later found that Laidlaw had violated the mercury limits on 489 occasions between 1987 and 1995.

[After filing a sixty-notice of their intent to sue], plaintiffs (collectively referred to as Friends of the Earth, or FOE) filed suit against Laidlaw in June, 1992. The District Court found that FOE had standing to bring suit, and in a judgment issued in January, 1997, assessed a civil penalty of $405,800. The court denied plaintiffs' request for injunctive relief, finding that Laidlaw had been in substantial compliance with its permit since August, 1992. The Court of Appeals reversed.]

According to Laidlaw, after the Court of Appeals issued its decision but before this Court granted certiorari, the entire incinerator facility in Roebuck was permanently closed, dismantled, and put up for sale, and all discharges from the facility permanently ceased....

Laidlaw contends first that FOE lacked standing from the outset even to seek injunctive relief, because the plaintiff organizations failed to show that any of their members had sustained or faced the threat of any "injury in fact" from Laidlaw's activities. In support of this contention Laidlaw points to the District Court's finding, made in the course of setting the penalty amount, that there had been "no demonstrated proof of harm to the environment" from Laidlaw's mercury discharge violations.

The relevant showing for purposes of Article III standing, however, is not injury to the environment but injury to the plaintiff. To insist upon the former rather than the latter as part of the standing inquiry (as the dissent in essence does) is to raise the standing hurdle higher than the necessary showing for success on the merits in an action alleging noncompliance with an NPDES permit. Focusing properly on injury to the plaintiff, the District Court found that FOE had demonstrated sufficient injury to establish standing. For example, FOE member Kenneth Lee Curtis averred in affidavits that he lived a half-mile from Laidlaw's facility; that he occasionally drove over the North Tyger River, and that it looked and smelled polluted; and that he would like to fish, camp, swim, and picnic in and near the river between 3 and 15 miles downstream from the facility, as he did when he was a teenager, but would not do so because he was concerned that the water was polluted by Laidlaw's discharges.....

Other members presented evidence to similar effect.... CLEAN [Citizens Local Environmental Action Network, Inc.] member Gail Lee attested that her home, which is near Laidlaw's facility, had a lower value than similar homes located further from the facility, and that she believed the pollutant discharges accounted for some of the discrepancy. Sierra Club member Norman Sharp averred that he had canoed approximately 40 miles downstream of the Laidlaw facility and would like to canoe in the North Tyger River closer to Laidlaw's discharge point, but did not do so because he was concerned that the water contained harmful pollutants.

These sworn statements, as the District Court determined, adequately documented injury in fact. We have held that environmental plaintiffs adequately allege injury in fact when they aver that they use the affected area and are persons "for whom the aesthetic and recreational values of the area will be lessened" by the challenged activity. Sierra Club v. Morton, 405 U.S. 727, 735, 31 L. Ed. 2d 636, 92 S. Ct. 1361 (1972). See also *Defenders of Wildlife*, 504 U.S. at 562–563 ("Of course, the desire to use or observe an animal species, even for purely esthetic purposes, is undeniably a cognizable interest for purposes of standing.")

Our decision in Lujan v. National Wildlife Federation, 497 U.S. 871, 111 L. Ed. 2d 695, 110 S. Ct. 3177 (1990), is not to the contrary. In that case an environmental organization assailed the Bureau of Land Management's "land withdrawal review program," a program covering millions of acres, alleging that the program illegally opened up public lands to mining activities. The defendants moved for summary judgment, challenging the plaintiff organization's standing to initiate the action under the Administrative Procedure Act, 5 U.S.C. § 702. We held that the plaintiff could not survive the summary judgment motion merely by offering "averments which state only that one of [the organization's] members uses unspecified portions of an immense tract of territory on some portions of which mining activity has occurred or probably will occur by virtue of the governmental action." 497 U.S. at 889.

In contrast, the affidavits and testimony presented by FOE in this case assert that Laidlaw's discharges, and the affiant members' reasonable concerns about the effects of those discharges, directly affected those affiants' recreational, aesthetic, and economic interests. These submissions present dispositively more than the mere "general averments" and "conclusory allegations" found inadequate in *National Wildlife Federation*, 497 U.S. at 888. Nor can the affiants' conditional statements—that they would use the nearby North Tyger River for recreation if Laidlaw were not discharging pollutants into it—be equated with the speculative "'some day' intentions" to visit endangered species halfway around the world that we held insufficient to show injury in fact in *Defenders of Wildlife*. 504 U.S. at 564....

Laidlaw argues next that even if FOE had standing to seek injunctive relief, it lacked standing to seek civil penalties. Here the asserted defect is not injury but redressability. Civil penalties offer no redress to private plaintiffs, Laidlaw argues, because they are paid to the government, and therefore a citizen plaintiff can never have standing to seek them....

We have recognized on numerous occasions that "all civil penalties have some deterrent effect." More specifically, Congress has found that civil penalties in Clean Water Act cases do more than promote immediate compliance by limiting the defendant's economic incentive to delay its attainment of permit limits; they also deter future violations. This congressional determination warrants judicial attention and respect....

It can scarcely be doubted that, for a plaintiff who is injured or faces the threat of future injury due to illegal conduct ongoing at the time of suit, a sanction that effectively abates that conduct and prevents its recurrence provides a form of redress. Civil penalties can fit that description. To the extent that they encourage defendants to discontinue current violations and deter them from committing future ones, they afford redress to citizen plaintiffs who are injured or threatened with injury as a consequence of ongoing unlawful conduct.

The dissent argues that it is the *availability* rather than the *imposition* of civil penalties that deters any particular polluter from continuing to pollute. This argument misses the mark in two ways. First, it overlooks the interdependence of the availability and the imposition; a threat has no deterrent value unless it is credible that it will be carried out. Second, it is reasonable for Congress to conclude that an actual award of civil penalties does in fact bring with it a significant quantum of deterrence over and above what is achieved by the mere prospect of such penalties. A would-be polluter may or may not be dissuaded by the existence of a remedy on the books, but a defendant once hit in its pocketbook will surely think twice before polluting again....

We recognize that there may be a point at which the deterrent effect of a claim for civil penalties becomes so insubstantial or so remote that it cannot support citizen standing. The fact that this vanishing point is not easy to ascertain does not detract from the deterrent power of such penalties in the ordinary case.... In this case we need not explore the outer limits of the principle that civil penalties provide sufficient deterrence to support redressability. Here, the civil penalties sought by FOE carried with them a deterrent effect that made it likely, as opposed to merely speculative, that the penalties would redress FOE's injuries by abating current violations and preventing future ones — as the District Court reasonably found when it assessed a penalty of $405,800.

Laidlaw contends that the reasoning of our decision in [*Steel Co. v. Citizens for a Better Environment*] directs the conclusion that citizen plaintiffs have no standing to seek civil penalties under the Act. We disagree. *Steel Co.* established that citizen suitors lack standing to seek civil penalties for violations that have abated by the time of suit. 523 U.S. at 106–107. We specifically noted in that case that there was no allegation in the complaint of any continuing or imminent violation, and that no basis for such an allegation appeared to exist. 523 U.S. at 108; *see also* Gwaltney [of Smithfield Ltd. v Chesapeake Bay Foundation], 484 U.S. [49], 59 [1987] ("the harm sought to be addressed by the citizen suit lies in the present or the future, not in the past"). In short, *Steel Co.* held that private plaintiffs, unlike the Federal Government, may not sue to assess penalties for wholly past violations, but our decision in that case did not reach the issue of standing to seek penalties for violations that are ongoing at the time of the complaint and that could continue into the future if undeterred....

\* \* \*

## Notes and Questions

1. In an important subsequent portion of its opinion, the Court addressed the related question of mootness. Defendant argued that plaintiffs' claim for penalties was moot because it had voluntarily come into substantial compliance with its permit after the complaint was filed, and later permanently closed the facility at which the violations had occurred. The Court ruled that a case "might become moot if subsequent events made it absolutely clear that the allegedly wrongful behavior could not reasonably be expected to recur," but that the "heavy burden" of demonstrating this rested with the

party asserting mootness. The Court found that the effects of Laidlaw's voluntary compliance and facility closure were disputed facts that had not been litigated at the trial court, and remanded this question to the lower courts. *Id.* at 189, 193–194.

2. *Laidlaw's* holding that establishing injury in fact does not require plaintiffs to prove harm to the affected environmental resource had the effect of overruling two contrary court of appeals decisions, Pub. Interest Research Group v. Magnesium Elektron, Inc., 123 F.3d 111 (3rd Cir. 1997), and Friends of the Earth v. Gaston Cooper Recycling Corp., 179 F.3d 107 (4th Cir. 1999). After *Laidlaw,* an en banc panel of the Fourth Circuit reversed its original decision in Gaston Copper, 204 F.3d 149 (4th Cir. 2000) and found injury in fact in a Clean Water Act enforcement case without requiring plaintiffs to demonstrate changes in the chemical content of waterways or harms to the ecosystem. The Fourth Circuit also made clear that proving the second prong of standing— that plaintiffs' injury was "fairly traceable" to defendant's actions—does not require proof to a scientific certainty that defendant's effluent caused the precise harm suffered by the plaintiffs. The court concluded that "[c]itizens may thus rely on circumstantial evidence such as proximity to polluting sources, predictions of discharge influence, and past pollution to prove both injury in fact and traceability." *Id.* at 161, 163.

3. Would community residents who live two miles from a power plant and allege that they are harmed by the plant's unlawful emissions be able to establish standing? How close a physical connection with a source of pollution do plaintiffs need in order to demonstrate injury in fact? In Ecological Rights Foundation v. Pacific Lumber Co., 230 F.3d 1141 (9th Cir. 2000), the Ninth Circuit reversed a district court's decision finding that plaintiffs lacked standing because they did not live sufficiently close to or use with sufficient regularity a creek allegedly harm by defendant's pollution. The Court explained: [t]he "injury in fact" requirement in environmental cases is not, however, reducible to inflexible, judicially mandated time or distance guidelines....An individual who visits Yosemite National Park once a year to hike or rock climb and regards that visit as the highlight of his year is not precluded from litigating to protect the environmental quality of Yosemite Valley simply because he cannot visit more often." *Id.* at 1148, 1150. Does the answer to the power plant hypothetical differ from the *Ecological Rights* fact situation because in the latter case plaintiffs allege harm from use of a resource rather than from ongoing emissions?

4. Constitutional standing is an issue that arises in cases filed in federal court as a result of Article III's limitation of federal court jurisdiction to "cases" and "controversies." In many states, there is no comparable limitation on hearing "cases" or "controversies," and establishing standing requires only a statutory right to sue. Many federal environmental laws do not provide for exclusive federal jurisdiction, and thus suits to enforce these laws can be filed in state court. Would you recommend this approach? What advantages or disadvantages are there to filing in state court?

5. Environmental groups also can press for legislative changes in Congress. For instance, Congress could authorize plaintiffs to sue for damages resulting from defendant's violations, or authorize courts to order mitigation measures that benefit plaintiffs. In the Clean Air Act Amendments of 1990, for example, Congress authorized courts to order that penalties up to $100,000 be used for beneficial mitigation projects that are consistent with the Clean Air Act's requirements and that enhance the public health or environment. *See* 42 U.S.C.§ 7604(g)(2). If plaintiffs are within the category of persons who benefit from these mitigation projects, the Supreme Court should have no difficulty in finding that the relief ordered redresses plaintiffs injuries. *See generally* Jim Hecker, *EPCRA Citizen Suits After Steel Co. v. Citizens for a Better Environment,* 28 Envtl. L. Rep. 10,306 (1998).

## 2.  The Practicalities of Private Enforcement

Apart from legal hurdles, numerous other practical considerations are implicated in bringing citizen suits. The following excerpt describes the potential promises and limits of using such suits to achieve environmental justice.

# Eileen Gauna,
# Federal Environmental Citizen Provisions: Obstacles and Incentives on the Road to Environmental Justice
## 22 Ecology Law Quarterly 1 (1995)

EPA, charged with enforcement of most federal environmental laws, lacks the ability to enforce all environmental laws to the maximum extent possible. Understanding that there would be undesirable underenforcement of environmental laws because of limited regulatory resources, Congress equipped many federal environmental laws with citizen suit provisions, which essentially confer "private attorney general status" on the citizenry.... After sufficient notice, and if a government agency is not already diligently prosecuting an action against the violator, any person may bring a private citizen enforcement action against a member of the regulated community to enforce requirements of the applicable law. Requirements are often, but not always, found in the permits required under the act in question. Some permit violations are easily proven, but other enforcement actions involve matters outside the ambit of clear violations of unambiguous permit requirements and standards....

Thus, the first crucial step in enforcement of environmental laws in poor and minority communities is that the citizens must have the knowledge and resources to detect noncomplying industrial activity within their community. Detecting noncompliance ranges from relatively easy to nearly impossible depending upon the type of polluting activity involved.

### Clean Water Act Enforcement Suits

Under the Clean Water Act, the detection and prosecution of permit violations are easy relative to other enforcement actions. As such, they constitute a disproportionately large percentage of citizen enforcement actions. Any facility discharging regulated pollutants into a body of water from a discrete conveyance must first obtain a Clean Water Act permit under the National Pollutant Discharge Elimination System (NPDES) program. In addition to limiting the amount of pollutant discharged with a facility's effluent, an NPDES permit requires its holder to test regularly its effluent and to submit reports with the recorded actual pollutant concentration. The reports are generally available to the public....

### Citizen Suits Under the Existing Clean Air Act Programs

Presently, not all facilities emitting air pollutants are subject to uniform national standards or require a permit under the Clean Air Act. Moreover, although one might think that an "emission standard or limitation" refers to a quantifiable, permitted concentration of a regulated pollutant emitted into the air at a particular rate, this is not always the case. The general definition of "emission standard or limitation" under the Clean Air Act also includes requirements that are not easily subject to measurement, such as requirements relating to operation or maintenance, design and equipment, work practices, and operational standards. As a result, identifying the enforceable requirements for a particular business operation is often difficult....

[T]he majority of stationary sources of air pollution (which includes small existing sources) has no uniform federal standards, does not require federal permits and, if regulated, is regulated primarily through state implementation plans. The regulation of small existing stationary sources emitting certain air pollutants will depend primarily upon how each state decides to achieve or maintain compliance with national ambient air quality standards (NAAQS)....

[E]ven where SIP standards are specific and monitoring is required, the problem of obtaining reliable data to detect and prove the violation remains.... A report by the Environmental Law Institute found that few Clean Air Act regulations "require periodic reports on emission levels and there is no uniform system of record keeping of hard, reliable compliance data. Tests are relatively expensive and obviously cannot be performed by prospective plaintiffs."... As a result of the difficulty in determining the nature and source of air pollution, isolating a federal requirement, and further proving the violation of an enforceable "standard or limitation," an attorney representing a citizens group in prosecuting a Clean Air Act enforcement action takes a substantial risk that after an expensive investigation, consultation with experts, and perhaps protracted litigation, a court would conclude that there was no enforceable standard or limitation, or that the defendant did not violate the permit or SIP requirement.... An additional disincentive to identifying and prosecuting violations, not applicable to national environmental groups prosecuting like cases, is that the facility in question might employ community residents. If this is the case, compliance monitoring might place some community residents in fear of losing their jobs and a citizens group might be reluctant to challenge the practices of local emitters....

*Comprehensive Environmental Response, Compensation and Liability Act Enforcement Suits*

The primary focus of the Comprehensive Environmental Response, Compensation and Liability Act (CERCLA), commonly known as Superfund, is to clean up contaminated sites. Enforcement actions under CERCLA do not involve violations of permit requirements as is common under environmental laws regulating the release of pollutants, like the Clean Air Act and Clean Water Act. Until EPA initiates an action to clean up a contaminated site, there are no "requirements" for the persons responsible for the contamination (potentially responsible parties) to violate. Citizen suit provisions under CERCLA, termed "one of the crueler farces of contemporary environmental lawmaking," limit enforcement actions to circumstances where the regulatory agency (EPA) first obtains an order against a potentially responsible party to abate an imminent and substantial endangerment, and the potentially responsible party subsequently violates the requirements stated in the order. As a practical result, citizens on or near contaminated areas can obtain relief under CERCLA citizen suit provisions only after EPA elects to take action....

*Resource Conservation and Recovery Act Enforcement Suits and Imminent Hazard Suits*

For communities located near solid waste and hazardous waste facilities, a citizen suit under the authority of the Resource Conservation and Recovery Act (RCRA) could provide a remedy in the event of regulatory inaction under CERCLA. RCRA is the federal statute that regulates the disposal, storage, and treatment of solid and hazardous wastes. Under RCRA citizen suit provisions, the citizen group may enforce any RCRA "permit, standard, regulation, condition, requirement, prohibition or order." In addition to enforcement suits, RCRA citizen suit provisions authorize private citizens to prosecute an action against any person who is contributing (or has contributed) to the handling of a solid or hazardous waste in a manner that presents an imminent and substantial endangerment to health or to the environment.

Each existing hazardous waste facility must have a RCRA permit to operate. A citizen group in a community located near a hazardous waste facility might choose to investigate the facility's compliance with RCRA and prosecute an enforcement action if the facility is violating its permit conditions....

A more promising avenue lies in the RCRA citizen suit imminent hazard authority. The standards to be applied under RCRA citizen suit imminent hazard provisions should be the same as the standards under the EPA Administrator's authority to address imminent hazards. EPA has taken the position that its authority under RCRA's imminent hazard provision may remedy hazards brought on by releases to land, water, or air. In this respect, RCRA's imminent hazard authority is "essentially a codification of common law public nuisance remedies." Unlike common law nuisance doctrine, however, RCRA's imminent hazard provisions may reach a broader range of defendants, specifically government agencies waiving sovereign immunity, and *past or present* generators, transporters, owners, or operators of waste facilities. Therefore, the advantage of RCRA citizen suit imminent hazard actions is that citizen groups may reach a wide range of defendants for dangerous conditions emanating from both operating and *abandoned* waste facilities....

### Attorney's Fees and Costs Under Citizen Suit Provisions

The citizen suit provisions of the Clean Air Act allow an award of attorney's fees and costs where appropriate. Citizen suit provisions of the Clean Water Act, RCRA, and CERCLA provide for an award of attorney's fees and costs to prevailing parties or substantially prevailing parties. Environmental "fee shifting" provisions are a necessary incentive to environmental enforcement because few private plaintiffs can afford to finance expensive environmental litigation that typically results in nonmonetary benefits to the public at large (rather than damage awards to the individual plaintiffs)....

The citizens group must find an environmental lawyer who is willing to take the case without any guarantee that the plaintiffs will prevail. Few private attorneys are willing to undertake expensive lawsuits on behalf of underfinanced citizens groups, especially without the incentive of a contingent fee arrangement or an hourly rate agreement backed by a retainer....

Underfinanced citizens groups face other practical problems. Recovery of legal costs occurs, if at all, at the end of the lawsuit. Meanwhile, the citizens group must be able to finance the lawsuit, which may require significant discovery costs, expert witness fees, and transportation costs (if the suit is not local). Although compensation for the delay factor may be subsumed in the lodestar amount if attorney's fees are awarded, the problem of up-front financing is still a significant obstacle for underfunded community groups.

Clearly, fee shifting is an incentive to private enforcement generally, although arguably not enough of an incentive considering the expense involved in undertaking complex environmental litigation. The Supreme Court has further limited the incentive structure by prohibiting contingency adjustments. The practical difficulty of financing complex environmental citizen suits, combined with substantive and procedural limitations of enforcement suits generally, presents substantial impediments to court access for community-based environmental justice groups in low income and minority communities. . . .

## Notes and Questions

1. As noted by Professor Gauna, many environmental statutes provide for an award of attorneys fees to "prevailing parties." In Buckhannon Board & Home Care v. West Virginia, 121 S. Ct. 1835 (2001), the Supreme Court held that a party is only "prevailing" when it obtains judicial relief from the court, either through a judgment on the merits or a court-ordered consent decree. The court rejected the view, which had been widely followed by the lower courts, that a plaintiff is entitled to fees where it achieves its desired result because the lawsuit brought about a voluntary change in the defendant's conduct (the so-called "catalyst theory"). The impact of the ruling may be to discourage a significant number of citizen actions from being brought, since defendants will be able to foreclose an award of fees by voluntarily agreeing to the relief requested by the plaintiffs and rendering the case moot.

2. One recurring issue in enforcement cases is the potential economic costs of enforcement actions to the regulated community. Community groups are often met with the response that stricter compliance with environmental requirements or payment of large penalties may result in fewer jobs or even the closure of a facility. Assume you are an attorney for a local community group. What issues would you want the group to discuss before bringing an enforcement action with possible job impacts in the community?

3. As the above excerpt indicates, private enforcement actions against noncomplying facilities may be financially infeasible for many groups. Professor Gauna also notes that action-forcing suits, such as suits against agencies for failure to adopt required regulations, "are often luxuries that underfunded citizen groups cannot afford to undertake . . . [since] they are often preoccupied attempting to remedy exigent local conditions." Gauna, *supra*, at 71. Can you think of some ways that underfinanced citizen groups can fund lawsuits, or alternatively, use their limited resources in other ways to achieve results similar to those obtainable through lawsuits?

4. In light of the above limits, are citizen suits an effective tool for community groups? Can they be? This issue is explored below.


## 3.  BUILDING COMMUNITY ENFORCEMENT CAPACITY

What approaches can be used to strengthen private enforcement in low income communities and communities of color? Consider the following suggestions:


### a. UPWARDLY ADJUSTING ATTORNEYS FEES

Most environmental statutes allow prevailing parties in enforcement actions to recover attorney's fees. The appropriate amount of fees is calculated as the product of a reasonable number of hours times a reasonable hourly rate, the so-called "lodestar" amount. Professor Gauna argues that courts should augment fees awarded to attorneys successfully prosecuting environmental justice enforcement cases:

> [J]udges could allow an upward lodestar adjustment, not as a contingency adjustment, but specifically to encourage and reward private attorneys who undertake enforcement actions in low income and minority neighborhoods (i.e., an "equity adjustment")....Fee shifting in the private attorney general context serves several important purposes, not the least of which is the incentive for citizens to bring suits that provide a recognized social benefit. In the case of environmental citizens suits, the recognized social benefit is the enforcement of environmental laws. One can assume that Congress (and the courts) had this general purpose in mind in developing the present fee shifting system based on a market rate lodestar calculation. However, in allowing attorney's fees based on the lodestar for environmental citizen suits across the board, Congress did not specifically address environmental justice concerns: that minority and low income communities suffer disparate environmental hazards due in part to a relative lack of resources as a class. Therefore, an upward adjustment is necessary to further another important policy objective that is not already subsumed in the lodestar calculation.

Gauna, *supra*, at 81. What do you think of this approach?

## b. TECHNICAL ASSISTANCE TO COMMUNITIES

Technical assistance to communities is another idea often advocated by environmental justice activists. Such assistance could take a variety of forms, as described below.

### i. SUPERFUND'S TECHNICAL ASSISTANCE PROVISIONS

Superfund mandates that EPA provide opportunities for public participation before it adopts final clean up plans. The 1986 Superfund amendments authorize EPA to make Technical Assistance Grants (TAGs) of up to $50,000 to citizens affected by sites listed on the National Priorities List. Communities can use the grants to hire independent technical advisors to help them understand and comment on technical aspects of the cleanup process. The TAG program has been criticized as unduly complex and imposing administrative barriers to participation, and observers have called for the grant process to be simplified and expedited, and the range of allowable expenditures by community groups broadened. Deeohn Ferris additionally argues "[t]o ensure effective public participation and to improve the pace and quality of the cleanup process, EPA should be required to work with communities to create Community Working Groups (CWGs) at each Superfund site. CWGs would consist of community leaders, community representatives, and, if desired by the community, other appropriate organizations....[The] CWGs would assume a key decision making role concerning health assessments, responses to hot-spots, remediation alternatives, cleanup schedules, and relocation decisions." Deeohn Ferris, *Communities of Color and Hazardous Waste Cleanup: Expanding Public Participation in the Federal Superfund Program*, 21 FORDHAM U. L. J. 671, 682 (1994). Community working groups, although perhaps not in the exact form envisioned by Ferris, were part of the consensus Superfund reform package that Congress came close to adopting at the end of the 1994 Congressional session. There has been little movement in Congress toward enacting Superfund reform since then.

## ii. COMMUNITY OUTREACH AND EDUCATION

Commentators also have argued that expanded government education and outreach can help environmental justice communities more effectively participate in the enforcement process:

> EPA is aware that low income and minority communities are less likely to be aware of the agency's activities and responsibilities and are, therefore, less likely to participate in the agency's decisionmaking process. The degree of attention paid by an agency to a violating facility or waste site can be strongly influenced by the amount of attention drawn to the site by the local community. The ability of an affected community to influence enforcement decisions takes both knowledge of the enforcement process and resources. Little information is provided by EPA, and probably less by states, identifying particular violations that have been detected and what enforcement responses the agency intends to pursue. Although EPA publishes its administrative penalties and proposed settlements in the Federal Register, this notice would not likely reach affected communities, particularly communities whose members lack knowledge of and access to the Federal Register....A requirement that agencies publish notice, in a timely and accessible manner, of all violations detected by inspectors and of the enforcement actions pending and concluded would foster greater community involvement.

Kuehn, *Remedying The Unequal Enforcement of Environmental Laws, supra*, at 659–661. Other environmental justice advocates have suggested that local residents be allowed to independently inspect facilities or to accompany agency staff on government inspections and that agencies provide local groups with enforcement information, such as inspection notices, notices of violations, and levels of pollutants being emitted, as they become available. (These and other recommendations can be found in the Report of the Environmental Justice Enforcement and Compliance Assurance Roundtable, available at <http://es.epa.gov/oeca/oej/nejac/pdf/1096.pdf>).

## iii. TRAINING COMMUNITIES TO DETECT NONCOMPLIANCE

Should state and federal agencies provide local community groups with funding, training and equipment to independently monitor the environment? Or is it inappropriate for government agencies to promote such capacity since it could lead to enforcement actions against regulated entities? Professor Gauna suggests that "EPA [and the states] could greatly enhance [private] enforcement in poor and minority neighborhoods by training community residents in sampling and monitoring techniques," enabling them to determine whether facilities are in compliance. Gauna, *supra*, at 80. EPA Region II's Interim Environmental Justice Policy, excerpted above, encourages settlement provisions that foster participation from the affected community in monitoring compliance at the facility. As Professors Robert Collin and Robin Morris Collin point out, citizen monitoring of environmental conditions has a well-respected tradition in this country (dating back to 1890 when the National Weather Service began training volunteers to report daily measurements of air temperatures and rainfall), and there are now hundreds of formal, volunteer water quality monitoring programs at the grassroots level. Many states rely upon volunteer citizen monitoring to meet the biennial water quality reporting requirements of section 305(b) of the Clean Water Act. Robert W. Collin & Robin Morris Collin, *The Role of Communities in Environmental Decisions: Communities Speaking for Themselves*, 13 U. OR. J. ENVTL. L. & LITIG. 37, 82–84 (1998).

## Notes and Questions

1. What do you think are the most effective ways to strengthen enforcement in environmental justice communities? Which are most feasible? What additional tools would you recommend?

2. Enforcement of pollution control laws is likely to remain of central importance in the effort to achieve environmental justice. Public agencies have a great deal of discretion to tailor their enforcement efforts to focus more on environmental justice communities, and EPA has taken some steps in this direction. Citizen enforcement can be a potent tool for community groups, but there are considerable legal and financial hurdles to bringing such actions, hurdles that will require creative new approaches to surmount.

# Chapter XII

# Planning, Environmental Review and Information Disclosure Laws as a Response

## A. Introduction

Overburdened communities can rely on a range of potential legal and political tools to remedy disproportionate environmental harms. These include challenging permitting decisions and pressing for brownfields redevelopment, as explored in Chapters VIII and IX, utilizing civil rights theories, including the Equal Protection Clause and Title VI of the Civil Rights Act, as discussed in chapters XIII and XIV, or seeking to enforce the requirements of pollution control statutes as discussed in Chapter XI. In many cases communities will rely on a combination of these (and other) strategies.

The tools outlined above are largely reactive—they are employed by a community to stop a proposal for an unwanted facility, or to mitigate harm at an existing site. This chapter examines several approaches that are more proactive. Section B looks at traditional land use planning and zoning mechanisms, as well as one of the favored solutions offered by academics: compensation for host communities. Sections C and D are applications of what Professor Zygmund Plater has characterized as "stop and think" statutes—they require information to be developed and disclosed about facilities or activities that cause environmental damage, but they do not prohibit such activities from going forward. Specifically, Section C looks at environmental review statutes such as the National Environmental Policy Act and state law equivalents, while Section D examines right to know laws such as the Toxics Release Inventory program and California's Proposition 65. To some extent, all of these approaches provide communities, government agencies, or businesses with the opportunity to plan and prevent disparate siting or other environmental harms from occurring.

# B. Planning, Land Use and Compensated Siting Approaches

## 1. PLANNING & ZONING CHANGES

The excerpt below advocates greater reliance on planning and zoning mechanisms to address disparate siting patterns.

## Craig Anthony Arnold, Planning Milagros: Environmental Justice and Land Use Regulation

### 76 Denver University Law Review 1 (1998)

The next frontier for both the movement and the focus of environmental justice scholarship... is land use planning by communities of color and low-income communities. Local neighborhoods can use land use planning to articulate visions for what they want their communities to be, and negotiate land use regulations to implement these visions. In other words, they would not be merely late participants in using existing rules to stop (or attempt to stop) current proposals for unwanted land uses, but also pre-siting participants in developing the rules that will determine what will and will not go in their neighborhoods....

### Land Use Planning & Regulation: Another Vision of Environmental Justice

Land use planning and regulation offer several advantages for achieving environmental justice goals. First, an owner or operator of a prospective [Locally Unwanted Land Use] LULU would have much more difficulty obtaining approval for siting the LULU in a minority or low-income neighborhood, if the comprehensive plan and zoning ordinances prohibited the LULU in that neighborhood than if they allowed the LULU, either by right or conditionally. Assume that a waste company wants to locate a hazardous waste incinerator in a low-income, Hispanic neighborhood. If the city zoning code prohibits hazardous waste incinerators in every zone except I-3, and the zoning map does not designate any land in the target neighborhood as I-3, the waste company will need a zoning amendment, as well as use-specific environmental permits. If the city's comprehensive plan provides for non-industrial uses only in the neighborhood or explicitly states that waste facilities are not appropriate for that neighborhood, the waste company also will need an amendment to the comprehensive plan. The waste company nonetheless might have enough political and economic power to obtain all the needed approvals, but it will face several obstacles.... Furthermore, the neighbors will have more government approvals to challenge in litigation....

### Comprehensive Plan

The first land use regulatory mechanism is the comprehensive plan. Zoning regulations that implement low-income and minority neighborhoods' goals may be legally ineffective if they are not preceded by amendments to the city's comprehensive plan to reflect those goals....

*Amendments to Zoning*

[T]he crux of land use regulation for environmental justice will be the amendment of existing zoning codes. Most low-income and minority communities that suffer or risk exposure to environmental harms exist in areas with zoning classifications that currently permit intensive uses. Because people of color and the poor live near and among a higher proportion of industrial and commercial uses than do white, high-income people, an appropriate land use regulatory response for cities would be to change the permitted uses in those areas to correspond more closely to the residents' desired neighborhood environment, as well as their health and safety needs. . . .

Zoning map amendments change the zoning district designation for a particular parcel, tract of land, or set of parcels. Although rezoning has been used to allow intensive uses in neighborhoods of color and low-income communities, grassroots environmental justice activists might seek zoning map amendments to change more intensive use designations in their neighborhoods to less intensive use designations, a technique known as "downzoning." For example, a low-income minority neighborhood might contain several parcels zoned for heavy industrial use in close proximity to residences, schools, churches, health care facilities, and the like. Residents might seek to rezone some or all of these parcels for less intensive, yet economically viable, commercial uses. . . .

Low-income and minority neighborhood groups will be most successful in achieving valid rezoning of neighboring properties from more intensive to less intensive uses if they follow four guiding principles: (1) seek rezoning before controversial specific land use proposals arise; (2) carefully document the incompatibility of existing high-intensity use designations and their impact or potential impact on the health and safety of local residents, as well as community character; (3) seek rezoning for all neighboring parcels with similar use designations and similar impacts (do not leave a landowner the argument that only his or her property has been downzoned while neighboring parcels remain zoned for more intensive uses); and (4) do not downzone so greatly that the landowner suffers a substantial diminution in the property's value (leave the owner some economically viable use—for example, downzone from an industrial use to a commercial use, instead of all the way to a single family residential use).

Perhaps the most successful strategy of all includes a comprehensive set of amendments to the zoning text, the zoning map, and the comprehensive plan. These combined text and map amendments often create new zoning designations and apply them to existing parcels, and they often receive judicial approval because of their comprehensive nature. . . .

*Flexible Zoning Techniques*

. . . Buffer zones, like performance zoning, both help and hurt low-income people and people of color. Buffer zones are use designations that create a buffer or transition between a less intensive use, such as single-family residential, and a nearby more intensive use, such as commercial or industrial. The buffer zone exists between the two areas to minimize the impact of the more intensive use on the less intensive, more sensitive use.

The most frequent type of buffer between single-family residential areas and industrial or commercial areas is medium-or high-density residential uses. . . . Buffer zones are perhaps one of the major reasons why low-income and minority neighborhoods have so much industrial and commercial zoning: the multi-family housing, where many low-income and minority people live, is purposefully placed near the industrial and commercial uses to create a buffer that protects high-income, white, single-family neighborhoods. Zoning practices place large numbers of poor and minority people near intensive uses because traditional zoning and planning theory values most the single-family residence, instead of the integrity and quality of all residential areas.

[L]ow-income and minority neighborhoods need buffers to protect them from intensive industrial and commercial activity. Buffer zones can also include physical screening, landscaping, significant set backs, open space, and even low-intensity commercial uses like offices, shops, churches, and medical care facilities. Environmental justice advocates can use the concept of buffer zoning but redefine it to protect low-income and minority residences....

### Exactions

...Exactions require the developer to provide the public either real property (land, facilities, or both) or monetary fees as a condition for permission to use land in ways subject to government regulation. These dedications and fees provide the public facilities necessitated by new development, including schools, parks, open space, roads, sidewalks, public utilities, fire and police stations, low-income housing, mass transit, day care services, and job training programs....Already, various federal, state, and local environmental regulatory programs require developers to dedicate land or pay fees to mitigate the environmental impacts of development in ecologically sensitive areas. A comprehensive environmental justice land use program, though, might include environmental impact fees and dedications for inner-city industrial and commercial development. The exactions would be based on the various environmental and social impacts of intensive uses and LULUs on the surrounding neighborhood(s), not just the publicly funded local infrastructure, and would be earmarked for ameliorating amenities in the affected neighborhood(s)....

### Limits to Land Use Regulations As Environmental Justice Tools

The land use regulatory model of environmental justice, while promising for many low-income communities of color, contains inherent limits. Among these limits are legal constraints on land use regulation that are largely designed to protect the private property rights of landowners. Courts, increasingly protective of private property rights and skeptical of local political processes, have eroded the well-established judicial presumption that zoning decisions are valid by imposing greater scrutiny on decisions about land use regulation....The final limits to land use regulation as an environmental justice strategy are political and economic. How successful, as a practical matter, will grassroots neighborhood groups be in changing land use patterns in low-income communities and communities of color? There is reason for a mix of sober realism and thoughtful optimism....Local government is likely to regard changes to existing industrial or commercial zoning as politically or fiscally inconvenient, especially when these uses cannot be relocated to higher-income, lower-minority areas without political conflict. Indeed, many local governments engage in "fiscal zoning," favoring industrial and commercial uses because these uses generate tax revenues without creating expensive demands for local services in the way that single-family residences do, particularly through public school costs....

* * *

## Notes and Questions

1. What is your response to Professor Arnold's question about the political obstacles to changing land use patterns? How successful are community activists likely to be in getting their neighborhoods rezoned to exclude industrial uses? What kind of an organizing strategy might accomplish these goals? Another approach suggested by Michael Gerrard is for local governments to focus attention on prior noncomforming uses. He argues that municipalities "may wish to survey their noncomforming uses and determine whether any of them pose such health and environmental problems that they should be targeted for closure, either immediately as public nuisances or later through an amortization process." Michael B. Gerrard, *Environmental Justice and Local Land Use Decisionmaking, in* TRENDS IN LAND USE LAW FROM A TO Z 148 (Patricia Salkin ed., 2001)

2. Exactions, such as the transfer of property interests or payment of fees that a municipality might require from the developer as a condition for granting permission to go forward with a project, often raise Fifth Amendment challenges if there is not a sufficient nexus between the exaction required and the activity regulated. What kinds of exactions could be imposed upon, for example, a manufacturing facility emitting toxic chemicals? A buffer zone, a park, a community center? How closely must the exaction mitigate the effects of the regulated activity to survive a takings challenge?

3. How would you recommend redefining the concept of buffer zoning to protect low income and minority residents, as Professor Arnold proposes?

4. Some states have passed statutes seeking to control the distribution of waste and other unwanted facilities, i.e., by prohibiting the placement of a waste facility where others exist, requiring plans that provide for a reasonable geographic distribution of facilities, or creating a rebuttable presumption against placing a waste facility where others exist. For example, Alabama statutes prohibit more than one commercial hazardous waste treatment facility or disposal site within each county. Ala. Code § 22-30-5.1. New York City's "Fair Share Ordinance" requires that the selection of sites for city facilities "further the fair distribution among communities of the burdens and benefits of these facilities." New York City Charter § 203. California law requires cities and counties to adopt a general plan guiding future development, composed of seven required elements (housing, transportation, open space, etc). Some local governments have added environmental equity elements to their general plans. For instance, the City of Los Angeles General Plan establishes as a goal of its land use policies a "physically balanced distribution of land uses." CITY OF LOS ANGELES GENERAL PLAN, Ch. 3, Goal 3A. As Professor Sheila Foster notes, more commonly found statutes require decision makers to consider "soft criteria" in permit decisions, such as the socioeconomic status of the host community, community perceptions, psychic costs, the potential for change in property values, and the cumulative health risks presented from other environmental sources in the host community. Typically, however, there is no statutory guidance for the weight decisionmakers must give these factors in the permitting process. Sheila Foster, *Impact Assessment, in* THE LAW OF ENVIRONMENTAL JUSTICE: THEORIES AND PROCEDURES TO ADDRESS DISPROPORTIONATE RISKS 287–289 (Michael Gerrard, ed. 1999). Are geographic constraints such as the Alabama and New York City statutes desirable? Recall Professor Kuehn's taxonomy of the four kinds of justice embodied in environmental justice principles (see Chapter I (B).) Is the distributive justice embodied by these laws easier to achieve than procedural, corrective, or social justice?

5. One spontaneous community-driven effort to alter local land use practices is embodied in New York City's "Green Thumb" program. During the 1970's, New York City became the owner, through tax foreclosure, of thousands of abandoned public and private lots in economically depressed neighborhoods. As described by Michael Gerrard, "[n]eighborhood groups began to clear these lots and turn them into community gardens, where neighborhood residents could stake out a few square feet and plant some vegetables or flowers. These makeshift plots became green oases in some rough neighborhoods." Michael B. Gerrard, *Environmental Justice and Local Land Use Decisionmaking, supra*, at 139. The City's Parks & Recreation Department formalized this arrangement in 1978 through the Green Thumb program, which grants vacant lots to communities and provides them with topsoil and other materials and technical support. There are currently over 650 gardens serving 20,000 city residents, with majority in economically disadvantaged communities. *See* City of New York Parks & Recreation, Green Thumb <http://www.greenthumbnyc.org>. In 1998, New York City decided to sell some of the gardens, arguing as justification that the land was needed for construction of low income housing. As Gerrard points out, however, "experience with other recent sales suggested that many of these lots would actually become parking lots, storage yards, and the like." Gerrard, *supra*, at 139. The proposed sales generated intense community opposition and protest, with dozens of activists in one case chaining themselves to cement blocks and fences in a garden to try and stop the City from bulldozing it. C.J. Chivers, *After Uprooting Gardeners, City Razes a Garden*, NY TIMES, Feb. 16, 2000, at B1. Consider that community groups generally lack legal rights to these spaces no matter how long they have used them because adverse possession does not generally run against the government. In this respect, is the Green Thumb program a governmental recognition of the legitimate reliance communities have come to place upon these spaces? Is the Green Thumb program an implicit recognition of the failure of the traditional zoning and planning process to create sufficient open space and other physical amenities needed to make urban communities liveable? Can you think of other "organic" responses by communities to change the land use patterns in their neighborhoods?

## 2.  COMPENSATED SITING PROPOSALS

As noted, one of the most discussed solutions for addressing the inequitable distribution of polluting facilities is the idea of compensating host communities. This reform is discussed below.

**Vicki Been,**
**Compensated Siting Proposals: Is it Time to Pay Attention?**
21 Fordham Urban Law Journal 787 (1994)

*The Theories Underlying Compensation Proposals*

The siting of LULUs...has become an extraordinarily difficult public policy challenge....A primary, although by no means the only, explanation for the vehemence with which communities protest proposed sites is that the benefits of LULUs are spread diffusely over an entire community, region, state, or nation, while their costs are concentrated upon the host neighborhood. Industry associations, academics, and public policy makers have responded with a seemingly simple solution: compensate host communities for the harms the LULU causes. Proponents advance several justifications for compensation programs. First, they argue that if a LULU's benefits to the community outweigh its costs, the community will have no reason to oppose the project, and indeed may welcome it.

Next, proponents justify compensation programs as an equitable solution to the siting problem.... Compensation schemes are advanced to redress that injustice in situations where it would be impractical to equitably distribute risks physically or spatially. It may be unwise, for example, to site a radioactive or hazardous waste facility in every community that produces such waste, because a few large centralized facilities generally are considered safer, more environmentally sound, and more efficient than many small facilities. Those communities that must serve as host to the larger centralized facilities should be compensated, however, for bearing the burden by those who enjoy the benefits.

A third major justification for compensation proposals is that compensation can help to make siting decisions more efficient. Compensation forces the facility's developer to internalize the costs of the facility, and therefore helps to ensure that only those facilities that are efficient will be built. In addition, liability for the costs of the facility gives the facility's developer a strong incentive to take precautions to avoid or reduce those costs. Moreover, a community's participation in negotiations over the facility may make the public more willing to accept the risks associated with its operation....

### Differences in Compensation Proposals

While the basic theoretical justifications for compensation tend to be relatively constant among proponents, the details of the proposals vary in several significant ways. This section offers a rough typology of the different types of proposals....

### Remedial Nature of the Compensation

As a remedy, compensation seeks to make a community whole for damages it will suffer as a result of the facility. Agreements to pay neighboring property owners for any decrease in the market value of their homes caused by the facility are an example of remedial compensation. Alternatively, compensation may seek to prevent or reduce the harm the facility will cause. Such compensation measures are often referred to as "mitigation." The provision of buffer zones between a facility and its residential neighbors is an example of mitigation. Finally, compensation may serve to reward the community for accepting the facility by providing funds or benefits in excess of those required to remedy any harms caused by the facility....

### Method of Compensation Proposed

Compensation either may be *ex ante* (before the facility is constructed or causes any harm to the community), on-going, or *ex post* (after the facility causes some harm). *Ex ante* compensation often takes the form of grants, which allow the host community to hire its own experts to evaluate the proposed facility. *Ex ante* compensation also may involve community participation in the design of the facility, selection of alternative facility operating procedures, or selection of the facility operator. Finally, *ex ante* compensation may consist of "risk substitution" rather than money, amenities, or rights of participation. Several academics have proposed, for example, that developers of waste disposal facilities offer to clean up all or some of a community's existing toxic waste sites in exchange for approval of the new facility.

On-going compensation often takes the form of special taxes or fees the facility regularly pays to the community, or services the facility regularly provides the community....In addition, on-going benefits may take the form of continuing opportunities for community participation in the management of the facility. Local community representatives may be guaranteed a role in site monitoring, or be allowed to have an independent third party serve as a monitor, or be given funds to buy monitoring equipment, for example. Moreover, the community may be given some role in decisions about whether to close a facility down in the event of an emergency, or...given representation on the facility's governing board.

*Ex post* compensation may include commitments to pay for, or insure against, future damages. Such commitments take the form of property value guarantees, local product price guarantees, agreements to indemnify local governments, or funds to compensate victims in the event of an accident.

### Determining the Compensation Package

Compensation proposals also differ in how the terms of the compensation package are determined. One approach is for the governing statute to establish the level of compensation applicable to all communities. Alternatively, the statute can authorize a regulatory agency to determine the compensation package on a case by case basis. Another technique is to allow the facility developer and the community to negotiate a mutually satisfactory package. A fourth approach is to auction the facility to the community willing to accept the least compensation....

### Theoretical Tests on the Proposals

Several scholars have attempted to test the likelihood that compensation programs will succeed through surveys asking people whether they would be willing to accept a facility in their community in exchange for some form of compensation. The surveys' results show that a relatively small number of people are willing to change their mind about a facility in exchange for compensation....[T]he studies provide substantial evidence that at least those compensation measures that guarantee local monitoring and control may sway a significant number of people to accept a facility. The studies also suggest that while compensation measures may not be sufficient to secure acceptance, they nevertheless may be necessary to gain sufficient support for the facility....

### State Negotiated Compensating Siting Programs for Hazardous Waste Facilities

Several states have adopted compensated siting as part of their hazardous waste siting programs....The Massachusetts program is highlighted because the Massachusetts Hazardous Waste Facility Siting Act ("the Massachusetts Act") was hailed as a major advance in siting policy by both industry and environmentalists. Moreover, it has served as a model for other states interested in compensated siting. Wisconsin is discussed because its program has enjoyed the greatest success of any compensated siting program.

### Massachusetts

Under the Massachusetts Act, any developer proposing to construct a hazardous waste facility must notify the chief executive officers of the proposed host community and of all adjoining communities of its plan. The developer is then prohibited from constructing the facility until the "local assessment committee" of the host community has accepted a "site agreement" for the facility.

Although the Massachusetts Act's siting agreement requirement affords potential host communities some protection against unwanted facilities, it also limits four significant tools that communities previously had used in excluding hazardous waste facilities from their neighborhoods. [These include imposing new permitting requirements on the facility or adopting zoning changes to exclude a proposed facility.] ...

The notice of intent that triggers the siting agreement negotiation process must include a description of the following: the proposed facility; the type of wastes it would accept; the processes that would be used for the treatment or disposal of the wastes; the developer's prior experience in the construction and operation of hazardous waste facilities; and the developer's plans for financing the project. In addition, the notice of intent may either name a specific proposed site, or describe the characteristics of a theoretically ideal site and ask for possible candidates.

[If the notice is deemed complete and feasible by the Hazardous Waste Facility Site Safety Council ("the Council")], the developer and the proposed host community's local assessment committee then begin negotiating the terms under which the proposed host community would agree to accept the facility. The local assessment committee consists of the chief executive officer and representatives of the proposed host community's board of health, conservation commission, planning board, and fire department. The committee members then elect four residents of the municipality to serve on the committee; three of the four must be residents of the area within the municipality most immediately affected by the proposed facility. In addition, the chief executive officer may appoint up to four additional members, whose appointments must be approved by the municipality's legislative body.

The local assessment committee is charged with representing the "best interests of the host community" by negotiating with the developer "to protect the public health, the public safety, and the environment of the host community, as well as to promote the fiscal welfare of said community through special benefits and compensation." The local assessment committee is authorized to negotiate over the facility's design, construction, maintenance, operating procedures, and monitoring practices. In addition, the committee may negotiate regarding the services the host community will provide the developer and the compensation, services, and special benefits that the developer will provide the host community. ...

If the negotiations fail the Council may declare an impasse and require the parties to submit the disputed issues to [binding] arbitration. ...

Since the Massachusetts Act was passed in 1980, it has been unsuccessful in encouraging communities to accept hazardous waste facilities. Although six different developers have attempted to site facilities under the terms of the Massachusetts Act, no facility has been sited. ...

The Massachusetts Act has been the subject of considerable criticism and many calls for change. ...

### Wisconsin

The siting process in Wisconsin proceeds on two independent tracks. The first track involves the state licensing process, and the second involves local approval of the facility. The local approval process begins when the developer applies for any permits ... or other approvals required by the proposed host community. Within sixty days of such applications, the host county, and any other "affected municipality" within 1,200 feet of the proposed facility, must elect whether to participate in negotiations with the developer. Those that do not elect to participate in the negotiations waive their right to require the developer to obtain any local permits or other approvals.

If a municipality elects to negotiate, it must pass a "siting resolution" stating its intention to negotiate, and if necessary to arbitrate, an agreement with the developer. The governing body of the municipality also must appoint members to the "local committee" that will conduct the negotiations. The host community may appoint four members, no more than two of whom are elected officials or municipal employees; the host county may appoint two members; and any other affected community may appoint one member.

The developer and the local committee may negotiate any subject except the need for the facility.... If the parties reach a settlement, the terms of the agreement must be approved by the governing body of each host municipality that has participated in the negotiations....

If the local committee and developer cannot reach a settlement, either or both parties may petition the Waste Facility Siting Board ("the Board") to submit the matter to arbitration.... The [arbitrator] must adopt, without modification, the final offer of either the local committee or the developer.

The Wisconsin siting statute has enjoyed moderate success. By the end of 1993, siting agreements had been entered into for five hazardous waste sites and forty-one solid waste sites. [It is unclear if the hazardous waste siting agreements actually resulted in any facilities being sited. Eds.] [The agreed-upon compensation included: for municipalities, annual monetary payments, free or discounted waste disposal services, reimbursement for costs of firefighting or lost revenues due to property tax exemptions; for individuals, monetary payments, property value guarantees, testing of private wells and replacement of damaged water supplies, and crop damage guarantees.]

### Solid Waste-Industry Compensation Programs

The solid waste industry also has turned to compensation in order to secure community acceptance of undesirable land uses such as solid waste landfills and incinerators. The programs have been successful in the sense that few communities now accept such facilities without bargaining for some form of compensation, and some communities do accept LULUs that they almost certainly would have rejected in the absence of compensation....

### Conclusion

...No compensated siting program has been a "success" in getting LULUs sited. But neither has any other siting program. The experience so far suggests that while compensation may not be sufficient to resolve siting impasses, it can't hurt, and indeed may be one of several necessary elements of a solution. Until some panacea for siting controversies comes along, the temptation to use compensation to reduce opposition to siting proposals will be too strong to resist without better evidence that it is ineffective or counter-productive....

Because the programs are here, and here to stay, the environmental justice movement should be prepared to meet them head on. It should begin to formulate a more thoughtful and comprehensive policy about compensated siting programs.

Several lines of questioning should be pursued. Initially, environmental justice advocates should seek to articulate the circumstances under which compensation schemes are morally objectionable, and why. There are at least four major moral questions that require further exploration. First, because the siting of noxious LULUs often involve risks to health and safety, the question arises whether compensation schemes commodify, or subject to the free market, matters that should not be bought and sold. Society has chosen not to allow people to sell their kidneys to the highest bidder; should a similar judgment be made about whether people can sell their freedom from the health risks posed by nearby LULUs?

Second, it is likely that the communities that accept LULUs under compensated siting programs will be our poorest communities, because those communities lack alternative sources of funds. The distributional consequences of compensated siting programs therefore raise fundamental questions about our treatment of the poor and about the voluntariness of any site accepted by the communities.

Third, compensated siting programs allow a community to trade away the rights of future generations, who aren't represented at the bargaining table.... Finally, compensation schemes are likely to be considered immoral unless the community voluntarily enters into the siting agreement. What are the essential elements of a voluntary agreement? Is an agreement voluntary, for example, if communities are, relative to site developers, ignorant about the risks and harms the facilities will impose?

[A]ssuming that at least some forms of compensation are moral in at least some circumstances, how do we structure compensation programs to be most fair? Those issues include, for example, the question of how to ensure that communities and siting officials have relatively equal bargaining power.... [C]ommunities are at a severe disadvantage in finding out about what other communities have bargained for. The industry sometimes imposes as a condition of the bargain that the community not reveal the terms of the agreement.... At the same time, there has been little research on how siting agreements have worked out in practice, so communities may find it hard to assess whether they should follow another community's example....

* * *

## Notes and Questions

1. Professor Been raises a host of difficult and important questions about compensation schemes. Additional difficult questions include: Who gets to negotiate and make these decisions on behalf of a community? If it is the community's elected officials, should a vote of the public be required to ratify the agreement? Should we give special weight to the interests of those community members most affected by the sitings? What do you think of the approaches followed by Massachusetts and Wisconsin? Professor Brad Mank advocates a system in which "the relative say that nearby residents, residents in a municipality, and regional neighbors have on a siting negotiation committee would depend on the relative amount of risk to which individuals are potentially or actually exposed, as determined by the risk assessment process," even if affected individuals live outside the host community's political boundaries. Bradford C. Mank, *Environmental Justice and Discriminatory Siting: Risk-Based Representation and Equitable Compensation* 56 Ohio. St. L. J. 329, 401 (1995).

2. Compensated siting approaches have been attractive to states, at least in theory. As of 1994, thirteen states mandated compensation for hazardous waste facilities, twelve offered compensation for low level radioactive waste facilities, and nineteen had procedures for negotiation between facility developers and proposed host communities.

Michael Gerrard, *Fear and Loathing in the Siting of Hazardous and Radioactive Waste Facilities: A Comprehensive Approach to a Misperceived Crisis*, 68 TUL. L. REV 1047, 1154, 1156 (1994). But as Professor Been points out, most compensated siting schemes have been unsuccessful, at least with respect to hazardous waste facilities. Why is that the case? Professor Joel Eisen argues that the negotiated schemes have failed largely because they have not provided opportunities for meaningful public participation. In Massachusetts, for example, many communities resisted proposed facilities because they had no input into the site selection process and because the negotiations process excluded discussion of the need for a facility, which to many communities is the central issue for negotiations. Joel B. Eisen, *Brownfields of Dreams?: Challenges and Limits of Voluntary Cleanup Programs and Incentive*, 1996 U. ILL. L. REV. 883, 998, 1005–1006, 1008. For a detailed examination of the Massachusetts law, see Michael Wheeler, *Negotiating NIMBYs: Learning from the Failure of the Massachusetts Siting Law*, 11 YALE J. ON REG. 241, 264–281 (1994). Michael Gerrard argues that monetary compensation will rarely gain acceptance of hazardous or radioactive waste facilities in places that do not want them. He maintains that "[t]he reason is clear: the opposition to these facilities stems mainly from concern over their impact on health, particularly children's health, and people will not accept any amount of money that will allow others to endanger their children. Individuals that perceive these facilities as dangerous will not change these perceptions when offered money, and they view the offer itself as immoral, 'bribery,' or 'blood money.'" Gerrard, *Fear and Loathing*, supra, at 1154–1155. He adds that compensation works when, and only when, the community does not believe the proposed facility poses an undue hazard. Compensation has accordingly been quite successful in siting municipal solid waste and incinerators, which have much lower perceived risks than hazardous waste and radioactive waste facilities (a point also made by Professor Been in the above excerpt). *Id.* at 1155.

3. Professor Been reports studies showing that compensation measures that guarantee local monitoring and control may sway a significant number of people to accept a facility. Michael Gerrard, however, believes that surveys suggesting that compensation can overcome public safety fears "do not seem to be translated into actual behavior." Gerrard, *Fear and Loathing*, supra, at 1155 n.692. Which view do you think is more plausible?

4. Professor Lynn Blais argues that "[r]ather than constituting an immoral buy-off of the residents of a host community, compensation can be understood as a mechanism for increasing the otherwise limited options faced by poor and minority communities and residents." She adds that "compensation can be used to finance the option most environmental racism scholars say is fatally lacking in siting decisions: the opportunity to leave the community if one does not agree with the risk/benefit analysis that led to the siting in the first place." Lynn E. Blais, *Environmental Racism Reconsidered*, 75 N.C. L. REV. 75, 149 (1996). Does the latter argument overlook racial barriers in the housing market that constrain the mobility of nonwhite families? Is it likely that the compensation offered would be sufficient to relocate to comparable yet safer neighborhoods? Even if sufficient compensation is offered, does relocation-oriented compensation address the threats to community stability that result if residents relocate? Relocation issues are discussed in more detail in Chapter IX.

5. Responding to critics who "argue that minority or poor residents should not be placed in the position of giving up their health in a devil's bargain for cash," Professor Mank advocates compensated siting proposals so long as appropriate safeguards are provided. He argues:

It is paternalistic and patronizing to presume that minority groups or the poor cannot make rational decisions even if they are fairly represented and have access to technical experts to assist them in understanding and questioning the developer's proposal. It should be assumed that poor or minority residents are as capable as wealthy persons of bargaining with developers, as long as the process for selecting the negotiating team adequately represents high-risk and minority residents and the team has access to adequate technical support selected by the team but paid for by the government or the developer.

Mank, *supra,* at 408. He further suggests that government agencies should establish maximum acceptable levels of risk and minimum levels of compensation to protect communities participating in the compensation process. *Id.* at 402–406. Do you agree with Professor Mank that it is paternalistic to preclude citizens from bargaining for hazardous waste or other unwanted facilities? Why or why not?

# C. Environmental Review: The National Environmental Policy Act and State Environmental Policy Acts

## 1.   A Note on NEPA And SEPAs

The National Environmental Policy Act (NEPA) is a cross-cutting statute that requires review of all environmentally significant decisions undertaken by federal agencies. NEPA requires that agencies prepare a detailed Environmental Impact Statement (EIS) discussing the environmental impacts of all federal projects that significantly affect the environment. Impacts are broadly defined to include ecological, aesthetic, historic, cultural, health, as well as cumulative effects. An EIS must also discuss alternatives to the proposed project and appropriate mitigation measures. In many cases an agency will prepare a less detailed Environmental Assessment (EA) to determine if an EIS is necessary. EAs are also prepared for projects with minor impacts, unless the projects are categorically excluded by agency regulation (i.e. minor maintenance operations). An EA is a "concise public document" that briefly discusses the need for the project, alternatives, and impacts of the project and alternatives. 40 C.F.R. § 1508.9.

While NEPA applies only to actions carried out by the federal government, sixteen states plus the District of Columbia and Puerto Rico have adopted similar statutes, known as state environmental policy acts (SEPAs), that govern projects approved by state or local agencies.

NEPA or its state analogues frequently will be implicated in environmental justice matters, particularly the siting of new facilities. Some of NEPA's provisions seem particularly well-suited for incorporating environmental justice concerns into the agency decision making process. For example, unlike most pollution control statutes, NEPA requires that agencies evaluate the cumulative impacts of proposed projects. This arguably imposes a duty on agencies to consider the pre-existing concentration of industrial facilities, health risks, and environmental exposures in a community.

Likewise, NEPA requires agencies to provide for meaningful public involvement in their environmental review process. Agencies must seek public input at various points in the NEPA process, such as when determining the scope of what matters are to be included in the EISs ("scoping"), after issuing draft EISs, and after issuing final EISs and before final decisions have been made about the project. They also are required to hold public hearings when there is substantial controversy surrounding a project or substantial interest in a hearing. Agencies also are required to respond to all public comments submitted on draft EISs. To facilitate public review, NEPA's regulations require that EISs must be written in "plain language...so that decisionmakers and the public can readily understand them." 40 C.F.R. § 1502.8. Some courts have invalidated EISs that were too dense for average persons to understand.

The public participation requirements of NEPA & SEPAs also may require translation for communities that do not speak English. One prominent case raising this issue involved a hazardous waste incinerator proposed by Chemical Waste for Kettleman City, a tiny farmworker community in California's San Joaquin Valley, where 95% of the residents are Latino, 70% speak Spanish at home, and 40% are monolingual Spanish speakers. Despite repeated requests, the local county permitting agency failed to translate into Spanish hearing notices, public testimony, or three versions of the Environmental Impact Report (EIR) prepared for the incinerator pursuant to the California Environmental Quality Act (CEQA). At the only public hearing on the project, the county refused to provide simultaneous translation of the proceedings or allow private translators (and ordered Spanish-speaking residents to sit in the back of the huge auditorium where the hearing took place). Residents sued, alleging that the County violated CEQA's public participation provisions, and a superior court ruled in their favor:

> [T]he strong emphasis in CEQA on environmental decisionmaking by public officials which involves and informs members of the public would have justified the Spanish translation of an extended summary of the [EIR], public meeting notices, and public hearing testimony in this case. The residents of Kettleman City, almost 40 percent of whom were monolingual in Spanish, expressed continuous and strong interest in participating in the CEQA review process for the incinerator project at [Chemical Waste's] Kettleman Hills facility, just four miles from their homes. Their meaningful involvement in the CEQA review process was effectively precluded by the absence of the Spanish translation.

El Pueblo Para el Aire y Agua Limpio v. County of Kings, 22 ENVTL L. REP. 20,357 (Super. Ct. Sacramento, Dec. 30, 1991).

NEPA has a number of important limitations, however. These limits include the following:

(1) NEPA's broad public participation requirements apply when an EIS is required, not when EAs are prepared—which is the level of review for approximately ninety-nine percent of projects subject to NEPA. Stephen Johnson, *NEPA and SEPA's In the Quest for Environmental Justice*, 30 LOY. L.A. L. REV. 565, 575 (1997). Agencies are required to notify the public only *after* the agency has completed the EA.

(2) NEPA only requires analysis of social and economic impacts in limited circumstances. This result is not self-evident from the face of the statute, which lists in its declaration of purpose the profound impact of man's activity on, among other things, "population growth, high density urbanization, and industrial expansion," NEPA, § 101(a), and which requires EISs for actions that significantly affect the "human environment." Some early cases held that NEPA requires agencies to evaluate urban environmental effects, including urban decay, crime and congestion. Subsequently, how-

ever, both case law and implementing guidelines adopted by CEQ have interpreted NEPA to focus primarily on impacts on the physical or natural environment; social and economic effects must be considered only to the extent that they are related to the physical effects of a proposed action. 40 C.F.R. § 1508.14. Thus, for example, when a project's physical environmental impacts lead to secondary socioeconomic impacts, these latter impacts must be evaluated. The Executive Order on Environmental Justice did not change the underlying trigger for such analysis, but some commentators suggest that it has prompted renewed agency attention to these socioeconomic effects.

Some SEPAs are broader than NEPA and require agencies to review social and economic impacts regardless of their link to physical impacts. In Chinese Staff & Workers Ass'n v. City of New York, 68 N.Y. 2d 359 (1986), for example, residents of challenged the proposed construction of a luxury condominium in New York's Chinatown on the grounds that it would displace local low income residents and businesses and alter the character of the community. The court held that under New York's environmental review statute, the city was required to evaluate these potential impacts from the luxury housing, noting that "land development impacts not only on the actual property involved but on the community involved." More recently, an administrative law judge in New York ruled that the broad ambit of the state statute appears to encompass environmental justice issues, and that these issues needed to be addressed in connection with a proposal to build a solid waste transfer station. In re American Marine Rail, LLC (ALJ Rulings on Issues and Party Status and Environmental Significance, Aug. 25, 2000, available at <http://www.dec.state.ny.us/website/ohms/decis/amrr.htm>)

(3) NEPA does not impose any substantive obligations on federal agencies, mandating only that agencies consider and fully disclose the environmental impacts of proposed projects. As the Supreme Court has explained, NEPA "merely prohibits uninformed—rather than unwise—agency action." Robertson v. Methow Valley, 490 U.S. 332, 351 (1989). Agencies are not obligated to choose less environmentally harmful alternatives, or adopt mitigation measures to reduce the impacts of a project. SEPAs vary in this regard, while many are similarly procedural, a few require state agencies to minimize or avoid significant adverse impacts

(4) The courts have held that EPA does not have to comply with NEPA when the environmental assessment and public participation procedures required by an EPA regulatory action are "functionally equivalent" to those mandated by the NEPA process. EPA thus does not comply with NEPA, when, for example, it issues hazardous waste permits under the Resource Conservation and Recovery Act (RCRA). EPA also has been successful in arguing that it does not have to prepare EISs in connection with cleanup orders under Superfund. Congress also has created express statutory exemptions from NEPA for a number of EPA programs, such as all actions under the Clean Air Act and many under the Clean Water Act.

(5) Most pollution control permits today are issued not by EPA, but by states that have been delegated authority to implement federal environmental programs in lieu of EPA. Since NEPA only applies to federal actions, the state permitting agency's actions are outside of NEPA's purview. This exemption is especially significant given the growing move to devolve greater environmental authority to the states, discussed in Chapters V & XI.

## Pathfinder on NEPA

For general background about NEPA, see DANIEL R. MANDELKER, NEPA LAW AND LITIGATION (2d ed. 2000). Regulations implementing NEPA that are binding on all federal agencies have been adopted by the Council on Environmental Quality ("CEQ Regulations"), and can be found at 40 C.F.R. § 1500 et. seq. (2001). For discussion of State Environmental Policy Acts (SEPAs), *see* DANIEL P. SELMI & KENNETH A. MANASTER, STATE ENVIRONMENTAL LAW, § 10 (2000). The CEQ's NEPA Environmental Justice Guidance can be found at <http://ceq.eh.doe.gov/nepa/regs/guidance.html>. EPA's Final Guidance for Incorporating Environmental Justice Concerns in EPA's NEPA Compliance Analyses can be found at http://es.epa.gov/oeca/ofa/ejepa.html. For a discussion of the extent to which NEPA and other environmental review statutes require consideration of environmental justice issues, *see* Sheila Foster, *Impact Assessment, in* THE LAW OF ENVIRONMENTAL JUSTICE: THEORIES AND PROCEDURES TO ADDRESS DISPROPORTIONATE RISKS 256 (Michael Gerrard ed., 1999).

## Notes and Questions

1. A new power plant, landfill, or factory may have social, psychological, economic or other impacts that are not directly related to physical effects from the facility. The facility may decrease the attractiveness of the neighborhood or lower property values. Community residents may worry about the threat of accidental releases or spills, or experience stress about harm to their families from exposure to a new source of pollution. Should agencies be required to evaluate these impacts under NEPA or state NEPA statutes, without regard to whether these impacts are related to physical impacts? For a discussion of the social psychological impacts that residents exposed to toxic chemicals experience, *see* MICHAEL EDELSTEIN, CONTAMINATED COMMUNITIES: THE SOCIAL PSYCHOLOGICAL IMPACTS OF RESIDENTIAL TOXIC EXPOSURE (1988).

2. Professor Stephen Johnson argues that the "functional equivalent" exemption improperly exempts from NEPA review many federal actions that have disparate impacts on low income and minority communities. He notes, for example, that when EPA issues a permit under RCRA, the agency does not have to consider socioeconomic impacts or project alternatives, as required by NEPA, and that the permitting process provides less opportunities for public participation than NEPA. Likewise, he argues, EPA's regulatory process for setting standards should not be considered the functional equivalent of NEPA when the agency is not required to consider the cumulative, indirect, or socioeconomic impacts of these standards. Johnson also argues that state agencies that have been given authority to administer a federal program in lieu of EPA should be required to provide for the same level of environmental impact review that the federal government would have to provide if it were implementing the program. Johnson, *supra*, at 590–596.

3. Although NEPA is often criticized as weak because it does not impose any substantive requirements on federal agencies, Professor Johnson contends that it can nonetheless be of considerable value to environmental justice communities as an information-gathering, educational, and organizational tool. For example, mandated disclosure of alternatives and mitigation measures can leave the agencies more vulnerable to criticism and result in pressure for them to take steps to mitigate adverse project impacts they might have otherwise overlooked. Likewise, the environmental review process can create important opportunities for organizing community opposition. Johnson, *supra*, at 572–580. How useful do you think NEPA's requirements are for communities engaged in environmental justice battles?

# 2. New Opportunities—CEQ and EPA Guidance

Many commentators have argued for a broader reading of NEPA to address environmental justice issues. In addition, since the Executive Order on Environmental Justice was issued in 1994, federal agencies have sought to expand the NEPA process to take into account environmental justice concerns.

The Executive Order and the accompanying Memorandum issued by President Clinton (both reprinted in Chapter XV) require agencies to identify disproportionately high and adverse human health or environmental effects of their programs. The Order specifically requires agencies to analyze environmental effects, including economic and social effects, and including effects on minority and low income communities, when such analysis is required by NEPA. The Executive Order also requires agencies, whenever feasible, to identify multiple and cumulative exposures in their environmental human health analyses and to identify mitigation measures that address significant and adverse environmental effects on minority and low income communities. Moreover, agencies must provide opportunities for community input in the NEPA process, including improving the accessibility of meetings, crucial documents, and notices.

The Council on Environmental Quality (CEQ), the agency created by Congress for coordinating federal agencies' compliance with NEPA, and EPA each responded to the Executive Order's requirements by promulgating NEPA environmental justice guidance. The CEQ guidance applies to all federal agencies in their implementation of NEPA. EPA's guidance applies only to internal projects initiated by EPA (with the exception of those agency activities exempted from NEPA requirements by the functional equivalency doctrine or by statute, as described above).

## a. CEQ's Guidance

NEPA documents traditionally have analyzed impacts on broadly defined affected areas and populations, without focusing on potential impacts to smaller subpopulations of minority or low income groups. CEQ's guidance, Environmental Justice Guidance Under the National Environmental Policy Act (1997), calls on agencies to determine whether an area impacted by a proposed project may include low income populations, minority populations, or Indian tribes, and whether the proposed action is likely to have a disproportionately high and adverse human health or environmental impact on these populations. Agencies should consider the potential for multiple or cumulative exposure, historical patterns of exposure to environmental hazards, and cultural differences which may lead certain communities to experience impacts more severely than the general population. For example, the Guidance notes, "data on different patterns of living, such as subsistence fish, vegetation, or wildlife consumption and the use of well water in rural communities may be relevant to the analysis."

With respect to alternatives, the Guidance instructs that the distribution and magnitude of any disproportionate adverse effects should be a factor in the agency's identification of the "environmentally preferable alternative" for a project (which agencies are required to identify in record of decisions following preparation of an EIS). Moreover, in developing mitigation measures, agencies should solicit the views of the affected populations throughout the public participation process, and mitigation measures should reflect the views of affected low income populations, minority populations, or Indian tribes to the maximum extent practicable.

The Guidance points out that encouraging the participation of low income populations, minority populations, or tribal populations in the NEPA process may require "adaptive or innovative approaches to overcome linguistic, cultural, economic, or other potential barriers." The Guidance suggests that agencies enhance their customary practices for public outreach—which often have included primary reliance on publication in the *Federal Register* or notice in local newspapers—by contacting a wide array of community, social service, homeowner, religious, civic, tribal, and other organizations. Agencies should take other steps to encourage effective public participation, including translation of major documents, provision of opportunities to participate other than through written communications, such as interviews or oral or video recording devices, provision of translators at meetings and other efforts to ensure that limited English speakers potentially affected have an understanding of the proposed actions and its potential impact, and use of locations and facilities that are local, convenient and accessible.

### b. EPA's GUIDANCE

EPA's Guidance parallels the CEQ's emphasis on more focused analysis, careful attention to cumulative impacts, and the need to enhance the participation of affected communities. EPA's Guidance also provides more elaboration on the identification of alternatives and mitigation measures and means to increase public involvement, as reflected in this excerpt.

## U.S. Environmental Protection Agency, Final Guidance for Incorporating Environmental Justice Concerns in EPA's NEPA Compliance Analyses
### (1998)

*Identification of Alternatives*

The EPA NEPA analyst should keep in mind that the goal of identifying and developing alternatives for mitigating disproportionately high and adverse effects is not to distribute the impacts proportionally or divert them to a non-minority or higher-income community. Instead, alternatives should be developed that mitigate or avoid effects to both the population at large and any disproportionately high and adverse effects on minority or low-income communities. [These include] the identification of alternate locations or sites where impacts to susceptible populations or environments will be avoided...[and]...pollution prevention practices and policies to reduce or mitigate emissions and/or impact....

*Mitigation Measures*

Regulations require that mitigation measures be developed to address environmental effects, including cumulative impacts, threatened by proposed actions (40 C.F.R. 1502.14(f) and 1502.16(h)). In addition, mitigation measures should be developed specifically to address potential disproportionately high and adverse effects to minority and/or low-income communities. [These include]: Reducing pollutant loadings through changes in processes or technologies.... Reducing or eliminating other sources of pollutants or impacts to reduce cumulative effects....Providing assistance to an affected community to ensure that it receives at least its fair (i.e., proportional) share of the anticipated benefits of the proposed action (e.g., through job training, community infrastructure improvements)....Relocating affected communities, upon request or with concurrence from the affected individuals...[and] [e]stablishment of a community oversight committee to monitor progress and identify potential community concerns....

### Mechanisms to Enhance Participation

[One] mechanism for providing information to the public is the establishment of information repositories which are accessible to members of the affected community. Locations can include libraries, churches, community centers, etc. Technical documents should contain a summary written to the lay public and translated, if necessary, into the dominant language of the affected community.

Meaningful public participation is based on the proposition that people should have a say in decisions which affect their lives in a significant way. Thus, for the public participation process to be effective, it must:

- Seek out and facilitate the involvement of those potentially affected;
- Contain the implicit commitment by decision makers to seriously consider the input of the public; and
- Communicate to participants how their advice was or was not utilized....

[Other recommended mechanisms include establishing Community Advisory Boards for the development of NEPA documents; employing community consultants; and providing technical assistance to affected communities to help them interpret scientific documents, develop potential alternatives and mitigation measures, and fully participate in the NEPA process.]

\* \* \*

## Notes and Questions

1. Are there other ideas that you think should be included in the CEQ or EPA Guidance to address environmental justice concerns?

2. Should EPA be required to translate NEPA documents whenever a project will impact a community that has a significant percentage of members that do not speak English? How large a percentage should this be? What if there are numerous, monolingual subpopulations within the affected community—should agencies be required to translate documents into multiple languages? Should entire documents be translated, or only summaries and/or important documents? (EISs can sometimes be several hundred pages long.) What other approaches should be explored? Should culturally sensitive outreach workers be hired? Under what circumstances? Should technical assistance be provided to help communities participate in the NEPA review process?

3. Some scholars and activists have argued that state and federal agency decisions should be required to prepare explicit "equity assessments," analyzing the relative harms and benefits from agency decisions on low income communities and communities of color. Professor Richard Lazarus notes that "EPA and other federal agencies are already required by various executive orders to account for the distributional impact of their rules on various interests, [including small] businesses, family, states rights, and private

property." Richard J. Lazarus, *Pursuing "Environmental Justice": The Distributional Effects of Environmental Protection*, 87 Nw. U. L. Rev. 787, 847 (1993).

## 3.  JUDICIAL REVIEW OF NEPA

What has been the impact of the Executive Order on Environmental Justice on agency adjudication involving NEPA? Thus far, few adjudicated cases have reached this question. One that did involves the Nuclear Regulatory Commission, an independent regulatory agency not technically covered by the Executive Order, but that nonetheless voluntarily agreed to be bound by it in 1994. In 1997, the Atomic Safety and Licensing Board (Board) of the NRC heard a challenge to a Final Environmental Impact Statement (FEIS) prepared for a proposal by Louisiana Energy Services (LES) to build an $855 million uranium-enrichment facility in the midst of two historically black communities in Claiborne Parish, Louisiana (the project was known as the Claiborne Enrichment Center, or CEC). The Board issued the following ruling.

## In the Matter of Louisiana Energy Services, L.P.,

### 45 N.R.C. 367, 1997 LEXIS 20, (May 1, 1997)

This Final Initial Decision addresses the remaining contention—environmental justice contention J.9—filed by the Intervenor, Citizens Against Nuclear Trash ("CANT"), in this combined construction permit-operating license proceeding.... The Applicant plans to build the CEC on a 442-acre site in Claiborne Parish, Louisiana, that is immediately adjacent to and between the unincorporated African-American communities of Center Springs and Forest Grove, some 5 miles from the town of Homer, Louisiana.... The site, called the LeSage property... is currently bisected by Parish Road 39 (also known as Forest Grove Road) running north and south through the property.... [Center Springs] lies along State Road 9 and Parish Road 39 and is located approximately 0.5 kilometers (about 0.33 mile) to the north of the LeSage property.... [Forest Grove] lies approximately 3.2 kilometers (about 2 miles) south of the site along Parish Road 39.... The two community churches, which share a single minister, are approximately 1.1 miles apart, with the LeSage property lying between them.

The community of Forest Grove was founded by freed slaves at the close of the Civil War and has a population of about 150. Center Springs was founded around the turn of the century and has a population of about 100. The populations of Forest Grove and Center Springs are about 97% African American. Many of the residents are descendants of the original settlers and a large portion of the landholdings remain with the same families that founded the communities. Aside from Parish Road 39 and State Road 9, the roads in Center Springs or Forest Grove are either unpaved or poorly maintained. There are no stores, schools, medical clinics, or businesses in Center Springs or Forest Grove. The Intervenor's evidence was undisputed that from kindergarten through high school the children of Center Springs and Forest Grove attend schools that are largely racially segregated. Many of the residents of the communities are not connected to the public water supply. Some of these residents rely on groundwater wells while others must actually carry their water because they have no potable water supply....

The Intervenor's environmental justice contention is grounded in the requirements of [NEPA].... Subsequent to... the Staff's issuance of the draft EIS, on February 11,

1994, the President issued Executive Order [on Environmental Justice No.] 12,898.... The President's memorandum accompanying the order...specifically states that, in conducting analyses required by NEPA, "[e]ach Federal agency shall analyze the environmental effects, including human health, economic and social effects, of Federal actions, including effects on minority communities and low-income communities."...Although Executive Order 12898 does not create any new rights that the Intervenor may seek to enforce before the agency or upon judicial review of the agency's actions, the President's directive is, in effect, a procedural directive to the head of each executive department and agency that, "to the greatest extent practicable and permitted by law," it should seek to achieve environmental justice in carrying out its mission by using such tools as [NEPA]. Pursuant to the President's order, there are two aspects to environmental justice: first, each agency is required to identify and address disproportionately high and adverse health or environmental effects on minority and low-income populations in its programs, policies, and activities; and second, each agency must ensure that its programs, policies, and activities that substantially affect human health or the environment do not have the effect of subjecting persons and populations to discrimination because of their race, color, or national origin. Thus, whether the Executive Order is viewed as calling for a more expansive interpretation of NEPA as the Applicant suggests or as merely clarifying NEPA's longstanding requirement for consideration of the impacts of major federal actions on the "human" environment as the Intervenor argues, it is clear the President's order directs all agencies in analyzing the environmental effects of a federal action in an EIS required by NEPA to include in the analysis, "to the greatest extent practicable," the human health, economic, and social effects on minority and low-income communities....

### Impacts of Road Closing/Relocation

The Intervenor [asserts] that the FEIS is deficient because if [sic] fails to address the impacts of closing Parish Road 39, which currently bisects the LeSage site and joins the communities of Forest Grove and Center Springs. Dr. Bullard [sociologist and prominent environmental justice scholar Robert Bullard] testified that in the FEIS the Staff assumed that Forest Grove Road would be relocated after it is closed. He claimed, however, that it is by no means clear that the road will be relocated because any decision about the road rests not with LES, but with the Claiborne Parish Police Jury that must pay for any road relocation. Dr. Bullard testified that if the road is not relocated it would impose upon the residents of Center Springs and Forest Grove an additional 8- or 9-mile trip by way of Homer to go from one community to the other.

Additionally, Dr. Bullard asserted that even if Parish Road 39 is relocated around the site, the Staff incorrectly concluded in the FEIS that the impacts would be very small and not pose unacceptable risks to the local community. According to Dr. Bullard, it is apparent that the Staff did not even consult with any of the residents of Forest Grove and Center Springs before reaching its conclusion for if it had, the Staff would have found that Forest Grove Road is a vital and frequently used link between the two communities, with regular pedestrian traffic.

For its part, the Staff does indeed state in the FEIS that Parish Road 39 will be relocated to pass to the west of the plant area and that the existing road will not be closed until the relocated road is fully constructed and open. Further, the FEIS indicates that the road relocation will add approximately 120 meters (0.075 mile) to the traveling distance between State Roads 2 and 9 and will add an additional 600 meters (0.38 mile) to the 1800 meter (1.1 mile) distance between the Forest Grove Church and the Center Springs Church, which are the approximate centers of the respective minority communities. The Staff also concludes in the FEIS that the impacts associated with the road relocation "are very small and would not impose unacceptable risks to the local community."...

[C]ontrary to the apparent belief of the Applicant and Staff witnesses, the police jury has only expressed a sentiment either to close or to relocate the segment of Parish Road 39 that crosses the LeSage property, but not necessarily to do both. The record before us thus does not support [applicant's] optimism that the parish will relocate the road.... Moreover, the record is clear that the Staff did not analyze the impacts on the communities of Forest Grove and Center Springs of closing Parish Road 39. This substantial shortcoming in the FEIS was remedied at the hearing, however, when LES indicated, for the first time, that it would relocate the road, if necessary.... Accordingly, we direct that a license condition to that effect must accompany any construction permit and operating license authorization.

The Intervenor also challenged the adequacy of the Staff's treatment in the FEIS of the impact from relocating (as opposed to closing) Parish Road 39 on the communities of Forest Grove and Center Springs and the Staff's conclusion that those impacts were very small....

The Staff's FEIS treatment of the impacts of relocating Parish Road 39 does not discuss Forest Grove Road's status as a pedestrian link between Forest Grove and Center Springs and the impacts of relocation on those who must walk the distance between the communities on this road. In the FEIS, the Staff calculates how much additional gasoline it will take to drive between the communities when the road is relocated and the added travel time the road relocation will cause for various trips....

Dr. Bullard testified, however, that Forest Grove Road is a vital and frequently used link between the communities with regular pedestrian traffic. Neither the Staff nor the Applicant presented any evidence disputing Dr. Bullard's testimony in this regard. Further, the Bureau of Census statistics introduced by the Intervenor show that the African American population of Claiborne Parish is one of the poorest in the country and that over 31% of black households in the parish have no motor vehicles. Again this evidence is undisputed. It thus is obvious that a significant number of the residents of these communities have no motor vehicles and often must walk. Adding 0.38 mile to the distance between the Forest Grove and Center Springs communities may be a mere "inconvenience" to those who drive, as the Staff suggests. Yet, permanently adding that distance to the 1- or 2-mile walk between these communities for those who must regularly make the trip on foot may be more than a "very small" impact, especially if they are old, ill or otherwise infirm. The Staff in the FEIS has not considered the impacts the relocation of Forest Grove Road will have upon those residents who must walk. Accordingly, we find that the Staff's treatment in the FEIS of the impacts on the communities of Forest Grove and Center Springs from the relocation of Parish Road 39 is inadequate and must be revised.

*Property Value Impacts*

Intervenor [also] asserts that property values in the neighboring communities will be adversely affected by the facility and that this economic effect will be borne disproportionately by the minority communities that can least afford it....

In support of his assertion that the Staff analysis [in the FEIS] is inadequate, Dr. Bullard stated that his research shows that negative impacts on property values will occur in the immediate area of the plant and that, because of the housing barriers faced by African Americans, the residents of Forest Grove and Center Springs will not have the same opportunities to relocate as do whites living in the parish. He asserted that the general beneficial effects on local housing values from the plant cited in the FEIS will have little, if any, effect on the minority communities of Forest Grove and Center Springs. In this regard, Dr. Bullard testified that the general "benefit streams" to counties with large industrial taxpayers do not have significant positive effects on low income minority communities, which are already receiving a disproportionately low share of the services offered by the county....

The Staff's treatment of the economic impacts of the CEC on property values in the FEIS does indeed recognize that the CEC will depress some property values while increasing others, but the Staff fails to identify the location, extent, or significance of impacts. Further, although, the FEIS generally indicates the CEC is likely to increase both housing and land prices because of increased demand and the benefits capture effect, the Staff makes no attempt to allocate the costs or benefits. Dr. Bullard directly challenges the Staff's failure to assess the impacts of the CEC on property values in the communities of Forest Grove and Center Springs asserting that when facilities like the CEC are placed in the midst of poor, minority communities, the facility has negative impacts on property values in the immediate area of the plant. For the reasons specified below, we find his testimony on the negative economic impact of the CEC on property values in these minority communities reasonable and persuasive....

Dr. Bullard explained that unlike white residents of the parish, the black residents of Forest Grove and Center Springs face substantial "housing barriers" that preclude them from leaving when a large industrial facility is sited in the midst of their residential area. As a consequence, these already economically depressed communities must fully absorb the further adverse impact of having a heavy industrial facility nearby making them even more undesirable. He testified that the beneficial effects on housing values from increased demand by new migrating employees and the benefit capture effect relied upon by the Staff in the FEIS will have no effect on these minority communities that currently receive almost no parish services, are virtually 100% African American, and are inhabited by some of the most economically disadvantaged people in the United States. As Dr. Bullard stated, it is "extremely unlikely" new workers to the area will seek to live in Forest Grove and Center Springs. Dr. Bullard concludes that these factors lead to an overall negative impact on property values in the minority communities that must host the CEC....

The Staff witnesses made no attempt to explain how or why Dr. Bullard might be mistaken....Indeed, given the Staff's recognition in the FEIS that there will be some negative impacts on property values from the CEC, it is difficult to envision an economic rationale that would demonstrate those adverse impacts from the CEC are likely to occur to properties well removed from the facility, such as in Homer or Haynesville, as opposed to the Forest Grove and Center Springs areas next to the facility....By the same token, the opinions of [two witnesses for the applicant that] the effect that industrial facilities often increase property values in the vicinity of a facility are far too general to draw any reasonable conclusions about the impacts on property values in the circumstances presented here. Likewise, Mr. LeRoy's [another witness for the applicant] testimony about the positive impact on lakefront vacation home values from the construction of nuclear power plants is neither useful nor reasonable in making a comparison with the economically disadvantaged minority communities of Forest Grove and Center Springs. Certainly, the reality of Forest Grove and Center Springs hardly seems comparable to the description of Lake Wylie in Applicant's Exhibit 19, which states that "the Catawba plant was built on a beautiful lake, dotted with hundreds of expensive homes and homesites." Nor do these communities resemble the description of Lake Keowee in Exhibit 19 as "one of the most prestigious resort/retirement communities in the United States [which] is less than a mile from Oconee Nuclear Station. At Keowee Key more than 1500 people golf, boat, fish, relax and retire next door to a nuclear plant."

On this basis, we find that the Staff's treatment in the FEIS of the impacts from the CEC on property values in the communities of Forest Grove and Center Springs is inadequate....

* * *

## Notes and Questions

1. What is different about the NEPA analysis demanded by the Board and the type traditionally prepared by federal agencies? Is it the particularized focus on how the project will impact very small subpopulations of larger communities? Is it the Board's careful attention to the project's social and economic impacts? The Board seems to embrace Dr. Bullard's longstanding view that achieving environmental justice requires examination of "who pays and who benefits" from industrial development. Note also that, although the Board requires an environmental justice analysis, it specifically declines to decide whether the Executive Order calls for a more expansive interpretation of NEPA or merely clarifies NEPA's existing requirement that impacts on the human environment be analyzed. Should it matter?

2. The Board's decision elsewhere quotes Dr. Bullard's testimony that the NRC Staff did not consult with any of the residents of Forest Grove and Center Springs before reaching its conclusion about the negative impacts of relocating the road, and that if it had "the Staff would have found that Forest Grove Road is a vital and frequently used link between the two communities, with regular pedestrian traffic." See Id. at *80. Does this in effect impose a duty to implement special outreach and public participation efforts in NEPA cases raising environmental justice concerns?

3. Apart from its claims relating to the FEIS' failure to analyze the project's social and economic impacts, the citizens group alleged that the NRC's siting process was racially discriminatory. The group presented testimony from Professor Bullard showing that at each successive stage of the siting process, the communities under consideration became poorer and more predominantly African American, culminating in the selection of a site that was 97 percent African American and extremely poor. Bullard also testified that the applicant's use of facially race-neutral siting criteria — such as eliminating sites close to sensitive receptors like hospitals, schools, and nursing homes — disadvantaged poor and minority communities by reinforcing the impacts of prior discrimination that had left them without such institutions. The Board found that this evidence raised a "reasonable inference that racial considerations played some part in the site selection process," and remanded for a more complete investigation. Responding to the agency's contention that its decision was based solely on technical and business criteria, and that there was no specific evidence that racial considerations motivated the decision, the Board wrote that racial discrimination "cannot be uncovered with only a cursory review of the description of the [site selection process]. If it were so easily detected, racial dis-

crimination would not be such a persistent and enduring problem in American society. Racial discrimination is rarely, if ever, admitted." The Board concluded that "for the [Executive Order] to have any meaning in this particular licensing action, the Staff must conduct an objective, thorough, and professional investigation that looks beneath the surface of the description of the site selection process in the [applicant's Environmental Report]. In other words, the Staff must lift some rocks and look under them." *See id.* at *53–55.

On appeal, a panel of the NRC reversed this part of the Board's order, holding that NEPA is not "a tool for addressing problems of racial discrimination." The Board noted that the CEQ's Guidance on Environmental Justice (discussed above) encourages agencies to consider impacts on low income and minority communities, but "neither states nor implies that if adverse impacts are found, an investigation into possible racial bias is the appropriate next step." In the panel's view, NEPA is limited to objective impacts rather than the subjective motives of the applicant or permitting agency. In short, "NEPA is not a civil rights law calling for full scale racial discrimination litigation in NRC licensing proceedings." *See* In the Matter of Louisiana Energy Services, L.P.,1998 NRC LEXIS 43, 60, 72 (April 3, 1998).

Is the NRC opinion sound? Should there be no recourse under NEPA against a decision that results from a racially biased decision making process? Recall the emphasis that NEPA places on procedure and meaningful public involvement in agency decisions. Could this be a basis for arguing that further review of the NRC's decision is warranted? As an attorney for a community group, how would you argue that consideration of possible racial bias is an appropriate consideration under NEPA?

4. The NRC panel upheld the part of the Board's NEPA decision that is reproduced above. In April, 1998, after this ruling, Louisiana Energy Services dropped its application to construct the CEC.

# D. Information Disclosure and Right to Know Laws

In recent years, information disclosure and right to know statutes have become increasingly popular as an alternative to conventional regulation. These laws serve numerous objectives. One, they improve the efficient functioning of the market by remedying information gaps facing consumers and workers. Such laws also are premised on an entitlement rationale; the underlying notion is that members of the public have a "fundamental right to know" what chemicals are "out there" and the chemicals to which they are being exposed. They also promote citizen power and advance democratic decision-making. Armed with more information, citizens can make better-informed decisions and are thus in a better position to bargain with private corporations and government. Finally, such measures provide indirect incentives for industry to undertake self-regulation and thereby reduce risky activities, help avoid accidents and facilitate emergency planning, and add to the data base that helps government agencies determine the need for additional regulation. The two most prominent information disclosure laws, the Emergency Planning and Community Right-to-Know Act (EPCRA), specifically its Toxics Release Inventory (TRI) program, and California's Proposition 65, are discussed below. The chapter ends with a discussion of the Environmental Scorecard, an interactive web site that is a powerful embellishment of the TRI concept.

## 1. THE TOXICS RELEASE INVENTORY

In 1986, spurred by a tragic toxic release from a chemical plant in Bhopal, India that killed 3,000 people and a similar (but far less damaging) accident in West Virginia, Congress adopted EPCRA. In part, to facilitate emergency planning, EPCRA requires companies to report annually to local emergency planning agencies information about the location, identity and amounts of hazardous chemicals used at their facilities. Since 1990, EPCRA also requires companies to report facility source reduction practices, recycling activities, and projected chemical releases for future years.

EPCRA also established the Toxics Release Inventory program. TRI requires manufacturing and certain other industrial facilities to annually disclose their releases and transfers of 654 specified toxic chemicals, subject to reporting thresholds. The information is provided on standardized reporting forms that are submitted to EPA and state officials. EPA is required to make the information available to the public through a national computerized database accessible through personal computers.

By all accounts, TRI has proven to be a major success. From 1988 to 1999, reported toxic releases (for chemicals reported in all years) dropped by 46 per cent. Moreover, releases of some chemicals that may pose particularly significant human threats (i.e. carcinogens) declined at a faster rate than other releases. EPA officials, as well as environmentalists and regulated entities, regularly tout TRI as one of the nation's most effective environmental laws.

Professor Bradley Karkkainen characterizes TRI as a "watershed," and explains that multiple factors explain its dramatic success.

## Bradley C. Karkkainen,
## Information as Environmental Regulation: TRI and Performance Benchmarking, Precursor to a New Paradigm?
### 89 Georgetown Law Journal 257 (2001)

TRI works by establishing an objective, quantifiable, standardized (and therefore comparable), and broadly accessible metric that transforms the firm's understanding of its own environmental performance, while facilitating unprecedented levels of transparency and accountability. Firms and facilities are compelled to self-monitor and, therefore, to "confront disagreeable realities" concerning their environmental performance "in detail and early on," even prior to the onset of market, community, or regulatory reactions to the information they are required to make public. Simultaneously, they are subjected to the scrutiny of a variety of external parties, including investors, community residents, and regulators, any of whom may desire improved environmental performance and exert powerful pressures on poor performers to upgrade their performance as measured by the TRI yardstick.

*Self-Monitoring: "You Manage What You Measure"*

TRI mandates a sharply focused form of environmental self-monitoring, compelling firms to produce a stream of periodic, quantified reports on releases of listed pollutants at each reporting facility. This information becomes available, inter alia, to the firm itself, which may use it to evaluate its own performance and production processes.... Many top corporate managers, previously unaware of the volumes of toxic pollutants their firms were generating, were indeed surprised by the information produced in the first rounds of TRI.... One chemical company official states that prior to TRI, his firm had never set internal pollution prevention goals because "we never had the information we needed to know if progress was being made."... This kind of careful self-monitoring may well be a necessary step toward improving the environmental performance of facilities and firms. As the well-worn adage has it, "what you don't know about, you can't manage," or yet more precisely, "you manage what you measure."

TRI-generated performance data are readily available to regulators, as well as to environmentalists and other citizen-critics of regulatory policy.... Adverse facility-, firm-, or industry-level TRI data thus carry the implicit threat that regulatory action may follow, whether at the initiative of regulators themselves or in response to rising political demand for regulatory action. But precisely because forward-thinking firms and investors anticipate that additional regulatory requirements may prove burdensome and costly, firms may come under self-imposed and market-driven pressures to undertake cost-effective, voluntary, pollution prevention measures....

Environmental and community organizations are among the principal users of TRI data, employing it in conscious efforts to pressure firms to raise environmental standards. At the national level, environmental organizations use TRI data to generate reports and profiles of toxic pollution and leading polluters, and to direct reputation-damaging publicity campaigns against polluting firms. TRI data are also used by both national and local organizations to produce community-level reports and profiles, and to single out the leading local sources of toxic pollution. Community groups use this information to educate and recruit community residents into local anti-pollution efforts, and to organize local campaigns seeking "good neighbor agreements" and similar commitments from polluting firms to reduce releases. And even where community residents do not explicitly put forth such demands, firms may self-regulate to preempt potentially costly and damaging attempts at informal regulation....

TRI's sponsors emphasized that it would encourage pollution prevention and enable communities to engage in local self-help—central themes of the "right-to-know" movement. The statute itself identifies informing the local citizenry and facilitating local action among TRI's core purposes. TRI has fulfilled those expectations, facilitating local organizing aimed at improving the environmental performance of polluting facilities. In recent years, TRI has taken on an "environmental justice" flavor as low-income and minority communities add complaints of disparate impact, backed by TRI-derived inter-community comparisons, to underlying concerns about toxic exposures....

### TRI and Capital Markets

Many investors use TRI data to monitor the environmental performance of firms.... Investors may interpret adverse TRI data as an indicator of a greater risk of future liability, remediation, or regulatory compliance costs; potential loss of consumer market share; or potentially costly and disruptive "informal regulation" by citizens. Alternatively, investors may simply conclude that poor TRI performance indicates that the firm is poorly managed, and thus may be likely to fare poorly in other critical performance areas such as product quality or cost control....

*Reputation*

Because TRI data allow easy comparisons among facilities, firms, and industries, a poor environmental performance record as reflected in TRI data can cause reputational damage, potentially affecting relations with customers, suppliers, employees, or investors. Unlike conventional regulations, which garner publicity for firms only in the breach, however, TRI may also generate opportunities for positive environmental image-building. No one credits a firm for being in compliance with mandatory environmental standards, but firms can use objective and comparable TRI data to document claims of "superior" performance or progress toward ambitious voluntary targets....

[Another advantage of TRI, according to Professor Karkkainen, is that it is very cost-effective.] TRI achieves all this at a relatively low cost to the agency. EPA's direct administrative costs are approximately $25 million, a modest fraction of its $7 billion annual budget. TRI does not require the agency to produce the extensive, costly, and time-consuming studies necessary to establish quantified exposure levels, dose-response curves, and threshold levels of "significant" or "unreasonable" risk that are often required under other environmental statutes. Under TRI, the agency normally only needs to make the (relatively) low-threshold determination that a pollutant "can reasonably be anticipated to cause" cancer or other chronic health effects at *some* level of exposure.... TRI is thus able to cast its regulatory net over a much larger number of pollutants and polluters in a much shorter period of time than conventional forms of regulation.... Direct compliance costs [with the reporting requirements] are also quite low.... [I]f TRI does induce real reductions in pollutant releases, then some firms must be incurring the costs of investing in new technologies or processes, even if these are not properly labeled "compliance costs." But since firms have absolute flexibility under TRI to determine how, when, and to what extent they will reduce emissions, they are generally free to adopt the improvement targets, timetables, and strategies that best suit their individual circumstances. This is almost certain to be cheaper than compliance with the costly "end-of-the-pipe" controls typically imposed by conventional regulation....

\* \* \*

## Notes and Questions

1. Is an information disclosure law like TRI likely to be useful in remedying disparate environmental burdens? Consider the following observations by Professor Karkkainen:

> TRI information is most likely to reach environmentalists, community activists, and other audiences that are already receptive to it. Arguably, it will also reach the relatively well-off and more highly educated citizens who are most likely to own and use computers, belong to environmental organizations, read newspapers, and view or listen to news broadcasts. In addition, information may be a more effective regulatory tool in some locations than others.... Beyond inequalities in the distribution of information, we should expect that some demographic groups and communities are more likely to act on TRI information once they acquire it. Some of these differences may arise from local and demographic differences in preferences with regard to environmental insults and amenities. For example, it is often argued that more affluent citizens value environmental amenities more highly than other groups. They may also have greater political efficacy—a mutually reinforcing combination of capacity

to effect change through political processes and confidence in their ability to do so. The expected result, then, would be that polluting firms in more affluent communities would come under greater pressure to reduce pollution levels, subjecting them to more stringent effective environmental standards. Empirical evidence indicates that this pattern is, in fact, emerging....Consequently, there is a danger that TRI and similar information-based regulatory approaches, especially if played out through "NIMBY"-like efforts at "informal regulation" by the most informed, affluent, and politically empowered, may reinforce existing inequalities in the social distribution of environmental risk.

*Id.* at 338–340. On the other hand, one benefit of information disclosure requirements is that the information generated can be effectively used by only a few, highly motivated individuals. As Professor Karkkainen points out, "in recent years some environmental justice advocacy groups have successfully used TRI data for precisely the opposite end, relying on community-level, TRI-based comparative data to advance claims that their communities are recipients of a disproportionate share of toxic pollution." *Id.* at 340.

2. One study looked at community characteristics influencing the substantial drop in nationwide TRI emissions and exposure to air toxics that occurred from 1988 to 1992. It determined that communities with higher African American populations were less likely to experience decreases in exposures in this period. (The opposite was true in communities where the likelihood of local collective action was high.) The study concludes that "[w]hile national attention [to publication of TRI data] does lead some firms to reduce exposure, this public pressure does not appear to impact high exposure communities uniformly. In particular, communities with a higher proportion of people of color are not as likely to experience decreases in exposure as other communities which are comparable with regard to their initial exposure levels." Nancy Brooks & Rajiv Sethi, *The Distribution of Pollution: Community Characteristics and Exposure to Air Toxics*, 32 J. ENVTL. ECON. & MGMT. 233, 248 (1997).

3. Another recent review of the TRI program by Mary Graham and Catherine Miller also finds a core of positive trends but argues that a closer analysis of the reductions reveals a more complex story. Specifically, Graham and Miller note that the rate of decline of toxic releases slowed markedly after the first five years of reporting, that the amount of toxic waste generated (as opposed to released) has continued to increase, and that few facilities have employed source reduction to cut releases. Moreover, they argue, the decline in releases "is not so much a national phenomenon as it is a media-, industry-, and often facility-specific phenomenon," which can be negated by specific economic forces and regulatory changes. Mary Graham & Catherine Miller, *Disclosure of Toxic Releases in the United States*, 43 ENV'T 8, 11–12 (Oct. 2001).

## 2.   PROPOSITION 65

## Clifford Rechtschaffen,
## The Warning Game: Evaluating Warnings
## Under California's Proposition 65
### 23 Ecology Law Quarterly 303 (1996)

In 1986, California voters overwhelmingly approved the Safe Drinking Water and Toxic Enforcement Act of 1986, an initiative better known as Proposition 65....[The statute] applies to a group of chemicals listed by the State of California as known carcinogens or reproductive toxicants. Over 500 carcinogenic substances and 153 reproductive toxicants have been listed. In part, the statute prohibits a person in the course of doing business from "knowingly" discharging or releasing any listed chemical "into water or onto or into land where such chemical passes or will probably pass into any source of drinking water." Proposition 65 also imposes a far-reaching warning requirement: businesses must provide a "clear and reasonable" warning prior to "knowingly and intentionally" exposing any individual to a listed chemical.... Once a chemical is listed and the statutory grace period elapses, Proposition 65's warning provisions take effect without specific administrative standards that specify acceptable levels of exposure. This contrasts with most environmental statutes, and reverses the usual industry incentives to delay the setting of administrative standards. Proposition 65 can be enforced by public prosecutors (the California Attorney General, district attorneys, and certain city attorneys) or by "any person in the public interest."...

In an enforcement action, the defendant bears the burden of proving that an exposure is exempt from the statute, another notable departure from other environmental laws. There are two main reasons underlying this provision. The first is that industry is in the best position to know about the chemicals it uses and the levels at which they are harmful. The second is that industry, rather than the public, should bear more of the risk of harm from chemicals about which there is limited knowledge....

### Objectives of Proposition 65's Warning Requirement

Consistent with the rationales underlying information disclosure statutes, Proposition 65 has two broadly expressed purposes: 1) to inform the public about exposures to toxic substances, and 2) to reduce exposures to toxic substances. As to the former, the statute is clearly intended to promote informed individual choice and decisionmaking.... [B]eyond simply informing people, Proposition 65 was intended to provide a "compelling incentive" for industry to remove nonessential carcinogens and reproductive toxins from its products and processes....

### Does Proposition 65 Satisfy Its Goal of Reducing Exposures to Hazardous Substances?

Proposition 65's warning requirement has stimulated significant consumer-product reformulation, due to a combination of industry concerns about liability and consumer reaction to warnings. In some instances, the reformulations have been close to industry-wide, reflecting the competitive pressures that arise once a portion of the industry alters its products. Almost all the reformulated products are being sold nationwide, giving the statute national effect. Moreover, the reported product reformulations probably represent only a portion of private businesses' actions....

Nearly forty manufacturers of glazed ceramicware (china) have agreed to reduce lead levels in their flatware by fifty percent and in their hollowware by twenty-five percent within five years.... The Environmental Defense Fund has estimated that the lead content of over 8000 patterns of china has been reduced.... A large segment of the nail polish industry agreed to remove toluene from dozens of consumer and professional nail polish products. Manufacturers have agreed to reformulate dozens of automobile paints, coatings, adhesives, and related products. Approximately three hundred wineries, representing a large share of the domestic wine industry, agreed to phase out their use of lead foil caps on wine bottles.... [T]welve major manufacturers of brass faucets agreed to reduce substantially the lead content of their products and make ninety-five

percent of their faucets virtually lead-free by 1999. These companies supply ninety percent of the California market and account for the bulk of faucet sales nationally....

The extraordinary steps taken by businesses to avoid consumer product warnings
can be partially explained by liability concerns. In Proposition 65 enforcement suits, the
California Attorney General's Office and private parties have been willing to forego imposing civil fines on defendant companies in exchange for product reformulation and
indeed have made this a goal of their enforcement policies. Facing statutory fines that
can be enormous, many companies have consented to reformulate their products in
order to reduce their potential liability....

More significant than the desire to minimize liability is corporate concern over consumer reaction to product warnings, and the power of green consumerism in the marketplace. Consumer demand can be extremely sensitive to the disclosure of adverse
health and safety product information, particularly in food products. Businesses perceive the possibility of significant sales losses by disclosing toxic chemical presence in
certain consumer products, and warnings for these products have, consequently, become anathema to business....At the same time, selling a reformulated product can
lead to a competitive market advantage. The explosive growth of consumer interest in
using everyday purchases as a means to achieve environmental goals has resulted in a
rush by businesses to market environmentally sound products....

The above discussion has focused on products for which substitutes exist. Where
there are no available substitutes, the marketplace has fared poorly as a mechanism for
achieving toxics reductions....

## Notes and Questions

1. Environmental attorney David Roe (one of the co-authors of Proposition 65) argues that Proposition 65 appears to be having an even greater impact on reducing toxic
air emissions than TRI. During the ten-year period 1988–1997, air emissions of TRI
chemicals that are also listed under Proposition 65 declined by approximately 85% in
California, as compared to 50% in the rest of the country (i.e. the U.S. not including
California). At the same time, Roe notes, decreases in emissions in California of all other
TRI chemicals, i.e. the air emissions in California of TRI chemicals that are not also covered by Proposition 65, are almost identical to the rest of the US. results, suggesting that
the differential between California and the rest of the U.S. is not due to other factors specific to California. Both TRI and Proposition 65 were enacted in 1986, and, for practical
purposes, both began taking effect in 1988. Roe contends that these large decreases
demonstrate that "conventional regulation of toxic chemicals achieves only a small fraction of readily available, acceptably low-cost reductions." David Roe, *Toxic Chemical
Control Policy: Three Unabsorbed Facts*, 32 ENVTL. L. REP. 10,232, 10,234 (2002).

2. Does the marketplace model, which in part underlies Proposition 65, serve low income communities and communities of color? In the consumer market place, for instance, many individuals may lack the time or interest to seek out information; less educated and limited-English speaking individuals are less likely to be able to read,
understand, and use information. Is it realistic to assume that workers will demand or
effect change in response to information about environmental risks? Consider in particular recent immigrant workers who are frequently unorganized, face substantial language and cultural barriers, and fear employer retaliation not only in terms of potentially losing a job but also their immigration status.

## 3. A Note on Environmental Scorecard and Other Mapping Tools

Something new in the evolution of disclosure tools is an interactive web site launched by the environmental group Environmental Defense in 1998, Scorecard (www.Scorecard.org). Scorecard compiles a variety of community environmental data and puts it in a user friendly format. (The information includes TRI data (supplemented to include the potential health risks of releases), air quality levels, impaired water bodies, estimated cancer risks from hazardous air pollutants, Superfund sites, land disposal facilities, and other environmental indicators). Users can obtain an environmental profile of their community by simply entering their zip code, including what chemicals are being emitted in their community and by whom; how these emissions compare to releases in other communities; and information about individual sources. Scorecard, moreover, is designed with a decidedly activist bent. There are links for users to email EPA or state regulators or to connect with local environmental groups; users can also send a free fax message to facilities. The website has generated enormous public interest; it received over 1 million hits alone during its first 24 hours on the web.

In 2001, Scorecard upgraded its web site to facilitate state and local-level environmental justice analyses. For every U.S. county, Scorecard compiled demographic and socioeconomic data as well as information about four environmental hazards. Scorecard can now calculate, within a given county or state, what the distribution of these hazards is across race, income, or other demographic or socioeconomic characteristics. For instance, Figure 1 depicts how these environmental burdens are distributed in Los Angeles County, and shows that people of color and low income groups bear greater burdens.[1]

---

### Figure 1

· **Distribution of Environmental Burdens in LOS ANGELES County**

**DISTRIBUTION OF BURDENS BY RACE/ETHNICITY**

| Releases of Toxic Chemicals | (indicator of chemical releases) | Ratio |
|---|---|---|
| People of Color | 37000 | 1.09 |
| Whites | 34000 | |

| Cancer Risks from Hazardous Air Pollutants | (added risk per 1,000,000) | Ratio |
|---|---|---|
| People of Color | 480 | 1.20 |
| Whites | 400 | |

| Superfund Sites | (sites per square mile) | Ratio |
|---|---|---|
| People of Color | .52 | 1.16 |
| Whites | .45 | |

| Facilities Emitting Criteria Air Pollutants | (facilities per square mile) | Ratio |
|---|---|---|
| People of Color | 150 | 1.63 |
| Whites | 92 | |

---

1. http://www.scorecard.org/community/ej-summary.tcl?fips_county_code=06037&backlink= tri-co#map (visited June 22, 2001).

Another example is provided in Figure 2 (see page 330). Scorecard can calculate how the environmental hazards and demographics of a given county compare to other counties within the state. The figure shows how Los Angeles County compares to the rest of California.[2]

This environmental justice overlay has its limits—it covers only four out of a wide range of environmental burdens (the only ones for which data for all counties in the U.S. is available); it doesn't control to determine which among various factors may best explain unequal distributions of environmental harm; and it doesn't allow for comparisons at levels smaller than the county. Nonetheless, by making sophisticated analytic tools accessible to ordinary individuals and community groups, it has great potential for environmental justice activists.

## Notes and Questions

1. Tools like Scorecard can be quite powerful for individuals with access to a computer and modem. On the other hand, many individuals in heavily burdened communities still do not have access to such equipment.

2. EPA has developed its own environmental justice mapping tool, known as Enviro-Justice Mapper, that allows users to obtain demographic information about communities surrounding EPA-permitted facilities. *See* <http://es.epa.gov/oeca/main/ej/ejmapper/>. The web site also contains links to community-specific health data such as cancer rates and cardiovascular disease, but in the face of industry opposition, EPA dropped its initial plans to allow users to view information on facility siting, demographics and health data together on a single map. *See New EPA Database Links Demographic Data, Facility Locations,* INSIDE EPA.COM (Aug. 17, 2001).

3. Should the government prepare more detailed environmental profiles about regulated entities? One modest attempt in this direction is the Sector Facility Indexing Project (SFIP) created by EPA. *See* <http://es.epa.gov/oeca/sfi/>. This database combines TRI data with air, water, and RCRA compliance information and reported chemical spills for about 650 facilities in five major industrial sectors, along with population estimates for a 3 mile radius surrounding the facility. Should EPA also rank or evaluate the facilities or publicize noncomplying or superior performance firms? Thus far, it has resisted such suggestions. Britain's Environmental Agency annually publishes a list of the country's worst complying companies, i.e. those with most violations and/or most penalties, which has been dubbed the "Hall of Shame."

4. Should companies be required to prepare environmental report cards documenting their compliance history and overall environmental performance? A few European countries mandate that companies prepare public reports documenting their emissions, waste generation, and consumption of resources. Is this a good idea?

---

2. http://www.scorecard.org/community/ej-report.tcl?fips_county_code=06037#risk (visited June 22, 2001).

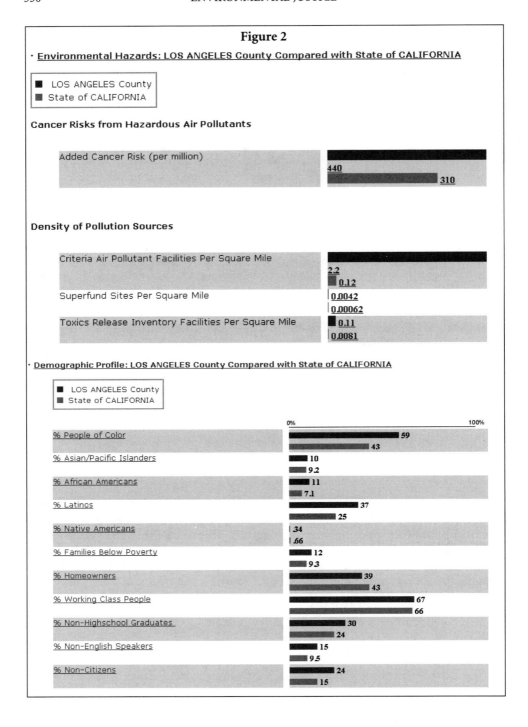

# Figure 2

· **Environmental Hazards: LOS ANGELES County Compared with State of CALIFORNIA**

■ LOS ANGELES County
■ State of CALIFORNIA

**Cancer Risks from Hazardous Air Pollutants**

Added Cancer Risk (per million)
440
310

**Density of Pollution Sources**

Criteria Air Pollutant Facilities Per Square Mile
2.2
0.12

Superfund Sites Per Square Mile
0.0042
0.00062

Toxics Release Inventory Facilities Per Square Mile
0.11
0.0081

· **Demographic Profile: LOS ANGELES County Compared with State of CALIFORNIA**

■ LOS ANGELES County
■ State of CALIFORNIA

0%                                                                    100%

% People of Color — 59 / 43

% Asian/Pacific Islanders — 10 / 9.2

% African Americans — 11 / 7.1

% Latinos — 37 / 25

% Native Americans — .34 / .66

% Families Below Poverty — 12 / 9.3

% Homeowners — 39 / 43

% Working Class People — 67 / 66

% Non-Highschool Graduates — 30 / 24

% Non-English Speakers — 15 / 9.5

% Non-Citizens — 24 / 15

# Chapter XIII

# Constitutional Claims as a Response

## A. Introduction

Some of the earliest legal challenges to the siting of undesirable land uses in communities of color were based on violations of the equal protection clause of the Fourteenth Amendment which provides in part that "[n]o State shall...deny to any person within its jurisdiction the equal protection of the laws." Professor Alice Kaswan provides background on this standard:

Facially discriminatory laws and actions have become rare in today's race-conscious society. It is inconceivable that a government body would declare that all landfills shall be sited in minority neighborhoods. Instead, equal protection claims in the environmental justice context are likely to allege that a governmental decision that is facially neutral is nonetheless discriminatory. The current understanding of when a facially neutral decision or action can be considered discriminatory was established in 1975 in Washington v. Davis [426 U.S. 229 (1976)]. Stating that the "central purpose of the Equal Protection Clause . . . is the prevention of official conduct discriminating on the basis of race," the Court held that a plaintiff must prove that the defendant acted with discriminatory intent.... The Court observed that a "racially disproportionate impact," standing alone, is generally insufficient to demonstrate a violation.... The Supreme Court did, however, recognize that since government actors rarely announce their intent to discriminate, discriminatory intent may not be explicit. The justifications presented by government actors may, in some instances, be pretexts for discriminatory conduct.... The Supreme Court addressed the question of what types of facts are relevant to inferring discriminatory intent in the 1976 case of Village of Arlington Heights v. Metropolitan Housing Development Corp. [429 U.S. 252 (1977)]....[T]he Court identified the following five factors as potentially probative of intentional discrimination: (1) disparate impact; (2) historical background to the decision; (3) history of the decision making process; (4) departures from normal substantive factors or procedures; and (5) legislative or administrative history. The Court made clear that its five-factor test was not "exhaustive." Nevertheless, courts have continued to use the five-factor test to determine whether direct and circumstantial evidence reveal that a facially neutral decision is discriminatory.

Alice Kaswan, *Environmental Laws: Grist for the Equal Protection Mill*, 70 U. COLO. L. REV. 387, 408–412 (1999).

### Pathfinder on Equal Protection and Environmental Justice

In addition to the articles by Professor Alice Kaswan and Edward Patrick Boyle excerpted in the text, the following articles discuss the equal protection doctrine in the environmental justice context: Robert W. Collin, *Environmental Equity: A Law and Planning Approach to Environmental Racism*, 11 VA. ENVTL. L. J. 495 (1992); Peter Reich, *Greening the Ghetto: A Theory of Environmental Race Discrimination*, 41 U. KAN. L. REV. 271 (1992); Robert M. Frye, *Comment, Environmental Injustice: The Failure of American Civil Rights and Environmental Law to Provide Equal Protection From Pollution*, 3 DICKINSON J. ENVTL. L. & POL'Y 53 (1993); Rodolfo Mata, *Comment, Inequitable Siting of Undesirable Facilities and the Myth of Equal Protection*, 13 B.C. THIRD WORLD L.J. 233 (1993), Donna Gareis-Smith, *Comment, Environmental Racism: The Failure of Equal Protection to Provide a Judicial Remedy and the Potential of Title VI of the 1964 Civil Rights Act*, 13 TEMP. ENVTL. L. & TECH. J. 57 (1994); and Jill Evans, *Challenging The Racism in Environmental Racism: Redefining the Concept of Intent*, 40 ARIZ. L. REV. 1219 (1998).

# B. The Equal Protection Cases

In several cases in the mid 1980's, courts inferred discriminatory intent and found violations of the equal protection clause based on the disparate provision of municipal services such as water hookups, street paving, and storm-sewer capacity to minority residents. One example is the case below:

## Dowdell v. City of Apopka
### 698 F.2d 1181 (11th Cir. 1983)

*Vance, Senior Circuit Judge:*

The situs of this case is the small city of Apopka, Florida located in the fern and foliage growing region north of Orlando. More specifically, it is the poor, geographically separate, black community of that city. The plaintiffs (appellees and cross-appellants here) are a Fed. R. Civ. P. 23(b)(2) class comprising the black residents of Apopka "who are, or have been, subjected to the discriminatory provision of municipal services."... Plaintiffs charged the City of Apopka, its mayor, and four council members with discrimination in the provision of seven municipal services: street paving and maintenance, storm water drainage, street lighting, fire protection, water distribution, sewerage facilities, and park and recreation facilities. After a preliminary finding by the Office of Revenue Sharing that the City was discriminatory in the provision of several of these services, an agreement was reached on improvements in street lighting and fire protection, and the district court filed an order settling these claims. The case went to trial on the remaining five issues.

The district court found intentional discrimination in the provision of street paving, the water distribution system, and storm drainage facilities in violation of the fourteenth amendment; Title VI of the Civil Rights Act of 1964, 42 U.S.C. § 2000d and the State and Local Fiscal Assistance Act of 1972, 31 U.S.C. § 1242 (Revenue Sharing Act).

To trigger strict scrutiny analysis under the fourteenth amendment, preliminary findings of both disparate impact and discriminatory intent are required. Appellants contend that the facts adduced in evidence do not support a finding of discriminatory intent....

We can reach no such conclusion. Substantial evidence, including video tapes, photographs, charts, and the testimony of community residents and of qualified experts who made on-site surveys revealed a disparity in the provision of street paving, water distribution, and storm water drainage.[3] Appellants do not question the accuracy of these statistical findings. Rather, they assert an absence of responsibility for them, claiming them, variously, to be beyond municipal jurisdiction or the result of historical and environmental forces. Their arguments are insubstantial and were properly rejected by the trial court.[4]

Refutation of Apopka's attempt to deny municipal responsibility for these services one by one does not conclude our inquiry into discriminatory intent. The gravamen of plaintiffs' claim is that Apopka has intentionally maintained a racially and geographically segregated system of municipal services as a result of which the disparities in the provision of street paving, water distribution, and storm drainage facilities have reached constitutional proportions. Discriminatory intent is not synonymous with a racially discriminatory motive. Neither does it require proof that racial discrimination is the sole purpose behind each failure to equalize these services. It is, rather, the cumulative evidence of action and inaction which objectively manifests discriminatory intent.

Although the fluid concept of discriminatory intent is sometimes subtle and difficult to apply, there is ample evidence in this case of the correlation between municipal service disparities and racially tainted purposiveness to mandate a finding of discriminatory intent. Nearly every factor which has been held to be highly probative of discriminatory intent is present.

---

3. The district court found that 42% of the street footage in the black community was unpaved as compared to 9% in the white community and that 33% of the black community residences fronted on such unpaved streets while only 7% of the residences in the white community did so. As regards storm drainage, the court found that while 60% of the residential streets in the white community had curbs and gutters, no streets in the black community had curbs and gutters. Additionally, it found that water service in many homes in the black community was so inadequate that at many times of the day there was insufficient water for such normal purposes as bathing.

4. For example, the city asserts that the unpaved streets are really "alleys" or "private driveways." But the district court properly found, after analysis of soil samples showing municipal road grading and intermittent repair, that there was sufficient evidence of municipal maintenance for the streets to be deemed dedicated to the City of Apopka by operation of Fla. Stat. § 95.361.

The city claims that the water distribution problem results from inadequacies in the privately owned water pipes running from the city's main supply lines to indoor plumbing facilities. But the district court properly found that the source of the water scarcity lies in the fact that the city's main lines are inaccessible to many residences because, unlike the situation in the white community, many streets in the black community are not serviced by municipal main lines so that special "service lines" must be run from main lines on remote streets to as many as sixteen black residences.

Finally, the city argues that storm water drainage is a problem throughout the municipality. However, the district court properly found that while the white community is substantially serviced by a curb and gutter system, the "alternate" drainage system in the black community consists only of ditches dug along the sides of the street which function improperly because they are not regularly maintained.

First, the magnitude of the disparity, evidencing a systematic pattern of municipal expenditures in all areas of town except the black community, is explicable only on racial grounds. Arlington Heights v. Metropolitan Housing Corp., 429 U.S. 252, 266, 97 S. Ct. 555, 564, 50 L. Ed. 2d 450 (1976). Second, the legislative and administrative pattern of decision-making, extending from nearly half a century in the past to Apopka's plans for future development, indicates a deliberate deprivation of services to the black community. A municipal ordinance restricting blacks to living only on the south side of the railroad tracks remained in force in Apopka until 1968. The ordinance contributed to the ghetto-like qualities of the black residential area. Blacks continue to be significantly under-represented in administrative and elective positions, and their requests for improved municipal services continue to be ignored while substantial funds are expended to annex and develop the new predominantly white sections of town. Third, the continued and systematic relative deprivation of the black community was the obviously foreseeable outcome of spending nearly all revenue sharing monies received on the white community in preference to the visibly underserviced black community. While voluntary acts and "awareness of consequences" alone do not necessitate a finding of discriminatory intent, "actions having foreseeable and anticipated disparate impact are relevant evidence to prove the ultimate fact, forbidden purpose."

Although none of these factors is necessarily independently conclusive, "the totality of the relevant facts," Washington v. Davis, 426 U.S [229], 242 [1976], amply supports the finding that the City of Apopka has engaged in a systematic pattern of cognitive acts and omissions, selecting and reaffirming a particular course of municipal services expenditures that inescapably evidences discriminatory intent. The finding of discriminatory intent by the district court is not clearly erroneous and therefore is affirmed....

\* \* \*

Plaintiffs have had far less success using the equal protection clause in the siting context. In the following trio of decisions, lower courts rejected equal protection challenges to siting decisions.

## Bean v. Southwestern Waste Management Corporation

482 F. Supp. 673 (S.D. Texas 1979)
affirmed without opinion, 780 F.2d 1038 (5th Cir. 1986)

*McDonald, District Judge*:

[Plaintiffs filed suit seeking to invalidate a decision by the Texas Department of Health (TDH) to grant a permit to Southwestern Waste Management to operate a Type I solid waste facility in the East Houston-Dyersdale Road area in Harris County, Texas. They sought a preliminary injunction to restrain the project from going forward.]

Before getting to the merits, the Court must address one other procedural matter. The plaintiffs did not name the Texas Department of Water Resources (TDWR) as a defendant in this case. That, of course, is not particularly surprising. That agency did not participate in the decision to grant Permit No. 1193 and nothing it did with respect to the issuance of that permit is being challenged here. The plaintiffs have, however, submitted a large quantity of data related to solid waste sites in Houston operating under the auspices of TDWR and a dispute has arisen as to the relevance of this data. The Court is of the opinion that the evidence as to TDWR's actions is entirely irrelevant to the question of whether it was an historical policy or practice of TDH to discriminate, since TDH should not be held responsible for the commission of acts, e.g., issuance of permits by TDWR, over which it had no control. Evidence as to TDWR's action is relevant, however, to the question of whether TDH, being aware of the placement of solid waste sites throughout the city of Houston, if it was so aware, discriminated by approving the permit for the East Houston-Dyersdale Road site, since a state agency must not put its stamp of approval on a discriminatory practice or policy even if it did not initiate the practice or policy.

[The court noted that to obtain a preliminary injunction, plaintiffs must establish (1) a substantial likelihood of success on the merits; (2) a substantial threat of irreparable injury; (3) that the threatened harm to plaintiffs outweighs the potential harm to defendants from an injunction; and (4) that the injunction is in the public interest. After concluding that plaintiffs had established a substantial threat of irreparable injury, the court then discussed the merits of plaintiffs' claims.]

The problem is that the plaintiffs have not established a substantial likelihood of success on the merits. The burden on them is to prove discriminatory purpose. That is, the plaintiffs must show not just that the decision to grant the permit is objectionable or even wrong, but that it is attributable to an intent to discriminate on the basis of race. Statistical proof can rise to the level that it, alone, proves discriminatory intent, as in Yick Wo v. Hopkins, 118 U.S. 356, 6 S. Ct. 1064, 30 L. Ed. 220 (1886), and Gomillion v. Lightfoot, 364 U.S. 339, 81 S. Ct. 125, 5 L. Ed. 2d 110 (1960), or, this Court would conclude, even in situations less extreme than in those two cases, but the data shown here does not rise to that level. Similarly, statistical proof can be sufficiently supplemented by the types of proof outlined in *Arlington Heights*, to establish purposeful discrimination, but the supplemental proof offered here is not sufficient to do that.

Two different theories of liability have been advanced in this case. The first is that TDH's approval of the permit was part of a pattern or practice by it of discriminating in the placement of solid waste sites. In order to test that theory, one must focus on the sites which TDH has approved and determine the minority population of the areas in which the sites were located on the day that the sites opened. The available statistical data, both city-wide and in the target area, fails to establish a pattern or practice of discrimination by TDH. City-wide, data was produced for the seventeen (17) sites operating with TDH permits as of July 1, 1978. That data shows that 58.8% of the sites granted permits by TDH were located in census tracts with 25% or less minority population at the time of their opening and that 82.4% of the sites granted permits by TDH were located in census tracts with 50% or less minority population at the time of their opening. In the target area, an area which roughly conforms to the North Forest Independent School District and the newly-created City Council District B and is 70% minority in population, two (2) sites were approved by TDH. One, the McCarty Road site, was in a census tract with less than 10% minority population at the time of its opening. The other, the site being challenged here, is in a census tract with close to 60% minority population. Even if we also consider the sites approved by TDWR in the target area, which, as discussed earlier, are not really relevant to TDH's intent to discriminate, no pattern or practice of discrimination is revealed. Of all the solid waste sites opened in the target area, 46.2 to 50% were located in census tracts with less than 25% minority population at the time they opened. It may be that more particularized data would show that even those sites approved in predominantly Anglo census tracts were actually located in minority neighborhoods, but the data available here does not show that. In addition, there was no supplemental evidence, such as that suggested by *Arlington*

*Heights, supra,* which established a pattern or practice of discrimination on the part of TDH.

The plaintiffs' second theory of liability is that TDH's approval of the permit, in the context of the historical placement of solid waste sites and the events surrounding the application, constituted discrimination. Three sets of data were offered to support this theory. Each set, at first blush, looks compelling. On further analysis, however, each set breaks down. Each fails to approach the standard established by *Yick Wo, supra,* and *Gomillion, supra,* and, even when considered with supplementary proof, *Arlington Heights, supra,* fails to establish a likelihood of success in proving discriminatory intent.

The first set of data focuses on the two (2) solid waste sites to be used by the City of Houston. Both of these sites are located in the target area. This proves discrimination, the plaintiffs argue, because "the target area has the dubious distinction of containing 100% of the type I municipal land fills that Houston utilizes or will utilize, although it contains only 6.9% of the entire population of Houston." There are two problems with this argument. First, there are only two sites involved here. That is not a statistically significant number. Second, an examination of the census tracts in the target area in which the sites are located reveals that the East Houston-Dyersdale Road proposed site is in a tract with a 58.4% minority population, but that the McCarty Road site is in a tract with only an 18.4% minority population. Thus, the evidence shows that, of the two sites to be used by the City of Houston, one is in a primarily Anglo census tract and one is in a primarily minority census tract. No inference of discrimination can be made from this data.

The second set of data focuses on the total number of solid waste sites located in the target area.[6] The statistical disparity which the plaintiffs point to is that the target area contains 15% of Houston's solid waste sites, but only 6.9% of its population. Since the target area has a 70% minority population, the plaintiffs argue, this statistical disparity must be attributable to race discrimination. To begin with, in the absence of the data on population by race, the statistical disparity is not all that shocking. One would expect solid waste sites to be placed near each other and away from concentrated population areas. Even considering the 70% minority population of the target area, when one looks at where in the target area these particular sites are located, the inference of racial discrimination dissolves. Half of the solid waste sites in the target area are in census tracts with more than 70% Anglo population. Without some proof that the sites affect an area much larger than the census tract in which they are in, it is very hard to conclude that the placing of a site in the target area evidences purposeful racial discrimination.

The third set of data offered by the plaintiffs focuses on the city as a whole. This data is the most compelling on its surface. It shows that only 17.1% of the city's solid waste sites are located in the southwest quadrant, where 53.3% of the Anglos live. Only 15.3% of the sites are located in the northwest quadrant, where 20.1% of the Anglos live. Thus, only 32.4% of the sites are located in the western half of the city, where 73.4% of the Anglos live. Furthermore, the plaintiffs argue, 67.6% of the sites are located in the eastern half of the city, where 61.6% of the minority population lives. This, according to the plaintiffs, shows racial discrimination.

---

6. It should be noted that there are some problems with the definition of the target area as selected and defined by the plaintiffs. There is some question as to whether the definition of the area was entirely scientific. Even so, the approach is a useful one and the target area data should be examined.

The problem is that, once again, these statistics break down under closer scrutiny. To begin with, the inclusion of TDWR's sites skew the data. A large number of TDWR sites are located around Houston's ship channel, which is in the eastern half of the city. But those sites, the Assistant Attorney General argues persuasively, are located in the eastern half of the city because that is where Houston's industry is, not because that is where Houston's minority population is. Furthermore, closer examination of the data shows that the city's solid waste sites are not so disparately located as they first appear. If we focus on census tracts, rather than on halves or quadrants of the city, we can see with more particularity where the solid waste sites are located. Houston's population is 39.3% minority and 60.7% Anglo. The plaintiffs argue, and this Court finds persuasive, a definition of "minority census tracts" as those with more than 39.3% minority population and Anglo census tracts as those with more than 60.7% Anglo population. Using those definitions, Houston consists of 42.5% minority tracts and 57.5% Anglo tracts. Again using those definitions, 42.3% of the solid waste sites in the City of Houston are located in minority tracts and 57.7% are located in Anglo tracts. In addition, if we look at tracts with one or more sites per tract, to account for the fact that some tracts contain more than one solid waste site, 42.2% are minority tracts and 57.8% are Anglo tracts. The difference between the racial composition of census tracts in general and the racial composition of census tracts with solid waste sites is, according to the statistics available to the Court, at best, only 0.3%. That is simply not a statistically significant difference. More surprisingly, from the plaintiffs' point of view, to the extent that it is viewed as significant, it tends to indicate that minority census tracts have a tiny bit smaller percentage of solid waste sites than one would proportionately expect.

In support of the proposition that there is a city-wide discrimination against minorities in the placement of solid waste sites, the plaintiffs also argue that the data reveals that, in 1975, eleven solid waste sites were located in census tracts with 100% minority population and none were located in census tracts with 100% Anglo population. There are problems with this argument, too, however. To begin with, the 1975 data is not entirely reliable. Compared with both the 1970 and the 1979 data, the 1975 data appears to overcount minority population. For example, of the eleven sites mentioned by the plaintiffs, only one had a 100% minority population in 1979. More importantly, there were, in fact, two sites located in 100% Anglo tracts in 1975. In addition, 18 other sites were located in tracts with a 90% or greater Anglo population in 1975. Thus, even according to the 1975 data, a large number of sites were located in census tracts with high Anglo populations.

Arlington Heights, *supra*, 429 U.S. at 267–268, suggested various types of non-statistical proof which can be used to establish purposeful discrimination. The supplementary non-statistical evidence provided by the plaintiffs in the present case raises a number of questions as to why this permit was granted. To begin with, a site proposed for the almost identical location was denied a permit in 1971 by the County Commissioners, who were then responsible for the issuance of such permits. One wonders what happened since that time. The plaintiffs argue that Smiley High School has changed from an Anglo school to one whose student body is predominantly minority. Furthermore, the site is being placed within 1700 feet of Smiley High School, a predominantly black school with no air conditioning, and only somewhat farther from a residential neighborhood. Land use considerations alone would seem to militate against granting this permit. Such evidence seemingly did not dissuade TDH.

If this Court were TDH, it might very well have denied this permit. It simply does not make sense to put a solid waste site so close to a high school, particularly one with no air conditioning. Nor does it make sense to put the land site so close to a residential neighborhood. But I am not TDH and for all I know, TDH may regularly approve of solid waste sites located near schools and residential areas, as illogical as that may seem.

It is not my responsibility to decide whether to grant this site a permit. It is my responsibility to decide whether to grant the plaintiffs a preliminary injunction. From the evidence before me, I can say that the plaintiffs have established that the decision to grant the permit was both unfortunate and insensitive. I cannot say that the plaintiffs have established a substantial likelihood of proving that the decision to grant the permit was motivated by purposeful racial discrimination in violation of 42 U.S.C. § 1983. This Court is obligated, as all Courts are, to follow the precedent of the United States Supreme Court and the evidence adduced thus far does not meet the magnitude required by *Arlington Heights, supra.*

### Permanent Relief

The failure of the plaintiffs to obtain a preliminary injunction does not, of course, mean that they are foreclosed from obtaining permanent relief. Because of the time pressures involved, extensive pre-trial discovery was impossible in this case. Assuming the case goes forward, discovery could lead to much more solid and persuasive evidence for either side. Ideally, it would resolve a number of the questions which the Court considers unanswered.

Where, for instance, are the solid waste sites located in each census tract? The plaintiffs produced evidence that in census tract 434, a predominantly Anglo tract, the site was located next to a black community named Riceville. If that was true of most sites in predominantly Anglo census tracts, the outcome of this case would be quite different.

How large an area does a solid waste site affect? If it affects an area a great deal smaller than that of a census tract, it becomes particularly important to know where in each census tract the site is located. If it affects an area larger than that of a census tract, then a target area analysis becomes much more persuasive.

How are solid waste site locations selected? It may be that private contractors consider a number of alternative locations and then select one in consultation with city or county officials. If that is so, it has tremendous implications for the search for discriminatory intent. It may be that a relatively limited number of areas can adequately serve as a Type I solid waste site. If that is so, the placement of sites in those areas becomes a lot less suspicious, even if large numbers of minorities live there. Either way, this is information which should be adduced. At this point, the Court still does not know how, why, and by whom the East Houston-Dyersdale Road location was selected.

What factors entered into TDH's decision to grant the permit? The proximity of the site to Smiley High School and a residential neighborhood and the lack of air conditioning facilities at the former were emphasized to the Court. It is still unknown how much, if any, consideration TDH gave to these factors. The racial composition of the neighborhood and the racial distribution of solid waste sites in Houston were primary concerns of the plaintiffs. It remains unclear to what degree TDH was informed of these concerns....

[P]laintiffs' Motion for a Preliminary Injunction...[is] denied.

* * *

## Notes and Questions

1. Consider the evidence analyzed by the Bean court in denying the preliminary injunction. Which of *Arlington Heights* factors does this evidence relate to? Consider also the additional evidence that the court suggests might have been persuasive to it, including where the solid waste sites were located in each census tract, how large an area a solid waste site affects, how solid waste sites are selected, and what factors entered the TDH's decision to grant the permit. How do each of the requested pieces of evidence relate to the *Arlington Heights* factors?

2. To what extent does the court find the actions of the Texas Department of Water Resources relevant to its analysis of the Texas Department of Health's discriminatory intent? To what extent should the decisions of agencies *other* than the immediate permitting agency be considered relevant in an analysis of the permitting agency? What factors would you consider pertinent to determining the relevance of other agencies' actions? How far back in time should a court look—5 years, 20 years, or longer? (This issue is also very briefly touched on in the *East Bibb* case excerpted below.)

3. How should discriminatory impact be measured? This threshold question, which also arises in the context of claims brought under Title VI of the Civil Rights, discussed in Chapter XIV, raises a host of difficult methodological questions. What is the definition of a "minority" community? Is it a community that is more than 50% minority? A community that has a higher percentage of minority residents than in the permitting jurisdiction generally? Than in the relevant city or state? Likewise, for purposes of determining whether a community has suffered a disparate burden, what should be the geographic scope of the impacted community? Should it be defined by city blocks, neighborhoods, zip code, census tracts, city quadrants, county lines? Or by a geographic radius extending from the land use? Should it vary depending on type of facility? As *Bean* demonstrates, the units chosen can have a huge impact on the outcome of a given case.

# East Bibb Twiggs Neighborhood Association v. Macon-Bibb County Planning & Zoning Commission
### 706 F. Supp. 880 (M.D. GA. 1989)

*Owens, Chief Judge*:

[Plaintiffs filed an equal protection challenge to a decision by the Macon-Bibb County Planning & Zoning Commission to allow Mullis Tree Service to build a waste landfill. The site in question was located in a census tract that was 60% black. The only other private landfill approved by the Commission, in 1978, was situated in a census tract that was 76% white. The proposed site was zoned A-Agricultural, which allows construction of landfills.]

The Commission reconvened on June 23, 1986, to consider petitioners' application. Petitioners were present and were represented by Mr. Charles Adams. Approximately one hundred fifty (150) individuals opposed to the landfill attended the Commission meeting. Numerous statements were made, and various opinions were offered. Included among those reasons offered in opposition to the landfill were the following: (1) threat to the residential character of the neighborhood; (2) devaluation of the residents' property; (3) danger to the ecological balance of the area; (4) concern regarding the possible expansion of the landfill into a public dump; (5) hazards to residents and children from increased truck traffic; and (6) dissatisfaction with the perceived inequitable burden borne by the East Bibb Area in terms of "unpleasant" and "undesirable" land uses.

Mr. Mullis and his representative, Mr. Adams, emphasized the need for an additional landfill and championed the free enterprise system as the appropriate developer and manager of such sites. They relied upon the reports supplied by Tribble & Richardson, Inc., an engineering concern with vast experience in examining proposed landfill sites, and upon the [Environmental Protection Division of the Georgia Department of Natural Resources] (EPD's) approval of the site. Petitioners further emphasized that the landfill would be managed pursuant to the existing regulations and under close supervision of the EPD.

After hearing the views of numerous individuals, the Commission voted to deny the application. The stated reasons were as follows: (1) the proposed landfill would be located adjacent to a predominantly residential area; (2) the increase in heavy truck traffic would increase noise in the area; and (3) the additional truck traffic was undesirable in a residential area.

Pursuant to a request from petitioners through both Tribble & Richardson and Mr. Charles Adams, the Commission voted on July 14, 1986, to rehear petitioners' application. The rehearing was conducted on July 28, 1986. Applicant Robert Mullis and his representatives addressed numerous concerns which had been previously raised by citizens opposed to the landfill and by members of the Commission. Specifically, Mr. Mullis informed those present that he had met all of the existing state, city, county and planning and zoning commission requirements for the approval of a permit to operate a landfill. He also reiterated that the site had been tested by engineers and that it had been found geologically suitable for a landfill. He explained that burning, scavaging, open dumping and disposal of hazardous wastes would be strictly prohibited, and he advised that this landfill would be regulated and inspected by the EPD. Mr. Mullis and Mr. Hodges of Tribble & Richardson pointed out that the site entrance would be selected by the EPD and that such selection would be subject to approval by the Commission. Mr. Mullis assured those present that the site would be supervised at all times. Finally, Mr. Mullis informed the Commission and the other participants that the buffer zone would be increased an additional fifty (50) feet, from one hundred (100) feet to one hundred fifty (150) feet, in those areas where the landfill site adjoined residences. Also included in the record was a letter dated July 15, 1986, in which Mr. Mullis stated that there existed only five residences contiguous to the proposed landfill site and only twenty-five houses within a one mile radius of the site.

The citizens opposing the landfill voiced doubts about the adequacy of the buffer zone and the potential health threats from vermin and insects. Concerns were expressed regarding the impact the landfill might have upon the water in the area in that many of the residents relied upon wells for their household water. Certain of the participants questioned whether the residents of this area were subject to the same considerations afforded residents in other areas of the city and county when decisions of this nature were made....

[The Commission then voted to approve the project subject to a number of conditions. Plaintiffs filed suit challenging the approval.]

Having considered all of the evidence in light of the above-identified factors, this court is convinced that the Commission's decision to approve the conditional use in question was not motivated by the intent to discriminate against black persons. Regarding the discriminatory impact of the Commission's decision, the court observes the obvious—a decision to approve a landfill in any particular census tract impacts more heavily upon that census tract than upon any other. Since census tract No. 133.02 contains a majority black population equaling roughly sixty percent (60%) of the total population, the decision to approve the landfill in census tract No. 133.02 of necessity impacts greater upon that majority population.

However, the court notes that the only other Commission approved landfill is located within census tract No. 133.01, a census tract containing a majority white population of roughly seventy-six percent (76%) of the total population. This decision by the Commission and the existence of the landfill in a predominantly white census tract tend to undermine the development of a "clear pattern, unexplainable on grounds other than race...." Village of Arlington Heights, 429 U.S. at 266.

Plaintiffs hasten to point out that both census tracts, Nos. 133.01 and 133.02, are located within County Commission District No. 1, a district whose black residents compose roughly seventy percent (70%) of the total population. Based upon the above facts, the court finds that while the Commission's decision to approve the landfill for location in census tract No. 133.02 does of necessity impact to a somewhat larger degree upon the majority population therein, that decision fails to establish a clear pattern of racially motivated decisions.

Plaintiffs contend that the Commission's decision to locate the landfill in census tract No. 133.02 must be viewed against an historical background of locating undesirable land uses in black neighborhoods. First, the above discussion regarding the two Commission approved landfills rebuts any contention that such activities are always located in direct proximity to majority black areas. Further, the court notes that the Commission did not and indeed may not actively solicit this or any other landfill application. The Commission reacts to applications from private landowners for permission to use their property in a particular manner. The Commissioners observed during the course of these proceedings the necessity for a comprehensive scheme for the management of waste and for the location of landfills. In that such a scheme has yet to be introduced, the Commission is left to consider each request on its individual merits. In such a situation, this court finds it difficult to understand plaintiffs' contentions that this Commission's decision to approve a landowners' application for a private landfill is part of any pattern to place "undesirable uses" in black neighborhoods. Second, a considerable portion of plaintiffs' evidence focused upon governmental decisions made by agencies other than the planning and zoning commission, evidence which sheds little if any light upon the alleged discriminatory intent of the Commission.

Finally, regarding the historical background of the Commission's decision, plaintiffs have submitted numerous exhibits consisting of newspaper articles reflecting various zoning decisions made by the Commission. The court has read each article, and it is unable to discern a series of official actions taken by the Commission for invidious purposes. Of the more recent articles, the court notes that in many instances matters under consideration by the Commission attracted widespread attention and vocal opposition. The Commission oft times was responsive to the opposition and refused to permit the particular development under consideration, while on other occasions the Commission permitted the development to proceed in the face of opposition. Neither the articles nor the evidence presented during trial provides factual support for a determination of the underlying motivations, if any, of the Commission in making the decisions. In short, plaintiffs' evidence does not establish a background of discrimination in the Commission's decisions.

"The specific sequence of events leading up to the challenged decision also may shed some light on the decisionmaker's purpose." Village of Arlington Heights, 429 U.S. at

267, 97 S. Ct. at 564, 50 L. Ed. 2d at 466.... In terms of other specific antecedent events, plaintiffs have not produced evidence of any such events nor has the court discerned any such events from its thorough review of the record. No sudden changes in the zoning classifications have been brought to the court's attention. Plaintiffs have not produced evidence showing a relaxation or other change in the standards applicable to the granting of a conditional use. Thus, this court finds no specific antecedent events which support a determination that race was a motivating factor in the Commission's decision....

The final factor identified in *Village of Arlington Heights* involves the legislative or administrative history, particularly the contemporary statements made by members of the Commission. Plaintiffs focus on the reasons offered by the Commission for the initial denial of petitioners' application, i.e., that the landfill was adjacent to a residential area and that the approval of the landfill in that area would result in increased traffic and noise, and they insist that those reasons are still valid. Thus, plaintiffs reason, some invidious racial purpose must have motivated the Commission to reconsider its decision and to approve that use which was at first denied. This court, having read the comments of the individual commissioners, cannot agree with plaintiffs' arguments.

Mr. Pippinger, who first opposed the approval of the conditional use, changed his position after examining the area in question and reviewing the data. He relied upon the EPD's approval of the site and upon his determination that the impact of the landfill on the area had been exaggerated. Mrs. Kearnes, who also inspected the site, agreed with Mr. Pippinger.

Dr. Cullinan also inspected the site. After such inspection and after hearing all of the evidence, he stated that, based "on the overriding need for us to meet our at large responsibilities to Bibb County I feel that [the site in question] is an adequate site and in my most difficult decision to date I will vote to support the resolution."

Both Dr. Cullinan and Mr. Pippinger were concerned with the problems of providing adequate buffers protecting the residential area from the landfill site and of developing an appropriate access to the site for the dumping vehicles. These concerns were in fact addressed by both the Commission and the EPD.

The voluminous transcript of the hearings before and the deliberations by the Commission portray the Commissioners as concerned citizens and effective public servants. At no time does it appear to this court that the Commission abdicated its responsibility either to the public at large, to the particular concerned citizens or to the petitioners. Rather, it appears to this court that the Commission carefully and thoughtfully addressed a serious problem and that it made a decision based upon the merits and not upon any improper racial animus.

For all the foregoing reasons, this court determines that plaintiffs have not been deprived of equal protection of the law. Judgement, therefore, shall be entered for defendants.

\* \* \*

## Notes and Questions

1. How significant is it that the Commission did not actively solicit the landfill application? Do you agree that it is irrelevant to assessing discriminatory intent?

2. The court concludes that decisions made by agencies other than the planning and zoning commission shed little light on the intent of the Commission. Is this consistent

with *Bean's* treatment of decisions by other regulatory agencies? This issue remains unsettled in equal protection case law. For further discussion, *see* Kaswan, *supra*, at 448–49, 453–454.

# R.I.S.E. v. Kay
## 768 F. Supp. 1144 (E.D. Va. 1991)

*Richard L. Williams, District Judge:*

[This case involved a regional landfill in King & Queen County, Virginia, proposed in a predominantly black area. The County initially sought to negotiate a joint venture landfill with the Chesapeake Corporation, in which Chesapeake would build the landfill and the County would operate it in exchange for free waste disposal. Chesapeake identified the "Piedmont Tract," as a potential site, and determined based on soil studies that it was suitable. Subsequently the County determined that it could not afford to operate a landfill on its own and decided to develop the landfill on its own by purchasing the Piedmont Tract. In response to community opposition, the County reviewed at least one alternative site, in an area that was 85% black, which was determined to be environmentally unsuitable. It is unclear if the County considered any other alternatives. The Piedmont Tract is located close to the Second Mt. Olive Baptist Church, founded in 1860 by recently freed slaves, and required rezoning from an agricultural to industrial area. The population of the county was approximately 50% black and 50% white. There were three existing landfills in the county. Plaintiffs brought suit under the equal protection clause challenging the County's approval of the landfill.]

*Demographic Analysis of County Landfill Sites*

...2. Thirty-nine blacks (64% of total) and twenty-two whites (36% of total) live within a half-mile radius of the proposed regional landfill site....

3. The Mascot landfill was sited in 1969. None of the present Board members were serving on the Board at that time. At the time the landfill was developed, the estimated racial composition of the population living within a one mile radius of the site was 100% black. The Escobrook Baptist Church, a black church, was located within two miles of the landfill.

4. The Dahlgren landfill was sited in 1971. None of the current Board members were on the Board at that time. An estimated 95% of the population living in the immediate area at the time the landfill was built were black. Presently, an estimated 90–95% of the residents living within a two-mile radius are black.

5. The Owenton landfill was sited in 1977. Supervisors Kay and Bourne were serving on the Board when the landfill was developed. In 1977, an estimated 100% of the residents living within a half-mile radius of the landfill were black. The area population is still predominantly black. The First Mount Olive Baptist Church, a black church, is located one mile from the landfill.

[The Court then discussed a controversy surrounding a private landfill opened in 1986 by King Land Corporation. Since the county did not have a zoning ordinance in 1986, the landfill did not require county approval. In response, the county implemented a zoning ordinance and successfully sued to bar the landfill from operating. The County subsequently denied King Land's application for a variance to use the property as a landfill, finding that the operation would result in a significant decline in property values of the adjacent properties, and that King Land had ignored environmental, health, safety and welfare concerns The racial composition of the residential area surrounding the King Land landfill is predominantly white.]

*Conclusions of Law*

...2. The placement of landfills in King and Queen County from 1969 to the present has had a disproportionate impact on black residents.

3. However, official action will not be held unconstitutional solely because it results in a racially disproportionate impact....

4. The impact of an official action—in this case, the historical placement of landfills in predominantly black communities—provides "an important starting point" for the determination of whether official action was motivated by discriminatory intent. Arlington Heights, 429 U.S. at 266.

5. However, the plaintiffs have not provided any evidence that satisfies the remainder of the discriminatory purpose equation set forth in *Arlington Heights*. Careful examination of the administrative steps taken by the Board of Supervisors to negotiate the purchase of the Piedmont Tract and authorize its use as a landfill site reveals nothing unusual or suspicious. To the contrary, the Board appears to have balanced the economic, environmental, and cultural needs of the County in a responsible and conscientious manner.

6. The Board's decision to undertake private negotiations with the Chesapeake Corporation in the hope of reaching an agreement to operate a joint venture landfill was perfectly reasonable in light of the County's financial constraints.

7. Once this deal fell through, the Board was understandably drawn to the Piedmont Tract because the site had already been tested and found environmentally suitable for the purpose of landfill development.

8. The Board responded to the concerns and suggestions of citizens opposed to the proposed regional landfill by establishing a citizens' advisory group, evaluating the suitability of the alternative site recommended by the Concerned Citizens' Steering Committee, and discussing with landfill contractor BFI such means of minimizing the impact of the landfill on the Second Mt. Olive Church as vegetative buffers and improving access roads.

9. Both the King Land landfill and the proposed landfill spawned "Not In My Backyard" movements. The Board's opposition to the King Land landfill and its approval of the proposed landfill was based not on the racial composition of the respective neighborhoods in which the landfills are located but on the relative environmental suitability of the sites.

10. At worst, the Supervisors appear to have been more concerned about the economic and legal plight of the County as a whole than the sentiments of residents who opposed the placement of the landfill in their neighborhood. However, the Equal Protection Clause does not impose an affirmative duty to equalize the impact of official decisions on different racial groups. Rather, it merely prohibits government officials from intentionally discriminating on the basis of race. The plaintiffs have not provided sufficient evidence to meet this legal standard. Judgment is therefore entered for the defendants.

\* \* \*

## Notes and Questions

1. Professor Alice Kaswan contends that the court's conclusion in *R.I.S.E.* that there were no procedural irregularities in the siting process is "somewhat glib" since the court failed to discuss the need to rezone the property from agricultural to industrial use, a factor considered relevant under *Arlington Heights*. Kaswan, *supra*, at 444–445. Professor Robert Collin also points to other evidence in the record suggesting that the rezoning was legally suspect. Robert Collin, *Environmental Equity: A Law and Planning Approach to Environmental Racism*, 11 VA. ENVTL. L. J. 495, 533 (1992). The *R.I.S.E.* court also did not discuss the project's legislative history, the fifth *Arlington Heights* factor, despite apparent evidence in the record suggesting some decisionmakers' discriminatory views. According to plaintiffs' appellate brief, for example, the County Administrator, after hearing the concerns about the landfill expressed by two African American ministers, told another party that the ministers "should be given a one-way ticket back to Africa." Another white member of the supervisors referred to the "niggers'" opposition to the landfill. *Id.,* at 532.

2. Did the courts in these three cases excerpted above find discriminatory impact? Could reasonable people have inferred discriminatory intent from the facts of the cases? Would you have?

3. Why are the courts (such as in the *Dowdell* case, excerpted at the start of this chapter) seemingly more willing to infer discriminatory intent on the part of government actors and find an equal protection violation when the issue is the inequitable provision of services, rather than when it is the inequitable siting of LULUs? In formulating your answer, consider the consequences that might follow from a successful equal protection claim under, respectively, the municipal services and the siting dispute cases.

4. Professor Michael Selmi has argued that the Supreme Court's reluctance to infer discrimination in equal protection cases is not a function of the *Arlington Heights* test itself, but is a consequence of the Court's underlying beliefs about the prevalence of racial discrimination. Professor Selmi argues that the Court has been very hesitant to infer discrimination in the absence of direct evidence because it is unwilling to accept that discrimination remains a vital explanation for social and political decisions, an unspoken explanation for facially neutral decisions. Michael Selmi, *Proving Intentional Discrimination: The Reality of Supreme Court Rhetoric*, 86 GEO. L. J. 279, 284–85, 332 (1997). Does this explain the results of the three lower court decisions ?

5. In Terry Properties, Inc. v. Standard Oil Co., 799 F.2d 1523 (11th Cir. 1986), the court rejected an equal protection challenge to the siting of a carpet-backing manufacturing facility next to an African American residential community. Plaintiffs argued that evidence of violations of local zoning laws that occurred in connection with the project were probative of discriminatory intent but the court noted that these standards had often been violated, and indeed that plaintiffs themselves had benefitted from such violations on other projects. Should the fact that plaintiffs might have benefitted from a locality's previous departures from its rules preclude the plaintiffs from using other violations as evidence of discrimination?

6. As a practical matter, do plaintiffs in equal protection cases need to show that alternative sites exist to prove discriminatory intent? Recall that in *Bean*, the court indicated that the lack of suitable alternative locations would make the placement of sites in minority communities "a lot less suspicious." Who should have the burden of showing the presence or absence of alternative sites, the plaintiff as part of its prima facie case, or

the defendant as part of its showing that there are legitimate nondiscriminatory reasons for the siting?

7. Are equal protection challenges a dead end for environmental justice plaintiffs? Professor Kaswan argues that "a wholesale abandonment of the equal protection approach is premature." Kaswan, *supra,* at 456. She contends that "[a]lthough the environmental [equal protection] cases confirm that the evidentiary burden for proving intentional discrimination is high, and the willingness of the courts to infer discrimination is low, the constitutional remedy should not be dismissed out of hand." She argues that the inquiry is highly fact-specific, and that while most cases may not be amenable to an equal protection claim, the facts of each case should be evaluated to determine whether they present the kind of evidence that would be considered probative under the demanding *Arlington Heights* test. *Id.* at 433–34, 456.

8. Equal protection clauses in some state constitutions have been interpreted to prohibit disparate impacts, not only actions that are intentionally discriminatory. For a discussion of these constitutional provisions, *see* Peter Reich, *Greening the Ghetto: A Theory of Environmental Race Discrimination,* 41 U. KAN. L. REV. 271, 301–304 (1992).

9. Professor William Treanor has suggested that communities of color bearing a disproportionate share of locally undesirable land uses should be entitled to compensation under the Fifth Amendment's taking clause. He provocatively argues that under an "original understanding" of the takings clause, courts should only award compensation in instances of physical appropriation or where the political process is unlikely to protect the property interests of particularly vulnerable groups. In Treanor's view, because minority communities are particularly likely to be victims of process failure in local siting decisions, which are likely to negatively impact their property interests, their interests warrant special judicial protection. He further explains:

> Previously, administrative siting decisions have been challenged on equal protection grounds, with a uniform lack of success. Under the approach suggested in this Article, they should be brought instead as takings claims. The possibility of process failure permits courts to be aggressive in evaluating environmental justice claims. Because the claims of minority groups are particularly unlikely to receive a fair hearing in the majoritarian process, it falls to courts to consider individual cases, weigh public need against private harm, and determine what remedy, if any, is appropriate.

> The teeth in a political process-based takings analysis would lie in the fact that courts, applying such an approach, should begin by looking at whether there has been disparate impact. In contrast, under current caselaw, equal protection analysis turns on whether there has been discriminatory purpose. Disparate impact is appropriate in the takings context because the kinds of process failures at issue in environmental justice claims are not simply that overtly-bigoted decisionmakers will fail to consider fairly the claims of minority communities. Rather, the political process failures giving rise to these claims also reflect the organizational difficulties that minority communities face (as well as more subtle biases of decisionmakers). That said, an anomaly that would be created should courts adopt this approach should be acknowledged: It would mean that, in a limited subset of property cases, minority groups would receive greater protection under the Takings Clause (which was not drafted to protect them) than under the Equal Protection Clause (which was).

William Michael Treanor, *The Original Understanding of the Takings Clause and the Political Process,* 95 COLUM. L. REV. 782, 876–877 (1995). What do you think of Treanor's argument? How likely are affected communities to be populated by property owners (as opposed to renters)?

# C. Rethinking the Intent Standard

## Edward Patrick Boyle,
## It's Not Easy Bein' Green: The Psychology of Racism, Environmental Discrimination, and the Argument for Modernizing Equal Protection Analysis
### 46 Vanderbilt Law Review 37 (1993)

*The Solution: Intermediate-Level Scrutiny For All State Actions with a Significant Disparate Impact on Suspect Classes*

Blacks and other disadvantaged groups have little recourse against aversive, institutional racism under current equal protection law because of the intent standard. In equal protection cases alleging environmental discrimination, the courts uniformly have ruled in favor of the defendants because the plaintiffs could not prove the requisite intent. This result is particularly unfortunate because the challenged siting decisions in these cases contained significant evidence of racial discrimination that was not properly considered and because victims of environmental discrimination have no alternative legal remedy available.

This Part suggests that the courts abandon the intent standard and apply an intermediate level of scrutiny to all legislative decisions that have a substantial disparate impact on suspect classes such as blacks. This approach, as detailed below, would reflect the understanding that racial discrimination may be unconscious and aversive as well as conscious and dominative. The focus, therefore, would not be on whether the decisionmakers *intended* to discriminate but on whether the structure of the decisionmaking process *was likely to generate* the disparate racial outcome.

Under an intermediate-level scrutiny approach, plaintiffs first would have to demonstrate that the government act had a significant disparate impact on a suspect class. Plaintiffs could meet this burden by showing that the act disadvantaged an inordinately large number or percentage of class members. A putative defendant could rebut plaintiffs' argument by showing that a substantial number or percentage of nonsuspect class members also were affected. In evaluating the persuasiveness of the defendant's proof, a court should be aware that institutionalized discriminatory acts are almost necessarily overinclusive because overt discrimination is no longer legal; thus, acts motivated by institutional discrimination often will affect a sizeable number of whites as well. Furthermore, when the evidence of impact is not conclusive, the court should examine past similar decisions by the government body to see whether other decisions had disparate racial impacts. If the plaintiffs failed to meet their burden on the disparate impact issue, the defendants would win.

If the plaintiffs can demonstrate disparate impact, the defendants then would bear the burden of proving that the affected group's interests were represented adequately in the decisionmaking process. They may make a prima facie showing by demonstrating that representative members of the minority group were part of the decisionmaking process and that these representatives were fully informed about the detriments and risks the decision would bring to bear on class members. The burden then would shift to plaintiffs to show that the representation was inadequate or that some other substantial process defect existed which could have undermined the effectiveness of the group's representation. Several factors can affect the adequacy of representation: the number of minority representatives who were actually decisionmakers or otherwise substantially part of the decisionmaking process; whether these representatives were chosen by the affected groups or by the decisionmakers; the amount of communication between the affected parties and the representatives; the completeness and accuracy of information made available to those affected and their representatives; the consideration given to less intrusive alternatives; and whether these representatives had incentives that ran counter to the interests of the affected group.

The court's finding on the representation issue would not dispose of the case, but it would determine how carefully the court should scrutinize the defendants' decision. If the court finds that the affected group had adequate representation and was not hampered by process defects, the state merely must demonstrate that a rational basis for its decision exists. On the other hand, if the court found that the process did not adequately include participation by suspect class representatives, it should carefully scrutinize the decision to see whether defendants had considered sufficiently the interests of those affected. The court should consider the severity of the disparate impact on the affected group and weigh that impact against the extent of the inadequacy of representation and the nature of the government interest at stake. Given that the plaintiff would lack access to evidence regarding the decisionmaking process, a court should presume that defendant's decision was discriminatory. The defendant could rebut this presumption with evidence that they considered the affected group's interests despite the representational inadequacy, or that the government interest was so high as to warrant a lack of representation. For their part, the plaintiffs could support their case with any evidence they had showing discrimination in the decisionmaking process, as well as evidence of a history of actual discrimination by defendants....

An examination of [the following situation] potentially involving environmental discrimination demonstrates that the intermediate-level approach is better suited for detecting racial discrimination than the intent standard....

### South Central Los Angeles and California Waste Management Board

In 1984, the California Waste Management Board decided that the Los Angeles area required new trash-burning facilities to handle its waste production. The Board hired a demographics consulting firm to determine which communities would greet the facilities with the least political resistance. The firm suggested the Board focus on "lower socio-economic neighborhoods" or "communities that conform to some kind of economic need criteria." Based on this recommendation, the Board planned to locate the first incinerator in South Central Los Angeles, a predominantly low-income, minority neighborhood that had the highest unemployment rate in the city.

After deciding to locate the incinerator in South Central, the city approached Gilbert Lindsay, an aging black city councilman who represented the neighborhood. The city proposed to place ten million dollars in a community betterment fund in exchange for Lindsay's support of the project. The betterment plan included a promise to revitalize a local community center and name it after Lindsay's wife. The representative supported the plan, and touted its economic benefits, but mentioned nothing about the dioxin, heavy metals, and vinyl chloride the facility would release into the local environment.

The South Central example illustrates how an intent-oriented focus fails to address racist decisionmaking. A court applying an intent analysis would not find an equal protection violation here because the Board manifested no intent to disadvantage minorities. Rather, the Board intended to construct a facility as quickly as possible to meet the waste disposal needs of the city. With timeliness in mind, the Board narrowed its list of potential sites to areas where the residents were not likely to delay the incinerator's construction with years of litigation and political maneuvering. The Board chose a lower-class minority neighborhood to realize its interest in time-efficiency and not to disadvantage lower-class minorities. Further, the city offered to spend ten million dollars to revitalize the depressed community in exchange for agreeing to host the incinerator, indicating that the city was concerned about the residents' interests. Therefore, plaintiffs would have difficulty obtaining relief under an intent-based equal protection analysis.

A court applying the intermediate-level scrutiny approach would begin, rather than end, its inquiry by noting that the Board chose a minority community for its disfranchisement. This fact raises suspicions that the residents' interests were not fully considered; other facts confirm these suspicions. First, the Board knew about the dioxin and vinyl chloride hazards, but attempted to conceal this knowledge from the community. The Board did not attempt to inform the community at all until after the siting proposal was finalized; even then, the Board only consulted an aged representative who seemingly had lost touch with the community. The Board's dealings with this representative indicate that real representation was lacking. The representative had personal motives that predisposed him to accept the proposal, and this personal benefit motivated him to disregard the residents' interests in health and safety.

The court additionally would take note of the high amounts of dioxin and vinyl chloride that the incinerator would release into the local environment, and of the fact that the Board must have known of these health risks when it selected this type of incinerator. The court would ask whether safer models were available given the Board's economic constraints. Depending on the costs of alternative disposal measures, the fact that the city was willing to spend ten million dollars on a community center in the neighborhood might indicate that economic constraints might not have been too great.

The South Central siting decision likely did not involve an intent to disadvantage minorities as much as an intent to avoid political controversy. Nevertheless, one cannot say that the minority neighborhood was only incidentally affected by the siting decision: the community was chosen because it had a high minority population. Accordingly, equal protection relief should be available in this case....

* * *

## Notes and Questions

1. What do you think of Boyle's argument for intermediate-level scrutiny? Do you think that heightened focus on the adequacy of representation of affected groups in the decisionmaking process sufficiently protects against discriminatory decisions, including the type of unconscious racism he suggests underlies siting decisions with disparate impacts?

2. Do you agree that equal protection relief should be available in the South Central incinerator case he describes?

# Chapter XIV

# Enforcement of the Civil Rights Act as a Response

## A. Introduction

### 1. AN INTRODUCTORY NOTE ON THE HISTORY OF ENVIRONMENTAL TITLE VI CLAIMS

Because of the apparent reticence of environmental agencies—at local and federal levels—to condition or deny permits on environmental justice grounds, activists and community residents have instead turned to Title VI, a non-environmental statute, as a potential redress for disparities. Title VI, promulgated in 1964, has been interpreted by the U.S. Supreme Court to give federal agencies the authority to promulgate regulations precluding recipients of federal funds from engaging in activities that have a discriminatory "effect," i.e., regulations that prohibit disparate impacts rather than regulations prohibiting only intentional discrimination. Following the practice of many federal agencies, in 1973 EPA promulgated regulations aimed at discriminatory effect rather than discriminatory intent. The most recent iteration specifically provides that "[a] recipient shall not use criteria or methods of administering its program which have the effect of subjecting individuals to discrimination because of their race." This standard is easier to satisfy than the intentional discrimination standard applicable to claims brought under the equal protection clause (see Chapter XIII).

However, it was not until almost twenty years later, in September, 1993, that the EPA saw the beginning of a steady stream of administrative complaints alleging Title VI violations by state and local environmental agencies. Typically, the remedy for a Title VI violation is for the federal agency to withdraw federal funds to recipients in violation, or alternatively, the federal agency may refer the matter to the Department of Justice, which may seek an injunction. Most of the complaints involved the permitting process. Initially, the EPA Office of Civil Rights had neither the resources nor the analytical framework to begin the task of investigating and deciding the claims. In 1996, the continuing institutional paralysis prompted activists to write to then EPA Administrator Browner about the lack of action on any of the pending complaints. The EPA committed to actively investigate at least 4 of the pending cases. Instead, in February of 1998, the Agency issued an 11-page document titled "Interim Guidance for Investigating Title VI Administrative Complaints Challenging Permits" (Interim Guidance). The Interim Guidance was received with lukewarm enthusiasm by environmental justice activists but sparked a firestorm of criticism from the industry/business sector and state/local regulatory agencies. Many of these stakeholders felt the Interim Guidance left too many unanswered questions, and complained that the ensuing uncertainty destabilized existing permit programs.

Partly in response to the strong criticism, in April of 1998 the EPA established the multi-stakeholder "Title VI Implementation Advisory Committee," which in March, 1999, submitted its report to the EPA. Although the mission of the Title VI FACA (so named because it is under the auspices of the Federal Advisory Committee Act) was to help the EPA provide guidance to state agencies on how to comply with Title VI, the discussions inevitably centered around the questions left unanswered by the Interim Guidance and plausible interpretations of a cognizable claim under Title VI. During the Committee deliberations, in October, 1999, the EPA Office of Civil Rights issued a ruling on the first administrative Title VI complaint decided on the merits after an investigation. In St. Francis Prayer Center v. Michigan Department of Environmental Quality (*Select Steel*), the EPA found no adverse impact from the project and dismissed the complaint (see Section C(3) below).

Meanwhile, the Title VI FACA had identified eight crucial substantive issues that the EPA needed to address, as well as several important procedural issues. The Agency responded in June of 2000 with lengthy draft guidances for investigating Title VI complaints and for recipients of EPA assistance. As of February 2002, these guidances had not been issued in final form.

But administrative complaints may not be the only way for a community group to prosecute a Title VI complaint. Community groups have tried to prosecute private lawsuits in court to enforce section 602, the section of Title VI under which EPA has promulgated its discriminatory effect regulations. With a private lawsuit, the community group may bypass the administrative process and ask the court for the appropriate relief.

We begin this Chapter with a discussion of the relative advantages and disadvantages of proceeding through a private right of action or an administrative complaint. Next, we discuss the alternative most often sought — the administrative process — including the development of the EPA's Draft Guidance for Investigating Title VI claims. This section includes the substantive issues identified by the Advisory Committee and, ultimately, the response to those issues as reflected in the EPA's Draft Guidance. We then discuss the potential for private lawsuits to enforce Title VI's regulations, first by examining the Supreme Court's ruling that no implied right of action exists under the statute, then looking at the possibility of using section 1983 to enforce Title VI. We then review a court case interpreting EPA's Title VI regulations.

## *Pathfinder on Title VI and Environmental Justice*

For those wishing to research this complex area in greater depth, in addition to the articles excerpted in this chapter, *see* Bradford C. Mank, *The Draft Recipient Guidance and Draft Investigation Guidance: Too Much Discretion for the EPA and a More Difficult Standard for Complainants?* 30 ENVTL. L. REP. 11,144 (2000); Bradford C. Mank, *Reforming State Brownfield Programs to Comply with Title VI*, 24 HARV. ENVTL. L. REV. 115 (2000); NATIONAL ADVISORY COUNCIL FOR ENVIRONMENTAL POLICY AND TECHNOLOGY, REPORT OF THE TITLE IV IMPLEMENTATION ADVISORY COMMITTEE: NEXT STEPS FOR EPA, STATE, AND LOCAL ENVIRONMENTAL JUSTICE PROGRAMS (1999); June M. Lyle, *Reactions to EPA's Interim Guidance: The Growing Battle For Control Over Environmental*

*Justice Decisionmaking*, 75 IND. L.J. 687 (2000); Julia B. Latham Worsham, *Disparate Impact Lawsuits Under Title VI, Section 602: Can a Legal Tool Build Environmental Justice?*, 27 B.C. ENVTL. AFF. L. REV. 631 (2000); Michael D. Mattheisen, *The U.S. Environmental Protection Agency's New Environmental Civil Rights Policy* 18 VA. ENVTL. L.J. 183 (1999); Richard Monette, *Environmental Justice and Indian Tribes: The Double-Edged Tomahawk of Applying Civil Rights Laws in Indian Country*, 76 U. DET. MERCY L. REV. 721 (1999); Kristen L. Raney, Comment, *The Role of Title VI in Chester Residents v. Seif: Is the Future of Environmental Justice Really Brighter?*, 14 J. NAT. RESOURCES & ENVTL. L. 135 (1998–1999); Maura Lynn Tierney, Comment, *Environmental Justice and Title VI Challenges to Permit Decisions: the EPA's Interim Guidance*, 48 CATH. U. L. REV. 1277 (1999); Jimmy White, Comment, *Environmental Justice: Is Disparate Impact Enough?*, 50 MERCER L. REV. 1155 (1999); Gilbert Paul Carrasco, *Public Wrongs, Private Rights: Private Attorneys General for Civil Rights*, 9 VILLANOVA ENVTL. L. J. 321 (1998); Wesley D. Few, *The Wake of Discriminatory Intent and the Rise of Title VI in Environmental Justice Lawsuits*, 6 S.C. ENVTL. L.J. 108 (1997); Michael Fisher, *Environmental Racism Claims Brought Under Title VI of The Civil Rights Act*, 25 ENVTL. L. 285 (1995); James H. Colopy, Comment, *The Road Less Traveled: Pursuing Environmental Justice Through Title VI of the Civil Rights Act of 1964*, 13 STAN. ENVTL. L. J. 125 (1994); Luke W. Cole, *Civil Rights, Environmental Justice And The EPA: The Brief History of Administrative Complaints Under Title VI of The Civil Rights Act of 1964*, 9 J. ENVTL. L. & LITIG. 309 (1994); and Richard J. Lazarus, *Pursuing "Environmental Justice": The Distributional Effects of Environmental Protection*, 87 NW. U. L. REV. 787 (1993).

# B. Administrative Complaints vs. Lawsuits in Court: A Brief Comparison

The administrative complaint process has several advantages over lawsuits. First, it is relatively easy to begin the process. The complainant need only send a letter to the EPA Office of Civil Rights alleging discrimination by an environmental regulatory agency that receives federal funds to administer its programs. The complainant does not need a lawyer, although one would be helpful. The EPA conducts the investigation at its own expense. Ideally, an EPA investigation might result in negotiations and a voluntary agreement to either locate a prospective facility elsewhere or mitigate the adverse effects of the agency action. The downside, however, is that the complainant has no right to participate in the investigation, although the EPA may request information from the complainant. Nor does the complainant have a right to an appeal within the administrative process. There is an elaborate procedure the EPA must go through before the agency can terminate funding. By contrast, the recipient of federal funds has substantial procedural rights in the administrative complaint process—including a right of appeal to an administrative law judge, the EPA Administrator, and eventually to a court.

A lawsuit, on the other hand, also has its advantages and disadvantages. The benefits to the plaintiff (usually a community-based organization) are that, through discovery procedures, the plaintiff has better control over the investigation. The plaintiff can call witnesses, give evidence and cross examine defendant's witnesses. A plaintiff can request injunctive relief to bar a state agency from granting a permit or taking other action. Attorney fees may be recoverable by the prevailing plaintiff, and a plaintiff who loses may appeal the decision. The disadvantages to the plaintiff are that it has to finance the investigation and litigation without assurances that it will be able to recover costs under attorney fee shifting provisions. In addition, and most significant, in 2001 the Supreme Court ruled that there is no private right of action available to enforce the §602 discriminatory effect regulations. In some circuits, plaintiffs may still be able to file claims alleging violations of §602 by suing under §1983. These issues are explored in detail in Section D below.

Given the substantial legal uncertainty over private remedies and the costs of prosecuting court cases, it is little wonder that most Title VI claims are brought administratively.

# C. Administrative Proceedings Under Title VI

## 1. Complaint Procedure

---

**Complaint Procedure**

Although the EPA has a more elaborate flowchart to explain the administrative procedure that is available on it's website, the crux of the administrative proceeding is the following:

A complaint letter is sent to the EPA Office of Civil Rights.

EPA undertakes preliminary review to determine if there is a valid claim (e.g., should be dismissed, investigated, or referred to another agency).

The EPA may accept the complaint for factual investigation to determine if the recipient agency's actions cause or contribute to an existing disparate impact. The investigation is conducted by the EPA.

If EPA makes an *initial finding of disparate impact*, the recipient can respond, either by rebutting, proposing a mitigation plan or justifying the impact.

If EPA makes *preliminary finding of a disparate impact*, EPA notifies the Award Official and Assistant Attorney General for Civil Rights. The EPA may include recommendations for recipient to comply.

If compliance fails, EPA makes a *formal determination of noncompliance*. The recipient has another chance to comply (10 days) or procedures to terminate financial assistance begin or EPA refers the matter to the Department of Justice for litigation (may include injunctive relief).

Appeal: If no impact is found, the complainant cannot seek an appeal within the administrative process; the recipient may appeal to an administrative law judge, then to the EPA Administrator and finally to a court.

---

As of February, 2002, there had been a total of 121 claims filed with the EPA Office of Civil Rights, but only one case has been decided on the merits after an investigation.

## 2.  STORIES OF FRUSTRATION[1]

*Padres has firsthand experience with the EPA on Title VI issues. Padres filed a Title VI complaint with EPA in December 1994, almost 6 years ago. Padres pointed out that all three of California's Class I toxic dumps are in or near Latino farmworker communities. Padres could be the poster child of EPA's civil rights enforcement orphans — the dozens of communities across the country facing massive civil rights violations that have been abandoned by EPA. In our community, as a direct result of EPA's failure to act, Laidlaw has secured all the permits it needs and is now expanding its toxic waste dump to double its former size, which will make it the largest capacity toxic dump in the entire United States.*

*- Rosa Solorio Garcia, Padres Hacia una Vida Mejor, Buttonwillow, CA*

*Our case has been pending for nearly eight (8) years. This continued lack of resolution is an injustice that our clients, Flint-Genesee United, the St. Francis Prayer Center and the residents of their community, face every day. We have been told repeatedly, for years, that a decision in this matter was imminent. As far back as November 1996, our clients were advised in writing that a decision had even been drafted. Yet, to date, we have no decision from EPA, and the facility in question is up and running, spewing pollutants into the community on a daily basis. Despite the numerous representations to us that an end was in sight, the "end" continues to be postponed. In one telephone conversation, well over a year ago, EPA indicated that it thought there would be a decision 45 days from the last week of March 1999. Again, in August 1999, we contacted EPA to inquire as to when a decision would be handed down and we were told, again, that a decision would be forthcoming within the next 45 days. Those 45 days have long since passed and we have not heard from EPA. As recently as November 1999, EPA indicated, in writing, to Congressman Dale Kildee that it hoped to make a decision within the coming months. Now, in August 2000, we still have no decision.*

*This facility has been at issue since 1992 and has been under supposedly active investigation by EPA since at least early 1995. We are now entering the new millennium, nearly eight years after the permit for Genesee Power Station was issued, and our clients are still uncertain whether or not EPA will enforce their civil rights. What is certain, however, is that during the pendency of this investigation, the Genesee Power Station has been built, is operating, has assumed a place on EPA's Significant Violators List, has been cited by the Michigan Department of Environmental Quality, has entered into a Consent Judgment based on those violations, and continues to adversely affect the health and*

---

1. From an August 26, 2000 comment letter to EPA on the Title VI Guidance from the Center for Race, Poverty and the Environment, California Rural Legal Association, signed by 125 community groups, environmental justice organizations, coalitions, networks, individuals, and an Indian nation, from 33 states and Puerto Rico. The signatories included 63 complainants in 59 of the Title VI complaints filed with EPA since December 1992, 41 of which are under consideration or have been accepted for investigation and 18 of which have been rejected on procedural or other grounds. The signatories include all six environmental justice networks in existence at the time, as well as 16 current or former members of EPA's National Environmental Justice Advisory Council and eight members of EPA's Title VI Implementation Committee. *See* <http://www.epa.gov/civilrights/docs/t6com2000_071.pdf>.

*welfare of the surrounding community. In fact, the incinerator has been in operation so long that the Title V Air Permit is now up for renewal.*

*- E. Quita Sullivan, Sugar Law Center, Detroit, MI*

## 3.   THE INTERIM GUIDANCE

In February of 1998, the EPA released its controversial Interim Guidance for Investigating Title VI complaints, which elaborates on the complaint procedure in EPA's regulations set forth above. Although the Interim Guidance was subsequently replaced by the Agency's Draft Guidance (discussed below), the Interim Guidance set forth the basic procedural framework that EPA will follow in investigating Title VI complaints. In addition, the arduous, conflict-ridden road to the development of a workable Title VI guidance is perhaps the best illustration of the difficulties encountered in reforming regulation to better respond to environmental disparities.

Substantively, the Interim Guidance follows a five step procedure to determine the existence of a disparate impact. The EPA Office of Civil Rights first identifies the affected population, then considers the demographics of the affected population, the universe of facilities and the total affected population. It proceeds to conduct a disparate impact analysis and determine the significance of the disparity, if any, between the affected population and the general population. If a disparate impact is found, the EPA will consider whether there is sufficient mitigation or whether a justification exists that will result in dismissal notwithstanding the disparate impact. A justification will not be considered acceptable, however, if there are less discriminatory alternatives demonstrated.

The Interim Guidance left many crucial terms unidentified and questions unanswered. State regulatory agencies, industry groups and public interest organizations criticized the Interim Guidance on numerous grounds, arguing that it lacked clear definitions, standards or methodologies, especially as to the determination of disparate impact; they also argued that the guidance intruded on state and local land use policy and conflicted with economic empowerment zones, brownfields initiatives, and other local efforts to foster urban revitalization; and they complained that EPA had failed to provide an opportunity for states and industries to participate throughout its development. *See* Cary Silverman, *EPA's Interim Guidance for Investigating Title VI Complaints Challenging Permits: The Bumpy Road Toward a Federal Environmental Civil Rights Policy,* 6 ENVTL. LAW 135 (1999). Following this controversy, Professor Bradford Mank made several suggestions for reworking the Interim Guidance. Although the Interim Guidance has been superceded, his recommendations are of relevance to EPA's later issued Draft Guidance.

# Bradford C. Mank,
# Environmental Justice and Title VI: Making
# Recipient Agencies Justify Their Siting Decisions
### 73 Tulane Law Review 787 (1999)

*Improving Title VI: Require Recipients to Identify Less Discriminatory Alternatives, Implement Mitigation Measures, and Provide for Public Participation, with the EPA to Provide Technical Assistance*

Title VI [court] cases have inappropriately followed Title VII law in placing the burdens of production and proof on plaintiffs to demonstrate that a less discriminatory alternative exists. In Title VI cases, if a defendant offers a legitimate nondiscriminatory business or educational justification for its actions, most courts have not required the defendant to consider alternative proposals with less disparate impact. Instead, courts have placed the burden on the plaintiff to demonstrate that a defendant failed to adopt an alternative practice with less discriminatory effect that would have met the defendant's legitimate business objectives. According to Title VI case law, if a defendant does present evidence that it chose the least discriminatory alternative, the plaintiff must demonstrate that the defendant in fact did not do so. Title VI case law suggests that a plaintiff must present a concrete alternative, rather than merely speculate that such an alternative might exist....

However, as Title VI recipients usually have greater expertise than complainants and have voluntarily accepted federal assistance, it is appropriate to place at least a limited burden on recipients to show no less discriminatory alternatives exist without interfering with recipient's legitimate policymaking discretion....Furthermore, the Interim Guidance's requirement that an alternative be "equally effective" makes it too easy for a permitting agency and permittee to use minor advantages to prefer their proposal to a reasonably effective alternative. Thus, the EPA should simply require that an alternative is "comparably effective" or reasonably similar in meeting any legitimate business needs of the permit applicant....

### Cost as a Factor

A difficult issue concerns the extent to which a recipient agency may use cost as a justification to exclude less discriminatory alternatives on the grounds that the proposed site is less expensive than any alternative site. Following *Wards Cove* [*Packing Co. v. Atonio*], Title VII cases generally require plaintiffs to demonstrate that an alternative is "equally effective" by showing that a less discriminatory alternative would not cost significantly more than the challenged policy. Similarly, in Title VI cases challenging allegedly discriminatory hospital closings or relocations, courts have allowed defendants to demonstrate that their proposals would save more money than less discriminatory alternatives.

If a low-income minority group lives in an area with significantly lower land prices, a recipient may argue that such lower land prices are a substantial business reason for selecting a site and, accordingly, that any disparate impacts on minority groups are justified. Because minority groups, on average, have lower incomes than whites and, as a result, often live in areas with lower land prices, allowing recipients and developers to use lower costs as a justification may place many minorities at risk....

*Safety as a Justification*

...The EPA should place the burden on the recipient to show that less discriminatory sites would be significantly less safe or efficient than the challenged proposal. While it is more difficult to reject safety as a justification in Title VI siting cases than in Title VII employment discrimination actions, the EPA should ensure that comparable less discriminatory sites do not exist that would provide similar advantages.

On the other hand, if a developer legitimately demonstrates that a minority site is safer than any less discriminatory alternative because, for example, there are unique geological formations in the minority area that inhibit spills from reaching underground aquifers, then such a justification should be allowed. There is no reason to believe that minority areas are disproportionately safer than majority areas. Indeed, to the extent that discriminatory siting has occurred in the past in areas such as Louisiana's "cancer alley," a policy focusing on safety should benefit minority groups more than hurt them....

*Requiring Legitimate Mitigation Measures*

The Congressional Black Caucus and environmental justice advocates have argued that the Interim Guidance is inconsistent with Title VI case law because it allows mitigation measures to be used to justify a project that would otherwise pose unacceptable risks to groups protected under the statute. While their fear that mitigation measures will be used to legitimate otherwise unacceptable projects raises genuine concerns, a total prohibition on considering mitigation measures is probably unrealistic. Instead, the permitting agency and permittee should bear the burden of establishing that any mitigation measures used to reduce disparate impacts to an acceptable level will in fact work....

*Technical Assistance Grants*

...[T]he EPA should take affirmative steps to ensure broad participation by minority and low-income populations by providing technical assistance to Title VI complainants and should also provide technical assistance grants so that complainants can hire their own technical experts or require recipients to provide them....

There are special reasons for providing technical assistance to Title VI complainants because of the complexities of demonstrating disparate impacts. These complexities include defining the relevant area and "affected populations," the appropriate facilities, and the amount and harmfulness of pollution involves complex scientific judgments....

If a state adopts effective and meaningful procedures encouraging early participation, the EPA should take such participation into account when reviewing a Title VI complaint....

*       *       *

As discussed previously, the EPA decided the *Select Steel* case prior to proposing the Draft Title VI Guidance. The following is a summary of the *Select Steel* decision, the only administrative complaint adjudicated on its merits as of December, 2001, which was decided based upon the Interim Guidance.

## (The *Select Steel* Administrative Decision) Letter to Father Phil Schmitter, Co-Director and Sister Joanne Chiaverini, Co-Director of St. Francis Prayer Center, and to Russell Harding, Director, Michigan Department of Environmental Quality, from Ann E. Goode, Director, EPA Office of Civil Rights

### *Alleged Discriminatory Effect Resulting from Air Quality Impacts*

As outlined in EPA's *Interim Guidance*, EPA follows five basic steps in its analysis of allegations of discriminatory effects from a permit decision. "The first step is to identify the population affected by the permit that triggered the complaint. . . . If there is no adverse effect from the permitted activity, there can be no finding of a discriminatory effect which would violate Title VI and EPA's implementing regulations. In order to address the allegation that MDEQ's [Michigan Department of Environmental Quality] issuance of a PSD [Prevention of Significant Deterioration] permit for the proposed Select Steel facility would result in a discriminatory effect, EPA first considered the potential adverse effect from the permitted facility using a number of analytical tools consistent with EPA's *Interim Guidance*. . . .

### *VOCs [Volatile Organic Compounds]*

To evaluate the impact of VOCs, EPA examined the permit application submitted by Select Steel and a variety of analyses conducted by MDEQ. . . . In examining VOCs as ozone precursors, EPA studied the additional contribution of VOCs from the proposed Select Steel facility and has determined those emissions will not affect the area's compliance with the national ambient air quality standards (NAAQS) [under the Clean Air Act] for ozone.

The NAAQS for ozone is a health-based standard which has been set at a level that is presumptively sufficient to protect public health and allows for an adequate margin of safety for the population within the area; therefore, there is no affected population which suffers "adverse" impacts within the meaning of Title VI resulting from the incremental VOC emissions from the proposed Select Steel facility. . . .

The Complainants also have alleged that failure to require immediate VOC monitoring for the proposed Select Steel facility will result in a discriminatory effect. Select Steel's permit condition regarding VOC monitoring allows Select Steel one year from plant start-up to implement a continuous emissions monitoring system ("CEMS") for VOCs. . . . As discussed above, there would be no affected population that suffers "adverse"impacts within the meaning of Title VI resulting from the incremental VOC emissions from the proposed Select Steel facility. For this reason, EPA finds that, with regard to VOC monitoring, MDEQ did not violate Title VI or EPA's implementing regulations.

### *Lead*

Similarly, to evaluate potential lead emissions from the facility, EPA studied the additional contribution of airborne lead emissions from the proposed Select Steel facility and has determined those emissions will not affect the area's compliance with the NAAQS for lead. As with ozone, there is a NAAQS for lead that has been set at a level presumptively sufficient to protect public health and allows for an adequate margin of safety for the population within the attainment area. Therefore, there would be no affected population which suffers "adverse" impacts within the meaning of Title VI resulting from the incremental lead emissions from the proposed Select Steel facility....

In this case, MDEQ also appropriately considered information concerning the effect of the proposed facility's lead emissions on blood lead levels in children in response to community concerns. EPA reviewed this information along with other available data on the incidence and likelihood of elevated blood lead levels in Genesee County, particularly in the vicinity of the site of the proposed facility. EPA considered this additional information in response to the Complainants' concerns that the existing incidence of elevated blood lead levels in children in the vicinity of the proposed facility were already high. Overall, EPA found no clear evidence of a prevalence of pre-existing lead levels of concern in the area most likely to be affected by emissions from the proposed facility....

### Air Toxics

For airborne toxics, EPA conducted its review based on information presented in the permit application, existing TRI data, and MDEQ documents. EPA reviewed MDEQ's analysis of Select Steel's potential air toxic emissions for evidence of adverse impacts based on whether resulting airborne concentrations exceeded thresholds of concern under State air toxics regulations. EPA also considered the potential Select Steel air toxic emissions together with air toxic emissions from Toxics Release Inventory (TRI) facilities, the Genesee Power Station, and other major sources in the surrounding area. EPA's review of air toxic emissions from both the proposed site alone, as well as in combination with other sources, found no "adverse" impact in the immediate vicinity of the proposed facility....

### Dioxin

The information gathered from the investigation concerning the monitoring of dioxin emissions is consistent with [EPA's Environmental Appeals Board's] EAB's analysis of the issue. No performance specifications for continuous emissions monitoring systems have been promulgated by EPA to monitor dioxins. Without a proven monitor, MDEQ was unable to impose a monitoring requirement on the source....

### Alleged Discriminatory Public Participation Process

To assess the allegations of discrimination concerning public process, EPA evaluated the information from interviews with Complainants and MDEQ, and from documents gathered from the parties. The first allegation was that the permit was "hastily sped through" by MDEQ to avoid permitting requirements (*i.e.*, conduct a risk assessment; provide opportunity for public comment on risk assessment; provide meaningful opportunity for all affected parties to participate in the permit process) imposed by a State trial court that are under appeal. The five months between receipt of the complete permit application and permit approval is actually slower than the average time of one and a half months for the past twenty-six PSD permits approved by MDEQ. EPA's review found that the public participation process for the permit was not compromised by the pace of the permitting process. MDEQ satisfied EPA's regulatory requirements concerning the issuance of PSD permits....

The Complainants alleged that the manner of publication of the notice of the permit hearing also contributed to the alleged discriminatory process. The Complainants allege that publication in newspapers was insufficient to inform the predominantly minority community because few community members have access to newspapers—something the Complainants allege was brought to MDEQ's attention during the permitting process for another facility in Genesee Township. EPA's regulations for PSD permitting require that notice of a public hearing must be published in a weekly or daily newspaper within the affected area. 40 C.F.R. § 124.10(c)(2)(i). In this case, MDEQ went beyond the requirements of the regulation and published notices about the hearing in three local newspapers.

Complainants also state that MDEQ's failure to provide individual notice of the hearing to more members of the community also contributed to the alleged discriminatory process. In addition to newspaper notice, EPA's regulations require that notice be mailed to certain interested community members. 40 C.F.R. § 124.10(c)(1)(ix). MDEQ mailed hearing notification letters a month in advance to Fr. Schmitter, Sr. Chiaverini, and nine other individuals in the community who had expressed interest in the Select Steel permit—an action which is consistent with the requirements of EPA's regulations. The mailing list that MDEQ developed was adequate to inform the community about the public hearing, in part, because the Complainants took it upon themselves to contact other members of the community.

The Complainants also alleged that the location of the public hearing (Mount Morris High School) made it difficult for minority members of the community to attend. Complainants felt that the hearing should have been held at Carpenter Road Elementary School. Both schools are approximately two miles from the proposed Select Steel site; however, the elementary school is located in a predominantly minority area, while the high school is in a predominantly white area. MDEQ explored other possible locations and chose the high school, among other reasons, because of its ability to accommodate the expected number of citizens and its close proximity to the proposed site. The high school also is accessible by the general public via Genesee County public transportation.

For all of these reasons, EPA finds that the public participation process for the Select Steel facility was not discriminatory or in violation of Title VI or EPA's implementing regulations....

\* \* \*

## Notes and Questions

1. Recall in the *AES Puerto Rico* case (Chapter VIII) that the Environmental Appeals Board refused to consider that an area designated as "in attainment" at the time of the permit proceedings, might not be in attainment as a factual matter due to recent exceedances of the NAAQ standards. In other words, the Appeals Board felt bound by the legal designation of the area. However, in the Title VI investigation, the EPA's Office of Civil Rights noted that the county hosting the facility had been formally designated nonattainment for ozone in 1978, but that it had demonstrated compliance with the 1-hour standard based upon three years of air quality data prior to 1998. Thus, reasoned the Office of Civil Rights, "[i]n practical terms, this means that the old classification of "nonattainment" has been superseded by a determination that Genessee County was meeting the old ozone standard." *See* Investigative Report, at 14 (a report that accompanied the decision). In other words, OCR did not feel bound by the legal designation of the area. Should the Environmental Appeals Board similarly disregard a current legal designation? Should the two adopt a consistent approach or is there a reason why the Office of Civil Rights might justifiably disregard a legal designation? Does it matter that the EAB is acting as a reviewing body while the EPA Office of Civil Rights is in an inves-

tigatory role? Environmental attorney Luke Cole is critical of this approach and has argued that, despite the EPA's contentions, as a legal *and* a factual matter Genessee County was not in attainment in 1998, the time of the permit proceeding in the Select Steel Title VI investigation:

> When the MDEQ made the decision to grant the permit to Select Steel on May 27, 1998, the area was not in attainment for the "old" one-hour ozone standard. In fact, less than two weeks earlier, on May 15, 1998, Flint hit a one-hour ozone level of 130 parts per billion (ppb) — a full 60 percent above EPAs health-based NAAQS of 80 ppb. On July 22, 1998 — after Michigan issued the permit and after the Title VI complaint had been filed — EPA revoked the one-hour NAAQS for the Flint area, and the area was then covered by the eight-hour ozone NAAQS. On both of these dates — May 27, 1998, for the permit decision and June 9, 1998, for the filing of the complaint — Flint was not in attainment with either the one-hour ozone standard or the eight-hour ozone standard.
>
> Nor is Flint in compliance with the new eight-hour ozone standard today. Flint was over the 0.080 parts per million (ppm) eight-hour NAAQS for ozone in 1996, 1997, and 1998. According to the MDEQ, Flints 1996 "Site Average" was 0.082 ppm, rising to 0.084 ppm in 1997, and then to 0.086 ppm in 1998. As the MDEQ was readying the Select Steel permit for issuance, on May 15, 1998, Flint hit an eight-hour ozone value of 105 ppb — 30 percent above EPAs health-based standards. Thus, the central underpinning of EPAs decision and theory of no adverse impact — that Flint was in attainment for ozone — is demonstrably false.

Luke W. Cole, *"Wrong on the Facts, Wrong on the Law": Civil Rights Advocates Excoriate EPA's Most Recent Title VI Misstep*, 29 Envtl. L. Rep. 10,775, 10,777–78 (1999).

2. Should a facility's compliance with existing regulatory requirements be sufficient to establish "no adverse impact" and defeat a Title VI claim? How effective would Title VI be under this view?

3. Postscript: the EPA denied a joint petition by environmental justice activists to reconsider the case based, in part, upon Cole's argument that the area was not in attainment as a factual or legal matter at the time of the permit. The company subsequently decided to locate in Lansing, Michigan. Executives cited objections from environmentalists as the reason for relocating. David Mastio, *EPA Race Policy Costs Flint Plant: Lansing Gains from Environmental Justice Controversy*, DET. NEWS, Mar. 2, 1999, at A1. Select Steel subsequently announced that it had been unable to secure financing for the project. As noted by Cole, "it is probable that Lansing's economic incentive package has more to do with the relocation than the civil rights complaint, which had been rejected five months before. The company's decision to move the plant, and its convenient statements blaming environmentalists, did give additional fodder to environmental justice foes in Michigan state government and the Detroit News. *See e.g.*, Editorial, *Killing Jobs in Genesee*, DET. NEWS, Mar. 4, 1999, at A10 ("environmental justice policies provide boundless opportunities for mischief," urging Congress to axe EPA's environmental justice initiatives)." Cole, *Wrong on Facts, supra*, at 10,780, n.50.

## 4.  THE TITLE VI FACA AND THE NEW DRAFT GUIDANCE

In June, 2000, the EPA published the long-awaited successor to the Interim Guidance, this time in a 147-page packet containing a "Draft Revised Guidance for Investigating

Title VI Administrative Complaints Challenging Permits" (known as the "internal guidance") and a "Draft Title VI Guidance for EPA Assistance Recipients Administering Environmental Permitting Programs" (known as the "external guidance"). 56 Fed. Reg. 39649 (June 27, 2000) (together *Draft Title VI Guidance*). As you read the following excerpt that explains the *Draft Title VI Guidance* in the context of the questions posed by the Title VI FACA Committee, also keep in mind the previous suggestions by Professor Mank.

# Eileen Gauna,
## EPA at Thirty: Fairness in Environmental Protection
### 31 Environmental Law Reporter 10,528 (2001)

*Defining and Evaluating Adverse Effects*

The first substantive issue presented by the [Title VI Advisory] committee was the difficulty in defining and evaluating effects. At its most narrow, an adverse effect could be construed to mean adverse health effects directly caused by the permitted releases only. A more expansive interpretation of adverse effect would include not only the newly permitted releases, but those changes to the community's well being that are related to the permit at issue, in light of the aggregate sources of pollutants and other adverse impacts existing at the time the permit is under consideration.... Also included would be all foreseeable adverse impacts that may befall the community as a result of the permitted operations. These facility-related (rather than solely emission-related) impacts could include increased traffic, odors, and noise....

Although it is somewhat unclear, the *Draft Title VI Guidance* appears to limit the types of recognized adverse effects to health impacts. First, the Guidance explains that in assessing whether an adverse impact exists, background sources of stressors may be considered. The definition of "stressor" in the glossary of terms includes "any substance introduced into the environment that adversely affects the health of humans, animals, or ecosystems." Although noise, odors, increased traffic are not always "introduced into the environment" by the permittee in the literal sense, the definition specifically lists "noise" as a factor that may adversely affect a receptor. Thus, to a limited degree the EPA intends to consider a range of cumulative impacts that affect health. To this baseline, the facility's impacts are added. However, it is less clear is whether the Agency will consider facility-related impacts that are not emission-related impacts. Equally surprising is that the Guidance does not explicitly address whether non-health related impacts can be the basis of a claim, as it focuses exclusively on health-related impacts....

A question related to evaluating an adverse impact is the type of proof that may be required to establish a violation under complaints grounded upon allegations of adverse health effects. The adverse effect might be established only by a strict test of causation similar to tests developed in toxic tort cases. This standard would probably require epidemiological studies demonstrating the presence of actual harm, and other evidence would need to be submitted to show an exposure pathway and the causal link between the demonstrated harm and the permitted activities. An adverse impact could also be established by evidence of differential risk. This standard would account for the potential latent effects of exposure to toxic chemicals but would likely require the use of comparative quantitative risk assessments. Given the number of complaints pending and the limited resources available to investigate the complaints, such a complicated and resource-intensive analysis does not seem feasible. An alternative test would be to infer an adverse effect based upon elevated levels of pollutants in the impacted area. The latter is a test essentially using differential exposure as an evidentiary surrogate for differential risk.

Before EPA addressed this issue in the *Draft Title VI Guidance*, it used a differential exposure test—or what it termed a "relative burden analysis"—in the Shintech case. The Shintech case involved a controversial Title VI administrative complaint [challenging a proposed polyvinyl chloride plant in Convent, Louisiana] that was under investigation at the time of the committee deliberations.... [The] EPA requested that the Science Advisory Board (SAB) review the methodology the Agency had used. The SAB in its report objected not only to the descriptive phrase "relative burden" but advised EPA that the consideration of differential exposure was too limited because *de minimis* risk could not be considered in such an analysis. However, the SAB also identified significant problems with a risk-based analysis as well, noting that both methodologies would tend to underestimate risks....

Ultimately, the *Draft Title VI Guidance* reveals that the Agency has endorsed a differential risk standard by its intent to use risk values as benchmarks for adverse impacts, adopting an acceptable cancer risk of less than one in one million and an acceptable non-cancer risk of less than one on the hazard index.... However, in also indicating its intent to consider "toxicity-weighted emissions" and "concentration levels," the Agency does appear to retain the option to rely solely upon differential exposure to determine whether an impact is adverse in some instances....

### Identifying the Community of Concern.

...EPA affirmed in the guidance [the Title VI FACA's understanding] that the reference area would be the recipient's jurisdiction under the relevant environmental statute. However, the comparison population would apparently depend upon the allegations of the case and could include either the general population of the reference area or only the non-affected portion of the reference area. In other words, one can compare the affected population with the general population (defined by the Agency's jurisdiction). Alternatively, one can compare the affected population with the unaffected population within the general population of the recipient agency's jurisdiction, or the most likely affected with the least likely affected (by percentage), or even the statistical probability of certain demographic groups within an affected population being affected.

Determining the "affected" population rather than the comparison population was more problematic to some [FACA] committee members. Some favored the use of monitoring data and computer modeling to determine the communities within the facility's exposure pathway. Environmental justice advocates were a bit more skeptical of this method because of their view that monitor placement is generally inadequate or nonexistent in many environmental justice communities. In the *Draft Title VI Guidance*, the EPA endorsed and preferred the use of monitoring data and modeled analysis, but recognized that the more simple proximity approach may be used where more detailed estimates cannot be developed....

### Determining the Degree of Disparity

...The committee discussed alternative descriptive measurements, such as "significant disparity," "substantial disparity," "above generally accepted norms," "appreciably exceeding the risk to (or the rate in) the general population," or "any measurable disparity." A statistical approach using two standard deviations or higher was discussed.

Some objected because of a perceived lack of connection between the statistical correlation and the actions of the facility at issue, others because the approach failed to account for communities that may be particularly vulnerable, for example, a community experiencing abnormally high rates of asthma.

Ultimately, EPA adopted a hybrid approach. First, "measures of the demographic disparity between an affected population and a comparison population would normally be statistically evaluated to determine whether the differences achieved statistical significance to at least 2 to 3 standard deviations." The Agency will then in some manner account for uncertainties such as population shifts, accuracy of predicted risk levels, population size, demographic composition of a general comparison population, and the proportion of the affected area within the recipient agency's jurisdiction. After a "demographic disparity" is examined, the agency will turn to examine the disparity in impact, considering other factors such as the level of adverse impact, its severity and frequency of occurrence. In one final balancing act, the EPA will weigh the demographic disparity against the disparity of impact and make a final determination whether the overall degree of disparity is enough to support a claim. The *Draft Title VI Guidance* cautions that there is no fixed formula or analysis to be applied and no single factor is applicable in all cases.

This convoluted approach is apparently designed to give the Agency wide latitude to address complicated situations, such as where the disparity of impact is large but the disparity in demographics is relatively slight, or vice versa. Other demographic complications may arise, for example one ethnic minority may be disparately impacted within the context of a general population having a relatively high percentage of a combination of ethnic minorities, such as where an African-American community is disparately impacted within an air shed that has a 90% ethnic minority population overall (African American, Hispanic, Native American and Asian combined)....

### The Role of Existing Environmental Standards

Industry representatives and some state regulators are strong adherents of the view that if a permit complies with all applicable requirements under the relevant environmental standards, there can be no violation of Title VI. The logic supporting this position is that environmental laws are designed to — and in fact do — accomplish an adequate level of protection for all members of society; thus, just because environmental burdens and benefits are not distributed evenly does not constitute illegal discrimination. During the Committee deliberations, EPA ruled on a Title VI administrative case that appeared to support this view to some degree. In what came to be called the *Select Steel* case [see excerpt above. Eds.], the EPA Office of Civil Rights dismissed a Title VI complaint...on the rationale that there was no adverse impact because the air shed was in compliance with the NAAQS. Apparently a bit wary that too much might be read into the *Select Steel* decision, EPA was quick to point out in the guidance...compliance with a health-based standard would raise a presumption that the impact, however disparate, was not adverse, a presumption which could be overcome.

Environmental justice representatives were adamantly opposed to using health-based standards in this manner....Such standards, they argued, were often insufficiently protective to begin with, had not been fully implemented, and did not take into account the particular vulnerabilities of a community. Moreover, the health-based ambient standards tended to cover large geographical regions (like an air shed); thus, while the geographical area might comply with the standards overall, toxic hot spots could well occur within those areas. The fact that such a presumption is rebuttable would be of little benefit to communities within the hot spot, as inadequate monitor placement (perhaps itself the result of discriminatory practices, unintentional or otherwise) would prevent the complainant or EPA from obtaining the data necessary to rebut the presumption. Rebutting such a presumption would also conceivably require additional empirical data such as information about home and workplace risks, exposures from other media, and information about atypical health problems the community may be experiencing, data that the Agency is unlikely to gather on its own....

### Agency Jurisdiction

Regulatory officials appear to have a range of views as to the appropriateness of addressing environmental justice issues in the course of issuing permits. However, even those that are open to the idea have expressed two concerns. First, that they may not have authority to condition or deny a permit on environmental justice grounds. After all, none of the federal environmental statutes mention environmental justice or grant explicit authority to go beyond typical requirements to protect heavily impacted communities. Moreover, the associated siting decisions are made in corporate boardrooms long before the recipient regulatory agency is involved and depend in large part upon local land use and zoning decisions, also outside the purview of these agencies. The second concern squarely presents a powerful and competing fairness claim by the regulatory agency: it would be unfair to hold recipient regulatory agencies accountable for impacts over which they have no control.

Responding to the second concern, EPA clearly agreed with the states.... [T]he guidance, in unequivocal terms [provided that only impacts within the recipient's jurisdiction would be considered in determining whether a violation occurred]. Unfortunately, this unequivocal position taken by the guidance only begged the more central questions. Exactly what impacts are within the recipient agency's jurisdiction?... Assuming there exists such authority, what is the scope of impacts that may be considered under the environmental statutes? Do agencies have authority to condition permits in order to mitigate or avoid nonemission-related impacts and nonhealth-related impacts? To take it one step further, do agencies have authority to deny a permit on similar grounds? If the answer is yes, then a related and critical question emerges under Title VI law: if a recipient agency fails to exercise this discretionary authority in response to a known significant racial disparity, has it violated its duty under Title VI by using methods of administering its program that has the effect of subjecting individuals to discrimination because of their race?...

### New Versus Renewal Permits

...When a project sponsor initially commits substantial capital to build a facility, it likely anticipates a useful life of the facility of at least 30 years. But a permit typically expires in five years. So there is a common understanding that these permits will be serially renewed as long as the facility complies with pollution control permit conditions that typically apply. Title VI destabilizes that compact. Consider, for example, a facility built in 1990, before the advent of permit-related Title VI complaints. It would be unfair to tell this facility owner, who expected routine permit renewals, that her multimillion dollar facility can no longer operate because a permit renewal would violate the regulator's Title VI duty by continuing to subject the host community to a racially disparate impact....

At the other end of the spectrum is the perspective of environmental justice advocates. They point out that the civil rights laws have been in effect for decades (prior to the building of many of the oldest facilities) and facility owners do not have an absolute right to a permit renewal.... In fact, permit applicants expect new requirements upon renewal as standards often change over time. Presenting their own fairness claims, they point out that a ton of pollution resulting from a permit renewal is just as harmful as a ton of pollution resulting from an initially granted permit.

In responding to this difficult issue, the Agency appears to have studiously steered a middle course. The *Draft Title VI Guidance* rejects the industry position that renewals should be treated differently categorically.... However, a potentially important and controversial exception was created...if an applicant for a renewal agrees to decrease emissions, the applicant may avoid a potential Title VI challenge to the agency based on its permit.

Environmental justice advocates criticized this position, reasoning that a comparatively small decrease in emissions will not help the overburdened community given the magnitude of the facility emissions overall and the cumulative effect of multiple-source impacts in the area. In addition, this provision disadvantages facilities with better control technology while benefitting older facilities with poor pollution control, as the latter can more easily reduce emissions....

### Mitigation

...In terms of how much mitigation should be required, the possibilities include mitigation sufficient to (a) eliminate the disparity, (b) reduce risk to acceptable levels, or (c) make reasonable progress in eliminating the disparity....

At its most narrow interpretation, mitigation could mean only those actions that reduce or eliminate the adverse impact at issue. A more moderate approach would allow mitigation measures that do not reduce the disparity, but address its effects, such as medical monitoring, research into cumulative risks and synergistic effects, or enhanced emergency response systems. The most expansive view of mitigation, termed by the Committee "loose nexus" mitigation, would include benefits to the host community that do not otherwise reduce the disparity or mitigate its effects, such as a day care center, for example. Loose nexus mitigation closely resembles proposals for compensated siting schemes....

[T]here were questions about the effect of agency-sponsored or facilitated mitigation measures taken in advance of any particular permit proceeding, termed by the Title VI FACA a "Track 1" approach. This latter pro-active approach was strongly recommended by the Committee overall as possibly the best means to address long-standing disparities caused by diverse and multiple sources, as well as addressing the entire range of community concerns, including nonhealth impacts and impacts beyond the jurisdiction of the environmental agency....

EPA, under the *Draft Title VI Guidance*, seized upon the Track 1 approach and assigned to it an extraordinary role in a Title VI investigation. Metamorphosed as an "Area Specific Agreement," this approach essentially became the centerpiece of the new *Draft Title VI Guidance*, as well as the means for the Agency to resolve all of the conflicting claims of fairness in one tidy package. The central idea was for the recipient agency to identify overburdened areas and enter into agreements among the residents and other stakeholders to eliminate or reduce adverse impacts "to the extent required by Title VI." The agreement might, for example, establish a ceiling on pollutant releases, with a steady reduction over time, i.e., a declining cap. Ideally, the process of arriving at such an agreement would include state and local governmental agencies, nongovernmental organizations and other stakeholders with the ability to help solve the identified problems. The guidance explains that if the analysis underlying the agreement supports the conclusions that there will occur "actual reductions over a reasonable time," the agreement will merit "due weight" in the course of a Title VI investigation and the EPA will close the pending Title VI investigation. This may occur even if the claimant was not included in the process and was not party to the area specific agreement. In addition, later-filed complaints concerning other permitting actions in the geographical area covered by the agreement will be similarly dismissed unless the agreement is "no longer adequate" or is "not being properly implemented." In substance, the area-specific agreement categorically constitutes adequate mitigation....

### Justification

[Finally,] proposed justification tests ranged from strict necessity with benefits flowing directly—and perhaps exclusively—to the impacted community, to less stringent tests justifying disparate impacts that would be too costly to mitigate or involve facilities that provide some public benefit.

The *Draft Title VI Guidance* first stated the Agency's seemingly strict position that the recipient would have to demonstrate that the challenged activity was "reasonably necessary to meet a goal that is legitimate, important *and* integral to the recipient's institutional mission." This appears to include only permitted operations that were designed primarily to provide environmental benefits, such as a waste water treatment plant. Anything else, such as a manufacturing facility, would not be integral to the mission of an environmental protection agency. Moreover, even if integral to the recipient's mission and therefore justified, such a justification would be rebutted if the EPA determined that a less discriminatory alternative exists.

Immediately following this conceptually straightforward test are provisions that call this interpretation into doubt. The guidance states that the Office of Civil Rights will "likely consider broader interests, such as economic development...if the benefits are delivered directly to the affected population and if the broader interest is legitimate, important *and* integral to the recipient's mission." Thus, the key to deciphering the twin provisions will lie in whether the Agency really meant to use the word "and" or whether it possibly meant to use a disjunctive for the three qualifiers. It seems odd that a broader interest like "economic development" would ever be an interest that is integral to the mission of an environmental protection agency. The grammatical ambiguity is important; if the *Draft Title VI Guidance* is ultimately implemented to allow goals or broader interests that are legitimate, important *or* integral to the recipient agency's institutional mission, that will justify virtually all disparate impacts. Anything less, however, makes the reference to economic development illogical....

* * *

## Notes and Questions

1. From each stakeholder position (environmental justice advocate, state regulator, industry/business), how would you make a case to the EPA Administrator that she should/should not adopt the *Draft Title VI Guidance* as final? From each stakeholder position, what would be the three most important issues to address (e.g., defining adverse effects, identifying the community of concern, determining the degree of disparity, what role existing standards should play, the extent of agency jurisdiction, treatment of renewal permits, mitigation, and justification)? Why?

2. To what extent do you think the *Select Steel* decision might differ under the *Draft Title VI Guidance*, if at all?

3. Under the new framework devised by the EPA, consider whether an Alabama state agency's approval of a landfill on the "Civil Rights Trail" might constitute a civil rights violation under Title VI:

The same U.S. Highway 80 that runs through Macon County also winds through Lowndes County past Montgomery and on to Selma. The 54-mile stretch of U.S. Highway 80 was made famous in 1965 by the historic "Selma-to-Montgomery March" for the right to vote. On March 7, 1965, civil rights marchers were savagely attacked with billy clubs and tear gas by the local Selma and Alabama state lawmen. By the time the marchers reached the state capitol in Montgomery on March 25, 1965, they were more than 25,000-strong. Lives were lost and blood was shed along that highway. One life was lost one month before the historic march and one a day after the march. The civil rights marches and ensuing state-sanctioned brutality moved President Lyndon Johnson to sign the Voting Rights Act of 1965.

Thirty-five years later, the Alabama Department of Environmental Management (ADEM) approved a 200-acre, $6.8 million landfill permit on the same U.S. Highway 80 that many consider "sacred ground." The landfill is being proposed by Alabama Disposal Solutions, a company owned by Montgomery businessman Lanny Young. Although Governor Siegelman spoke out against the Macon County dump, he has remained noncommittal on the Lowndes County landfill controversy.

In 1996, the 54-mile stretch along U.S. Highway 80 was designated the "Selma to Montgomery Historic Trail." Congress under the National Trails Systems Act of 1968 created the trail. The trail is also designated an "All-American Road" under the Federal Highway Administration's National Scenic Byways Program, created under the Intermodal Surface Transportation Efficiency Act of 1991 or ISTEA. Despite these federal government designations and strong sentiment held by black people, ADEM moved forward in approving the landfill permit.

*See* Robert D. Bullard, *Environmental Racism in the Alabama Blackbelt, available at* http://www.ejrc.cau.edu/envracismalablackbelt.htm (visited October 1, 2001).

# D. Private Rights of Action Under Title VI Regulations

Given the backlog of administrative complaints pending at the EPA's Office of Civil Rights and a remedy that, from the community's perspective, is not sufficiently protective (i.e., the potential withdrawal of federal funding to the recipient state environmental protection agency), some communities have turned instead to the courts to seek an injunction against activities causing or exacerbating racial inequities. The U.S. Supreme Court put a serious, if not deadly, roadblock in their way.

## Alexander v. Sandoval
### 532 U.S. 275 (2001)

*Justice Scalia delivered the opinion of the Court:*

This case presents the question whether private individuals may sue to enforce disparate-impact regulations promulgated under Title VI of the Civil Rights Act of 1964.

The Alabama Department of Public Safety (Department), of which petitioner James Alexander is the Director, accepted grants of financial assistance from the United States Department of Justice (DOJ) and Department of Transportation (DOT) and so subjected itself to the restrictions of Title VI of the Civil Rights Act of 1964, 78 Stat. 252, as amended, 42 U.S.C. § 2000d *et seq.*... Section 602 authorizes federal agencies "to effectuate the provisions of [ § 601]...by issuing rules, regulations, or orders of general applicability," 42 U.S.C. § 2000d-1, and the DOJ in an exercise of this authority promulgated a regulation forbidding funding recipients to "utilize criteria or methods of administration which have the effect of subjecting individuals to discrimination because of their race, color, or national origin...." 28 C.F.R. § 42.104(b)(2) (1999). *See also* 49 C.F.R. § 21.5(b)(2) (2000) (similar DOT regulation).

The State of Alabama amended its Constitution in 1990 to declare English "the official language of the state of Alabama." Pursuant to this provision and, petitioners have argued, to advance public safety, the Department decided to administer state driver's license examinations only in English. Respondent Sandoval, as representative of a class, brought suit in the United States District Court for the Middle District of Alabama to enjoin the English-only policy, arguing that it violated the DOJ regulation because it had the effect of subjecting non-English speakers to discrimination based on their national origin....

[W]e must assume for purposes of deciding this case that regulations promulgated under § 602 of Title VI may validly proscribe activities that have a disparate impact on racial groups, even though such activities are permissible under §601. Though no opinion of this Court has held that, five Justices in *Guardians [Assn'n v. Civil Service Comm'n of New York City]* voiced that view of the law at least as alternative grounds for their decisions.... We therefore assume for the purposes of deciding this case that the DOJ and DOT regulations proscribing activities that have a disparate impact on the basis of race are valid....

It is clear now that the disparate-impact regulations do not simply apply § 601 — since they indeed forbid conduct that § 601 permits — and therefore clear that the private right of action to enforce § 601 does not include a private right to enforce these regulations. That right must come, if at all, from the independent force of § 602. As stated earlier, we assume for purposes of this decision that § 602 confers the authority to promulgate disparate-impact regulations; the question remains whether it confers a private right of action to enforce them. If not, we must conclude that a failure to comply with regulations promulgated under § 602 that is not also a failure to comply with § 601 is not actionable.

Implicit in our discussion thus far has been a particular understanding of the genesis of private causes of action. Like substantive federal law itself, private rights of action to enforce federal law must be created by Congress. The judicial task is to interpret the statute Congress has passed to determine whether it displays an intent to create not just a private right but also a private remedy. Statutory intent on this latter point is determinative. Without it, a cause of action does not exist and courts may not create one, no matter how desirable that might be as a policy matter, or how compatible with the statute....

We therefore begin (and find that we can end) our search for Congress's intent with the text and structure of Title VI. Section 602 authorizes federal agencies "to effectuate the provisions of [§ 601] . . . by issuing rules, regulations, or orders of general applicability." 42 U.S.C. § 2000d-1. It is immediately clear that the "rights creating" language so critical to the Court's analysis in *Cannon [v. University of Chicago]* of § 601, *see* 441 U.S., at 690 n. 13, is completely absent from § 602. Whereas § 601 decrees that "[n]o person . . . shall . . . be subjected to discrimination," 42 U. S. C. § 2000d, the text of § 602 provides that "[e]ach Federal department and agency . . . is authorized and directed to effectuate the provisions of [§ 601]," 42 U.S.C. § 2000d-1. Far from displaying congressional intent to create new rights, § 602 limits agencies to "effectuating" rights already created by § 601. And the focus of § 602 is twice removed from the individuals who will ultimately benefit from Title VI's protection. Statutes that focus on the person regulated rather than the individuals protected create "no implication of an intent to confer rights on a particular class of persons." Section 602 is yet a step further removed: it focuses neither on the individuals protected nor even on the funding recipients being regulated, but on the agencies that will do the regulating. Like the statute found not to create a right of action in Universities Research Assn., Inc. v. Coutu, 450 U.S. 754 (1981), § 602 is "phrased as a directive to federal agencies engaged in the distribution of public funds," id., at 772. When this is true, "[t]here [is] far less reason to infer a private remedy in favor of individual persons," So far as we can tell, this authorizing portion of § 602 reveals no congressional intent to create a private right of action.

Nor do the methods that § 602 goes on to provide for enforcing its authorized regulations manifest an intent to create a private remedy; if anything, they suggest the opposite. Section 602 empowers agencies to enforce their regulations either by terminating funding to the "particular program, or part thereof," that has violated the regulation or "by any other means authorized by law," 42 U.S.C. § 2000d-1. No enforcement action may be taken, however, "until the department or agency concerned has advised the appropriate person or persons of the failure to comply with the requirement and has determined that compliance cannot be secured by voluntary means." Ibid. And every agency enforcement action is subject to judicial review. § 2000d-2. If an agency attempts to terminate program funding, still more restrictions apply. The agency head must "file with the committees of the House and Senate having legislative jurisdiction over the program or activity involved a full written report of the circumstances and the grounds for such action." § 2000d-1. And the termination of funding does not "become effective until thirty days have elapsed after the filing of such report." Ibid. Whatever these elaborate restrictions on agency enforcement may imply for the private enforcement of rights created outside of § 602 . . . they tend to contradict a congressional intent to create privately enforceable rights through § 602 itself. The express provision of one method of enforcing a substantive rule suggests that Congress intended to preclude others. Sometimes the suggestion is so strong that it precludes a finding of congressional intent to create a private right of action, even though other aspects of the statute (such as language making the would be plaintiff "a member of the class for whose benefit the statute was enacted") suggest the contrary. . . .

Both the Government and respondents argue that the regulations contain rights-creating language and so must be privately enforceable, but that argument skips an analytical step. Language in a regulation may invoke a private right of action that Congress through statutory text created, but it may not create a right that Congress has not. Thus, when a statute has provided a general authorization for private enforcement of regulations, it may perhaps be correct that the intent displayed in each regulation can determine whether or not it is privately enforceable. But it is most certainly incorrect to say that language in a regulation can conjure up a private cause of action that has not been authorized by Congress. Agencies may play the sorcerer's apprentice but not the sorcerer himself. . . .

*Justice Stevens, with whom Justices Souter, Ginsburg and Breyer, joined, dissenting:*

. . . At the time of the promulgation of [disparate impact] regulations, prevailing principles of statutory construction assumed that Congress intended a private right of action whenever such a cause of action was necessary to protect individual rights granted by valid federal law. Relying both on this presumption and on independent analysis of Title VI, this Court has repeatedly and consistently affirmed the right of private individuals to bring civil suits to enforce rights guaranteed by Title VI. A fair reading of those cases, and coherent implementation of the statutory scheme, requires the same result under Title VI's implementing regulations.

In separate lawsuits spanning several decades, we have endorsed an action identical in substance to the one brought in this case, *see* Lau v. Nichols, 414 U.S. 563 (1974); demonstrated that Congress intended a private right of action to protect the rights guaranteed by Title VI, *see* Cannon v. University of Chicago, 441 U.S. 677 (1979); and concluded that private individuals may seek declaratory and injunctive relief against state officials for violations of regulations promulgated pursuant to Title VI, *see* Guardians Assn. v. Civil Serv. Comm'n of New York City, 463 U.S. 582 (1983). Giving fair import to our language and our holdings, every Court of Appeals to address the question has concluded that a private right of action exists to enforce the rights guaranteed both by the text of Title VI and by any regulations validly promulgated pursuant to that Title, and Congress has adopted several statutes that appear to ratify the status quo....

The majority acknowledges that *Cannon* is binding precedent with regard to both Title VI and Title IX, but seeks to limit the scope of its holding to cases involving allegations of intentional discrimination. The distinction the majority attempts to impose is wholly foreign to *Cannon*'s text and reasoning. The opinion in *Cannon* consistently treats the question presented in that case as whether a private right of action exists to enforce "Title IX" (and by extension "Title VI"), and does not draw any distinctions between the various types of discrimination outlawed by the operation of those statutes. Though the opinion did not reach out to affirmatively preclude the drawing of every conceivable distinction, it could hardly have been more clear as to the scope of its holding: A private right of action exists for "victims of *the* prohibited discrimination." 441 U. S. at 703 (emphasis added). Not some of the prohibited discrimination, but all of it....Moreover, *Cannon* was itself a disparate impact case....

As I read today's opinion, the majority declines to accord precedential value to *Guardians* because the five Justices in the majority were arguably divided over the mechanism through which private parties might seek such injunctive relief. This argument inspires two responses. First, to the extent that the majority denies relief to the respondents merely because they neglected to mention 42 U.S.C. §1983 in framing their Title VI claim, this case is something of a sport. Litigants who in the future wish to enforce the Title VI regulations against state actors in all likelihood must only reference §1983 to obtain relief; indeed, the plaintiffs in this case (or other similarly situated individuals) presumably retain the option of rechallenging Alabama's English only policy in a complaint that invokes §1983 even after today's decision....

Beyond its flawed structural analysis of Title VI and an evident antipathy toward implied rights of action, the majority offers little affirmative support for its conclusion that Congress did not intend to create a private remedy for violations of the Title VI regulations. The Court offers essentially two reasons for its position. First, it attaches significance to the fact that the "rights-creating" language in §601 that defines the classes protected by the statute is not repeated in §602. But, of course, there was no reason to put that language in §602 because it is perfectly obvious that the regulations authorized by §602 must be designed to protect precisely the same people protected by §601. Moreover, it is self evident that, linguistic niceties notwithstanding, any statutory provision whose stated purpose is to "effectuate" the eradication of racial and ethnic discrimination has as its "focus" those individuals who, absent such legislation, would be subject to discrimination.

Second, the Court repeats the argument advanced and rejected in *Cannon* that the express provision of a fund cut-off remedy "suggests that Congress intended to preclude others." In *Cannon*, 441 U.S. at 704–708, we carefully explained why the presence of an explicit mechanism to achieve one of the statute's objectives (ensuring that federal funds are not used "to support discriminatory practices") does not preclude a conclusion that a private right of action was intended to achieve the statute's other principal objective ("to provide individual citizens effective protection against those practices"). In support of our analysis, we offered policy arguments, cited evidence from the legislative history, and noted the active support of the relevant agencies. *Ibid.* In today's decision, the Court does not grapple with—indeed, barely acknowledges—our rejection of this argument in *Cannon*.

Like much else in its opinion, the present majority's unwillingness to explain its refusal to find the reasoning in *Cannon* persuasive suggests that today's decision is the unconscious product of the majority's profound distaste for implied causes of action rather than an attempt to discern the intent of the Congress that enacted Title VI of the Civil Rights Act of 1964. Its colorful disclaimer of any interest in "venturing beyond Congress's intent" has a hollow ring.

\* \* \*

## Notes and Questions

1. Left undecided by the Supreme Court, for the moment at least, is the validity of the underlying Title VI discriminatory impact regulations. Some hints of the Court's position on this issue appear in *Sandoval*. Justice Scalia seems to suggest that it is inconsistent to allow regulations under Section 602 to prohibit conduct having a discriminatory impact when that same conduct is permitted by Section 601, which bars only intentional discrimination. *Sandoval,* 121 S. Ct. 1511, at 1519 n.6. It is likely that this issue will eventually be resolved by the Supreme Court as well.

2. Does the *Sandoval* case absolutely preclude lawsuits based upon Title VI's disparate impact regulations? Professor Bradford Mank argues that recipients of federal funds acting under color of state law may be subject to a § 1983 action for failure to comply with § 602 of Title VI, a possibility raised, and arguably encouraged, by Justice Stevens' dissent. Section 1983, which originated in the Civil Rights Act of 1871, allows suits for violations of the Constitution and other federal laws against persons acting under color of law. 42 U.S.C. § 1983.

# Bradford C. Mank,
# Using Section 1983 to Enforce
# Title VI's Section 602 Regulations
### 49 University of Kansas Law Review 321 (2001)

While many commentators have discussed whether there is a private cause of action under Title VI's implementing regulations, there has been little attention to whether suits under § 1983 could enforce the same regulations. Courts have become increasingly reluctant to recognize implied rights of action because they require proof that Congress intended to create such a private remedy.

By contrast, because § 1983 already authorizes private rights of action to enforce federal statutory rights, a plaintiff suing under § 1983 need merely comply with a three-part test that focuses on whether a statute contains a right that is sufficiently definite to be capable of judicial enforcement and on whether Congress intended to benefit a class including the plaintiff. Once a court recognizes that a federal statute creates a "right" that Congress intended to benefit persons like the plaintiff, there is a presumption that the right is enforceable under § 1983. Accordingly, the standard for recognizing a § 1983 suit based on a statutory violation of a federal statute is generally less than that for implying a private right of action under the same underlying statute. The burden is then on the defendant to show that Congress expressly prohibited a suit under § 1983 or implicitly did so by enacting a comprehensive remedial scheme incompatible with a § 1983 suit. There is a strong presumption against using a statute's remedial scheme to preclude § 1983 suits. Accordingly, courts have recognized that a valid § 1983 cause of action may exist even where there is no private right of action under the same statutory provision.

Whether agency regulations alone may create a federal right is more controversial, and there is a split in the circuits on this issue. However, even the Eleventh Circuit in Harris [v. James, 127 F.3d 993 (11th Cir. 1997)] recognized that a regulation may flesh out rights that are implicit in the underlying statute.

Even under the Eleventh Circuit's restrictive test that agency regulations may only "define" statutory rights that are enforceable under § 1983, Title VI's administrative regulations merely flesh out the anti-discrimination rights Congress established in the statute. In section 602, Congress expressly directed federal funding agencies to promulgate regulations that forbid recipients from engaging in discrimination and to establish enforcement mechanisms to prevent such discrimination. In *Guardians*, the Supreme Court held that agency regulations issued pursuant to section 602, which prohibit recipients from engaging in activities that cause disparate impacts, are valid. Subsequently, Congress amended the statute to make it clear that Title VI forbids any discriminatory actions by a recipient even if the conduct occurs in a program that is not funded by the federal government. Accordingly, even in the Eleventh Circuit, the district court in *Sandoval* concluded that section 602 regulations simply "further define" or "flesh out" the anti-discrimination right that Congress clearly created in Title VI. While the *Sandoval* case addressed whether there is a private right of action under Title VI's section 602 regulations, that court's analysis strongly supports a finding that those regulations are also enforceable under § 1983.

Furthermore, in Powell [v. Ridge, 189 F.3d 387 (3d Cir. 1999), *cert. denied*, 528 U.S. 1046 (1999)], the Third Circuit correctly concluded that Title VI's express remedy of funding termination does not preclude § 1983 suits. Several Supreme Court decisions have emphasized that preclusion of § 1983 suits is limited to exceptional cases in which such suits would interfere with a federal statute's comprehensive remedial scheme. Title VI's administrative remedies do not protect the rights of individuals, which is one of the two major purposes of the statute, and therefore do not preclude the use of § 1983 to enforce Title VI's section 602 regulations. Furthermore, there is no evidence in Title VI's legislative history that Congress intended to create a private right of action that might arguably preclude suits under § 1983. Accordingly, even if the Supreme Court eventually refuses to recognize a private right of action under Title VI's section 602 regulations, there is a strong argument that the disparate impact test used in those regulations is enforceable through a § 1983 suit....

Section 1983 is a powerful tool for vindicating both constitutional and federal statutory rights, including regulations such as those issued pursuant to section 602 that "flesh out" existing statutory rights. In light of Title VI's limited explicit remedies, there is no basis to find that the statute precludes § 1983 claims. Title VI plaintiffs should be able to use § 1983 suits to raise constitutional claims and sue officials in their individual capacities because Title VI itself does not provide such remedies.

\* \* \*

Shortly after the publication of Professor Mank's article, a federal district judge in New Jersey agreed with his position.

## South Camden Citizens in Action v. New Jersey Department of Environmental Protection
145 F. Supp. 2d 505 (N.J.D.C. 2001) (Supplemental Opinion)

*Orlofsky, District Court Judge:*

On April 19, 2001, this Court granted Plaintiffs' request for a preliminary injunction and a declaratory judgment based upon the allegation that the New Jersey Department of Environmental Protection ("NJDEP") and NJDEP Commissioner Robert Shinn ("Shinn") had violated § 602 of Title VI of the Civil Rights Act of 1964, 40 U.S.C. § 2000d-1, and the EPA's implementing regulations thereto, codified at 40 C.F.R. § 7.10 *et seq.*, by failing to consider the potential adverse, disparate impact of their decision to grant St. Lawrence Cement Co.'s ("SLC") application for air permits to operate its proposed facility. *See* South Camden Citizens in Action ("SCCIA"), et al. v. New Jersey Department of Environmental Protection, et al., ("SCCIA I"), 145 F. Supp. 2d 446 (D.N.J. April 19, 2001) [Excerpted below. Eds.] That determination was based upon the assumption that an implied private right of action existed under § 602 of Title VI, a cause of action which had recently been recognized in this Circuit in Powell v. Ridge, 189 F.3d 387 (3d Cir. 1999), *cert. denied*, 528 U.S. 1046 (1999). I noted in *SCCIA I* that the precise question of whether an implied private right of action was available to enforce disparate impact regulations promulgated under Title VI was pending before the Supreme Court. *Id.* I concluded, however, in *SCCIA I*, that I was bound by the Third Circuit's decision in *Powell* to recognize such a claim.

On the morning of April 24, 2001, five days after this Court filed its Opinion and Order in *SCCIA I*, the Supreme Court held that § 602 does not provide an implied private right of action to enforce disparate impact regulations promulgated by federal agencies pursuant to § 602. *See* Alexander v. Sandoval, 532 U.S. 275 (2001)....

The Supreme Court's decision in *Sandoval* clearly held that private individuals can no longer sue directly under § 602 to enforce the disparate impact regulations promulgated under Title VI of the Civil Rights Act of 1964. The question presented to this Court for the first time, and perhaps for the first time to any federal court, is whether the same disparate impact regulations which can no longer be enforced through a private right of action brought directly under § 602 of Title VI, can be enforced pursuant to 42 U.S.C. § 1983.

For the reasons set forth below, I conclude that: (1) the Supreme Court's decision in *Sandoval* does not preclude Plaintiffs from pursuing their claim for disparate impact discrimination, in violation of the EPA's implementing regulations to Title VI, under 42 U.S.C. § 1983; and (2) Plaintiffs are entitled to preliminary injunctive relief based upon a claim for disparate impact discrimination in violation of the EPA's implementing regulations to Title VI, brought under 42 U.S.C. § 1983....

[U]pon a careful review of Justice Scalia's majority opinion in *Sandoval*, it is clear that the impact of the Supreme Court's holding in *Sandoval* on this case is limited to its holding that § 602 of Title VI does not create an implied private cause of action to en-force agency regulations promulgated under § 602 which prohibit disparate impact dis-crimination.... Justice Scalia took pains to point out that because the validity of the Title VI implementing regulations promulgated by the DOJ and DOT were not con-tested in *Sandoval*, the Court's holding in *Sandoval* does not address or invalidate the disparate impact regulations promulgated under § 602 of Title VI, or the many cases in which the Supreme Court has assumed such a right exists....

[T]he Court limited the question decided in *Sandoval* to determining whether Con-gress intended to create a private *remedy* to enforce § 602, while assuming that in fact Congress intended that statute, to create a substantive *right*: "The judicial task is to in-terpret the statute Congress has passed to determine whether it displays an intent not just to create a private right, but also a private remedy." Finally, a careful review of the Supreme Court's jurisprudence on the issue of implied remedy, beginning with the Court's holding twenty years ago in Middlesex County Sewerage Auth. v. Nat'l Sea Clammers Assoc., 453 U.S. 1 (1981), cited by the Supreme Court in Sandoval, 532 U.S. 275, reveals the Court's recognition of the critical distinction in the judicial analysis re-quired to divine Congressional intent to create such a private right of action, and the very different question of Congressional intent to create such a remedy via, for example, § 1983....

The Supreme Court has explained that, once plaintiffs seeking a remedy under § 1983 demonstrate that they can meet the requisite statutory elements for a § 1983 claim:

> [A] determination that § 1983 is available to remedy a statutory or constitu-tional violation involves a two-step inquiry. First, the Plaintiff must assert the violation of a federal right. . . . Second, even when the plaintiff has asserted a federal right, the defendant may show that Congress "specifically foreclosed a remedy under § 1983," by providing a "comprehensive enforcement mecha-nism for protection of a federal right."

Golden State Transit Corp. v. City of Los Angeles, 493 U.S. 103, 106 (1989). With respect to the first part of this inquiry, the Court has emphasized that "in order to seek redress through § 1983, [] a plaintiff must assert the violation of a federal right, not merely a viola-tion of federal law."... Describing this analysis in *Livadas v. Bradshaw*, the Court explained that "apart from [some] exceptional cases, § 1983 remains a generally and presumptively available remedy for claimed violations of federal law." 512 U.S. 107, 132 (1994)....

The Third Circuit, applying Blessing [v. Freestone, 520 U.S. 329, 340 (1997)], has ex-plained the two conditions which are sufficient to rebut this presumption: "the pre-sumption is rebutted 'if Congress specifically foreclosed a remedy under § 1983, [either] expressly, by forbidding recourse to § 1983 in the statute itself, or impliedly, by creating a comprehensive enforcement scheme that is incompatible with individual enforcement under § 1983.'"... [T]he burden is upon the defendant, to "make the difficult showing that allowing a § 1983 action to go forward in these circumstances 'would be inconsis-tent with Congress' carefully tailored scheme.'"...

[Section] 1983 is limited to claims alleging the deprivation, under color of state law, of "any rights, privileges, or immunities secured by the Constitution and laws." 42 U.S.C. § 1983. Plaintiffs may only bring suit under § 1983 to enforce rights secured by the Constitution "and laws."...

The Supreme Court has held that the plain meaning of the phrase "and laws" in § 1983 authorizes plaintiffs to bring § 1983 claims based on alleged violations of federal statutes. The Court has, however, limited the prospective reach of its holding in [Maine v. Thiboutot, 448 U.S. 1 (1980)] by emphasizing, in subsequent decisions construing that case, that §1983 may only be invoked to assert a violation of a federal *right*, not merely a violation of federal *law*. The Court developed the analysis articulated in *Blessing* [] as a means of distinguishing those statutes which create rights within the meaning of §1983 from those which merely provide guidance or state policy preferences.

In this case, Plaintiffs contend that the EPA's implementing regulations, promulgated pursuant to §602 of Title VI, create "rights," within the meaning of §1983.... I must first consider Plaintiffs' contention, that, as a general proposition, agency regulations may create "rights" within the meaning of §1983.

The Supreme Court has answered this question in the affirmative....

[In *Wright v. City of Roanoke*,] the Court held that the regulations created rights enforceable under §1983 because they conferred benefits on tenants, which were "sufficiently specific to qualify as enforceable rights under Pennhurst [State School & Hospital v. Halderman, 451 U.A. 1 (1981)] and §1983," and were not beyond the competence of the judiciary to enforce. *Wright*, 479 U.S. at 432....

The fact that federal regulations may have the force of law has been confirmed by the Supreme Court in other contexts. In Chrysler Corp. v. Brown, 441 U.S. 281 (1979), the Supreme Court held that regulations have the "force and effect of law" if they: (1) are substantive, meaning they function as a "legislative-type rule" which affects individual rights and obligations; (2) Congress granted the agency which issued the regulations the authority to promulgate such regulations; (3) the regulations were promulgated in accordance with any procedural requirements imposed by Congress, e.g., the Administrative Procedure Act. *Chrysler*, 441 U.S. at 301–03....

Applying the *Chrysler* inquiry to the regulations at issue in this case, I conclude that the EPA's §602 regulations satisfy the *Chrysler* criteria, and therefore have the "force and effect of law." The regulations, insofar as they explicitly prohibit recipients of federal funding from using "criteria or methods of administering [their] programs which have the effect" of subjecting individuals to discrimination, create obligations which directly affect individuals. 40 C.F.R. §7.35 (b). Furthermore, Congress granted the agency which issued the regulations not merely the authority to promulgate such regulations, but a directive to do so....

The inquiry I must now undertake is whether the EPA's Title VI implementing regulations, codified at 40 C.F.R. §7.1 *et seq.*, create rights enforceable under §1983....

Significantly, Congress, in enacting Title VI, did not define "discrimination," nor does §602 contain an explanation of what constitutes "discrimination." Rather, as Justice Brennan explained, "the legislative history shows that Congress specifically eschewed any static definition of discrimination in favor of broad language that could be shaped by experience, administrative necessity, and evolving judicial doctrine." [Regents of Univ. of Cal.] v. Bakke, 438 U.S, [265], 337 [1978].

Congress chose to delegate this duty to the federal agencies....

The frequency with which federal courts have had occasion to review [disparate impact] claims, and the proficiency with which they have done so, leads this Court to conclude that the right(s) created by Title VI implementing regulations are not so "vague and amorphous" as to be unenforceable, but rather, are clearly within the competence of the judiciary to enforce....

[F]or the reasons I have already set forth above, the EPA's implementing regulations must be considered in the context of the broader legislative and regulatory initiative mandated by Congress through the Civil Rights Act in general, and Title VI in particular, of which the EPA's implementing regulations are but a small part. "[To determine] whether a statute creates a right, courts must look to the entire statute and its policy objective." In enacting Title VI, Congress intended to benefit individuals who were subjected to discrimination....

The Supreme Court has also summarized the intent of Congress when it enacted Title VI, as follows:

> Title IX, like its model Title VI, sought to accomplish two related, but nevertheless somewhat different, objectives. First, Congress wanted to avoid the use of federal resources to support discriminatory practices; second, it wanted to provide individual citizens effective protection against those practices. Both of these purposes were repeatedly identified in the debates on the two statutes.

Cannon v. Univ. of Chicago, 441 U.S.[677], 704 [1979].

Of the ten individual plaintiffs in this case, seven are African-American and two are Hispanic. The organizational plaintiff, South Camden Citizens In Action, draws its membership from a neighborhood, Waterfront South, which is 91% persons of color. Plaintiffs in this case clearly belong to the class of persons Congress intended to benefit in Title VI by prohibiting programs and activities which receive federal funds from discriminating against persons based on their race, §601, and authorizing federal agencies to promulgate regulations to effectuate this prohibition, §602....

In addition to this general prohibition, the EPA's Title VI implementing regulations specifically forbid recipients of federal funds from "using criteria or methods of administering [their] program[s] which have the effect of subjecting individuals to discrimination because of their race, color, national origin, or sex, or have the effect of defeating or substantially impacting the accomplishment of the objectives of the program with respect to individuals of a particular race, color, national origin, or sex." 40 C.F.R. §7.35(b). The EPA's regulations, promulgated at the express instruction of Congress in §602, are "undoubtedly intended to benefit individuals such as the plaintiffs."

I find SLC's argument, that neither §602 nor the EPA's implementing regulations were intended to benefit Plaintiffs, unpersuasive. SLC argues that "[a]s a preliminary matter, Congress did not intend for Section 602 to benefit Plaintiffs." SLC contends that both §602 and the EPA's implementing regulations are too broadly worded to invoke individual rights, that they create a "yardstick" for the "system-wide measurement" of services as opposed to an "individual entitlement," and are focused on funding recipients. To support this contention, SLC relies on the Supreme Court's decision in *Blessing*, in which the Court held that a particular provision of Title IV-D of the Social Security Act "does not give individual rights to force a state agency to substantially comply with Title IV-D." Blessing, 520 U.S. at 333. As the following analysis makes clear, however, *Blessing* is clearly distinguishable from this case on both the facts and the law....

Plaintiffs in this case have asserted a simple and specific right under the EPA's Title VI implementing regulations: to be free of disparate impact discrimination caused by the use, by a recipient of federal funds, of "criteria or methods" which have a discriminatory "effect" on individuals based on their race, color, or national origin. Plaintiffs assert that by undertaking an adverse disparate impact analysis prior to permitting the operation of polluting facilities, NJDEP would avoid such a discriminatory "effect." Indeed, in accordance with the specific language of the regulations, as a condition of receiving federal funds, NJDEP had given its *assurance* that it will conduct a disparate impact analysis. Unlike the plaintiffs in *Blessing*, Plaintiffs in this case have not merely requested "substantial compliance" with a "general provision," but rather, have identified with precision both the regulatory provisions upon which they base their claim, 40 C.F.R. §7.35(b), and the compliance they seek, namely, the performance of an adverse disparate impact assessment and consideration of the cumulative environmental burdens and community-specific health problems, as part of the NJDEP's permitting process. And unlike the defendant state agency in *Blessing*, which was at least attempting to comply with the obligations it had assumed as a condition of accepting federal funds, though the *Blessing* plaintiffs alleged its attempt was insufficient, the NJDEP in this case has flatly denied that it has any obligations whatsoever to Plaintiffs beyond ensuring that permitted facilities comply with environmental emissions standards....

The second part of the *Blessing* test requires an analysis of whether the right which Plaintiffs are asserting is "so vague and "amorphous" that its enforcement would strain judicial competence. *Blessing*, 520 U.S. at 341. There is no ambiguity in the EPA's Title VI implementing regulations....

This Court need not speculate about judicial competence to enforce federal regulations prohibiting disparate impact discrimination, promulgated pursuant to Title VI, because a substantial body of case law already exists which demonstrates the capacity of the federal judiciary to perform exactly this analysis....

The final factor in the *Blessing* analysis requires this Court to consider whether the provision in question "unambiguously imposes a binding obligation on states." *Blessing*, 520 U.S. at 341. "In other words, the provision giving rise to the asserted right must be couched in mandatory, rather than precatory, terms" to create a right enforceable under §1983. *Id.* Provisions which indicate "no more than a confessional preference — at most a 'nudge' in the preferred direction" are not intended to, and therefore, according to the Supreme Court, cannot, rise to the level of an enforceable right.

An analysis of the language of Title VI and of the EPA's implementing regulation reveals that Congress intended to place mandatory obligations on recipients of federal funding. Section 601 states that "no person *shall*, on the ground of race, color, or national origin" be subjected to discrimination under any program which receives federal funding. 42 U.S.C. §2000d (emphasis added)....

The use of the term "shall" indicates a mandatory obligation....

Because I have concluded that Plaintiffs have asserted the violation of a "federal right," the Plaintiffs are entitled to a "rebuttable presumption that the right is enforceable under §1983." *Powell*, 189 F.3d at 401 (citing *Blessing*, 520 U.S. at 341).... [T]he Third Circuit recently explained,

> The presumption is rebutted if Congress specifically foreclosed a remedy under §1983...either expressly, by forbidding recourse to §1983, or impliedly, by creating a comprehensive enforcement scheme that is incompatible with individual enforcement under §1983....

Defendants argue that Plaintiffs are foreclosed from seeking a remedy under §1983 because: (1) the EPA's §602 regulations require recipients to provide grievance proceedings (which the NJDEP did not), *see* 40 C.F.R. §7.90; (2) the regulations define "Agency Compliance Procedures" which EPA will utilize to secure compliance, *see* 40 C.F.R. §7.105 *et seq.*; and (3) the EPA Administrator is authorized, under §602, to withdraw federal funding from a recipient in the event of noncompliance, *see* 42 U.S.C. §602....

Given the presumption of enforceability under § 1983, however, it is perhaps not surprising that the Court recently acknowledged that "only twice have we found a remedial scheme sufficiently comprehensive to supplant § 1983." *Blessing*, 520 U.S. at 347 (citing *Sea Clammers*, 453 U.S. 1, and Smith v. Robinson, 468 U.S. 992 (1984), *superceded by statute*, 20 U.S.C. § 1415)....

After reviewing *Sea Clammers* and *Smith v. Robinson*, the Court cautioned that "we have [] stressed that a plaintiff's ability to invoke § 1983 *cannot be defeated simply by 'the availability of administrative mechanisms to protect the plaintiff's interests.'*" *Id.* (quoting *Golden State*, 493 U.S. at 106)(emphasis added)....

Based on my review of applicable Supreme Court precedent, I conclude that the enforcement scheme created by the EPA hardly qualifies as "an elaborate enforcement provision" such as those which the Supreme Court considered in *Sea Clammers* and *Robinson v. Smith*. For example, the statute which was the subject of the litigation in *Sea Clammers* [the Clean Water Act] contained detailed procedural provisions for citizen suits to be brought under the statute, which plaintiffs in that case had ignored, including notice requirements which mandated that plaintiffs notify the EPA before filing suit. *Sea Clammers*, 453 U.S. at 8; *see also* 28 U.S.C. § 1331, 33 U.S.C. §§ 1415(g) and 1365(b)(1)(A). In contrast, Congress did not create such a scheme in Title VI, but instead included a general provision for the termination of federal funding, and deferred to federal agencies to articulate standards for compliance with Title VI's anti-discrimination provisions. *See* 42 U.S.C. § 2000d-1. In *Wright*, 479 U.S. at 428, the Supreme Court specifically held that the power to terminate funding is a "generalized power" which is "insufficient to indicate a congressional intention to foreclose § 1983 remedies." *Id.*; *see also Blessing*, 520 U.S. at 348 (rejecting defendants' claim that Title IV-D of the Social Security Act precluded individual enforcement under § 1983 because it provided only the "limited powers to audit and cut funding").

Furthermore, the EPA's Title VI implementing regulations, while establishing an administrative mechanism for the review of complaints, do not contain any provisions which demonstrate an intent to foreclose individuals from pursuing remedies for alleged violations under § 1983. *See* 40 C.F.R. §§ 7.105–7.135. In fact, EPA's recently issued Draft [Title VI Guidance] recognizes and specifically addresses the possibility that individuals will seek judicial relief to vindicate their right to be free of discrimination caused by the adverse disparate impact of a facially neutral environmental permitting policy implemented by a federally funded agency. *Id.* Paraphrasing the Supreme Court's conclusion in *Wright*, I conclude that not only are Title VI and the EPA's implementing regulations "devoid of any express indication that exclusive enforcement authority was vested in" the EPA, but also that the EPA's actions "indicate that enforcement authority is not centralized and private actions were anticipated." *Wright*, 479 U.S. at 424....

\* \* \*

## Notes and Questions

1. During the Clinton Administration, EPA filed amicus briefs supporting a private right of action to enforce its Title VI regulations, arguing that such a right would not interfere with the agency's enforcement program, and that the remedy will advance the statute's purposes in light of the agency's limited resources. How, if at all, would this be relevant to a court's determination of whether section 1983 permits actions to enforce Title VI's regulations?

2. Other commentators have proposed the possibility of using Title VIII of the Civil Rights of 1968, the Fair Housing Act, to remedy environmental inequities. Professor Colin Crawford has made several observations concerning this potential strategy. Colin Crawford, *Other Civil Rights Titles,* in THE LAW OF ENVIRONMENTAL JUSTICE: THEORIES AND PROCEDURES TO ADDRESS DISPROPORTIONATE RISKS 69 (Michael Gerrard, ed. 1999).

3. As this book went to press, the Third Circuit, upon an expedited review of an appeal of Judge Orlofsky's Supplemental Opinion, reversed his order granting a preliminary injunction against St. Lawrence Cement Company and ruled that § 602 of Title VI cannot be enforced through a private action under § 1983. South Camden Citizens in Action v. New Jersey Department of Environmental Protection, 274 F.3d 771 (3rd. Cir. 2001).

# E. Judicial Interpretation

Assuming that other circuits allow actions under § 1983 alleging that recipient environmental agencies failed to comply with Section 602 of Title VI, are courts likely to find violations of the regulations? If an agency is found in violation, do you think the courts will be more or less inclined to issue injunctive relief than the EPA would be inclined to withdraw funding for it, including funding to administer delegated federal environmental programs? In the Camden case, Judge Orlofsky, applying the *Draft Title VI Guidance,* found a disparate impact and issued an injunction.

## South Camden Citizens in Action v. New Jersey Department of Environmental Protection
### 145 F. Supp. 2d 446 (2001)

*Orlofsky, District Court Judge*

[The case involves an application by SLC for an air permit to operate a facility in the Waterfront South neighborhood of South Camden, New Jersey, that would grind and process granulated blast furnace slug [GBFS]. Plaintiffs had already constructed the facility when the lawsuit was filed.]

*Introduction*

...SLC's proposed facility will emit certain pollutants into the air. These pollutants will include particulate matter (dust), mercury, lead, manganese, nitrogen oxides, carbon monoxide, sulphur oxides and volatile organic compounds. The GBFS will arrive by barge at a Camden port facility. Trucks will then deliver the GBFS to SLC's proposed facility in Waterfront South, a distance of approximately three miles. The GBFS will then be processed and transported back to the port by truck. Annually, there will be approximately 35,000 inbound delivery trucks arriving at SLC's proposed facility and approximately 42,000 outbound truck deliveries departing from the facility. Inbound truck deliveries will occur on about eighty days per year with approximately 500 truck deliveries per day. Outbound truck departures from the SLC facility will occur on approximately 225 days per year, with about 200 trucks departing per day. The contemplated truck routes pass through the Waterfront South Community.

The population of Waterfront South is 2,132, forty-one percent of whom are children. Ninety-one percent of the residents of Waterfront South are persons of color. Specifically, sixty-three percent are African-American, twenty-eight percent are Hispanic, and nine percent are non-Hispanic white. The residents of Waterfront South suffer from a disproportionately high rate of asthma and other respiratory ailments.

The Waterfront South neighborhood is already a popular location for the siting of industrial facilities. It contains the Camden County Municipal Utilities Authority, a sewage treatment plant, the Camden County Resource Recovery facility, a trash-to-steam plant, the Camden Cogen Power Plant, a co-generation plant, and two United States Environmental Protection Agency ("EPA") designated Superfund sites. Four sites within one-half mile of SLC's proposal facility are currently being investigated by the EPA for the possible release of hazardous substances. The NJDEP has also identified fifteen known contaminated sites in the Waterfront South neighborhood.

As described in greater detail in this Court's Findings of Fact and Conclusions of Law set forth below, the NJDEP granted the necessary air permits to SLC to allow its proposed facility to begin operations. In doing so, the NJDEP considered only whether the facility's emissions would exceed technical emissions standards for specific pollutants, especially dust. Indeed, much of what this case is about is what the NJDEP failed to consider. It did not consider the level of ozone generated by the truck traffic to and from the SLC facility, notwithstanding the fact that the Waterfront South community is not currently in compliance with the National Ambient Air Quality Standard ("NAAQS") established by the EPA for ozone levels, nor did it consider the presence of many other pollutants in Waterfront South. It did not consider the pre-existing poor health of the residents of Waterfront South, nor did it consider the cumulative environmental burden already borne by this impoverished community. Finally, and perhaps most importantly, the NJDEP failed to consider the racial and ethnic composition of the population of Waterfront South....

For the reasons which follow in this Court's Findings of Fact and Conclusions of Law made pursuant to Fed. R. Civ. P. 52(a), I conclude that: (1) The NJDEP's failure to consider any evidence beyond SLC's compliance with technical emissions standards, and specifically its failure to consider the totality of the circumstances surrounding the operation of SLC's proposed facility, violates the EPA's regulations promulgated to implement Title VI of the Civil Rights Act of 1964; and (2) Plaintiffs have established a prima facie case of disparate impact discrimination based on race and national origin in violation of the EPA's regulations promulgated pursuant to section 602 of the Civil Rights Act of 1964....

*Findings of Fact and Conclusions of Law*

[The following are selected findings of facts and conclusions of law from the Court's 257 findings and conclusions. Eds.]

- Air contaminant emissions will be generated at the following stages of GBFS processing: (1) fugitive dust emissions will be generated from the handling and movement of GBFS when it is offloaded from trucks, piled, and then placed in the hopper; (2) GBFS particles may be blown into the ambient air once on the conveyor belt; (3) various air pollutants will be produced during the heating and grinding processes; and (4) GBFS emission may occur when the GBFS is stored and offloaded for delivery off-site.

- The City of Camden recently commissioned a study of Waterfront South, and, after analyzing the study results, designated Waterfront South as "an area in need of redevelopment," pursuant to N.J.S.A. §40A:12A-3. The study found that:

  > Properties in [unsanitary, dilapidated or obsolete] condition are not only harmful to themselves, but also constitute a clear and present danger to the surrounding community.... Properties which are deleterious in their use, or are poorly arranged have— or threaten to—become safety and health hazards to their users as well as to those who come in contact (even incidentally) with such properties. Buildings and land which produce air, land or water pollution—particularly radiation—are prime examples of property uses which are detrimental to the community's welfare. Additionally businesses which generate excessive noise, dust, odors, etc. or cause immoderate vehicle traffic (especially trucks) which introduces safety hazards for pedestrians (especially children and the elderly) and other motorist [sic]; and such truck traffic which produce noise and vibrations harmful to the mostly residential structures found on unintended truck routes . . . are examples not only of deleterious land uses but show how faulty or obsolete site design can prove harmful to the rest of the community . . . The dense arrangement of buildings, the close proximity of residential and industrial uses, and unregulated truck traffic makes the spillover effects of noxious manufacturing or related industrial activity . . . detrimental to surrounding property users and residents throughout Waterfront South.

- In his deposition testimony, Dr. [Irwin] Berlin [a health expert] testified that he had been asked by Morris Smith, Esq., consultant for SLC, on behalf of the CAP, to evaluate the overall SLC facility design and emission protections, with specific attention to particulate emissions. In the letter he submitted to Mr. Smith documenting his findings, Dr. Berlin identifies Camden County as a "Community of Concern" ("COC") based on initial findings of a study Dr. Berlin is currently performing regarding the bronchial and lung cancer and asthma rates of residents of New Jersey. The initial findings of Dr. Berlin's study, which are not challenged, indicate that in Camden County:

  1) The age-adjusted cancer rate for black females is higher than 90% of the rest of the state;

  2) The age-adjusted cancer rate for black males is higher than 70% of the rest of the state;

  3) The rate of cancer is significantly higher for black males than for white males;

  4) The age-adjusted rate of death of black females in Camden County from asthma is over three times the rate of death for white females from asthma in Camden County;

  5) The age-adjusted rate of death of black males in Camden County from asthma is over six times the rate of death for white males from asthma in Camden County.

- It is undisputed that, with all proposed emissions controls in place as stated in the permit applications, the SLC facility will emit 59.1 tons of particulate matter size PM-10 or smaller per year. The SLC facility will therefore be in compliance with the current NAAQ standard for PM-10 emissions.

- Plaintiffs contend, however, that mere compliance with the NAAQ standard for PM-10 does not result in the avoidance of adverse health consequences for the residents of Waterfront South who will be exposed to the particulate emissions of the proposed SLC facility. Rather, Plaintiffs argue that: (1) when the totality of the circumstances are considered, the addition of the SLC facility's PM-10 emissions to the existing environmental conditions in Waterfront South will have an adverse impact on the health of residents of Waterfront South; and (2) the portion of PM-10 emitted by the SLC facility which is composed of particulate matter 2.5 microns in diameter or smaller (PM-2.5), although it is not currently regulated by a NAAQ standard, will adversely affect the health of residents of Waterfront South.

- With respect to PM-10 emissions, Dr. Lavietes testified that there is a statistically significant relationship between PM-10 emissions and mortality, even where PM-10 emissions are *well below* the level set by NAAQS. Dr. Lavietes based this conclusion on the results of a recent study conducted by researchers at Johns Hopkins University, published in the New England Journal of Medicine ("Hopkins Study"). (Jonathan Samet, M.D., Francesca Dominici, M.D., Frank C. Curriero, M.D., Ivan Coursac, M.S., and Scott L. Zeger, Ph.D., *Fine Particulate Air Pollution and Mortality in 20 U.S. Cities, 1987–1994*, 343 New Eng. J. Med. 1742 (2000)). According to this study, for every 10 microgram increase per cubic meter of PM-10 levels in a twenty-four hour period, the increase in relative rate of death from all causes was .51 percent, and the increase in rate of death from cardiovascular and pulmonary cases was .68 percent.

- In his certification, Dr. Lavietes testified that PM-2.5, because it is smaller, can lodge more deeply in the lungs than coarser components of PM-10. Dr. Lavietes also testified that it is the most dangerous component of PM-10, and is likely responsible for most of the negative health consequences associated with PM-10.

- The NJDEP responds to Plaintiffs' concerns regarding the SLC facility's potential PM-2.5 emissions by emphasizing that there is currently no NAAQ standard for PM-2.5. Essentially, the NJDEP argues that unless and until the EPA issues a NAAQ standard for PM-2.5, the NJDEP cannot be held responsible for failing to consider whatever adverse health consequences might result from PM-2.5 exposure. The NJDEP maintains this position despite the fact that the NJDEP has noted that "ozone and particulates are New Jersey's two most pervasive air quality problems and more measures need to be taken to ensure that those health standards are attained in future years."

- [T]he NJDEP's argument that it need not consider the adverse effects of PM-2.5 because the EPA has not defined PM-2.5 as dangerous and promulgated a NAAQS is disingenuous. As the NJDEP is well aware, on July 18, 1997, the EPA issued a final agency rule setting new NAAQS for particulate matter, and specifically setting NAAQS for PM-2.5. National Ambient Air Quality Standards for Particulate Matter; Final Rule, 62 Fed. Reg. 38652 (July 18, 1997)(to be codified at 40 C.F.R. §50). Stating that '[t]hese decisions are based on a thorough review…of the latest scientific information on known and potential human health effects associated with exposure to PM at levels typically found in ambient air," the EPA explained that "the most significant new evidence on the health effects

of PM is the greatly expanded body of community epidemiological studies...
[which] provide 'evidence that serious health effects (mortality, exacerbation of
chronic disease, increased hospital admissions, etc.) are associated with exposures to ambient levels of PM found in contemporary U.S. urban airsheds even
at concentrations below current U.S. PM standard." 62 Fed. Reg. 38,652, 38,655.

- The EPA specifically noted that "sensitive subpopulations [] appear to be at
  greater risk to such effects, specifically individuals with respiratory disease and
  cardiovascular disease and the elderly (premature mortality and hospitaliza-
  tion), children (increased respiratory symptoms and decreased lung function),
  and asthmatic children and adults (aggravation of symptoms)." 62 Fed. Reg.
  38,652, 38,656.

- SLC, through the CAP TAG, commissioned a study of existing and carbon
  monoxide emissions along the truck route to be used by the SLC delivery
  trucks. The study found that the SLC truck traffic would not cause an exceedence of the carbon monoxide NAAQS in the area. The study did not analyze
  the impact of the SLC facility or the SLC truck traffic on ozone.

- Given the large volume of truck traffic which will be traveling to and from the
  SLC facility, NJDEP's failure to give any consideration whatsoever to the potential increase in ozone levels in an area which is in non-attainment with the existing ozone NAAQS, I find NJDEP's argument to be disingenuous. In these
  circumstances, it is clear that ozone levels will only get worse, not better.

- The results of the modeling revealed that the PM-10 emissions generated by
  the proposed SLC facility would not exceed the NAAQS for PM-10 established
  by the EPA....

- SLC was not required to, nor did it, model the emissions of particulate matter
  2.5 microns or less, or PM-2.5. As I explained earlier, PM-2.5 is a smaller component of PM-10. PM-2.5 is included in any measurement of PM-10, however,
  SLC did not collect or analyze data which would indicate what percentage of
  SLC's PM-10 emissions is composed of PM-2.5 or less. Nonetheless, SLC estimates that "approximately half" of the PM-10 emissions which the proposed
  facility will generate will be PM-2.5 emissions....

- [The] NJDEP's insistence that its obligation to Plaintiffs under Title VI does
  not go beyond ensuring compliance with the NAAQS is completely undermined by the NJDEP's own recognition, in numerous fora, that it has precisely such an obligation under Title VI. On October 22, 1998, NJDEP Commissioner Shinn issued the first of several Administrative Orders
  acknowledging the NJDEP's obligation under Title VI. In this Administrative
  Order, Commissioner Shinn established the NJDEP's "Advisory Council on
  Environmental Equity" ("Advisory Council"). The NJDEP defined "environmental equity" as "the fair and equitable treatment in environmental decision-making of the citizens of all New Jersey communities regardless of race,
  color, income, or national origin. Fair and equitable treatment means that no
  population should bear disproportionate amounts of adverse health and environmental effects."...

- Furthermore in early 2000, Commissioner Shinn issued Administrative Order
  2000–01, which took effect immediately. In this Administrative Order, Commissioner Shinn discussed responsibilities of the Advisory Council and identi-

fied "environmental equity implementation strategies" to be implemented by the NJDEP....

- It is the Court's understanding that none of the policies or procedures referred to in the Administrative Orders have been implemented. Counsel for the NJDEP did not cite or otherwise describe or refer to any of the policies, the grant, or the administrative orders the Court has just described above. Indeed, when asked if she had any understanding of New Jersey's Environmental Equity Program, Dr. Atay, Chief of the NJDEP's Bureau of Air Quality Control and Hearing Officer for the SLC permit, stated that she had "none."

- It is uncontested that the NJDEP's permitting policy is facially neutral. The NJDEP uses a complicated system, including air dispersion modeling, to predict the level and pattern of pollutant emissions from a proposed facility such as the SLC facility. The NJDEP then compares these results to the federally established NAAQS, set by the EPA, for the particular pollutants which will be produced by the facility. As counsel for the NJDEP explained at oral argument, once the NJDEP reaches the conclusion that a proposed facility will be in compliance with the NAAQS, the NJDEP's inquiry into the environmental impacts of the facility stops, and the NJDEP will issue a permit to operate the proposed facility.

- Plaintiffs contend that the operation of the proposed facility will adversely impact them in several ways. After reviewing the record, I have determined that the primary adverse impacts of which Plaintiffs complain are impacts to the health of the residents who live in the Waterfront South neighborhood where the proposed SLC facility is located. While Plaintiffs also complain of adverse effects to their quality of life, caused by the noise, vibrations and dirt associated with the truck traffic which will traverse the neighborhood if the facility becomes operational, I have concluded that the record in this case is insufficient to support such a claim. Accordingly, I shall deny Plaintiffs' request for a preliminary injunction to the extent that it is based on the alleged adverse impact of the operation of the SLC facility on Plaintiffs' quality of life.

- While the EPA's method of analysis in *Select Steel* is instructive here, the circumstances of *Select Steel*, which led the EPA to conclude there was no adversity, are entirely distinguishable from the present case. First, the area of concern in *Select Steel* was in compliance for all relevant NAAQS; in contrast, it is undisputed that Camden County is in "severe nonattainment" of the established ozone NAAQS. Second, both MDEQ and the EPA OCR [Office of Civil Rights], in investigating the complainants' Title VI concerns, looked beyond mere compliance with the NAAQS and considered community-specific health data before determining that the facility would not adversely affect the residents' health. Third, the EPA examined the cumulative environmental burdens on the community, based on data from the TRI, before concluding that the aggregate effect of these pollutants would not adversely effect the residents' health. Only after this comprehensive review of community-specific data did the EPA OCR reach its conclusion that the MDEQ's decision to permit the facility did not violate Title VI.

- ...Specifically, the Draft Revised Investigation Guidance advises that the EPA OCR will begin investigation of Title VI complaints by determining the "universe of sources" affecting the complainant community, including not only those pollutants identified with the permitted activities, but also other sources of environmental stressors. 65 Fed. Reg. 39,650, 39,678. Significantly, the Guidance notes that even actions which are not explicitly covered by the permitting program, such as, for example, the diesel truck emissions in the present case, should be considered as part of the adverse disparate impact analysis, as long as the recipient of EPA funds, in this case, the NJDEP, has some obligation or authority concerning those sources. 65 Fed. Reg. 39,650, 39,678.

- The NJDEP did not oppose Plaintiffs' claim of disparity, nor did the NJDEP respond to the data submitted by Dr. Gelobter. The NJDEP simply terminated its analysis of Plaintiffs' disparate impact claim at the point that the NJDEP determined that the SLC facility would not have an "adverse" impact because it would not cause an exceedence of the PM-10 NAAQS.

- SLC, however, briefed the causation issue at length. SLC contends that based on Dr. Gelobter's analysis, Plaintiffs make an "unsubstantiated leap" to the conclusion that the NJDEP's permitting process is causally linked to the admitted disparity in the distribution of industrial facilities in the State of New Jersey. According to SLC, this Court must reject Dr. Gelobter's data on causation because he failed to consider all of the factors that could account for the siting of industrial facilities in particular areas, such as access to transportation, existing infrastructure, and available labor force. Thus, SLC asserts that "even assuming the statistical evidence that Plaintiffs have produced is accurate, those statistics are not the result of some defect in NJDEP's permitting process, but are rather the result of hundreds, if not thousands, of individual siting decisions made by private entities searching on the basis of sound business principles for the most appropriate locations for their industrial facilities."

- I reject SLC's argument for several reasons. First, this Court has already concluded that there is in fact a severe "defect" in the NJDEP's permitting process, namely, that the NJDEP relies exclusively on compliance with environmental regulations such as the NAAQS, without considering its obligations under Title VI, in issuing permits such as those it issued for the proposed SLC facility.

- [A] review of the applicable regulations promulgated by the EPA clearly indicates that the EPA has determined that there is a causal connection between recipients' permitting practices and the distribution of polluting facilities, and enacted the implementing regulations to Title VI to ensure that recipients consider the potential disparate impact of their permitting decisions. *See* 40 C.F.R. § 7.1 *et. seq.* In other words, the EPA has acknowledged that because recipients are responsible for permitting, they are also responsible for considering the distribution of the facilities which they permit with respect to the classes protected by the Civil Rights Act of 1964. The regulations therefore support the conclusion that a recipient's permitting decisions are causally linked to the distribution of facilities as a matter of law.

- [A]fter reviewing the expert testimony submitted by both Plaintiffs and SLC on the issue of causation, and the facts of this case, I have concluded that the Plaintiffs have carried their prima facie burden of demonstrating that the NJDEP's permitting practices are causally linked to the adverse, disparate impact about which Plaintiffs complain.

- The NJDEP did not specifically address the issue of justification, again, because it terminated its disparate impact analysis, with the conclusion that the proposed SLC facility would not violate the PM-10 NAAQS and therefore would not "adversely" affect Plaintiffs. To the extent that the NJDEP might argue that the proposed facility's compliance with the NAAQS constitutes a substantial, legitimate justification for its permitting decision, I have already explained that I reject that reasoning because it is based exclusively on an analysis of environmental regulations and does not include considerations required by Title VI.

- Plaintiffs contend that the NJDEP will not be harmed by the issuance of an injunction, because the injunction which Plaintiffs request only requires the NJDEP to meet its existing obligations under Title VI. Plaintiffs concede that SLC will suffer economic injury if an injunction issues, but argue that SLC assumed this risk by beginning construction of the proposed facility over a year before the NJDEP issued the permits, which were not issued until October 31, 2000. Furthermore, Plaintiffs argue that SLC was aware, due to Plaintiffs' frequent protests, that Plaintiffs believed the NJDEP had not complied with the requirements of Title VI and that disagreements over the permitting process raised the possibility of civil rights litigation. Finally, Plaintiffs note that the NJDEP advised SLC, by letter dated September 2, 1999, well before SLC began construction, that "due to the fact that St. Lawrence will be operating in an economically depressed area which has a substantial minority population, the Department will evaluate the need to conduct a Environmental Justice analysis."

- SLC argues that the granting of preliminary injunctive relief as requested by Plaintiffs will cause immeasurable harm to SLC and will "thwart" the public interest. The harm alleged by SLC is entirely economic. Specifically, SLC argues that it has expended more than $50 million to construct the facility, and will lose $200,000 for each week that the facility does not operate. The Third Circuit has held, however, that purely economic injury is not irreparable harm....

- ...SLC's argument misconstrues the relief which Plaintiffs have requested and which I am granting. I am not "revoking" SLC's permits, but rather enjoining SLC from operating under the permits until the NJDEP performs an appropriate adverse disparate impact analysis in compliance with Title VI. While I have concluded, based on the evidence in the record before me, that Plaintiffs have established a likelihood of success on the merits that the permitting of the SLC facility will have an adverse, disparate impact in violation of Title VI, I have done so only in the context of issuing a preliminary injunction. It is now up to the NJDEP in the first instance to reevaluate its permitting decision with respect to the SLC facility after conducting the requisite adverse, disparate impact analysis.

* * *

## Notes and Questions

1. The court in *South Camden Citizens* says that the case is distinguishable from EPA's *Select Steel* administrative ruling, excerpted above. Do you agree? Or do you think that the court interpreted Title VI differently than EPA's Office of Civil Rights, for instance rejecting the NJDEP's argument that because the project would not result in a violation of the NAAQS for particulate emissions, there was no adverse impact on community members?

2. What factors are most significant in the Court's holding that defendant likely violated Title VI? The Court at one point notes that it is undisputed that the NJDEP's per-

mitting policy is facially neutral, yet it later finds that NJDEP's permitting activities have contributed to the racially disparate distribution of industrial facilities in New Jersey. How could the court reach both of these conclusions?

3. *South Camden Citizens* is one of the most important Title VI environmental justice cases decided by the courts as of December 2001, and the only one that specifically applies EPA's *Draft Title VI Guidance* to the facts at issue. Two other Title VI decisions are Goshen Road v. USDA, 1999 U.S. App. Lexis 6135 (an unpublished 4th Circuit decision), in which the court rejected a Title VI challenge to a wastewater treatment siting because plaintiffs failed to identify equally effective alternatives, and New York City Environmental Justice Alliance v. Giuliani, 214 F.3d 65 (2d Cir. 2000), in which the court rejected a Title VI challenge to New York City's sale of city-owned lots containing community gardens because plaintiffs failed to show adequately measured adverse impacts from the City's actions, or the existence of less discriminatory alternatives.

4. As you contemplate the arduous attempt to develop standards and a methodology to determine the point where disparate environmental impacts become actionable as a civil rights issue—in light of the significantly different processes and remedies afforded under administrative investigations and court adjudications—how do you rate the success of civil rights laws in addressing environmental justice?

# Chapter XV

# Interagency Initiatives and Collaboration as a Response

Because environmental justice is such a cross cutting issue, addressing the roots of environmental disparities requires a broad effort encompassing public and private actors in many fields and at different levels of governance. Some view these voluntary collaborative efforts as a welcome alternative to litigation, while others view such strategies as a complement to but not replacement of more traditional methods of enforcement of laws through litigation. In any event, there are special problems encountered when agencies reach across jurisdictional lines, when public and private actors attempt to jointly address difficult problems, and when problems are addressed on a local or regional scale. This chapter examines the emergence of this strategy and some of the interagency and collaborative initiatives that have been undertaken to date. We begin with the Executive Order on Environmental Justice, which seeks to enlist all federal agencies in the battle to achieve environmental justice. We then examine what the responses of federal agencies has been so far to the Order. The second section looks at some specific collaborative multiple agency and public/private demonstration projects. We then take a brief look at steps that various states have taken in the environmental justice area, and conclude with a proposal for environmental justice legislation.

## A. The Executive Order on Environmental Justice

### Executive Order 12898:
### Federal Actions To Address Environmental Justice in Minority Populations and Low-Income Populations
February 11, 1994

*Section 1-1. Implementation.*

1-101. Agency Responsibilities. To the greatest extent practicable and permitted by law, and consistent with the principles set forth in the report on the National Performance Review, each Federal agency shall make achieving environmental justice part of its mission by identifying and addressing, as appropriate, disproportionately high and adverse human health or environmental effects of its programs, policies, and activities on minority populations and low-income populations in the United States and its territories and possessions, the District of Columbia, the Commonwealth of Puerto Rico, and the Commonwealth of the Mariana Islands.

1-102. Creation of an Interagency Working Group on Environmental Justice.

(a) Within 3 months of the date of this order, the Administrator of the Environmental Protection Agency ("Administrator") or the Administrator's designee shall convene an interagency Federal Working Group on Environmental Justice ("Working Group"). The Working Group shall comprise the heads of the following executive agencies and offices, or their designees: (a) Department of Defense; (b) Department of Health and Human Services; (c) Department of Housing and Urban Development; (d) Department of Labor; (e) Department of Agriculture; (f) Department of Transportation; (g) Department of Justice; (h) Department of the Interior; (i) Department of Commerce; (j) Department of Energy; (k) Environmental Protection Agency; (l) Office of Management and Budget; (m) Office of Science and Technology Policy; (n) Office of the Deputy Assistant to the President for Environmental Policy; (o) Office of the Assistant to the President for Domestic Policy; (p) National Economic Council; (q) Council of Economic Advisers; and (r) such other Government officials as the President may designate. The Working Group shall report to the President through the Deputy Assistant to the President for Environmental Policy and the Assistant to the President for Domestic Policy.

(b) The Working Group shall:

(1) provide guidance to Federal agencies on criteria for identifying disproportionately high and adverse human health or environmental effects on minority populations and low-income populations;

(2) coordinate with, provide guidance to, and serve as a clearinghouse for, each Federal agency as it develops an environmental justice strategy as required by section 1-103 of this order, in order to ensure that the administration, interpretation and enforcement of programs, activities and policies are undertaken in a consistent manner;

(3) assist in coordinating research by, and stimulating cooperation among, the Environmental Protection Agency, the Department of Health and Human Services, the Department of Housing and Urban Development, and other agencies conducting research or other activities in accordance with section 3-3 of this order;

(4) assist in coordinating data collection, required by this order;

(5) examine existing data and studies on environmental justice;

(6) hold public meetings as required in section 5-502(d) of this order; and

(7) develop interagency model projects on environmental justice that evidence cooperation among Federal agencies.

1-103. Development of Agency Strategies.

(a) Except as provided in section 6-605 of this order, each Federal agency shall develop an agency-wide environmental justice strategy, as set forth in subsections (b)–(e) of this section that identifies and addresses disproportionately high and adverse human health or environmental effects of its programs, policies, and activities on minority populations and low-income populations. The environmental justice strategy shall list programs, policies, planning and public participation processes, enforcement, and/or rulemakings related to human health or the environment that should be revised to, at a minimum:

(1) promote enforcement of all health and environmental statutes in areas with minority populations and low-income populations;

(2) ensure greater public participation;

(3) improve research and data collection relating to the health of and environment of minority populations and low-income populations; and

(4) identify differential patterns of consumption of natural resources among minority populations and low-income populations. In addition, the environmental justice strategy shall include, where appropriate, a timetable for undertaking identified revisions and consideration of economic and social implications of the revisions.

(b) Within 4 months of the date of this order, each Federal agency shall identify an internal administrative process for developing its environmental justice strategy, and shall inform the Working Group of the process.

(c) Within 6 months of the date of this order, each Federal agency shall provide the Working Group with an outline of its proposed environmental justice strategy.

(d) Within 10 months of the date of this order, each Federal agency shall provide the Working Group with its proposed environmental justice strategy.

(e) Within 12 months of the date of this order, each Federal agency shall finalize its environmental justice strategy and provide a copy and written description of its strategy to the Working Group. During the 12 month period from the date of this order, each Federal agency, as part of its environmental justice strategy, shall identify several specific projects that can be promptly undertaken to address particular concerns identified during the development of the proposed environmental justice strategy, and a schedule for implementing those projects.

(f) Within 24 months of the date of this order, each Federal agency shall report to the Working Group on its progress in implementing its agency-wide environmental justice strategy.

(g) Federal agencies shall provide additional periodic reports to the Working Group as requested by the Working Group.

1-104. Reports to the President. Within 14 months of the date of this order, the Working Group shall submit to the President, through the Office of the Deputy Assistant to the President for Environmental Policy and the Office of the Assistant to the President for Domestic Policy, a report that describes the implementation of this order, and includes the final environmental justice strategies described in section 1-103(e) of this order.

*Sec. 2-2. Federal Agency Responsibilities for Federal Programs.*

Each Federal agency shall conduct its programs, policies, and activities that substantially affect human health or the environment, in a manner that ensures that such programs, policies, and activities do not have the effect of excluding persons (including populations) from participation in, denying persons (including populations) the benefits of, or subjecting persons (including populations) to discrimination under, such programs, policies, and activities, because of their race, color, or national origin.

*Sec. 3-3. Research, Data Collection, and Analysis.*

3-301. Human Health and Environmental Research and Analysis.

(a) Environmental human health research, whenever practicable and appropriate, shall include diverse segments of the population in epidemiological and clinical studies, including segments at high risk from environmental hazards, such as minority populations, low-income populations and workers who may be exposed to substantial environmental hazards.

(b) Environmental human health analyses, whenever practicable and appropriate, shall identify multiple and cumulative exposures.

(c) Federal agencies shall provide minority populations and low-income populations the opportunity to comment on the development and design of research strategies undertaken pursuant to this order.

3-302. Human Health and Environmental Data Collection and Analysis. To the extent permitted by existing law, including the Privacy Act, as amended (5 U.S.C. section 552a):

(a) Each Federal agency, whenever practicable and appropriate, shall collect, maintain, and analyze information assessing and comparing environmental and human health risks borne by populations identified by race, national origin, or income. To the extent practical and appropriate, Federal agencies shall use this information to determine whether their programs, policies, and activities have disproportionately high and adverse human health or environmental effects on minority populations and low-income populations;

(b) In connection with the development and implementation of agency strategies in section 1-103 of this order, each Federal agency, whenever practicable and appropriate, shall collect, maintain and analyze information on the race, national origin, income level, and other readily accessible and appropriate information for areas surrounding facilities or sites expected to have a substantial environmental, human health, or economic effect on the surrounding populations, when such facilities or sites become the subject of a substantial Federal environmental administrative or judicial action. Such information shall be made available to the public, unless prohibited by law; and

(c) Each Federal agency, whenever practicable and appropriate, shall collect, maintain, and analyze information on the race, national origin, income level, and other readily accessible and appropriate information for areas surrounding Federal facilities that are: (1) subject to the reporting requirements under the Emergency Planning and Community Right-to-Know Act, 42 U.S.C. section 11001–11050 as mandated in Executive Order No. 12856; and (2) expected to have a substantial environmental, human health, or economic effect on surrounding populations. Such information shall be made available to the public, unless prohibited by law.

(d) In carrying out the responsibilities in this section, each Federal agency, whenever practicable and appropriate, shall share information and eliminate unnecessary duplication of efforts through the use of existing data systems and cooperative agreements among Federal agencies and with State, local, and tribal governments.

*Sec. 4-4. Subsistence Consumption of Fish and Wildlife.*

4-401. Consumption Patterns. In order to assist in identifying the need for ensuring protection of populations with differential patterns of subsistence consumption of fish and wildlife, Federal agencies, whenever practicable and appropriate, shall collect, maintain, and analyze information on the consumption patterns of populations who principally rely on fish and/or wildlife for subsistence. Federal agencies shall communicate to the public the risks of those consumption patterns.

4-402. Guidance. Federal agencies, whenever practicable and appropriate, shall work in a coordinated manner to publish guidance reflecting the latest scientific information available concerning methods for evaluating the human health risks associated with the consumption of pollutant-bearing fish or wildlife. Agencies shall consider such guidance in developing their policies and rules.

*Sec. 5-5. Public Participation and Access to Information.*

(a) The public may submit recommendations to Federal agencies relating to the incorporation of environmental justice principles into Federal agency programs or policies. Each Federal agency shall convey such recommendations to the Working Group.

(b) Each Federal agency may, whenever practicable and appropriate, translate crucial public documents, notices, and hearings relating to human health or the environment for limited English speaking populations.

(c) Each Federal agency shall work to ensure that public documents, notices, and hearings relating to human health or the environment are concise, understandable, and readily accessible to the public.

(d) The Working Group shall hold public meetings, as appropriate, for the purpose of fact-finding, receiving public comments, and conducting inquiries concerning environmental justice. The Working Group shall prepare for public review a summary of the comments and recommendations discussed at the public meetings.

*Sec. 6-6. General Provisions.*

6-601. Responsibility for Agency Implementation. The head of each Federal agency shall be responsible for ensuring compliance with this order. Each Federal agency shall conduct internal reviews and take such other steps as may be necessary to monitor compliance with this order.

6-602. Executive Order No. 12250. This Executive order is intended to supplement but not supersede Executive Order No. 12250, which requires consistent and effective implementation of various laws prohibiting discriminatory practices in programs receiving Federal financial assistance. Nothing herein shall limit the effect or mandate of Executive Order No. 12250.

6-603. Executive Order No. 12875. This Executive order is not intended to limit the effect or mandate of Executive Order No. 12875.

6-604. Scope. For purposes of this order, Federal agency means any agency on the Working Group, and such other agencies as may be designated by the President, that conducts any Federal program or activity that substantially affects human health or the environment. Independent agencies are requested to comply with the provisions of this order.

6-605. Petitions for Exemptions. The head of a Federal agency may petition the President for an exemption from the requirements of this order on the grounds that all or some of the petitioning agency's programs or activities should not be subject to the requirements of this order.

6-606. Native American Programs. Each Federal agency responsibility set forth under this order shall apply equally to Native American programs. In addition, the Department of the Interior, in coordination with the Working Group, and, after consultation with tribal leaders, shall coordinate steps to be taken pursuant to this order that address Federally-recognized Indian Tribes.

6-607. Costs. Unless otherwise provided by law, Federal agencies shall assume the financial costs of complying with this order.

6-608. General. Federal agencies shall implement this order consistent with, and to the extent permitted by, existing law.

6-609. Judicial Review. This order is intended only to improve the internal management of the executive branch and is not intended to, nor does it create any right, benefit, or trust responsibility, substantive or procedural, enforceable at law or equity by a party against the United States, its agencies, its officers, or any person. This order shall not be construed to create any right to judicial review involving the compliance or noncompliance of the United States, its agencies, its officers, or any other person with this order.

* * *

President Clinton issued the following memorandum simultaneously with the Executive Order.

# Memorandum on Environmental Justice
## February 11, 1994

*Memorandum for the Heads of All Departments and Agencies*

*Subject:* Executive Order on Federal Actions To Address Environmental Justice in Minority Populations and Low-Income Populations

Today I have issued an Executive order on Federal Actions to Address Environmental Justice in Minority Populations and Low-Income Populations. That order is designed to focus Federal attention on the environmental and human health conditions in minority communities and low-income communities with the goal of achieving environmental justice. That order is also intended to promote nondiscrimination in Federal programs substantially affecting human health and the environment, and to provide minority communities and low-income communities access to public information on, and an opportunity for public participation in, matters relating to human health or the environment.

The purpose of this separate memorandum is to underscore certain provisions of existing law that can help ensure that all communities and persons across this Nation live in a safe and healthful environment. Environmental and civil rights statutes provide many opportunities to address environmental hazards in minority communities and low-income communities. Application of these existing statutory provisions is an important part of this Administration's efforts to prevent those minority communities and low-income communities from being subject to disproportionately high and adverse environmental effects.

I am therefore today directing that all department and agency heads take appropriate and necessary steps to ensure that the following specific directives are implemented immediately:

In accordance with Title VI of the Civil Rights Act of 1964, each Federal agency shall ensure that all programs or activities receiving Federal financial assistance that affect human health or the environment do not directly, or through contractual or other arrangements, use criteria, methods, or practices that discriminate on the basis of race, color, or national origin.

Each federal agency shall analyze the environmental effects, including human health, economic and social effects, of Federal actions, including effects on minority communities and low-income communities, when such analysis is required by the National Environmental Policy Act of 1969 (NEPA), 42 U.S.C. section 4321 *et seq.* Mitigation measures outlined or analyzed in an environmental assessment, environmental impact statement, or record of decision, whenever feasible, should address significant and adverse environmental effects of proposed Federal actions on minority communities and low-income communities.

Each Federal agency shall provide opportunities for community input in the NEPA process, including identifying potential effects and mitigation measures in consultation with affected communities and improving the accessibility of meetings, crucial documents, and notices.

The Environmental Protection Agency, when reviewing environmental effects of proposed action of other Federal agencies under section 309 of the Clean Air Act, 42 U.S.C. section 7609, shall ensure that the involved agency has fully analyzed environmental effects on minority communities and low-income communities, including human health, social, and economic effects.

Each Federal agency shall ensure that the public, including minority communities and low-income communities, has adequate access to public information relating to human health or environmental planning, regulations, and enforcement when required under the Freedom of Information Act, 5 U.S.C. section 552, the Sunshine Act, 5 U.S.C. section 552b, and the Emergency Planning and Community Right-to-Know Act, 42 U.S.C. section 1104....

This memorandum is intended only to improve the internal management of the Executive Branch and is not intended to nor does it create, any right, benefit, or trust responsibility, substantive or procedural, enforceable at law or equity by a party against the United States, its agencies, its officers, or any person.

/s/ William J. Clinton

## Notes and Questions

1. An important limitation of the Executive Order on Environmental Justice (EJ Executive Order) is section 6-608, an express provision stating that the Order does not create any new rights enforceable at law or equity, a provision common to such orders. Of what practical value is the Order given this limitation? Assuming the order is intended to signal administrative policy at the highest level, do you think it will accomplish its goal?

2. Section 1-103 of the EJ Executive Order sets forth a strict initial time table for federal agencies to develop an environmental justice strategy. Thereafter, the order require "periodic" reporting to the Interagency Working Group. Why do you think these provisions were included?

3. If the executive order is not rescinded, are federal officials under administrations subsequent to President Clinton's obligated to follow it?

4. In the memorandum accompanying the EJ Executive Order, former President Clinton indicated that use of existing environmental and civil rights statutes is an important part of his Administration's efforts to promote environmental justice. How do you assess the success of this effort? At the end of the Clinton Administration, a group of law professors sought to survey the actions of federal agencies in responding to the

executive order. The survey, intended to provide information that was descriptive rather than analytical, nonetheless provided interesting insights into the ways agencies sought to accomplish the goals of the Order, as reflected in the excerpt below.

# Denis Binder, Colin Crawford, Eileen Gauna, M. Casey Jarman, Alice Kaswan, Bradford C. Mank, Catherine A. O'Neill, Clifford Rechtschaffen, and Robert R. M. Verchick, A Survey of Federal Agency Responses to President Clinton's Executive Order 12898 on Environmental Justice,

### 31 Environmental Law Reporter 11,133 (2001)

[Executive Order 12898 (EO)] has been in effect for seven years.... [A group of environmental law professors] prepared a survey for selected federal agencies to assess the governmental response to the EO. The agencies surveyed are the Departments of Agriculture (USDA), Energy (DOE), Interior (DOI) Justice (DOJ), and Transportation (DOT), EPA, the Department of Housing and Urban Development (HUD), and the National Institute of Environmental Health Sciences (NIEHS)....The purpose of the survey is not only to measure the response of selected federal agencies, but also to assess the impact of the EO, to wit, has it had a substantive impact, or is it merely of symbolic significance?...

A preliminary caveat is necessary. The agency responses are self-reporting and self-described. We accepted their responses and reports at face value and did not seek to independently verify whether they were accurate, inaccurate, or over- or under-inclusive....Several other preliminary observations are in order. First, no agency claims to have dropped any specific environmentally harmful project because of environmental justice (hereinafter EJ) concerns. However, the situation may be, as expressed by the DOT, that EJ concerns are considered in the front end of the planning process. In this respect, increased sensitivity, at the beginning of the planning stage, will result in EJ benefits, which might not otherwise have occurred....

Second,...the effectiveness of a program or goal often depends upon the tone set at the top of the agency....Clear leadership and direction at the Secretarial level is important both in implementing the goals of the EO and in being able to assess the effectiveness of the agency's response....

Third, most agency efforts are directed at the broader definition of EJ—the delivery of environmentally related services to poor and minority communities. Many of these activities seem to partake more of the nature of traditional anti-poverty efforts and the providing of services aimed at everyday environmental problems and children's health issues, such as lead paint poisoning, rather than the large siting problems. These efforts are a significant step in furthering the goals of the EO. The EO was a catalyst in getting agencies to assess what they were doing—a necessary, preliminary step. Such actions are, however, only the first in a series of actions envisioned by the EO.

Fourth, federal agencies have clearly made substantial progress to increase, improve, or refine public participation in information gathering and dissemination, if not in decisionmaking. Almost every agency reports substantial community outreach and involvement in the form of workshops, information sessions, publications, and grants.

EPA, HUD, NIEHS and USDA publish materials in languages other than English. EPA, DOE, and DOI have web pages that address EJ. DOE and USDA have provided computers and technical training to low-income and minority communities.

Fifth, the number of federal employees working full-time on EJ issues appears very limited—indeed, almost non-existent. Many agencies, however, report that a number of employees spend a greater or lesser amount of their work on EJ issues....Finally, and significantly, the number of agencies reporting assessments of their EJ activities was small. Even when an annual report was initially prepared, follow up reports were lacking. This lack of assessment makes it difficult to fully evaluate how agencies are implementing the EO, and to compare agencies....

### Interagency Coordination

Section 1-102 of the EO created the Federal Interagency Working Group on Environmental Justice (IWG), which is chaired by the Administrator of EPA. The IWG, in 1999, established an Integrated Federal Interagency Environmental Justice Action Agenda (Action Agenda), pursuant to which a number of demonstration projects have been undertaken to promote EJ. EPA's Office of Environmental Justice (OEJ) published, in November 2000, a report on the success of the Action Agenda. The report describes 15 demonstration projects in which two or more federal agencies are working together with state, local and tribal governments, private partners, and community representatives to address EJ challenges in meaningful ways....

All the federal agencies identified in the EO (the USDA, the U.S. Departments of Commerce and Defense, DOE, the U.S. Department of Health and Human Services (HHS), HUD, the DOI, the DOJ, the DOT, EPA, and the U.S. Department of Labor) are meeting regularly to exchange information on how they can work together and implement EJ initiatives within their respective programs....

### Programmatic Impacts

The programmatic impacts of EO 12898 have varied by agency. For example, EPA views Title VI [of the Civil Rights Act] as the center of the Agency's EJ programs. Significantly, EPA created the OCR [Office of Civil Rights] to address Title VI and other discrimination issues. On the other hand, no consistent EJ program or programs are characteristic of the DOI. The DOT issued a department-wide order incorporating Title VI as part of its official policy and practices. EJ concerns are incorporated into the decision-making processes of the Federal Highway Administration (FHwA) and the Federal Transportation Administration (FTA). The DOT's emphasis is to put EJ considerations into the front end of the planning process....Similar to the DOT, HUD integrates EJ considerations into existing programs....

### Grants

A strong overlap exists with community outreach programs and agency grants. DOE, EPA, HUD, and NIEHS report the issuance of scores of grants to community-based organizations and academic institutions....

### Individual Federal Agencies

#### EPA

...EPA's OEJ plays a primary role in implementing the EO by providing grants to community groups, assisting other EPA departments with equity issues, and coordinating a large number of interagency activities. For example, OEJ has provided over 800 EJ grants of between $10,000 and $20,000 to local community-based groups since 1994....

EPA has awarded several larger grants as part of its brownfield programs to promote voluntary private cleanups of moderately contaminated properties....The Agency has awarded over $157 million for various brownfield projects since 1993, not including additional millions for revolving loan funds or job training.

EPA has initiated many actions to increase public participation by low-income and minority groups, including translating documents into languages other than English.... On December 28, 2000, EPA published a Draft Public Involvement Policy (*Draft Policy*), which is intended to update the Agency's 1981 *Public Participation Policy*. For example, the new *Draft Policy* discusses the use of the internet and web pages to disseminate information. The *Draft Policy* is designed to encourage public participation. It is not binding, however; instead, it "relies heavily on the sound use of discretion by Agency officials." The six-step public participation process described in the *Draft Policy* is similar to that established in 1981, but the new approach places greater emphasis on early outreach and consultation actions by Agency officials with a broad range of stakeholders....

Many of EPA's activities entail noncontroversial activities, such as awarding community grants and translating documents. The Agency has been less likely to take stands that industry or state officials might oppose. EPA has, for example, spent much more on brownfield redevelopment than on EJ projects, or on reform of the permitting process and the establishment of more protective standards.

EJ became a significant component of EPA's permit review process when the independent U.S. Environmental Appeals Board (EAB) held EPA has a duty to apply EJ whenever it has the discretionary authority to do so. The EAB has reviewed 10 cases involving the EO. [See Chapter VIII. Eds.]...Although the board allowed affected citizens to raise EJ issues in the appeals, the EAB denied relief to them in every case....

EPA's 1995 Environmental Justice Strategy represented that the Agency would use its enforcement discretion to focus on EJ issues raised by violations in communities disproportionately harmed by environmental pollution....However, NEJAC's enforcement subcommittee pointed out that no empirical evidence shows EPA is actually increasing its enforcement efforts in these areas....

[E]PA has not published a comprehensive review of its compliance with the EO since the 1996 report....

## USDA

The USDA promulgated a departmental regulation (DR) on December 15, 1997, DR 5600-2, which outlines the Agency's strategy....DR 5600-2...commits the USDA to providing opportunities for minority and low-income populations to participate in planning and decisionmaking on matters that affects their health or environment....[U]SDA noted it has partially implemented its EO strategy by expanding the criteria for its impact analysis to include racial and ethnic demographics, income levels, health sensitivity, environmental exposures, past regulatory actions and interactions with communities, integration of land use management systems, and subsistence consumption patterns. The Agency has also reported integrating EJ criteria into its technical and financial assistance programs, facility management programs, hazardous materials transportation use and disposal practices, Agency reinvention initiatives, and its Five-Year Strategic Plan and Long-Term Strategic Plan under the Forest and Rangeland Renewable Resources Act....

## DOE

Public participation and EJ were not historically part of DOE's culture. DOE's response to the EO has been to make EJ "part of the fabric of DOE's programs and policies." DOE refocused a number of relevant program activities and implemented procedural changes to meet the challenge of the EO.... [DOE's 1996 Progress Report] listed a large number of environmental cleanup and other projects undertaken or complete, which the DOJ [sic] claimed would benefit the affected communities. However, many of these efforts are traditional environmental cleanup programs mandated by statutes that predate the EO. In addition, some of the projects may have been initiated prior to the issuance of the EO....

## HUD

HUD highlighted four program areas in which EJ considerations are incorporated. The first is its Empowerment Zone and Enterprise Communities (EZ/EC) program, which encourages development in low-income and minority areas suffering from pervasive poverty, high unemployment, and other social ills.... The second area incorporating EJ concerns is HUD's lead-based paint initiative, to which HUD devotes substantial resources.... In general, HUD strives to reduce lead risks to protect children's health, but in a manner that will not jeopardize the availability of low-income housing or cause property owners to abandon high-risk residential properties.... The third area incorporating EJ concerns is that of brownfield cleanups and redevelopment projects. Many poor and minority populations reside in close proximity to abandoned industrial facilities. Efforts to clean up and redevelop these properties are considered critical to improving environmental conditions and revitalizing depressed communities. HUD has therefore worked closely with EPA in various initiatives associated with the cleanup and redevelopment of brownfields. For example, the agencies provide technical assistance to communities on financial, technical, and environmental issues.... The fourth program HUD highlights in connection with EJ is its Colonias program, which aims to provide housing and development needs to the impoverished areas along the U.S.-Mexico border. Many of these communities suffer from a lack of adequate sewer systems, water services, and housing....

## DOI

...Due in part to DOI's decentralized structure, no centralized process is in existence for identifying and tracking EJ-related matters within [the Department's] jurisdiction. The eight bureaus are individually responsible for oversight of EJ matters within their respective jurisdictions. No consistent EJ policies, programs, or themes are characteristic of DOI as a department. Significant variation exists in the way each bureau approaches EJ. The bureaus share information among themselves about their different initiatives....

Many times the EO was a reason, but not the sole reason, a program [by a DOI bureau] was initiated. EJ was simply a piece of the larger whole. For example, the U.S. Geological Survey's annual effort to train faculty at historically black colleges and universities in Geologic Information Systems and other developments in cartography may have been given a push by the existence of the EO, but it was the kind of thing that DOI bureaus were already on schedule to do....

## DOJ

The DOJ's Environmental Justice Strategy, adopted in 1995, sets forth a broad array of lofty objectives for the DOJ, including development of an enforcement strategy "to help ensure that all communities and persons live in a safe and healthful environment"...[and] working with communities so that enforcement actions respond directly to environmental risks....

Efforts in implementing EO 12898 have been modest, but DOJ does sensitize its employees to EJ issues in their case investigation and handling. The DOJ's efforts tend therefore to be ad hoc, depending in considerable degree on the judgment and initiative of individual attorneys. The 1995 Environmental Justice Strategy stated that the DOJ would develop a list of EJ enforcement priorities and a strategy for addressing these priorities. However, it apparently has not done so....

Much of the legal implementation is left to the individual federal attorneys assigned to specific cases. DOJ attorneys are instructed to review each case to determine if it raises EJ issues. They may request more information from a referral agency or obtain relevant demographic data. Attorneys have used SEPs [Supplemental Environmental Projects] in case settlements to mitigate environmental harms in EJ communities.... With the exception of a lead-based paint enforcement initiative, however, the DOJ has not undertaken any targeted EJ investigations or formalized efforts to focus on compliance in EJ communities....

### DOT

The DOT has identified EJ as a "flagship initiative" to ensure it remains a departmental priority. The DOT has created the Environmental Justice Review Committee, which includes senior DOT officials, to further EJ concerns and review the impact of transportation projects on minority communities. The Committee has encouraged other units of DOT to be aware of EJ issues, including the Federal Maritime Administration and the Federal Aviation Administration (FAA), which oversees airport expansion plans....

The DOT has also revised its highway regulations to incorporate EJ concerns into city planning. Metropolitan Planning Organizations (MPO) are now required to incorporate EJ issues in their annual certifications. The addition of EJ concerns to the written MPO certification is a significant step. MPOs must, for example, certify to FHwA and FTA that "the planning process is addressing the major issues facing the areas," that the planning process complies with Title VI and other statutes, and that the metropolitan transportation planning process includes a "proactive public involvement process" that seeks out and considers the needs of those traditionally underserved by existing transportation systems.

While EJ concerns did not appear to play a significant role in the DOT's decision-making in the past, the recent priority given EJ has affected at least two important decisions. Two local MPOs have received conditional certifications, and will not be certified unless they satisfy the DOT as to how they propose to incorporate EJ concerns into the analysis of transportation projects in their region.

The DOT issued a department-wide order on EJ, DOT Order 5610.2, making Title VI part of its official policy and practices.... The most significant and controversial part of the Order,... is §8.... Pursuant to §8, the head of each DOT administration or component must be wary of "adverse effects" on EJ populations, must "determine whether programs, policies, and activities, for which they are responsible, will have an adverse impact on minority and low-income populations, and, if so, whether that adverse impact will be disproportionately high."...

If DOT activity would create such adverse effects, then the conduct may not be pursued unless "further mitigation measures or alternatives, that would avoid or reduce the disproportionately high or adverse effects, are not practical." Agency officials must also show that "less harmful alternatives" would impose other adverse social, economic, environmental, or human health impacts that are more severe or would involve increased costs of "extraordinary magnitude."

The FHwA issued its own EJ order on December 2, 1998, closely paralleling its parent's DOT order. FHWA's order requires its own officials and staff to identify risks of discrimination early so that corrective actions can be taken. The DOT shall inquire into the racial and socio-economic status of affected populations where practical and appropriate, and will consider steps to guard against discriminatory unfairness. The FHA will collect and maintain needed EJ data.

### NIEHS

NIEHS, which is an agency of the HHS [Department of Health and Human Services], had initiated EJ programs prior to the issuance of EO 12898. Programs and conferences have been organized for the past decade. The NIEHS does not conduct specific EJ projects. Instead, it awards grants to community-based organizations and academic institutions. The purposes of the NIEHS-funded EJ research and educational programs are to bring together communities, scientists, and health care providers to improve public health outcomes in at-risk neighborhoods. The NIEHS has four professional level staff, along with additional support staff, primarily engaged in implementation of EJ research programs. Staff have both attended and organized numerous EJ-related programs over the past decade.... 

The NIEHS regularly evaluates the work of its grantees, and significantly, has conducted an evaluation of its total EJ program. It concluded that "the program has been successful in promoting novel community-university partnerships and enabling them to develop future research and intervention strategies....

Community outreach and public participation are key components of the EJ grant programs. EJ related workshops, professional society conferences, and town meetings are regularly sponsored. All-day town meetings are held at least four times a year. Local residents can share their environmental health concerns with high-level staff of NIEHS, including the Director....

### Conclusion

All of the federal agencies surveyed pay homage to EJ to some extent. A few have made major institutional investments in promoting and achieving EJ. Clearly, substantial federal environmental resources are now directed at minority and low-income communities, especially in brownfield development and lead-based paint remediation efforts.... [On the other hand] [m]eaningful community participation in decisionmaking is still lacking in some agencies.

All agencies had an initial burst of energy upon issuance of the EO. Carry through, though, has sometimes been problematic. Perhaps the most critical factor is the level of commitment at the highest levels of an agency. A Secretary or Administrator who makes EJ a priority, follows through with a commitment of resources and strong leadership, and requires accountability by agency employees, will see the agency respond accordingly. No agency has apparently been dragging its feet on the issue, but clearly some stand out in their level of success. EPA, HUD, DOT, and the NIEHS have consistently performed at a higher level. The record at the DOJ and at the DOI has been sporadic. DOE is somewhere in between....

Every agency has considerable discretionary authority to implement measures that will reduce existing environmental disparities. Agency responses may be conceptualized as a continuum: On the one end we see "repackaging" of normal agency activities as "EJ programs." The next strategy is to undertake discrete environmental projects, such as pilot projects and initiatives that lie outside the purview of broadly applicable requirements. The third and more advanced strategy is to design explicit EJ protections into the core design of major regulatory programs and activities. The fourth and last strategy on the continuum would be to undertake a comprehensive review of all agency EJ efforts to determine their effectiveness in impacted communities. The agencies vary in how far they have progressed. Repackaging and identifying existing programs was the norm, with a trend towards undertaking discrete new projects. Integrating EJ into program design has been relatively rare, and comprehensive assessment and analysis exceedingly uncommon. Based upon the agency responses, there appears to be only a few instances in which agencies have incorporated EJ principles and protections into programmatic design. Of course, we are at the early stages of federal agencies redirecting their efforts in light of the EO. Seven years cannot be expected to change decades, if not generations, of agency attitudes and approaches. While all agency actions that reduce disparities are admirable and constitute an advance, clearly full integration is the strategy most likely to result in significant, long-term progress....

\* \* \*

### Notes and Questions

1. What does the response of the federal agencies surveyed suggest about the degree to which environmental justice concerns have become part of their normal activities? Has the Executive Order changed agency behavior in any significant way? Is this perhaps too much to ask of an executive order?

2. In light of the findings above, what steps would you recommend for President Bush to take to see that the goals of the Executive Order are fully realized?

# B. Interagency Collaborations

## 1.   AN INTRODUCTORY NOTE ON COLLABORATION

The concept of a collaborative process is a deceptively simple one. Although it makes eminent good sense, there are a variety of reasons why well-meaning collaborative processes may fail and end up doing more harm than good. Although collaborations can take various forms—from advisory groups to oversight groups—most in the environmental justice context involve public and private actors attempting to identify and address interrelated environmental problems on a local scale. These "place-based" efforts often require some devolution of authority in order to implement more innovative strategies, but at the same time must maintain accountability to traditional regulatory authorities. As explained by Professor Sheila Foster,

> There are at least two recognizable strands of devolved collaboration currently in practice. The first involves mostly ad hoc local groups that are concerned with diverse issues in natural resources planning and management. The

second features more formalized, local working groups and a focus on land use and pollution control decisions. Both strands expand the influence of, and demand deeper participation by, public and private local actors in environmental and natural resource decisions. Yet, neither strand requires a complete abdication of government authority and responsibility over those decisions. Accountability to central government decision makers is preserved through a multilateral relationship whereby local actors supplement central regulatory authorities, and those authorities, in turn, support local efforts. In both strands, regulators (and sometimes legislators) expect to, and often do, use the proposals and recommendations of community-based participants to manage natural resources in line with local values, reformulate minimum performance standards, and/or impose additional conditions and monitoring requirements on regulated sources.

Sheila Foster, *Environmental Justice in an Era of Devolved Collaboration*, 26 HARV. ENVT. L. REV. (2002).

One important collaborative effort has been spearheaded at the federal level. As noted above, in 1999 the Interagency Working Group on Environmental Justice (IWG) established an Integrated Federal Interagency Environmental Justice Action Agenda. The Action Agenda has led to a number of interesting demonstration projects involving collaboration among government agencies, communities, and other private parties. Some of these projects, and the philosophy underlying the collaborative approach of the Action Agenda, are described in the excerpt below by Charles Lee, author of the landmark Toxic Waste and Race study (see Chapter III), and presently a high-ranking official in EPA's Office of Environmental Justice.

# Charles Lee, Submission to the National Environmental Policy Commission*
(May 15, 2001)

*IWG Interagency Action Agenda*

...Because of the enormous complexity and interrelated/multi-faceted nature of the issues that make up the concept of environmental justice, a primary challenge facing the IWG was to develop a mechanism which can leverage the benefits of many important federal initiatives and public-private partnerships. For example, Christine Todd Whitman, the new EPA Administrator, speaks of brownfield revitalization as "a way to merge environmental justice, environmental policy and economic growth." The Action Agenda and its demonstration projects is the right response to that challenge:

> Across the nation, communities are working hard to address a range of environmental, public health, economic and social concerns, known as environmental justice issues. They are struggling to better understand the complex relationships between environment, economy and equity. Through the efforts of many governmental and non-governmental organizations, communities are

---

* These written comments were submitted in connection with a presentation made on December 15, 2000, at the Newark, New Jersey Listening Session of the National Environmental Policy Commission.

beginning to fashion strategies that result in healthy and sustainable communities which are environmentally sound and economically revitalized.

Environmental justice is a complicated issue and the concept is not yet well understood. It is not a static concept but a dynamic process. However, important lessons are emerging. One such lesson is the need for greater Federal Agency collaboration. Without focused and concerted efforts on the part of multiple agencies, singularly directed initiatives, no matter how well intentioned, fall short in the face of the overwhelming challenges presented by the combined ills of environmental, social and economic distress. Another lesson is the need to involve all stakeholders in the development of the solutions. All groups in a community must be mobilized to truly make a lasting difference.

*(Preface of the Action Agenda, p.1)*

From the recognition of complex and challenging issues which surround the quality of life of disadvantaged communities, the Action Agenda is spearheading the development of a distinctively new collaborative model for achieving environmental justice. The Action Agenda is a "living" framework to ensure greater utilization of federal resources, which will support and promote local community problem-solving. In order for this model to work, it requires not only cooperation and coordination among Federal agencies, but leadership and direction from place-based partnerships of all relevant stakeholder groups.

The Action Agenda has four major goals:

- Promote greater coordination and cooperation among Federal agencies....
- Make the Federal government more accessible and responsive to communities....
- Ensure integration of environmental justice in policies, programs and activities of Federal agencies....
- Initiate "environmental justice demonstration projects" to develop integrated place-based models for addressing community livability issues.

To test and develop the collaborative model of the Action Agenda, the IWG has sponsored 15 demonstration projects, almost all of which [sic] is geographically based and which embrace a plethora of environmental justice issues and stakeholder communities. Presently, the IWG is developing, with input from all stakeholders, criteria for evaluating these current projects and criteria for selecting possible future projects....

### Background: IWG Collaborative Model

Collaborative processes require the building of genuine partnerships among all relevant parties, and the process results in better understanding for all participants of the perspectives and concerns of each party. Constructive processes are geared toward local solving problems, which require proactive, pragmatic and innovative strategies. The resulting action must be solution-oriented and of benefit to impacted communities (who must be at the center of the decision making process) and relevant stakeholders.

The collaborative model promoted by the Action Agenda also flows from an understanding that issues confronting environmentally and economically distressed communities are multi-faceted. Environmental health and quality of life concerns which often spark environmental justice disputes more often than not include issues of environment, housing, transportation, urban sprawl, community infrastructure, economic development, capacity building and others. In addition, there are special concerns with respect to Tribes and indigenous populations. A collaborative model must, therefore, be holistic and comprehensive, as well as proactive and continuous. No single agency can adequately address the multi-faceted dimensions of any environmental justice situation. This has been an important criticism from environmental justice communities for many years; the need for greater collaboration among Federal agencies to address the concerns of environmentally and economically distressed communities. Without focused and concerted efforts on the part of multiple agencies, the singularly directed initiatives of a given agency, no matter how well intentioned, fall short in the face of the overwhelming challenges presented by the combined ills of environmental, social and economic distress on impacted communities.

A cautionary note: The collaborative model is not appropriate for all environmental justice situations. Some of the most intractable and difficult issues affecting impacted communities may in fact only be resolved in litigation. Nonetheless, the absence heretofore of a well articulated model for collaborative and constructive problem solving has resulted unfortunately in parties not attempting to pursue this route. As a result, opportunities to collaborative [sic] address problems in a proactive manner are lost as well as opportunities to prevent disputes and the litigation associated with them. Experience and the overwhelming consensus to date from all stakeholders underscores the judgement that this effort to promote the collaborative process has broad support and is both timely and appropriate....

On May 24, 2000, EPA formally announced the [Action Agenda] on behalf of the eleven participating Federal departments and agencies, including the initial round of fifteen National Demonstration Projects. [Below are selected examples of some of the projects. Note the diversity of the issues addressed. Eds.]

*Selected Demonstration Projects*

*Re-Genesis: Environmental Cleanup and Community Revitalization*
Location: Spartanburg, South Carolina
Population: African American
Issue: Environmental cleanup and community revitalization
Partners: Re-Genesis, Forest Park Neighborhood Assoc., City of Spartanburg, County of Spartanburg, DHEC, SC EDA, USC, Clemson, IMC-Global, 4 Banks, Senator Hollings, Rep. DeMint, EPA, DOE, HUD, DOT, DOL, ATSDR, DOJ, NIEHS, DOI
Activities:
- Re-Genesis built broad based public-private partnership
- Ensure cleanup of two Superfund sites and other contaminated industrial properties
- Developed vision of holistic redevelopment to include: housing, technology & job-training center, health clinic
- Conduct planning charettes [sic] to turn vision into plan
- Secured more than $1 million in federal-private funding, including Ford Foundation

*Protecting Children's Health & Reducing Lead Exposure Through Collaborative Partnerships*
Location: East St. Louis, Illinois
Population: African American
Issue: Lead Screening and Abatement

Partners: Involve 17 different organizations, including St. Mary's Hospital, East St. Louis, St. Clair County, EPA, HUD, USDA, USACE
Activities:
- Screening over 3,000 children for blood lead
- Conduct lead based paint assessments
- Conduct site assessments in abandoned lots where children play
- Participate in worker training program
- Initiated phytoremediation project
- Develop outreach and education, including video
- Leveraged over $4 million in federal funding
- Designated a National Brownfields Showcase Community

*Metlakatla Indian Community Unified Interagency Environmental Management Task Force*
Location: Annette Islands, Alaska
Population: Alaska Native
Issue: Environmental cleanup and restoration
Partners: Tlingit & Haida Indian Tribes, BIA, DOD, EPA, FAA-DOT, USCG-DOT; Metlakatla Indian Community Unified Interagency Environmental Management Task Force
Activities:
- Develop Master Plan for cleanup and restoration of Metlakatla Peninsula
- DOD anticipates commitment of $2.5 million for site assessment
- Protect traditional use of food resources
- Planning to promote economic development through tourism and commercial fishing
- Designated a National Brownfields Showcase Community

*Addressing Asthma Coalition in Puerto Rico: A Multi-Faceted Partnership for Results*
Location: Puerto Rico
Population: Children in Puerto Rico
Issue: Protect children's health
Partners: PR Dept of Health, Pediatric Pulmonary Program, PR Lung Association, others HRSA, ATSDR, CDC, EPA
Activities:
- Two strategic planning conferences involving over 1000 people in NYC and Puerto Rico
- Support development of the Asthma Coalition of Puerto Rico
- Increase public awareness and professional training
- Coordinate better between asthma care providers and insurance companies
- Institute asthma research and surveillance programs

*New York City Alternative Fuels Summit*
Location: New York, New York
Population: People of Color and Low Income Communities
Issue: Reduce respiratory illnesses and improve air quality
Partners: NYC EJ Alliance, The Point, WHEACT, UPROSE, NYCDOT, NYS Environmental Business Assoc., etc.
DOE, EPA, DOI, GSA, FHWA-DOT, USPS

Activities:

- Communities identify vehicular fleets for fuel conversion projects
- Citywide effort involving community-based organizations in all planning meetings and design charettes
- Outreach to NYC to participate in DOE Clean Cities Program
- USPS committed $1.93 million for fleet conversion

*Easing Troubled Waters: Farm Worker Safe Drinking Water Project*
Location: State of Colorado
Population: Migrant Farm workers
Issue: Public Health
Partners: Plan de Salad del Valle, High Plains Center for Agricultural Health and Safety, National Center for Farmworker Health, CO DPH, CO DOL, CO DOA HRSA, EPA, DOL, USDA Colorado State Agricultural Extension
Activities:

- Develop GIS maps of migrant farmworker camps and drinking water sources
- Assess water quality data for camps
- Recommend changes to federal policy regarding testing of migrant worker water sources
- Develop interagency and community plan to address communication and education needs
- Build sustainable network to implement policy and communications changes

* * *

## Notes and Questions

1. As the demonstration pilot projects vividly illustrate, there are a variety of agencies that can participate, both "horizontally" and "vertically." Sister federal agencies often agree to participate, initially because of the mandate of the EJ Executive Order. However, because environmental hot spots implicate local land use decisions, the participation of municipal, county, regional and state agencies is indispensable. The participation of the business sector is also key. Yet, how do these various agencies and stakeholders get together in a collaborative effort, and what is the framework that is most likely to result in tangible results to the impacted area?

A May, 2001 forum convened by the International City/County Management Association (ICMA), entitled Building Collaborative Models to Achieve Environmental Justice, provided interesting insights into the successes and failures of the IWG demonstration projects. At the conference, long-time environmental justice activists began by explaining why collaborative efforts were necessary, but extraordinarily difficult to implement. Richard Moore of the Southwest Network for Environmental and Economic Justice (SNEEJ) described the initial days of "pounding at the doors" of the federal agencies, constantly having to dispute the frequent response by the agencies that there was a "lack of evidence" of contamination, as well as the tendency of each agency to identify the problem as one lying beyond the scope of its jurisdiction (and pointing instead to another agency). He noted that from the point of view of the frustrated community residents, it was all one interrelated problem. Tom Goldtooth of the Indigenous Environmental Network (IEN) concurred, noting that the term "collaboration" raised trust issues with Native American tribes given the history of colonization and deception on the part of the U.S. government. Charlotte Keyes, who represented Jesus People Against Pollution (JPAP), noted that the initiatives that have taken place on the federal level were the direct result of unrelenting pressure put on government by community and other grassroots activists. Government regulators responded that the task was difficult initially because the federal government operates on big issues and big policies, while communities work on a different scale and the "levers of decision-making" were necessarily different and not subject to coordination easily.

The participants appeared to agree that certain components are critical to successful collaborative partnerships. Among them are:

(a) There must be a high level of community education and empowerment about the issues. Environmental justice advocates, in particular, argued that a well-organized community group was a critical component of the process;

(b) Early resident and community involvement and visioning is key. All other stakeholders participants should recognize that the community is different than all other stakeholder groups;

(c) There must be a development of a clear action plan;

(d) The partnership must include the community, businesses and government agencies;

(e) Collaborating must include "win-win" scenarios for many stakeholders;

(f) There must be a commitment to facilitate conflict resolution, where appropriate. Sometimes, parties engaged in a conflict cannot work their way through the conflict by themselves and may need to find a third-person that has a sensitivity to the issues; and

(g) There must be sufficient resources to address the problem. One can better leverage available resources by interagency coordination.

Perspectives differed, however, concerning the interplay between collaborative partnerships and collateral adversary proceedings, such as litigation. Environmental justice advocates were clear in their view that there must be a recognition that the collaborative process has limitations. Thus, they maintained that there are some issues that require resolution by litigation or other methods. They see no problem with these proceedings occurring simultaneously and collaterally to the collaborative processes. In fact, one activist noted that her organization had collaterally participated in proceedings that resulted in a $150,000 fine against one of the partners. Business stakeholders, on the other hand, viewed collateral litigation as disruptive of and counterproductive to the collaborative effort. Some questioned whether litigation might preclude potential partners from joining a collaboration.

2. What is your view about the interplay between these approaches? Should groups forego litigation where they are involved in collaborative projects such as those described above?

3. Professor Foster also probes the collaborative process—one strongly oriented towards consensus—for potential bias. She introduces the following note of caution:

> Even with broad representation, however, devolved collaborative processes can be highly problematic from a substantive point of view. As critics of consensus aptly observe, the theory of consensus itself contains an inherent ideological bias. Its emphasis on securing unanimous agreement through the identification of common interests ("win-win") can be antithetical to achieving substantive justice. Such emphasis can skew the process in favor of the outcome which reflects the lowest common denominator acceptable to all parties.

The problem with outcomes reflecting the lowest common denominator is that, while the process can be deemed "legitimate" in a democratic process sense, its outcome may reflect a type of "domination by means of leveling." That is, it tends to leave out difficult and unpopular or minority concerns, and may orient the process away from sorely needed innovative solutions which address these concerns.

The substantive bias also reveals itself in the very mechanisms upon which consensus depends. Consensus simultaneously stresses agreement and compromise, while "veiling the increased potential for coercion by leaders" of collaborative groups. The primary mechanism through which this coercion is operationalized is the veto power possessed by each participant. This veto power can force agreement by threatening complete failure of the process if it is exercised. Given current disparities in material resources and social capital, "those with greater power possess and [will] frequently use their prerogative to exert substantial influence over other member[s] and, through them, the content of group decisions." In this way, by forcing agreement through coercion, more powerful/knowledgeable participants are able to co-opt dissident viewpoints which may be critical to seeking more creative, and just, decisions.

By ignoring, marginalizing or co-opting difficult questions of distributional justice, or other pressing policy dilemmas, consensus processes at their most benign replicate the status quo. That is, communities disproportionately bearing the costs of current environmental policy and natural resources management may not be left any worse off by consensus solutions, but they will likely not be helped by them either. At their most dangerous, consensus solutions may change the status quo for the worse, exacerbating existing distributional disparities. In the final analysis, the outcomes from some consensus-based process will no more reflect the "public interest" than do the problematic pluralistic processes they replace.

Sheila Foster, *Environmental Justice in an Era of Devolved Collaboration*, 26 Harv. Envt. L. Rev. 459, 493–494 (2002). Do you agree with Professor Foster that collaboration will simply replicate the problematic processes they replace and are unlikely to promote substantive justice? In light of these potential biases, is collaboration worth the effort? What are the potential gains?

4. One interesting pilot project that was discussed at the forum and that illustrates many of the ingredients for success noted above is the "Barrio Logan" project in San Diego, California. Like many other projects, this one included numerous federal and non-federal agencies as well as participants from the business sector. However, not all governmental agencies participated. There was a mix of interesting strategies attempted, with varying degrees of success, as discussed in the note below. As you read the note, consider to what extent, if any, the project was designed to avoid some of the problems identified by Professor Foster.

## 2. A Collaborative Project in Detail: The Case of Barrio Logan

Barrio Logan in San Diego is a low income, urban community, whose residents are primarily Latino. The area is beset with a variety of incompatible land uses and suffers poor air quality. Many of the sources that contribute to environmental problems are exempt from major provisions of federal environmental laws, such as nearby military operations and vessels in the port area. Children's health is the issue that appears to be of primary concern to the residents. As explained by Diane Takvorian of the Environmental Health Coalition (EHC), a sophisticated environmental justice organization in the San Diego area, 65 million pounds of hazardous waste are generated per year in the area. Shipyards, chrome platers, chemical supply facilities, and the U.S. Navy are all sources of toxic pollution. Navy operations are problematic because the Navy repairs and changes out components of its nuclear carriers in the area. Moreover, in some instances plating shops are located right next to homes and schools. Takvorian noted that, based on data from EPA's Cumulative Exposure Project, EHC created a Geographic Information Systems [GIS] map demonstrating higher risks of respiratory illnesses, cancer, and reproductive problems within the Barrio Logan area. An EHC survey of 800 families disclosed that 20% of children and 17% of the adults in the neighborhood had asthma or probable asthma.

Dr. Clarice Gaylord, who worked with the US EPA on the project, noted that many of the main players had a complicated and adversarial history with each other prior the start of the project. They had engaged in scientific debates with each other on committees and other fora, and various other "political showdowns," and were often seen "in front of TV cameras yelling at each other." As noted by Gaylord, "everyone had to agree to leave that stuff out of the room." Takvorian noted that her organization was skeptical initially because of a 20-year history of bad partnerships and a perceived reluctance on the part of various agencies to deal with the problems in the area. For example, she explained that in 1994–95, the EHC had to sue the county air pollution control district to get it to release information to her organization. This county agency also reportedly refused to act on EHC's health survey and in 1999 it refused EHC's request for an air monitoring station in the area. In 1999–00, the California Air Resources Board (CARB) conducted an audit of the county agency and found poor compliance rates by regulated entities and infrequent agency inspections. Thus, as Takviorian candidly admitted, EHC was "not interested in being on yet another committee that would not get anything done." It had to be convinced that this was a solution-oriented process.

The initial federal agencies involved were EPA, the office of Housing and Urban Development (HUD) and the National Institute of Environmental Health Services (NIEHS). At the EHC's request, CARB was also invited to participate. The Office of Congressman Bob Filner, whose district includes Barrio Logan, also became active in the project. Mary Knees from his office noted that from their perspective, indispensable to the project was the participation of a credible organization, like EHC, that included local PTA members, school nurses, families with sick children and other families. Several small businesses joined the collaboration. But not all stakeholders agreed to participate. The EPA reportedly attempted to bring in the Navy and work with it on the project, but Navy officials did not want to "talk to a non-cabinet agency" and attempted to persuade the EPA's Office of Environmental Justice to exclude Barrio Logan from the demonstration pilot projects.

Despite the absence of the Navy and other sources of pollution, in relative terms the participation was remarkable. Louis Michaelson, who acted as a facilitator to the project, explained that he knew from his work with previous EPA-sponsored grant programs in the area that achieving a successful collaboration faced significant uphill battles. In his view, previous attempts at partnerships had been unsuccessful because industry stakeholders tended to dominate the process and resources went into debating the data rather than solving the problems. In an attempt to avoid this dynamic, a decision was made early on that all potential partners would be required to "apply" to participate in the process. They had to agree to problem statements and goal statements, and had to describe the types of resources they could bring to the process. From Michaelson's perspective, this turned the dynamic around. All partners had to agree to act rather than debate, focus on goals rather than individual agendas, and reach an early consensus on the problems to be addressed. The partnership agreed that the primary goals were threefold: to address air pollution, address incompatible land uses, and improve children's health. According to Michaelson, the language describing the goals was critical. The focus on health and wellness served to avoid the "data wars."

As noted earlier, some agencies refused to participate. However, stakeholders that did come to the table were serious and had a commitment to action. Michaelson noted that some stakeholders had applied but did not become partners for various reasons, however, they still participated in workgroups. While the partnership had an initial session on how participants were going to work together, members wanted to avoid endless meetings on process, thus the importance of the initial agreement letter to lay out the framework in written form. A separate workgroup was established to address each goal. Each workgroup developed a set of options and prioritized them, leading eventually to a single action plan by the partnership.

To deal with the air pollution goal, for example, CARB committed substantial resources. Linda Murchison from CARB explained the sensitive situation facing her agency. As she stated, CARB needed to be very careful. Agency staff didn't know what they would find, but at the same time they needed to be very clear about what they could and could not do for the community in order to maintain CARB's credibility. According to her, CARB also needed to be prepared to take action, for example by promoting greater enforcement of regulated entities and developing guidance to prevent problems in the future. She noted that a process of "personalization" was a key component of the agency's participation. This occurred when CARB members took tours (conducted by EHC community leaders and organizers) through the area, then went back and took higher level personnel with them. These "toxic tours" served to put a face on the issue and increased the commitment of agency personnel.

CARB's initial involvement began with a serious attempt to gather information. The agency set up a monitor and monitored for a year and a half to get seasonal data about ambient pollution levels in the community. Stakeholder groups selected a contractor to look at the data, and there were community meetings to talk about the results. Meanwhile, other studies were continuing. As noted by Murchison, it was important to consider and explain that air monitoring only picks up pollution levels in air at a particular spot. While such an endeavor is a good first step, additional monitoring and modeling is needed. She also noted that inventorying smaller, neighborhood sources of pollution, (like chrome platers and auto body shops) that collectively can be significant contributors requires different approaches and assumptions than inventorying large facilities. With these caveats in mind, she explained that CARB now plans to undertake a comprehensive inventory of all area sources, including smaller sources, and model all emissions to predict where there might be pockets of toxics, and where future monitor placement might be most appropriate. As of the end of 2001, the partnership continues, not without controversy or problems, but with moderate success and good potential. Although significant concrete results have yet to be realized, the partners remain committed, and are still striving to make improvements in the community's environmental health.

## Notes and Questions

1. What lessons do you draw from the description of Barrio Logan initiative? Are the process innovations used in this project replicable to other communities?

2. Although undoubtedly a potent strategy for addressing community impacts, a collaborative project is a complementary strategy. As noted by several environmental justice activists at the ICMA conference, it does not replace the types of organizing and policy advocacy efforts undertaken by community residents, leaders and community-based organizations. For example, the efforts to address environmental problems in Barrio Logan began long before its selection as a IWG demonstration pilot project, and many of those earlier efforts were successful. Thus, a credible community-based organization with a demonstrated track record is often necessary to bring other stakeholders to the collaborative project in the first instance. In fact, activists maintain that it is their success in using more adversarial processes that may provide an incentive for some stakeholders to remain engaged in (the sometime arduous) process.

3. One drawback to the Barrio Logan and other collaborative projects is that not all relevant agencies and private businesses necessarily participate. Not surprisingly, agencies and private entities have varying degrees of commitment to addressing environmental inequities. Participation and nonparticipation can influence the scope of the collaborative project, and may affect the ultimate outcomes. What role do existing stakeholders have in prompting sister agencies or other polluting businesses to participate? What role do oversight agencies (like the EPA in many instances) have in prompting such participation?

4. If successful, a collaborative project may represent a viable model for addressing specific community problems. However, it may also illustrate a transition from a more utilitarian, pluralistic approach to environmental decisionmaking either to a civic republican approach (described in Chapter V) or an empowerment approach as described by Luke Cole (see Chapter X).

5. The Barrio Logan campaign also includes the active participation of political actors, such as Congressman Filner, and strong advocacy for changes in the law, including legislation proposed by Filner that would tighten environmental controls on the military, as well as locally-introduced buffer ordinances. Because of the multi-jurisdictional nature of environmental justice problems, changes in the law at all levels often becomes necessary to fully address the problem. We now turn to responses to environmental justice taken by various states.

# C. A Sampling of State Responses

States have responded in a variety of ways to the challenges raised by the environmental justice movement. Some—about fourteen according to a survey completed in late 2000—appear to have taken few if any concrete steps. On the other hand, the survey reported that:

> Numerous states have been active in pursuing environmental justice, while a handful of states have been especially active. Those active states (Florida, Maryland, New Jersey, New York, Oregon, and Tennessee) have all employed similar strategies. First, each state created a commission, task force, or advisory

council, usually through legislative action. The advisory groups consisted of representatives from various stakeholder groups, including industry, community groups, government representatives, and other interested parties. Second, in addition to holding internal meetings, the advisory groups often held public meetings throughout the state to gather public input. After this "information gathering" stage, the advisory group usually presented the results of its findings, with recommendations, to the state's legislature and/or governor. While the results of these reports varied by state, some common themes emerged. Most reports recommended changing various internal policies (i.e. permitting) to include environmental justice issues, establishing an office or program within the state's environmental department to continue addressing environmental justice concerns, and creating a separate institution (often at a university) to study environmental justice concerns and provide the general public with an outlet for their concerns.

Hilary Gross et al., Environmental Justice: A Response to State Responses, Public Law Research Institute, University of California, Hastings College of Law (Dec. 2000) (available at <http://www.uchastings.edu/plri/PDF/environjustice.pdf>). Various state programs are also discussed in Chuck D. Barlow, *State Environmental Justice Programs and Related Authorities* in THE LAW OF ENVIRONMENTAL JUSTICE: THEORIES AND PROCEDURES TO ADDRESS DISPROPORTIONATE RISKS 140 (Michael Gerrard, ed. 1999).

As of early 2001, however, California was the only state with general environmental justice legislation in effect. California's statute, SB 115, requires the California Environmental Protection Agency (Cal/EPA) to follow principles that closely parallel the provisions of President Clinton's Executive Order. The bill was passed in 1999 after five other environmental justice statutes were vetoed by former Governor Pete Wilson in the prior seven years. Cal/EPA is required to promote enforcement of health and environmental statutes and conduct its programs and policies "in a manner that ensures the fair treatment of people of all races, cultures, and income levels." It is also required to develop a model environmental justice mission statement for its constituent departments. CAL PUB. RES. CODE § 71110-71116; CAL. GOVT. CODE § 65040.12. Subsequent legislation also requires Cal/EPA to ensure that environmental justice considerations are addressed in carrying out reviews by the agency under the California Environmental Quality Act (the state version of NEPA), and to make recommendations for ensuring that public documents, notices and hearings are understandable and accessible to the public, including translation for limited-English-speaking populations. *See* Ellen M. Peter, *Implementing Environmental Justice: the New Agenda for California State Agencies*, 31 GOLDEN GATE U.L. REV 529 (2001).

The responses of other states fall into a few general categories. Several states have statutes that seek to limit the geographic concentration of waste facilities or that allow decision makers to consider "soft" criteria such as the socioeconomic status of the host community in permit decisions about waste facilities. (Some of these are discussed in Chapter XII(B)). A number of states have sought to increase public participation in their programs. For example, the Arizona Department of Environmental Quality has adopted a policy of notifying affected "environmental justice populations"after receipt of major permit applications. Louisiana's Department of Environmental Quality established a community-industry relations group "to address the concerns of community members about industrial pollution and health," and to improve industry-community communication. Tennessee and Texas set up toll-free numbers to assist citizens with environmental justice concerns.

A number of states have convened environmental justice task forces or advisory groups. The recommendations of these tasks forces include increasing public participation in agency decisions, improving public education and outreach by agencies, heightening awareness among agency staff about environmental justice issues, collecting better data about environmental disparities, facilitating community-industry dialogue, and in at least one case, targeting enforcement in environmental justice communities. A smaller number of states have gone further and adopted formal environmental justice policies or established environmental justice positions within state government. For example, under New Hampshire's Department of Environmental Quality's equity policy, the agency will incorporate equity considerations into every applicable decision or action. Connecticut's environmental equity policy commits the Department of Environmental Protection to review its activities in light of impacts to minority and lower income residents. Georgia has created a position of Outreach Coordinator to act as a clearinghouse for environmental justice matters.

Finally, in several states the primary response has been to conduct research into the extent of environmental disparities. For example, legislation in Louisiana requires the environmental agency to study air and water discharges and determine any correlations between discharges and residential areas in the state. Florida legislation likewise mandated a study of environmental risks by race and income, which concluded that minority and low income communities are disproportionately impacted by hazardous sites. Florida since has established two institutions to address environmental justice issues: a Center for Environmental Equity and Justice to conduct research, education, community outreach, and develop policies about environmental justice, and a Community Environmental Health Program to ensure that health services are available to low income communities that may be affected by contaminated sites.

### Notes and Questions

1. Overall, the survey of state responses indicates that relatively few have adopted comprehensive environmental justice legislation or changed their permitting, standard setting, or enforcement policies. The most popular responses seem to be creating environmental justice advisory committees or environmental justice policies, and enhancing public participation programs. Why do you think this is the case? Which approaches—of those tried by the states or other ones—would you like to see adopted?

2. Assume that you are counsel to Cal-EPA and asked to draft a model environmental justice mission statement. What would you recommend? How would you define "fair treatment" for purposes of implementing this bill?

# D. A Model Environmental Justice Framework?

We conclude this chapter with an excerpt from Professor Robert Bullard, one of the pioneering researchers and leading scholars in the field of environmental justice.

## Robert D. Bullard,
## A Model Environmental Justice Framework in Confronting
## Environmental Racism: Voices from the Grassroots
### 203 (Robert D. Bullard, ed. 1993)

The question of environmental justice is not anchored in a debate about whether or not decisionmakers should tinker with the EPA's risk-based management paradigm. Distribution of burdens and benefits is not random. Reliance solely on "objective" science for environmental decisionmaking, in a world shaped largely by power politics and special interests, often masks institutional racism. A national environmental justice framework is needed to begin addressing environmental inequities that result from social oppression.

The environmental justice framework implicit throughout this book rests on an ethical analysis of strategies to eliminate unfair, unjust, and inequitable conditions and decisions. The framework also seeks to prevent the threat before it occurs. It does so by incorporating the concerns of social movements that seek to eliminate harmful, discriminating practices in housing, land use, industrial planning, health care, and sanitation services. Thus, the environmental justice framework attempts to uncover the underlying assumptions that contribute to and produce unequal protection. This framework brings to the surface the blunt questions of "who gets what, why, and how much." To be specific, the environmental justice framework:

- incorporates the principle of the right of all individuals to be protected from environmental degradation;
- adopts a public health model of prevention (that eliminates the threat before harm occurs) as the preferred strategy;
- shifts the burden of proof to polluters/dischargers who do harm, discriminate, or who do not give equal protection to racial and ethnic minorities, and other "protected" classes; and
- redresses disproportionate impact through "targeted" action and resources.

The lessons from the civil rights struggles around housing, employment, education, and public accommodations over the past four decades suggest that environmental justice will need to have a legislative foundation to ensure its principle of across-the-board environmental rights. It is not enough to demonstrate the existence of unjust and unfair conditions; the practices that caused the conditions must be made illegal. In cases where applicable laws already exist, the environmental justice framework demands that they are enforced in a nondiscriminatory fashion. Yet, much more is needed than better enforcement of existing laws. Unequal protection needs to be attacked via a Fair Environmental Protection Act that moves protection from a "privilege" to a "right."

A Fair Environmental Protection Act would need to address both *the intended* and *unintended* effects of public policies, land-use decisions, and industry practices that have a disparate impact on racial and ethnic minorities, and other vulnerable groups. The purpose of this act would be to prohibit environmental discrimination based on race and class. The precedents for this framework are the Civil Rights Act of 1964, which attempted to address both *de jure* and *de facto* school segregation, the Fair Housing Act of 1968 and as amended in 1988, and the Voting Rights Act of 1965.

The struggle for new legislation will also need to be directed at the state level. Since many of the decisions and problems lie with state actions, states will need to model their legislative initiatives (or even develop stronger initiatives) on the needed federal legislation. States that are initiating "fair share" plans to address *interstate* waste conflicts (siting equity) need also to begin addressing *intrastate* siting equity concerns being raised by impacted local communities.

The public health principle of our framework suggests further that impacted communities should not have to wait until conclusive "proof" of causation is established before preventive action is taken. For example, the framework offers a solution to the lead problem by shifting the primary focus from *treatment* (after children have been poisoned) to *prevention* (elimination of the threat via abating lead on the human body. However, very little action has been taken to rid the nation of lead poisoning in housing.

This suggests the need for the burden-of-proof principle. Under the current system, individuals who challenge polluters must "prove" that they have been harmed, discriminated against, or disproportionately impacted. Few impacted communities have the resources to hire lawyers, expert witnesses, and doctors needed to sustain such a challenge.

The environmental justice strategy would require that entities applying for operating permits (landfills, incinerators, smelters, refineries, chemical plants, etc.) prove that their operations are not harmful to human health and will not disproportionately impact racial and ethnic minorities and other protected groups. This principle would also require proven statistics of disparate impact to constitute proof of discrimination in legal proceedings instead of using "intent" as the relevant criteria. Proving intentional or purposeful discrimination in a court of law is next to impossible. Yet, numerous empirical studies point to disparate public and private waste facility siting where African Americans and Latino Americans are disproportionately impacted. These statistical analyses should be given the greatest weight in legal decisionmaking.

The targeted resources principle of the environmental justice framework would also mean providing the most resources where environmental and health problems are greatest. Reliance solely on "objective" science disguises the exploitative way the polluting industries have operated in some communities and condones a passive acceptance of the status quo....

Environmental justice targeting would channel resources to the "hot spots," communities that are burdened with more than their "fair share" of environmental problems. For example, the EPA's Region VI has developed a Geographic Information System and comparative risk methodologies to evaluate environmental equity concerns in the region. The methodologies combines susceptibility factors (i.e., age, pregnancy, race, income, pre-existing disease, and lifestyle) with chemical release data (i.e., Toxic Release Inventory and monitoring information), geographic and demographic data (i.e., site-specific areas around hazardous waste-sites, census tracts, zip codes, cities, and states), and state health department vital statistics data for its regional equity assessment....

An environmental justice framework would allow us to identify such communities nationally. Yet, as we have seen, a key question remains resource allocation—the level of resources that will be channeled into solving the pollution problem in communities that have a disproportionately large share of poor people, working-class people, and people of color. This will be an important arena of struggle in the coming decades.

*Conclusion*

Environmental philosophy and decisionmaking has often failed to address the "justice" question of who gets help and who does not; who can afford help and who cannot; why some contaminated communities get studied while others get left off the research agenda; why industry poisons some communities and not others; why some contaminated communities get cleaned up while others do not; and why some communities are protected and others are not protected.

The grassroots environmental justice movement chronicled in this book seeks to strip away the ideological blinders that overlook racism and class exploitation in environmental decisionmaking. From this critical vantage point, the solution to unequal environmental protection is seen to lie in the struggle for justice for all Americans. No community, rich or poor, black or white, should be allowed to become an ecological "sacrifice zone."

Saying "NO" to the continued poisoning of our communities of color is the difficult first step in this struggle. Yet, our long-range vision must also include institutionalizing sustainable and just environmental practices that meet human needs without sacrificing the land's ecological integrity. If we are to succeed, we must be visionary as well as militant. Our very future depends on it.

## Notes and Questions

1. Should the "Fair Environmental Protection Act" proposed by Professor Bullard be enacted nationally? At the state or local level? In light of the various other legislative, administrative and other responses to environmental injustices that are discussed in this book, do you think Professor Bullard is correct that a more firm legislative foundation is needed to ensure across the board environmental rights?

# Chapter XVI

# Native American Issues

## A. Introduction

### 1. An Introductory Note on Native American Legal Issues

Indian communities share many of the environmental burdens of other communities of color. However, environmental justice issues in Indian country take on a character special to Native American tribes. As Professor Judith Royster points out,

> Indian tribes connect to their lands not only on economic and emotional levels, but also on the levels of culture, religion and sovereignty. Environmental degradation may, for example, affect land that is sacred to tribes, or pose a threat to the entire territory in which the tribe as government operates. And for Native American tribes, land is not fungible. Most tribes today occupy reservations carved out of their aboriginal territory, lands that the tribes occupied before white contact. The reservations are "place": a homeland, a source of physical subsistence and spiritual sustenance. The loss of place may impact the identity and destiny of the tribe itself.

> Moreover, environmental degradation may impact tribal cultures in special ways because of the limited size of the territory or subsistence or religious practices of the tribes. Oil pollution may irreparably damage the only source of drinking water on a reservation, or a radioactive spill may contaminate the primary source of drinking and stock water in an arid land. Pollution of fisheries has a far greater effect on Indian communities that historically depend upon the fish for their main food source than it does on the population at large....

Judith V. Royster, *Native American Law, in* The Law of Environmental Justice: Theories and Procedures to Address Disproportionate Risks, 157–158 (Michael B. Gerrard. ed., 1999).

Environmental justice issues also are more complex in Indian country because of the governmental status of tribes and their authority to manage environmental matters within their jurisdiction. Indian tribes are sovereign governments, and as such, retain broad sovereign authority to regulate activities within their territories, including enacting tribal environmental codes and permit requirements regulating tribal lands and resources subject to their jurisdiction. Like states, moreover, Indian tribes can also receive authorization to administer most federal environmental statutes in lieu of EPA, provided they satisfy minimum federal criteria. Once they receive authorization, like states, they can also adopt stricter standards. For example, as seen in the Chapter VII excerpt of *Albuquerque v. Browner*, tribes can adopt water quality standards more stringent than federal minimum standards, for instance to protect unique tribal values and use for water resources. As of March 1998, EPA had approved some twenty tribes for setting water quality standards, and another fifteen applications were pending. Dean B. Suagee & James J. Havard, *Tribal Governments and the Protection of Watersheds and Wetlands in Indian Country*, 13 ST. THOMAS L. REV. 35, 44 (2000). However, as Professor Dean Suagee notes, "when tribal governments become engaged in environmental federalism, they do not act exactly like state governments. Perhaps the most significant distinction between the two is that tribal policy decisions tend to reflect tribal cultural values. Tribal cultures are deeply rooted in the natural world; therefore, protecting the land and its biological communities tends to be a prerequisite for cultural survival. " Dean B. Suagee, *Legal Structure and Sustainable Development: Tribal Self-Determination and Environmental Federalism: Cultural Values As a Force for Sustainability*, 3 WIDENER L. SYMP. J. 229, 233–34 (1998).

On the other hand, tribal sovereignty may result in tribes promoting natural resources extraction or accepting environmentally harmful activities. Indian tribes own approximately 56.6 million acres of land in the lower forty-eight states. Some of these lands are rich in hard rock minerals, timber, oil, natural gas, wildlife, and other natural resources. For instance, underlying Indian reservations is approximately half of all uranium deposits, one-third of all western low sulfur coal, and twenty percent of all known oil and natural gas reserves in the U.S. Mary Christina Wood, *Indian Land and the Promise of Native Sovereignty: The Trust Doctrine Revisited*, 1994 UTAH L. REV. 1471, 1481. In 1990, over 15 million barrels of oil, 135 million cubic feet of natural gas, and 27 million tons of coal were produced from Indian lands. Robert Laurence, *American Indians and the Environment: A Legal Primer for Newcomers to the Field*, 7 NAT. RESOURCES & ENV'T 3, 3 (Spring 1993). Moreover, the open spaces and grinding poverty present on many reservations has made them attractive targets for siting noxious facilities that other jurisdictions have rejected.

The federal government's relationship with Indians also is significantly shaped by treaties signed with the United States, and by the federal trust doctrine. In exchange for Indians ceding vast amounts of their original lands to the U.S, the treaties reserved tribal rights on lands outside reservation borders, including the right to hunt, fish, and access water and other resources. The treaties may also impose affirmative obligations on governmental agencies to protect tribal resources. Professor Catherine O'Neill, for example, argues that treaties between the U.S. and various Pacific Northwest tribes "support an interpretation that not only recognizes Indians' reservation of their right to take fish 'at all usual and accustomed grounds and stations,' but also includes some guarantee that there be fish for taking (and consuming), that is, that the fishery habitat be protected from degradation or contamination." Catherine A. O'Neill, *Variable Justice: Environmental Standards, Contaminated Fish, and "Acceptable" Risk to Native Peoples*, 19 STAN. ENVTL. L.J. 3, 98 (2000).

The federal trust doctrine imposes an obligation on the federal government to manage Indian lands, funds and resources that are held "in trust" by the federal government for the benefit of tribes and individual Indians. As currently interpreted, a central purpose of the trust responsibility is to further tribal sovereignty and cultural integrity. A number of scholars have called for greater reliance on the trust doctrine to protect Indian lands and resources from environmental harm, arguing that traditional environmental statutes do not adequately meet the needs of the tribes. *See, e.g.* Mary Christina Wood, *Fulfilling the Executive's Trust Responsibility Toward the Native Nations on Environmental Issues: A Partial Critique of the Clinton Administration's Promises and Performance*, 25 ENVTL. L. 733, 745 (1995). Finally, there are a growing number of international norms that pertain to Indians. For example, international human rights instruments increasingly recognize the rights of indigenous peoples to self-government and cultural integrity.

This chapter examines several important environmental justice issues in Indian country. The first section explores issues involving tribes as sovereign governments, including tribal decisionmaking about environmental and natural resource protection. It continues with an examination of conflicts that may stem from (1) a western (mis)perception of Indian identity, culture and values, and (2) fundamentally different conceptions of land held by Indian and the dominant western cultures in the United States. The second part of the chapter continues this exploration with an examination of how the courts have resolved conflicts between Indian sacred sites and management of federal public lands.

## *Pathfinder on Native Americans*

A concise discussion of governmental authority of Indian tribes to manage environmental matters within their jurisdiction can be found in Judith V. Royster, *Native American Law, in* THE LAW OF ENVIRONMENTAL JUSTICE: THEORIES AND PROCEDURES TO ADDRESS DISPROPORTIONATE RISKS (Michael B. Gerrard ed., 1999). Comprehensive background on Indian law is provided in FELIX S. COHEN'S HANDBOOK OF FEDERAL INDIAN LAW (Rennard Strickland ed., 1982). The federal trust obligations are discussed in a trilogy of articles by Mary Christina Wood, *Indian Land and the Promise of Native Sovereignty: The Trust Doctrine Revisited*, 1994 UTAH L. REV. 1471; *Protecting the Attributes of Sovereignty: A New Trust Paradigm for Federal Actions Affecting Tribal Lands and Resources*, 1995 UTAH L. REV. 109; and *Fulfilling the Executive's Trust Responsibility Toward the Native Nations on Environmental Issues: A Partial Critique of the Clinton Administration's Promises and Performance*, 25 ENVTL. L. 733 (1995). Some key federal regulatory documents include EPA's Policy for the Administration of Environmental Programs on Indian Reservations <http://www.epa.gov/indian/1984.htm> (1984); the Memorandum on Government-to-Government Relations With Native American Tribal Governments, 59 Fed. Reg. 22,951 (May 4, 1994); the Executive Order on Indian Sacred Sites, Exec. Order No. 13,007, 61 Fed. Reg. 26,771 (May 29, 1996); and the Executive Order on Consultation and Coordination With Indian Tribal Governments, Exec. Order No. 13,175, 65 Fed. Reg. 67,249 (Nov. 9, 2000).

In addition to the articles excerpted in this chapter, other articles include Williamson B. C. Chang, *The "Wasteland" in the Western Exploitation of "Race" and the Environment*, 63 U. COLO. L. REV. 849 (1992); James L. Huffman, *An Exploratory Essay on Native Americans and Environmentalism*, 63 U. COLO. L. REV. 901 (1992); Kevin Gover & Jana L. Walker, *Escaping Environmental Paternalism: One Tribe's Approach to Developing a Commercial Waste Disposal Project in Indian Country*, 63 U. COLO. L. REV. 933 (1992); RACE, POVERTY & THE ENVIRONMENT (Fall 1992) (Special issue on Native Nations in 1992: 500 Years of Cultural Survival); Dean B. Suagee, *Turtle's War Party: An Indian Allegory on Environmental Justice*, 9 J. ENVTL. L. & LITIG. 461 (1994); Richard Monette, *Environmental Justice and Indian Tribes: The Double-Edged Tomahawk of Applying Civil Rights Laws In Indian Country*, 76 U. DET. MERCY L. REV. 721 (1999); John P. LaVelle, *Achieving Environmental Justice by Restoring the Great Grasslands and Returning the Sacred Black Hills to the Great Sioux Nation*, 5 GREAT PLAINS. NAT. RESOURCES J. 40

(2001). A host of information about environmental issues facing Indians and local campaigns can be found on the website of the Indigenous Environmental Network, a national network of indigenous groups working on environmental issues *available at* http://www.ienearth.org/.

* * *

The following article discusses some of the prevailing cultural stereotypes facing Indians in U.S. society.

# Paul Smith,
# Lost in America
## Border/Lines (Winter 1991/1992)

*Four Key Points About Indians*

First, North America is Indian country. A very short history of North America: For thousands of years, as long as people have lived in Europe, hundreds of distinct peoples numbering in the tens of millions lived in North America. Europeans invaded and after centuries of war and disease the Native American population dropped to as few as three hundred thousand. The U.S. and Canada are nations created on the destruction of Indian people and the theft of Indian land....

Second, Indians live under a colonial system. The Bureau of Indian Affairs [BIA] in the U.S. and the Department of Indian Affairs in Canada have almost total control over the lives of Indians living on reservations and reserves. Indian language and culture was forbidden until just 50 years ago. Under a system established in the U.S. in 1934, each federally recognized tribe has an elected tribal council that makes decisions for the tribe, as long as the BIA Area Superintendent agrees. Jobs, health care, housing, all social services are provided by this agency, which was originally under the War Department. All leases for mineral, oil and gas and grazing rights are managed by the BIA. This system has produced astonishing results: we are by far the poorest people in the United States. We have our own health system called the Indian Health Service: with a budget of $1 billion a year, a third of us die by the age of 45, we suffer from diseases unheard of anywhere else in North America, and a staggering percentage of Native women have been sterilized.

Third, Indians face a particular, highly developed and highly ideological kind of racism. Chief, tribe, warrior, medicine man; these are all terms invented by Europeans to objectify Indians (as is the term Indian itself). For chief, president or prime minister would be equally accurate. Why tribe instead of nation? Warrior instead of fighter or soldier? Medicine man instead of religious leader or minister? Because it makes Indians strange and primitive. These terms make us the "other." These terms make it impossible to imagine us as contemporary human beings, or players in our own destiny.

Indian names were usually translated into English. Sitting Bull, not the Lakota language name, is what is used. But Beethoven is not translated into English; if so it would be Beet Patch's Fifth Symphony and sound as ridiculous as Sitting Bull. But only Indian names are translated....

Recently someone gave me a fundraising letter that discussed the terrible conditions on reservations in South Dakota. This letter, written by a white person, advocated a project called "Adopt an Elder." Now, there are old people in West Virginia that could talk about wars between coal miners and the companies, or who embody Appalachian culture and oral tradition. But would anyone seriously argue that the way to solve the problems of the region would be for people in New York to adopt a hillbilly? Is the most effective way to fight stripmining really to send $20 a month to an Appalachian elder? Why would this be suggested for Indians when it seems absurd for others?

Fourth, Indians are just plain folks.... We are not an impenetrable mystery, and for non-Indians to support us does not require an advance [sic] appreciation of our religions, or culture.... Since we are just plain folks, we also have differences just like other people. Among Afro-Americans today you find a Marxist left, Louis Farrakhan, the Republic of New Africa, Jesse Jackson and Republicans. Why should it surprise anyone that we, who in many ways come from more diverse histories than any other minority group, also have a wide range of political views?...

\* \* \*

### Notes and Questions

1. Paul Smith's observations raise difficult questions. How does the dominant culture's tendency to view Indians as exotic directly impact decisions about environmental protection? When is it appropriate to view Native American situations as special, if not unique, without stereotyping or patronizing entire groups of people? For example, does acting to protect sacred sites or approve higher water quality standards for ceremonial use involve undue special treatment of Native peoples or is it simply a recognition of a fundamentally different conception of land and natural resources? Is questioning nuclear or hazardous waste sites in Indian Country always patronizing? How should these questions be decided? Do they matter if the resolution of the environmental law issue ultimately enures to the benefit of the tribes? Many of these issues are explored in the readings below.

2. The process of interacting with Native Americans—simultaneously as tribal sovereign governments, a people with a fundamentally different conception of man's relationship to nature, and a people subjected to environmental disparities—is a particularly tricky endeavor, as the next section illustrates.

# B. Tribes as Environmental Regulators

The following excerpt describes how tribes fit into the inter-governmental structure governing federal environmental law.

## Dean B. Suagee,
## The Indian Country Environmental
## Justice Clinic: From Vision to Reality
### 23 Vermont Law Review 567 (1999)

Something remarkable is happening in the environmental law system in the United States—something that has virtually escaped notice by the mainstream environmental community and by the legal educational establishment. Indian tribal governments are building their own environmental protection programs, and they are doing so with a sense that this mission is a sacred trust. Tribes are building their programs within the general framework of the federal environmental statutes, but also within the framework of cultural traditions that have ancient roots in this land. These cultural traditions generally hold that human beings have important responsibilities, including responsibilities to the communities of nonhuman living things with whom we share this Earth....

Part I of the Essay examines the concept of environmental justice as it might be applied to Indian country. In my view the concept holds great potential for protecting communities of Indian country from environmental degradation and for helping the people of these communities to bring about healing where Mother Earth has been injured. This potential will not be realized by simply taking the concept of environmental justice from the context in which it arose and assuming that it fits in Indian country. Indian country is different....

The potential of the environmental justice movement for helping the communities of Indian country lies, I believe, in its ability to help the larger American society understand the need for commitment to the tribal right of self-government. I believe that the existence of exemplary tribal environmental programs will be essential in building this commitment. As the American people become more aware that tribes are in fact protecting the environment, they will be grateful that tribes are still around....

### The Concept of Environmental Justice in Indian Country

...Civil rights laws generally prohibit discriminatory treatment based on race, color, religion, sex, or national origin. Most people probably think that at least some of these classifications include Indians. Not surprisingly, a handful of decisions by federal courts have ruled that discriminatory treatment against Indians is prohibited, although the reasoning has varied. But the Supreme Court has held that, at least for certain purposes, being an Indian is *not* a racial classification, but rather a political classification. Being an Indian is primarily defined by being a member of a tribe that is recognized by the federal government. Some individuals who are Indian by ancestry are not members of federally recognized tribes, and many tribal members have a high degree of non-Indian ancestry. It is because of the relationship between the federal government and the tribes that it is constitutionally permissible for Congress to enact laws that treat Indians differently from any other group of American citizens.

Regardless of whether Indians fit within a protected class, in the context of Indian country, I think that the concept of environmental justice is not very useful unless it is broader than just the intersection of civil rights and environmental law. Instead, I think that in Indian country a vision of environmental justice must also include the tribal right of self-government. Unless the larger American society honors the tribal right of self-government, the word "justice" as applied to Indian communities simply does not have much meaning. This means that tribal governments must be involved in performing the full range of functions that governments are expected to do in protecting the environment: making the law, implementing the law, and resolving disputes....

### Measured Separatism Rather than Equal Treatment under the Law

Indian tribes differ from other minority groups in modern day America in one very significant respect—tribes are sovereign governments. They have the power to make and enforce laws to govern their reservations. Within our federal system, tribal governments have a status roughly comparable to that of the states, although people in the larger American society tend to ignore this status. The status of tribes as governments is based on the fact that tribes were recognized as sovereigns by European governments during the colonial era and by the United States during its period of westward expansion. The status of tribes as governments is woven into the body of federal Indian law in treaties, acts of Congress and court decisions dating from the earliest years of the Union....

Environmental protection in Indian country does raise some challenging questions, and some of these questions are too important to ignore even if they do not have easy answers. For example, is it fair for a tribe whose members comprise less than half the population of its reservation to set water quality standards for all surface waters within its reservation? Answering this question requires an acknowledgment that opening the reservation to settlement by non-Indians in the late nineteenth or early twentieth century was accomplished over the objections of tribal leaders and in violation of the promises made in a treaty half a century earlier, and that these actions were done with the intent of destroying the tribe. If we are really concerned with fairness, then we must consider not only the rights of non-Indians to representative government, but also the right of the tribe to continue to exist as a distinct culture. And we must recognize that the tribe's identity as a distinct culture is inextricably interwoven into the portion of its homeland that it reserved to itself in its treaty (or that was otherwise set aside for it)....

### Tribes as Partners in Environmental Federalism

Environmental law in the United States exists within a federalist framework. For the most part, the basic policies and mechanisms have been established by federal laws, but these laws provide major roles for the states.... In the 1970s, Congress enacted several environmental statutes, and the EPA issued a host of regulations. Most of these statutes and regulations either totally overlooked Indian tribes or barely mentioned them.

Beginning in the mid-1980s, Congress has amended most of the major federal environmental statutes to authorize tribal governments to become treated like states for a variety of purposes. For example, under the Clean Water Act, tribes can adopt water quality standards, and they can take over the permit program that regulates point sources of water pollution. Under the Clean Air Act, tribes can adopt tribal implementation plans for their reservations. Under the Comprehensive Environmental Response, Compensation and Recovery Act, tribes can act as trustees for natural resources damage claims....

Over the next several decades, tribal leaders and staff, along with their lawyers and consultants, will be working to build environmental programs for their reservations. A flowering of tribal environmental programs on reservations across this land could be a very good thing for the American environment and for the American people. Tribal programs carried out within the federalist framework could help to bring tribal cultural values into environmental protection, values such as what Professor David Getches has called the tribal "philosophy of permanence."...

### Building Tribal Programs

If we accept that tribal self-government is essential to any meaningful notion of environmental justice, we might also be tempted to assume the existence of tribal environmental programs that are comparable to those of the states. That would be a big leap of faith. Tribal programs do in fact exist, but most are very new, understaffed, and underfunded.

There are some 555 federally recognized tribes, including 329 in the contiguous states and 226 in Alaska. The tribes exhibit a great deal of diversity. Indian reservations can be found in thirty-three of the states. Some twenty-four reservations are larger in area than the smallest state (Rhode Island); many other reservations are only a few hundred acres in size. Only one of the tribes in Alaska has a reservation. About two-thirds of the tribes have fewer than 1000 members.

As of March 1998, 146 tribes had received program authorization from EPA (or a determination of eligibility to be treated like a state) for at least one purpose under a federal statute, though the vast majority of these were for the purpose of receiving grants under section 106 of the Clean Water Act (CWA). In terms of assuming regulatory roles, the most popular program is the Water Quality Standards (WQS) program under section 303 of the CWA. Tribes that are approved for this program are also approved for the section 401 certification program. As of March 1998, some twenty tribes had been approved for setting WQSs, and applications from some fifteen other tribes were pending. The number of tribes setting WQSs is substantial, but these numbers also mean that nearly 300 other tribes that are eligible to take this step have not done so....

* * *

## Notes and Questions

1. Implicit in Professor Suagee's comments is the idea that a tribal environmental regulator cannot be neatly analogized to a state environmental regulator, although both are operating under a regime of cooperative federalism. Tribes have only recently been recognized as potential regulators under environmental laws and have far fewer resources to set up an environmental protection infrastructure. On the other hand, tribes have a larger, and perhaps different, mission as an environmental protection agency. Many tribes are operating in a cultural context where land is not often viewed as a commodity but is more linked with social, cultural and religious values. Thus, the idea of stewardship may be much stronger in Indian country. But to complicate matters, past treaty violations and governmental allotment policies have resulted in substantial numbers of non-Indians living within tribal jurisdictional boundaries, thus setting the stage of conflict over regulatory options. How should these problems be addressed by the federal government? Should tribes be treated exactly like states or given additional assistance? If so, how should this be done? Should they have additional leeway in setting standards?

2. As Professor Suagee notes, Indians are not a protected racial class under the Constitution. One difficult set of questions thus concerns the application of Title VI to Indians. EPA has been wrestling with the related questions of whether tribes that receive financial assistance from EPA are subject to the requirements of Title VI, and whether individual members of tribes in Indian country are within the class of minority groups protected classes by Title VI. Professor Richard Monette argues that:

> These two questions illustrate the impossibly difficult, sometimes ironic, position of Indians in America. To put it bluntly, if Tribes answer "no" to the first question, their arguments will inevitably mirror the federalism arguments of Mississippi or Alabama fighting against federal civil rights for minorities within their borders. In other words, "Tribes' rights" will sound like "states' rights." The irony is that, in the larger scheme of things, tribal members are also minorities in America. Thus, if Tribes answer "yes" to the second question, their arguments will sound like those of the civil rights leaders who rose against Mississippi and Alabama. The irony here is, as sovereign entities, Tribes

have civil rights complaints leveled against them, like any other government.... [These] questions force Tribes to choose between identifying as their own autonomous government, on the one hand, or as an aggregate racial group under another government's rule on the other.

Richard Monette, *Environmental Justice and Indian Tribes: The Double-Edged Tomahawk of Applying Civil Rights Laws in Indian Country*, 76 U. Det. Mercy L. Rev. 721, 724–25 (1999). EPA's *Draft Title VI Guidance* issued in 2000 (see Chapter XIV) does not address the first question. As to the second issue, since EPA's Title VI implementing regulations define a "racial classification" to include an American Indian or Alaskan native, *see* 40 C.F.R. § 7.25, it appears that Native Americans may file Title VI complaints against states or off-reservation entities. How should Title VI be interpreted with respect to Indians? For example, should a white citizen living in Indian country be able to assert a Title VI claim against a tribe as regulator for allegedly causing a disparate impact to white residents living within the reservation boundaries? Of what relevance is the fact that, historically, whites have not been subject to discrimination?

# Rebecca Tsosie,
# Tribal Environmental Policy in an Era of
# Self-Determination: The Role of Ethics, Economics
# and Traditional Ecological Knowledge
## 21 Vermont Law Review 225 (1996)

As Indian nations assume greater responsibility for managing tribal lands under the rubrics of tribal sovereignty and the federal self-determination policy, they are able to exercise more autonomy over environmental decision-making. That decision-making process, however, raises significant legal issues, ethical conflicts, and economic considerations.... [T]ribal environmental policy must be responsive to the interacting forces of traditional ecological knowledge, western science, economics, and tribal systems of ethics....

### Tribal Environmental Authority in the Era of Self-Determination

...In 1970, President Richard Nixon called for a new federal policy of self-determination for American Indians. The self-determination policy represented a welcome change from the previous federal policy of "termination," which sought to abolish the federal trusteeship over Indian tribes, dismantle the reservations, and end the Indian tribes' unique status as "domestic, dependent nations." The self-determination policy, intended to "strengthen the Indian's sense of autonomy without threatening his sense of community," encouraged tribes to assume control over many of the federal programs being administered on the reservation....

The federal policy of self-determination has also encouraged tribes to consolidate their land bases and exercise control over their natural resources, thereby reversing earlier federal policies that placed control over land and resources with the Bureau of Indian Affairs, often to the clear detriment of the tribes. These newer policies are significant because natural resource development has long been a predominant means of economic development on many reservations. In particular, the extractive industries, such as coal, uranium, oil, and gas, have played a major role in reservation economic development. Along with their fiscal contributions, however, the extractive industries have brought mining, milling, and smelting operations to Indian lands, causing pollution of reservation lands, waters, and air passages....

Environmental conditions on the reservation are therefore subject to a dual legal structure of federal and tribal law, providing added complexity to the notion of "environmental self-determination." Although tribal values and norms regarding environmental use should serve as the basis for tribal environmental policy under the principle of "self-determination," tribal policy is in fact heavily impacted by the values and norms of Anglo-American society, embodied in federal environmental law and policy....

### The Role of Indigenous Land Ethics in Guiding Tribal Environmental Law and Policy

The diversity among American Indian people makes defining an "indigenous land ethic" somewhat difficult. Nevertheless, the similarities among indigenous world views regarding the environment cannot be discounted....

### Traditional Indigenous Environmental Ethics: Finding the Common Ground

"[I]ndigenous" people...generally refers to the "original inhabitants of traditional lands" who maintain their traditional values, culture, and way of life. Those collective values and ways of life are encompassed within the notion of "traditional ecological knowledge," which is "the culturally and spiritually based way in which indigenous peoples relate to their ecosystems." Thus, the concept of traditional ecological knowledge comprises both indigenous systems of environmental ethics and the group's scientific knowledge about environmental use that has resulted from generations of interaction.... Many of these principles, such as the concept of caring for the land for the benefit of future generations, have parallels among other Native American peoples throughout Canada and the United States. The similarities among American Indian environmental perspectives may stem from the fact that virtually all traditional Indian cultures had "land-based" rather than "industrial" or "market" economies.... A central feature of many indigenous world views is found in the spiritual relationship that Native American peoples appear to have with the environment....

Professor Ronald Trosper has drawn on several tribal traditions to construct a model of "traditional Indian world views" premised on four basic principles: "community," "connectedness," "the seventh generation," and "humility."...Trosper's model of traditional world views, as affirmed by other scholarship, has several important aspects: a perception of the earth as an animate being; a belief that humans are in a kinship system with other living things; a perception of the land as essential to the identity of the people; and a concept of reciprocity and balance that extends to relationships among humans, including future generations, and between humans and the natural world.

### Living in an Animate Universe

A central belief among many Native American cultures is that Earth is a living, conscious being that must be treated with respect and care....Many Native American groups describe the earth as being a mother or grandmother, a source of life for the people....One significant feature of this understanding of the relationship of the people to the earth is that the earth preceded the people, both in time and ultimate power....

### Human Kinship with the Natural World

In a way of thinking that sees man and nature as part of one ordered, balanced, and living whole, humans have social and kinship relationships with other beings....The indigenous understanding of the relationships between man and the natural environment is radically different from the Western understanding of such relationships. Euro-American values stemming from Christianity, capitalism, and technology promote a view of nature as a commodity, "as wilderness to be tamed," and as a "nonliving collection of natural resources to be exploited." Although European traditions may speak of the need to maintain balance in nature, these traditions do not suggest that humans are in a kinship relation with animals, or that humans owe a duty to animals....

### Land, Place, and Human Identity

Vine Deloria has noted that a central difference between indigenous and Western belief systems is in the use of history to document the spiritual development of the people.... Under the Native American perception of reality, which is "bound up in spatial references," specific natural areas are imbued with complex significance. Thus, a tribe may speak of its "origin place"—such as a river, mountain, plateau, or valley—as a central and defining feature of the tribal religion. The tribe may also depend on a number of "sacred" places for practice of religious activities. These spatial references orient the people and place them within the land; they give a sense of history, rootedness, and belonging....

### Reciprocity and Balance as Guiding Ethics

The interrelationship of people and land, combined with the deeply rooted ethics of reciprocity and balance, lead to a long-term view of ecological stability or, in contemporary terms, a concern with "sustainability." Traditionally, the relationships between indigenous peoples and their traditional lands were largely seen as permanent and stable. This perception has only intensified with the diminishment of the land base through the reservation system....

For Indian peoples, who traditionally interpreted their relationship with the land and with future generations as holistic, cyclical, and permanent, sustainability was the natural result, if not the conscious goal, of deeply rooted environmental ethics and traditional land-based economies. Many contemporary indigenous peoples thus advocate a Native concept of sustainability that "means ensuring the survival of the people, the land and the resources for seven generations." Although the indigenous understanding of sustainability is promoted by traditional land-based economies, the incorporation of Indian nations into the larger industrial and market economy of the United States, with its attendant value systems, has facilitated pressures to engage in commercial resource extraction and other nontraditional economic development. This has often precipitated intratribal disputes over land use and resource development and has raised the question of whether non-traditional economic development will undermine the indigenous commitment to sustainability....

### The Role of Indigenous Ethics in Guiding Tribal Environmental Policy

The influence of traditional ethics and environmental knowledge on contemporary tribal policy cannot be underestimated. Indeed, there are many examples of successful implementation of traditional ethics in contemporary tribal environmental management. However, there are also many examples of tribal policy built on what appear to be Anglo-American norms, particularly in the case of industries such as mining and waste disposal, which also serve non-Indian interests....

### Incorporation of Traditional Values into Environmental Policy

...The Confederated Salish and Kootenai Tribes of the Flathead Reservation in Montana have developed a comprehensive environmental regulatory and land use management scheme that rests heavily on traditional values. For example, the Salish and Kootenai Natural Resources Department developed the "Mission Mountains Tribal

Wilderness Management Plan" ("Wilderness Plan")....An important part of the Wilderness Plan is the preservation of cultural and historical resources. The Flathead Culture Committee was given a critical role in determining specific policies and actions to govern specific sites. In some cases this has resulted in barring public access to certain ceremonial and religious sites. The Flathead Culture Committee explains the importance of the Mission Mountains:

> Our elders have many stories to tell about experiences in the mountains in hunting, berry picking and about Indian people seeking their powers in the mountains. They have become for us, the descendants of Indians, sacred grounds. Grounds that should not be disturbed or marred. We realize the importance of these mountains to our elders, to ourselves, and for the perpetuation of our Indian culture because of these stories. They are lands where our people walked and lived. Lands and landmarks carved through the minds of our ancestors through Coyote stories and actual experiences. Lands, landmarks, trees, mountain tops, crevices that we should look up to with respect.

A central purpose of the Wilderness Plan is to preserve the wilderness for future generations. As one tribal Committee noted: "These mountains belong to our children, and when our children grow old they will belong to their children. In this way and for this reason these mountains are sacred."...

The Northern Cheyenne Tribe is another example of an Indian nation that has applied traditional norms both to overcome the detrimental impacts of previous federal policies and to set a more positive direction for future policies. The Northern Cheyenne Reservation sits over the Fort Union coal formation, which stretches from northern Colorado to Canada, and houses an estimated 5 billion tons of coal worth approximately $400 billion. A significant number of the Northern Cheyenne Tribe are committed to maintaining traditional values and have resisted efforts to strip-mine the vast coal reserves, even though tribal unemployment rates continue to hover at 50%. During the 1970s, the Bureau of Indian Affairs leased more than half of the Cheyenne Reservation in Montana for coal mining. The leases provided for minimal lease royalties (17 cents per ton) and had no environmental safeguards. The Northern Cheyenne Tribe formed a committee to study ways to void the leases. After the Tribe brought its first lawsuit, federal legislation cancelling the leases was enacted in 1980. The Northern Cheyenne Tribe's resistance to coal mining provides a sharp contrast to the neighboring Crow Tribe which is heavily engaged in coal mining and has opposed the Northern Cheyenne Tribe's attempts to secure enhanced protection for air quality.

The Northern Cheyenne Tribe was the first Indian nation to petition the EPA under regulations to the Clean Air Act to redesignate the reservation air quality as "Class I," a class reserved for near-pristine air quality. This was an important step in mitigating the air quality impacts of the two power plants directly north of the Reservation at Colstrip, Montana. The need for pristine air quality was a means of perpetuating the Northern Cheyenne commitment to the holistic preservation of the Cheyenne "environment, culture, and religion."...

### Tribal Environmental Policy That Departs from Traditional Norms

There are several categories of land use that appear to be inconsistent with the traditional environmental norms that we have explored, including coal strip-mining, uranium mining, and siting solid, hazardous, or nuclear waste repositories on tribal land. Both the mining industry and the waste industry carry the potential of severe environmental degradation and, as a result, would appear to be diametrically opposed to traditional indigenous land ethics. Yet both industries have found homes on some Indian reservations. Why?

### The Mining Industry and Indian Reservations

[T]o a large extent, all Indian nations have been subjected to successive federal policies which encouraged the exploitation of mineral resources on Indian lands. In the late nineteenth century and early twentieth century, Indian treaty lands were often removed from Indian ownership and trust status to facilitate mineral exploitation. For example, the Crow Reservation once encompassed 39 million acres, including vast stores of coal, oil, and natural gas. After several land cessions, the Crow Reservation now encompasses only 2.2 million acres, although the Tribe has reserved mineral rights in certain of the ceded lands. Other lands remained in tribal ownership but were leased out for mineral development by BIA officials convinced, as was Commissioner of Indian Affairs Cato Sells, that it is "an economic and social crime...to permit thousands of acres of fertile land belonging to the Indians and capable of great industrial development to lie in unproductive idleness."...

Without direct policy control over mineral development, Indian nations were exploited financially and their lands and people were subjected to severe environmental contamination. By the 1970s, the beginning of the era of "self-determination," Indian nations could only hope to control the damage by renegotiating lease terms that practically gave away their mineral resources and by seeking remediation for the environmental degradation....

[M]any tribal members continue to protest mining operations on reservation lands, contending that such industry dries up precious water supplies, pollutes water, and endangers the health of people and livestock. The mining companies, however, point to the economic benefits they have offered to tribal communities, including increased funding for education. Given these competing claims, tribal decisions on mining policy are not clearly "right" or "wrong." Nor can tribal governments be faulted for trying to maximize the gain from on-going resource development by renegotiating lease agreements. In many cases, after nearly a century of mineral exploitation, there was no realistic opportunity to go back to a pristine natural world that would enable a traditional land based economy to flourish. The traditional land bases had been badly eroded, open mines and mineral tailings were located throughout many reservations, and many tribal members were dependent upon jobs with the local mines. [Marjane] Ambler notes that in the thirty years that the Anaconda Minerals Company operated a uranium mine on Laguna Pueblo lands in New Mexico, it "had completely changed the local economy from agriculture to mining, employing thousands of tribal members over the years." After Anaconda pulled out, the Pueblos had to pressure the company to provide funds to remediate the massive contamination at Laguna....

### The Waste Industry and Indian Reservations

The "Not in My Backyard" movement among urban environmentalists and concerned citizens and increasingly stringent state environmental regulations have promoted the recent trend of waste disposal companies to approach tribal governments. The quasi-sovereign trust status of Indian lands has long exempted them from many types of state regulation, and the remote locations of many reservations appeal to the waste industry. From 1990 to 1992, many tribes were approached by waste disposal companies with proposals to site hazardous and solid waste repositories on tribal lands. In some cases, such as the Campo case, these proposals have been enthusiastically accepted by tribal leaders as providing economic hope to desperately impoverished reservations. In other cases the proposals have been greeted by community outrage and allegations of genocide. As one Navajo leader commented, it is often hard to tell whether such a project represents "economic development or genocide."

In 1989, for example, officials from High Tech Recycling and Waste Tech, Inc. of Colorado arrived in the community of Dilkon on the Navajo Reservation, proposing to lease 100 acres of land for a hazardous waste disposal plant that would include an incinerator and landfill. At the time, the community had an unemployment rate of 75%. The company offered to "invest $35 million, bringing millions in revenue for the local economy, a new hospital and 175 jobs." Local tribal officials initially approved the project, but other community leaders formed a chapter of Dine CARE ("Citizens Against Ruining Our Environment"), a grassroots environmentalist movement. Dine CARE educated the community about the dangers of the project, not an easy task, as one Navajo activist noted, when "there are no words in the Navajo language to describe the kind of poisons that technology has enabled man to produce." The community eventually defeated the proposal....

However, not all tribes agree that the waste business imperils Indian lands and communities. The Salt River Pima-Maricopa Community in Arizona has opened a second phase of its solid-waste landfill, established in the early 1980s. The Campo Band in California is proceeding with its landfill project after a heated battle with local non-Indians who opposed the project. Interestingly, by 1993, all members of the Campo Band supported the waste project and its only opposition has been from non-Indian residents of the adjacent community. Why was the sentiment at Campo different from Dilkon, Rosebud, or the Los Coyotes Reservation, also located in Southern California, where tribal members finally rescinded the Tribal Council's approval of a waste facility?

Poverty is obviously a factor in Campo's decision, but it is a factor that Campo shares with the tribes that have defeated such proposals. In 1987, when Campo first started considering the landfill proposal, the tribal unemployment rate was 79%, and more than half of those who were employed earned less than $7,000 per year.... Another factor in Campo's decision was that the Tribe's relatively small, remote, and arid reservation offered no other realistic opportunities for economic development. In the late 1800s, the Tribe was removed from its arable traditional lands to an area that one BIA official at the time described as "so nearly worthless that a living by farming is out of the question."...

[Another factor,] tribal sovereignty, raises different issues: that is, whether opposition by non-Indians is seen as an attack on the tribe's ability to engage in self-determination as a sovereign government. In the Campo case, non-Indian activists pressured state legislators to introduce legislation that would extend state regulation to waste facilities on Indian land, constituting a blatant attempt to intrude on tribal sovereignty. [Daniel] McGovern suggests that if tribal members perceive a threat to their sovereignty, they tend to unite against the off-reservation forces, even if that means supporting a decision that may be contrary to certain traditional norms about appropriate land use. Thus, the value of maintaining tribal sovereignty may prevail over the value of protecting the integrity of the land. In fact, the Campo landfill represents some risk of permanent groundwater contamination, and thus, potential loss of the ability to even live on the reservation. However, the risk to sovereignty appears to have been perceived as the more immediate threat....

*Concluding Thoughts*

...Tribal governments who depart from traditional norms to engage in nontraditional economic development are responding to a complex history and set of realities.

As the above cases demonstrate, these departures may be caused by a lengthy history of competing values imposed by federal policy, by values formulated as a protective response to ensure the continuation of tribal sovereignty, by values stemming from economic dependency on earlier development decisions, and by the cultural loss that has become endemic to many reservations as a result of loss of traditional lands, resources, and a certain measure of sovereignty....

\* \* \*

## Notes and Questions

1. Is there a difference between the Native American conception of sustainability as articulated in Professor Tsosie's article above, and the western view of sustainability? Is the western view of sustainability more akin to a philosophy of conservation, presumably conservation for the purposes of resource extraction in a market economy?

2. Professor Tsosie gives several specific examples of how Indian-style environmental regulation deviates from western norms. Is this deviation a difference in degree only (quantitative) or is it more qualitative? For example, when environmental regulators elevate environmental values over economic development, is there something going on other than a strict cost-benefit calculation that the anticipated (economic) benefits of resource extraction do not outweigh the (environmental) costs? Conversely, when tribes choose development projects, Tsosie suggests that such decisions may be more complicated than simply a decision that economic benefits outweigh environmental consequences. These decisions may be premised in part upon a perceived threat to sovereignty and self-determination. What implications flow from the observation that tribal decisions about environmental protection reflect the resolution of a complicated mix of factors? Should these decisions be treated any differently on review by an administrative review board or the courts? What happens when the environmental decision has effects beyond the boundaries of tribal land? Does this mean that non-Indian residents adjacent to tribal land must sustain environmental impacts in part to protect the self-determination and sovereignty of the tribe? By what (or whose) standards should we resolve these issues?

3. Professor Tsosie notes that in some instances it is no longer possible for Indian tribes to resume a land-based economy, often because of environmental degradation caused by past extractive uses promoted by federal government agencies. What are possible remedies in such a situation?

4. Professor James Huffman argues that traditional environmentalism assumes a biocentric and anti-growth approach fundamentally opposed to economic development, even when necessary for Native survival. He writes that Native Americans "will suffer at the altar of environmentalism worshiped in their name." He argues that environmental protection is a "luxury good" enjoyed by wealthier societies, and contends that " [l]ike other people living in poverty and circumstances of scarcity, Native Americans will take greater interest in the environment when their material circumstances are improved. Until then, they should be expected to be desirous of resource exploitation and economic development on their reservations." James L. Huffman, *An Exploratory Essay on Native Americans and Environmentalism*, 63 U. Colo. L. Rev 901, 902, 914–919 (1992). Do you agree? Does Professor Huffman give enough weight to the multifaceted nature of the decision making process in Indian country described by Professor Tsosie?

5. In a situation where a tribe is divided regarding a potentially noxious or polluting facility, how can national environmental organizations (including environmental justice

organizations) offer legal, technical or scientific assistance, while still respecting tribal sovereignty? For example, tribal members who dissent from a tribal council decision to site a waste dump may lack the resources to critique the proposal from a legal or scientific perspective, but if they are given help from "outsiders," they may be accused of being manipulated by other organizations' agendas. What advice would you provide to outside environmental groups in these situations?

6. Professor Suagee notes that many Indians view environmental groups with some suspicion. The primary reason for this, he argues, is that "many environmentalists, like most people in the dominant American society, just do not know much about basic principles of federal Indian law, such as the doctrine of retained sovereignty." He further contends that "[g]iven the significant differences between the status of Indian tribes under federal law and minority communities in the United States, minority community activists and their advocates should exercise caution in making statements that may be taken as speaking for reservation Indians." Dean B. Suagee, *Turtle's War Party: An Indian Allegory on Environmental Justice*, 9 J. ENVTL. L. & LITIG. 461, 463, 465 (1994). Some of the tensions Professor Suagee describes are reflected in following article.

## Robert Williams, Large Binocular Telescopes, Red Squirrel Pinatas, and Apache Sacred Mountains: Decolonizing Environmental Law in a Multicultural World
### 96 West Virginia Law Review 1133 (1994)

*Introduction*

For two years, as Director of the Office of Indian Programs at the University of Arizona, I was involved on a near-daily basis with what has come to be known throughout the southwestern United States, and in other parts of the country and world, as the Mt. Graham controversy. The controversy centers around the efforts of the University of Arizona, together with a consortium of foreign astronomers from the Vatican, the Max Planck Institute in Germany, and Arcetri astrophysical observatory of Florence, Italy, to build an astronomical observatory on the peaks of Mt. Graham in southeastern Arizona. Because of my personal involvement, I cannot claim a detached neutrality in my recitation of the facts, or for my very tentative legal-cultural analysis of the controversy. But I do believe that as a minor bit-player in this multi-layered, multicultural drama involving large binocular telescopes, red squirrel pinatas, and Apache sacred mountains, I gained some valuable first-hand knowledge of how our environmental law has been colonized by a perverse system of values which is antithetical to achieving environmental justice for American Indian peoples....

One point which I want to develop in this essay is that any efforts aimed at decolonizing our environmental law must first identify and confront this perverse value system. As I attempt to illustrate, American Indian peoples possess their own unique visions of environmental justice which are capable of inaugurating this decolonization process. The values animating these American Indian visions are typically reinforced throughout tribal culture by myths and narratives which seek to invoke our imaginative capacities to see the social, physical, and spiritual worlds we inhabit as connected and interdependent....

As the Mt. Graham controversy demonstrates, however, the perverse system of values which has colonized our environmental law subjects these Indian visions of environmental justice to a political process, which presents these myths and narratives in a simplified and pejorative way. Indian resistance to the threats posed to our social, physical, and spiritual world by our environmental law are dismissed as attributable to "religious, magical, fanatical behavior."...

### A Layer Cake of Lifezones

...[T]he southernmost forest of spruce and fir in North America grows on Mt.Graham's peaks, and the ecological diversity of the mountain marks it as one of the truly unique environmental resources on the continent. It is reputed as the only mountain range to stack five of the seven major ecosystems of North America in one place...But it is at Mt. Graham's summit, where you find a boreal zone of virgin spruce-fir forest standing yet untouched by the Forest Service's devouring lessees, that it becomes clear what makes this mountain worth fighting for. Wild nature still controls the desert sky-island at the top of Mt. Graham. Mountain lions and black bears roam freely atop the mountain's peaks. The Mexican Spotted Owl and goshawk, two gravely threatened species in the southwest, are found here as well....

### The Universe is Expanding Constantly

...At least eighteen species and subspecies of plants and animals are reputed to be found nowhere else but on Mt. Graham's sky-island peaks. Among the creatures unique to the mountain is the appropriately named Mt. Graham Red Squirrel, a genetic variant of the North American red squirrel....

In the mid-1980s, an international consortium led by the University of Arizona had first proposed construction of 13 telescopes, support facilities, and an access road on Mt. Graham's peaks. The proposal drew protests from a number of environmental groups, forcing the Forest Service in 1985 to begin the Environmental Impact Statement (EIS) process under the National Environmental Protection Act (NEPA) for the project.

The draft Environmental Impact Statement that the agency released the following year identified a "preferred alternative" in which only five telescopes would be constructed on High Peak, one of the various peaks of Mt. Graham. Meanwhile, in 1987, the U.S. Fish and Wildlife Service listed the Mt. Graham Red Squirrel as endangered. This action, not wholly unexpected, required the Forest Service to initiate "formal consultation" [under the Endangered Species Act, (ESA)] with the Fish and Wildlife Service regarding the suitability of an astrophysical complex on Mt. Graham given the endangered status of the red squirrel....The Fish and Wildlife Service then issued a Biological Opinion in 1988, which found that "establishment of the seven telescope observatory on Emerald and High Peaks is likely to jeopardize the continued existence of the endangered red squirrel because this plan significantly increases the existing jeopardy status of this squirrel."...

Given the language of Section 7 of the ESA, that forbids federal agencies from taking action "likely to jeopardize" or endanger species, and a federal agency's biological opinion that the university's telescopes would "likely jeopardize the continued existence" of the Mt. Graham Red Squirrel, the university recognized that its project could be interminably delayed by legal and political challenges from environmentalists, and perhaps even killed....

A new strategy was developed to conquer Mt. Graham—simply exempt the entire project from NEPA and the Endangered Species Act. This stroke of brilliance was legislated into law in 1988, when Congress passed the Arizona-Idaho Conservation Act. In Section VI of the Act, Congress essentially assumed the role the Forest Service would ordinarily have played and [selected the alternative] that permitted construction on Emerald Peak, the most vital portion of the red squirrel's habitat....

### Barometer Functions

Even up to this point in the story, the symbology generated by the Mt. Graham controversy is irresistible to the cultural critic. Like the Northern Spotted Owl, which has pitted environmentalists against the logging industry of the Pacific Northwest, endangered species like the Mt. Graham Red Squirrel perform a valuable "barometer function" in alerting humans to environmental threats. Our modern environmental law, however, as is evidenced by the Mt. Graham controversy, has generally done a poor job of explaining the basic importance to us, as human beings connected to our ecosystems, of protecting endangered species. Using an endangered species such as the Mt. Graham Red Squirrel or the Northern Spotted Owl as a symbol of the need for preserving biological diversity and respecting its importance translates poorly in the public imagination.... In the press and even on the campus, the environmentalists involved in the Mt. Graham controversy were caricatured as groups of slightly unbalanced tree-huggers and wildly unbalanced eco-terrorists of the Earth First! variety, who preferred saving a subspecies of an otherwise ubiquitous rodent, as opposed to constructing a multi-million dollar astronomical observatory devoted to the highest causes of science. Given this symbology, the Mt. Graham Red Squirrel never had a chance of surviving unmolested in its mountain habitat....

### The GAANS' Emergence

The first stage of the Mt. Graham controversy came to a close in October of 1989, when the university was given the go-ahead by a federal district court to cut an access road to the proposed telescope site on the mountain....

It was during this same period that the Mt. Graham controversy entered its second stage, with the appearance of a group called the Apache Survival Coalition. The Coalition claimed that Mt. Graham was sacred according to traditional Apache spiritual and ritual beliefs because it was the home of the Gaans. The Gaans, as members of the Coalition explained, represented the elemental forces of the Universe according to traditional Apache belief. The Gaans had emerged from Mt. Graham many ages ago to give the original medicine to an Apache medicine person. After performing this service for the Apaches, the Gaans had then gone back into Mt. Graham to rest. The university's telescopes, it was declared, would not only destroy the ability of traditional Apaches to worship on the mountain and give thanks to the Gaans, but if the Gaans were now disturbed by the university's digging and blasting on the top of the mountain, there would be a great cosmic disturbance in the universe....

### A Prayer to Mt. Graham

It should come as little surprise to find out that Indian values and belief systems are not reflected in or accepted by our environmental law. The point that I have learned from working and talking with many Indian people is that this is precisely what is wrong with our environmental law.

In many Indian belief systems, you will find an intimate relation between the spiritual world, the physical world, and the social world. These three dimensions of human experience are all closely integrated in most Indian belief systems, an integration which is totally alien to our environmental law. Indians have many ways to imagine and act upon this intimate relation between the spiritual, physical, and social worlds, but all of them basically boil down to a deep and abiding reverence for the land that sustains the interconnected worlds of the tribe. Without the land, in other words, there is no tribe. That is why tribal land is sacred land, because it has been given by the Creator to sustain the tribe. That is why tribal values seek to cultivate an attitude of respect for the land and the resources it yields....

It is difficult for environmentalists to deal with tribal governments who seriously consider siting hazardous waste dumps in their reserves and for scientists to deal with a group of Indians opposed to siting a telescope on top of a mountain because neither group is capable of understanding the Indian vision of environmental justice which underlies all land use planning decisions in a tribal community—whether or not a particular use of land will be good for the people physically, socially, and spiritually. The tribe's determination will turn on the nature of the people's connection to that land resource; a connection which Indian people can more easily visualize through sacred stories and myths like the story of the Gaans....

Thus, according to this Indian way of looking at Mt. Graham, you protect what a modern environmentalist might call the biodiversity of the mountain because it is that biodiversity which physically sustains you and the members of your tribe. It is a source of food and other forms of sustaining nourishment. It provides herbs and healing medicines. The Gaan story teaches that not only does Mt. Graham sustain you physically, but socially as well, because the sacred story of the Gaans connects the tribal community around a set of cohesive values which define tribal social life. The tribal society is sustained by the mountain's life-giving forces. Protecting Mt. Graham fulfills our obligations to the future generations which will constitute the tribal society....

What I found most depressing about the Mt. Graham controversy is that the perverse system of values which has colonized our environmental law has so little difficulty in dismissing the relevance of Indian visions of environmental justice embodied in stories like the Gaans on Mt. Graham. It dismisses these visions through various mechanisms which have institutionalized environmental racism against Indian peoples at the deepest levels of our society....

### The San Carlos Apache "Community"

From the university's perspective, any rights—moral or legal—that the Apaches might have had to protest the telescope project on Mt. Graham had been waived by the San Carlos Apache Tribal governments' failure to formally respond in a timely fashion, or even at all, to the various Forest Service initiatives designed to inform the tribe about the project....In reality, the process by which Indians peoples, be they Apaches or members of other tribes, were supposed to voice their visions on their connections to Mt. Graham had been, in effect, colonized by a system of values antithetical to achieving environmental justice for Indian peoples.

The San Carlos Apache Community is not a "community" at all, at least in the way that a non-Indian would normally understand that concept. The reservation is comprised of an amalgamation of Western Apache bands—Arivaipa, Tontos, Yavapais, Coyoteros, Chiricahuas, Mimbrenos—that were placed on the San Carlos reservation by the United States Army in the nineteenth century....Factionalism was further inbred from the start of the reservation's creation because many of these Apache groups had never been associated with each other. Even to this day, factionalism has never been eliminated as a dominant, defining fact of "community" life on the San Carlos reservation....

The fact is that the Apaches had never ruled themselves according to the type of "tribal government" that the BIA had provided for them, at least prior to their colonization by the United States. Apaches traditionally organize themselves at the band level, and to many Apaches, the idea that a BIA-created "tribal government" represents their interests generally, or particularly on issues of religious belief, is offensive and resisted in the extreme....

### Invasion of the Lutheranizers

...[T]he various laws and regulatory procedures designed to incorporate Indians into the federal environmental and land use planning process need a point of access to identify tribal interests. Who do you contact if you are the University of Arizona or the United States Forest Service? Why, the tribal government, of course; but who is the tribal government, and where does tribal sovereignty reside? These are questions that our environmental law, colonized by the same system of values which colonized Indian tribes, does not bother to even ask.

The Mt. Graham controversy illustrates perfectly how the processes of our environmental law subtly perpetuate colonialism against Indian peoples. The history of treaties between tribes and the federal government teaches us how the United States would frequently designate a tribal "chief" to sell out the territorial interests of his people, or how the BIA would form a tribal government to facilitate surrender of tribal resources. From the perspective of the white man's law, these "chiefs" and these "governments" represented the Indians. In truth, these processes had little to do with how Indians actually governed themselves....

Thus, our environmental law tells Indians that they must run their governments the same way that the dominant society runs its governments. This means that when the tribal government in a fractionalized Indian community fails to respond to a request from the Forest Service about the tribal community's religious interests in a mountain, our environmental law can treat the tribe as having no religious interests in that mountain at all. Indians can only engage in the federal land use and environmental regulatory process through cultural and political institutions determined by the dominant society....

### Conclusion: Religious, Magical, Fanatical Behavior

...For Indians, stories and narratives like the Gaan creation myth invoke the imaginative capacity to visualize the connections between the physical environment, the social welfare of the community, and the spiritual values that create the consensus in Indian communities as to whether a particular use of the environment is beneficial or harmful to the human community. For non-Indians, there are no stories and myths which can help us imagine why preserving biodiversity is something deeply connected to who and what we are in the world—only science, economic analysis, vaguely stated appeals to aesthetic sensibility, and symbols generated by the Endangered Species Act such as the red squirrel. None of these has proven capable of generating consensus in our society about the importance of environmental values such as biodiversity to the human community.

Our technological society has lost its sense of reliance on nature for survival, and therefore, we have lost our sense of respect for the world we inhabit. We have thus lost those stories and myths which once must have helped us see our connections to our own world. And so our environmental law has been impoverished of such metaphors as the Gaans on Mt. Graham. Indian resistance to siting a telescope on Mt. Graham seems like "religious, magical, fanatical behavior." The price we pay for maintaining our dying colonialism is to dismiss the decolonizing potential of these Indian visions of environmental justice. And until we do decolonize our environmental law, we always risk the danger of the Gaans reemerging from Mt. Graham to wreak havoc upon our world.

\* \* \*

## Notes and Questions

1. What does Professor Williams mean by the term "colonized" and how does that term apply to environmental law? In what respect do Professor Williams' comments about a colonizing process that describes Indian resistance as magical and fanatical echo Paul Smith's points about the power of language? For example, Smith notes the use of the words chief and tribe instead of president and nation, respectively. Williams points out how the Native American belief system is characterized as "myth." Thus, in a dispute over resources, the tribal position is rendered strange, exotic, primitive, or otherwise marginalized. How does one begin to decolonize such a process? Does it matter whether we view environmental law as a set of rules emanating from a particular set of values concerning the natural world, or simply a legal mechanism to resolve disputes over natural resources?

2. In Professor Williams' view, why does environmental law do a poor job of safeguarding the interests of Indians? Why, in his view, does environmental law do a poor job of protecting ecosystems and biodiversity? Professor Williams is as unsparing in his criticism of the environmentalists who opposed the Mt. Graham telescopes as he is of the scientists, university administrators and politicians who pushed it forward. He writes of his experience:

> On the whole, the environmentalists I dealt with spoke passionately about the need to protect Mt. Graham, but they never connected that passion to any particular vision or ethic of how we as human beings ought to relate to the mountain. Nor could they articulate any set of values not connected to some sterile form of economic calculus that made it clear to me why siting telescopes on Mt. Graham would be wrong.

*Id.* at 1140–41. Is this critique a reaction to the professionalization and insider status of conventional environmental organizations that is similar to the sentiments expressed by environmental justice activists in the "group of ten letter" to environmental organizations excerpted in Chapter I? If so, where do you think the tensions might lie between Native American environmental justice activists and non-Native environmental justice activists?

3. Do you agree that traditional practices of public notice and consultation are inapt when dealing with Indians? Can you suggest ideas for better models that should be used?

# Eric K. Yamamoto & Jen-L W. Lyman, Racializing Environmental Justice
## 72 University of Colorado Law Review 311 (2001)

"[Racial c]ommunities are not all created equal." Yet, the established environmental justice framework tends to treat racial minorities as interchangeable and to assume for all communities of color that health and distribution of environmental burdens are main concerns. For some racialized communities, however, environmental justice is not only, or even primarily, about immediate health concerns or burden distribution. Rather, for them, and particularly for some indigenous peoples, environmental justice is mainly about cultural and economic self-determination and belief systems that connect their history, spirituality, and livelihood to the natural environment....

### The Established Environmental Justice Framework

...The roots of environmental injustice lie in what the Reverend Benjamin Chavis termed "environmental racism." Environmental racism is described as the "nationwide phenomenon" that occurs when "any policy, practice, or directive...differentially impacts or disadvantages [whether intended or unintended] individuals, groups, or communities based on race or color." For most scholars, this "differential effect," measured against white communities, results in the unfair distribution of environmental hazards. The established environmental justice framework addresses this problem of environmental racism and seeks to achieve healthy and sustainable communities.

This vision of environmental justice has four general characteristics. First, it focuses on traditional environmental hazards such as waste facilities and resulting pollution.... Second, and closely related, the environmental justice framework focuses on the disproportionate distribution of hazardous facilities and on the re-siting of those facilities.... Third, the established environmental justice framework seeks to ensure that communities of color have equal representation in the administration of environmental laws and policies....Fourth, environmental justice framework emphasizes "a community-based movement to bring pressure on the person or agency with decisionmaking authority."...

### Limits

The established framework sometimes furthers, and at times undermines, environmental justice. It furthers environmental justice when it provides racial and indigenous communities the concepts and language they need to advocate effectively for the siting and health outcomes they desire.

The framework, however, at times also undercuts environmental justice struggles by racial and indigenous communities because it tends to foster misassumptions about race, culture, sovereignty, and the importance of distributive justice. Those misassumptions sometimes lead environmental justice scholars and activists to miss what is of central importance to affected communities.

The first misassumption is that for all racialized groups in all situations, a hazard-free physical environment is their main, if not only, concern. Environmental justice advocates foster this notion by placing emphasis on "high quality environments" and the adverse health effects caused by exposure to air pollutants and hazardous waste materials.

Not all facility sitings that pose health risks, however, warrant full-scale opposition by host communities. Some communities, on balance, are willing to tolerate these facilities for the economic benefits they confer or in lieu of the cultural or social disruption that might accompany large-scale remedial efforts. Other communities, struggling to deal with joblessness, inadequate education, and housing discrimination, indeed with daily survival, prefer to devote most of their limited time and political capital to those challenges. In these situations, racial and indigenous communities may have pressing needs and long-range goals beyond the re-siting of polluting facilities....

*An Emerging Native American Framework*

As part of a critical re-examination, Native American legal scholars are attempting to develop an integrated environmental, race, and sovereignty framework by approaching environmental justice with greater cultural and historical depth....

Although illuminating in important respects, the emerging Native American framework itself is limited. It reconstructs environmental justice in terms of a more or less singular indigenous perspective of the environment. This perspective is important for indigenous groups facing environmental injustice—or seeking to define for themselves how "the environment" and "justice" connect. But to a large extent, the writings overlook salient differences among Native American groups and subgroups and wide differences among traditionally classified "racial minorities" in terms of understandings of environmental injustice and how to deal with it....

[William] Shutkin and [Charlie] Lord suggest that "the legal system has perpetuated environmental injustice by misreading or disregarding [a] community's history." These scholars urge "a more complete history that incorporates not only a view of the past, present, and future, but also the question of justice."...

This suggested contextual approach moves closer to treating racial and indigenous groups and their relationships to the environment in light of cultural and social differences. The approach, however, needs both expansion and refinement in order to: (1) address explicitly how racial categories are constructed, racial identities forged, and racial meanings developed; (2) account for significant differences between groups traditionally described as racial minorities (African Americans, Asian Americans, Latinas/os, and indigenous peoples (including American Indians, Aleuts, Eskimos, Native Hawaiians)); and (3) recognize and deal more directly with the influences of whiteness in the formation and implementation of environmental law and policy. What is needed, then, is a framework that more subtly interrogates social, political, historical, cultural, and power interactions among whites and racial and indigenous groups.

*Racializing Environmental Justice*

Critical race theory offers communities and environmental justice proponents important critical tools for evaluating past experiences and present conditions. Beginning with a skepticism of legal impartiality common to all legal realists, critical race theory pays particular attention to the roles that race, racism, and nativism play in the formation of legal norms and the administration of justice. Recognizing the law as a "text" written by society, critical race theory looks beyond the law's main story to those "outsider" accounts that the legal system suppresses or ignores. Critical race theory thus examines power in social relationships and seeks to reframe legal concepts of justice by challenging and reworking their implicit biases. It offers an approach for integrating key aspects of the established environmental justice framework and the emerging Native peoples' framework with new insights into racial differentiation and empowerment, the influences of whiteness, and the importance of praxis. That approach is what we call "racializing environmental justice."

*Racialization and Differentiation*

...Critical race theory challenges the very concept of "race" as "immutable" or biological, as something objective and largely devoid of social content or historical context. It moves analytical understandings of "race" beyond its conception as "an independent variable requiring little or no elaboration." For Michael Omi and Howard

Winant, race is understood "as an unstable and 'decentered' complex of social meanings constantly being transformed by political struggle." Race, and, more particularly, racial categories and identities, are continually formed and reformed through social and political struggle. This process of racialization extends "racial meaning to a previously racially unclassified relationship, social practice, or group." Racializing environmental justice thus entails interrogation into the ways evolving public perceptions and the particular struggles of a community have generated racial or cultural meanings for that community....

The racialization process, furthermore, "fixes status and allocates power differentially among and within racial groups." So, for instance, more "'established' immigrant groups, with greater resources and access to political power may organize around mobility issues ('glass ceiling'), while recent immigrant groups may focus on 'survival issues' (funding for language classes and job-training programs)." As a result, differential racialization primarily pursues a framing of race that acknowledges that historical and contemporary social and cultural influences have important consequences for "individual identity and collective consciousness, and political organization."

For Native peoples, differential racialization fosters another kind of inquiry, one that addresses often substantial differences among immigrant racial populations in America, imported slaves, and conquered indigenous peoples. The inquiry focuses on the effects of land dispossession, culture destruction, loss of sovereignty, and, in turn, on claims to self-determination and nationhood (rather than to equality and integration)....

[E]nvironmental justice must recognize that each racial or Native group is differently situated and that differing contexts contribute to differing group goals, identities, and differential group power.... When applied, this framework illuminates the underlying racialized character of environmental justice claims and treats each racial or Native community separately according to its specific socio-economic needs, cultural values, and group goals.

For example, environmental racism may be different for Latina/o or African Americans residing in a low-income area with a toxic waste dump than it is for Native Hawaiians or Native Americans faced with problems of cultural destruction and loss of spiritual connection to the land. Their goals, needs, and racial identities differ. Latinas/os and African Americans may be mainly concerned about health risks associated with exposure to toxic pollutants, while Native Hawaiians and Native Americans may be primarily concerned about cultural survival, economic self-sufficiency, political self-governance, and the maintenance of a spiritual connection to the environment....

* * *

## Notes and Questions

1. Yamamoto and Lyman urge the environmental justice community to rethink what they suggest is an undue emphasis on the distributional aspects of traditional environmental hazards, an emphasis they argue may promote a misconception that facility siting and environmental hazards are of primary concern and that communities of color will always forego economic development to resist the risks generated by these facilities. As noted in Chapter I, however, the principles of environmental justice reflect a much broader view by environmental justice activists, emphasizing fair process, self-determination, cultural and spiritual values, and sustainability. Is there a disjunction between the values as articulated in those principles and the various environmental justice cam-

paigns undertaken throughout the United States and beyond? Some suggest there is, while others argue that the diversity of environmental justice campaigns and presence of stable coalitions among diverse environmental justice organizations (including Native American organizations) suggests a much broader range of values is at play. If the latter is more accurate, the perception that environmental justice activists unduly emphasize siting challenges may be due to frequent media portrayals of environmental justice campaigns as single-mindedly anti-development and anti-siting. On the other hand, if the environmental justice movement is in fact too preoccupied with distributional issues and traditional pollution-generated risk, how can the broad group of community-based movements that comprise the environmental justice movement reorder its collective priorities or broaden its collective mission?

2. Yamamoto and Lyman advocate for the use of critical race theory to "racialize" environmental justice, meaning in part the process of using techniques such as outsider accounts to analytically investigate the way in which different groups—variously situated historically, economically, culturally, and politically—are racialized, and how that process of racialization may generate different cultural meanings and political goals for different groups. In what ways might their approach be different or similar to one of the stronger tenets that has emerged from the environmental justice movement: that impacted communities should "speak for themselves?" One of the most effective political strategies used by environmental justice activists is a variant of the outsider account. Community residents tell their own stories through compelling testimony or by physically taking participants to the affected area. The experiential value of a site tour has proven a powerful counter narrative to the dominant discourse of "negligible risk" or "trivial impact." In a similar vein, Professor Robert Verchick has described how women of color in the environmental justice movement, in the course of their activism and leadership roles, employ various techniques long advanced by feminist theorists, such as consciousness raising and unmasking. Robert R. M. Verchick, *In a Greener Voice: Feminist Theory and Environmental Justice*, 19 HARV. WOMEN'S L.J. 23, 73–74 (1996). However, as remarkable a process as this is, it typically occurs in an ad hoc and inconsistent manner in the field. Given the theoretical depth evident in critical race writings, a collaborative project between the critical race theorists and environmental justice activists may have its own beneficial brand of synergy. How might this collaboration occur given the environmental justice principle that "we speak for ourselves?"

3. As Yamamoto and Lyman suggest, the cultural context in which environmental harms occur can be of central importance to Indians. For example, Professor Catherine O'Neill explains that "[f]ish, especially salmon, are necessary for the survival of the native peoples of the Pacific Northwest, both as individuals and as a people. Fish are crucial for native peoples' sustenance, in the sense of a way to feed oneself and one's family. Fish are also crucial for subsistence, in the sense of a culture or way of life with economic, spiritual, social, and physical dimensions—a way to be Yakama, or to be Tulalip. Salmon, especially, are central to the belief systems, identities, and social relationships that define these peoples." O'Neill, *supra* at 5–6.

# C. Protection of Sacred Sites on Public Lands

Many sites of great religious and cultural importance to Indians are found on public lands managed by the federal government. Approximately 662 million acres of land are owned by the federal government, approximately 29 percent of all the land in this country. Federal public land laws establish different governing regimes depending on how the lands are classified (i.e., as a wilderness area, national park, national forest, etc), but most vest significant discretion in agency land managers. Many public lands must accommodate multiple and sometimes competing uses, including timber harvesting and mineral development, recreation, wildlife protection, preservationist interests, and others. Inevitably, some of these uses occur on sites that are sacred to Indians, raising two types of important constitutional questions under the First Amendment: do agency activities that interfere with Indian religious practices violate their free exercise of religion ("free exercise claims"), and do governmental efforts to protect Indian religious practices violate the establishment clause? The cases below reveal how the courts have attempted to resolve these conflicts, starting with the leading Supreme Court decision on this issue.

## Lyng v. Northwest Indian Cemetery Protective Association
### 485 U.S. 439 (1988)

*Justice O'Connor delivered the opinion of the Court*:

This case requires us to consider whether the First Amendment's Free Exercise Clause forbids the Government from permitting timber harvesting in, or constructing a road through, a portion of a National Forest that has traditionally been used for religious purposes by members of three American Indian tribes in northwestern California....

As part of a project to create a paved 75-mile road linking two California towns, Gasquet and Orleans, the United States Forest Service has upgraded 49 miles of previously unpaved roads on federal land. In order to complete this project (the G-O road), the Forest Service must build a 6-mile paved segment through the Chimney Rock section of the Six Rivers National Forest. That section of the forest is situated between two other portions of the road that are already complete.

In 1977, the Forest Service issued a draft environmental impact statement that discussed proposals for upgrading an existing unpaved road that runs through the Chimney Rock area. In response to comments on the draft statement, the Forest Service commissioned a study of American Indian cultural and religious sites in the area. The Hoopa Valley Indian reservation adjoins the Six Rivers National Forest, and the Chimney Rock area has historically been used for religious purposes by Yurok, Karok, and Tolowa Indians. The commissioned study, which was completed in 1979, found that the entire area "is significant as an integral and indispensible [sic] part of Indian religious conceptualization and practice." Specific sites are used for certain rituals, and "successful use of the [area] is dependent upon and facilitated by certain qualities of the physical environment, the most important of which are privacy, silence, and an undisturbed natural setting." The study concluded that constructing a road along any of the available routes "would cause serious and irreparable damage to the sacred areas which are an integral and necessary part of the belief systems and lifeway of Northwest California Indian peoples." Accordingly, the report recommended that the G-O road not be completed.

In 1982, the Forest Service decided not to adopt this recommendation, and it prepared a final environmental impact statement for construction of the road. The Regional Forester selected a route that avoided archeological sites and was removed as far as possible from the sites used by contemporary Indians for specific spiritual activities. Alternative routes that would have avoided the Chimney Rock area altogether were rejected because they would have required the acquisition of private land, had serious soil stability problems, and would in any event have traversed areas having ritualistic value to American Indians. At about the same time, the Forest Service adopted a management plan allowing for the harvesting of significant amounts of timber in this area of the forest. The management plan provided for one-half mile protective zones around all the religious sites identified in the report that had been commissioned in connection with the G-O road.

[Plaintiffs then filed suit in federal court challenging the road-building and timber-harvesting decisions, and after a trial, the district court granted an injunction barring those actions from going forward.]

While an appeal was pending before the United States Court of Appeals for the Ninth Circuit, Congress enacted the California Wilderness Act of 1984, Pub. L. 98-425, 98 Stat. 1619. Under that statute, much of the property covered by the Forest Service's management plan is now designated a wilderness area, which means that commercial activities such as timber harvesting are forbidden. The statute exempts a narrow strip of land, coinciding with the Forest Service's proposed route for the remaining segment of the G-O road, from the wilderness designation....

The Free Exercise Clause of the First Amendment provides that "Congress shall make no law...prohibiting the free exercise [of religion]." U. S. Const., Amdt. I. It is undisputed that the Indian respondents' beliefs are sincere and that the Government's proposed actions will have severe adverse effects on the practice of their religion. Respondents contend that the burden on their religious practices is heavy enough to violate the Free Exercise Clause unless the Government can demonstrate a compelling need to complete the G-O road or to engage in timber harvesting in the Chimney Rock area. We disagree.

In Bowen v. Roy, 476 U. S. 693 (1986), we considered a challenge to a federal statute that required the States to use Social Security numbers in administering certain welfare programs. Two applicants for benefits under these programs contended that their religious beliefs prevented them from acceding to the use of a Social Security number for their two-year-old daughter because the use of a numerical identifier would "rob the spirit' of [their] daughter and prevent her from attaining greater spiritual power." Id., at 696.... The Court rejected [this challenge]:

> "The Free Exercise Clause simply cannot be understood to require the Government to conduct its own internal affairs in ways that comport with the religious beliefs of particular citizens. Just as the Government may not insist that [the Roys] engage in any set form of religious observance, so [they] may not demand that the Government join in their chosen religious practices by refraining from using a number to identify their daughter." [Id. at 699–700.]...

The building of a road or the harvesting of timber on publicly owned land cannot meaningfully be distinguished from the use of a Social Security number in Roy. In both cases, the challenged government action would interfere significantly with private persons' ability to pursue spiritual fulfillment according to their own religious beliefs. In neither case, however, would the affected individuals be coerced by the Government's action into violating their religious beliefs; nor would either governmental action penalize religious activity by denying any person an equal share of the rights, benefits, and privileges enjoyed by other citizens....

It is true that this Court has repeatedly held that indirect coercion or penalties on the free exercise of religion, not just outright prohibitions, are subject to scrutiny under the First Amendment.... This does not and cannot imply that incidental effects of government programs, which may make it more difficult to practice certain religions but which have no tendency to coerce individuals into acting contrary to their religious beliefs, require government to bring forward a compelling justification for its otherwise lawful actions....

Whatever may be the exact line between unconstitutional prohibitions on the free exercise of religion and the legitimate conduct by government of its own affairs, the location of the line cannot depend on measuring the effects of a governmental action on a religious objector's spiritual development. The Government does not dispute, and we have no reason to doubt, that the logging and road-building projects at issue in this case could have devastating effects on traditional Indian religious practices. Those practices are intimately and inextricably bound up with the unique features of the Chimney Rock area, which is known to the Indians as the "high country." Individual practitioners use this area for personal spiritual development; some of their activities are believed to be critically important in advancing the welfare of the tribe, and indeed, of mankind itself. The Indians use this area, as they have used it for a very long time, to conduct a wide variety of specific rituals that aim to accomplish their religious goals. According to their beliefs, the rituals would not be efficacious if conducted at other sites than the ones traditionally used, and too much disturbance of the area's natural state would clearly render any meaningful continuation of traditional practices impossible. To be sure, the Indians themselves were far from unanimous in opposing the G-O road, and it seems less than certain that construction of the road will be so disruptive that it will doom their religion. Nevertheless, we can assume that the threat to the efficacy of at least some religious practices is extremely grave.

Even if we assume that we should accept the Ninth Circuit's prediction, according to which the G-O road will "virtually destroy the Indians' ability to practice their religion," (opinion below), the Constitution simply does not provide a principle that could justify upholding respondents' legal claims. However much we might wish that it were otherwise, government simply could not operate if it were required to satisfy every citizen's religious needs and desires. A broad range of government activities — from social welfare programs to foreign aid to conservation projects — will always be considered essential to the spiritual well-being of some citizens, often on the basis of sincerely held religious beliefs. Others will find the very same activities deeply offensive, and perhaps incompatible with their own search for spiritual fulfillment and with the tenets of their religion. The First Amendment must apply to all citizens alike, and it can give to none of them a veto over public programs that do not prohibit the free exercise of religion. The Constitution does not, and courts cannot, offer to reconcile the various competing demands on government, many of them rooted in sincere religious belief, that inevitably arise in so diverse a society as ours....

One need not look far beyond the present case to see why the analysis in *Roy*... offers a sound reading of the Constitution. Respondents attempt to stress the limits of the religious servitude that they are now seeking to impose on the Chimney Rock area of the Six Rivers National Forest. While defending an injunction against logging operations and the construction of a road, they apparently do not at present object to the area's being used by recreational visitors, other Indians, or forest rangers. Nothing in the principle for which they contend, however, would distinguish this case from another lawsuit in which they (or similarly situated religious objectors) might seek to exclude all human activity but their own from sacred areas of the public lands. The Indian respondents insist that "privacy during the power quests is required for the practitioners to maintain the purity needed for a successful journey." Similarly: "The practices conducted in the high country entail intense meditation and require the practitioner to achieve a profound awareness of the natural environment. Prayer seats are oriented so there is an unobstructed view, and the practitioner must be surrounded by undisturbed naturalness." No disrespect for these practices is implied when one notes that such beliefs could easily require de facto beneficial ownership of some rather spacious tracts of public property. Even without anticipating future cases, the diminution of the Government's property rights, and the concomitant subsidy of the Indian religion, would in this case be far from trivial: the District Court's order permanently forbade commercial timber harvesting, or the construction of a two-lane road, anywhere within an area covering a full 27 sections (i.e. more than 17,000 acres) of public land.

The Constitution does not permit government to discriminate against religions that treat particular physical sites as sacred, and a law forbidding the Indian respondents from visiting the Chimney Rock area would raise a different set of constitutional questions. Whatever rights the Indians may have to the use of the area, however, those rights do not divest the Government of its right to use what is, after all, its land.

Nothing in our opinion should be read to encourage governmental insensitivity to the religious needs of any citizen. The Government's rights to the use its own land, for example, need not and should not discourage it from accommodating religious practices like those engaged in by the Indian respondents. It is worth emphasizing, therefore, that the Government has taken numerous steps in this very case to minimize the impact that construction of the G-O road will have on the Indians' religious activities. First, the Forest Service commissioned a comprehensive study of the effects that the project would have on the cultural and religious value of the Chimney Rock area. The resulting 423-page report was so sympathetic to the Indians' interests that it has constituted the principal piece of evidence relied on by respondents' throughout this litigation.

Although the Forest Service did not in the end adopt the report's recommendation that the project be abandoned, many other ameliorative measures were planned. No sites where specific rituals take place were to be disturbed. In fact, a major factor in choosing among alternative routes for the road was the relation of the various routes to religious sites: the route selected by the Regional Forester is, he noted, "the farthest removed from contemporary spiritual sites; thus, the adverse audible intrusions associated with the road would be less than all other alternatives." Nor were the Forest Service's concerns limited to "audible intrusions." As the dissenting judge below observed, ten specific steps were planned to reduce the visual impact of the road on the surrounding country.

Except for abandoning its project entirely, and thereby leaving the two existing segments of road to deadend in the middle of a National Forest, it is difficult to see how the Government could have been more solicitous. Such solicitude accords with "the policy of the United States to protect and preserve for American Indians their inherent right of freedom to believe, express, and exercise the traditional religions of the American Indian...including but not limited to access to sites, use and possession of sacred objects, and the freedom to worship through ceremonials and traditional rites." American Indian Religious Freedom Act (AIRFA), Pub. L. 95-341, 92 Stat. 469, 42 U. S. C. § 1996.

Respondents, however, suggest that AIRFA goes further and in effect enacts their interpretation of the First Amendment into statutory law. Although this contention was rejected by the District Court, they seek to defend the judgment below by arguing that AIRFA authorizes the injunction against completion of the G-O road. This argument is without merit.... Nowhere in the law is there so much as a hint of any intent to create a cause of action or any judicially enforceable individual rights....

*Justice Brennan, with whom Justice Marshall and Justice Blackmun Join, dissenting:*

For at least 200 years and probably much longer, the Yurok, Karok, and Tolowa Indians have held sacred an approximately 25 square-mile area of land situated in what is today the Blue Creek Unit of Six Rivers National Forest in northwestern California. As the Government readily concedes, regular visits to this area, known to respondent Indians as the "high country," have played and continue to play a "critical" role in the religious practices and rituals of these tribes....

In marked contrast to traditional western religions, the belief systems of Native Americans do not rely on doctrines, creeds, or dogmas.... Native American faith is inextricably bound to the use of land. The site-specific nature of Indian religious practice derives from the Native American perception that land is itself a sacred, living being. Rituals are performed in prescribed locations not merely as a matter of traditional orthodoxy, but because land, like all other living things, is unique, and specific sites possess different spiritual properties and significance. Within this belief system, therefore, land is not fungible....

For respondent Indians, the most sacred of lands is the high country where, they believe, pre-human spirits moved with the coming of humans to the earth. Because these spirits are seen as the source of religious power, or "medicine," many of the tribes' rituals and practices require frequent journeys to the area.... Among the most powerful of sites are Chimney Rock, Doctor Rock, and Peak 8, all of which are elevated rock outcroppings....

The Court does not for a moment suggest that the interests served by the G-O road are in any way compelling, or that they outweigh the destructive effect construction of the road will have on respondents' religious practices. Instead, the Court embraces the Government's contention that its prerogative as landowner should always take precedence over a claim that a particular use of federal property infringes religious practices. Attempting to justify this rule, the Court argues that the First Amendment bars only outright prohibitions, indirect coercion, and penalties on the free exercise of religion. All other "incidental effects of government programs," it concludes, even those "which may make it more difficult to practice certain religions but which have no tendency to coerce individuals into acting contrary to their religious beliefs," simply do not give rise to constitutional concerns. Since our recognition nearly half a century ago that restraints on religious conduct implicate the concerns of the Free Exercise Clause, we have never suggested that the protections of the guarantee are limited to so narrow a range of governmental burdens. The land-use decision challenged here will restrain respondents from practicing their religion as surely and as completely as any of the governmental actions we have struck down in the past, and the Court's efforts simply to define away respondents' injury as nonconstitutional is both unjustified and ultimately unpersuasive....

In the final analysis, the Court's refusal to recognize the constitutional dimension of respondents' injuries stems from its concern that acceptance of respondents' claim could potentially strip the Government of its ability to manage and use vast tracts of federal property. In addition, the nature of respondents' site-specific religious practices raises the specter of future suits in which Native Americans seek to exclude all human activity from such areas. These concededly legitimate concerns lie at the very heart of this case, which represents yet another stress point in the longstanding conflict between two disparate cultures—the dominant western culture, which views land in terms of ownership and use, and that of Native Americans, in which concepts of private property are not only alien, but contrary to a belief system that holds land sacred. Rather than address this conflict in any meaningful fashion, however, the Court disclaims all responsibility for balancing these competing and potentially irreconcilable interests, choosing instead to turn this difficult task over to the federal legislature. Such an abdication is more than merely indefensible as an institutional matter: by defining respondents' injury as "non-constitutional," the Court has effectively bestowed on one party to this conflict the unilateral authority to resolve all future disputes in its favor, subject only to the Court's toothless exhortation to be "sensitive" to affected religions. In my view, however, Native Americans deserve—and the Constitution demands—more than this....

Similarly, the Court's concern that the claims of Native Americans will place "religious servitude" upon vast tracts of federal property cannot justify its refusal to recognize the constitutional injury respondents will suffer here. It is true, as the Court notes, that respondents' religious use of the high country requires privacy and solitude. The fact remains, however, that respondents have never asked the Forest Service to exclude others from the area. Should respondents or any other group seek to force the Government to protect their religious practices from the interference of private parties, such a demand would implicate not only the concerns of the Free Exercise Clause, but those of the Establishment Clause as well. That case, however, is most assuredly not before us today, and in any event cannot justify the Court's refusal to acknowledge that the injuries respondents will suffer as a result of the Government's proposed activities are sufficient to state a constitutional cause of action.

Today, the Court holds that a federal land-use decision that promises to destroy an entire religion does not burden the practice of that faith in a manner recognized by the Free Exercise Clause. Having thus stripped respondents and all other Native Americans of any constitutional protection against perhaps the most serious threat to their age-old religious practices, and indeed to their entire way of life, the Court assures us that nothing in its decision "should be read to encourage governmental insensitivity to the religious needs of any citizen." I find it difficult, however, to imagine conduct more insensitive to religious needs than the Government's determination to build a marginally useful road in the face of uncontradicted evidence that the road will render the practice of respondents' religion impossible. Nor do I believe that respondents will derive any solace from the knowledge that although the practice of their religion will become "more difficult" as a result of the Government's actions, they remain free to maintain their religious beliefs. Given today's ruling, that freedom amounts to nothing more than the right to believe that their religion will be destroyed....

* * *

## Notes and Questions

1. In *Lyng*, the Court allowed the Forest Service to greatly threaten, and possibly destroy, a tribal religion by building a road, on the grounds that the construction would

not coerce Indian religious practitioners into actively violating their own beliefs. Yet in other free exercise cases not involving public lands, non-Indian plaintiffs need only show that a governmental action places a substantial burden on the free exercise of their religion in order for the government to be required to demonstrate a compelling interest in limiting religious practices. What explains the difference?

2. The dissent argues that the majority opinion is best explained by "its concern that acceptance of respondents' claim could potentially strip the Government of its ability to manage and use vast tracts of federal property." *Id.* at 473. In your view, how much was the court's decision influenced by this concern?

3. Are there other statutes that can protect sacred sites from development? The American Indian Religious Freedom Act (AIRFA) provides that it is the "policy of the United States to protect and preserve" tribal freedom of religion, including access to sacred sites. As the *Lyng* court noted, however, AIRFA is not judicially enforceable. Professor Royster points to other mechanisms:

> [In 1996], President Clinton issued Executive Order 13,007-Indian Sacred Sites, mandating federal land agencies to accommodate tribal access to and use of sacred sites, and to avoid adverse impacts on the physical integrity of sacred sites. Executive Order, 13,007, however, like all executive orders, does not create a cause of action and is not enforceable by the tribes.
>
> A number of federal agencies with management responsibilities for federal lands, however, have attempted to accommodate Indian rights in federal lands, including the protection of religious practices and sacred sites. Several of the agencies have issued policy statements and agency guidelines calling for consultation with tribes and cooperation and accommodation in agency decision making and implementation. Moreover, and more generally, Executive Order 13,084 requires federal agencies to respect tribal rights and establish procedures for tribal input on federal regulatory policies "on matters that significantly or uniquely affect their communities." [Executive Order 13,084 was superceded and strengthened by Executive Order 13,175, adopted in 2000. Eds.]

Royster, *supra*, at 171. Professor Royster notes that three other statutes offer some protection for places and objects of religious, cultural or historical importance to Indian tribes: the National Historic Preservation Act, the Archaeological Resources Protection Act, and the Native American Graves Protection and Repatriation Act. *Id.* at 172–174. Several states also have similar, and in some cases more protective, statutes.

4. *Lyng* clearly upheld the ability of federal agencies to factor tribal religious practices into land use decision-making, if at their discretion they choose to do so. Such protective steps by the government, however, may be challenged as violating the establishment clause, as seen in the two cases below. In the first case, *Badoni v. Higginson,* which was decided before the Supreme Court's decision in *Lyng,* Navajo Indians alleged that the government's management of the Rainbow Bridge Reservoir and Glen Canyon Dam and Reservoir violated their freedom to practice religion. After rejecting the claim that the government had impermissibly burdened plaintiffs' religious practices (i.e., the free exercise claim), the court discussed whether the affirmative steps requested by plaintiffs violated the establishment clause.

# Badoni v. Higginson
## 638 F.2d 172 (10th Cir. 1980)

*Logan, Circuit Judge*:

The Rainbow Bridge National Monument is a 160-acre tract of land in southern Utah, set aside by executive order for scientific and historical purposes. Within this parcel is Rainbow Bridge, a great sandstone arch 309 feet high with a span of 278 feet. The Monument, which is surrounded by the Navajo reservation, is administered by the National Park Service. Glen Canyon Dam, located on the Colorado River fifty-eight miles below the Monument, is a 710-foot high structure built pursuant to Congressional authorization. Glen Canyon Reservoir, known as Lake Powell, formed behind the dam after its completion in 1963. By 1970 the lake had entered the 160-acre tract of the Monument and by 1977 the water had a peak depth of 20.9 feet directly under the Bridge. If the lake fills to its maximum capacity, the water apparently will be 46 feet deep under the Bridge....

Prior to the creation of Lake Powell, Rainbow Bridge National Monument was isolated and was visited by few tourists. The lake now provides convenient access to the Monument....

The individual plaintiffs are Indians residing in the general area of Rainbow Bridge National Monument in southern Utah and are enrolled members of the Navajo Tribe.... Rainbow Bridge and a nearby spring, prayer spot and cave have held positions of central importance in the religion of some Navajo people living in that area for at least 100 years. These shrines are regarded as the incarnate forms of Navajo gods, which provide protection and rain-giving functions. For generations Navajo singers have performed ceremonies near the Bridge and water from the spring has been used for other ceremonies. Plaintiffs believe that if humans alter the earth in the area of the Bridge, plaintiffs' prayers will not be heard by the gods and their ceremonies will be ineffective to prevent evil and disease. Because of the operation of the Dam and Lake Powell, the springs and prayer spot are under water. Tourists visiting the sacred area have desecrated it by noise, litter and defacement of the Bridge itself. Because of the flooding and the presence of tourists, plaintiffs no longer hold ceremonies in the area of the Bridge....

[Plaintiffs' free exercise claim is that government action has infringed the practice of their religion in two respects: (1) by impounding water to form Lake Powell, the government has drowned some of plaintiffs' gods and denied plaintiffs access to a prayer spot sacred to them; and (2) by allowing tourists to visit Rainbow Bridge, the government has permitted desecration of the sacred nature of the site and has denied plaintiffs' right to conduct religious ceremonies at the prayer spot.]

[The court first holds that the government's interest in impounding water in Lake Powell and maintaining its capacity to provide water supplies to several states outweighed the burden on the Navajo religion that resulted from drowning the Navajo gods in the area.]

The second basis for plaintiffs' free exercise claims concerns management of the Monument by the National Park Service. Specifically, plaintiffs assert that tourists visiting the Monument desecrate the area by noisy conduct, littering and defacement of the Bridge and that the presence of tourists prevents plaintiffs from holding ceremonies near the Bridge.

The gravamen of plaintiffs' claim is that by permitting public access and the operation of commercial tour boats the government has burdened the practice of plaintiffs' religion.... In their brief-in-chief, plaintiffs state they "seek only some measured accommodation to their religious interest, not a wholesale bar to use of Rainbow Bridge by all others." They suggest some specific types of relief, such as prohibiting consumption of beer at the Monument and closing the Monument on reasonable notice when religious ceremonies are to be held there....

The government here has not prohibited plaintiffs' religious exercises in the area of Rainbow Bridge; plaintiffs may enter the Monument on the same basis as other people. It is the presence of tourists at the Monument and their actions while there that give rise to plaintiffs' complaint of interference with the exercise of their religion. We are mindful of the difficulties facing plaintiffs in performing solemn religious ceremonies in an area frequented by tourists. But what plaintiffs seek in the name of the Free Exercise Clause is affirmative action by the government which implicates the Establishment Clause of the First Amendment. They seek government action to exclude others from the Monument, at least for short periods, and to control tourist behavior.

Unquestionably the government has a strong interest in assuring public access to this natural wonder. Congress has charged the Park Service with the duty to provide "for the enjoyment of (parks and monuments)...by such means as will leave them unimpaired for the enjoyment of future of the generations." 16 U.S.C. § 1....

Issuance of regulations to exclude tourists completely from the Monument for the avowed purpose of aiding plaintiffs' conduct of religious ceremonies would seem a clear violation of the Establishment Clause.

> The test [of the Establishment Clause] may be stated as follows: what are the purpose and the primary effect of the enactment? If either is the advancement or inhibition of religion then the enactment exceeds the scope of legislative power as circumscribed by the Constitution. That is to say that to withstand the strictures of the Establishment Clause there must be a secular legislative purpose and a primary effect that neither advances nor inhibits religion.

School Dist. of Abington v. Schempp, 374 U.S.[203 ], 222 [1963]....

We must also deny relief insofar as plaintiffs seek to have the government police the actions of tourists lawfully visiting the Monument. Although Congress has authorized the Park Service to regulate the conduct of tourists in order to promote and preserve the Monument, we do not believe plaintiffs have a constitutional right to have tourists visiting the Bridge act "in a respectful and appreciative manner."

> The First Amendment protects one against action by the government, though even then, not in all circumstances; but it gives no one the right to insist that in the pursuit of their own interests others must conform their conduct to his own religious necessities.... We must accommodate our idiosyncrasies, religious as well as secular, to the compromises necessary in communal life.

Otten v. Baltimore & O. R. Co., 205 F.2d 58, 61 (2d Cir. 1953). Were it otherwise, the Monument would become a government-managed religious shrine.

The Park Service already has issued regulations applicable to the Monument prohibiting disorderly conduct, 36 C.F.R. § 2.7 (1979), intoxication and possession of alcoholic beverages by minors, *id.* § 2.16, defacement, *id.* § 2.20, littering, *id.* § 2.24, and tampering with personal property, *id.* § 2.29. These regulations no doubt would be justified as authorized under its charge to conserve and protect the scenery, natural and historic objects for the enjoyment of the public. See 16 U.S.C. § 1. These regulations also provide the relief plaintiffs request as to control of tourist behavior, except perhaps for a total ban on beer drinking.

What of the request stated in the appellant's reply brief for access "on infrequent occasions" to conduct religious ceremonies in private? The government asserts that plaintiffs, in common with other members of the public, may apply for a public assembly permit to hold religious ceremonies at the Bridge. No one suggests such a permit could not be used to permit access after normal visiting hours when privacy might be assured....

\* \* \*

## Notes and Questions

1. The court suggests that to grant plaintiffs their requested relief would turn Rainbow Bridge Monument into a "government-managed religious shrine." Do you agree? Could the government impose short term visitation restrictions without violating the Establishment Clause?

2. Although plaintiffs lost their legal challenge in *Badoni*, the Park Service has taken more steps in recent years to protect Rainbow Bridge and other sacred Indian sites. For example, in 1995, the agency built a shin-high rock wall to discourage visitors from leaving the viewing area of Rainbow Bridge and walking directly under the arch. Likewise, Park Service signs now explain that the area is sacred to some American Indians and ask visitors not to walk any farther. In 1996, park officials closed the "great kiva" at Chaco Culture National Historical Park after Navajos and Pueblo Indians complained it had been defiled by tourists leaving everything from crystals to cremated human remains. And at New Mexico's Bandelier National Monument, park rangers now do not publicize the existence of Stone Lions, two volcanic rocks carved into the shape of lions. The shrine is sacred to members of nearby Pueblos. Chris Smith & Elizabeth Manning, *The Sacred and Profane Collide in the West*, HIGH COUNTRY NEWS, *available at* http://www.hcn.org/servlets/hcn.Article?article_id=3424) (May 26, 1997). Such protective measures have led to challenges by non-Indian users, who want access to these same spectacular sites for recreational and other users, as seen in the case below.

## Bear Lodge Multiple Use Association v. Babbitt
### 2 F. Supp. 2d 1448 (D.C.W.Y. 1998), *affirmed* 175 F.3d 814 (10th Cir. 1999)

*Downes, District Judge:*

[Devils Tower is a National Monument located in northeast Wyoming. Indian tribes have long viewed Devils Tower as a sacred site of special religious and cultural significance. At Devils Tower, Indians partake in Sun Dances and individual Vision Quests. The Sun Dance is a group ceremony of fasting and sacrifice which leads to spiritual renewal of the individual and group as a whole. Sun Dances are performed around the summer solstice. Vision Quests are intense periods of prayer, fasting, sweat lodge purification, and solitude designed to connect with the spiritual world and gain insight. These and other ceremonies require solemnity and solitude.]

[Devils Tower is also world famous for its rock climbing. Over the past thirty years the number of climbers has increased dramatically, to over 6,000 annual recreational climbers. During the last ten years route development and bolt placement on the monument have accelerated, and there are about 220 named climbing routes. Approximately 600 metal bolts are embedded in the rock along with several hundred metal pitons. June is the most popular month for climbing Devils Tower.]

[Recognizing that increasing climbing activity affects the environment as well as "the ability of American Indians to engage in their ceremonial activities in peace," the National Park Service (NPS) began preparing a draft climbing management plan in 1992. In 1995, it issued a Final Climbing Management Plan [FCMP].]

The FCMP "sets a new direction for managing climbing activity at the tower for the next three to five years," its stated purpose being, "to protect the natural and cultural resources of Devils Tower and to provide for visitor enjoyment and appreciation of this unique feature." To protect against any new physical impacts to the tower, the FCMP provides that no new bolts or fixed pitons will be permitted on the tower, and new face routes requiring new bolt installation will not be permitted. The FCMP does allow individuals to replace already existing bolts and fixed pitons. In addition, the plan calls for access trails to be rehabilitated and maintained, and requires camouflaged climbing equipment, and climbing routes to be closed seasonally to protect raptor nests. The FCMP further provides that "in respect for the reverence many American Indians hold for Devils Tower as a *sacred* site, rock climbers will be asked to *voluntarily* refrain from climbing on Devils Tower during the culturally significant month of June [when American Indians engage in the Sun Dance and other ceremonies]." ...

The NPS represents that it will not enforce the voluntary closure, but will instead rely on climbers' self-regulation and a new "cross-cultural educational program" "to motivate climbers and other park visitors to comply." The NPS has also placed a sign at the base of the Tower in order to encourage visitors to stay on the trail surrounding the Tower. Despite the FCMP's reliance on self-regulation, it also provides that if the voluntary closure proves to be "unsuccessful," the NPS will consider taking several actions including: (a) revising the climbing management plan; (b) reconvening a climbing management plan work group; (c) instituting additional measures to further encourage compliance; (d) change the duration and nature of the voluntary closure; (e) *converting the June closure to mandatory*; and (f) writing a new definition of success for the voluntary closure. Factors indicating an unsuccessful voluntary closure include, little to no decrease in the number of climbers, an increase in the number of unregistered climbers and increased conflict between user groups in the park. The NPS, however, states that the voluntary closure will be "fully successful" only "when every climber personally chooses not to climb at Devils Tower during June out of respect for American Indian cultural values."

The NPS plans to fully comply with its own June closure by not allowing NPS staff to climb on the tower in June except to enforce laws and regulations or to perform emergency operations. Originally the plan also contained a provision stating that commercial use licenses for June climbing guide activities would not be issued by the NPS for the month of June. Plaintiffs filed a Motion for Preliminary Injunction seeking to enjoin Defendants from the commercial climbing ban during the month of June. This Court granted that motion in June of 1996. In December of that year, Defendant issued a decision revoking the commercial climbing ban.

[P]laintiffs [Bear Lodge Municipal Use Association and several climbers] contend that the NPS has stepped outside of the bounds imposed by law.... [T]hey allege that the NPS's plan wrongfully promotes religion in violation of the establishment clause of the first amendment. ...

*Voluntary Climbing Ban*

The Establishment Clause of the First Amendment states that "Congress shall make no law respecting an establishment of religion...." U.S. Const. amend. I. The Courts of this country have long struggled with the type and extent of limitations on government action which these ten words impose. At its most fundamental level, the United States Supreme Court has concluded that this provision prohibits laws "which aid one religion, aid all religions, or prefer one religion over another."...In Lemon v. Kurtzman, 403 U.S. 602 (1971), the court established a three part test for delineating between proper and improper government actions. According to this test a governmental action does not offend the Establishment Clause if it (1) has a secular purpose, (2) does not have the principal or primary effect of advancing or inhibiting religion, and (3) does not foster an excessive entanglement with religion. *Lemon*, 403 U.S. at 612–13. In a concurring opinion in the case of Lynch v. Donnelly, 465 U.S. 668 (1983), Justice O'Connor sought to clarify the *Lemon* analysis by focusing on whether the government action endorsed religion....

The Supreme Court "has long recognized that the government may (and sometimes must) accommodate religious practices and that it may do so without violating the Establishment Clause." The Constitution actually "mandates accommodation, not merely tolerance, of all religions, and forbids hostility toward any."... This Court must look beyond the plain language establishing the climbing ban and examine its purpose and effects in order to determine if it is appropriate accommodation or if it breaches the necessary gap between state and religion fusing the two into one.

*Purpose*

The ability to accommodate religious practices is an important consideration in determining what constitutes a proper purpose under the *Lemon* test and Justice O'Connor's endorsement test. The Plaintiffs can succeed on this prong only if they show that the action has no clear secular purpose or that despite a secular purpose the actual purpose is to endorse religion....

In this case the Defendants contend that the climbing plan was designed, in part, to eliminate barriers to American Indian's free practice of religion. They argue that this type of accommodation is particularly appropriate in situations like this where impediments to worship arise because a group's sacred place of worship is found on property of the United States. Defendants assert that their actions are also aimed at fostering the preservation of the historical, social and cultural practices of Native Americans which are necessarily intertwined with their religious practices. While the purposes behind the voluntary climbing ban are directly related to Native American religious practices, that is not the end of the analysis. The purposes underlying the ban are really to remove barriers to religious worship occasioned by public ownership of the Tower. This is in the nature of accommodation, not promotion, and consequently is a legitimate secular purpose.

*Effect*

Accommodation also plays a role in considering whether the principal effect of a policy is to advance religion. The Supreme Court has said; "[a] law is not unconstitutional simply because it allows churches to advance religion, which is their very purpose. For a law to have forbidden 'effects' under *Lemon*, it must be fair to say that the government itself has advanced religion through its own activities or influence."...

The record clearly reveals that climbing at the Devils Tower National Monument is a "legitimate recreational and historic" use of Park Service lands. If the NPS is, in effect, depriving individuals of their legitimate use of the monument in order to enforce the tribes' rights to worship, it has stepped beyond permissible accommodation and into the realm of promoting religion. The gravamen of the issue then becomes whether climbers are allowed meaningful access to the monument. Stated another way, is the climbing ban voluntary or is it actually an improper exercise of government coercion?

Plaintiffs argue that the "voluntary" ban is voluntary in name only. In support of their argument Plaintiffs note that the NPS has established a goal of having every climber personally choose not to climb at the Tower during June. Plaintiffs also cite to possible modifications to the FCMP if the NPS deems the voluntary ban unsuccessful. Specifically,... the NPS may convert the closure to a mandatory closure.

Neither of these factors is sufficient to transform the voluntary ban into a coerced ban. The Park Service's stated goals are not the measure of coercion, rather the implementation of those goals. The goal of reducing the number of climbers to zero may or may not be a desirable one, but coercion only manifests itself in the NPS's actions, not in its aspirations. The Park Service's stated goals would not be advanced at all by mandating that climbers not scale the Tower. Instead, it has stated that the "voluntary closure will be fully successful when every climber *personally chooses* not to climb at Devils Tower during June." Ordering climbers not to climb or deterring climbing through intimidation undermines this goal and robs individuals of the personal choice necessary to accomplish it. Yet, the Park Service's hopes that climbers will adhere to the voluntary climbing ban cannot be viewed as coercive....

Although the NPS has stated that an unsuccessful voluntary ban may lead it to make the ban mandatory, that is far from an inevitable result. To the contrary, the conversion to a mandatory ban is only one of eight options which the NPS may consider in the event of a failed voluntary ban....

*Excessive Entanglement*

The Court concludes that the voluntary climbing ban also passes muster when measured against the excessive entanglement test. To determine whether a given policy constitutes an excessive entanglement the Court must look at "the character and purposes of the institutions that are benefitted, the nature of the aid that the State provides, and the resulting relationship between the government and religious authority." Lemon, 403 U.S. at 615.... The organizations benefitted by the voluntary climbing ban, namely Native American tribes, are not solely religious organizations, but also represent a common heritage and culture. As a result, there is much less danger that the Government's actions will inordinately advance solely religious activities.... The government is merely enabling Native Americans to worship in a more peaceful setting. In doing so, the Park Service has no involvement in the manner of worship that takes place, but only provides an atmosphere more conducive to worship. This type of custodial function does not implicate the dangerously close relationship between state and religion which offends the excessive entanglement prong of the *Lemon* test....

\* \* \*

## *Notes and Questions*

1. On appeal, the 10th Circuit affirmed on the grounds that plaintiffs lacked standing to sue, since they remained free to climb Devils Tower and thus had not demonstrated harm from the Park Service's voluntary ban.

2. What explains the different outcome in this case with the Rainbow Bridge Monument case immediately above? Is it the voluntary nature of the ban on climbing Devils Tower?

3. Does the Park Service's management plan violate the establishment clause by establishing religion? Or it is an appropriate plan to eliminate barriers to Indians' free practice of religion on federal public lands? Consider the following comments:

> [L]awyers from the Cheyenne River Sioux tribe, an intervenor on behalf of the Park Service [argue] that if the Park Service has established religion at Devils Tower, it has also done so at other national monuments and parks. The Cheyenne lawyers point out that twice a year at Tumacacori National Historical Park in Arizona, the Park Service sponsors a Catholic mass reenacting 18th-century religious traditions. And in Texas, at San Antonio Missions, the park's official brochure states the following: "Please be considerate. The historic structures are fragile resources. Help us preserve them for future generations. Remember also that these are places of worship. Parish priests and parishioners deserve your respect; please do not disrupt their services." The question, then, is why should a butte that is sacred to Native Americans be treated differently than a mission or a church managed by the Park Service? Because the butte is a natural feature and Native American religions are harder to understand than Western ones? Or because hundreds of thousands of tourists come to Devils Tower each summer to see the nation's first monument — and the place where spaceships landed in Steven Spielberg's Close Encounters of the Third Kind?

*See,* Smith & Manning, *supra.* Where do you come out in this debate? Is it possible for the courts to engage in a value free analysis under either the free exercise clause or establishment clause of the Constitution? Do the outcomes of these types of cases hinge more upon individual judges' sensitivities to Native Americans than on objectively applied constitutional doctrine? Assuming that true objectivity is a chimera, should courts be more forthright in admitting a greater understanding of and ability to appreciate the types of accommodations necessary for western religious beliefs?

4. Part of the rationale of the district court's opinion was that religious values were not the only values at stake, but that the spiritual significance of Devils Tower was inextricably bound to the cultural and social fabric of the affected tribes. Is this true, and should these factors matter?

5. As noted above, federal authority over Native Americans is subject to the federal government's trust responsibility to manage Indian lands, funds and resources for the benefit of Indians. Before the court issued the ruling excerpted above, it had issued a preliminary injunction barring the National Park Service from implementing a temporary commercial climbing moratorium on Devils Tower during the month of June (subsequently dropped by the Forest Service). The court's preliminary injunction order makes no mention of the federal trust responsibility to the affected tribes, an omission criticized in the following commentary:

> The significance of this choice is that applying an exclusively Establishment Clause frame of reference operates by trying to demonstrate similarities in law

between tribal spiritualism and Anglo-American religious denominations, while the trust responsibility approach instead emphasizes the uniqueness of the federal government relationship to the tribes as semi-sovereign peoples rather than religious practitioners. As applied in the Devils Tower trial court decision, pure Establishment Clause analysis seeks to accommodate pluralism by focusing on perceived sameness, while trust responsibility doctrine seeks the same objective by focusing on difference.

The distinction between the two is more than strictly academic. Confining the analysis solely to Establishment Clause discourse denies both the NPS and the affected tribes the moral authority to seek any accommodation beyond that allowed by the decision (such as the temporary mandatory commercial climbing ban the superintendent first tried to impose at the Tower). Following this approach, the superintendent may have potent discretionary authority to prohibit all commercial and recreational activity in order to protect the physical integrity of the monument or the well-being of its wildlife, but not to assure the unimpeded replication of spiritual aspects of tribal culture.

Lloyd Burton & David Ruppert, *Bear's Lodge or Devils Tower: Inter-Cultural Relations, Legal Pluralism, and the Management of Sacred Sites on Public Lands,* 8 CORNELL J. L. & PUB. POL'Y 201, 231 (1999). For more discussion of the federal government's trust responsibility to Indians, see the articles cited in the pathfinder at the start of this chapter.

# Index